Splendid Legacy

SPLENDID LEGACY
THE HAVEMEYER COLLECTION

ALICE COONEY FRELINGHUYSEN   GARY TINTEROW
SUSAN ALYSON STEIN   GRETCHEN WOLD
JULIA MEECH

With contributions by
Maryan W. Ainsworth, Dorothea Arnold, Katharine Baetjer,
Janet S. Byrne, Keith Christiansen, Hyung-min Chung, Barbara B. Ford,
James H. Frantz, Maxwell K. Hearn, Colta Ives, Marilyn Jenkins,
Walter Liedtke, Joan R. Mertens, Helen B. Mules, Morihiro Ogawa, Hiroshi Onishi,
Rebecca A. Rabinow, Suzanne G. Valenstein, Clare Vincent,
Daniel Walker, James C. Y. Watt, H. Barbara Weinberg

THE METROPOLITAN MUSEUM OF ART, NEW YORK

This publication is issued in conjunction with the exhibition *Splendid Legacy: The Havemeyer Collection*, held at The Metropolitan Museum of Art, New York, from March 27 to June 20, 1993.

The exhibition is made possible by The Annenberg Foundation, The Dillon Fund, Cowen & Company, the William Randolph Hearst Foundation, and The Real Estate Council of The Metropolitan Museum of Art. The exhibition catalogue is made possible by generous grants from Janice H. Levin, the Frelinghuysen Foundation, and The Peter Jay Sharp Foundation Fund.

Published by The Metropolitan Museum of Art, New York

John P. O'Neill, Editor in Chief
Carol Fuerstein, Editor
Bruce Campbell, Designer
Gwen Roginsky and Rachel M. Ruben, Production

New photography of Metropolitan Museum works of art by Joseph Coscia, Jr., Anna Marie Kellen, Oi-Cheong Lee, Patricia Mazza, Karen L. Willis, Carmel Wilson, Katherine Dahab, Bruce Schwarz, and Eileen Travell of the Photograph Studio, The Metropolitan Museum of Art

Set in Sabon and Benguiat by U.S. Lithograph, typographers, New York
Separations by Arnoldo Mondadori, S.p.A., Verona, Italy, and Professional Graphics, Rockford, Illinois
Printed and bound by Arnoldo Mondadori, S.p.A., Verona, Italy

Jacket/Cover Illustration
Detail, Manet, *Boating*, 1874. Plate 31

Frontispiece
Louisine and H. O. Havemeyer in Paris, 1889

LIBRARY OF CONGRESS CATALOGING IN PUBLICATION DATA

Splendid legacy : the Havemeyer collection / Alice Cooney
Frelinghuysen . . . [et al.].
p.   cm.
Includes bibliographical references and index.
ISBN 0-87099-664-9. — ISBN 0-87099-665-7 (pbk.)
1. Havemeyer, Henry Osborne, 1847–1907—Art collections—Catalogs.
2. Havemeyer, Louisine Waldron Elder—Art collections—Catalogs.
3. Art—Private collections—New York (N.Y.)—Catalogs. 4. Art—New
York (N.Y.)—Catalogs. 5. Metropolitan Museum of Art (New York,
N.Y.)—Catalogs. I. Metropolitan Museum of Art (New York, N.Y.)
N5220.H295S65 1993   92-45902
708.147'1—dc20   CIP

Contents

Foreword

The Metropolitan Museum of Art became the splendid encyclopedia of world art that it is today without the advantage of a great royal or princely collection. This is largely due to the taste, intelligence, and generosity of numerous collectors who chose to share their possessions with the public. Even counted in a roster that includes such legendary collections as J. Pierpont Morgan's, Benjamin Altman's, Jules Bache's, and Robert Lehman's, the Havemeyer collection remains one of the most noteworthy, not only in size and scope but also in quality. Nearly two thousand works of art entered the Museum in 1929 with the Havemeyer bequest, paintings and objects brought together as the result of many years of enthusiastic and judicious activity on the part of the subjects of this exhibition and publication, Louisine and Henry Osborne Havemeyer. Amazingly, these gifts joined a significant number of other objects that had been given to the Museum earlier, while the Havemeyers were alive, and the collection has continued to grow in ensuing decades, to reach a total approaching 4,500. The scope of the collection is such that it enriches nearly every department of the Museum—American decorative arts, American paintings and sculpture, arms and armor, Asian art, drawings, Egyptian art, European sculpture and decorative arts, Greek and Roman art, Islamic art, Medieval art, and prints and illustrated books—but none more brilliantly than that of European paintings.

The current project, conceived over a decade ago, sheds much light on a collection that is perhaps more famous than really known and provides new insight into the Havemeyers' collecting methods. It holds up a mirror to the last decades of the nineteenth century and to the early twentieth century, a time when great fortunes were made and great quantities of art were available to the discerning buyer. It also reflects our perennial desire to look at the Museum's collections for the purpose of special exhibition and explication.

The exhibition comprises over 450 works of art in various media that at one time were owned by the Havemeyers, including paintings, drawings, prints, sculpture, ceramics, glass, metalwork, lacquerwork, and textiles. Many of these undoubtedly will be familiar, as they have been on view almost continually since they entered the Museum, but others will surprise, as Havemeyer objects have not been shown as a group since 1930, when the entire bequest was put on view. The exhibition has been selected and arranged to underscore the richness and diversity of this collection, and some of the surviving architectural details from the Havemeyers' New York house, at 1 East 66th Street, have been brought together in order to suggest its original context.

It is to the Metropolitan that the large part of the Havemeyers' holdings was given. A number of important works did, however, find their way to other public collections and to private hands, and some are still in the possession of family descendants; the owners of many of these works have generously lent them to the Metropolitan for this show. The lenders, except those who wished to remain anonymous, are listed elsewhere in the catalogue. We are grateful to all of them and particularly wish to thank the staff and trustees of the Shelburne Museum, Shelburne, Vermont, the single largest lender to the show, the National Gallery of Art, Washington D. C., for parting with its great Manet and Goya paintings; and the University of Michigan Museum of Art, Ann Arbor, for allowing us to borrow architectural elements from the Havemeyer house.

The history of the Havemeyer gifts to the Metropolitan spans a period of over one hundred years and demonstrates that much of the collection was amassed with the Museum in mind. As early as 1888 H. O. Havemeyer gave the Museum its first portrait of George Washington by Gilbert Stuart. Mr. Havemeyer had learned that the Metropolitan was eager to acquire the portrait but lacked the necessary funds, whereupon he purchased the painting himself and presented it to the Board of Trustees. In 1896 Mr. Havemeyer gave an extensive collection of favrile glass made specially for him and his wife by Louis Comfort Tiffany, as well as some two thousand Japanese textile fragments that he had bought from the Parisian dealer Siegfried Bing. The Havemeyer gifts generally were made without restrictions or fanfare; indeed some remained anonymous until the time of the 1929 bequest. For example, in 1923 Louisine Havemeyer made the notable gift of Giovanni Battista Tiepolo's painted ceiling for the Palazzo Barbaro in Venice as an anonymous donation in memory of her close friend and neighbor Col. Oliver H. Payne.

The Havemeyers' belief in sharing their art with the public embraced loans as well as gifts, and they lent extensively to exhibitions over the years. Among those held at the Metropolitan to which they contributed were the 1909 *Hudson-Fulton Celebration*, an exhibition of Chinese pottery and sculpture in 1916 and one of Japanese screens and paintings in 1917, the Courbet exhibition of 1919, which Mrs. Havemeyer actually helped organize, the *Fiftieth Anniversary Exhibition* in 1920, an exhibition of French Impressionist and Post-Impressionist paintings and prints in 1921, one of paintings by J. Alden Weir in 1924, and another of Spanish painting in 1928. The range of these exhibitions of course parallels the range of the Havemeyers' collecting interests.

Only when Louisine Havemeyer's will was read after her death in 1929—she had inherited the entire collection when her husband died in 1907—did it become clear that most of the greatest treasures would be given in public trust to the Metropolitan. In her will Louisine had left everything to her three children. However, she had added three codicils making the following provisions: in the first, that 113 works of art, about half of which were pictures and the remainder sculpture and decorative objects, would go outright to the Metropolitan; in the second, that 28 paintings and 1 drawing would be added to the gift; and in the third, that Horace Havemeyer, as her son and executor, would be authorized to give the Museum any works not specifically mentioned in the will. Horace Havemeyer and his two sisters, Adaline Havemeyer Frelinghuysen and Electra Havemeyer Webb, followed their parents' initiative, and by the time the gift was complete, it totaled

nearly two thousand works of art. Only a relatively small selection of paintings was set aside specifically for various family members, and when the bequest was made, the Metropolitan's curators were given virtually free choice in selecting works that would enhance the Museum's holdings. The three children did their utmost to carry out what they felt was their mother's wish, namely that the Museum have the best of everything she left. At the same time they showed their self-effacement and true concern for the public by refusing to insist that the Museum accept objects it did not want. The additions made to the bequest comprised paintings, drawings, and pastels, as well as prints, Spanish ceramics and other decorative arts, and an impressively large collection of the arts of China and Japan, including screens, paintings, sculpture, porcelains, pottery, swords and sword fittings, bronzes, lacquers, and textiles. The collection grew from the original 142 works specified in the first two codicils to an aggregate of 1,967 items. The single condition imposed on this gift was that each object bear the credit line "H. O. Havemeyer Collection."

In the decades following the 1929 bequest, members of the Havemeyer family have continued the tradition of commitment begun by Louisine and H. O. Havemeyer by sharing their collections with the public. Horace Havemeyer made frequent gifts from his collection of Islamic pottery and textiles to the Museum from the 1930s until his death in 1956. In addition Horace Havemeyer and Mrs. Peter H. B. Frelinghuysen gave Japanese screens in 1949 and 1962, respectively, and *The Dance Lesson*, a superb pastel by Edgar Degas, was donated anonymously by a family member in 1971, and J. Watson Webb, Jr., donated an exceptional Japanese dagger in 1972. The most recent example of this tradition was the splendid gift presented in 1992 by the family of Adaline Havemeyer Frelinghuysen of Cassatt's portrait *Adaline Havemeyer in a White Hat*.

Mr. and Mrs. Havemeyer not only donated specific works of art but also helped the Museum in indirect ways. Many of Col. Oliver H. Payne's pictures were acquired on the advice of the Havemeyers, for example, and some of them, notably Goya's *Don Ignacio Garcini y Queralt* and *Doña Josefa Castilla Portugal de Garcini*, gifts of his nephew Harry Payne Bingham, hang regularly in the Museum's primary galleries. In 1891 H. O. Havemeyer donated funds to help keep the

Museum open on Sundays, a practice initiated in May of that year.

In spite of Mr. and Mrs. Havemeyer's generosity, H. O. Havemeyer was never elected to the Board of Trustees. The reasons for this are not known, but it has been speculated that he was passed over because he was notoriously hard to get along with. The unfavorable publicity surrounding the investigation of the Sugar Trust and the subsequent Federal suit against the Havemeyers' firm toward the end of his life may also have influenced the board's decision. The Havemeyers rose above such matters, however, and their desire to share their art survived; this public-spiritedness resulted in the bequest and the gifts described in this catalogue, benefactions that gave extraordinary depth to the Metropolitan's collections.

We had planned to mount a Havemeyer exhibition for over a decade, but it was only with the two-year closing of the nineteenth-century galleries for renovations that the project could realistically be envisaged, and we are indebted to Gary Tinterow and Alice Cooney Frelinghuysen for taking on the challenge of this enormously complicated task. They were aided in the project's initial stages of organization by Mahrukh Tarapor and Martha Deese and were soon joined by nearly thirty curators from twelve departments, many of whom contributed to this catalogue. We are all grateful for their help, and I refer the reader to the title page for the list of the authors' names. I should like to single out for special recognition Susan Alyson Stein and Gretchen Wold for providing the scholarly backbone of this book, Carol Fuerstein for shaping this avalanche of information into a reference work that can be consulted easily, and, once again, Gary Tinterow and Alice Cooney Frelinghuysen for their industry and determination in the production of what is a definitive collection catalogue designed to satisfy scholar and amateur alike.

We would not be able to publish this book without the support of Janice H. Levin, the Frelinghuysen Foundation, and The Peter Jay Sharp Foundation Fund, and we would have no exhibition to celebrate without the support of The Annenberg Foundation, The Dillon Fund, Cowen & Company, The William Randolph Hearst Foundation, and The Real Estate Council of The Metropolitan Museum of Art.

Philippe de Montebello
Director

Acknowledgments

The book and exhibition *Splendid Legacy: The Have-meyer Collection* reflects the combined efforts of many people whose participation calls for recognition and thanks: the reevaluation of the enormous and diverse collection amassed by the Havemeyers required the collaboration of many departments within the Metropolitan and of numerous individuals, both within and outside the Museum.

It seems a fitting tribute to the breadth of the Havemeyer collection that twenty-seven experts were required to assess it for the purpose of this publication. We extend sincere thanks to all of the authors, whose names are listed on the title page, for making this catalogue so informative and stimulating. A number of them have made exceptional contributions, and it is our pleasure to offer particular acknowledgment of their labors. Julia Meech generously agreed to interrupt her research on other subjects to write her fascinating account of the Havemeyers' involvement with Asian art. Susan Alyson Stein, aided by Rebecca A. Rabinow, devoted an entire year to researching and writing her exhaustive chronicle of the Havemeyers' lives. We can say with assurance that she now knows more about the Havemeyers and their collection than they knew about themselves and their possessions, and that her Chronology has opened a new and highly illuminating perspective on the process of building a major collection at the turn of the century. Many of the authors have relied on her work, and we thank her on their behalf as well as on our own. An equally significant contribution to the catalogue, and to our knowledge of the Havemeyer collection, has been made by Gretchen Wold, who devoted the past year to her work on the Appendix. Her illustrated checklist of all the known Western paintings, watercolors, pastels, and drawings owned by the Havemeyers will be an invaluable resource for scholars for generations to come. Roberta Wue and Christine Scornavacca helped sift through mountains of information to compile this impressive document.

The authors extend their deepest gratitude to Carol Fuerstein, who gracefully coped with the deluge of material and in record time crafted it into a very readable and important book. We also thank John P. O'Neill, Editor in Chief, and Barbara Burn for their guidance and support. Joanne Greenspun, Tonia Payne, Barbara Cavaliere, and Joan Holt assisted with the editing of this enormous manuscript. We are grateful to Gwen Roginsky and Rachel M. Ruben for skillfully seeing the book through all its stages of production. Victoria Ross helped assemble and organize the masses of photographic material, and Steffie Kaplan executed the mechanicals. Bruce Campbell was responsible for the handsome design.

Many members of the Museum's various departments contributed to *Splendid Legacy* in a number of other capacities, and they all deserve our thanks. Philippe de Montebello, Director, who initiated Museum-wide discussions on the Havemeyer collection in March 1990, not only offered his leadership throughout all phases of the project but also demanded a sense of discipline that proved essential in shaping the publication and exhibition. Mahrukh Tarapor, Assistant Director, provided most welcome advice and encouragement, and we depended on Martha Deese for important administrative work and coordination during the early phase of the project. Emily Kernan Rafferty, Vice President for Development and Membership, and her very competent staff, Nina McN. Diefenbach, Carol D. Ehler, Lynne M. Winter, and Nancy McLaughlin worked conscientiously to secure the funding for the show. Jeanie M. James, Archivist, and Barbara W. File endlessly procured Havemeyer documents from the Museum's archives and read and checked for accuracy innumerable quotes included in the catalogue. We are immensely indebted to the staff of the Museum's Photograph Studio for efficiently and expertly taking hundreds of color and black-and-white photographs of objects in the Metropolitan's collection. In addition to the photographers listed on the copyright page, we thank Barbara Bridgers, Manager, Kenneth Campbell, Robert L. Goldman, Mark D. Herdter, Caitlin McCaffrey, Teri Aderman, and Josephine Freeman of that department.

The members of the Museum's conservation departments performed crucial services, particularly checking incoming loans and cleaning works of art before they were photographed as well as preparing them for exhibition; in this context we express our appreciation to Hubert von Sonnenburg, Sherman Fairchild Chairman of Paintings Conservation, Dorothy Mahon, and Maryan W. Ainsworth in Paintings Conservation; James H. Frantz, Conservator in Charge, Antoine M. Wilmering, Yale Kneeland, Nancy C. Britton, and Mark D. Minor of Objects Conservation; Helen K. Otis, Conservator in Charge, and Marjorie N. Shelley in Paper Conservation; and Nobuko Kajitani and Elena Phipps in Textile Conservation. Herbert M. Moskowitz, Registrar, with the help of Kären Anderson and Nina S. Maruca, made the arrangements necessary for insurance, packing, and shipping of the objects that were borrowed for the exhibition. David Harvey, Senior Exhibition Designer, was responsible for the complicated and handsome installation, which so sympathetically displays the many kinds of art in the exhibition. Jill Hammerberg conceived the attractive design of the exhibition graphics, and Zack Zanolli was in charge of the lighting of the galleries. Kent Lydecker, Deputy Director for Education, and his staff, notably Aline Hill-Ries, Nicholas Ruocco, Peter L. Donhauser, Mary Grace Whalen, Stella Paul, and Linda Komaroff, coordinated the educational programs accompanying the exhibition. The resources of the Museum's Thomas J. Watson Library were consulted daily by curators, authors, and editors throughout the course of the project's preparation, and we are grateful for the help of William B. Walker, Arthur K. Watson Chief Librarian, and his entire staff, the members of which are too numerous to cite individually. Donna Manetta provided computer assistance helpful in the compilation of the Appendix.

Because of the encyclopedic scope of the Havemeyer collection, members of the staffs of a wide range of curatorial departments deserve special mention for their research and administrative help. Three of these should be singled out above all: Susan Alyson Stein, in the Department of European Paintings, not only provided her extraordinary Chronology but also tirelessly contributed to the exhibition and book in countless other ways, for which we are greatly indebted; Rebecca A. Rabinow, in European Paintings, was indefatigable in her hunt for elusive newspaper articles and periodical references and helped write labels for the paintings in the exhibition; Susan H. Barto, in American Decorative Arts, enthusiastically performed numerous tasks relating to ordering photographs and gathering from the Museum's disparate curatorial departments information for exhibition labels and captions for the catalogue. We also thank all the other individuals in the Museum's curatorial departments who assisted us, especially the following: in the Departments of American Art, H. Barbara Weinberg, Elisabeth Agro, Seraphine Wu, Ellin Rosenzweig, Donald E. Templeton, Gary Burnett, Edward Di Farnecio, and Sean Farrell; in the Department of Arms and Armor, Stuart W. Pyhrr and Morihiro Ogawa; in the Department of Asian Art, James C. Y. Watt, Judith G. Smith, Hiroshi Onishi, Suzanne G. Valenstein, Barbara B. Ford, Maxwell K. Hearn, Masako Watanabe, and Martin Fleischer; in the Drawings Department, Helen B. Mules, Calvin D. Brown, and Henrietta Susser; in Egyptian Art, Dorothea Arnold; in European Paintings, Everett Fahy, Katharine Baetjer, Keith Christiansen, Walter Liedtke, Dorothy Kellett, Anne M. P. Norton, Samantha Sizemore, Gary Kopp, Theresa King-Dickinson, Kathryn Butler, and Sarah Ganz; in European Sculpture and Decorative Arts, James David Draper, Jesse McNab, Clare Vincent, and Alice Zrebiec; in Greek and Roman Art, Carlos A. Picón and Joan R. Mertens; in Islamic Art, Daniel Walker, Marilyn Jenkins, and Stefano Carboni; in Medieval Art, Charles T. Little, and in Prints and Illustrated Books, Colta Ives, Janet S. Byrne, David W. Kiehl, Elliot Davis, and Elizabeth Wyckoff.

Many individuals outside the Museum assisted us in our research on the Havemeyer collection. The archives of dealers in New York and Paris were invaluable to the research effort. The authors are especially indebted to the archives of Durand-Ruel in Paris and to Caroline Durand-Ruel Godfroy; Stephen Bendixson, who sifted through The Dieterle Archives, Goupil/Boussod, Valadon et Cie stockbooks, The Resource Collections of the Getty Center for the History of Art and the Humanities, Malibu; Melissa De Medeiros, Librarian, M. Knoedler and Co., New York; Manuel Schmit, Galerie Schmit, Paris; Noriko Adachi, Galerie Nichido, Tokyo; Ay-Whang Hsia, Wildenstein and Co., Inc., New York; and Hiroko Yoda Saeki, Hiroko Saeki, Inc., New York. We have also turned to the auction houses, and in this context we extend our thanks to Michael Findlay, Polly J. Sartori, and Nancy McClelland of Christie's, New York, and David Nash and Thomas Cashin of Sotheby's, New York.

Many museums and libraries helped us by making their collections accessible and by answering numerous inquiries about works in their collections. We are grateful for the cooperation of the Shelburne Museum, Shelburne, Vermont, which houses many of the works that were inherited by the Havemeyers' daughter Electra Havemeyer Webb, particularly John Wilmerding, Chairman of the Board, David Sheldon, Director, Eloise Beil, Director of Collections, Celia Y. Oliver, Curator, Lauren B. Hewes, Assistant Curator, and Pauline H. Mitchell, Registrar. William Hennessey, Director, and Lori A. Mott, Assistant Registrar, of the University of Michigan Museum of Art, Ann Arbor, facilitated the loans of surviving architectural fragments from the Havemeyers' house and helped provide information about these objects. Sally E. Mansfield, The Denver Art Museum, and David Brooks, the Sterling and Francine Clark Art Institute, Williamstown, Massachusetts, kindly shared information relating to their collections.

The authors extend additional thanks to Frances Beatty, Richard L. Feigen and Co., Inc., New York; Celine Blair, Glasgow Art Gallery and Museum; Philippe Brame, Hector Brame-Jean Lorenceau, Paris; Janet M. Brooke, The Art Gallery of Ontario, Toronto; Laurene Buckley, Memorial Art Gallery of the University of Rochester; Elena Calvillo, The Detroit Institute of Arts; Sara Campbell, Norton Simon Museum of Art, Pasadena; Florence E. Coman, National Gallery of Art, Washington, D.C.; E. Jane Connell, Columbus Museum of Art; Anne Cullimore, Alex Reid and Lefevre, Ltd., London; Guy-Patrice Dauberville, Bernheim-Jeune et Cie, Paris; Professor Hamid Dabashi, Columbia University, for his translation of an Islamic inscription; Jacqueline Dugas, Henry E. Huntington Library and Art Gallery, San Marino, California; Jean Edmondson and Esperanza Sobrino, Acquavella Galleries, New York; Walter Feilchenfeldt; Patricia J. Fidler, Nelson-Atkins Museum of Art, Kansas City; Ileen Sheppard Gallagher, John and Mable Ringling Museum of Art, Sarasota;

Thomas H. Gibson and Alison Sherlock, Thomas Gibson Fine Art Ltd., London; Deborah Goodman, Yale University Art Gallery, New Haven; Stephen B. Jareckie, Worcester Art Museum, Massachusetts; Evie T. Joselow, Forbes Magazine Collection, New York; Katherine Kaplan, Kraushaar Galleries, Inc., New York; Nanette Kelekian; Steven Kern, Sterling and Francine Clark Art Institute, Williamstown, Massachusetts; Linda Krenzin, Walker Art Center, Minneapolis; Dr. Christian Lenz, Bayerische Staatsgemäldesammlungen, Munich; Margaret MacDonald, Hunterian Art Gallery, University of Glasgow; Irene Martin, Fondazione Thyssen-Bornemisza, Lugano; Linda Merrill, Freer Gallery of Art, Smithsonian Institution, Washington, D.C.; Linda Muehlig, Smith College Museum of Art, Northampton, Massachusetts; Mary Murphy, Jennifer Stone, and Martha Wolff, The Art Institute of Chicago; Terri O'Hara, The Brooklyn Museum; Carolyn B. Padwa, New Britain Museum of American Art, Connecticut; JoAnne C. Paradise, The Getty Center for the History of Art and the Humanities, Malibu; Kelly M. Pask and Perrin Stein, The J. Paul Getty Museum, Malibu; Nancy Ames Petersen, The Putnam Foundation/Timken Museum of Art, San Diego; Simon de Pury, Sotheby's, London; Susan Richardson, The Historical Society of the Town of Greenwich; Anne Roquebert, Musée d'Orsay, Paris; Betsy Rosasco, The Art Museum, Princeton University, New Jersey; Irene Roughton, The Chrysler Museum, Norfolk, Virginia; Robert Schmit, Galerie Schmit, Paris; David Scrase, The Fitzwilliam Museum, Cambridge; John Wilson, Cincinnati Art Museum; Alison Winter, Agnew's, London; Sachi A. Yanari, Allen Memorial Art Museum, Oberlin College, Ohio; and Sylvia Yount, Philadelphia Museum of Art.

We would like to single out for special mention the contributions of Frances Weitzenhoffer, who made the formation of the Havemeyers' collection of paintings the subject of her doctoral dissertation for City University of New York. Her 1982 dissertation, "The Creation of the Havemeyer Collection, 1875–1900," written under John Rewald's guidance, and her 1986 book, *The Havemeyers: Impressionism Comes to America*, were the basis for all of our work. Ms. Weitzenhoffer encouraged us when the project was first broached but tragically and to our most profound regret did not live to see the exhibition become a reality. Before her death in 1991, she gave all of her notes and papers relating to her work on the Havemeyers and their collecting to the Museum's Department of European Paintings, an act of extraordinary generosity. We are grateful to her husband, Max Weitzenhoffer, and to her colleague Frances Nauman for helping to facilitate her gift.

A number of Louisine and H. O. Havemeyer's descendants have helped us immeasurably by sharing their photographs of the family and their houses, lending works of art for exhibition and photographing, confirming details of family and business history, and relating reminiscences that furnish this extraordinary couple with a personal dimension. In this respect we extend our sincere thanks to Adaline Havemeyer Rand, Harry W. Havemeyer, Mrs. Horace Havemeyer, Jr, J. Watson Webb, Jr., Dr. Fletcher McDowell, George G. Frelinghuysen, the Honorable Peter H. B. Frelinghuysen, H.O.H. Frelinghuysen, Christian Havemeyer, Linden Havemeyer Wise, Adaline Havemeyer, Dundeen Catlin, Elliot Davis, Peter Frelinghuysen, Beatrice Frelinghuysen Van Roijen, Rodney P. Frelinghuysen, Adaline Havemeyer Ogilvie-Laing, Frederick Frelinghuysen, and George L. K. Frelinghuysen.

Although the Museum's Havemeyer holdings number in the thousands, we felt from the beginning that we would not do justice to the Havemeyers and their collection if we did not include many of the important works that did not come to the Metropolitan. We therefore express our deep appreciation of the generosity of the lenders, public and private, who agreed to share their works of art with the many visitors to the exhibition *Splendid Legacy: The Havemeyer Collection*. All of the lenders who do not wish to remain anonymous are listed elsewhere in this catalogue, but we would like to single out the Shelburne Museum for parting with paintings and objects normally on display in their Memorial Building for this landmark show, the National Gallery of Art for the loan of several of its most popular works of art, and The University of Michigan School of Art and College of Architecture and Urban Planning and the University of Michigan Museum of Art for allowing us to borrow many of the architectural elements from the Havemeyer house.

Finally, we are most grateful for the contributions of Janice H. Levin, the Frelinghuysen Foundation, and The Peter J. Sharp Foundation Fund to defray the enormous costs of this extensive catalogue. We also extend our sincere gratitude to the funders who made the exhibition possible, The Annenberg Foundation, The Dillon Fund, Cowen & Company, the William Randolph Hearst Foundation, and The Real Estate Council of The Metropolitan Museum of Art.

Alice Cooney Frelinghuysen and Gary Tinterow, Co-curators of the Exhibition

Lenders to the Exhibition

The Art Museum, Princeton University, Princeton

The Brooklyn Museum, New York

The Chrysler Museum, Norfolk

Sterling and Francine Clark Art Institute, Williamstown

The Denver Art Museum, Denver

National Gallery of Art, Washington, D.C.

Philadelphia Museum of Art, Philadelphia

Shelburne Museum, Shelburne

Smith College Museum of Art, Northampton

The Putnam Foundation/Timken Museum of Art, San Diego

University of Michigan Museum of Art, Ann Arbor

Walters Art Gallery, Baltimore

Worcester Art Museum, Worcester

Yale University Art Gallery, New Haven

Private collections

Note to the Reader

Titles are given in English except when the foreign-language form represents the official title used by a museum in an English-speaking country. For more on titles and attributions, see the note at the beginning of the Appendix.

Japanese personal names appear in Japanese style, surname first, except in the case of individuals living in and writing for the West who have chosen to adopt the Western order.

Numbers preceded by the letter "A" given after titles of paintings, watercolors, and drawings refer to listings in the Appendix.

The Havemeyers acquired works of art in the United States and abroad. Quotations of asking and purchase prices are given in the currency used. Prior to World War I the exchange rates for the French franc, Spanish peseta, and Italian lira were equivalent—roughly one-fifth or 20 percent of a dollar. An English pound was roughly five times the value of a dollar.

For full listings of abbreviated references used in notes and the Appendix, see the Bibliography and Key to Exhibition Abbreviations.

Abbreviations used for names in citations of correspondence are: MC, Mary Cassatt; CD-R, Charles Durand-Ruel; D-R, Durand-Ruel; GD-R, George Durand-Ruel; JD-R, Joseph Durand-Ruel; PD-R, Paul Durand-Ruel; TD, Théodore Duret; CLF, Charles Lang Freer; RdM, Ricardo de Madrazo; AEH, A. E. Harnisch; EH, Electra Havemeyer; HH, Horace Havemeyer; HOH, H. O. Havemeyer; LWH, Louisine W. Havemeyer; DK, Dikran Kelekian

In the Chronology, sources are not given for acquisition information derived exclusively from files on individual paintings in the MMA Department of European Paintings Archives or from Gretchen Wold's research notes for the Appendix.

Unpublished sources and archives consulted

The Dieterle Archives, Getty Center, Malibu: The Dieterle Archives, Goupil/Boussod, Valadon et Cie, stock books, The Resource Collections of the Getty Center for the History of Art and the Humanities, Malibu

Durand-Ruel Archives

Havemeyer correspondence: letters to the Havemeyers on deposit in the MMA Department of European Paintings Archives

Knoedler sales books

Weitzenhoffer files: the archives of Frances Weitzenhoffer, which include unpublished notes, newspaper clippings, photographs, and originals, copies, or transcriptions of legal documents, correspondence, publications, and gallery records, notably from Durand-Ruel and Knoedler stock books, on deposit in the MMA Department of European Paintings Archives

THE HAVEMEYER COLLECTION

European and American Pictures

Plate 1. J.-A.-D. Ingres. *Joseph-Antoine Moltedo*, ca. 1807–14. Oil on canvas, 29⅝ x 22⅞ in. (75.3 x 58.1 cm). H. O. Havemeyer Collection, Bequest of Mrs. H. O. Havemeyer, 1929 (29.100.23) A330

THE HAVEMEYER PICTURES

GARY TINTEROW

"One of the most magnificent gifts of works of art ever made to a museum by a single individual,"[1] the 1929 bequest of Louisine Havemeyer transformed the collections of the Metropolitan Museum. Ultimately, two years were required to settle Mrs. Havemeyer's estate, during which time her three children, Horace Havemeyer, Electra Havemeyer Webb, and Adaline Havemeyer Frelinghuysen, augmented from their own inheritances the 142 works that she specifically designated for the Museum as a memorial to her husband, H. O. Havemeyer. The children donated another 111 paintings, pastels, and drawings, 213 prints, including 34 by Rembrandt, and vast quantities of Oriental ceramics, Japanese armor, textiles, and bronzes.[2] This is a collection called by the Metropolitan's director "invaluable . . . in its range and the high quality of its specimens," sufficient to "furnish a museum in itself."[3]

At the Museum the impact of the Havemeyer bequest was immediate and profound. It "doubles the prestige of the Metropolitan Museum in painting," wrote the critic and art historian Frank Jewett Mather in 1930. Finding real strength in the Metropolitan's collection of European painting only in the Dutch and Flemish schools and noting that its holdings of modern European painting were inferior to those of Chicago and Boston, Mather observed that the bequest instantly made the institution "the premier Museum for nineteenth century French art in America, and one of the two or three most distinguished in this branch in the world." Thanks to the great depth of the Havemeyer collection of French painting of the second half of the nineteenth century—its Corots, Courbets, Manets, Degases, and works by the Impressionists—the Metropolitan has retained this preeminence in the United States and in the world is second in this area only to the collection of the French state at the Musée d'Orsay in Paris. Mather perceived a further advantage conferred by the bequest: the release of considerable acquisition funds that otherwise would have been devoted to

French painting and could subsequently be applied to filling the "lamentable gaps in the older schools, particularly in the Italian field."[4] And the Havemeyers' gift has yielded another result, one that Mather could not have anticipated, for the quality of the French pictures has attracted the donation of smaller but no less choice collections of French nineteenth- and twentieth-century art—Stephen C. Clark's twenty pictures in 1961 and the extraordinary group of fifty-three paintings that the Honorable Walter H. Annenberg has announced he will bequeath to the Museum.

A legendary assemblage, the Havemeyer collection is known throughout the world for its obvious strengths: the unparalleled group of figure paintings by Corot, the magnificent nudes and portraits by Courbet, the masterpieces by Manet, the exhaustive series of paintings, pastels, drawings, and bronzes by Degas, the great landscapes and still lifes by Cézanne, the pivotal canvases by Monet. Today many observers rightly associate the Havemeyer pictures with Mary Cassatt, the expatriate American who painted in France, whom Mrs. Havemeyer called the godmother of the collection, even though Cassatt's own work is not, in fact, extensively represented in it. But the true depth and range of the Havemeyer collection are still not well known, largely because one part of it is dispersed throughout the Museum, and the other part is dispersed throughout the world. Few know that the Metropolitan received only the glorious tip of the Havemeyer iceberg, and that some of the finest French pictures at the National Gallery of Art in Washington, D.C., The Brooklyn Museum, The Denver Art Museum, the J. Paul Getty Museum in Malibu, and Kansas City's Nelson-Atkins Museum of Art were formerly owned by the Havemeyers. Few know that the pictures Electra Havemeyer Webb put on display in the Shelburne Museum, which she founded in Shelburne, Vermont, were a legacy inherited from her parents. Few realize that the Havemeyer bequest established the core of the Metropolitan Museum's collection of Japanese decorative arts and

Plate 2. Edgar Degas. *Ballet Rehearsal*, ca. 1876. Gouache and pastel over monotype, 21¾ x 26¾ in. (55.3 x 68 cm). Nelson-Atkins Museum of Art, Kansas City, Missouri, Acquired through the Kenneth A. and Helen F. Spencer Foundation Acquisition Fund (F73–30) A215

greatly expanded the representation of its Oriental ceramics. And even fewer are aware that the Havemeyers owned highly important old masters—a distinguished group of paintings by Rembrandt and Hals, the greatest Bronzino in America, and two of the finest canvases El Greco ever executed. Thus the Havemeyers were not only the premier American patrons of French painting of the late nineteenth century, they were also pathbreaking collectors in uncharted fields for which they created a demand and established a taste among contemporary collectors like Henry Clay Frick or Col. Oliver Payne.

Upon examination we come to see that if the range of the Havemeyers' collecting was surprising, so too were their motives—nothing more than pure enjoyment of art and deep respect for the artist's work. Mrs. Havemeyer could have been describing herself when

she wrote admiringly of the French: "The people love art, the people know art, the people buy art, the people live with their art."[5] Unlike so many of their wealthy peers—Sugar King H. O. Havemeyer was certainly an extremely rich man at the turn of the century—the Havemeyers did not collect to attain social standing: they set themselves apart from Mrs. Astor's "four hundred" and did not move in fashionable social circles. Nor did they attempt to create a monument to their taste and erudition. Unlike J. Pierpont Morgan, Frick, William T. Walters, William Wilson Corcoran, or Isabella Stewart Gardner, they did not establish a museum to bear their name. With characteristic modesty and reasonableness, Mrs. Havemeyer wrote her children before her death, "I have made very few stipulations in my will in regard to the placing or care of the Collection because I believe there are those who are as

4

Plate 3. Claude Monet. *The Drawbridge*, 1874. Oil on canvas, 21 x 25 in. (53.3 x 63.5 cm). Shelburne Museum, Shelburne, Vermont (27.1.2–109). A395

Plate 4. Camille Pissarro. *The Cabbage Gatherers*, ca. 1878–79. Gouache on silk, 6½ x 20½ in. (16.5 x 52.1 cm). Private collection. A427

5

intelligent and as interested as I, in the care and conservation of a valuable gift." [6]

The Havemeyer collection, very much a joint creation, was fifty years in the making. Louisine Elder and Henry O. Havemeyer made their first important purchases individually about 1876–77, some years before they were married to each other.[7] From their marriage in 1883 until Mr. Havemeyer's death in 1907, all decisions regarding acquisitions were taken jointly. Although her emphasis shifted slightly away from the old masters after 1907, Mrs. Havemeyer continued faithfully along the course they had charted together, at first buying paintings that her husband had known and liked, later acquiring some of the Spanish masters he had admired, in addition to the modern French paintings he had come to love. But the two did have distinct interests and preferences that were apparent from the beginning. When he was twenty-nine, Harry Havemeyer bought a large group of Japanese decorative arts at the 1876 Centennial Exhibition in Philadelphia, thereby announcing his affinity with three-dimensional objects and works from the Far East and particularly Japan, which was opened for trade with the West only in the previous decade. Artists and advanced collectors in Paris, London, and New York were fascinated by the art that suddenly had become available from the East, and Havemeyer's interest in it placed him if not in the vanguard at least close to sophisticates with a taste for what was currently fashionable.

Louisine Elder struck out on a more adventurous path. After meeting Cassatt while she attended a kind of finishing school in Paris, the twenty-two-year-old Miss Elder scraped together funds from her allowance to purchase a pastel Cassatt had pointed out to her, probably in the window of an artists' supplier such as Père Tanguy or Lochard, Degas's *Ballet Rehearsal* (pl. 2),[8] which she bought for Fr 500, about $100. By 1877 Degas had only recently begun to sell his works with any regularity, and he had just suffered a huge financial reversal as a result of his brother's bad investments with family money. He was so happy about the sale that he wrote Cassatt to thank her for her help. As Mrs. Havemeyer reminisced in her memoirs: "Five hundred francs was a large sum for me to spend in those days, and represented many little economies and even some privations; also it was just half my art balance and I still wanted a Monet and a Pissarro." [9] She probably bought the Monet (pl. 3) in the same year and the

Figure 1. Edouard Manet. *Boy with a Sword*, 1861. Oil on canvas, 51 ⅝ x 36¾ in. (131.1 x 93.3 cm). Gift of Erwin Davis, 1889 (89.21.2)

Pissarro (pl. 4) shortly thereafter. (Pissarro was even more grateful for his sale to "la Demoiselle américaine" than Degas had been for his own. In a letter to a friend he called it only a "drop of water against a large fire," but it assuaged his despair over his finances.)[10] These purchases were prescient in several respects. The Havemeyers would assemble the world's largest and most complete collection of Degas's work, and many of their choices, like Louisine's first, would be guided by Cassatt. Thus Mrs. Havemeyer recalled, "As always, Miss Cassatt was firm in her judgment." [11] Louisine Havemeyer remained true to her interest in the Impressionists and their predecessors Corot and Courbet, and, like Cassatt, she was indifferent to the talents of such younger artists as Gauguin, van Gogh, and, later, Matisse and Picasso.

Harry Havemeyer was still acting on the taste of the previous generation of collectors when he made his first purchases of paintings, in the early 1880s: academic Salon pictures and works by the Barbizon school artists Corot, Diaz, Millet, and Rousseau. But the fact that he was looking at French rather than American or German paintings is evidence of a certain discrimination. The majority of American collectors bought American paintings; those who were interested in European art generally bought paintings of the School of Düsseldorf. And of course he could buy only what was available. The Goupil, Vibert Gallery, founded in New York in 1847 and later called M. Knoedler and Co., specialized in importing Barbizon pictures into the United States, where the demand for them had been increasing since the 1850s, especially among such discerning Boston collectors as Quincy Adams Shaw and Thomas Gold Appleton. New York collectors like August Belmont, John Wolfe, Alexander Stewart, and Cornelius Vanderbilt also owned Barbizon paintings, but they tended to favor the flashier, often erotically charged work of French

Salon artists like Couture and Cabanel, which was also sold by Goupil, over the earnest peasants and rural landscapes of Millet, Troyon, Diaz, and Rousseau. (In fact, the appeal of European art to the new American collectors was so strong that American artists and their dealers organized several—ultimately unsuccessful—attempts to impose duties and trade restrictions.)[12] However, the work of younger French artists such as those Louisine Elder patronized in Paris was not yet available in New York. Paintings by Courbet, Manet, and the Impressionists were shown in America only in a few isolated instances before Durand-Ruel mounted his large exhibition in New York in the spring of 1886.

Prior to 1886 the one notable showing of avant-garde French painting in the United States had been organized by Alfred Cadart, the founder of the Société

Plate 5. Edouard Manet. *The Salmon*, 1869. Oil on canvas, 28 ¼ x 35 ⅜ in. (71.8 x 89.9 cm). Shelburne Museum, Shelburne, Vermont (27.1.3–24) A350

des Aquafortistes in Paris. For an exhibition held in Boston and in New York in 1866, he brought over a group of etchings by contemporary artists as well as paintings by Boudin, Corot, Jongkind, and the young Monet. Also included was Courbet's imposing hunt scene *The Quarry*, which was bought from the show for the Museum of Fine Arts in Boston. Critics were extremely receptive, and numerous other sales were made. It was logical then for Paul Durand-Ruel, who had been dealing in works by Degas, Monet, Pissarro, and Renoir since the 1870s, to attempt to capitalize on the vogue for French painting in America. To this end the dealer, still in difficult financial straits after enduring the deep recession of the early 1880s in France, organized his 1886 exhibition, sending 264 works on paper—pastels, watercolors, and drawings—to James F. Sutton's American Art Association. The newspapers were extraordinarily enthusiastic. "There are technical lessons to be learned from the pictures of Manet and Degas which are worth something to every artist who has the power of intelligent discrimination," wrote the critic for the *New York Tribune*. Collectors were exhorted to take the plunge:

> These pictures represent an interesting movement in foreign art, and the time has gone by for Americans to wait to learn of art movements from ancient history. When Delacroix and Gericault were leading the "romantic" movement, and when Constable was influencing French art, Americans, placidly indifferent, collected "old masters." When Couture was in his prime, we were collecting Dusseldorf pictures, and there was no general enthusiasm over Millet and Rousseau until their works were skillfully "boomed" after their deaths. M. Durand Ruel may be anxious to "boom" the paintings of the impressionists in which, however, we imagine that he sincerely believes. . . . Despite the bizarre effects and violent contrasts of crude colors which the impressionists have found in nature, and despite the speechless indignation of staid Academicians who beheld these effects yesterday, these versatile and technically clever painters have done some work of fine quality.[13]

When Durand-Ruel moved the exhibition from its commercial venue to an educational one, the National Academy of Design, in order to evade duties, Mrs. Havemeyer lent two of her paintings, the Monet and the Pissarro she had bought before she married, to the slightly expanded presentation of 287 works. For the first time Mr. Havemeyer strongly considered purchasing a Manet, the *Boy with a Sword* (fig. 1), lent to the

enlarged show by Erwin Davis, a speculative collector. He told his wife that it was "too much" for him,[14] but he did buy Manet's still life *The Salmon* (pl. 5), no doubt encouraged by the many reviews that singled it out. One critic, for example, wrote: "Manet's 'Still Life,' again, is one of the natures mortes in which he was confessedly incomparable, and is one of his best and most easily understood; it contains a specimen of his capitally scaly fish, and a cut lemon, surely the most cruelly sour lemon ever painted."[15] With the single exception of *By the Seashore* (pl. 6), their only painting by Renoir, acquired in 1889, the Havemeyers would not buy modern French paintings again until 1894, the year they purchased three Monets, a Sisley, and another Manet. Nevertheless, the 1886 exhibition had an extremely important effect on the formation of the Havemeyers' collection. For one, it allowed them to survey a wide spectrum of Impressionist art—for the last time, because the Impressionists would no longer exhibit together. Although Mr. and Mrs. Havemeyer bought only one painting from the show, they kept others such as Degas's *Ballet from "Robert le Diable"* (pl. 7) in mind and eventually acquired them. The exhibition also gave the Havemeyers the opportunity to acquaint themselves with Paul Durand-Ruel, who, with his sons, would become their almost exclusive purveyor of pictures. Finally, it enabled them to have their interest in contemporary art ratified by the leading critics of the day. In this context and in light of the knowledge that the Havemeyers would form important collections of Spanish painting and Japanese art as well as of modern French painting, it is fascinating to read that a reviewer of the 1886 exhibition believed that the most important influences on the Impressionists were Spanish painting, "Manet—that latter-day Velasquez," and "color and composition . . . borrowed from Japan."[16]

In 1886 Mr. Havemeyer bought not only his first Manet but also his first Rembrandts—two etchings out of a New York auction. For the next six years the Havemeyers focused their collecting on the work of Dutch and Flemish artists of the seventeenth century: van der Capelle, Codde, Cuyp, Hals, de Hooch, Metsu, Mettling, van der Neer, van Ostade, and Teniers, in addition to Rembrandt.[17] These relics of the prosperous mercantile culture of the Netherlands were the perfect accompaniment to Mr. Havemeyer's meteoric rise as a merchant prince: the Sugar Trust, organized in 1887, posted profits of twenty-five million dollars in its first

Plate 6. Pierre-Auguste Renoir. *By the Seashore*, 1883. Oil on canvas, 36¼ x 28½ in. (92.1 x 72.4 cm). H. O. Havemeyer Collection, Bequest of Mrs. H. O. Havemeyer, 1929 (29.100.125) A460

Plate 7. Edgar Degas. *The Ballet from "Robert le Diable,"* 1871. Oil on canvas, 26 x 21 3/8 in. (66 x 54.3 cm). H. O. Havemeyer Collection, Bequest of Mrs. H. O. Havemeyer, 1929 (29.100.552) A202

two and one-half years. The nineteenth-century paintings the Havemeyers bought in the late 1880s were closely akin to the old master paintings they concurrently pursued: "brown" paintings of the Barbizon school or the so-called generation of 1830—landscapes by Rousseau, Millet, Dupré, and Troyon, figure paintings and watercolors by Barye, Decamps, and Daumier, the last a Rembrandt of the nineteenth century. Not until two years after the interiors of the Havemeyers' new house at 1 East 66th Street were completed in 1892[18] did they begin to purchase contemporary art in quantity.

With the acquisition in 1892 of *Portrait of a Young Man in a Broad-Brimmed Hat* (A459), then thought to be by Rembrandt, Harry Havemeyer declared his Rembrandt Room (the library, in which his Dutch pictures hung) (fig. 30) complete. After his death Mrs. Havemeyer's sole move in the field of Rembrandt's art was

a regrettable purchase of a fake (A455) in 1922. After 1892 Mr. Havemeyer's interests shifted toward nineteenth-century painting, especially Courbet: "Next to the Rembrandts—my favorite," Mrs. Havemeyer overheard him say.[19] He continued to buy works by Barye, Corot, Decamps (pl. 8), Dupré, Millet (pl. 9), and Troyon through 1895, but thereafter narrowed his focus in mid-century painting to Corot and Courbet, with an occasional purchase of a Daumier or a Millet. In 1897 the Havemeyers began pursuing old master paintings again, but they no longer looked at Northern European artists; instead they bought Italian and Spanish masters, with an occasional Clouet, Poussin, or Cranach (pl. 56). Typically, a trip to Italy or to Spain would result in numerous acquisitions, or at least the beginning of negotiations for sought-after works. And visits to the great princely collections and museums in Paris, Florence, Rome, and Madrid encouraged the

Plate 8. Alexandre-Gabriel Decamps. *The Experts*, 1837. Oil on canvas, 18 ¼ x 25 ¼ in. (46.4 x 64.1 cm). H. O. Havemeyer Collection, Bequest of Mrs. H. O. Havemeyer, 1929 (29.100.196) A183

Plate 9. J.-F. Millet. *Peasant Children at Goose Pond*, ca. 1865–68. Pastel on paper, 15 ¼ x 20 ½ in. (38.7 x 52.1 cm). Yale University Art Gallery, New Haven, Gift of J. Watson Webb, B.A. 1907, and Electra Havemeyer Webb (1942.298) A377

Plate 10. Francisco de Goya y Lucientes. *Bartolomé Sureda y Miserol*, ca. 1803/4. Oil on canvas, 47⅛ x 31¼ in. (119.7 x 79.4 cm). National Gallery of Art, Washington, D.C., Gift of Mr. and Mrs. P.H.B. Frelinghuysen in memory of her father and mother, Mr. and Mrs. H. O. Havemeyer (1941.10.1) A291

Havemeyers to refine their tastes and to lift to a higher plane the ambitions they harbored for their own collection. Louisine and Harry Havemeyer acquired many works specifically because they reminded them of paintings seen elsewhere:

> Our collecting . . . took us abroad into lands little frequented by travelers in those days; into out-of-the-way places, where no one would imagine art treasures could be found; into unknown bypaths where, high among the hills, a painter had left a

Madonna to hang unknown and unobserved in the little chapel among the trees; into palaces which had been adorned by works of the great masters; into the villas of the *signori*, or into the tiny apartments of the impoverished nobility, where just an heirloom or two remained unsold. It brought us into contact with people of many nationalities, with collectors and with critics, with gentile and with Jew. It enabled us to penetrate into some vast estates where the dealer had not been permitted to apply his rake. . . . As the French say, Miss Cassatt had the "flair" of an old hunter,

Plate 11. Francisco de Goya y Lucientes. *Thérèse Louise de Sureda*, ca. 1803/4. Oil on canvas, 47 ⅛ x 31 ¼ in.(119.7 x 79.4 cm). National Gallery of Art, Washington, D.C., Gift of Mr. and Mrs. P.H.B. Frelinghuysen in memory of her father and mother, Mr. and Mrs. H. O. Havemeyer (1942.3.1) A292

and her experience had made her as patient as Job and as wise as Solomon in art matters; Mr. Havemeyer had the true energy of a collector, while I— well, I had the time of my life.[20]

The Havemeyers' Goyas can be used to illustrate the procedure they followed to build a collection, the nature of the collection they were attempting to assemble, and the pitfalls encountered when their method was applied to artists who were no longer living. In all they acquired seventeen paintings ascribed to Goya. Their first

purchase, a pair of portraits of Bartolomé and Thérèse Sureda (pls. 10, 11), made in September 1897 for under Pts 50,000, less than $10,000, was their best. Obtained through Durand-Ruel before the collectors took their first trip to Spain in 1901, these handsome portraits of about 1803/4 were bought not because they were reminiscent of pictures previously seen but because they appealed to the Havemeyers' sensibilities. The young man, Sureda, an engineer who had worked in England and then returned to Madrid to direct the royal furnishings factory, is shown to be sincere, informal, confident of his place among his peers. The young woman is erect and proud, with the almost audacious stare of a *maja*, the kind of impudent regard Manet used in paintings like *Mlle V . . . in the Costume of an Espada* (pl. 25), which the Havemeyers would buy the next year. These features notwithstanding, the most exceptional quality the two portraits possess, in terms of the Havemeyer collection, is their authenticity. Of the fifteen Havemeyer Goyas, these are two of only four that generally are accepted by authorities. *Young Lady Wearing a Mantilla and a Basquiña* (A293), now in the National Gallery of Art, is unquestioned, and one other work, *Doña Narcisa Barañana de Goicoechea* (pl. 233), is widely regarded as authentic, although doubts about it have been raised. The remaining eleven are certainly not by Goya. Some have been attributed to other known artists, such as Eugenio Lucas, but most are simply copies of authentic paintings or, worse, outright forgeries.

How is it that the Havemeyers could have bought eleven questionable Goyas? Some of them, Louisine Havemeyer admitted, were taken simply for the fun of it: Mr. Havemeyer "appeared delighted when one morning Miss Cassatt and I said we were going out in quest of a Greco. 'You had better add a Goya while you are about it,' said my husband."[21] Their second purchase in the realm of Goyas, a portrait of the Duke of Wellington (pl. 226), illustrates the problem. Joseph Wicht, a dealer with entrée to Spanish society who was known to Cassatt, brought this painting to the attention of the Havemeyers and Cassatt during the collectors' first sojourn in Spain. Normally quite circumspect and often suspicious, the Havemeyers seemed to suspend judgment of anyone introduced by Cassatt. Mrs. Havemeyer wrote that they had found Wicht "perfectly straight" and seemed to admire that he "said frankly that he knew little about pictures."[22] Yet, in spite of the latter remark, she maintained that Wicht's premature death in a hunting accident "was a great loss to us" and was sure that their "collection would have been far richer in Spanish art if he had lived."[23] The Wellington portrait came complete with an impressive provenance, presumably supplied by Wicht: the Duke of Montalava, a friend of Wellington's, had commissioned it while the English commander was routing the French army from Spain. "Wellington became dissatisfied with it and insisted . . . that Goya must change his face. . . . Words ran high and weapons were

drawn."[24] Mrs. Havemeyer even imagined "Goya tossing his artistic little nose in the air in defiance of Wellington's red cloth and gold braid."[25] When the painting was finally acquired—Cassatt continued negotiations in the Havemeyers' absence, setting a price of Fr 17,975 (about $3,600)—the collectors were supplied with documents certifying the apocryphal story, and another of their agents, Ricardo de Madrazo, went so far as to profess that his grandfather had actually separated the quarreling duo![26] Needless to say, the painting is a fake.

Because she wished to assemble a complete and representative collection of Goyas, Mrs. Havemeyer fell prey to untrustworthy purveyors who knew she had a set list of categories that she was determined to fill. "Everyone who collects Goya must have a portrait of the Queen and one of the Duchess of Alba," she maintained.[27] The execrable fake portrait of María Luisa (A299), for example, was purchased from Théodore Duret, a good critic but a dishonest dealer, who surely could not have been deceived by this painting as he deceived Mrs. Havemeyer.

The Havemeyers' problems with fakes did not arise because they considered their judgment infallible— they had evidence to the contrary: by the time of Mrs. Havemeyer's death in 1929, three of their supposed Goyas—*Doña Maria Teresa de Borbón y Vallabriga, Condesa de Chinchón (The Princesa de la Paz)* (pl. 12), *Portrait of a Lady with a Guitar* (pl. 240), and *Portrait of an Officer on Horseback* (A298)—already had been demoted. Nor were they novices ignorant of the tricks of the trade. Mrs. Havemeyer's memoirs contain a passage, fittingly included in her chapter on Spain, on the custom of having a painting copied before selling the original and the practice of later generations of selling the copy as if it were the genuine article.[28] (Several such copies gravitated to the Havemeyer collection, and the Havemeyers, in turn, paid to have a copy of *Young Lady Wearing a Mantilla and a Basquiña* made for its owner before they took possession of the picture.) Rather, they were fooled because they followed their enthusiasms and, even more, those of Cassatt. Sadly, Cassatt was an aficionada but no connoisseur of old master painting. And there were few reputable experts and virtually no scholarly books to consult—art history was in its infancy. Yet Mrs. Havemeyer was conscious of the risk. She wrote, "In art . . . believe nothing that you hear and still less of what you

Figure 2. Francisco de Goya y Lucientes. *Condesa de Chinchón*, 1800. Oil on canvas, 85 ⅛ x 56 ¾ in. (216 x 144 cm). Private collection, Madrid

Plate 12. Attributed to Francisco de Goya y Lucientes. *Doña Maria Teresa de Borbón y Vallabriga, Condesa de Chinchón (The Princesa de la Paz)*. Oil on canvas, 40 x 31 in. (101.6 x 78.7 cm). Shelburne Museum, Shelburne, Vermont (27.1.1–153) A295

see, and then pray the gods to protect you. . . . I firmly believe there is nothing under the sun that cannot be imitated, and with such consummate deceit that it is necessary to know the art of the imitator to discover the imitation."[29]

The Goya of which the Havemeyers were most proud, the *Majas on a Balcony* (pl. 13), has recently been challenged by this author.[30] Mrs. Havemeyer recorded in her memoirs that three years were needed to negotiate the purchase of the picture.[31] Paul Durand-Ruel undertook several trips to Madrid specifically to procure it. When they finally succeeded in October 1904, they could rightly rejoice in the acquisition of a celebrated work. The painting came from the collection of the son of a royal prince, the Infante Don Sebastian Gabriel de Borbón, himself the son of Queen Isabella, and Don Sebastian had acquired it before 1835 and probably after the artist's death in 1828. Don Sebastian's painting was often on display in Madrid, where it was photographed in the 1860s; there was, however, another version of the picture (fig. 3), which

had belonged to the French king Louis Philippe and had been exhibited in the Galerie Espagnole in Paris, where Manet, among many others, could have seen it. Reproductions of both versions appeared in publications from the 1860s on, and no one disputed the authenticity of either—although copies of both paintings were known and known to be false. Today, we can conjecture that Xavier Goya likely had the Havemeyer version of the *Majas* made for sale to Don Sebastian and kept the original available for future sale; in fact, Xavier sold the authentic canvas to Louis Philippe's agent, Baron Taylor, in 1836.

After the Havemeyers acquired it, "*Las Majas al Balcón* for some reason went to Paris, and remained a while with Miss Cassatt and was greatly admired by the critics who dropped into her apartment to see it."[32] We now know that the painting went to Paris because it was in problematic condition. Photographs in the Durand-Ruel Archives of the *Majas on a Balcony* before and after treatment show that there were extensive losses in the background and a certain amount of re-

Plate 13. Attributed to Francisco de Goya y Lucientes. *Majas on a Balcony*. Oil on canvas, 76¾ x 49½ in. (195 x 125.7 cm). H. O. Havemeyer Collection, Bequest of Mrs. H. O. Havemeyer, 1929 (29.100.10) A296 (Here called copy after Goya, ca. 1827–35)

Figure 3. Francisco de Goya y Lucientes. *Majas on a Balcony*, 1808–12. Oil on canvas, 63⅞ x 42⅛ in. (162 x 107 cm). Private collection

painting in the foreground. The repairs were done well and resulted in a convincing picture, but an unusual quality in the manner of execution nevertheless remained. The French critic and collector Roger Marx noticed something peculiar, although it did not lead him to question the attribution. Cassatt reported that "Marx congratulates you on the possession of this Goya which he considers very fine, and says it is extraordinary for Goya to paint the women's faces as if they were miniatures."[33] Today we can understand Marx's remark as an insight into the overly meticulous execution of a copyist. By contrast the original, which is now in a private collection in Switzerland, is masterfully painted in broad strokes. The faces are strongly built up of flesh tones mixed with white, resulting in masklike visages very different in effect from the faces in the Havemeyer painting, which are laid in with thin washes. The dresses in the Swiss canvas are rendered freely and summarily in an almost slapdash manner, without any niggling detail. The author of the Havemeyer picture mimicked Goya's bravura brushwork in the dresses as in other features, but was overly descriptive. Even more important, he misunderstood the point of the Swiss painting—the exchange of a confidence between the two women—and depicted two figures that lean toward each other without purpose. When the copy was exhibited at the Metropolitan in the great Havemeyer exhibition of 1930, Mather, like Marx before him, discerned weaknesses that he had not previously noticed when he had viewed it in the Havemeyer house. He called it "a picture that has lost by coming nearer the light of day . . . an incomplete impressionist picture."[34] In retrospect, it is all the more frustrating to read in Mrs. Havemeyer's memoirs that she and her husband had attempted but failed to see in Cadiz the authentic version of the *Majas*, which was then in the Montpensier family collection and which they had vainly hoped to buy.[35]

The Havemeyers' Spanish pictures paradoxically include their greatest paintings—El Greco's *Portrait of a Cardinal* and *View of Toledo* (pls. 59, 60)—and their worst—the putative Goya said to represent Vicente Lopez (pl. 256). Louisine and Harry Havemeyer discovered El Greco at the Prado: "It was these portraits [in the Prado] that first attracted Miss Cassatt and Mr. Havemeyer to Greco. . . . always the fascination of that painter threw a spell over us. We could not resist his art; its intensity, its individuality, its freedom and its color attracted us with irresistible force."[36] The Havemeyers bought photographs of as many El Grecos (and Goyas) as they could find, set out to meet Manuel Cossío, the author of the single monograph on El Greco in existence at the time—evidence of their somewhat scholarly approach to collecting—and made a pilgrimage to Toledo to see the *Burial of the Conde de Orgaz*. Both were deeply moved, and Mr. Havemeyer resolved to acquire an important picture by the master. He scoffed when Cassatt first informed him of a portrait of a cardinal wearing spectacles but he came around, and four years of negotiations ensued before he could call it his own. Cassatt informed Mrs. Havemeyer: "My head is set on you having that picture for the new gallery. . . . It would be rather a triumph to possess a really fine Greco."[37] At some point during those four years, Durand-Ruel presented Mr. Havemeyer with the opportunity to acquire the portrait *Fray Hortensio Félix Paravicino* (fig. 4), now at the Museum of Fine Arts in Boston, a painting we would be hard-pressed to call inferior to the portrait of the cardinal. But Mr. Havemeyer was characteristically steadfast when he was in pursuit of an object and declined *Hortensio*. Mrs. Havemeyer recorded his reply to Durand-Ruel, "Why buy a monk when you [can] have a cardinal?"[38]

The merits of both *Portrait of a Cardinal* and *View of Toledo*, as well as of the Havemeyers' authentic Goyas, are indisputable, but the list of other fine Spanish paintings that eluded them is a sad one to record. Goya's *Family of the Infante Don Luis de Borbón*, his *Condesa de Chinchón* (fig. 2), and his portrait of the Duchess of Alba that is now the pride of the Hispanic Society of America in New York are just three of the extraordinary Spanish pictures that were offered to the Havemeyers but not purchased for one reason or another. Some were too expensive, others were not to their taste, others were proposed yet were not available. But it is truly lamentable that they did succeed in buying a fake portrait of La Chinchón (pl. 12), a fake portrait of the Duchess of Alba (pl. 240), and a hideous fake portrait of Queen María Luisa (A298).

Their lapses in discrimination notwithstanding, the Havemeyers were prescient in their taste for Spanish painting and instrumental in introducing the fashion for this kind of art to America. This was a role of which they were quite conscious: "We were, so to speak, to open the market for Grecos and Goyas, at least in the United States."[39] To cite one example, Mr. and Mrs. Havemeyer were responsible for securing and bringing to this country El Greco's monumental *Assumption of the Virgin* (fig. 66), now at The Art Institute of Chicago. Durand-Ruel had an option to buy the altarpiece, but insufficient reserves to purchase it for stock, so Mr. Havemeyer advanced the money. At thirteen feet in height the painting was too large for the Havemeyers' picture gallery, and the Metropolitan, which was in the

Figure 4. El Greco (Domenikos Theotokopoulos). *Fray Hortensio Félix Paravicino*, 1609. Oil on canvas, 44 ⅛ x 33 ⅞ in. (112 x 86.1 cm). Museum of Fine Arts, Boston, Isaac Sweetser Fund (04.234)

Plate 14. Camille Corot. *The Destruction of Sodom*, 1843/57. Oil on canvas, 36⅜ x 71⅜ in. (92.4 x 181.3 cm). H. O. Havemeyer Collection, Bequest of Mrs. H. O. Havemeyer, 1929 (29.100.18) A100

midst of negotiations for a smaller but more expensive El Greco, *The Adoration of the Shepherds*, made a mistake and turned it down. Thus the *Assumption* passed to Chicago, where it is one of the best old master paintings at the Art Institute.

When Cossío published his catalogue of El Greco's works in 1908, Mrs. Havemeyer was among a mere handful of Americans who owned paintings by the master—Charles Deering of Chicago, Henry Clay Frick of New York, and Joseph Widener of Philadelphia were the others—and he was represented in only three museums—those of Boston, Chicago, and New York. In France, however, works by El Greco were in the hands of a number of advanced collectors, typically individuals with close contacts to artists: the painter Zuloaga had a large group in his studio in Paris, as did Raimundo de Madrazo; Degas and his friends Henri Rouart and Michel Manzi each owned two works; dealers such as Durand-Ruel, Trotti, and the Prince de Wagram all had El Grecos in stock; and the Russian collector Ivan Shchukin, brother of Matisse's patron Serge, bought three paintings.[40] In importing El Grecos to America, then, the Havemeyers were importing a sophisticated French taste, a taste also reflected in the kind of French painting they were acquiring concurrently.[41]

Plate 15. Camille Corot. *Portrait of a Child*, ca. 1835. Oil on wood, 12⅝ x 9¼ in. (32.1 x 23.5 cm). H. O. Havemeyer Collection, Bequest of Mrs. H. O. Havemeyer, 1929 (29.100.564) A98

Plate 16. Camille Corot. *Mlle Dobigny—The Red Dress*, ca. 1865–70. Oil on wood, 30¾ x 18½ in. (78.1 x 47 cm). Shelburne Museum, Shelburne, Vermont (27.1.1–154) A110

Plate 17. Camille Corot. *Bacchante in a Landscape*, ca. 1865. Oil on canvas, 12⅛ x 24¼ in. (30.8 x 61.6 cm). H. O. Havemeyer Collection, Bequest of Mrs. H. O. Havemeyer, 1929 (29.100.598) A107

Plate 18. Camille Corot. *Sibylle*, ca. 1870. Oil on canvas, 32¼ x 25½ in. (81.9 x 64.8 cm). H. O. Havemeyer Collection, Bequest of Mrs. H. O. Havemeyer, 1929 (29.100.565) A114

The Havemeyer collection of works by Corot perfectly illustrates the impact of current French taste, most probably transmitted through Cassatt's recommendations and Durand-Ruel's good offices. For unlike every other American collector of Corot, and there were many, the Havemeyers bought figure painting to the virtual exclusion of landscapes. They ignored the sylvan scenes bathed in Corot's famous silvery light in favor of a difficult but important Salon painting, *The Destruction of Sodom* (pl. 14), a child's portrait of infinite charm (pl. 15), a costume piece posed by Emma Dobigny (pl. 16), a favorite model of Corot's who was taken up by Degas, a startlingly frank nude (pl. 17), and a great, late, unfinished studio piece in which the painter almost achieves the poise and balance of a Raphael (pl. 18). It cannot be a coincidence that Degas, Cassatt's close friend and mentor, often asserted that Corot's genius lay in his figures. If Degas did not make this remark in the presence of the Havemeyers, we can be sure that Cassatt did. Although it seems that all

twenty-five Corots in the collection were acquired before Mr. Havemeyer's death, Mrs. Havemeyer prized them as well. According to her grandson George G. Frelinghuysen, she hung one of her two recumbent nudes (pl. 17 or pl. 207) in her sitting room.

The Havemeyer holdings in Courbet, Manet, and Degas as well as in Corot were particularly strong. Mrs. Havemeyer systematically set out to acquire comprehensive collections of the work of each of these three artists, just as she did in the case of Goya, starting in the early 1890s and not resting satisfied until the early 1920s. In the beginning it was more difficult for her and Cassatt to persuade Mr. Havemeyer to live with Courbets than with other modern paintings because the best examples available—like *Landscape with Deer* (fig. 52), on the one hand, and *Woman with a Parrot* (pl. 19), on the other—often were very large or provocative. As Mather put it, "Zola [writing in the 1860s] had to prove that Courbet and Manet were great as painters, and not immoral. Nobody believed him on

Plate 19. Gustave Courbet. *Woman with a Parrot*, 1866. Oil on canvas, 51 x 77 in. (129.5 x 195.6 cm). H. O. Havemeyer Collection, Bequest of Mrs. H. O. Havemeyer, 1929 (29.100.57) A145

either score." [42] By the 1890s, however, Courbet's importance was not in dispute, although his imagery tested propriety. When Durand-Ruel placed the *Woman with a Parrot* on view in his New York gallery in 1896, Alfred Trumble wrote in the *Collector* that "it was more than a pity" that the painting did not belong to the Metropolitan. "The subject is, to be sure, not of the most puritanical order, for it might be the portrait of some Creole Messalina, sporting with her shrill-voiced pet in an interval of her siesta, but as a powerful piece of painting, and as a priceless lesson to the student, it deserves rank with anything produced by modern art." [43] When the unsold painting was about to be returned to France in 1898 to escape duties that were to be levied by the United States,[44] Mrs. Havemeyer "begged Mr. Havemeyer to buy the picture, not to hang it in our gallery lest the anti-nudists should declare a revolution and revise our Constitution, but just to keep it in America, just that such a work should not be lost to future generations." [45] Harry Havemeyer did acquire *Woman with a Parrot*, but whether the painting indeed hung in his house is not known. In 1909 Mrs. Havemeyer placed the picture on long-term loan to the Metropolitan, where it has remained ever since. That such a large painting was kept in a closet for the eleven years prior to its display at the Museum—as legend holds—seems unlikely.

Despite their initial squeamishness, the Havemeyers assembled the largest collection in the world of Courbet's nudes, which range from the sensational *Woman with a Parrot*, to the prurient *Woman in the Waves* (pl. 20), "a strange combination of sea and nude," [46] to the suggestive *Woman with a Dog* (A149), "the way the little white poodle is painted [is] excuse enough for the tender adoration of its mistress," [47] to the disappointing *Source* (pl. 21). The last painting, one of the weakest of the group, inexplicably was one of Mrs. Havemeyer's favorites. Like many of her mistakes, it was purchased because it reminded her of a greater work that was not available. "Her back is toward us and she looks, as we do, into the dark green woods frankly enjoying the sunlight that sparkles on her back, revealing the same modeling, the same drawing, as one sees in the more celebrated picture of 'La Source' [fig. 5]. . . . My nude is pearly and gray and the half-tones luminous and bewitching." [48] Mrs. Havemeyer was such an enthusiastic admirer of Courbet that she did not see the base quality of some of his nudes and

was thus able to write: "I think I know most of Courbet's nudes, they are realistic and frank, but never vulgar; he never even, like that crushing cynic Degas, treats them with brutal force nor reveals the degradation of their class. . . . You always feel his respect for women." [49] Mather, like other modern critics, disagreed: "There was hope in a nude of Cabanel or Lefèvre; in real life one could buy the like. There was no such stimulation in a nude of Courbet, Manet or Degas. In real life one wouldn't want to buy her." [50] Mather, of course, brings home the point that Mrs. Havemeyer ignored in the case of Courbet—that many of the women he, Manet, and Degas portrayed were represented not as ordinary women but as prostitutes, and were intended to shock. Mrs. Havemeyer looked the other way: "The French girl of Paris was [Courbet's] model, and is it our affair if he mixed a little romance with his colors?" [51]

Unlike their Corots, the Courbets bought by the Havemeyers represent every genre in which the artist worked. Portraits of men and women, landscapes of winter and summer, mountain and sea, still lifes, and scenes of daily life, as well as nudes, were acquired with equal deliberation. Louisine Elder's first encounter with Courbet's work had been at an 1881 exhibition in the Théâtre de la Gaîté in Paris of thirty-three pictures from the artist's estate that were to be sold at auction.[52] The experience defined her notion of Courbet's career. The exhibition included great works like *The Painter's Studio* and *The Burial at Ornans* (both now in the Musée d'Orsay) as well as less important ones, and it gave a complete overview of his achievement. Over the following years Mrs. Havemeyer seems almost to have attempted to acquire paintings that had been exhibited at the Théâtre de la Gaîté or that resembled ones she had seen there. Posterity is fortunate that the Havemeyers passed up the opportunity to buy *The Painter's Studio* from Victor Desfossés, who used it as the stage curtain for his private theater, since they considered improving it: "Mr. Havemeyer thought he would buy it and take out the center group, for the rest of the picture was never finished, but—a composition is a composition—my husband could not make up his mind to do it, and decided not to buy it." [53] Years later they did purchase the beautiful *Portrait of Jo (La Belle Irlandaise)* (pl. 211), which had been shown at the Gaîté, and Mrs. Havemeyer thought that her first nude by Courbet, *Torso of a Woman* (pl. 194) had also been

Plate 20. Gustave Courbet. *The Woman in the Waves*, 1866. Oil on canvas, 25 ¾ x 21 ¼ in. (65.4 x 54 cm). H. O. Havemeyer Collection, Bequest of Mrs. H. O. Havemeyer, 1929 (29.100.62) A148

included in the 1881 exhibition under the title *The Cherry Branch*, but that, in fact, was a different work. In a similar vein, Mr. and Mrs. Havemeyer often sought Courbets that were like others they had seen and sometimes pursued: their first Courbet landscape (*Landscape with Cattle* [A130]) was acquired because they had lost the *Landscape with Deer* (fig. 52) in the 1889 Secrétan sale;[54] *The Knife Grinders* (pl. 266) was acquired because it resembled *The Stone Breakers*, which they had seen at the 1889 World's Fair;[55] *Hunting Dogs* (A128) was acquired because the subjects recalled the dogs in *The Quarry* at the Museum of Fine Arts in Boston; *The Stream* (A126) was acquired because it "rivaled the one [Mr. Havemeyer] lost [the

Secrétan painting], being possibly more juicy and verdant, more suggestive of the charm and solitude of the forest and of the mossy brook, than the one which hangs in the Louvre."[56]

Whether or not the results were always fortunate, then, the Havemeyers, inspired by their own experiences of Courbet's work, were not dumbly following the example of other collectors and of connoisseurs. Their interest in Courbet's portraits, for instance, led them to buy paintings that set their collection apart. Ranging from sensitive and informal interpretations of male sitters, *Portrait of a Man* (pl. 237) and *Alphonse Promayet* (pl. 23), to a smartly fashionable female portrait, *Woman in a Riding Habit* (pl. 24), much admired

23

Plate 21. Gustave Courbet. *The Source*, 1862 Oil on canvas, 47¼ x 29¼ in. (120 x 74.3 cm). H. O. Havemeyer Collection, Bequest of Mrs. H. O. Havemeyer, 1929 (29.100.58) A135

Figure 5. Gustave Courbet. *The Source*, 1868. Oil on canvas, 50⅜ x 38³⁄₁₆ in. (128 x 97 cm). Musée d'Orsay, Paris (RF 2240)

by Cassatt,[57] to a brooding and enigmatic depiction of *Mme de Brayer* (pl. 244), which reminded Degas of a Rembrandt,[58] to an extraordinary period piece, *Mme Auguste Cuoq* (pl. 246), these works are testimony that the Havemeyers, especially Louisine, truly appreciated Courbet's talent. "Mr. Havemeyer and I collected over thirty Courbets and our good fortune as usual was due to Miss Cassatt, the godmother who took me to see that exhibition in the foyer of the Gaîté in Paris, and said to me: 'Some day *you* must have a Courbet.'"[59]

Perhaps even more than the building of their Courbet holdings, the making of their Manet collection gave the Havemeyers the thrill of defying popular convention. Courbet was long dead and his reputation established when they bought his works. Manet had died only three years before Mr. Havemeyer brought home *The Salmon* from Durand-Ruel's 1886 exhibition in New York. Manet's death came early—he was only fifty-one—and the recognition of his genius came late: while

he was mourned by advanced collectors and artists in France, his name was little known to the general public, which still found his pictures queer and controversial—controversial not so much because they dealt with touchy subjects like prostitutes, but because many people thought they were badly painted. Mrs. Havemeyer always remembered the derisive remarks she overheard when she stood in front of the *Portrait of M. Pertuiset, the Lion Hunter* (Museu de Arte Moderna de São Paolo) and the *Portrait of M. Henri Rochefort* (Hamburger Kunsthalle), the pictures Manet showed at the Salon of 1881. "'Ah, ah' and 'Ma foi' and 'Oh, là, là.' The public made frank fun of the lion hunter but the portrait of Rochefort came in for the largest share of ridicule."[60] One person remarked that Manet painted Rochefort as if his subject had smallpox.

Mrs. Havemeyer seemed to revel in the critical opprobrium generated by the next purchase she and her husband made, *Ball at the Opera* (pl. 196). "How the

Plate 22. Gustave Courbet. *Hunter on Horseback*, 1867. Oil on canvas, 46 ¹³⁄₁₆ x 38 in. (118.9 x 96.5 cm). Yale University Art Gallery, New Haven, Gift of J. Watson Webb, B.A. 1907, and Electra Havemeyer Webb (1942.301) A138

Plate 23. Gustave Courbet. *Alphonse Promayet (1822–1872)*, 1851. Oil on canvas, 42 ⅛ x 27 ⅝ in. (107 x 70.2 cm). H. O. Havemeyer Collection, Bequest of Mrs. H. O. Havemeyer, 1929 (29.100.132) A124

Plate 24. Gustave Courbet. *Woman in a Riding Habit*, 1856. Oil on canvas, 45 ½ x 35 ⅛ in. (115.6 x 89.2 cm). H. O. Havemeyer Collection, Bequest of Mrs. H. O. Havemeyer, 1929 (29.100.59) A127

Plate 25. Edouard Manet. *Mlle V. . . in the Costume of an Espada*, 1862. Oil on canvas, 65 x 50¼ in. (165.1 x 127.6 cm).
H. O. Havemeyer Collection, Bequest of Mrs. H. O. Havemeyer, 1929 (29.100.53) A344

critics whistled and hissed [and] found the masked ball . . . indecent and a menace to society."[61] She marveled at the sea of hats in the picture—"hats with springs, hats open, hats shut, hats in the hand, hats on the head, hats tilted, tipped, tossed, thrown upon the head, hats on straight, hats on crooked"[62]—and delighted in the "woman's leg ending in a pretty shoe [that] was thrown over the marble stairway to let us know that the frolic was going on above as well as in the scene before us."[63] It was no surprise to her that the painting excited criticism when she hung it in her own gallery, so she removed it to her bedroom, where she "studied and enjoyed it, hour after hour, year after year," and came to think it "one of Manet's best if not his greatest work."[64] Similarly, Mrs. Havemeyer recorded in her memoirs that the portrait *George Moore* (pl. 26) "attracted more attention than any Manet in our gallery. I grew accustomed to the exclamations I would hear as soon as visitors saw it. . . . The echo of raillery and laughter in the casual observations made me certain that Manet's portrait was considered a huge joke on George Moore."[65]

With their Manet collection, the Havemeyers got off to a start consistent with their usual pattern. They bought a fine painting, *The Salmon*, but passed over a better one, *Boy with a Sword*, in 1886. When they returned to the pursuit of modern painting in 1894, Mr. and

Mrs. Havemeyer made a more daring choice, the *Ball at the Opera*; this was an excellent work, but, once again, not as important as the *Boy with a Sword*, the loss of which the collectors by now sorely regretted. However, they made up for their mistake in 1895, when they bought at least five—and perhaps six—capital paintings: the grand *Luncheon in the Studio* (pl. 201), the spectacular *The Grand Canal, Venice (Blue Venice)* (pl. 30), and the famous *Boating* (pl. 31), in addition to a flower piece (A366), an early student work, *Copy after Delacroix's "Bark of Dante"* (A343), and, probably, *Manet's Family at Home in Arcachon* (pl. 27). They owned *Luncheon in the Studio* for less than seven months: "For some reason I never understood—Mr. Havemeyer asked me if I objected to his returning it to the Durand-Ruels. I never questioned my husband's decisions, and I acquiesced, of course. Manet's still life in the picture, and the boy with the black jacket and straw hat were lost to us forever."[66]

Mr. Havemeyer's objection may well have concerned the picture's size. The *Luncheon* would have been one of the largest paintings in their collection at the time, and he may have felt it was out of scale with the rest of their possessions. We do know that when Mrs. Havemeyer, almost on a lark, had *A Matador* (pl. 212) sent home from Durand-Ruel, she worried about her husband's response not to the price but to its

Plate 26. Edouard Manet. *George Moore (1852–1933)*, 1879. Pastel on canvas, 21 ¾ x 13 ⅞ in. (55.3 x 35.2 cm). H. O. Havemeyer Collection, Bequest of Mrs. H. O. Havemeyer, 1929 (29.100.55) A360

Plate 27. Edouard Manet. *Manet's Family at Home in Arcachon*, 1871. Oil on canvas, 15 ½ x 21 ⅛ in. (39.4 x 53.7 cm). Sterling and Francine Clark Art Institute, Williamstown, Massachusetts (552) A352

Plate 29. Edouard Manet. *Gare Saint-Lazare*, 1872–73. Oil on canvas, 36 ¼ x 45 ⅛ in. (92.1 x 114.6 cm). National Gallery of Art, Washington, D.C., Gift of Horace Havemeyer in memory of his mother, Louisine W. Havemeyer (1956.10.1) A356

Plate 28. Edouard Manet. *In the Garden*, 1870. Oil on canvas, 17 ½ x 21 ¼ in. (44.5 x 54 cm). Shelburne Museum, Shelburne, Vermont (27.1.1–200) A351

size—it is five feet seven inches high. "'I fear Mr. Havemeyer would think it too big.' . . . 'Don't be foolish,' said Miss Cassatt, 'It is just the size Manet wanted it, and that ought to suffice for Mr. Havemeyer; besides, it is a splendid Manet and I am sure he will like it if you buy it.'"[67] This time it was Mr. Havemeyer who acquiesced. Not only did he like it, he also decided to buy the equally large, and greater, *Mlle V . . . in the Costume of an Espada* (pl. 25). Indeed, on the last day of 1898, Mr. Havemeyer agreed to purchase simultaneously the *Matador*, *Mlle V*, and *Gare Saint-Lazare* (pl. 29) from Durand-Ruel's New York gallery. On the strength of this sale, Durand-Ruel bought from the French collector Jean-Baptiste Faure the *Young Man in the Costume of a Majo* (A345) on the same day and shipped it to New York in January. By the end of February this picture too was in the Havemeyer house. Mr. Havemeyer had quickly accustomed himself to Manets on the grand scale and could now boast a collection second only to that of Faure. Over the next few years a significant portion of Faure's holdings would be acquired by the Havemeyers.[68]

"The 'Gare St. Lazare' Mr. Havemeyer bought to please himself, for the painter had become an open book to [him] and he recognized [it] as one of Manet's greatest achievements," wrote Mrs. Havemeyer, who was as proud of the acquisition as her husband was. "It is as realistic as any picture Manet ever painted. . . .

Plate 30. Edouard Manet. *The Grand Canal, Venice (Blue Venice)*, 1875. Oil on canvas, 23 ⅛ x 28 ⅛ in. (58.7 x 71.4 cm). Shelburne Museum, Shelburne, Vermont (27.1.5–30) A359

Plate 31. Edouard Manet. *Boating*, 1874. Oil on canvas, 38¼ x 51¼ in. (97.2 x 130.2 cm). H. O. Havemeyer Collection, Bequest of Mrs. H. O. Havemeyer, 1929 (29.100.115) A358

He concentrated all his art, all his ability, on that which he wished to paint and was still able—what a gift to a painter—to eliminate all unnecessary details." [69] She was no less impressed with *Mlle V*, "one of the greatest and most difficult things Manet ever did." But she was at a loss to match it in words: "I recognize my inability to give you an adequate idea of the beauty of the picture." [70] Her commitment to Manet was such that she undertook a campaign to persuade her husband to buy the enormous *Dead Christ and the Angels* (pl. 32), a painting she knew was not suitable for their house:

> It went begging both here and abroad . . . and let the public galleries explain it if they can, for if ever there was a museum Manet, it seems to me it is his "Christ with the Angels." . . . to please me Mr. Havemeyer bought it, saying as he gave it to me: "I really do

not know what you will do with it." . . . I found it crushed everything beside it and crushed me as well. Finally I concluded it would be impossible to live with that mighty picture. . . . For several years I put it away, but after my husband's death, when Manet was better understood, I sent it to the Metropolitan Museum, where it hangs beside the Manet Mr. Havemeyer saw and rejected because it was "too much for him," the splendid "Boy with a Sword." [71]

In all, Mr. Havemeyer bought twenty-five Manets before his death, and Mrs. Havemeyer did not add a single picture to the collection afterward. There were mistakes among their Spanish paintings and Courbets but none among the Manets. Some are less important than others, but there is not one disputed work. As Mather put it, even "the minor pictures of Manet are admirable." [72]

Plate 32. Edouard Manet. *The Dead Christ and the Angels*, 1864. Oil on canvas, 70⅝ x 59 in. (179.4 x 149.9 cm).
H. O. Havemeyer Collection, Bequest of Mrs. H. O. Havemeyer, 1929 (29.100.51) A346

The thirty Monets assembled by the Havemeyers are as comprehensive in scope as, say, their Courbets or Manets. However, today they are the least well-known group of paintings in the collection because many have remained out of public view: Mrs. Havemeyer and her three children gave only eight Monets to the Metropolitan, in contrast, for example, to twenty of forty-five Courbets or ten of twenty-five Manets. Undoubtedly the primary reason so many Monets were given to the children and kept by them is that they are all of domestic scale and comfortable subject matter, easy to introduce into city apartments or country houses, and agreeable to live with. (It is difficult to imagine a modern living room that could sustain Courbet's *Woman with a Parrot* over the sofa, and we know that even Mrs. Havemeyer's large rooms were crushed by Manet's *Dead Christ and the Angels*.) The Havemeyer Monets range from a powerful early marine, *The Green Wave* (pl. 210), executed when the artist was only twenty-five years old, to masterpieces of his proto-Impressionist style, *Garden of the Princess, Louvre* (A388) and *La Grenouillère* (pl. 33), to works that literally define Impressionism of the 1870s, *In the Garden* (pl. 34) and *The Drawbridge* (pl. 3), to ambitious and relatively large paintings of the 1880s, *Floating Ice* (pl. 36) and *Bouquet of Sunflowers* (pl. 38), to key examples from his various series of the 1890s, Haystacks (A402, pl. 200, A406), Poplars (pl. 35), Morning on the Seine (A412), the Japanese Bridge (pls. 219, 220), Charing Cross Bridge (pl. 37), and the Houses of Parliament (pl. 238).

Although *The Drawbridge* was probably the second purchase made in Paris by the young Louisine Elder in the late 1870s—and perhaps the first Monet bought by an American—she would not acquire another painting by the artist until 1894, when the Havemeyers began concentrating in earnest on modern art. They bought three Monets that year and four the next. These were mostly recent works, such as *Morning on the Seine*, 1893 (A410), and *Haystacks*, 1891 (A406), obtained from Monet's principal dealer, Durand-Ruel, but also included earlier pictures on the secondary market, such as *View of Rouen*, 1872 (A393), and *Floating Ice*, 1880, purchased at the liquidation auction of the American Art Association, a commercial gallery that often worked closely with Durand-Ruel. Indeed from 1894 until just before Mr. Havemeyer's death in 1907, each year save 1902, 1904, and 1905 would bring at

least one, usually two, and sometimes three Monets into the collection, from every possible source in Paris or America. A number of their pictures were acquired, through Durand-Ruel, from American collectors—an indication that Monet had found a responsive audience of some size in the United States. *The Green Wave* came from Cassatt's brother Alexander; *Garden of the Princess, Louvre* and *Old Church at Vernon* (A411) from New Yorker Frederic Bonner's sale; *Bouquet of Sunflowers* from Catholina Lambert of the Patterson silk merchant family;[73] *Haystacks in the Snow* (pl. 200) from the Cleveland steel industrialist Alfred Pope; *Haystacks (Effect of Snow and Sun)* (A406) from the Chicago collector Berthe Honoré (Mrs. Potter) Palmer. One work, *Ice Floes* (A408), was specifically chosen by Monet for the Havemeyers. On the whole, however, the Havemeyers resisted works that were designated for them by anyone other than Cassatt. In 1904, for example, Durand-Ruel insisted that they buy a work from Monet's 1903 campaign in London, and Mr. Havemeyer informed him that he wanted more Goyas, not Monets. They did reluctantly agree to purchase one of the London series, *The Houses of Parliament, Sea Gulls* (pl. 238), in 1906, although Mrs. Havemeyer decided to return it to Durand-Ruel in 1908. Nevertheless, Monet was one of the few Impressionists whose work Mrs. Havemeyer continued to seek out after Mr. Havemeyer's death. She acquired four more of his paintings between 1911 and 1917: *In the Garden*; *Garden of the Princess, Louvre*; *Germaine Hoschedé in the Garden at Giverny* (pl. 260); and *Morning Haze* (A403).

At the turn of the century Monet and Rodin were perhaps the most famous artists alive. Monet in particular was widely shown in France and abroad, with displays of contemporary work staged almost yearly and retrospective exhibitions at frequent intervals. The Havemeyers were able, therefore, to achieve an overview of his career more complete than that of the other artists whose work they acquired. This advantage is manifest in the consistently high quality of the Monet collection, a level that is perhaps unmatched even in their Manets. And the eight Monets chosen by Mrs. Havemeyer for the Metropolitan—*The Green Wave*, *La Grenouillère*, *Bouquet of Sunflowers*, *Chrysanthemums* (A400), *Haystacks (Effect of Snow and Sun)*, *Poplars*, *Ice Floes*, *Bridge over a Pool of Water Lilies* (pl. 219)—were "simply made for a Museum," to quote Mather. "The representation is so complete, joyous and instructive

Plate 33. Claude Monet. *La Grenouillère*, 1869. Oil on canvas, 29⅜ x 39¼ in. (74.6 x 99.7 cm). H. O. Havemeyer Collection, Bequest of Mrs. H. O. Havemeyer, 1929 (29.100.112) A389

Plate 34. Claude Monet. *In the Garden*, 1872. Oil on canvas, 25 x 31¼ in. (63.5 x 79.4 cm). Private collection. A392

Plate 35. Claude Monet. *Poplars*, 1891. Oil on canvas, 32¼ x 32⅛ in. (81.9 x 81.6 cm). H. O. Havemeyer Collection, Bequest of Mrs. H. O. Havemeyer, 1929 (29.100.110) A407

that it becomes really a matter of indifference to the Metropolitan Museum whether it acquires further Monets or not."[74] Today curators might regret the absence of the tightly constructed *Garden of the Princess, Louvre*, the pristine *In the Garden*, or the magnificent *Floating Ice*. They might debate whether the Japanese bridge the Havemeyers kept (pl. 219) or the one they sold (pl. 220) is the finer picture. But they could not accuse the Havemeyers of buying a bad Monet.

The irascible Degas was the living artist whom Mrs. Havemeyer valued most, and her collection gives generous proof of her respect for this exceptional man. That her first and her last important purchases—*Ballet Rehearsal* (pl. 2), probably bought in 1877, and *A Woman Seated Beside a Vase of Flowers* (pl. 39), acquired in 1921—were both works by Degas is no coincidence. It was for a Degas, *Dancers Practicing at the Bar* (pl. 40), that she paid, at auction in 1912, the highest price ever attained by a living artist—Fr 478,500, nearly $100,000—a price dearer than that commanded by any other work in the collection, save perhaps Rembrandt's *Herman Doomer* (pl. 63), which

Plate 36. Claude Monet. *Floating Ice*, 1880. Oil on canvas, 38¼ x 58¼ in. (97.2 x 148 cm). Shelburne Museum, Shelburne, Vermont (27.1.2 108) A398

Plate 37. Claude Monet. *The Thames at Charing Cross Bridge*, 1899. Oil on canvas, 25½ x 35⅜ in. (64.8 x 89.9 cm). Shelburne Museum, Shelburne, Vermont (27.1.4–70) A415

Plate 38. Claude Monet. *Bouquet of Sunflowers*, 1881. Oil on canvas, 39¾ x 32 in. (101 x 81.3 cm). H. O. Havemeyer Collection, Bequest of Mrs. H. O. Havemeyer, 1929 (29.100.107) A399

Plate 39. Edgar Degas. *A Woman Seated Beside a Vase of Flowers (Mme Paul Valpinçon?)*, 1865. Oil on canvas, 29 x 36½ in. (73.7 x 92.7 cm). H. O. Havemeyer Collection, Bequest of Mrs. H. O. Havemeyer, 1929 (29.100.128) A196

was bought for between $70,000 and $100,000. (In an exception to the Havemeyers' self-imposed restriction against imprudent spending, Mrs. Havemeyer left instructions to purchase the picture at any cost, and not even Cassatt was consulted or informed.[75]) And it was to obtain one of Degas's greatest nudes, *Woman Having Her Hair Combed* (pl. 48), at the 1914 sale in Paris of the collection of Roger Marx that Mrs. Havemeyer hastily rearranged her travel plans in the face of the sudden death of her sister-in-law in Switzerland. Rushing to Montreux in the midst of the emerging war in Europe to pick up her relative's visiting grandson, she immediately returned to Paris, telegraphing Durand-Ruel along the way that under no circumstances was she to lose the pastel to a competitor.[76] "I entered the auction room just in time to see the picture knocked down to me, and I knew I possessed one of Degas's

finest pastels."[77] She recalled that "for many years had we admired this wonderful picture of woman just out of a bath, seated upon a yellow divan, pressing her hands against her sides to steady herself while her maid lifts up her head and draws it back as she brushes the masses of heavy hair."[78] Yet at the same sale she was also eager to buy a small thing, an early self-portrait etching that was particularly fine and rare (*Self-Portrait*, 1857 [pl. 43]). It was Mrs. Havemeyer who, in 1903, encouraged Degas to repair the original wax *Little Fourteen-Year-Old Dancer* (fig. 67), the sculpture that had been the sensation of the 1881 Impressionist exhibition; and it was her order, after Degas's death, for the first complete set of his bronzes that helped guarantee that they, as well as the little dancer, would be cast.[79]

By the time Mrs. Havemeyer wrote the chapter on Degas in her memoirs—we know it was in 1916 or 1917,

Plate 40. Edgar Degas. *Dancers Practicing at the Bar*, 1876–77. Mixed media on canvas, 29¾ x 32 in. (75.6 x 81.3 cm). H. O. Havemeyer Collection, Bequest of Mrs. H. O. Havemeyer, 1929 (29.100.34) A216

for he was still alive but very ill—she had formed a clear understanding of the artist's career and a strong sense of the chronology of his work:

It matters little whether or not I recall the order in which we collected Degas's pictures, for like Brahms in music he began by doing his best, and his early works are among his greatest. Whether we admire the exquisite precision of his drawing, the light and air with which he envelops his compositions in the eighties and early nineties, or the broader touch and the glowing color of his later years, we can never forget that from first to last the eye of the philosopher is penetrating the innermost depth of his subject and

that whether he works by analysis or synthesis, his vision reveals to us nature in its truth.[80]

Her understanding was no doubt enhanced by the experience of organizing the 1915 suffrage exhibition, which featured many works by Degas and Cassatt. But, as Mrs. Havemeyer said, "it takes special brain cells to understand Degas,"[81] and she clearly had them in ample quantities at an early stage.

In all the Havemeyers bought some sixty-four paintings, pastels, drawings, and fans, a complete set of seventy bronzes, in addition to the *Little Fourteen-Year-Old Dancer* (pl. 78), and a large number of etchings,

Plate 41. Edgar Degas. *Dancer Tying Her Slipper*, 1887. Pastel and black chalk on buff-colored paper mounted at the edges on board, 18⅝ x 16⅞ in. (47.3 x 42.9 cm). Private collection. A233

Plate 42. Edgar Degas. *The Rehearsal on the Stage*, 1874? Pastel over brush-and-ink drawing on thin cream-colored wove paper, laid on bristol board and mounted on canvas, 21 x 28½ in. (53.3 x 72.4 cm). H. O. Havemeyer Collection, Bequest of Mrs. H. O. Havemeyer, 1929 (29.100.39) A211

Plate 43. Edgar Degas. *Self-Portrait*, 1857. Etching and drypoint, third state, plate: 9 1/16 x 5 5/8 in. (23 x 14.3 cm); sheet: 13 3/4 x 10 1/8 in. (34.9 x 25.7 cm). H. O. Havemeyer Collection, Bequest of Mrs. H. O. Havemeyer, 1929 (29.107.53)

Plate 44. Edgar Degas. *The Collector of Prints*, 1866. Oil on canvas, 20 7/8 x 15 3/4 in. (53 x 40 cm). H. O. Havemeyer Collection, Bequest of Mrs. H. O. Havemeyer, 1929 (29.100.44) A197

lithographs, and monotypes by Degas. Theirs was the largest and most complete collection of Degas's work ever formed. It was not as choice as the much smaller collection of Count Isaac de Camondo, to whom they lost several of Degas's great works, including *The Pedicure* (fig. 60). (A backer of Durand-Ruel's gallery who was not reluctant to pay ever higher prices, Camondo sometimes succeeded in snatching a masterpiece from the hands of the Havemeyers.) The Havemeyers were honored when, on a visit to Degas's studio, the artist produced a portfolio of drawings—"What treasures he revealed!"[82]—and thrilled when he selected three works for them (*Dancer Adjusting Her Slipper* [A206], *Seated Dancer* [A208], and *Little Girl Practicing at the Bar* [A221]). They acquiesced when Degas asked to keep *The Collector of Prints* (pl. 44) for retouching after they had bought it and paid up when, three years later, he decided it was worth much more money than he had asked originally. "Degas's ideas of a bargain were more picturesque than businesslike,"[83] recalled Mrs. Havemeyer about this incident. With a healthy

regard for Degas's difficult nature, they did not act as patrons—a role that had cost Faure the artist's friendship. Nor did they attempt to commission new works or extract old ones from him: "No one knew him better than we did in that respect."[84]

In fact, the majority of the works the Havemeyers bought had already been owned by one, two, and sometimes three other collectors. Many of Degas's first clients were French businessmen, like Ernest May and Albert Hecht, whose fortunes tumbled in the financial upheavals of the 1870s and 1880s and whose collections, consequently, were dispersed as quickly as they were formed. The Havemeyers' Degas collection, however, remained intact until Mrs. Havemeyer's death. With the single exception of a small landscape (A248) returned to Durand-Ruel soon after it was bought in 1894, everything they acquired by Degas was kept. And upon Mrs. Havemeyer's death, thirty-five of the sixty-four pictures, in addition to the prints and sculpture,[85] came to the Museum. All the rare pictures completed before 1872, such as *Sulking* (pl. 45), were

Plate 45. Edgar Degas. *Sulking*, ca. 1869–71. Oil on canvas, 12¾ x 18¼ in. (32.4 x 46.4 cm). H. O. Havemeyer Collection, Bequest of Mrs. H. O. Havemeyer, 1929 (29.100.43) A201

Plate 46. Edgar Degas. *Racehorses in Training*, 1894. Pastel on tracing paper, 19¼ x 24¾ in. (48.9 x 62.9 cm). Thyssen-Bornemisza Collection. A255

Plate 47. Edgar Degas. *At the Milliner's*, 1882. Pastel on pale gray wove paper (industrial wrapping paper), adhered to silk bolting in 1951, 30 x 34 in. (76.2 x 86.4 cm). H. O. Havemeyer Collection, Bequest of Mrs. H. O. Havemeyer, 1929 (29.100.38) A236

Plate 48. Edgar Degas. *Woman Having Her Hair Combed*, ca. 1886–88. Pastel on light green wove paper now discolored to warm gray, affixed to original pulpboard mount, 29 ⅛ x 23 ⅞ in. (74 x 60.6 cm). H. O. Havemeyer Collection, Bequest of Mrs. H. O. Havemeyer, 1929 (29.100.35) A242

Plate 49. Edgar Degas. *Dancers, Pink and Green*, ca. 1890. Oil on canvas, 32⅜ x 29¾ in. (82.2 x 75.6 cm).
H. O. Havemeyer Collection, Bequest of Mrs. H. O. Havemeyer, 1929 (29.100.42) A252

given to the Metropolitan, and of the later works, only a few isolated pictures—*Little Milliners* (A235), *Waiting: Dancer and Woman with Umbrella on a Bench (L'Attente)* (A237), and *Racehorses in Training* (pl. 46)—are missed at the Museum.

Although the Havemeyers are associated with the majestic paintings by Cézanne that came to the Metropolitan—*Mont Sainte-Victoire and the Viaduct of the Arc River Valley* (pl. 51), *Still Life with a Ginger Jar and Eggplants* (pl. 243), and *Rocks in the Forest* (pl. 52)—they in fact owned a group of his pictures that was both surprisingly large (it numbered thirteen works) and wide-ranging. Mr. and Mrs. Havemeyer no doubt had noticed works by Cézanne in the studios of Degas, Cassatt, and Monet but did not purchase any until they became acquainted, in the first years of this century, with his dealer, Ambroise Vollard. Cézanne was considered a recluse and an eccentric; his pictures sold for very little (one-fifth the price of a Monet) until the collection of his principal patron, Victor Chocquet, was auctioned in 1899 and prices suddenly jumped. At this point Durand-Ruel, always cautious, saw new potential in Cézanne, but the young Vollard invested much more heavily in his reputation and his art. Vollard had consistently bought the strident late works by Degas that Durand-Ruel thought too risky, and this met with the approval of the Impressionists of Degas's generation. Mr. Havemeyer must also have approved, because, according to Cassatt, he entered into a financial arrangement that saved Vollard from ruin in 1901.[86]

Plate 50. Paul Cézanne. *Still Life: Flowers in a Vase*, ca. 1885–88. Oil on canvas, 18¼ x 21⅞ in. (46.4 x 55.6 cm). Private collection. A76

Plate 51. Paul Cézanne. *Mont Sainte-Victoire and the Viaduct of the Arc River Valley*, ca. 1885–87. Oil on canvas, 25¾ x 32⅛ in. (65.4 x 81.6 cm). H. O. Havemeyer Collection, Bequest of Mrs. H. O. Havemeyer, 1929 (29.100.64) A74

Among the first Cézannes the Havemeyers acquired were unexpected choices—atypical still lifes (pl. 224, A73), thickly painted and rather awkwardly composed, that were bought from Vollard in 1901. Even more surprising was their purchase two years later of *The Abduction* of 1867 (A67), a robust picture charged with sexual tension that had belonged to Cézanne's childhood friend Emile Zola. In 1868 they bought a rather brutal early self-portrait (pl. 236), and in about 1906, the year of Cézanne's death, two splendid works of the 1880s, *Still Life: Flowers in a Vase* (pl. 50) and *The Banks of the Marne* (A77). After Cézanne died, the cost of his pictures increased enormously and the Havemeyers stopped buying them. Cassatt, who had admired Cézanne's painting (if not his table manners),[87] resented the boom in prices and began encouraging Mrs. Havemeyer, newly widowed, to sell. After initial resistance, she relented in 1909 and consigned

two paintings (A71, 77) to Durand-Ruel. It was a mistake she greatly regretted and that thereafter colored her dealings with the firm that had always served her so well: "I shall leave it to my readers to say what [Durand-Ruel] lacked when I tell them that I sold him three [*sic*] of my best Cézannes, for which he paid me only three thousand dollars."[88] In fact, Durand-Ruel bought the pictures for Fr 7,500 apiece, about $1,500, and within two months sold both to Ivan Morosov for Fr 30,000.

Mrs. Havemeyer understandably felt unfairly treated in this transaction. However, Durand-Ruel paid her an amount that only a year or two before would have been considered very generous, and it is possible that he did not anticipate the high price he could obtain for resale. She almost certainly never discovered what Durand-Ruel charged Morozov. Yet had she done so, she probably would have been more alarmed by that figure than

Plate 52. Paul Cézanne. *Rocks in the Forest*, ca. 1893–94. Oil on canvas, 28⅞ x 36⅜ in. (73.3 x 92.4 cm). H. O. Havemeyer Collection, Bequest of Mrs. H. O. Havemeyer, 1929 (29.100.194) A79

by the amount of money she did not realize, for the Havemeyers never fully accustomed themselves to the dramatic rise in the cost of paintings to which they contributed by creating such a large demand. For exceptional pieces they were sometimes willing to pay dearly: Rembrandt's *Herman Doomer*, El Greco's *Portrait of a Cardinal*, Degas's *Two Dancers at the Bar* were all more expensive than the Havemeyers had expected, yet they paid record prices in order not to lose the works for their collection. Unfortunately Mr. and Mrs. Havemeyer did fail to obtain a number of highly desirable pictures because they felt that dealers were attempting to bilk them.

The case of the Manets from the Faure collection illustrates the problem. A baritone at both Covent Garden and the Paris Opera, Faure had formed a staggering collection of modern French painting with his hard-earned income: over the years he owned some

sixty-seven Manets, nearly sixty Monets, two dozen Pissarros, and almost as many Sisleys and Degases. Since he lacked the millions that the Havemeyers, the Potter Palmers, or the Camondos had at their disposal, he amassed his pictures by driving hard bargains with the painters and by selling whenever the opportunity was ripe. He bought and sold Degas's *Ballet from "Robert le Diable"* (pl. 7) twice, to cite one example, before the Havemeyers finally acquired it. After his wife died in 1905, Faure decided to sell his collection en bloc. He sold a large group of Manets to Durand-Ruel, who in turn offered a selection to Mr. Havemeyer. Durand-Ruel paid just under Fr 500,000 for some twenty Manets and seventeen Monets, but he asked the Havemeyers for Fr 300,000 ($60,000) for three Manets— the great *Bon Bock* (fig. 69), *Springtime* (private collection), and an early work, *The Virgin with the Rabbit* (location unknown). Mr. Havemeyer found the

Plate 53. Alfred Sisley. *Allée of Chestnut Trees*, 1878. Oil on canvas, 19¾ x 24 in. (50.2 x 61 cm). Robert Lehman Collection, 1975 (1975.1.211) A478

proposal "preposterous" and offered Fr 150,000. Although Durand-Ruel had already purchased the Manets, he informed the Havemeyers that Faure would not look kindly on their offer.[89] Exasperated, Mr. Havemeyer offered Fr 250,000 (about $50,000) for the three paintings under discussion plus another Manet, *The Port of Bordeaux* (fig. 64). Durand-Ruel demurred, aware that he could sell them elsewhere. What he did not know was that his heretofore constant ally, Cassatt, did not favor the new speculative prices. She informed Mrs. Havemeyer: "Durand-Ruel wants to see me to talk about the Faures' Manets to impress upon Mr. Havemeyer that the offer he makes is too low and he may miss the three he wants. Now Mr. Havemeyer has seen the pictures and therefore is perfectly able to judge for himself. I must confess personally I would not 'faire des folies' for the Bon Bock."[90]

The *Port of Bordeaux* and *Bon Bock*, like the Have-meyers' *Luncheon in the Studio* (pl. 201), were sold to collectors in Germany, while *Springtime* was bought by their neighbor Payne. The Havemeyers had already purchased some of the important Manets that Faure had sold earlier: *Young Man in the Costume of a Majo* (A345), *Mlle V. . . in the Costume of an Espada* (pl. 25), *Ball at the Opera* (pl. 196), *Gare Saint-Lazare* (pl. 29). But other great works by the artist that came from Faure's collection, such as *The Street Singer* (Museum of Fine Arts, Boston), were lost on account of the new high prices. And, as Mrs. Havemeyer admitted to herself, Manet's *Olympia* might today be in New York rather than Paris had she acted more aggressively.[91] It is revealing of the Havemeyers' great concern with prices that when Mrs. Havemeyer referred in her memoirs to Frick's collection, she made mention of its cost as well as its quality.[92]

How does the Havemeyer collection compare with

Plate 54. Camille Pissarro. *Flood at Pontoise*, 1882. Oil on canvas, 20 ½ x 25 in. (52.1 x 63.5 cm). Private collection. A430

the collections formed by their peers—in character and quality, that is, if not in cost? The boom period at the turn of the century enabled a select few to amass stupendous wealth, a wealth enhanced by the trusts they established and by the absence of income tax. Almost all of the new tycoons acquired works of art. Some, like the Potter Palmers in Chicago, collected to further themselves socially: Mr. and Mrs. Palmer wanted to have important advanced art in place in the house in which they would entertain visitors to the World's Columbian Exposition. Others, like Morgan or William Randolph Hearst, bought older art on a gargantuan scale in order to display their tremendous power and to equate themselves with the great princes of history. A few, like Gardner, John G. Johnson, Charles Lang Freer, and Frick, bought judiciously, acting with advisers to create collections based on erudition and elevated taste. In terms of their knowledge and choices, the Havemeyers are close to the latter camp, but the scale on which they collected brought them perilously near the likes of Morgan. The Havemeyer collection is distinguished by its comprehensive groups of the work of specific artists: Goya, Corot, Courbet, Manet, Monet, Degas. It is perhaps not so refined as the collections of Frick or Freer but is far larger and more specialized. In the last two respects, it is rivaled by only one other collection—that of Faure, whose house Mr. and Mrs. Havemeyer visited many times and whose decision to focus on particular artists they either consciously or unconsciously seem to have adopted.

Hindsight enables us to assess readily the quality of the Havemeyer collection. The artists they valued are precisely those whom history has identified as great. Of the second rank of the Impressionists—Sisley, Pissarro, Caillebotte, Bazille—only the first two were given representation, and this was minor. Sisley's *Allée of Chest-*

nut Trees (pl. 53) and Pissarro's *Flood at Pontoise* (pl. 54) are typical of the fine but modest paintings acquired. Of the work of Renoir, who was not always a great painter, there is only one superb canvas, *By the Seashore* (pl. 6), with an additional pastel and a drawing. If the Havemeyers were taken in by the vagaries of scholarship on Dutch and Spanish painting, they made up for it with their understanding of modern French painting. In the years between Mr. Havemeyer's death and that of Mrs. Havemeyer, theirs was the most important collection of its kind in the world. A budding collector of the next generation, Albert C. Barnes, summed up the position of the Havemeyer collection in 1915:

> For instruction, one naturally turns to the great private collections like Weidener's [*sic*], Johnson's, Havemeyer's, Frick's, Altman's (now in the Metropolitan Museum), most of which are to be freely seen by applicants. They are all superb, with the Havemeyer easily first in importance in art rather than names, and each collection reflects its owners predominant characteristic. The Weidener and Frick are swagger, the former excelling in blue-bloodedness of great pictures by names conjured with by the experts and dealers in old masters. In these two collections, especially the Weidener, almost every painting is pedigreed, catalogued, and certified by experts. They contain, in best examples, the great art of the past only. They are essentially millionaires' collections. . . . Havemeyer's is the best and wisest collection in America. There are less old masters there than in the others, but that is more than compensated for by the large number of paintings by the men that make up the greatest movement in the entire history of art—the Frenchmen of about 1860 and later, whose work is so richly expressive of life that means most to the normal man alive today. One could study art and its relations to life to better advantage in the Havemeyer collection than in any single gallery in the world.[93]

1. The Metropolitan Museum's official comment when Louisine Havemeyer's bequest was accepted by the trustees, quoted in "$3,489,461 Art Left Museum by Mrs. Havemeyer," *New York Herald Tribune*, March 24, 1931.

2. Some of the 142 works of art specified in Mrs. Havemeyer's will were not accepted by the Museum and substitutions were made. Of the 111 paintings given by her children, 5 were substitutions for works not accepted. See Chronology, April 6, 1929–January 7, 1930, this catalogue. My essay is heavily dependent on the impressive work of Susan Alyson Stein, author of the Chronology, and Gretchen Wold, author of this catalogue's Appendix, and all three of us, in turn, have relied on Frances Weitzenhoffer's book, Weitzenhoffer 1986, her dissertation, Weitzenhoffer 1982, and her extraordinary archives, which she, in an act of great generosity, lent to the Museum expressly for our use in this catalogue.

3. Edward Robinson, "Introduction: The H. O. Havemeyer Collection," *The H. O. Havemeyer Collection: A Catalogue of the Temporary Exhibition*, exh. cat., MMA, New York, 1930, p. ix.

4. Frank Jewett Mather, Jr., "The Havemeyer Pictures," *The Arts* 16 (March 1930), p. 452.

5. Havemeyer 1961, p. 193.

6. Havemeyer "Notes" [1974], quoted in Weitzenhoffer 1986, p. 253.

7. Harry Havemeyer's first marriage was to Mary Louise Elder, the aunt of his second wife, Louisine Waldron Elder. This marriage was childless and ended in divorce. See Chronology, March 1, 1870, this catalogue.

8. For further information on the circumstances of all of the recorded purchases made by the Havemeyers, see Chronology and Appendix.

9. Havemeyer 1961, p. 250.

10. Letter from Pissarro to Eugène Murer, in *Correspondance de Camille Pissarro*, ed. Janine Bailly-Herzberg, vol. 1, Paris, 1980, pp. 119–20.

11. Havemeyer 1961, p. 250.

12. See Lois Marie Fink, "French Art in the United States, 1850–1870, Three Dealers and Collectors," *Gazette des Beaux-Arts* 92 (September 1978), pp. 87–100.

13. "The French Impressionists," *New York Tribune*, April 10, 1886, p. 4.

14. Havemeyer 1961, p. 221.

15. "Exhibition of the 'Plein-Airistes,'" *The Nation* 42 (April 15, 1886), p. 328.

16. "The Fine Arts: The French Impressionists," *Critic* 5 (April 17, 1886), p. 195.

17. See Walter Liedtke, "The Havemeyer Rembrandts," this catalogue.

18. See Alice Cooney Frelinghuysen, "The Havemeyer House," this catalogue.

19. Havemeyer 1961, p. 193.

20. Ibid., pp. 83–84.

21. Ibid., p. 132.

22. Ibid., p. 158.

23. Ibid., p. 156.

24. Ibid., pp. 156–57.

25. Ibid., p. 157.

26. Ibid.

27. Ibid., p. 162.

28. Ibid., p. 159.

29. Ibid., p. 145.

30. The attribution of the painting was officially changed at the Metropolitan in 1990, after it had been examined in the company of related works on view in the exhibition *Goya and the*

Age of the Spanish Enlightenment. Goya scholars Jeannine Baticle, Eleanor Sayre, and Juliet Wilson Bareau are also of the opinion that the painting is not from Goya's hand. However, others, including Hubert von Sonnenburg, who cleaned the picture in 1971, believe that it is authentic. It is listed as Attributed to Goya in Katharine Baetjer's *European Paintings in The Metropolitan Museum of Art*, New York, 1993. I am still investigating the issue and will publish a full explication of it in the near future.

31. Havemeyer 1961, p. 157.
32. Ibid., p. 158.
33. Ibid.
34. Mather 1930, p. 468.
35. Havemeyer 1961, p. 144.
36. Ibid., p. 131.
37. MC to LWH, 11/20/03, Havemeyer correspondence.
38. Havemeyer 1961, p. 156.
39. Ibid., p. 135.
40. The direct relationship between modern artists and the rediscovery of El Greco would be recognized by 1930, when a critic noted: "The appreciation of El Greco in modern times developed almost contemporaneously with that of the XIXth century painters, and though he painted more than three hundred years ago, his work has been so closely associated with the modern school that it seems to belong more to the XIXth and XXth centuries than to the XVIth and XVIIth" ("Havemeyer Collection at Metropolitan Museum," *Art News* 28 [March 15, 1930], p. 43).
41. For futher discussion of the Havemeyers' El Grecos, see Katharine Baetjer, "A Portrait and a Landscape by El Greco of Toledo," this catalogue.
42. Mather 1930, p. 472.
43. Alfred Trumble, "News and Views," *Collector* 8 (December 15, 1896), p. 49.
44. Paintings imported to the United States were taxed from 10 to 30 percent from 1790 to 1894. There were no duties from 1894 to 1897. From 1897 to 1909 duties were 20 percent; from 1909 to 1915, 15 percent. There have been no duties on imported art since World War I. (See Hans Huth, "Impressionism Comes to America," *Gazette des Beaux-Arts* 29 [1946], p. 248, no. 47.)
45. Havemeyer 1961, p. 196.
46. Ibid.
47. Ibid., p. 197.
48. Ibid., pp. 197–98.
49. Ibid., p. 198.
50. Mather 1930, p. 472.
51. Havemeyer 1961, p. 196.
52. *Catalogue de trente-trois tableaux et études par Gustave Courbet et dépendant de sa succession*, Hôtel Drouot, Paris, December 9, 1881.
53. Havemeyer 1961, pp. 183–84.
54. Ibid., pp. 191–92; see also Chronology, June 29–30, 1889.
55. It was not exhibited, as Mrs. Havemeyer wrote, at the 1900 World's Fair in Paris (Havemeyer 1961, p. 193).
56. Ibid., p. 194.
57. Ibid., pp. 201–2.
58. Ibid., p. 188.
59. Ibid., p. 203.

60. Ibid., p. 218.
61. Ibid., p. 219.
62. Ibid.
63. Ibid.
64. Ibid., p. 220.
65. Ibid., p. 235.
66. Ibid., p. 225. For further details regarding the purchase and return of this painting, see Chronology, April 8, October 28, 1895.
67. Havemeyer 1961, p. 223.
68. The following works from the Faure collection were bought by the Havemeyers: Courbet, *The Deer* (A144), *The Woman in the Waves* (A148); Degas, *The Ballet from "Robert le Diable"* (A202), *A Woman Ironing* (A205); Manet, *Mlle V. . . in the Costume of an Espada* (A344), *Young Man in the Costume of a Majo* (A345), *Matador Saluting* (A348) (owned jointly with Durand-Ruel), *Luncheon in the Studio* (A349), *The Salmon* (A350), *The Port of Calais* (A353), *Gare Saint-Lazare* (A356), *Ball at the Opera* (A357); Millet, *Girl with Sheep* (A382); Monet, *The River Zaan at Zaandam* (A390).
69. Havemeyer 1961, pp. 237–38.
70. Ibid., p. 224.
71. Ibid., pp. 236–37.
72. Mather 1930, p. 478.
73. Lambert, who had a large and fairly impressive collection of French painting, also owned Renoir's *By the Seashore* (A460).
74. Mather 1930, pp. 479, 481.
75. See Chronology, December 10, 1912.
76. See Chronology, By May 7, 1913.
77. Havemeyer 1961, p. 262.
78. Ibid., p. 261.
79. See Clare Vincent, "The Havemeyers and the Degas Bronzes," this catalogue.
80. Havemeyer 1961, p. 257.
81. Ibid., p. 249.
82. Ibid., p. 252.
83. Ibid.
84. Ibid., p. 253.
85. Two of the bronzes are missing from the set bequeathed to the Metropolitan.
86. MC to LWH, 7/6/13, Havemeyer correspondence.
87. Weitzenhoffer 1986, p. 142.
88. Havemeyer 1961, p. 8.
89. Weitzenhoffer states that Durand-Ruel bought the Faure Manets and Monets for Fr 800,000, the figure that Durand-Ruel gave the Havemeyers (1986, p. 161). Anne Distel gives the price of Fr 500,000 (*The First Collectors of Impressionism*, New York, 1990, p. 93). Information in the Durand-Ruel Archives strongly suggests that the dealer had concluded his purchase from Faure while he was still negotiating with the Havemeyers. See Chronology, March 29, 1905.
90. MC to LWH, n.d. [7/05], quoted in the unpublished chapter on Cassatt from Louisine Havemeyer's memoirs, MMA Archives.
91. Havemeyer 1961, p. 236.
92. Ibid., p. 32.
93. Albert C. Barnes, "How to Judge a Painting," *Arts and Decoration* 5 (April 1915), p. 246.

Plate 55
Hugo van der Goes

PORTRAIT OF A MAN, ca. 1475

Oil on wood, 12 ½ x 10 ½ in. (31.8 x 26.7 cm)
H. O. Havemeyer Collection, Bequest of
Mrs. H. O. Havemeyer, 1929
29.100.15
A290

Commenting on Mrs. Havemeyer's purchase of the *Portrait of a Man*, in which the background and hands had been completely overpainted, the noted critic Frank Jewett Mather, Jr., remarked, "It took a fine and daring sense of quality to buy it in this condition," because "the portrait had been Holbein-ized."[1] After a careful cleaning and a brief period in which the painting was thought to be by Antonello da Messina, both Max J. Friedländer and Georges Hulin de Loo properly attributed this fine portrait to van der Goes.[2]

This is one of only two independent portraits in existence by van der Goes; the other is in the Walters Art Gallery in Baltimore. The Havemeyer panel was not originally oval in shape but has been cut down from a rectangular format. The concentrated gaze of this unknown man with his hands in an attitude of prayer doubtless centered on a half-length representation of the Virgin. As he would thus have appeared to the left of the Virgin, the painting probably would have been balanced at the far right by a portrait of the man's wife.

Because Hugo made use of dramatic lighting and depicted his sitters in a less idealized manner than his contemporary Memling, his portraits convey a sense of fervent devotional piety and strength of character. His bold representation here can be compared favorably with the donor portraits in van der Goes's greatest work, the *Portinari Altarpiece* in the Galleria degli Uffizi in

Florence. A date for the Havemeyer portrait of about 1475, corresponding to that of the *Portinari Altarpiece*, is most likely.

MWA

1. F. J. Mather, Jr., "The Havemeyer Pictures," *The Arts* 16 (March 1930), p. 455.
2. See B. B[urroughs], "Loan Exhibition of the Arts of the Italian Renaissance," *Metropolitan Museum Bulletin* 18 (May 1923), p. 109; B. Burroughs, "Un Portrait inédit attribué à Hugo van der Goes," in *Mélanges Hulin de Loo*, Brussels and Paris, 1931, pp. 71–73.

Plate 56
Lucas Cranach the Elder

PORTRAIT OF A MAN WITH A ROSARY

Oil on wood, 18 ¾ x 13 ⅞ in. (47.7 x 35.2 cm)
H. O. Havemeyer Collection, Bequest of
Mrs. H. O. Havemeyer, 1929
29.100.24
A168

Often prized for their decorative qualities and fanciful themes, paintings by Cranach have been favored by American collectors. The Havemeyer *Portrait of a Man with a Rosary* stands apart in its characteristics, however. The image is as compelling in its forthright record of the sitter's features as it is sensitive in the expression of his reflective mood. The man holds a rosary in his hands, his fingers pausing on one of the beads as he perhaps silently recites a prayer.

A pendant for the Havemeyer painting, a *Portrait of a Lady*, is in the Kunsthaus Zürich. The paintings are similar in size and in the decoration of the reverse sides; an unidentifiable male saint and a Saint Catherine, each in a niche, may represent the names or patron saints of the male and female sitters. The lady faces left, her hands joined in prayer, suggesting that a missing painting of the Virgin Mary may have been the object of devotion between the two portraits. However, it would be highly unusual and disrespectful to cover one's head in the presence of the Virgin, and our man with a rosary wears a hat. Thus it is likely that Cranach was emphasizing the personal piety of the portrait pair, rather than showing the subjects in a specific act of devotion.

Certain details help to locate the paintings historically. The man's signet ring shows the coat of arms of the Dutch family Six te Hillegom, and the lady's Dutch hood is a type that was commonly worn in the first decades of the sixteenth century. Perhaps Cranach painted the likenesses of these two members of the wealthy bourgeoisie on his trip to the Netherlands in 1508.

MWA

Plate 57
Paolo Veronese (Paolo Caliari)
BOY WITH A GREYHOUND

Oil on canvas, 68⅜ x 40⅛ in.
(173.7 x 101.9 cm)
H. O. Havemeyer Collection, Bequest of
Mrs. H. O. Havemeyer, 1929
29.100.105
A503

It is traditionally thought that this portrait, owned by the eminent Martinengo family in the Lombard city of Brescia, portrays a member of the Colleoni family, to whom the Martinengo were related by marriage. Whether this is true or not cannot be said. The picture, which shows the youth full-length, standing before a door opening onto a distant landscape, was intended to be viewed at eye level and was probably part of a larger decorative scheme. At the Villa Barbaro at Maser, Veronese included similar portraits in his illusionistic fresco decoration. The work has been dated to the 1570s, when Veronese was at the peak of his powers.

The picture has suffered somewhat, with the most significant changes caused by the alteration of some of the pigments the artist used: the sky is painted in a fugitive smalt blue that now reads as gray, and the copper resonate green of the landscape has oxidized brown, thereby depriving the work of the plein air quality that the artist intended. The Havemeyers were shown the portrait twice and purchased it only after a rather liberal "restoration" in which egregious highlights were added. These were removed by a cleaning carried out at the Metropolitan in 1989–90. To the left of the greyhound can now be seen the outlines denoting an earlier position of the animal. The cleaning has confirmed Veronese's authorship and greatly enhanced the virtuosic, proto-Impressionist execution (particularly in the beautiful striped sleeve).

KC

55

Plate 58
Bronzino (Agnolo di Cosimo di Mariano)

PORTRAIT OF A
YOUNG MAN, ca. 1540

Oil on wood, 37 ⅝ x 29 ½ in.
(95.5 x 74.9 cm)
H. O. Havemeyer Collection, Bequest of
Mrs. H. O. Havemeyer, 1929
29.100.16
A45

This painting, probably dating from about 1540, is among Bronzino's greatest portraits. The self-possessed aloofness of the sitter and the austere elegance of the palace interior are hallmarks of the courtly portrait style Bronzino created for Medicean Florence.

Although the sitter cannot be identified, he is probably a member of the close circle of literary friends that Bronzino formed in Florence around the historian Benedetto Varchi. Varchi was a staunch supporter of Dante, Petrarch, and the Florentine dialect as the basis of a vernacular (as opposed to Latin) literary style. Bronzino himself composed Petrarchan verse, some of which was addressed to Varchi, and between 1541 and 1547 he was a member of the Accademia Fiorentina (to which Michelangelo also belonged). Among his circle of friends were Lorenzo Lenzi, Ugo Martelli, Luca Martini, and the poetess Laura Battiferri, all of whom he portrayed. Bronzino's portrait of Ugo Martelli (Gemäldegalerie, Staatliche Museen Berlin) provides the closest point of comparison with the Metropolitan picture. In it Martelli is shown seated next to a table in a Florentine palace interior, indicating the Greek text of the *Iliad*. Doubtless, the book held by the sitter in the Metropolitan portrait alludes to his literary interests, and the fanciful table and chair, with their grotesque decorations, are visual analogues to the sorts of literary conceits enjoyed by this young man's cultivated group of friends. The suggestion has been made that the picture is a self-portrait, but confirmation for this is lacking.

During its genesis, the painting underwent numerous changes, some of which are still visible on the surface. The position of the hand holding the book was altered, the face was turned differently, and the whole of the background architecture—originally shown as a vaulted corridor in diagonal recession—was redesigned. Much of the table was drawn in with the butt of the brush.

KC

Pl. 57

56

Pl. 58

A PORTRAIT AND A LANDSCAPE
BY EL GRECO OF TOLEDO

Domenikos Theotokopoulos, called El Greco, was born in Crete, then a Venetian colony, where he was first recorded as a master icon painter in 1566.[1] Two years later he was living in Venice and by 1570 in Rome, so that at the age of thirty he had studied both Venetian color and Tuscan drawing, the poles of Italian High Renaissance style. In the absence of important patronage in Rome, El Greco looked to Spain, and, failing to find favor with King Philip II, he settled by 1577 in Toledo, where he remained until his death. Circumstance as well as talent contributed to the uniqueness that is one of the fascinations of El Greco's art. He was not bound by the strictures of nature or by the properties of natural light, and he was ceaselessly inventive and a brilliant colorist. He ran afoul of—but refused to be shackled by—the requirement that religious content be precisely depicted in support of the orthodox goals of the Counter-Reformation, and thus it was fortunate that he worked in Toledo, away from the center of power.

The Toledan school was remarkable only for its lack of distinction, but in Toledo the artist found sympathetic local patronage, and his cosmopolitan background, uncompromising originality, and innate technical gifts combined to produce a body of work set apart from the severe and rather pedestrian naturalism that characterized the art of his contemporaries. El Greco's hybrid and very personal style was, however, inimitable, and so he left no talented followers. With the passage of time he was seen as an eccentric, and then forgotten, only to be redis-

covered after two hundred years as a painter's painter whose work appealed to Delacroix and Manet and was copied by Cézanne.

During their trip to Spain in 1901 Mr. and Mrs. Havemeyer had heard about El Greco's *Portrait of a Cardinal* (pl. 59) from Manuel Cossío, the scholar who in 1908 would publish the first catalogue raisonné of El Greco's paintings.[2] The fervor born of religious conviction that characterizes the art of the Spanish church is not easily accommodated in a domestic environment, and the Havemeyers were among many private collectors who preferred secular subjects. They were, however, drawn to this ecclesiastical portrait, which was acquired through Paul Durand-Ruel in 1904. One of only three full-lengths by El Greco, it is remarkable for both the painterly quality of its handling and the compelling characterization of the sitter. The force of the cardinal's convictions is announced by his piercing, dominant stare and talonlike grip. The sharp, angular shapes of the stiffened watered silk and lace of his costume overwhelm his slight body while drawing attention to the spiritual power of his office. The canvas is unmatched among El Greco's portraits for the elaborately appointed interior—embossed and gilt leather wall hangings, stained woodwork, colored marbles, and velvet upholstery—and for its brilliant hues and stabbing, rapid-fire technique.

For the last seventy-five years El Greco has been the object of intense scholarly scrutiny, but the Havemeyer portrait has resisted elucidation. The character of the cardinal was long interpreted in accordance

with the identification of the sitter first proposed by Cossío in 1908.[3] Cossío thought he was Don Fernando Niño de Guevara (1541–1609), who returned to Spain from Rome in 1599 to take up the post of inquisitor general and who served from 1601 as archbishop of Seville. A native of Toledo, he was a distinguished jurist known for his piety and integrity. If, as seems likely, the cardinal is Guevara, a date of about 1600 for the portrait can be assumed. However, it is possible that he is Cardinal Gaspar de Quiroga, archbishop of Toledo from 1577 until his death in 1594, or Cardinal Bernardo de Sandoval y Rojas (d. 1618), archbishop from 1599.[4] In paintings and engravings by other Toledan portraitists of the later sixteenth century the several candidates are all represented as elderly and bearded, but each of them lacks distinguishing physical characteristics. By contrast El Greco's sitter, with his extraordinary eyeglasses, conforms to an elongated physical type that must owe more to the artist's style than to literal appearance. It is thus unlikely that the sitter's identity will ever be established with absolute certainty.

In 1901 Mr. and Mrs. Havemeyer had also heard, in this case from Cassatt, about the *View of Toledo* (pl. 60). They did not see the picture

Plate 59. El Greco (Domenikos Theotokopoulos). *Portrait of a Cardinal, Probably Cardinal Don Fernando Niño de Guevara*, ca. 1600. Oil on canvas, 67 ¼ x 42 ½ in. (170.8 x 108 cm). H. O. Havemeyer Collection, Bequest of Mrs. H. O. Havemeyer, 1929 (29.100.5) A304

while they were in Spain, and Mr. Havemeyer did not respond to Durand-Ruel's offer of sale in 1907. However, Mrs. Havemeyer acquired El Greco's only pure landscape when she saw it in Paris in 1909. *View of Toledo* is a hypnotic, symbolic, and very unusual picture. Insofar as there was any landscape painting in the sixteenth century, the bird's-eye view, a sort of three-dimensional map presented as if seen from above, was the norm; but El Greco shows only the Alcazar, the approach from the west by the Alcántara Bridge over the Tagus River, and the bell tower of the cathedral, dramatically displaced from the center of the city. He emphasizes the vertical dimension, so that the buildings seem to spring upward into the dome of the sky from the very unrealistically painted green landscape. The light, equally unnaturalistic, glows from within with a sort of ominous combustible force.

In deliberately denying the true appearance of Toledo, El Greco required that his canvas be understood in some other, less literal terms. Perhaps the *View of Toledo* is an emblem of the city's former glory as the seat of both church and state. It is difficult to imagine the circumstances that might have inspired him to paint this landscape, which seems to have remained in his possession until his death, and impossible to construe its meaning in the absence of contemporary evidence. The canvas is conspicuously signed but undated, although it is believed to have been painted about 1600. There are buildings in it that may have some particular significance but have not as yet been securely identified. The limits of scholarly endeavor have never hampered our appreciation of El Greco's gifts as represented by the landscape and the portrait. Their compelling interest may be enhanced by the critical uncertainty that surrounds them, and since 1930 they have been among a half-dozen works by which the Metropolitan is best known to the museum-going public.

KB

1. The El Greco literature is vast. The standard work of reference is the catalogue raisonné by Harold E. Wethey, *El Greco and His School*, 2 vols., Princeton, N.J., 1962. For a recent scholarly overview, see Jonathan Brown et al., *El Greco of Toledo*, exh. cat., Boston, 1982, and for the *Portrait of a Cardinal*, which was not included in the Toledo Museum of Art exhibition this catalogue accompanied, see Jonathan Brown and Dawson A. Carr, "Portrait of a Cardinal: Niño de Guevara or Sandoval y Rojas?," *Studies in the History of Art* 11 (National Gallery of Art, Washington, D.C., 1982), pp. 33–42.
2. This monograph was revised and updated by the author's daughter: Manuel B. Cossío, *El Greco*, ed. Natalia Cossío de Jiménez, Barcelona, 1972.
3. Ibid., pp. 250–53, pl. 97, pp. 293–94, cat. no. 354.
4. In addition to Brown and Carr, "Portrait," see Brown et al., *El Greco*, p. 54, fig. 19. The late Xavier de Salas proposed to identify the sitter as Quiroga in 1982 (unpublished opinion).

Plate 60. El Greco (Domenikos Theotokopoulos). *View of Toledo*, ca. 1600. Oil on canvas, 47¾ x 42¾ in. (121.3 x 108.6 cm). H. O. Havemeyer Collection, Bequest of Mrs. H. O. Havemeyer, 1929 (29.100.6) A303

THE HAVEMEYER REMBRANDTS

Dutch paintings in the Havemeyer collection, and especially the Rembrandts, were Harry Havemeyer's pictures. He bought his first three paintings by Rembrandt—the van Beresteyn pendant portraits (pls. 61, 62) and *Herman Doomer*, then known as *The Gilder* (pl. 63)—in December 1888 and in March 1889, respectively. Havemeyer paid nearly record prices on both occasions, which he could do thanks to his central role in forming the Sugar Trust in 1887. The large pair of portraits was acquired from the Fifth Avenue firm of Cottier and Co. for $60,000, and another New York dealer, William Schaus, received at least $70,000 for *Herman Doomer* (the pendant to which was sold separately about 1750 and is now in the State Hermitage Museum in St. Petersburg).

H. O. Havemeyer had earlier collected fine Chinese and Japanese decorative wares and Barbizon landscapes. The influence of Louisine Havemeyer, whom he married in 1883, may have encouraged Harry's purchase, with the van Beresteyn portraits, of Delacroix's *Expulsion of Adam and Eve* (A265), but he had bought the same painter's *Arab Rider* (A262) at Knoedler's in New York in 1882. In all his acquisitions of the 1880s Havemeyer revealed considerable discernment, although his taste was entirely consistent with that of polite East Coast society at the time. It may be said that the Rembrandts also reflected conventional taste, but they were recognized as in another class, that of great old master paintings. There can be little doubt that Harry, who had recently turned forty and be-

Plate 61. Rembrandt Harmensz. van Rijn. *Portrait of a Man*, 1632. Oil on canvas, 44 x 35 in. (111.8 x 88.9 cm). H. O. Havemeyer Collection, Bequest of Mrs. H. O. Havemeyer, 1929 (29.100.3) A445

come a much wealthier man, was placing himself in a more venerable category when he embraced the class of paintings represented by his first three Rembrandts. As it happens, this was more true than Havemeyer ever knew: of the eight "Rembrandts" that he had assembled in his library, the Rembrandt Room (fig. 30), by the fall of

1892—less than four years after the van Beresteyn purchase—only the first three acquisitions are autograph works by the master himself.

The five other pictures were all supplied by the Durand-Ruels, effectively on just two occasions. In November 1890 they brought three then unquestioned Rembrandts to New York. Havemeyer immediately

Plate 62. Rembrandt Harmensz. van Rijn. *Portrait of a Woman*, 1632. Oil on canvas, 44 x 35 in. (111.8 x 88.9 cm). H. O. Havemeyer Collection, Bequest of Mrs. H. O. Havemeyer, 1929 (29.100.4) A446

bought the *Portrait of a Man—The Treasurer* (A456), dated 1632, which in composition bears a striking resemblance to the so-called *Christian Paul van Beresteyn* (pl. 61). The latter and its pendant, which possibly represent some as yet unidentified members of the van Beresteyn family, have themselves lately but wrongly been described by a small minority of Rembrandt scholars as studio works and stand at the center of a lively dispute. *The Treasurer*, by contrast, dropped completely out of the flourishing literature on the artist after Horst Gerson, in 1969, followed Kurt Bauch in rejecting it from Rembrandt's oeuvre.[1]

In February 1891 Havemeyer paid $50,000 for the *Portrait of an Old Woman* (A11), which is falsely signed and dated 1640. The panel, possibly an old copy or a studio version of a portrait by Jacob Backer (Rembrandt's independent colleague in the early 1630s), would at best bring the same amount today. The third Rembrandt offered by Durand-Ruel in 1890–91, a picture declined by Harry, was the famous *David Playing Before Saul* now in the Mauritshuis in The Hague. The painting may be partly by Rembrandt and, like *The Polish Rider* in the Frick Collection in New York, will remain an ardently contested work for some time to come.

Havemeyer wanted a critical mass of Rembrandts to decorate the library in his new house on Fifth Avenue. The same approach produced very similar results for Benjamin Altman, who, as John G. Johnson acidly remarked in 1909, "cannot get too much of a good thing [Rembrandt portraits]. He now has eight."[2] It was at Havemeyer's request that Paul Durand-Ruel followed the Princesse de Sagan to Trouville and secured another pair of portraits, called "The Admiral and His Wife" (pls. 192, 193), in June 1892. In 1969 Gerson, following A. Burroughs, considered the canvases "certainly by F. Bol,"[3] but that artist no longer is counted among the Rembrandt followers who are now thought possibly to be responsible for these Amsterdam products of the mid-seventeenth century. Havemeyer's last "Rembrandt," *Portrait of a Young Man in a Broad-Brimmed Hat* (A459), is a vaguely Bol-like work that has not entered

into serious discussions of Rembrandt during the past fifty years.

Rembrandt scholars of Havemeyer's day would not have questioned for a moment any of the eight portraits constituting the Rembrandt Room. In 1893 the preeminent authority, Wilhelm von Bode, praised the Havemeyer Rembrandts as beyond equal in private collections, and in an article written in 1902 Bode remembered generously "nine portraits from Rembrandt's hand" that "Henry Havemeyer has assembled within a few years."[4] Bode himself was eagerly buying Rembrandts for the Kaiser-Friedrich-Museum in Berlin, which, like the comparable institutions in Amsterdam, London, New York, and Paris, has since the 1930s seen about half of its Rembrandts reassigned to other artists and in some cases to other centuries. Of the 643 Rembrandts catalogued by America's leading expert, Wilhelm Valentiner, in the 1909 *Klassiker der Kunst* volume, less than half are accepted today, and over 90 percent of the 108 "rediscovered" Rembrandts published in Valentiner's supplementary volume, *Wiedergefundene Gemälde* (1923), are no longer listed under Rembrandt's name.

As Johnson noted, it was portraits by Rembrandt that Americans wanted, and this was largely the case also with respect to English painters, who in their view included van Dyck. The interiors of Anglo-Saxon mansions, not Roman palazzi, were the essential models for American home decoration on the grand scale. Harry's rejection of the celebrated *David Playing Before Saul* was a typical exercise in American taste, which did not extend to another culture's mythology (much less religion) or to tragic encounters with weak-willed individuals. There was a strong element of self-identification and a quest for surrogate ancestry in the American admiration of sober portraits by Rembrandt and by other masters of the Old World. The Rembrandt Room was Harry's study and the usual setting for dignified entertainments. The Rembrandts and the two small and earnest portraits by Hals (pls. 64, 65) that hung there established an air of propriety that somehow became the collector's own.

Similarly, Havemeyer's other Dutch pictures—two de Hoochs (pl. 187, A327) and works by or attributed to Cuyp, Kalf, and familiar contemporaries (A172, 173, 336, 372, 498)—were painted by some of the dozen or so most desired Dutch artists in America during the 1890s. On the whole these landscapes and interior views suggested pastoral or domestic tranquillity and enhanced one's sense of the home as a refuge from public life.

The inevitable pressures of big business were intensified for Havemeyer between 1888 and 1891, when antitrust sentiment and legislation were repeatedly in the news. It has been suggested that "Harry's public manner became noticeably more severe" as a result and that he was not named a trustee of the Metropolitan Museum because other businessmen and collectors (in particular Henry Marquand) considered Havemeyer's image insufficiently reserved.[5] When Harry retired to the Rembrandt Room, he must have felt a great relief from the outside world for reasons he would not have been able to articulate clearly and would not care to if he could.

WL

1. Bredius/Gerson 1969, no. 168; Kurt Bauch, *Rembrandt: Gemälde*, Berlin, 1966, p. 47.
2. See Walter Liedtke, "Dutch Paintings in America: The Collectors and Their Ideals," in *Great Dutch Paintings from America*, exh. cat., Mauritshuis, The Hague, and The Fine Arts Museums of San Francisco, 1990, p. 48.
3. Bredius/Gerson 1969, p. 566, under no. 223; A. Burroughs, *Art Criticism from a Laboratory*, Boston, 1938, p. 157.
4. Weitzenhoffer 1986, p. 63.
5. Ibid., p. 69.

Plate 63. Rembrandt Harmensz. van Rijn. *Herman Doomer*, 1640. Oil on wood, 29 5/8 x 21 3/4 in. (75.2 x 55.3 cm). H. O. Havemeyer Collection, Bequest of Mrs. H. O. Havemeyer, 1929 (29.100.1) A449

Plate 64. Frans Hals. *Petrus Scriverius*, 1626. Oil on wood, 8¾ x 6½ in. (22.2 x 16.5 cm). H. O. Havemeyer Collection, Bequest of Mrs. H. O. Havemeyer, 1929 (29.100.8) A320

Plate 65. Frans Hals. *Anna van der Aar*, 1626. Oil on wood, 8¾ x 6½ in. (22.2 x 16.5 cm). H. O. Havemeyer Collection, Bequest of Mrs. H. O. Havemeyer, 1929 (29.100.9) A319

Plate 66
Rembrandt Harmensz. van Rijn

A COTTAGE AMONG TREES

Pen and brown ink on tan laid paper,
6¾ x 10⅞ in. (17.2 x 27.5 cm)
H. O. Havemeyer Collection, Bequest of
Mrs. H. O. Havemeyer, 1929
29.100.939
A450

When Mr. Havemeyer purchased eight Rembrandt drawings at the Seymour Haden sale in London on June 15, 1891, preparations were

under way for the Havemeyers to move into their splendid new residence at 1 East 66th Street. In the following year he acquired three portrait paintings, then attributed to the great Dutch master, to complete the extraordinary display of eight Rembrandt portraits in his new library, the Rembrandt Room (fig. 30).

The drawings he selected represent the range of Rembrandt's subject matter. They include figure studies, a biblical scene, and landscapes. One of the drawings, *Interior of a Picture Gallery* (A335), has since been reassigned to Hans

Jordaens III (Flemish, fl. 1619–43). The remaining seven have retained their attribution, although recent opinion has cast some doubts on the superbly drawn *Seated Man Wearing a Flat Cap* and *Nathan Admonishing David* (2 Samuel 12:1–15) (A448, 453), suggesting they may be the work of Rembrandt's ablest pupils.

Not surprisingly, *A Cottage Among Trees* was recognized at the sale as the finest among the twenty-five Rembrandt drawings there. It alone fetched £130, whereas the others averaged £30. The drawing be-

longs to the artist's mature period, when his interest turned briefly to the landscape. This exceptional work is one of a group of landscape studies that were executed about 1650–51 (the high point of Rembrandt's classical period). In technique and poetic mood it shows a strong indebtedness to the sixteenth-century Venetian masters, whose landscape prints he collected. With a fine quill pen Rembrandt transformed this solitary cottage, partially hidden by trees, into an image of pictorial richness and monumental grandeur. Alternating be- tween broad strokes and tightly rendered ones, he captured the movement in the trees as the wind blew across the lowlands. The spectator is drawn to the firmly rooted dwelling receding into the space of the composition; cast in shadow, it seems shrouded in mystery.

HBM

Plate 68
Rembrandt Harmensz. van Rijn

CHRIST WITH THE SICK AROUND HIM, RECEIVING LITTLE CHILDREN (THE "HUNDRED GUILDER PRINT"), ca. 1649

Etching, drypoint, and burin on paper watermarked with a lily in a shield, countermark IV, second state of two, plate: 11 x 15 ½ in. (28 x 39.4 cm); sheet: 11 ⅛ x 15 ⅝ in. (28.3 x 39.8 cm)
H. O. Havemeyer Collection, Bequest of Mrs. H. O. Havemeyer, 1929
29.107.35

Rembrandt combined several stories from the life of Christ in this image and used a dramatic composition with strong shadows and with light concentrated on the central figure. A street crowd of Christ's followers is immobilized for a magic moment; each character is a real and expressive individual with a personal story.

Working on the copperplate of the "Hundred Guilder Print" for some ten years, Rembrandt experimented with the inking and printed on different kinds of paper. He did not sign the copperplate, perhaps indicating that he was reluctant to think he had finished it.   JSB

Plate 67
Rembrandt Harmensz. van Rijn

PORTRAIT OF THOMAS JACOBSZ. HAARINGH (THE "OLD HAARINGH"), ca. 1655

Drypoint and burin on paper, second state of two, plate: 7 ¾ x 5 ¹³⁄₁₆ in. (19.5 x 14.7 cm); sheet: 7 ⅞ x 5 ¹⁵⁄₁₆ in. (20 x 15 cm)
H. O. Havemeyer Collection, Bequest of Mrs. H. O. Havemeyer, 1929
29.107.23

Two portraits of men from the Haaringh family, etched about 1655–56, were in the Havemeyer collection. The father, "Old Haaringh," shown here, was bailiff to the Amsterdam Court of Insol- vency and was later responsible for the sale of Rembrandt's house and possessions. His son, the "Young Haaringh," was a lawyer and was also involved with Rembrandt's bankruptcy.

By 1655 Rembrandt was a distin- guished portrait painter and etcher. His early etched heads, those from the 1630s and the 1640s, were often not portraits but studies of his own head, made while he sat in front of a mirror, wearing different caps, hats, or hairstyles. By the time he etched the Haaringhs, experience gained from his continual experi- ments in the etching and drypoint techniques allowed him to concen- trate on the character and emotions of his sitters to produce portraits that are masterpieces.   JSB

Plate 69
Rembrandt Harmensz. van Rijn

LANDSCAPE WITH THREE GABLED COTTAGES BESIDE A ROAD, 1650

Etching and drypoint on paper watermarked with a foolscap, third state of three, plate: 6 ⅜ x 8 in. (16.3 x 20.3 cm); sheet: 6 ⁹⁄₁₆ x 8 ¼ in. (16.7 x 20.9 cm)
Signed and dated l.l.: *Rembrandt f 1650*
H. O. Havemeyer Collection, Bequest of Mrs. H. O. Havemeyer, 1929
29.107.33

From time to time after producing an etching, Rembrandt returned to his copperplate and made changes. Shadows were often introduced or strengthened, as in the *Landscape with Three Gabled Cottages Beside a Road*. Three times Rembrandt added shadows to this plate, but he did not change the entire composition, as he did most notably in his *Three Crosses*, where figures disappear in new shadows under a sky darkening in cataclysm. Recognizing that he had said all that he wanted to say about the three gabled cottages in a landscape endowed with the pervasive smells of chilly dampness—of mud, of wet grass, of woodsmoke—Rembrandt signed his copperplate and dated it 1650.

JSB

THE HAVEMEYERS AND ANTOINE-LOUIS BARYE

In 1906, when the American sculptor Daniel Chester French was Chairman of The Metropolitan Museum of Art's recently formed Trustees' Committee on Sculpture, he reported that the Museum had "few or no examples of Barye, Rodin, St. Gaudens and other modern sculptors of the first importance."

He went on to add that "the expenditure of a sum equal to the cast of one work of antiquity, of historic or archaeological value, would create a collection of popular interest and would tend to stimulate this important art."[1] French was speaking of the Metropolitan's holdings, but a few blocks away from the Museum in the house of Henry O. and Louisine Havemeyer, a collection of small bronzes by one of the three artists mentioned in his report, Antoine-Louis Barye, the animal sculptor par excellence of nineteenth-century Paris, had long been cherished.

A photograph (fig. 6) made in 1892 of the dining room of the

Havemeyers' Tiffany-designed house documents the collection as it existed at the time.[2] A veritable menagerie of small bronze animals inhabited the mantelpiece above the fireplace, while miniature versions of two of Barye's most successful monumental sculptures perched on the andirons below. Atop the left andiron stood one of the reductions of the *Lion Crushing a Serpent*, initially commissioned by the French government for the gardens of the Tuileries as a lifesize bronze from a plaster model exhibited in the Paris Salon of 1833. On the right andiron was a tiny *Seated Lion*, first modeled in 1835, which in its original

Figure 6. Dining room, 1 East 66th Street

70

Plate 70. Antoine-Louis Barye. *Lion Crushing a Serpent*, cast after 1848 from model in reduced size of ca. 1832. Bronze with greenish patina, h. 10⅛ in. (25.4 cm). Signed on base: *BARYE*. Shelburne Museum, Shelburne, Vermont, Gift of the Webb Estate (26–26)

Plate 71. Antoine-Louis Barye. *Jaguar Devouring a Crocodile*, cast at unknown date from model probably of ca. 1858–60. Bronze with dark brown patina on wood base, l. 9⅞ in. (25.1 cm). Signed on base: *BARYE*. Shelburne Museum, Shelburne, Vermont, Gift of the Webb Estate (26–28)

Plate 72. Antoine-Louis Barye. *Wolf Seizing a Stag by the Throat*, cast ca. 1875 from model of ca. 1830–43. Bronze with green patina, l. 17½ in. (44.5 cm). Signed on base: *BARYE*. Shelburne Museum, Shelburne, Vermont, Gift of the Webb Estate (26–24)

Plate 73. Antoine-Louis Barye. *Elephants by a Pool*. Watercolor on wove paper, 13 x 19⅝ in. (33.1 x 49.9 cm). H. O. Havemeyer Collection, Bequest of Mrs. H. O. Havemeyer, 1929 (29.100.593) A19

size now guards the portal of the Pavillon de Flore on the side of the Louvre that fronts on the Seine. On the mantel itself two smaller reductions of the *Lion Crushing a Serpent* (pl. 70) flanked, from right to left, the *Jaguar Devouring a Crocodile* (pl. 71), the *Panther of Tunis*, the *Indian Mounted on an Elephant Crushing a Tiger*, the *Asian Elephant* or *Elephant of Cochin China*, and what is probably the *Python Swallowing a Doe*. The cornice above supported the *Walking Lion* and the *Walking Tiger* and still another cast of the *Lion Crushing a Serpent*.[3]

Not all of the Havemeyers' bronzes were present, however, in the 1892 photograph of the dining room. A letter preserved in the Shelburne Museum in Vermont informs us that the bronze *Wolf Seizing a Stag by the Throat* (pl. 72) was purchased by Henry O. Havemeyer in 1895 from one Edward Sutton Smith, who had ordered it from Barye shortly before the sculptor's death in 1875.[4]

Barye, whose early career was furthered greatly by commissions from the French royal family, lost his most important French patrons with the downfall of King Louis-Philippe in 1848. The blow was made more severe by his artistic differences with the neoclassically oriented officials of the French Academy. Even before the monarchy collapsed, however, Barye had turned to making small bronzes in quantity for middle-class collectors, setting up a short-lived partnership for the purpose with the entrepreneur Emile Martin in 1845.[5] Barye later marketed his bronzes with the aid of a series of catalogues that permitted the purchaser to order from a variety of available models.

The earliest catalogue, published in 1847,[6] divided the sculpture into four categories and noted that those in category two would be suitable for the decoration of clocks for offices and bedrooms, while others in category three, among them the reduced version of the *Lion Crushing a Serpent*, would be appropriate for formal drawing rooms. The fourth category included candle-sticks, candelabra, an inkwell, and other decorative objects, though not andirons like those in the Havemeyer dining room, which may have been a conceit specially assembled for the Havemeyers. Thus, while Barye produced some of the best monumental sculpture of the Romantic period in nineteenth-century French art, much of which is still to be seen in present-day Paris, he also made small bronzes for collectors; moreover, his ideas about the use of these small pieces as decorative elements were, in fact, not far removed from the way the Havemeyers displayed them.

The Havemeyers were delighted by Barye's watercolors as well as by his small sculpture, and their purchases in the former category constitute a sizable portion of the surviving oeuvre of the artist. Among the twenty-five Barye watercolors that were part of the Havemeyer gift to the Metropolitan Museum are such choice examples as the *Elephants by a Pool* (pl. 73), the *Tiger Rolling on Its Back* (A39), and the *Vultures on a Tree* (pl. 74).[7] These display the same consummate skill in rendering animals and birds found in Barye's modeling of sculpture and are the fruit of his years of observation in the menagerie of the Jardin des Plantes in Paris, where he sketched and modeled from life, sometimes in the company of his old friend Delacroix.

Barye's art was greatly admired by nineteenth-century Americans. The wealthy Baltimore collector William T. Walters was the most prominent patron of the sculptor in his later years. Walters, on the advice of the American expatriate George A. Lucas, began buying Barye's bronzes in 1861.[8] His collection, now in the Walters Art Gallery in Baltimore, contains a number of the finest small bronzes that Barye produced, notably some of those intended for the *surtout de table* commissioned by the French king's eldest son, the Duke of Orléans (1810–1842). In

Plate 74. Antoine-Louis Barye. *Vultures on a Tree*. Watercolor on wove paper, 10 ¹¹⁄₁₆ x 15 ⅛ in. (27.2 x 38.4 cm). H. O. Havemeyer Collection, Bequest of Mrs. H. O. Havemeyer, 1929 (29.100.596) A41

1874 Walters was instrumental in commissioning an example of each of Barye's bronzes for William Wilson Corcoran's newly established Corcoran Gallery of Art in Washington, D.C., where he was a trustee.[9]

Walters and Lucas were zealous fund-raisers for a monument that was to be erected in Barye's honor on the rue Sully in Paris. As head of the American Barye Monument Association, Walters not only formulated the plans but also lent generously to an exhibition of Barye's art in American collections organized to raise money for the monument, which opened at the American Art Galleries in New York on November 15, 1889. (The Metropolitan Museum lent the bronze *Theseus Fighting the Centaur Bianor* that had been the gift of its trustee Samuel P. Avery in 1885. Avery was another enthusiastic collector of Barye's art and the lender of thirty of his own Baryes to the exhibition in New York.) The catalogue, which included more than five hundred works by the artist, was written by Cyrus J. Lawrence, whose own considerable collection formed an even larger portion of the exhibition than Avery's and is now the nucleus of The Brooklyn Museum's Barye holdings.

Henry O. Havemeyer had bought at least one of Barye's bronzes, as well as an unidentified oil painting by him, through Lucas in 1886.[10] Another bronze, a *Lion Crushing a Serpent*, was purchased for $675 at the American Art Galleries nine months before the Barye exhibition opened there.[11] These were not among the works in the November exhibition. However, that exhibition evidently reinforced the Havemeyers' interest in Barye and prompted their purchases of additional bronzes and watercolors from Durand-Ruel, which included the andirons.[12]

The *Seated Lion* and the *Lion Crushing a Serpent* are now in the collection of the Shelburne Museum, as are the *Walking Lion*, the *Walking Tiger*, the *Indian Mounted on an Elephant Crushing a Tiger*, the *Asian Elephant*, and the *Jaguar Devouring a Crocodile*. In Louisine Havemeyer's "Notes to Her Children," four Barye bronzes were earmarked for Electra Havemeyer, an enthusiastic sportswoman. None were among the gifts to The Metropolitan Museum of Art.

CV

1. Reports: Sculpture Committee 1906–1907, 1/15/06, MMA Archives.
2. See Weitzenhoffer 1986, p. 59.
3. See Pivar 1974, p. 64, fig. F-14; p. 122, fig. A-37; p. 126, fig. A-41; p. 131, fig. A-48; p. 141, fig. A-58; p. 150, fig. A-73; p. 155, fig. A-85; p. 157, fig. A-88; p. 236, fig. A-196. See also Jeanne L. Wasserman and Arthur Beale, *Sculpture by Antoine-Louis Barye in the Fogg Art Museum*, Cambridge, Mass., 1982, pp. 82–83.
4. Mrs. Edward Sutton Smith to HOH, 2/28/95, Shelburne Museum, Shelburne, Vermont. According to this letter, the bronze had been cast while Smith was away from Paris, and as he was not in the city when Barye died, the piece was sold in the auction of the sculptor's estate held at the Hôtel Drouot, Paris, in 1876. However, Smith traced the bronze to the purchaser, George E. Woodward, in 1879 and recovered it. I would like to thank Eloise Beil and Lauren Hewes of the Shelburne Museum for bringing this letter, as well as the bill of sale from the American Art Galleries (see n. 11), to my attention.
5. See Glenn F. Benge, *Antoine-Louis Barye, Sculptor of Romantic Realism*, University Park, Pa., 1984, p. 155.
6. Reproduced by Roger Ballu, *L'Oeuvre de Barye*, Paris, 1890, pp. 161–63, and by Martin Sonnabend, *Antoine-Louis Barye (1795–1875)*, Munich, 1988, pp. 266–68.
7. See Zieseness 1953, p. 77, no. F-8, pl. 28; p. 65, no. B-19, pl. 12; p. 79, no. G-3, pl. 31.
8. See Lilian M. C. Randall, *The Diary of George A. Lucas: An American Art Agent in Paris, 1857–1909*, Princeton, N.J., 1979, vol. 1, p. 13.
9. See ibid., p. 14, and Lilien Filipovitch Robinson, "Barye and Patronage," in *Antoine-Louis Barye: The Corcoran Collection*, exh. cat., The Corcoran Gallery of Art, Washington, D.C., 1988, pp. 66–70.
10. See Randall, *Diary of Lucas*, vol. 2, p. 628.
11. Bill of sale, 2/1/89, Shelburne Museum, Shelburne, Vermont.
12. See Weitzenhoffer 1986, p. 61.

Plate 75
Honoré Daumier

THE CONNOISSEUR, 1860–65

Pen and ink, wash, watercolor, conté crayon, and gouache over black chalk on wove paper, 17¼ x 14 in. (43.8 x 35.5 cm)
H. O. Havemeyer Collection, Bequest of Mrs. H. O. Havemeyer, 1929
29.100.200
A179

Daumier spent most of his life drawing for the wide audience reached by France's popular press. But when he was temporarily let go from the magazine *Le Charivari* in 1860, he began to produce highly finished watercolors designed particularly for collectors. The Paris art market of the late nineteenth century, no longer the exclusive realm of princes and barons, flourished thanks to the keen interest of art-loving lawyers, bankers, industrialists, and merchants. Daumier often pictured the broad spectrum of enthusiasts attending exhibitions or visiting artists' studios; here he portrayed the model connoisseur engaged in the rapt contemplation of his collection.

The special object of this collector's appreciation is a tabletop replica of the Venus de Milo, the monumental Greek marble that came to symbolize the beauty of antique art upon its installation in the Louvre in 1821. As if aware of the admiration directed toward her (by the sculpted and painted men in the room as well as by the connoisseur), the statuette returns the collector's gaze, somewhat impudently, it seems, and with exaggerated body torsion—which was modified in the original sculpture when its upper and lower parts were readjusted in 1871.

Among the five known preparatory sketches for this finely worked watercolor, one concentrates on the Venus alone, and another is a charcoal study of the composition dedicated to the actor-producer Alfred Baron (Cléophas), a friend of the artist's.[1] The present work belonged to another of Daumier's friends, the landscape painter Jules Dupré. On September 19, 1895, the Havemeyers purchased the picture from Durand-Ruel,[2] in whose Paris galleries it first had been displayed in 1878, in the only one-man exhibition given to Daumier during his lifetime.

CI

1. Maison 1968, 2, nos. 113, 114, 368, 369, 806; the Havemeyer watercolor is no. 370. See also Jacob Bean, *100 European Drawings in The Metropolitan Museum of Art*, New York, 1964, no. 71.
2. Purchase no. 3367 P.

Plate 76
Honoré Daumier

A MAN READING IN A GARDEN, 1860–65

Watercolor over black chalk, with pen and ink, wash, and conté crayon on wove paper, 13 5/16 x 10 5/8 in. (33.8 x 27 cm)
Verso: preliminary study in pen and brown ink, gray wash, and conté crayon
H. O. Havemeyer Collection, Bequest of Mrs. H. O. Havemeyer, 1929
29.100.199
A178

Daumier was introduced to the pleasures of the countryside by his friends the Barbizon painters Corot, Millet, Dupré, and especially Daubigny, who brought him to the village of Valmondois, a short train ride northwest of Paris. It was there that Daumier spent much of his old age, taking a lease on a cottage in 1865, while retaining a studio in Paris.

There is no reason to believe that the sitter in this watercolor is Corot, as once was thought. The man might just as well be Daumier himself settled down with a good book in the embrace of branching trees and dappled sunlight. The superb structure of the composition and its finely tuned transparency are compelling enough to have attracted the attention of Cézanne; such focus and balance were achieved only after Daumier completed at least

two preliminary studies, one worked on the back of this same sheet.[1]

The Havemeyers purchased *Man Reading in a Garden*, as they did Daumier's *Connoisseur*, from the dealers Durand-Ruel.[2] The two works might have been displayed attractively side by side as pendant scenes of contemplative life agreeably pursued indoors and out, the man-made order of the furnished interior in marked contrast to the fluctuations of nature and the open air.

CI

1. Maison 1968, 2, nos. 359, 360; the Havemeyer watercolor is no. 361. See also Jacob Bean, *100 European Drawings in The Metropolitan Museum of Art*, New York, 1964, no. 70.
2. The exact date of the drawing's purchase is not known. It was lent by Durand-Ruel to an exhibition at the Union League Club in New York in 1890 and mentioned in a review of that show published in *Art Amateur* 22 (May 1890), p. 122.

Plate 77
William Merritt Chase

AZALEAS (VASE OF FLOWERS), ca. 1882

Oil on canvas, 31 x 37 in. (78.7 x 94 cm)
Private collection
A81

An 1892 photograph of the balcony of the skylit gallery of the Havemeyer house shows Chase's *Azaleas (Vase of Flowers)* prominently displayed next to a tall case filled with Chinese porcelain vases. This opulent still-life painting portrays on a narrow table covered with a peacock-blue cloth a highly glazed rustic green pottery jar filled with pink and white azaleas. To the right of the jar is a shiny glass bowl lying on its side against the mottled dark background wall. A pair of ladies' kidskin gloves and a pale pink ladies' handkerchief are casually laid on the table toward the right.

The jar and the bowl echo objects that the Havemeyers collected. Azaleas, shrubs that are often hybrids of American and Asian strains, reflect the dual taste for the Occidental and

Oriental that guided their acquisitions. The gloves and handkerchief suggest the elegant and active life that they pursued and announce a woman's presence in relation to the objects assembled on the tabletop.

As it bespeaks the Havemeyers' cosmopolitan taste and social life, Chase's floral still life was an appropriate exception to their indifference to American painting. (Other than works by their friend Cassatt, the Havemeyers owned only a few American canvases, most of which were landscapes.) Completed about 1882, *Azaleas* typifies key aspects of Chase's work. The dark tonalities of the background and the bold brushwork recall the contemporary painting of Munich, where he studied in the 1870s. The extraordinary freedom with which he constructed the gloves and handkerchief out of shards of pale paint proclaims his admiration for the style of Manet, whose *Woman with a Parrot* and *Boy with a Sword* (fig. 1) he had helped New York collector Erwin Davis acquire from the artist in

1881. The rapid rendering of the mass of flowers and the play of complementaries in the jar and the flowers anticipate Chase's experiments in Impressionism in the mid-1880s. While fewer than 10 canvases among Chase's 120 still-life paintings depict floral subjects, flowers and bric-a-brac challenged him to produce some of his most successful still lifes and allude to his own passionate collecting.

The catalogue of the sale of paintings from Mrs. Havemeyer's estate indicates that Chase's *Azaleas* was purchased from the artist himself. Although Cassatt, whom Chase had met in Paris in June 1881, might have encouraged the acquisition, that Tiffany proposed it is just as likely. Tiffany was closely involved with Chase in organizing and installing the 1883 Bartholdi Pedestal Fund Art Loan Exhibition in New York, and he may have recognized how appropriate *Azaleas* would be to the spirit and the decorative needs of his leading clients' gallery.

HBW

THE HAVEMEYERS AND THE DEGAS BRONZES

If the Havemeyers were not remarkably daring in their collecting of small bronzes by Antoine-Louis Barye, the case was quite different when it came to acquiring the sculpture of Edgar Degas. Degas's sculpture is essentially a private art, akin to the sketch or drawing, and it remained largely unknown during the artist's lifetime. The only sculpture that Degas ever exhibited, *The Little Fourteen-Year-Old Dancer* (fig. 67), was shown in the sixth Impressionist exhibition, held in Paris in 1881, but the work has little to do with Impressionism. Modeled in wax and wearing a real bodice, stockings, shoes, cotton skirt, and horsehair wig with satin ribbon, the figure astonished Degas's contemporaries, not only for its unorthodox use of materials and colors but also and above all for its realism, judged brutish by some.[1] *The Little Fourteen-Year-Old Dancer* was not again seen publicly until April 1920.[2]

The remaining examples of Degas's surviving sculpture, for the most part modeled in wax, clay, and plastiline, are essentially intimate in character, evidently intended for the artist's own pleasure; indeed, it was not until Degas's death in 1917 that their existence became common knowledge. Many were by that time in advanced stages of decay, but illustrations of *The Little Fourteen-Year-Old Dancer*, as well as of some of the other better-preserved examples, were soon published in French journals,[3] and several even appeared in the March 1919 issue of *Vanity Fair*.[4] The debate about their preservation and ultimate disposition began.

Among those who had long known of this sculpture trove was Louisine Havemeyer. Louisine's first purchase, made in 1877, was a Degas pastel titled *Ballet Rehearsal* (now in the Nelson-Atkins Museum of Art in Kansas City) (pl. 2).[5] In 1894 she and Harry began collecting Degas's paintings in earnest, but not until 1903, on a visit to Degas's studio with the indefatigable Mary Cassatt, did she see *The Little Fourteen-Year-Old Dancer* and decide that she wanted to buy it. Letters written about 1903 indicate that Degas seriously contemplated making repairs to the sculpture, as well as the possibility of having it cast in bronze, in preparation for its sale.[6] However, nothing came of these considerations, perhaps because Degas was notoriously ambivalent about preserving his sculpture in the relatively permanent medium of bronze.

Louisine seems to have bided her time until 1917, after the artist's death, when a flurry of letters about the availability and condition of the figure commenced between Louisine and Cassatt. Degas's heirs were in disagreement about a great many things, however, and the price of *The Little Fourteen-Year-Old Dancer* kept rising. The price of Fr 500,000 quoted in 1919[7] was doubled in 1920.[8] The condition of the sculpture was far from certain and the price was too high for Louisine. How amazed she might have been had she lived to see *one* of the multiple posthumous bronzes cast from the original figure auctioned for $10,120,000.[9]

In the meanwhile the heirs of Degas had decided to authorize a series of casts or editions of bronzes to be made from seventy-two of the small figures. These were chiefly dancers, bathers, and horses: many repetitions of the same subject, but with subtle transformations in composition or in the dynamics of movement within the figure. Paul-Albert Bartholomé, a sculptor and Degas's longtime friend, was to prepare the figures for casting, and the execution of the editions to be put into the hands of the Paris foundry A.-A. Hébrard et Cie.

In the contract, which is dated May 13, 1918, it was stipulated that each edition would be limited to twenty casts, plus one for Adrien Hébrard, head of the foundry, and one for Degas's heirs.[10] All the bronzes were to be stamped *Degas*, and a method of marking the individual casts was outlined, but it was not, in fact, the one actually used. Instead, as the catalogue for the first exhibition of the bronzes in Paris stated, each sculpture was to be assigned a number (1–73, although, in actual practice, 73, *The Little Fourteen-Year-Old Dancer* [pl. 78], was not numbered) and each series of casts a letter (A–T).[11] For example, the first sculpture, a small dancer titled *Arabesque over the Right Leg* (pl. 79), was numbered 1 and the first cast of the figure given the letter A. The completed bronze thus bore the inscribed identification *1/A* in addition to the stamp *Degas* and the seal of the founder (*CIRE/PERDUE/A.-A. HEBRARD*, raised within a rectangle). The series cast for the Degas family was to be marked *HER.D*, and the series cast for Hébrard *HER*. Despite some puzzling evidence to the contrary, this system seems to have been followed by Hébrard.[12]

The first, or A letter, series (see fig. 7) was reserved for Mrs. Havemeyer by Cassatt for the sum of Fr 60,000.[13] This series was certainly completed before May 1921, when it was exhibited in Paris. It was in New York by 1922, when it was shown, attributed to an anonymous lender, at the Grolier Club,[14] and twelve of the bronzes were lent anonymously to the Metropolitan Museum in 1923. A second loan was made in 1925.[15]

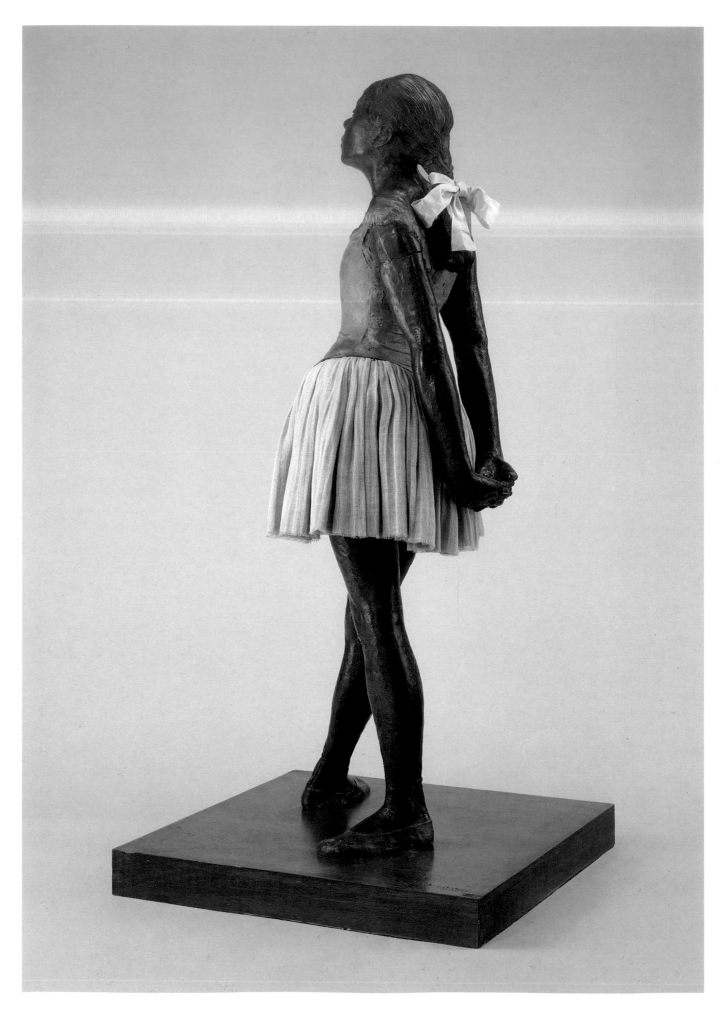

Plate 79. Edgar Degas. *Arabesque over the Right Leg, the Left Arm in Front*, cast 1920 from wax sculpture probably modeled 1877/85. Bronze, h. 11⅜ in. (28 cm). Signed on base: *Degas*; founder's marks on base: *CIRE/PERDUE/A.A. HEBRARD* (stamped within rectangle), *r/A* (incised). H. O. Havemeyer Collection, Bequest of Mrs. H. O. Havemeyer, 1929 (29.100.401)

The actual casting of the bronzes seems to have been chiefly the work of one of Hébrard's employees, Albino Palazzolo (b. 1883).[16] Palazzolo was entrusted with the difficult process of making molds of the delicate originals without destroying them. The molds were then used for casting master models in bronze, and these, in turn, were used to make the molds necessary for casting the individual waxes for the lost-wax casting of each of the twenty-two bronzes in an edition, thus sparing the fragile originals.

The Little Fourteen-Year-Old Dancer had a somewhat different and quite complex casting history.[17] It is not certain how many casts were made in bronze, but two examples cast by Palazzolo in plaster are known.[18] In any case, the first example in bronze, lettered A but not numbered, is the cast that would have been sent to New York for de-

Figure 7. Installation view showing a selection of Degas bronzes, *The H. O. Havemeyer Collection*, The Metropolitan Museum of Art, 1930

Plate 78. Edgar Degas. *The Little Fourteen-Year-Old Dancer*, cast 1922 from wax sculpture of ca. 1880. Bronze, partly tinted, with cotton skirt and satin hair ribbon, on wood base, h. 41¼ in. (104.5 cm). Signed on base: *Degas*; founder's marks on base: *CIRE/PERDUE/A.A. HEBRARD/A* (stamped within rectangle of bronze let into wood); founder's marks on left thigh: *CIRE/PERDUE/A.A. HEBRARD* (stamped within rectangle) *A* (incised). H. O. Havemeyer Collection, Bequest of Mrs. H. O. Havemeyer, 1929 (29.100.370)

livery to Mrs. Havemeyer.[19] Still another of the original sculptures, *The Schoolgirl*, was omitted from the initial series of editions. It had a separate and rather complicated casting history but was never acquired by Mrs. Havemeyer.

The original sculptures, long thought to have been destroyed, had, in fact, been preserved by Hébrard. They came to light in 1955 when they appeared in New York at Knoedler's, where they were offered for sale.[20] The master models, which were completely unknown until 1955 when Palazzolo revealed their existence and explained their function,[21] began appearing on the market in the early 1970s. The majority of the originals were acquired by Paul Mellon and ultimately given to the National Gallery of Art in Washington, D.C.[22] The master models were bought by Norton Simon and can be seen today in the Norton Simon Museum of Art in Pasadena.

Under the terms of the third codicil to her will, dated August 18, 1922, Mrs. Havemeyer bequeathed all the bronzes in the A series with the exception of 19/A, *Dancer Moving Forward*, and 41/A, *Dancer at Rest*, to the Metropolitan. The account books of the Hébrard foundry reveal that Louisine bought a cast that was not in the A series, 15/G, *Grand Arabesque, Second Time*.[23] Its present location, like that of 19/A and of 41/A, is not known. Electra Havemeyer Webb bought an additional dozen bronzes, which included 4/O, *Rearing Horse*; 25/G, *Horse with Jockey*; 32/C, *Horse Galloping*; and 48/G, *Horse Clearing an Obstacle*, now in the collection of the Shelburne Museum in Vermont, along with the bronze cast J of *The Little Fourteen-Year-Old Dancer*, also the gift of the Webb Estate.

GV

1. See Michael Pantazzi's summary of contemporaneous criticism in Boggs et al. 1988, p. 343.
2. See Pingeot 1991, p. 189.
3. See Paul Gsell, "Edgar Degas, Statuaire," *La Renaissance de l'art français et des industries de luxe* 1 (December 1918), pp. 373–78; Paul-André Lemoisne, "Les Statuettes de Degas," *Art et Décoration* 36 (July–August 1919), pp. 109–17.
4. *Vanity Fair* (March 1919), p. 50.
5. For more on this subject, see Gary Tinterow, "The Havemeyer Pictures," and Susan Alyson Stein, Chronology, this catalogue.
6. See Pantazzi in Boggs et al. 1988, p. 343; Pingeot 1991, p. 189.
7. MC to LWH, 12/10/19, Havemeyer correspondence.
8. MC to LWH, 4/18/20, Havemeyer correspondence.
9. Sale catalogue, Sotheby's, New York, May 10, 1988, lot no. 14.
10. The contents of the contract appear in Pingeot 1991, p. 194.
11. See Galerie A.-A. Hébrard, Paris, *Exposition des Sculptures de Degas*, exh. cat., May–June 1921.
12. See Patricia Failing, "The Degas Bronzes Degas Never Knew," *Art News* 78 (April 1979), pp. 38–41; Pingeot 1991, p. 29.
13. See Pingeot 1991, p. 130.
14. Grolier Club, New York, *Catalogue of Prints, Drawings, and Bronzes by Degas*, exh. cat., 1922.
15. See Joseph Breck, "Sculptures by Degas on Loan," *Bulletin of The Metropolitan Museum of Art* 18 (March 1923), p. 59; "A New Loan of Degas Bronzes," *Bulletin of The Metropolitan Museum of Art* 20 (February 1925), p. 58.
16. See Jean Adhémar, "Before the Degas Bronzes," *Art News* 54 (November 1955), pp. 34–35, 70. See also Patricia Failing, "Cast in Bronze: The Degas Dilemma," *Art News* 87 (January 1988), pp. 136–41; Pingeot 1991, pp. 23–28.
17. For details of this history, see Pingeot 1991, pp. 188–90.
18. Ibid., p. 188.
19. GD-R to Gallery Durand-Ruel, New York, 11/10/22, quoted in ibid., p. 190.
20. John Rewald, "Foreword," in *Edgar Degas 1834–1917: Original Wax Sculptures*, exh. cat., M. Knoedler and Co., New York, 1955, n.p.
21. See Adhémar, "Before the Degas Bronzes," p. 70.
22. For the present location of each, see Pingeot 1991, pp. 153–91.
23. See ibid., p. 196.

Plate 80
Edgar Degas

A GIRL PUTTING ON HER STOCKING, 1876–77

Monotype in black ink on china paper, plate:
6 ¼ x 4 ⅝ in. (159 x 118 cm); sheet:
7 ¾ x 6 ³⁄₁₆ in. (197 x 157 cm)
H. O. Havemeyer Collection, Bequest of
Mrs. H. O. Havemeyer, 1929
29.107.54

The heavily inked drawings Degas made on metal plates and then printed on paper with a press are among his most ingenious productions. He printed about four hundred such pictures, evidently thinking himself the inventor of the monotype process, although the technique is traceable to the seventeenth century.[1]

It is likely that Degas began making monotypes in the summer of 1876, during a period of intense printing activity that resulted in (at least) the three individual sets of monotypes he contributed to the third Impressionist exhibition of 1877. *A Girl Putting on Her Stocking* undoubtedly dates to this first wave of monotype work. The careful and varied handling of the ink — alternately brushed, wiped, and scumbled — suggests an exploratory approach to the description of human contours and the textures of interior furnishings.

Although by this time Degas had begun to peer at the workaday world of prostitutes, the young woman seen here has all the earmarks of a ballerina, in her physical delicacy and agility and in her attention to her feet. (Her only element of costume, a black-ribbon choker, was a fashionable accessory in the late nineteenth century for women both onstage and in the brothel.)

The fact that this impish nude would seem more at home in a boudoir decorated by Boucher than in one of the back rooms of a *maison*

close probably endeared her to both Cassatt and Louisine Havemeyer. A note written by Mrs. Havemeyer in pencil on the monotype's original mount reads: *Given to me by Mary Cassatt 1889.*

CI

1. Michael Pantazzi, "The First Monotypes," in Boggs et al. 1988, pp. 257–60.

Plate 81
Edgar Degas

ACTRESSES IN THEIR DRESSING ROOMS, 1879–80

Etching and aquatint on heavy wove paper, fourth state of five, plate: 6 ¼ x 8 ⅜ in. (159 x 213 cm); sheet: 8 ⅞ x 12 ¼ in. (225 x 311 cm)
H. O. Havemeyer Collection, Bequest of Mrs. H. O. Havemeyer, 1929
29.107.51

Of the five etchings by Degas in the Havemeyer bequest, this is the most disconcertingly modern; unlike the other intaglio prints in the donation, which are all portraits, it lends veracity to Louisine Havemeyer's remark: "I believe it takes special brain cells to understand Degas."[1] A memento of an evening's intrusion behind the scenes at the theater, this grainy, snapshot-style picture reveals the special vantage point of the artist, who, Mrs. Havemeyer observed, "did not mince matters" and "frankly exposed poor human nature in its vulgar banality."[2]

Degas was a longtime aficionado of backstage life, which he depicted most vividly between 1876 and 1877 in a series of monotypes based on Ludovic Halévy's stories about two young dancers at the Opéra, Pauline and Virginie Cardinal. It was at this time, too, that he began to study the everyday business of the brothel, engaging in the kind of voyeurism that came to empower Lautrec's work and then Picasso's. But unique to Degas's private spectacle of two women getting dressed at the theater is his exacting control of pictorial composition that fixes the structure of doors, floors, and walls as a backdrop for human forms, ghostly shadows, and reflected light.

Although only fifteen impressions of this etching are thus far known,[3] Degas may have considered including it in the periodical illustrated with prints that he planned to publish in 1880 under the title *Le Jour et la nuit*. Illumination and night effects, which are here strikingly simulated by means of aquatint, preoccupied him during much of the late 1870s. CI

1. Havemeyer 1961, p. 249.
2. Ibid., p. 261.
3. Sue Welsh Reed and Barbara Stern Shapiro, *Edgar Degas: The Painter as Printmaker*, exh. cat., Museum of Fine Arts, Boston, 1984, no. 50, IV.

Plate 82
Mary Cassatt

HELENE OF SEPTEUIL, 1889–90

Drypoint on laid paper, third state of five, plate: 9 ⅜ x 6 ³⁄₁₆ in. (240 x 160 cm); sheet: 12 ¼ x 9 ⅜ in. (311 x 238 cm)
Stamped l.r.: *CM* (in monogram); signed and inscribed l.r.: *Mary Cassatt Hélène de Septeuil*
H. O. Havemeyer Collection, Bequest of Mrs. H. O. Havemeyer, 1929
29.107.89

Mary Cassatt adopted the technique of drypoint on the strength of Edgar Degas's advice. The practice of sketching on a polished copperplate with a sharpened needle was a severe discipline, but it won her the Frenchman's disbelieving praise: "This back, did you draw this?"[1]

Cassatt began making etchings about 1879, the year she first exhibited with the Impressionists and about the time her friend Degas entered what was then laughingly called his "metallurgical phase." It was at this moment too that Cassatt began to portray children (usually in the company of their mothers or nursemaids) with a clear-eyed scrutiny that even now is disarming. The double challenge of capturing uncooperative subjects in an unforgiving medium proved a test of her draftsmanship.

With her discovery of Japanese prints, Cassatt's work became much more clearly defined; thus, when she took up drypoint about 1889, she began to draw in open curves like those in Utamaro's woodcuts of women and infants, which manage to look elegant and unpretentious at the same time (see pl. 147). Her vision focused in concentrated studies like this depiction of the innkeeper's daughter at Septeuil, a village west of Paris, where Cassatt spent the summers of 1889 and 1890 with her family. Hélène and her mother, Mathilde, are portrayed in two other closely related works: a pastel (The William Benton Museum of Art, The

University of Connecticut, Storrs) and an experimental color etching (The New York Public Library).[2]

Hélène of Septeuil was one of twelve drypoints Cassatt showed in Paris in the March 1890 Exposition de Peintres-Graveurs. All twelve are represented among the twenty-three prints by Cassatt bequeathed to the Museum by the Havemeyers. Their gift probably also would have in-

cluded Cassatt's more famous suite of ten color prints (1890–91) had Paul J. Sachs not already donated the set to the Metropolitan in 1916.

CI

1. Quoted in Nancy Mowll Mathews and Barbara Stern Shapiro, *Mary Cassatt: The Color Prints*, exh. cat., Williams College Museum of Art, Williamstown, Mass., 1989, p. 39.
2. Ibid., pp. 97–98.

FOUR CASSATT PASTELS OF HAVEMEYER WOMEN: LOUISINE, ELECTRA, ADALINE

Mary Cassatt rarely accepted portrait commissions, preferring to depict family members and friends with whom she felt a personal bond. Four portraits of Louisine Havemeyer and her two young daughters, Electra and Adaline, executed in pastel between 1895 and 1898, suggest the

mutual affection felt by the artist and her sitters and evoke the pleasure of their encounters.

By the 1890s Cassatt was working more and more in pastel, finding the colored chalks most suitable for capturing candid glimpses and most expedient in that they allowed her to avoid elaborate preparations, paint mixing, and studio setups. Yet, under the influence of her friend Edgar Degas, she created her pastels with as much care and intensity as her oils, building up layers of color and letting the figures fill up the large-scale sheets of wove paper and press out at their edges.

The Havemeyers spent the summer of 1895 visiting London, Paris, and Switzerland, purchasing Re-

naissance and modern works. In August the family—or perhaps only Mrs. Havemeyer and her daughters—went to stay with Cassatt at Mesnil-Théribus, about fifty miles northwest of Paris in the Oise region. Cassatt had acquired the Château de Beaufresne—a seventeenth-century manor house with forty-five acres of fields and woods—a year earlier. This country retreat permitted the artist to create and cultivate a garden and to entertain friends away from the bustle of Paris.

At Beaufresne Cassatt produced two fine pastel portraits of Louisine Havemeyer and her children. The image of Louisine and Electra (pl. 83) is a sympathetic description

Plate 83. Mary Cassatt. *Louisine Havemeyer and Her Daughter Electra*, 1895. Pastel on wove paper, 24 x 30½ in. (61 x 77.5 cm). Private collection. A55

Plate 84. Mary Cassatt. *Adaline Havemeyer*, 1895. Pastel on wove paper, 28⅞ x 23¾ in. (73.4 x 60.4 cm). Private collection. A54

of the sitters and an eloquent characterization of maternal affection, reflecting Cassatt's devotion to the mother-and-child theme in the 1890s. On a bright red sofa Louisine sits with young Electra, just past her seventh birthday, snug and comfortable on her lap. Rather than looking at each other, at the artist, or at any spectator, the two are absorbed in thought. The echo of the mother's pensiveness in the daughter's, the arm of the one encircling the shoulders of the other, the merging of

their hands in the foreground, the migration of color and thick stroke across the edges of their garments all suggest the deepest bonds between them.[1]

For a pastel portrait of Adaline (pl. 84), Cassatt employed both the pose and the mood of self-absorption she used in the depiction of Electra on her mother's lap. Then eleven years old, the wistful Adaline simultaneously evokes a sense of unself-conscious girlhood, with her scrubbed cheeks and simple coiffure,

and the dignity of approaching young womanhood.

During the Havemeyers' visit to France in the spring of 1896, Cassatt began a portrait of Louisine alone (pl. 85). As the image could not be finished before Mrs. Havemeyer's return home, Cassatt was obliged to refer to a photograph to complete it. The result reveals the artist's struggle to capture the face of her forty-one-year-old friend, now appearing more monumental and less tranquil than she

Plate 85. Mary Cassatt. *Louisine Havemeyer*, ca. 1896. Pastel on wove paper, 29 x 24 in. (73.7 x 61 cm). Shelburne Museum, Shelburne, Vermont, Gift of J. Watson Webb, Jr., 1973 (27.3.1–1) A56

the fact that she made a very similar drypoint etching—possibly as a sketch for the pastel or as a reiteration of it—relying on line alone. In the pastel Cassatt found great chromatic variety within a restricted palette of chalks. While she brought the face to a high level of definition, Cassatt indicated the hat and especially the dress much more cursorily. She took the drawing away, possibly intending to complete it by reference to a photograph of Adaline in the same ruffled hat (fig. 9). But in the winter of 1911–12 she delivered it unfinished to Adaline, then Mrs. Peter H. B. Frelinghuysen, for her daughter Frederica's nursery. In a letter to Louisine, Cassatt excused the fact that the pastel was still incomplete and referred to its documentary value and its charm: "it is like Adaline & between you and me it may be the F[relinghuysen]'s like it better than a stronger thing."[2] The lack of finish is, in fact, one of the most felicitous aspects of the image, especially in the areas where Cassatt enlisted the color of the paper to support and define form and to unify the composition. The coincidence between vivacious expression and vivacious execution makes this one of Cassatt's most successful portraits in any medium.

HBW

The author acknowledges with gratitude the advice of Nancy Mowll Mathews, whose biography of Cassatt is scheduled for publication in 1993 by Villard Books, New York.

1. Breeskin noted that the pastel was inscribed *Vichy* (1970, no. 248). In turn, Weitzenhoffer posited a visit to the French spa by the artist and the sitters in 1895 (1982, p. 250, n. 48; 1986, p. 107). Rather than *Vichy*, the inscription is a preliminary signature—*Mary*—which the artist seems to have effaced with chalk when she chose to sign and date the drawing in the upper right corner of the sheet.
2. MC to LWH, n.d. [after 12/14/11], Havemeyer correspondence.

had in the less labored portrait of the prior year.

By the time of Cassatt's trip to the United States in early 1898, she was working in pastel even more often than in oils, and she brought with her only her pastel equipment. In her image of Adaline in a fluffy white hat (fig. 8), probably begun during her visit with the Havemeyers in New York, Cassatt caught the vivacity of a bright and lively thirteen-year-old. Although the drawing is unfinished, Cassatt's handling of the pastel medium is particularly masterful here.

In contrast to the linear restraint and emphasis on form seen in her 1895 pastel portrait of Adaline—which the Havemeyers lent to the artist's February 1898 exhibition at Durand-Ruel in New York—Cassatt exploited a wide range of strokes, from the delicate touches in the flesh of the face to the rapid and definitive calligraphy in the hat. Cassatt's interest in the element of draftsmanship in this pastel is underscored by

Figure 8. Mary Cassatt. *Adaline Havemeyer in a White Hat*, probably begun 1898. Pastel on wove paper, 25 ¼ x 21 ⅛ in. (63.5 x 54 cm). Signed u.r.: *Mary Cassatt*. Gift of members of the family of Adaline Havemeyer Frelinghuysen, 1992 (1992.235)

Figure 9. Adaline in the hat in which she posed for Cassatt

Plate 86. Mary Cassatt. *Young Mother Sewing*. Oil on canvas, 36⅛ x 29 in. (92.4 x 73.7 cm).
H. O. Havemeyer Collection, Bequest of Mrs. H. O. Havemeyer, 1929 (29.100.48) A59

THE SUFFRAGE EXHIBITION OF 1915

REBECCA A. RABINOW

Louisine Waldron Havemeyer today is best remembered for the art collection she assembled. Less well known, though, is the active role she undertook in support of the woman suffrage movement. Mrs. Havemeyer joined these two passions by organizing "one of the choicest exhibitions of the season,"[1] the *Loan Exhibition of Masterpieces by Old and Modern Painters*, held from April 6 to 24, 1915, in the New York galleries of M. Knoedler and Co. She was adamant that her "art collection . . . take part in the suffrage campaign,"[2] and almost half of the more than fifty-nine works in this show, the proceeds from which were earmarked for the suffrage campaign of 1915, were borrowed from her collection.[3]

Louisine Havemeyer recalled that she became aware of the woman's rights movement at a young age.[4] Years later, after her husband's death in 1907, she became increasingly involved in the cause. Her interest surely was fanned by her longtime friend Mary Cassatt, who was outspoken in her belief that "women need the vote."[5] In 1912 Mrs. Havemeyer lent works from her collection to Knoedler's *Loan Exhibition of Paintings by El Greco and Goya*, a show that benefited "the cause of woman's suffrage,"[6] and by May of the following year she was participating in suffrage marches up Fifth Avenue. In 1914 Cassatt advised Mrs. Havemeyer to continue to "work for the suffrage. If the world is to be saved, it will be the women who save it."[7] Mrs. Havemeyer heeded her friend's advice—in fact, the exhibition she already had begun to plan was intended to serve the movement.

Exhibiting art in support of a cause, even woman suffrage, was hardly a novel idea in 1915. However, in the eyes of the *New York Times* art critic, the *Loan Exhibition of Masterpieces by Old and Modern Painters* was distinguished from other recent loan exhibitions in that it offered "as a special feature the work of two modern painters . . . Edgar Degas and Mary Cassatt."[8] In her earliest plans Mrs. Havemeyer had foreseen an exhibition of paintings and pastels by Degas, to be held

at Durand-Ruel's New York gallery. Because there were insufficient works available in 1914, the gallery asked to postpone the show a year.[9] Mrs. Havemeyer spent the spring of 1914 vacationing in southern France with Cassatt; at this time her vision of the exhibition evolved, and a two-artist show, featuring works by both Cassatt and Degas, took shape. Cassatt was pleased with the thought of showing alongside the French artist, but she also felt strongly that "if such an exhibition is to take place I wish it to be for the cause of Women Suffrage."[10] Urged by Mrs. Havemeyer to clean out the closets of her Parisian apartment to "see what would come forth,"[11] Cassatt salvaged a number of pictures. These included the portrait of Mrs. Riddle, *Lady at the Tea Table* (fig. 95), about which the artist mused, "I wonder if any one will care for it at the Exhibition. I doubt it."[12] (It turned out to be one of the more popular paintings in the show.) Cassatt promised to send Louisine Havemeyer all of the works still in her possession, "four in all, three paintings and a pastel,"[13] via her dealer, Durand-Ruel. Although the artist was apprehensive about shipping her pictures to the States during the war, she did so, knowing that Mrs. Havemeyer would attend to them once they arrived.[14]

Sometime between November 25 and December 29, 1914, Mrs. Havemeyer relocated the exhibition from Durand-Ruel's gallery to M. Knoedler and Co.[15] This change presumably occurred when she decided to expand the show to include old master paintings. Although the press reported that the works were chosen by a "Committee of Ladies," it is more likely that the selection was made by Mrs. Havemeyer, with a good amount of overseas advice from Cassatt. In January 1915 Cassatt wrote Mrs. Havemeyer, suggesting that she "get the Colonel [Oliver Payne, Mrs. Havemeyer's next-door neighbor] to lend his Degas, if you could get someone to lend a Vermeer for the Old Masters, it would show Degas superiority."[16] The colonel, however, was unwilling to lend, due to his antisuffrage position. Frustrated by Payne's attitude, Cassatt wrote to him

Figure 10. Installation view, 1915 suffrage exhibition, showing Havemeyer old master loans: l. to r., Rembrandt, "The Gilder, Herman Doomer" (A449); de Hooch, "The Visit" (A326); Rembrandt, "Portrait of An Old Woman" (A11)

Figure 11. Installation view, 1915 suffrage exhibition, showing Cassatts, including Havemeyer loans: far l., "Mère et Enfant" (A64); third from l., "Mother and Child" (A52); fifth from l., "Little Girl Leaning upon Her Mother's Knee" (A59); fourth from r., "Mother and Son with Mirror" (A58); third from r., "Mother and Baby in Pink and Lilac" (A61); far r., "Mother with Baby Reflected in Mirror" (A60)

directly, appealing to him in vain as "a patriotic American," to lend his Degas. "The sight of that picture may be a turning point in the life of some young American painter," she wrote. "Never mind the object of the exhibition. Think only of the young painters. As to the suffrage for women it must come as a result of this awful war."[17]

That none of Mrs. Havemeyer's fine El Grecos were included among the old master paintings exhibited in her own show is hardly surprising, considering that just three months earlier Knoedler's had exhibited a number of El Grecos and Goyas (including four from the Havemeyer collection) to benefit the American Women War Relief Fund and the Belgian Relief Fund. Of the eighteen old masters that were displayed in the 1915 suffrage exhibition, Mrs. Havemeyer owned six (a Bronzino, a Coello, a de Hooch, two Rembrandts, and a Rubens) (see fig. 10).[18] The others were lent by Mrs. Elizabeth Milbank Anderson, Watson B. Dickerman, Henry Clay Frick, Philip Lehman, William H. Moore, Mrs. John W. Simpson, Mrs. Herbert L. Terrell, and Joseph Widener. The old masters were outnumbered by the modern works of Cassatt and Degas. In addition to a photograph of Cassatt and a portrait of Degas, the walls of Knoedler's large gallery featured at least nineteen paintings and pastels by Cassatt and twenty-seven by Degas (see pls. 86, 87, figs. 11, 12, 13).[19] At least twenty-two of these works were lent by Mrs. Havemeyer; the others came from Cassatt, Durand-Ruel, Henry Clay Frick, William Van Horne, Mrs. Henry Munn (Louisine Havemeyer's sister), Mrs. J. Montgomery Sears, Harris Whittemore, and Joseph Widener.[20] All loans, both of the old master and the modern works, were made anonymously.

Mrs. Havemeyer's responsibilities relating to the exhibition were varied. In addition to making the selection, she may well have determined the placement of the works in the three galleries—Cassatts and Degases in the large gallery, old masters in the two smaller ones.[21] Moreover, Roland Knoedler, the head of Knoedler's, was willing to present the exhibition to the press in whatever way she desired.[22] Mrs. Havemeyer's goals were twofold: to show great works of art and to garner support, both moral and financial, for the suffrage cause. At an early stage she considered the fundraising potential of raffling a picture, but Cassatt vetoed the idea. "I really cannot give any of [my works] to be raffled for nor do I think it a good thing, it is

lowering Art. . . . I would far rather give $5000 than one of my pictures."[23] Ultimately it was decided to institute an admission fee of one dollar, and, to keep the gallery's overhead costs to a minimum, lenders such as Mrs. Terrell generously offered to defray the insurance premiums on works in the show.

Knoedler's was in charge of the practical aspects of the exhibition: handling the insurance, arranging for the transportation of the paintings and pastels, overseeing the printed matter (such as admission cards), photography, and publicity. As all of the proceeds were to benefit the suffrage cause, it may seem curious that the gallery agreed to host the show. Contemporary correspondence indicates, however, that business was slow, and it is possible that Knoedler's was attempting to gain publicity by exhibiting such spectacular museum-quality art.[24] It is also likely that the gallery was attempting to court Mrs. Havemeyer: she and her husband had been good clients before they transferred their business to Durand-Ruel. In fact, many of the other lenders were patrons of Knoedler's—the majority of the old master paintings exhibited in the show had, at some point, passed through the gallery's hands.[25]

A freak snowstorm, which hit the New York area with ten inches of snow on April 3, delayed the arrival at the gallery of five old master paintings: Rembrandt's *Portrait of Himself*, the two ter Borchs, Vermeer's *Woman Weighing Pearls*, and van Dyck's *Marchesa Giovanna Cattaneo*. Whittemore, who did not want his Degas pastels to be late, personally brought them through the snow, delivering them in time for the press preview on the afternoon of Monday, April 5. The only other work absent from the press preview was Van Horne's Cassatt, which, due to a delay at the customhouse, did not arrive at Knoedler's until April 12.

The *Loan Exhibition of Masterpieces by Old and Modern Painters* opened on Tuesday, April 6. A five-dollar entry fee was charged for the private preview, where one could hear Mrs. Havemeyer's late-afternoon speech, a lecture that had caused her some anguish. "It was very easy to talk about the emancipation of women," she later said, "but art was a very different and difficult subject."[26] Mrs. Havemeyer had consulted with the art critic of the *New York Tribune*, Royal Cortissoz, who suggested that she write down her words, and although she did pen a draft, she later ignored it. Mrs. Havemeyer's concern was so great that she insisted that Harriet Stanton Blatch, her friend and

Plate 87. Edgar Degas. *A Woman Ironing*, 1873. Oil on canvas, 21 ⅜ x 15 ½ in. (54.3 x 39.4 cm). H. O. Havemeyer Collection, Bequest of Mrs. H. O. Havemeyer, 1929 (29.100.46) A205

the president of the Women's Political Union, listen to her read it in advance. Mrs. Havemeyer need not have worried; her anecdotal speech was well received by both the audience and the press. As she spoke of her encounters with Cassatt and Degas, she singled out works in the large gallery to illustrate her points and to identify those Cassatt had created specifically for the exhibition (fig. 13).[27] Excerpts from Louisine Havemeyer's speech were quoted in almost every account of the opening, and within ten days Knoedler's sold all its printed copies of it, at twenty-five cents apiece. The interest in Mrs. Havemeyer's talk crossed the Atlantic, and Joseph Durand-Ruel requested her permission to publish an abridged edition of the lecture for distribution abroad.

Evidently there was some negative reaction to the show. In July Cassatt informed Mrs. Havemeyer that, according to Joseph Durand-Ruel, "it was the cause which kept many people away, 'society' it seems is so against suffrage. Many regretted to him that they

missed seeing a fine exhibition but their principles forbade their going."[28] Mrs. Havemeyer must have realized that not everyone would take kindly to her use of art to further a hotly debated political issue. Gustav Kobbe of the *New York Herald* remarked on the exhibition of Rembrandts for the suffrage cause: "Could there be greater contrast than that between the conditions under which Rembrandt produced [his portraits] and the circumstances under which they are now exhibited? Who heard of suffrage in 1654? Saskia? Hendrikje? . . . Hardly."[29] Cassatt was aware of a similar incongruity in regard to Degas. On occasion she had been the butt of Degas's derogatory jokes concerning the abilities of women painters and now was amused that his works were included in a suffrage benefit. "[It is] rather piquant," she observed. "If only Degas knew!"[30] One wonders how Cassatt's pictures of modern mothers and children were viewed in relation to the antisuffragists' claims that the women's movement would destroy the family unit.

Although the works by Degas and Cassatt were contemporary, they were hardly considered shockingly modern and were met with public acceptance.[31] Nonetheless, it was the old masters that lent a certain respectability to the undertaking, signaling the support of their upper-class owners for the suffrage cause. The extensive press coverage of the art, both modern and older, led a writer in the *Sun* to lament that the suffrage campaign was being overlooked. "The primal cause of an event is sometimes lost in the importance of the event itself. . . . These wonderful pictures . . . create so much comment of an artistic nature that for the moment the question of votes for women will be relegated to the background, although undoubtedly the purse for 'the cause' will be plentifully filled before the exhibition has run its course."[32]

The exhibition was a critical success. Soon after it closed, Cassatt wrote Mrs. Havemeyer, "My dear I am so very glad about the exhibition. . . . you deserve all the credit. . . . The time has finally come to show that women can do something."[33] Financially the show was a triumph as well. According to the *World*, the private preview of April 6 raised more than $1,100 "to start the Woman Suffrage Campaign Fund,"[34] and at the end of April Knoedler's presented Mrs. Havemeyer with a check for $1,375.10, "which with our receipted account of $907.91 form a total of $2,283.01 being amount of the receipts from the recent exhibition."[35]

Figure 12. Installation view, 1915 suffrage exhibition, showing Degases, including Havemeyer loans: far l. and second from l., two versions of "The Ballet Rehearsal" (A212, 211); far r., "The Milliners" (A233)

Figure 13. Installation view, 1915 suffrage exhibition, showing Cassatts created for the exhibition and Degases, including Havemeyer loans: far l., Cassatt, "Child Asleep on Mother's Shoulder" (A65); second from l., Cassatt, "Family Group" (A63); third from r. top, Degas, "The Dispute" (A201); far r. top, Degas, "The Laundress" (A205). A photograph of Cassatt and a Guys ink drawing of Degas frame the door.

In May of 1915 Knoedler's sent Mrs. Havemeyer installation photographs of the show. She responded, "They will be a pleasant souvenir of our exhibition which interested me during an entire winter & which I trust, has not only helped my cause but has done much good in the artistic world."[36] In the following months Mrs. Havemeyer became increasingly involved in the suffrage campaign, lecturing and traveling around the New York area to garner support for passage of the woman-suffrage referendum. On election day, November 2, the referendum was defeated in New York State by approximately two hundred thousand votes. It would be almost four more years before American women won the right to vote, years during which Louisine Havemeyer continued to be a leading figure in the suffrage fight.

I would like to thank Melissa De Medeiros of M. Knoedler and Co. for her kind assistance and Susan Alyson Stein and Anne M. P. Norton for their helpful comments.

1. "News of the Art World, Notable Exhibition of Work of Old and Modern Painters for Benefit of Woman Suffrage Cause to Open Wednesday," *World*, April 4, 1915, section N, p. 2.

2. Havemeyer 1922a, p. 529.

3. Fifty-nine works are listed in the catalogue of the exhibition, but it is possible to identify at least nine others that were included *hors catalogue* by consulting installation photographs and illustrated reviews of the show. See essay appendix.

4. Havemeyer 1922a, p. 528.

5. MC to LWH, 2/4/[14], Havemeyer correspondence.

6. M. Knoedler and Co., New York, *Loan Exhibition of Paintings by El Greco and Goya*, April 2–20, 1912. Two different catalogues accompanied this show, one listing fourteen works, the other fifteen. In any case, Louisine Havemeyer lent all the paintings except no. 2, El Greco, *St. Peter*, and no. 13, Goya, *Senorita Juanita of Mazarredo*, both of which belonged to her daughter Electra.

7. Louisine W. Havemeyer, "The Waking Up of Women," in Weitzenhoffer 1986, p. 220.

8. "Exhibition for Suffrage Cause. Pictures Representing Many Phases of the Art of Edgar Degas and Mary Cassatt in Exhibition for the Suffrage Cause," *New York Times Magazine*, April 4, 1915, p. 14.

9. JD-R to MC, 2/11/14, Durand-Ruel Archives, book 32, letter 283, correspondence, Weitzenhoffer files.

10. MC to LWH, 5/30/[14], Havemeyer correspondence.

11. Louisine W. Havemeyer, "Remarks on Edgar Degas and Mary Cassatt," text of lecture, New York, April 6, 1915, n.p.; subsequently quoted in a number of newspaper reviews.

12. MC to LWH, 2/4/15, in Mathews 1984, pp. 320–21. The letter reads more fully: "George D.R has just written to me about Mrs R's portrait [*Lady at the Tea Table*]. My dear I would give it to you at once, (of course to be left to a Museum.) only I have more than half promised it to the Petit Palais. . . . I wonder if any one will care for it at the Exhibition. I doubt it, its home ought to be in Paris where I painted it."

13. MC to George Biddle, 7/3/[14], in ibid., pp. 315–16. JD-R to MC, 11/25/14, Durand-Ruel Archives, book 33, letter 325, correspondence, Weitzenhoffer files, lists three paintings and a pastel that the gallery was preparing to ship to New York for the exhibition: "Portrait de dame agée," 1885 essay appendix, no. 44, "Femme et enfant vu de dos," no. 43, "Femme en robe jaune et deux enfants," no. 42, and "Mère et enfant," pastel, no. 54.

14. MC to LWH, 12/3/14, Havemeyer correspondence: "I hope my pictures will get over safely. Won't you see that the round 'tonda' is framed properly in white and gold, or solely in gold, it is ruined in its present frame. It was intended for a decoration over a door, at Harrisburg." The "tonda" was shown as no. 42.

15. Durand Ruel, New York, however, remained interested in showing Cassatt's work, and while the suffrage exhibition was on view at Knoedler's, the exhibition *Water Colors and Dry Points by Mary Cassatt* was featured at Durand-Ruel. The latter closed on April 20, 1915.

16. MC to LWH, 1/20/[15], Havemeyer correspondence. Cassatt also encouraged Mrs. Havemeyer to procure loans from Mrs. Alfred Pope and Mr. Walters. (MC to LWH, 2/15/[14], Havemeyer correspondence; MC to LWH, 3/12/[15], in Mathews 1984, p. 322).

17. MC to Oliver Payne, 2/28/[15], in Mathews 1984, p. 321.

18. For identification of works in the exhibition, see essay appendix.

19. See n. 3. The catalogue lists twenty-three works by Degas and eighteen by Cassatt. For documentary purposes a photograph of Cassatt and a drawing, by Guys, of Degas were also included in the show. Louisine Havemeyer recalled borrowing the Guys drawing in her memoirs (Havemeyer 1961, p. 251).

20. Knoedler loan books, loan receipt no. 4480, list Mrs. Henry Munn as having lent one Cassatt pastel for the duration of the exhibition. This work, as yet unidentified, is cat. no. 55 or was exhibited *hors catalogue*. The Degas pastel, *Dancer with a Bouquet* (no. 30), was lent by Whittemore, not Havemeyer, as has been suggested in the literature. Whittemore's ownership of this pastel is confirmed by Knoedler stock books nos. A2268 and CA 948.

21. Roland Knoedler sent Mrs. Havemeyer a "rough sketch" showing the dimensions of the galleries in a letter of 1/2/15, Knoedler correspondence, domestic letter book, and the two met on the premises on numerous occasions.

22. C.R. Henschel to LWH, 3/20/15, Knoedler correspondence, domestic letter book.

23. MC to LWH, 2/1/15, in Mathews 1984, p. 320.

24. The newspaper reviews made much of the fact that many of the old masters had been seen in the 1909 *Hudson-Fulton Celebration* exhibition at The Metropolitan Museum of Art.

25. The old master works that had passed through Knoedler's were: no. 3, van Dyck, *Marchesa Giovanna Cattaneo*; no. 4, Holbein the Younger, *Sir Brian Tuke*; no. 10, Rembrandt, *Portrait of Himself*; no. 11, Rembrandt, *Portrait of a Man*; no. 12, Rembrandt, *Portrait of a Woman*; no. 13, Rembrandt, *Portrait of an Elderly Man*; no. 15, Rubens, *The Triumphal Entry of Henry IV into Paris After the Battle of Ivry*; no. 16, ter Borch, *Portrait of Burgomaster Jan van Duren*; no. 17, ter Borch, *Portrait of Margaretha van Haexbergen*; and no. 18, Vermeer, *Woman Weighing Pearls*. A number of the Cassatts and Degases had been handled by Knoedler's as well.

26. Havemeyer 1922a, p. 529.

27. Cassatt's most recent works, presumably made for the exhibition, included no. 43, *Femme et enfant vu de dos*; no. 54, *Mère et enfants*; no. 55, *Mother Playing with Her Baby*; no. 56, *Family Group*; and no. 57, *Child Asleep on Mother's Shoulder*.

28. MC to LWH, 7/5/15, in Mathews 1984, p. 324.

29. Gustav Kobbe, "Painted by Rembrandt in 1634, First Exhibited in New York 1915," *New York Herald*, April 4, 1915, section 3, p. 1.

30. MC to JD-R, 2/12/[14], Durand-Ruel Archives, book 32, letter 283, correspondence, Weitzenhoffer files. In MC to LWH, 2/15/[14], Havemeyer correspondence, she repeats the sentiment. although Degas (1834–1917) was alive at the time of Cassatt's statement, the elderly artist was not a lender to the show.

31. According to the *World*, "in recent years . . . others have crowded the scene with extremes of view and style to which Miss Cassatt and M. Degas would hardly subscribe" ("News of the Art World," *World*, April 4, 1915, section N, p. 2). For a similar view, see Royal Cortissoz, "M. Degas and Miss Cassatt, Types Once Revolutionary Which Now Seem Almost Classical," *New York Tribune*, April 4, 1915, section 3, p. 3.

32. "Loan Exhibition in Aid of Suffrage, Behind the Scenes Types Shown To-day With Miss Cassatt's Work, Impressionist Works," *Sun*, April 6, 1915, p. 7.

33. MC to LWH, 4/29/15, Havemeyer correspondence.

34. "Suffrage Art Show Nets $1,100 in a Day, Mrs. H.O. Havemeyer Opens Display With Talk on Miss Cassatt and Degas," *World*, April 7, 1915, p. 7.

35. Knoedler Gallery to LWH, 4/30/15, Knoedler correspondence, domestic letter book.

36. LWH to Raymond Knoedler, 5/8/15, Knoedler correspondence, Knoedler files.

APPENDIX: IDENTIFICATION OF WORKS IN THE EXHIBITION AND THEIR LENDERS

Cat. no.	Lender*	Work†
1	Havemeyer	Bronzino, A45
2	Havemeyer	Coello, A280
3	Frick	Van Dyck, Larsen 1988, no. 337
4	Dickerman	Holbein the Younger, Rowlands 1985, no. 64
5	Havemeyer	de Hooch, A326
6	Dickerman	Von Kulmbach, Stadler 1936, no. 71
7	Anderson	Lawrence, Garlick 1989, no. 182 fragment
8	Havemeyer	Rembrandt, A11
9	Havemeyer	Rembrandt, A449
10	Terrell	Rembrandt, Bredius/Gerson 1969, no. 36
11	Moore	Rembrandt, Bredius/Gerson 1969, no. 177
12	Moore	Rembrandt, Bredius/Gerson 1969, no. 344
13	Lehman	Rembrandt, Bredius/Gerson 1969, no. 215
14	Havemeyer	Rubens, A472
15	Simpson	Rubens, Held 1980, no. 85
16	Lehman	Terborch, Gudlaugsson 1959, no. 201
17	Lehman	Terborch, Gudlaugsson 1959, no. 202
18	Widener	Vermeer, Blankert 1978, no. 15
19	Whittemore	Degas, Lemoisne 1946, supplement no. 60
20	Durand-Ruel	Degas, Lemoisne 1946, no. 258
21	Durand-Ruel	Degas, Lemoisne 1946, no. 333
22	Widener	Degas, Lemoisne 1946, no. 941
23	Widener	Degas, Lemoisne 1946, no. 317
24	Frick	Degas, Lemoisne 1946, no. 537
25	Havemeyer	Degas, A201
26	Havemeyer	Degas, A205
27	Sears	Degas, Lemoisne 1946, no. 971
28	Sears	Degas, probably Lemoisne 1946, no. 966
29	Sears	Degas, Lemoisne 1946, no. 1221
30	Whittemore	Degas, Lemoisne 1946, no. 650
31	Whittemore	Degas, Lemoisne 1946, no. 334
32	Durand-Ruel	Degas, Lemoisne 1946, no. 521
33	Havemeyer	Degas, A215
34	Havemeyer	Degas, A237
35	Havemeyer	Degas, A217
36	Havemeyer	Degas, A235
37	Havemeyer	Degas, A241
38	Havemeyer	Degas, A211 or A212
39	Havemeyer	Degas, A257
40	Havemeyer	Degas, A204
41	Havemeyer	Degas, A230
42	Cassatt	Cassatt, Breeskin 1970, no. 472‡
43	Cassatt	Cassatt, Breeskin 1970, no. 550
44	Cassatt	Cassatt, Breeskin 1970, no. 139
45	Durand-Ruel	Cassatt, Breeskin 1970, no. 336
46	Havemeyer	Cassatt, A58
47	Havemeyer	Cassatt, A59
48	Havemeyer	Cassatt, A52
49	Havemeyer	Cassatt, A61
50	Havemeyer	Cassatt, A60
51	Sears	Cassatt, Breeskin 1970, no. 224
52	Sears	Cassatt, Breeskin 1970, no. 577
53	Sears	Cassatt, Breeskin 1970, no. 489
54	Cassatt (Havemeyer by 4/13/14)	Cassatt, A64
55	Havemeyer	Cassatt, Breeskin 1970, no. 604§
56	Havemeyer	Cassatt, A63
57	Havemeyer	Cassatt, A65
58	Havemeyer	Cassatt, A53
59	Van Horne	Cassatt, Breeskin 1970, no. 195‖

Hors catalogue:

Havemeyer	Degas, A212 or 241
Havemeyer	Degas, A228
Durand-Ruel(?)	Degas, Lemoisne 1946, no. 614
Havemeyer	Degas, A209
Durand-Ruel(?)	Cassatt, Breeskin 1970, no. 281
	Barye, Pivar 1974, no. A86
	Barye, Pivar 1974, no. A197

Hors catalogue works exhibited for documentary purposes:

Durand-Ruel	Guys, ink drawing of Degas
Durand-Ruel	photograph of Mary Cassatt

* All loans were anonymous.

† Artists' names are taken verbatim from the 1915 catalogue; some works have since been reattributed.

‡ At least four of the Cassatts marked Durand-Ruel in a partially annotated catalogue of the exhibition (in the Knoedler library)—nos. 42–44, 54—still belonged to the artist in April 1915; Durand-Ruel arranged for their transportation. See n. 13.

§ Although the annotated catalogue indicates this Cassatt pastel to be a Havemeyer loan, no evidence supporting Havemeyer ownership of the work has been found. This may be the pastel lent by Anne Munn, Louisine Havemeyer's sister; if not, the Munn work was exhibited *hors catalogue*.

‖ The annotated catalogue lists "Havemeyer" as the lender of cat. no. 59, a Cassatt pastel. However, in a letter of 4/12/15, Roland Knoedler informs Van Horne that his Cassatt painting "is No. 59, 'Mother and Child.'" Knoedler correspondence, domestic letter book.

Decorative Arts

Plate 88. *Jar*, Syria, late 12th–early 13th century. Underglaze-painted composite body, h. 11 ½ in. (29.2 cm). H. O. Have-meyer Collection, Bequest of Horace Havemeyer, 1956 (56.185.15)

THE FORGOTTEN LEGACY: THE HAVEMEYERS' COLLECTION OF DECORATIVE ARTS

ALICE COONEY FRELINGHUYSEN

The Havemeyers' collection of decorative arts is not as well known as their prodigious assemblage of old masters and Impressionists, yet it was an integral part of their extraordinary efforts. As is handsomely demonstrated by the Havemeyer bequest, which benefited almost every department at the Metropolitan, their collecting zeal extended to a far broader range of objects and materials than works on canvas and paper. Louisine and Henry Osborne Havemeyer had extremely catholic tastes in the decorative arts. They did not restrict themselves to objects from one time or one country—as did many of their affluent peers—but rather cast a wide net over different cultures, periods, and media. In addition to their extensive collection of Asian art—a particular passion of Harry's and the subject of another section of this publication—they pursued with equal vigor and enthusiasm the acquisition of Egyptian sculpture, Roman glass, Islamic rugs and pottery, Tanagra figurines, Hispano-Moresque pottery, and Tiffany favrile glass.

By the time of Louisine's death in 1929, the Havemeyer collection of decorative arts was far from modest. Aside from the Asian material—over 4,000 pieces—the objects, including those bequeathed to the Metropolitan or given to family members and the items that would be sold at auction in 1930, totaled over 1,000. This number comprised 419 examples of Roman glass, 424 Islamic and 81 Hispano-Moresque ceramics, about 58 Islamic carpets and runners, and 55 pieces of Tiffany glass (not counting the 56 vessels donated to the Metropolitan by Mr. Havemeyer in 1896).[1] In addition there were some 25 examples of Italian majolica, 15 Tanagra terracotta groups, 10 pieces of Greco-Roman glazed pottery, 2 Greek helmets, 2 Egyptian sculptures, 2 Venetian glass vessels, 4 early European textiles, and a large group of gold coins.

The Havemeyers were inspired to acquire their diverse and numerous decorative arts by an astonishing renewal of interest in art objects of every kind that took place during the 1870s and 1880s, a period that encompassed the Aesthetic Movement. Decorative arts in many media were the necessary accoutrements for furnishing one's home in the taste of the day. Cabinets and overmantel shelves became repositories for all sorts of art objects and bric-a-brac. Artists and craftsmen—Louis Comfort Tiffany (1848–1933), Samuel Colman (1832–1920), and Edward C. Moore (1827–1891) among them—surrounded themselves with various decorative items, whether used as showpieces, as props in their studios, or as inspirations for their own designs.[2] It was an era when a plethora of collectors' magazines were filled with discussions of Persian pottery, Chinese porcelains, and Venetian glass. Decorative-arts societies were founded in cities across the nation. The period also witnessed the birth of the nation's great art museums, where decorative arts were given representation in the galleries equal to that of the fine arts of painting, architecture, and sculpture.

In the nineteenth century many individuals made their initial purchases of decorative arts in order to "accessorize" their paintings collections. Harry Havemeyer, on the other hand, embarked on his collecting career by focusing on the decorative arts for themselves. He and Louisine, unlike some of their contemporaries, did not follow patriotic instincts and buy American colonial or contemporary objects, favrile glass by Tiffany

Figure 14. Interior view of the West Room, Pierpont Morgan Library, courtesy of the Archives of The Pierpont Morgan Library, New York

being the exception. Nor did the Havemeyers seek out works from the European past, as did many prominent collectors of the 1880s and 1890s. J. Pierpont Morgan, who formed most of his collection after 1890, probably epitomized the "old master" approach. Morgan concentrated on the most luxurious articles of historic European cultures, amassing, among other objects, Renaissance and Baroque silver and silver gilt, Renaissance majolica, eighteenth-century French and German porcelain, and medieval, Renaissance, and Baroque ivories (see fig. 14).[3] With only a few exceptions— some Italian majolica, two pieces of Venetian glass, and a fifteenth-century Italian cope—the Havemeyers did not own the requisite European articles such as the Italian Renaissance bronzes and eighteenth-century porcelains favored by their more conservative New York neighbors and social and business peers such as Mor-

gan. Instead the couple directed their attention to the exotic works of foreign cultures that were being sought primarily by the artistic communities of New York and Paris.

Whereas the Havemeyers' paintings collection is well documented in the letters of Mary Cassatt, in Louisine's published memoirs, and in the archives of the Durand-Ruel gallery, little recorded information survives regarding the acquisition of their decorative arts. Therefore it is difficult, perhaps impossible, to determine the exact chronology of the Havemeyers' purchases in this area. There are no organized dealer archives to shed light on the matter, but a careful study of both the published and unpublished sources provides a basic outline of their collecting activities.

It remains something of a mystery how H. O. Havemeyer, who began to collect even before his marriage

Plate 89. Tiffany and Co., New York. *Flatware from a sixty-two piece service made for Louisine Havemeyer*, ca. 1883. Silver, copper, and brass, r. to l.: l. 10½ in. (26.7 cm); l. 8¾ in. (22.2 cm); l. 8⅛ in. (20.6 cm); l. 6 in. (15.2 cm); l. 4¾ in. (12.1 cm); second from bottom: l. 11½ in. (29.2 cm); bottom: l. 11¼ in. (28.6 cm). Marked: TIFFANY & CO./STERLING SILVER/AND OTHER METALS PAT. 1880; LWE (monogram). Private collection

to Louisine, first became drawn to the arts. There is little in his background to suggest any significant early contact with art. He apparently was an average student, abandoning his education after high school in order to enter the family sugar-refining business.[4] The skills that he demonstrated in his strategic handling of the financial interests of the sugar company, Havemeyers and Elder, later the American Sugar Refining Co., as well as his firm determination and courage, which also accounted for some of his great success in business, carried over into his modus operandi for collecting.[5] Rather than seek tried-and-true documented works, he entered relatively uncharted territory, preferring to spend his wealth on objects yet to be proven.

Although Harry did not attend college, the Havemeyer family was highly cultured. Through his father he was exposed to literature and the study of Latin,

and at an early age he developed a love of music and became accomplished on the violin. Other family members, also involved in the sugar company, had pursued artistic interests and may have influenced the young Harry. His brother Theodore A. Havemeyer (1839–1897) collected paintings, primarily works of minor European artists, some of which were exhibited in New York in 1876.[6] His cousin William F. Havemeyer (1850–1913) preferred American paintings and may have been responsible for introducing him to Colman, a landscape artist, perhaps in 1875, after Colman had returned from an extended painting trip in Africa and Europe.[7] It was with Colman that H. O. Havemeyer, a mature young man of twenty-nine, visited the 1876 Centennial Exhibition in Philadelphia, an event later recorded by Louisine and the first documented instance of Havemeyer's interest in art of any kind.

Plate 90. *Dish*, Spain, 1st half of 17th century. Glazed and lustered earthenware, diam. 15 ¼ in. (38.7). H. O. Havemeyer Collection, Bequest of Mrs. H. O. Havemeyer, 1929 (29.100.138)

Plate 91. *Armorial dish*, Spain (Valencia), 1st half of 16th century. Molded, glazed, and lustered earthenware, diam. 17 ⅝ in. (44.8 cm). H. O. Havemeyer Collection, Bequest of Mrs. H. O. Havemeyer, 1929 (29.100.140)

The Philadelphia Centennial was a stupendous event. It comprised material from virtually every foreign nation and covered approximately 260 acres. There were hundreds of ceramics exhibits alone.[8] The presentations were seen by thousands of visitors and kindled the enthusiasm of collectors, craftsmen, and the general public for art objects from exotic cultures.[9] Louisine relates that at the Centennial, Havemeyer, in Colman's company, purchased a large quantity of Japanese textiles and other Oriental decorative arts.[10]

Beginning at the time of the Centennial, Colman and Tiffany seem to have been the Havemeyers' primary tastemakers in the area of decorative arts.[11] Both Colman and Tiffany had already started their extensive collections of exotic art, which they selected for their decorative qualities. Colman amassed a sizable number of Asian art objects, as did Tiffany. In addition Tiffany acquired Islamic, Hispano-Moresque, and Near Eastern pottery and tiles, ancient glass, and Native American pottery and baskets.[12] Colman's large collection incorporated rare plates of various origins as well as Persian pottery, antique Greek and Roman glass, and Oriental rugs.[13] It is interesting to note that in spite of Tiffany's and Colman's influence and friendship, the Havemeyers did not patronize either for their paintings, never owning a picture by Tiffany and only a few by Colman.

Another adviser to the Havemeyers was undoubtedly Edward C. Moore, chief designer of Tiffany and Co. Moore accrued impressive personal holdings of Chinese and Japanese decorative objects, many of which he used as inspiration for his own designs, as well as Egyptian, Syrian, and Mesopotamian metalwork and glass, and Persian and Hispano-Moresque pottery. He bequeathed his extensive collection to the Metropolitan Museum in 1891.

At the time he married Louisine in 1883, Harry Havemeyer commissioned Moore to design a silver flatware service for his bride, giving Moore "carte blanche" in its creation (pl. 89).[14] This service consisted of sixty-two pieces, no two alike, in the Japanese style that had become popular for Tiffany silver as early as 1878. The style incorporated designs in which plant, bird, insect, fish, and animal forms made of various colored metals—especially brass and copper— were applied to the handles of the knives, forks, and spoons, in emulation of the metalwork on Japanese sword fittings. This rather startling service helps to establish that the Havemeyers were willing to experiment and take risks despite prevailing conservative taste while at the same time demanding the highest quality of design, materials, and craftsmanship, standards that they would thereafter consistently maintain.

From about the time of their marriage to about

1892, it appears that the Havemeyers' interest in the arts may have been focused primarily on items used to furnish the house that Tiffany and Colman were designing for them. Each had employed unusual art objects in the decoration of his own residence, and the two undoubtedly steered the Havemeyers to their own dealers. Like the other decorators of the day, Tiffany and Colman may have sold them pieces, especially Islamic carpets, from showrooms of the Tiffany studios or works of art from their own collections. It is tempting to speculate that when Louisine wrote that the Hispano-Moresque plate with "the Arabic star design in blue" (pl. 90) over the glass cabinet in the dining room had come from "Tom. Colman's" collection, she may actually have been referring to that of Samuel Colman.[15] The Havemeyers decorated the walls of their dining room (fig. 33) with Hispano-Moresque pottery (see pl. 91), and when this collection is considered as a whole, a general similarity of palette and decoration becomes apparent, suggesting that they were purchased with the idea of displaying them as a group in the house. Indeed, several of the Museum's Hispano-Moresque dishes can be matched up with those that appear in the 1892 photographs of the dining room.[16] From whom these works were purchased is not known, but Tiffany may well have selected them: the patterning of various colored lusters in abstract designs on a cream-colored ground recalls the kind of metallic stenciled walls that he used in several commissions, notably the Veterans' Room of the Seventh Regiment Armory in New York and Mark Twain's house in Hartford. Hispano-Moresque pottery continued to interest the couple: for in 1901, some years after their house was completed, they bought two plates, "one with a copper and the other with a moonlight luster . . . [from an] owner [who] had taken them from off his walls."[17] These plates, too, were supposed to have hung in the dining room.

The Havemeyers, unlike many of their wealthy contemporaries—such as Morgan, Marquand, or Vanderbilt—did not favor buying en bloc an entire collection of one kind that had been put together by another individual. Rather, they carefully considered objects that were offered to them by various dealers, primarily those located in Paris and to a lesser extent in New York, or made purchases at auction. They undoubtedly attended most of the important auctions of the day, particularly on their trips abroad. For example, in Paris in 1905 Mr. and Mrs. Havemeyer obtained three Hispano-Moresque pottery plates at the sale of the M. Boy collection, which also included Renaissance enamels, ivories, and antiquities.[18]

For a brief period the Havemeyers collected Italian Renaissance majolica. They probably responded to the lustrous qualities of this ware, whose development was sparked by the enthusiasm for Hispano-Moresque pottery in the fifteenth century. That the couple did not pursue majolica with greater vigor is perhaps due to its strong pictorial content. Mr. and Mrs. Havemeyer may have purchased examples prior to the completion of their house, for they bought a sixteenth-century plate (pl. 92) in 1892 in London at the sale of the Magniac collection.[19] If they acquired the rest of their majolica at about the same time, they soon abandoned it in favor of the more unconventional ceramic arts from medieval Spain, Syria, and Persia.

Both Tiffany and Moore probably stimulated the Havemeyers' interest in Roman glass (see pls. 93, 94), of which Tiffany himself had put together a large collection. At the time of his death in 1933, ancient pieces formed the greatest component of Tiffany's impressive assemblage of glass. The appeal for him of these glasses, which were not always of the first quality, lay in the colorful iridescent surfaces produced by centuries of burial in moist earth. As the artist wrote in an

Plate 92. *Dish*, Italy (probably Gubbio), ca. 1530–40. Tin-enameled, painted, and lustered earthenware, diam. 17 ¼ in. (43.8 cm). H. O. Havemeyer Collection, Bequest of Mrs. H. O. Havemeyer, 1929 (29.100.95)

Plate 93. *Two-handled flask*, Roman, 4th century A.D. Glass, h. 8%6 in. (21.8 cm). H. O. Havemeyer Collection, Bequest of Mrs. H. O. Havemeyer, 1929 (29.100.72)

Plate 94. *Beaker and handled cup*, Roman. Glass, l.: 1st century A.D., h. 5½ in. (14 cm); r.: 4th century A.D., h. 2⅝ in. (6.1 cm). H. O. Havemeyer Collection, Bequest of Mrs. H. O. Havemeyer, 1929 (29.100.80,90)

article published at the time of the World's Columbian Exposition in 1893, he attempted to develop "a material . . . which rivaled the painter's palette in its range of tones and eclipsed the iridescence and brilliancy found in the Roman and Egyptian glass."[20] It was this effect that he would later strive to replicate in glass of his own making.

The Havemeyers acquired their ancient glass from about 1890 to 1910, during the period when most of the earliest and in many cases the finest American and European collections, both private and public, of ancient glassware were created.[21] We know that the size of the Havemeyer collection was impressive, but to assess its merits is difficult now because the objects were never individually documented before their dispersal. Fourteen pieces (see pls. 104, 105), each a superb example of its kind, were selected for the Museum in 1929 by Gisela M. A. Richter, then Curator of the Museum's Classical department. These glasses suited

the Havemeyers' taste for highly decorative objects, and they particularly liked the many-hued iridescent surfaces and the Roman gold-band and mosaic vessels. At Louisine's death, the collection contained over four hundred pieces described as Roman or Syrian.

Evidence that ancient glass may have been a relatively early interest for H. O. Havemeyer is a notice that appeared in an 1890 art periodical of the loan of some of his objects to a special exhibition of "artistic glassware," held at the Union League Club in New York, which included wares of all periods, from Roman to modern Venetian and German. Of all the lenders Havemeyer was the only one singled out by the reviewer in a description of the Roman glass: "But among the (originally) clear Roman pieces were several of very beautiful form, notably a large urn belonging to Mr. Havemeyer, and many of them showed the most beautiful iridescent effects."[22]

Mr. Havemeyer undoubtedly purchased his first

pieces of ancient glass from Tiffany's and Moore's sources, but beginning in the early 1890s he apparently obtained wares primarily from Azeez Khayat (1875–1943), one of the best-known dealers of ancient glass in New York. Khayat was a Lebanese who at an early age, in 1892, established his Ancient Arts Gallery at 366 Fifth Avenue, across from the Waldorf-Astoria Hotel.[23] Havemeyer was among his first clients, buying glass from him even before he had opened his shop.[24] After the Museum acquired its selection of glass from the Havemeyer bequest, Khayat reviewed the items and determined that they had all been sold by him.[25] Other sources for the Havemeyers' ancient glass certainly included Dikran Kelekian, who also sold the couple other kinds of objects, including most of their Islamic pottery. On one occasion in 1906 Cassatt recalled visiting Kelekian, who had made some purchases with Havemeyer in mind. She wrote to Louisine that "he showed me several most *exquisite* pieces of glass (Cyprian) oh! *such* beauties so dainty so *lovely* in color, one a blue small [?] looks like pottery glorified, he says he is going to keep them until Mr. Havemeyer comes over, if he sends them they may be stolen at the Custom House."[26] In addition they may have purchased glass from the Paris and New York gallery known as Kouchakji Frères, founded in the 1890s, and from one or more of the important collections sold at auction in the early 1900s.[27]

Although most of the glass the Havemeyers acquired was Roman, they had at least two Venetian examples as well. One of these was a small, mold-blown beaker with enamel decoration (pl. 95), which was purchased from Kouchakji Frères as early Syrian and which has since been reattributed by the Museum to Venice.[28] Louisine recalled that the other piece, a Venetian tazza that was displayed in the music room under the lacquer cabinet, was probably purchased at the Emile Gavet sale held in Paris in 1897.[29] Although the Havemeyers may well have bought some other Venetian glass at the sale, which included a large group, the tazza in the Museum's collection (pl. 96) does not match any described or illustrated in the catalogue.

Not surprisingly, the only contemporary glass that the Havemeyers collected seriously was that by Tiffany. They were patrons and close friends of the artist long before 1893, when he began to produce glass vessels. Mr. and Mrs. Havemeyer became immediate admirers of his glass, for they appreciated the sensitive color har-

monies and iridescent surfaces that had appealed to them in their quest for ancient glass. The couple continued to acquire Tiffany's favrile pieces even after H. O. Havemeyer's substantial donation of vessels to the Metropolitan in 1896 (see pls. 114, 115, 117). A number of gold and "kingfisher-blue" iridescent pieces obtained after this gift included tablewares, such as goblets, cordials, compotes, and finger bowls.[30] In addition there were numerous cabinet vases, which revealed the full range of Tiffany's luster and color effects (see pl. 97).[31] The largest of these, at seventeen and a half inches high, was a "'Persian' Rose Vase . . . of reeded lily form rising from a bulbous base, in amethyst and emerald-green glaze."[32] Theirs seems to have been a highly individualized collection: in the auction catalogue of the Havemeyers' decorative arts published at the time of Louisine's death, the Tiffany glass was described as "having been made for the owners personally by Mr. Louis Comfort Tiffany."[33]

Although the Havemeyers surely knew the production of modern European glassmakers, it is surprising that they seem not to have acquired glass by any of them, not even the work of Emile Gallé. The only evidence that they purchased any other contemporary glass is a 1901 reference in the Cassatt correspondence to a comb that Louisine ordered from René Lalique. It was apparently specially made for her because when Cassatt began to try to arrange for its delivery to Lou-

Plate 95. *Beaker*, Italy (Venice), ca. 1500. Molded, enameled, and gilded glass, h. 3¼ in. (8.3 cm). H. O. Havemeyer Collection, Bequest of Mrs. H. O. Havemeyer, 1929 (29.100.92)

Plate 96. *Tazza*, Italy (probably Venice), 2nd half of 16th century. Molded, gilded, and cold-painted glass, diam. 10½ in. (26.7 cm). H. O. Havemeyer Collection, Bequest of Mrs. H. O. Havemeyer, 1929 (29.100.146)

isine in New York, she commented that Lalique "remembered you [Louisine] very well and no doubt would get *just* what would suit you." However, Cassatt was not favorably impressed with Lalique and described him as "rather common & full of airs."[34]

Captivated by their elegance and decorative quality, H. O. Havemeyer purchased some "delightful terracotta Asia Minor groups" at the Spitzer collection sale in 1891.[35] The same year a critic admired them during a visit to the Havemeyers' newly furnished home: "When Mr. Havemeyer enters his new Fifth Avenue residence, art lovers will be astonished to see how . . . liberal and discriminating his purchases of Greek art objects have been. His cabinets will show, in particular, some fine terra cotta groups of figures that are not even generally known to be in this country."[36]

During the 1870s these delicate terracotta statuettes, principally of draped women, were excavated at the site of Tanagra, in Greece, and they soon developed into a vogue among collectors. Mr. and Mrs. Havemeyer may have become acquainted with them through their interest in the art of Whistler, for he admired the elegant stance and garb of these statuettes and often used them as subjects for his paintings and pastels. The great appeal of Tanagra figures and groups, however, inspired unscrupulous individuals to produce replicas that were sold as authentic, and they fooled many an

Plate 97. Tiffany Glass and Decorating Co. and Tiffany Studios, New York. *Vase*, 1896–1905. Favrile glass, h. 10%16 in. (26.8 cm). University of Michigan Museum of Art, Ann Arbor, transfer from the College of Architecture and Design (1972/2.217)

unsuspecting collector as the demand for them grew. The Havemeyers were no exception: all of their fifteen figure groups are today thought to be probable late nineteenth-century copies (see pl. 98). Mrs. Havemeyer was clearly aware that there were numerous frauds on the market, and this subject came up in her correspondence with Cassatt. In 1906, in response to a letter from Louisine, Cassatt wrote that she had heard that such copies were also being made in the United States.[37] By the time that Louisine thought seriously about giving the collection to the Metropolitan, she felt apprehensive about the groups, which were housed in a cabinet in the third-floor hall, and wrote, "Don't give if their genuineness are doubted."[38]

In addition to Tiffany, Colman, and Moore, another influential source of decorative arts for the Havemeyers was the Armenian dealer Dikran Kelekian (1868–1951) (fig. 15), who formed numerous collections for himself and others from about 1900 into the early years of the twentieth century and is mentioned above in the context of the couple's acquisition of ancient glass. Kelekian had a strong interest in the arts of Persia and devoted himself to putting together a sizable collection to promote them and to educate collectors and the general public on the subject. Although he was an American citizen, he was recognized for his efforts through his appointments as Persian Ambassador to the United States and as Commissioner-General for Persia at the Saint Louis Panama–Pacific International Exposition of 1904. Kelekian may have first met the Havemeyers in 1893, when he brought a large exhibit to the World's Columbian Exposition in Chicago and acquainted Americans with Persian art on a grand scale.[39] It is likely that Kelekian's long-term friendship with Cassatt may have prompted the introduction. Cassatt traveled with Kelekian and they often exchanged visits in France, and she painted four portraits of members of his family. The Havemeyers acquired many different kinds of objects from Kelekian, primarily from his Paris shop, and even when the Havemeyers were not touring abroad, between 1906 and 1919 Cassatt kept her friend Louisine abreast of the dealer's new finds through frequent correspondence. Kelekian had a passion for Egypt and its art, eventually establishing a gallery in Cairo. Before opening his gallery, Kelekian traveled extensively in Egypt, even accompanying the Havemeyers on their trip there and offering them several pieces of Egyptian sculpture. Although Cassatt

Plate 98. *Leda and the Swan*, 19th century. Terracotta, h. 9 ¼ in. (23.5 cm). Shelburne Museum, Shelburne, Vermont (31.10.1 125)

never collected such exotic items herself, living instead with more traditional eighteenth-century French furnishings, she often saw and critiqued the works that were shown to the Havemeyers by Kelekian. In one instance, in about 1906, Cassatt brought to their attention the fact that a fine Egyptian statuette that Kelekian had acquired, possibly for them, was slightly odd in that "the head and base of the kneeling figure are so finished and the hands [only] sketched in."[40] This piece is probably the statuette of Khnumhotep (pl. 103) now in the Museum's collection.

On a few occasions Kelekian tempted the Havemeyers with early European decorative arts in addition to his objects from Egypt, Syria, and Greece. The Italian Gothic blue velvet cope (MMA 29.100.147) bought by the Havemeyers in 1906 was claimed by Kelekian to be "dear and unique." Louisine later recalled that he had hunted a long time to find it for her.[41] Unfortunately, the collectors accorded this object a value that far exceeds its actual worth—current scholarship has determined the cope to be a reconstructed vestment composed of pieces of fifteenth-century ferronerie vel-

Figure 15. Dikran Kelekian, ca. 1904, frontispiece from *Kelekian Exhibit at the Louisiana Exposition, 1904*

vet and lacking its ornate orphrey band and hood. At the turn of the century it was popular to hang articles of this kind in lavish interiors. This one, fitted along its long straight side with rings, was intended for such use.[42]

Beginning in the 1890s, the Havemeyers developed a deep appreciation of Persian lusterware, an appreciation that grew out of their admiration for the lusterware of southern Spain that they had already collected. One piece in the Havemeyer collection that was continually praised by Kelekian was the large blue Persian jar with a date and an inscription molded in relief (pl. 99).[43] This object's size and quality lend it prestige, and the charm of the inscription confers additional appeal. This inscription reads, "The clouds pregnant with life-giving rain, the meadows in full bloom/Merry be he who drinks and forgets the gloom." The dealer was particularly proud of this piece and selected it for inclusion in *The Potteries of Persia*, a history of Near Eastern ceramics that he compiled in 1909.[44] That Kelekian and H. O. Havemeyer developed a strong relationship can be ascertained by Kelekian's reflections on Havemeyer shortly after he died. In a letter the dealer wrote to Louisine a few years after her husband's death, he reminisced that he "took such a personal pleasure in helping Mr. Havemeyer form his collection."[45] Commenting later, he expressed his admiration for Mr. Havemeyer, calling him "the ablest and most intelligent

collector I ever knew. His nobility of character served him well in matters where weaker people lose their way."[46]

By the time of Harry Havemeyer's death in 1907, Louisine had clearly learned to love the decorative arts. She initially may have confronted her husband's collections with little knowledge or interest, but she soon absorbed a great deal from him and from the objects he had gathered together for their New York home. One particularly telling incident in this gradual process occurred about 1884, shortly after their marriage. Mrs. Havemeyer recounted that her husband announced one morning that a case of tea jars would arrive and instructed her to make a selection for display. Expressing her total ignorance of the subject, she innocently asked, "But what is a tea jar?"[47] However, before the day was over, Louisine had caressed a caseful of such jars and had completely succumbed to their charms, exclaiming, "What pretty, dainty things they appeared to me."[48]

After her husband's death, Louisine maintained the dealer contacts that Harry had made, especially that with Kelekian. Kelekian continued his close friendship with Cassatt, and his name appears frequently in her letters to Louisine. In addition, Kelekian carried on his own correspondence with Louisine, especially to encourage her to acquire his important collection of thirteenth-century Persian pottery. As he confided to Cassatt in a letter dated November 15, 1909, "They [the Havemeyers] absolutely own the finest collection in the world and yet they do not realize. What is missing in the Havemeyer collection is the 13th century potteries which unfortunately Mr. Havemeyer did not understand to buy."[49] Harry Havemeyer may have felt such works too intellectually demanding, for according to conversations he often had with Kelekian, "he considered them more fitting for a public museum than for a private collection."[50] Although Mr. Havemeyer had resisted buying thirteenth-century ceramics, Kelekian continued to appeal to Louisine on the basis that they would fill a gap in her collection. By 1909, when he was making his overtures to Louisine, Kelekian had put together what he claimed were "the best specimens known of the 12th and 13th century potteries."[51] He first made her an exclusive offer of fifty pieces for a special price and then stated that he would consider selling her just forty-nine, reserving his "blue vase," which would represent a fifty-thousand-dollar deduc-

Plate 99. *Jar*, Iran, A.D. 1282–83 (dated A.H. 681). Composite earthenware body, molded, with monochrome glaze, h. 21½ in. (54.6 cm). H. O. Havemeyer Collection, Gift of Horace Havemeyer, 1956 (56.185.3)

tion.[52] This concession was undoubtedly made because Louisine already owned an important blue jar (probably pl. 99), which was one of the most expensive items in her collection.[53] Louisine must have decided against purchasing Kelekian's thirteenth-century Persian pottery at this time, for there is no further correspondence regarding it. In fact, the fifty objects proposed to Louisine formed the core of a larger collection Kelekian assembled between 1885 and 1910 and published in a folio volume, *The Kelekian Collection of Persian and Analogous Potteries, 1885–1910*, about which he wrote regretfully, "how glad he [Havemeyer] would have been to see this *triumph* of the art he was one of the first to understand and support."[54] Shortly thereafter Kelekian lent his collection to the Victoria and Albert Museum in London, giving the museum the option to buy it at the end of two years.[55]

Louisine and Harry's interest in Syrian and Persian pottery was embraced even more enthusiastically by their son, Horace. Horace frequented Kelekian's New York gallery and on his own purchased Syrian and Persian examples.[56] It was clearly a source of pleasure to his mother that Horace was putting together a collection, and the two shared this activity during their travels. Louisine encouraged Horace by giving him pottery. One late twelfth-century Raqqa vase (MMA 48.113.1), which has an iridescent turquoise blue glaze over carved relief decoration, bore the legend: "I give

Plate 100. *Vase*, Syria, late 12th–early 13th century. Underglaze-painted composite body, h. 5 in. (12.7 cm). H. O. Havemeyer Collection, Gift of Horace Havemeyer, 1945 (45.153.3)

this jar to Horace as a wedding Present Feb. 1911 L. W. Havemeyer." Another, of approximately the same date with an Arabic inscription painted in black under the glaze (pl. 100), has a paper label with the inscription: "To Horace from Mother/Xmas 1916." Although it is unclear how many examples Horace purchased on his own and how many he inherited from his mother, he had a sizable collection of Islamic pottery in 1931, when he lent 66 objects—literally one-third of those in the show—to the Museum for its *Loan Exhibition of Ceramic Art of the Near East*.[57] From 1929 until his death in 1957, Horace Havemeyer donated, either by gift or bequest, to the Metropolitan 109 pieces of Islamic pottery and 2 Persian rugs. His collection was particularly rich in Raqqa ware with painted decoration, mostly in black under a turquoise blue glaze (see pl. 88) or luster-painted, making the Museum's holdings of Raqqa ware the finest in the world.[58]

In addition, the Havemeyer gifts strengthened other areas of the Metropolitan's Islamic pottery holdings. One notable example is an early fourteenth-century Persian bowl (pl. 101), which is clearly indebted to the highly prized Chinese celadon-glazed wares. It shows a radiating petal pattern on the exterior and is also ornamented on the interior—an unusual feature—with three fish in relief, recalling similar Chinese celadon-glazed bowls. This acquisition filled a major gap and remains the only example of the rare imitation celadon pieces among the Museum's Islamic ceramics.

A certain fastidiousness marked the Havemeyers' collecting of decorative arts. Harry Havemeyer was used to acquiring large numbers of objects, but the job of organizing and inventorying them was apparently delegated to his wife. Probably sometime in the 1920s, Louisine Havemeyer had a special HOH Collection label designed and produced (fig. 16). She placed it on virtually every one of her thousands of objects, and at the same time inscribed it with an inventory number, date, or attribution. She added a paper label marked "Z" on all the ones she felt were worthy of the Metropolitan Museum. Louisine's meticulous record keeping was also demonstrated in her "Notes to Her Children," in which she wrote of many of the objects she intended to give to them and to the Museum. In the brief entries she typically included the location—the room and the cupboard—in which each vase or jar might be found. "Italian and Gnahio[?] plates," she

Plate 101. *Bowl*, Iran, 1st half of 14th century. Glazed composite body with applied decoration, diam. 11 ⅛ in. (28.3 cm). Gift of Mrs. Horace Havemeyer, in memory of her husband, 1959 (59.60)

Figure 16. HOH Collection label, paper, on the underside of a 17th century Spanish dish (see plate 90)

wrote, could be found "on the high shelves in store room by rug chest," adding that "some of the finest hispagno moresque plates are there marked."[59]

In spite of the fact that paintings were clearly their mother's first love, all the Havemeyer children gravitated more to the decorative arts. Horace, as mentioned above, carried on his father's interest in Persian pottery. The Havemeyers' daughter Adaline displayed an acquisitive nature by at least 1919, after her children were born. As Cassatt commented in a letter to Louisine: "Adaline was sure to collect she is her Father's daughter & yours."[60] Adaline furnished her house in

Morristown, New Jersey, with simple seventeenth- and eighteenth-century English furniture, Chinese export porcelain, eighteenth- and early nineteenth-century English pottery, and antique printed textiles. As she was fond of saying, she "would much prefer owning an eighteenth-century textile than a Rembrandt."[61] She also purchased American furniture, quilts, hooked rugs, and pressed glass, objects that suited her house in Manchester, Vermont.[62]

Adaline's younger sister, Electra, developed the collecting fever at an early age. She amassed American decorative arts on a scale that would have been best understood by her father.[63] Like her parents, Electra struck out on her own, in opposition to the conventional taste of the day; she pursued American folk art rather than traditional high-style eighteenth and early nineteenth-century furniture and other objects. Her extraordinary assemblages included great quantities of trade signs and figures, decoys and other wood carvings, scrimshaw, weather vanes (see fig. 17), quilts, and hooked rugs. With the same enlightened spirit that motivated her parents to share their collections with the public, Electra eventually displayed her multitude of objects in a group of old Vermont houses and other buildings that she brought together as the Shelburne Museum in the town of Shelburne.

The Havemeyers were typical of their time in the sense that they were attracted to the decorative arts, which were vigorously sought during the last quarter of the nineteenth century. Yet they stood apart from the majority of their economic peers in their intensely serious pursuit of advanced, somewhat avant-garde areas of collecting, purchasing objects that suited their private and highly cultured life. Louisine and Harry Havemeyer were also distinguished from many of their contemporaries because their decisions were influenced by their associations with and advice from artist friends—particularly Cassatt, Tiffany, Colman, and Moore. Their decorative arts collection reveals that they were drawn to the artistic merit of objects and responded far more to color, especially the rainbow hues of iridescent surfaces or luster glazes, than they did to qualities of form or rarity. As A. Hyatt Mayor, Curator of Prints at the Metropolitan, wrote about the Havemeyers in 1957, assessing their major gifts to the Museum:

> They had in the highest degree the indispensable requirement for a great collector—the courage of perception—and this rare quality makes a Havemeyer object recognizable no matter where it turns up. Their things do not look rich materially but each one identifies itself in any gallery by its accent of imagination.[64]

Figure 17. *TO, TE—Indian Hunter*. America, ca. 1860. Polychromed sheet iron, h. 51 in. (129.5 cm). Shelburne Museum, Shelburne, Vermont (FW–4)

1. See Havemeyer 1931, pp. 228–33, 457–71, 516–18, and *The Estate of Mrs. H. O. Havemeyer: [Part II] Roman, Syrian, & Egyptian Glass, Hispano-Moresque Lustre Ware, Mohammedan Pottery and Italian Majolica, Fine Rugs*, sale cat., American Art Association, Anderson Galleries, New York, April 10, 11, 12, 1930.
2. See Doreen Bolger Burke et al., *In Pursuit of Beauty: Americans and the Aesthetic Movement*, exh. cat., MMA, New York, 1986, pp. 19–21, 131–33, 199–201.
3. For further material on J. Pierpont Morgan's decorative arts collection, see Linda Horvitz Roth, ed., *J. Pierpont Morgan, Collector: European Decorative Arts from the Wadsworth Atheneum*, exh. cat., The Wadsworth Atheneum, Hartford, 1987. See also William George Constable, *Art Collecting in the United States of America*, London, 1964, pp. 91–140.
4. Weitzenhoffer 1986, p. 30.
5. One event that helps characterize Havemeyer's courage in business dealings was a joint decision with his brother Theodore in 1882 to risk a considerable amount of the family fortune to rebuild the family's sugar refinery, which had been destroyed in a disastrous fire, into the largest in the country. (See Daniel Catlin, Jr., *Good Work, Well Done: The Sugar Business Career of Horace Havemeyer, 1903–1956*, New York, 1988, p. 8.)
6. See James L. Yarnall and William H. Gerdts, comps., *The National Museum of American Art's Index to American Art. Exhibition Catalogues*, Boston, 1986, vol. 1, pp. 51, 155, 281; vol. 2, p. 1239; vol. 3, p. 2241; vol. 4, p. 2380; vol. 5, pp. 3385, 3675, 3916.
7. See *Catalogue of Oil Paintings by American Artists Belonging to William F. Havemeyer*, exh. cat., Fifth Avenue Art Galleries, New York, 1899.
8. James D. McCabe, *The Illustrated History of the Centennial Exhibition . . .* , 1876; repr. Philadelphia, 1975.
9. Alice Cooney Frelinghuysen, "Aesthetic Forms in Ceramics and Glass," in Bolger et al., *In Pursuit of Beauty*, pp. 199–229.
10. Havemeyer 1961, p. 16.
11. J.B.T., "A Great Art Collector Passes," *American Art News* 6 (December 14, 1907), p. 1.
12. *Objects of Art of Three Continents and Antique Oriental Rugs: The Extensive Collection of the Louis Comfort Tiffany Foundation*, sale cat., Parke-Bernet Galleries, New York, September 24–28, 1946.
13. *Catalogue of the Valuable Art Collection Recently Contained in the Newport Residence of Samuel Colman, N.A. . . .* , sale cat., American Art Association, New York, March 19–22, 1902.
14. Havemeyer "Notes" [1974], p. 9. Louisine wrote that "the hammered silver set was made for me by Tiffany['s] 'Moore' who adopted [*sic*] it from the Japanese. . . . Father gave him 'carte blanche' to make me a set." She also recorded that Moore made her twelve fish forks by mounting the tines onto actual Japanese knife handles from her collection. In addition, there were "a fine salad bowl and spoons, a tea pitcher and cady [*sic*], etc."
15. Havemeyer "Notes" [1974], p. 28. Although Louisine indicated that the plate came from "Tom. Colman's Collection," this is most likely a typographical error.
16. The plate over the cabinet at one end of the dining room and

the plate second from left on the wall above the buffet illustrated in fig. 33, and the plate on the far left seen over the mantelpiece in fig. 6 can be identified as MMA 29.100.138, 140, and 144, respectively. In addition, two others, lots 570 and 603 in *The Estate of Mrs. H. O. Havemeyer, Part II*, can be matched with plates on the far left and the second from the right, respectively, over the buffet seen in fig. 33.

17. Havemeyer 1961, pp. 153–56, 179.

18. *Catalogue des Objets d'Art et de Haute Curiosité de l'Antiquité, du Moyen Age et de la Renaissance Composant la Collection de feu M. Boy*, sale cat., Galerie Georges Petit, Paris, May 15–24, 1905, nos. 45, 54, 65 (MMA 29.100.96, 142, 99, respectively).

19. *Catalogue of the Renowned Collection of Art by the Late Hollingworth Magniac, Esq. (Known as the Colworth Collection)*, sale cat., London, Christie, Manson and Woods, July 2–15, 1892, p. 120, lot 481.

20. Louis Comfort Tiffany, "American Art Supreme in Colored Glass," *Forum* 15 (July 1893), pp. 621–28.

21. David Frederick Grose, *Early Ancient Glass*, New York, 1989, p. 375, n. 2.

22. Montezuma, "My Note Book," *Art Amateur* 22 (May 1890), p. 112.

23. Grose, *Early Ancient Glass*, p. 20.

24. Sidney M. Bergman, "Azeez Khayat (1875–1943): A Noted Collector of Ancient Glass," *Carnegie Magazine* 48 (1974), p. 242.

25. Azeez Khayat to Gisela M. A. Richter, 5/12/30, MMA Greek and Roman Department Archives.

26. MC to LWH, 6/2/06, Havemeyer correspondence.

27. Havemeyer may have bought examples at one or both of the Henry De Morgan sales in 1901 and 1909. (See *The Collection of Henry De Morgan, Greek Art, Fine Iridescent Glass, Greek Vases, Terracotta Figurines and Groups*, sale cat., American Art Galleries, New York, March 12, 13, 1901; *Greek Vases, Also Iridescent Glass, Cameos, Intaglios and Silver Coins Selected and Catalogued by H. De Morgan*, sale cat., Fifth Avenue Art Galleries, New York, January 16, 1909.)

28. Gustavus Augustus Eisen and Fahim Kouchakji, *Glass, Its Origin, History, Chronology, Technic and Classification to the Sixteenth Century*, vol. 2, New York, 1927, pp. 690, 703 (ill.). This beaker is illustrated and described as "from Damascus, Syria," and discussed with others of a group called Arab glass of the fifteenth through the seventeenth century.

29. The tazza is described as "Class [sic] dish decorated with gold I think fr. Ganet [sic] Sale" in Havemeyer "Notes" [1974], pp. 24, 27. According to the Museum catalogue card, the tazza was said to be from the Ganary collection, but it does not appear in the sale catalogue of that collection. The entry on the card further states that it was said to have been purchased through Durand-Ruel, Sr.

30. *Estate of Mrs. H. O. Havemeyer: [Part II]*, sale cat., p. 34, lot 228.

31. The vase shown in pl. 97 was illustrated in the 1930 Havemeyer estate sale catalogue and described as "Iridescent 'Quartz' vase, signed, ovoid shape simulating richly variegated carnelian quartz, with brilliant kingfisher-blue, silver and fiery opal iridescence. Fine specimen." (Ibid., p. 36, lot 248.)

32. Ibid., p. 39, lot 258.

33. Ibid., p. 34.

34. MC to LWH, 8/9/01, Havemeyer correspondence.

35. Montague Marks, "My Note Book," *Art Amateur* 29 (September 1893), p. 80.

36. "Notes for Collectors," *Art Courier*, an occasional supplement to the *Art Amateur* 24 (March 1891), p. 2.

37. MC to LWH, 10/17/06, Havemeyer correspondence.

38. Havemeyer "Notes" [1974], p. 22.

39. In a 1907 letter to the editor commenting on H. O. Havemeyer's obituary, the author claimed that Havemeyer had been purchasing works of art from Kelekian "during the past eighteen years," which would mean that his first purchases dated to about 1889 or 1890. (See T.[homas] B. C.[larke], "The Havemeyer Collections," *American Art News* 6 [December 21, 1907], p. 4.) Unfortunately, there is no documentation of Havemeyer and Kelekian's first meeting.

40. MC to LWH, 7/19/06 [or 07], Havemeyer correspondence. For other decorative arts and sculpture that Cassatt brought to Mrs. Havemeyer's attention, see Chronology, late April, early May 1906, September 5, 1910, December 14, 1911, July 31, 1916, December 14, 1919.

41. Havemeyer "Notes" [1974], p. 21.

42. I am grateful to Alice Zriebec for her information concerning this cope. A related example, probably used in the same way, is in the National Gallery of Art, Washington, D.C., and was originally owned by Joseph E. Widener.

43. T.[homas] B. C.[larke], "The Havemeyer Collections," p. 4.

44. Dikran Khan Kelekian, *The Potteries of Persia: Being a Brief History of the Art of Ceramics in the Near East*, Paris, 1909, pp. 20, 25, 26.

45. DK to LWH, 6/7/09, MMA Archives.

46. DK to LWH, 12/16/10, MMA Archives.

47. Havemeyer 1961, p. 73.

48. Ibid., p. 74.

49. DK to MC, 11/15/09, MMA Archives.

50. DK to LWH, 6/7/09, MMA Archives.

51. Ibid.

52. Ibid.

53. The blue vase that Kelekian referred to in his correspondence with Louisine Havemeyer is most likely the "large Persian vase" included as the frontispiece and pl. 111 in *The Kelekian Collection of Persian and Analogous Potteries, 1885–1910*, Paris, 1910.

54. DK to LWH, 12/16/10, MMA Archives.

55. Ibid.

56. Kelekian expressed understandable pleasure in Horace's "continuing in his father's footsteps as a great lover and connoisseur of art," and wrote to Louisine that he "shows the greatest taste and understanding in the pieces he admires and buys." (Ibid.)

57. *Loan Exhibition of Ceramic Art of the Near East*, exh. cat., MMA, New York, 1931.

58. See Maurice S. Dimand, "The Horace Havemeyer Bequest of Islamic Art," *Metropolitan Museum of Art Bulletin* 15 (May 1957), pp. 208–12.

59. Havemeyer "Notes" [1974], p. 24.

60. MC to LWH, 8/26/19, Havemeyer correspondence.

61. George G. Frelinghuysen to Alice Cooney Frelinghuysen, 8/7/92, correspondence.

62. This collecting spirit was inherited by the next generation as well. See, for example, the various collections of Adaline's eldest son, George G. Frelinghuysen, that included Americana, African and Oceanic carvings, and Native American artifacts, sold at auction: sale cats., Sotheby–Parke Bernet, New York, March 4, 5, 1974; April 29, 1974; May 27, 1974; June 10, 1974; January 22, 23, 1975; Los Angeles, February 4, 1975; November 18, 1975; June 6, 1975.

63. For one of the best accounts of Electra Webb's collecting, see Aline B. Saarinen, *The Proud Possessors*, New York, 1958, pp. 287–306. See also Benjamin L. Mason, "A 'Simple' Vision," in *An American Sampler: Folk Art from the Shelburne Museum*, exh. cat., National Gallery of Art, Washington, D.C., 1987, pp. 8–22.

64. A. Hyatt Mayor, "The Gifts That Made the Museum," *Metropolitan Museum of Art Bulletin* 16 (November 1957), p. 100.

Plate 102
FACE OF A PHARAOH

Egyptian, provenance unknown, end of
Dynasty 12, ca. 1800 B.C.
Shelly gray limestone, h. 3 ½ in. (8.9 cm)
H. O. Havemeyer Collection, Bequest of
Mrs. H. O. Havemeyer, 1929
29.100.150

The Metropolitan owes its prominent position as a repository of
Egyptian Middle Kingdom sculpture
in general and royal portraiture in
particular to a combination of fortunate acquisitions and excavations
carried out by the Museum at foremost Middle Kingdom sites. When
Louisine Havemeyer's bequest
brought this dark marblelike face of
a pharaoh to the Museum in 1929,
the collection was already crowned
by the superb quartzite head of
Senwosret III (MMA 26.7.1394), an
image that epitomizes the burden of
royal power and responsibility as
does no other work of ancient art.
Four more royal heads were acquired in the 1940s and 1960s, enriching the holdings so that they
became an assemblage of Middle
Kingdom royal sculpture unsurpassed in any other museum.

The Havemeyer head of a pharaoh was once shown wearing the
royal headcloth (*nemes*), only fragments of which remain above both
sides of the face. This face is remarkable for its serene expression; no
wrinkles mar the austere beauty of
the evenly rounded features. The
chronological placement of the sculpture at the very end of Dynasty 12
(ca. 1800 B.C.) is based on the
rather advanced schematization of
the facial features, especially noticeable in the abstract almond shape of
the eyes. Since the Havemeyer face
has an unmistakable feminine character, it is tempting to identify the
pharaoh represented as Queen
Sobekneferu, the last ruler of Dynasty 12, who—like Queen Hat-

shepsut more than three hundred
years later—reigned in her own
right.[1]   DA

1. The head is published in Cyril Aldred,
   "Some Royal Portraits of the Middle
   Kingdom in Ancient Egypt," *Metropolitan Museum Journal* 3 (1970), pp. 46–
   47, figs. 29-31, and Janine Bourriau,
   *Pharaohs and Mortals: Egyptian Art in
   the Middle Kingdom*, exh. cat., Fitzwilliam Museum, Cambridge, 1988,
   p. 45. The usual attribution to
   Amenemhat III is suggested in each.

Plate 103
STATUETTE OF KHNUMHOTEP

Egyptian, provenance unknown, Dynasty 13,
1800–1750 B.C.
Basalt, h. 7 ½ in. (19.1 cm)
H. O. Havemeyer Collection, Bequest of
Mrs. H. O. Havemeyer, 1929
29.100.151

The Havemeyer basalt statuette of
Khnumhotep was made sometime
after the royal head (between 1800
and 1750 B.C.). Khnumhotep is represented in a squatting posture that
was often used in the Middle King-

dom to show figures seated at a meal. His long cloak covers the left shoulder and is drawn demurely over the knees and lower legs. Khnumhotep's left hand lies flat on the chest in a gesture of piety. A striped kerchief covers the head. Statuettes of this type were set up as recipients of funerary offerings. An example excavated by the Museum (MMA 22.1.107a,b) shows such a statuette set into an offering table of

white stone. The inscription on Khnumhotep's lap fittingly invokes the god Ptah Sokar to guarantee eternal provisions. Although the statuette was made at a somewhat later date than the royal head, Khnumhotep's face is, nevertheless, rendered according to an earlier artistic tradition. The large ears, forcefully compressed lips, and heavy-lidded eyes are features first conceived for royal sculpture of mid-Dynasty 12.

By Dynasty 13 these features had acquired emblematic significance: Khnumhotep is thus characterized as a wise and responsible person of high rank.[1]

DA

1. The statuette is published in William C. Hayes, *The Scepter of Egypt*, 5th printing, New York, 1990, vol. 1, p. 213, fig. 130, and Janine Bourriau, *Pharaohs and Mortals: Egyptian Art in the Middle Kingdom*, exh. cat., Fitzwilliam Museum, Cambridge, 1988, no. 43, pp. 56–57.

Plate 104. *Modiolus, bowl, and bottle*, Roman, 1st century A.D. Glass, l.: h. 4⅞ in. (12.3 cm); c.: h. 1¾ in. (4.5 cm); r.: h. 4⅛ in. (10.5 cm). H. O. Havemeyer Collection, Bequest of Mrs. H. O. Havemeyer, 1929 (29.100.71, 86, 88)

ROMAN GLASS AND LEAD-GLAZED POTTERY

Nineteen pieces of glass make up the largest single group of antiquities received by the Museum's Greek and Roman department from the Havemeyer bequest. The family did not collect glass exclusively, however. The privately printed Havemeyer collection catalogue of 1931 mentions the Greek and Roman coins of Horace Havemeyer as well as so-called Tanagra terracottas belonging to Adaline Havemeyer Frelinghuysen and Electra Havemeyer Webb. Terracotta figures, moreover, are already cited in the *Art Courier* for March 1891 as occupying a prominent place in the Havemeyers' new residence on Fifth Avenue. The auction catalogue of the Havemeyer sale in April 1930 includes one marble, eight pieces of pottery—and a total of four hundred pieces of glass.

From the Havemeyers' appreciable assemblage, Gisela M. A. Richter, Curator of the classical department, made her selection of glass for the Museum. Of the nineteen examples chosen, four were subsequently transferred to the departments responsible for ancient Near Eastern, Medieval, and European decorative arts. The fifteen Greek and Roman pieces strengthened already remarkable holdings founded upon the glass from Cyprus that came to the Museum with the Cesnola Collection between 1874 and 1876, the Charvet Collection donated by Henry G. Marquand in 1881, and the Gréau Collection given by J. Pierpont Morgan in 1917. All of the pieces in the Havemeyer bequest had been purchased by Mrs. Havemeyer from Azeez Khayat, a major dealer in ancient glass from the turn of the century until World War II, with establishments in New York, Haifa, and Cairo. The material he sold to the Havemeyers is predominantly Roman from the eastern Mediterranean.

Without parallel in the Museum's collection is a one-handled cup, or *modiolus*, datable to the first century A.D. (pl. 104). The shape is known from counterparts in terracotta and silver; there are, however, few other examples in such blobbed blown glass. Supplementing fine pieces that already belonged to the Museum are the bottle of gold-band glass and the bowl made in a variant of the mosaic technique that produces a pattern of flowing stripes (pl. 104). Both of these works are datable to the end of the first century B.C. Of exceptional interest is the mold-blown beaker (pl. 105) that bears the inscription: *let the buyer remember, Jason made it*. Jason was active during the first century A.D. in one of the many glass-producing centers of the Levant. A beaker from the same mold was acquired in 1959 (MMA 59.11.3).

The other ancient glasses in the Havemeyer bequest provide an excellent representation of major techniques and types current in Roman times. The emphasis is on mold-blown pieces and on those decorated with applied glass threads.

The lead-glazed pottery in the Havemeyer bequest is a natural concomitant of the glass, for the objects are roughly contemporary and come from the eastern Mediterranean world. The two green-glazed skyphoi (pl. 106) represent the most common shape for this ware. They were made in Tarsus (southeastern Turkey), a center of production that has been studied quite fully. Both are datable to between the end of the first century B.C. and the middle of the first century A.D. The very characteristic foliate decoration consists of tendrils with rosettes and *korymboi*, the fruit of the ivy plant, on one example (pl. 106, at right), and sprigs of a plane tree on the other (pl. 106, at left).

JRM

Plate 105. *Beaker*, Roman, 1st century A.D. Glass, h. 3⅝ in. (9.1 cm). H. O. Havemeyer Collection, Bequest of Mrs. H. O. Havemeyer, 1929 (29.100.82)

Plate 106. *Skyphoi*, Roman, late 1st century B.C.–mid-1st century A.D. Terracotta, l.: h. 3⅛ in. (7.8 cm); r.: h. 3¼ in. (8 cm). H. O. Havemeyer Collection, Bequest of Mrs. H. O. Havemeyer, 1929 (29.100.77,78)

Plate 107
HELMET

Greece, 2nd half of 7th century B.C.
Bronze, h. 8⅝ in. (22.7 cm)
H. O. Havemeyer Collection, Bequest of
Mrs. H. O. Havemeyer, 1929
29.100.488

Among the classical antiquities in the Havemeyer bequest, the Greek bronze helmet stands out as exceptionally severe, especially in comparison to the colorful decorative glass. Its presence in the Museum's collection reflects the wide-ranging expertise of Gisela M. A. Richter, who chose the Greek and Roman objects for the bequest. The helmet is of the Corinthian type, open at the eyes and the front of the face and provided with a nosepiece. The small holes around the edges served to attach a lining of leather or, perhaps,

fabric. The stylistic evolution of the Corinthian helmet is best known from the hundreds of examples dedicated at the Greek sanctuary site of Olympia. The Havemeyer example belongs with those of the second half of the seventh century B.C. The bent-up nosepiece occurs on other helmets that were offered as dedications. The selection of the helmet may document not only Miss Richter's but perhaps also the Havemeyers' interest in Greek armor, kindled by the finds made at Olympia from the 1870s on.   JRM

CARVED CERAMICS FROM THE ARAB WORLD

The principal decoration of the first brightly glazed vessel (pl. 108) proclaims *Glory* (*al-ʿizz*) in the Arabic language, executed in ornamental foliated Kufic script on a ground of undulating arabesques. The dish is one of eleven objects in the category of carved and monochrome-glazed ware that came to The Metropolitan Museum of Art from the Havemeyers. It must be assumed that the type was highly prized early in this century, as one of the group, a large vase in less than perfect condition (MMA 48.113.1), bore a label with the following information: "I give this jar to Horace as wedding present Feb. 1911 L.W. Havemeyer. . . ."

Laqabi, another type of Islamic pottery that is well represented in the Havemeyer collection, is very closely related to the carved and monochrome-glazed ware. One of the nine examples of *laqabi* in the Havemeyer gift to the Museum is a bowl that bears a lively antlered quadruped as its main design (pl. 109). Both the monochrome-glazed and the *laqabi* wares are decorated by carving away the entire background, so that the design is left in relief, which is then highlighted with deeply incised lines. In vessels of the former category, the deeply carved design is simply covered with a monochrome

Plate 108. *Dish*, Syria, 11th century. Carved and glazed composite body, diam. 12 in. (30.5 cm). H. O. Havemeyer Collection, Gift of Horace Havemeyer, 1929 (29.160.8)

Plate 109. *Bowl*, Syria, 11th century. Carved composite body with colored and colorless glazes, diam. 12 ⅝ in. (32.1 cm). H. O. Havemeyer Collection, Gift of Horace Havemeyer, 1929 (29.160.15)

Plate 110. *Ewer*, Syria, late 12th–1st half of 13th century. Underglaze- and luster-painted composite body, h. 7 ½ in. (19.1 cm). H. O. Havemeyer Collection, Gift of Horace Havemeyer, 1948 (48.113.16)

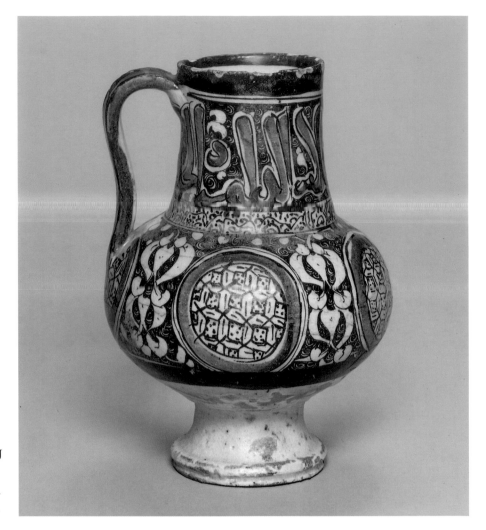

glaze; in the *laqabi*, however, various colored glazes are painted within the cloisons created by the incised lines, which act as dikes to keep the different colors from running together. The two shapes exhibited in the *Glory* and quadruped examples exist in both types, and the most common rim design in either group is that seen on the *Glory* dish.

Although such wares were long considered to have been produced in Iran in the twelfth and thirteenth centuries, only recently the excavation of a shipwreck off the Turkish coast has helped determine, rather, that they originated in the Arab world during the eleventh century.[1]

MJ

1. Marilyn Jenkins, "Early Medieval Islamic Pottery: The Eleventh Century Reconsidered," *Muqarnas* 9 (forthcoming).

LUSTER-PAINTED POTTERY

Luster-painted decoration originated in the Muslim world as a means of embellishing glass. Not long after its invention, this completely new creation of Islamic artisans was applied to ceramics, a medium in which it is better known, more common, and much longer-lived. It was on pottery that the technique passed from ninth-century Iraq to Egypt, North Africa, Syria, Iran, and Spain and from the Islamic world to Italy, and then to the rest of Europe and America. In this extremely difficult process, designs are painted on a vessel in silver and copper oxides, each mixed with a medium. When the vessel is placed in a reducing

atmosphere, oxygen is drawn out of the metallic oxides, leaving the metal suspended on the surface to refract light and create a lustrous appearance.

Thanks to the Havemeyers' taste for Early Medieval Islamic pottery from Syria, the Metropolitan Museum has the world's largest and most important collection of luster-painted pottery from the Syrian city of Raqqa, on the Euphrates. The handled drinking vessel (pl. 110) typifies the luster-painted production of Raqqa as well as the characteristic decorative vocabulary of Islamic art: its bands bear geometric patterns, highly stylized vegetal forms, and

calligraphy, three of the four basic Islamic motifs (the fourth being figural designs).

Kashan, in central Iran, was another major center in the Islamic world for the manufacture of luster-painted pottery. This Iranian city was so well known for its tiles that the word *kashi* came to mean "tile" in Persian. The decoration of the vessels and tiles produced in this city often incorporates figural and animal motifs. A particularly fine example of the type shows two figures seated outdoors under tall checkerboard-patterned trees (pl. 111). In what is probably a vignette of courtly life, the person on the left, who is clothed in a garment covered with arabesques, plays an *ʿud* (lute), and the second figure, whose dress is adorned with haloed harpies, listens attentively.

Another example of Kashan luster-painted ware consists of two tiles from a frieze (pl. 112). After these tiles were formed in a mold, their bold inscriptions were painted in cobalt and their broad upper borders were highlighted in turquoise. Then the glaze was applied and the tiles were fired. Finally, the luster-painted decoration was added and the pieces were refired.

Of the 147 Islamic objects that came to the Metropolitan from the Havemeyers, 53 are luster-painted ceramics produced in Kashan and 45 of the latter are tiles. The large number of tiles in the collection not only indicates a predilection for such ware on the part of the donors but also suggests that they may have used them as wall decoration.

MJ

Plate 111. *Bowl*, Iran (Kashan), late 12th–early 13th century. Glazed, luster-painted, and incised composite body, diam. 8 ½ in. (21.6 cm). H. O. Havemeyer Collection, Bequest of Horace Havemeyer, 1956 (56.185.13)

Plate 112. *Two tiles from a frieze*, Iran (Kashan), 1st half of 14th century. Molded, glazed, stain- and luster-painted composite body, each 17 ½ x 15 ½ in. (44.5 x 39.4 cm). H. O. Havemeyer Collection, Gift of Horace Havemeyer, 1940 (40.181.5,6)

Plate 113
CARPET WITH A COMPARTMENT DESIGN

Iran, Safavid period, 17th century
Wool pile on foundation of cotton, silk, and
wool, ca. 270 asymmetrical knots per square
in., 15 ft. 8 in. x 10 ft. 6 in. (4.7 x 3.2 m)
H. O. Havemeyer Collection, Bequest of
Horace Havemeyer, 1956
56.185.1

This carpet is a splendid example of
seventeenth-century Persian pile
weaving. It features a continuous re-
peating field pattern that lacks both
the central focus or medallion of
many classical Persian pieces and
the directional orientation found in
pictorial types; in this sense it is reminiscent of a loom-woven textile.
The pattern consists of overlapping
cartouches organized in columns
and rows. Within the compartments
are various palmettes and blossoms
linked by a scrolling vine system.
The palette is rich and varied and,
contrary to usual practice, no single
ground color predominates. The
field is framed by a narrow border
with a reciprocal arabesque whose
undulations allow the use of two
contrasting ground colors.

The Havemeyer piece belongs to a
class known as vase carpets, named
for the vases incorporated into the
floral patterns of some of the best-
known examples.[1] Carpets of this
group have much more in common
than vase motifs (which many, in
fact, lack): a broad palette of unusually crisp and bright colors, very fine
wool, and a distinctive weave. The
carpets tend to be thick and unpli-
able because of the extreme depression of alternate warps, and the wefts
are an unusual combination of wool
and silk or cotton; these features
yield a recognizable wear pattern.
Vase carpets most frequently display
floral lattice patterns; the compart-
ment pattern of the Havemeyer example, while known in other types of
classical Persian carpets, is unique
among vase carpets.

The question of the provenance
of vase carpets has yet to be resolved
conclusively, but a number of scholars have assigned them to the city
of Kirman, in southeastern Iran. The
evidence is largely circumstantial:
Kirman is named in sixteenth- and
seventeenth-century sources as a
major carpet-weaving center and was
also famous for fine wool.

When or where Harry Havemeyer
purchased this fine carpet is not
known,[2] but it was in the collection
of his son, Horace, by 1931, when it
was exhibited in London. The acquisition suggests a sophisticated taste,
since it is neither a routine example
of the vase type nor a typical reflec-
tion of the grand furnishing taste for
giant Indo-Persian carpets demonstrated by other collectors of the
late nineteenth and early twentieth
centuries.

DW

1. For discussion of this and other vase
   carpets and for bibliography, see M.
   Beattie, *Carpets of Central Persia*,
   London, 1976 (Havemeyer carpet is
   no. 67), and M. S. Dimand and Jean
   Mailey, *Oriental Rugs in The Metropolitan Museum of Art*, New York, 1973,
   pp. 72–77 (Havemeyer carpet is no. 39).
2. In *Oriental Rugs in The Metropolitan
   Museum of Art*, Dimand says the rug
   was formerly in the collection of
   Dikran Kelekian (no. 39, p. 111), but it
   has not been possible to verify this.

FAVRILE GLASS

Louisine and Henry Osborne Have-meyer were among the earliest individuals to admire and seriously collect the favrile glass, or hand-made iridescent blown colored glass, vessels made by Louis Comfort Tiffany and the talented artists of his studio; indeed the sizable holdings they acquired probably represent the first private collection of these precious, fragile objects. Tiffany, who had been producing leaded-glass windows since the late 1870s, began to make blown-glass vessels only two years after he decorated the interiors of the Havemeyers' Fifth Avenue mansion; he added them to his studio's repertoire in 1893, when he completed construction of his glass furnace in Corona, New York.

Undoubtedly prompted by the artist, the Havemeyers gave their favrile collection to the Metropolitan Museum in 1896, a mere three years after Tiffany had begun to produce this glass. When he offered the Museum fifty-six Tiffany vases and roundels—the first examples of American glass of any kind to enter the collection—Harry Havemeyer wrote, "Since the Tiffany Glass Co. have been making favrile glass, Mr. Louis Tiffany has set aside the finest pieces of their production, which I have acquired for what I consider their artistic value. Their number now is such that I am disposed to offer the collection, which is one of rare be[a]uty, to the Metropolitan Museum of Art."[1] At the time he offered the gift, which was delivered to the Metropolitan in January 1897, Havemeyer specified that Tiffany, with the help of Samuel Colman, personally arrange the pieces in the cabinet chosen for their display.[2]

Although Tiffany placed collections of his new glass vessels in museums in the United States and abroad during the mid-1890s, the assem-

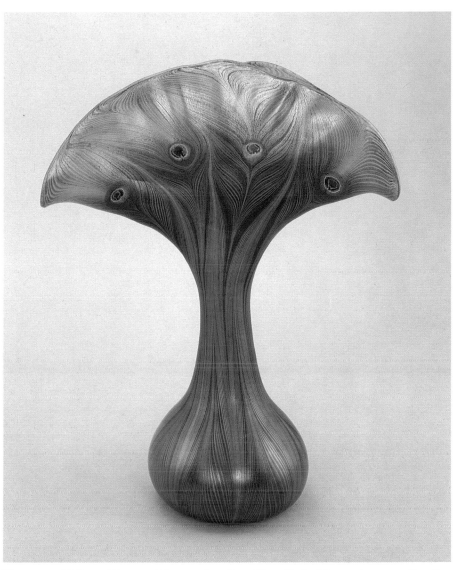

Plate 114. Tiffany Glass and Decorating Co., New York. *Vase*, 1893–96. Favrile glass, h. 14⅛ in. (35.9 cm). Inscribed on base: *01600*; paper label on base: *conjoined TGDCo*. Gift of H. O. Havemeyer, 1896 (96.17.10)

blage that came to the Metropolitan from Harry Havemeyer remains the largest group in any institution.[3] The collection at the Metropolitan is significant not only for the number of very impressive vessels it encompasses but also because it documents a group of glasses that can be pinpointed precisely to the first three years of Tiffany's production: many of the vases bear their original Tiffany Glass and Decorating Co. paper labels, and some also retain their original price stickers.

A survey of the Havemeyer gift allows us to draw certain conclusions about the early Tiffany wares: most notably that the artist was preoccu-

pied with both color and nature and also that an extraordinary variety of glasses was produced within a very short period. An aspect of the material that is well represented in the Havemeyer donation is the perfection of iridescent effects, often simulating the surfaces of long-buried ancient glass. This iridescence is realized superlatively in the peacock vase (pl. 114), whose fan profile echoes the shape of spread-out feathers; here the veins and eyes of the peacock feathers, as well as their oily sheen, are captured brilliantly in glass.

Another iridescent vessel is a large vase with rainbow hues and a pitted surface (pl. 115) that more closely re-

Plate 115. Tiffany Glass and Decorating Co., New York. *Vase*, 1893–96. Favrile glass, h. 11½ in. (29.2 cm). Inscribed on base: *Louis C. Tiffany L. C. T. D1765*; paper label on base: *conjoined TGDCo.* Gift of H. O. Havemeyer, 1896 (96.17.13)

Plate 116. Tiffany Glass and Decorating Co., New York. *Punch bowl with three ladles*, 1900. Favrile glass and silver gilt, diam. 24 in. (61 cm). Impressed on base: *April 1900/Tiffany/G. & D. Co./1282.* Virginia Museum of Fine Arts, Richmond, The Sydney and Frances Lewis Art Nouveau Fund

sembles excavated Roman glasses. This is among the earliest and largest of the so-called Cypriote glasses, a group that Tiffany must have begun making during 1895 or 1896. At this same time Tiffany also initiated production of the willowy vases that look like flowers. The earliest examples (see pl. 117) are delicate, narrow vessels with leaf motifs drawn in glass threads of different hues of green and red.

After 1896 the Havemeyers continued to associate with Tiffany—they attended parties at the artist's home and went to the lectures he gave in New York—and to patronize his work. In 1900 Harry commissioned him to fabricate an extraordinary punch bowl for the Paris International Exposition of that same year (pl. 116).[4] The bowl is made of iridescent gold favrile glass mounted on a gilt silver base whose form evokes waves; three glass and

gilt-silver ladles are suspended from favrile glass hooks near the top of the bowl. This unique object was exhibited in America the year after the International Exposition, at the 1901 Pan-American Exposition held in Buffalo, New York.

Louisine kept many examples of Tiffany's work; when the portion of her estate that was not willed to her children or given to museums was sold at auction in 1930, Tiffany objects were still placed next to ancient glasses in display cases on the third-floor balcony of the Havemeyer home.[5] Although Tiffany glass had fallen out of favor by the 1920s, it maintained its appeal for Louisine. In the notes she left for her three children regarding the dispersal of her estate, she indicated that her Tiffany glass would be given to Horace, who, she felt, would appreciate it. She wrote of this glass in particularly touching

words: "It was made especially for me—and will be beautiful always."[6]

ACF

1. HOH to Henry G. Marquand, President, The Metropolitan Museum of Art, 12/8/96, MMA Archives.
2. Ibid.
3. In America the Smithsonian Institution in Washington, D.C., acquired thirty-nine examples in 1896, and the Cincinnati Art Museum obtained twenty-seven in 1897 and 1898. In Europe smaller groups went to the Musée des Arts Décoratifs in Paris and the Musée du Luxembourg, both in 1895, to the Museum für Kunst und Gewerbe in Hamburg in 1896, and to the Österreichisches Museum für Angewandte Kunst in Vienna in 1898. In addition, a collection was placed in the Imperial Museum in Tokyo in 1895.
4. "A Tiffany Masterpiece," *Buffalo Express*, May 1900.
5. Much of the Tiffany favrile glass sold at auction in 1930 was bought by the Museum of Art, University of Michigan, Ann Arbor (1972.2.200–226).
6. Havemeyer "Notes" [1974], p. 9.

Plate 117. Tiffany Glass and Decorating Co., New York. *Flower-form vases*, 1893–96. Favrile glass, l.: h. 13 ⅛ in.
(33.3 cm). Inscribed on base: *01315*; original paper label on base: *conjoined TGDCo*; original price label on base: *15°°*;
c.: h. 12 ¾ in. (32.4 cm). Inscribed on base: *01218*; original paper label on base: *conjoined TGDCo*; original price label on
base: *12°°*; r.: h. 13 ⅜ in. (34 cm). Inscribed on base: *01892*. Gift of H. O. Havemeyer, 1896 (96.17.41,36,39)

Asian Art

Plate 118. Kitagawa Utamaro. *Geisha Dressed for a Niwaka Performance*, Japan, Edo period, ca. 1794. Color woodblock print, 15 ⅛ x 10 1/16 in. (38.4 x 25.6 cm). H. O. Havemeyer Collection, Bequest of Mrs. H. O. Havemeyer, 1929 (JP 1667)

THE OTHER HAVEMEYER PASSION: COLLECTING ASIAN ART

JULIA MEECH

 "Mr. Havemeyer always bought the best," wrote Louisine Havemeyer, reminiscing about their Chinese tea bowls.[1] A man of his times, the Sugar King can certainly be said to have bought in bulk, whether or not he bought the best; roughly two thousand Asian works were sold in the 1930 Havemeyer auction, and there were another two thousand Japanese, Chinese, and Korean objects of almost every medium in the collection when it was unveiled at the Metropolitan Museum in 1930.[2] Harry Havemeyer had the habit of dropping in on art dealers on Fifth Avenue as he walked to work in the morning. Mrs. Havemeyer's vivid description of the arrival of a shipment of tea caddies (ceramic containers for the powdered green tea served during a tea ceremony) perfectly illustrates his style of acquisition:

> How well I remember my first acquaintance with a tea jar! I think it was in 1884, and as usual, done in Mr. Havemeyer's grand style. My husband said to me one morning:
> "A case of tea jars will arrive today. You'd better unpack them; make a selection; take out what you want and put the rest in the storeroom."
> "But what is a tea jar?" I asked innocently.
> Mr. Havemeyer looked at me curiously, as if amused that my question could puzzle him, and then said frankly:
> "Well, I don't know much about them myself. They are little brown jars that hold tea. I guess that covers it, but they are very beautiful, so soft you want to hold them in your hand, and so lovely in color you cannot but admire them; just sober dark brown."[3]

She opened the case and was soon surrounded by rows of dainty "brownies." Eventually she counted 475 tea jars![4]

The Havemeyer taste in Asian art was unusually broad, encompassing objects ranging from sword guards to folding screens, from Nō robes to peachbloom vases. Mr.

and Mrs. Havemeyer were ahead of their time in some respects—they favored Chinese tomb vessels of the Han dynasty (206 B.C.–A.D. 220) over more fashionable, multicolor enameled porcelains of the seventeenth and eighteenth centuries, for example. In fact, the collection is virtually devoid of overglaze enamel wares. Unlike so many of their contemporaries, they eschewed cloisonné as well, and, as Mrs. Havemeyer pointed out, "The highly esteemed Chinese bronzes in the form of grotesque animals never appealed to Mr. Havemeyer; the reason is obvious."[5]

But was Havemeyer taste "the best"? Viewed from the perspective of modern scholarship, the Havemeyers' Asian art, with very notable exceptions, was essentially decorative (Mr. Havemeyer's purchases were intended "to beautify his home"[6]) and sometimes downright mediocre. Mrs. Havemeyer was no doubt misled on the matter of the importance of her Chinese and Japanese collection by dealers who catered to their clients' taste. Two of the *temmoku* tea bowls she praises as unique Song dynasty (960–1279) masterpieces—one with a leaf and one with plum blossoms in the interior ("the bowl Mr. Eumorfopoulos says he is coming to America to see"[7])—are now considered late nineteenth-century Japanese copies. To be fair, the Havemeyers were not the only collectors to be deceived by modern replicas: few people were competent to judge attributions in those days, and even fewer were attracted by the unassuming charm of these simple brown bowls. Ordinary as they may seem to us now, they were still quite a novelty at the time. The Havemeyers had the money to buy pieces of the highest quality, but they lacked advisers and depth of knowledge, and, of course, they never traveled to Asia and so were not exposed to the truly great works of art.

Like most Americans, Harry Havemeyer was introduced to Chinese and Japanese art at the 1876 Philadelphia Centennial Exhibition (fig. 18). The textiles he purchased there were used fourteen years later by Samuel Colman to decorate the ceiling of the Havemeyer library (fig. 30) and the walls of the music room (fig. 32) and the reception room (fig. 29).[8] Colman, who had accompanied Havemeyer to the fair in Philadelphia, was himself a collector of all forms of Japanese decorative arts, as well as prints—he gave 250 Japanese ceramics to the Metropolitan Museum in 1893 and sold another 1,370 lots of Asian art, mostly Japanese, at auction in 1902.[9]

For Mrs. Havemeyer the spark that ignited an interest in Asian art was a visit to Whistler's studio in London as a teenager. "Two objects in the room arrested the eye," she recalled. " Near the window stood a blue and white hawthorn jar which held one or two sprays of long reedy grass, and in the center of the room there was a huge Japanese bronze vase; it loomed up in that mellow light with the solemnity of an altar."[10] The Whistler aesthetic of subdued, subtle color harmonies, typified by his preference for later Chinese blue-and-white (available in large quantities in both Europe and America), left its mark on a generation of Western collectors. Such wares have fallen out of favor now, but there was enough underglaze blue-and-white in the Havemeyer collection (see pl. 119)—including hawthorn vases—to have filled an entire room. Most were sold in the 1930 auction.

The Havemeyers began collecting Asian art just as the cult of Japan was reaching its peak. From the late 1860s government-sponsored international expositions in Paris, Vienna, London, Philadelphia, Chicago, and St. Louis promoted contemporary Japanese crafts in the form of pottery and porcelain, lacquer, bronzes, textiles, and cloisonné. When railroad magnate William T. Walters (1820–1894) opened a private gallery behind his home in Baltimore in 1884, examples of Meiji-era (1868–1912) craftsmanship acquired in Vienna and Philadelphia constituted the nucleus of the nearly 4,100 Asian objects on view (fig. 19)—there were only a few paintings and no prints.[11] George Walter Vincent Smith (1832–1923) retired at age thirty-five, having made a fortune in manufacturing carriages in New York, and devoted the remainder of his life to collecting Asian art. Without ever having visited Asia, he accumulated almost 6,000 objects, primarily Japanese decorative arts, and opened his own museum in Springfield, Massachusetts, in 1896. He was a compulsive buyer and the level of quality of his acquisitions is relatively low, but the museum and collection are still preserved intact, encapsulating permanently one aspect of Victorian taste. The ostentatious Japanese parlor in William H. Vanderbilt's house on Fifth Avenue, designed by Herter Brothers between 1879 and 1882, is the classic example of Japonism run amok (fig. 20). Art

Figure 18. The Empire of Japan exhibition at the Philadelphia Centennial, 1876

magazines brought the idea of Japan into hundreds of thousands of American households, and there were enterprising dealers in Chinese and Japanese art to be found on both Broadway and Fifth Avenue as early as the 1870s. The 4,000 items collected by British designer Christopher Dresser in Japan, for example, were offered for sale by Tiffany and Co. in New York in 1877.[12] At a time when crafts in general were held in high esteem, the Orient was a fresh discovery.

By the 1890s it was not uncommon for wealthy Americans to travel to Japan. Two New York philanthropists, Valentine Everit Macy (1871–1930) and Charles Stewart Smith (1832–1909), went to Japan within four years of each other on honeymoon trips. Smith shipped a collection of 468 Japanese ceramics back to the Metropolitan Museum in 1893 and gave his collection of 1,763 ukiyo-e prints to the New York Public Library in 1901. Macy purchased 429 pieces of Japanese porcelain on his wedding trip in 1896 and likewise shipped them directly to the Metropolitan Museum.

Plate 119. *Vase*, China, Qing dynasty, Kangxi period, late 17th–early 18th century. Porcelain with slight relief decoration, painted in underglaze blue, h. 18 in. (45.7 cm). H. O. Havemeyer Collection, Bequest of Mrs. H. O. Havemeyer, 1929 (29.100.308)

Figure 19. Chinese and Japanese metalwork and porcelain displayed in William T. Walters's private gallery, Baltimore, ca. 1884

131

Figure 20. The Japanese parlor in William H. Vanderbilt's house, Fifth Avenue and 51st Street, New York, 1879–82. Published in Edward Strahan [Earl Shinn], *Mr. Vanderbilt's House and Collection*, New York, 1883–84

Figure 21. Charles Lang Freer and his two Japanese ricksha men in Kyoto, 1895. Charles Lang Freer Papers, Freer Gallery of Art/Arthur M. Sackler Gallery Archives, Smithsonian Institution, Washington, D.C.

A triumvirate of Bostonians—Edward Sylvester Morse, William Sturgis Bigelow, and Ernest F. Fenollosa —constituted the serious scholars and pioneer educators in the field of Asian art and culture in America. Edward Sylvester Morse (1838–1925), a zoologist, spent nearly three years in Japan in the late 1870s and early 1880s teaching Darwinian evolutionary theory at Tokyo University. His interest turned to ceramics, and from kilns all over Japan he systematically assembled more than five thousand pieces, which he sold to the Museum of Fine Arts in Boston, where his title was Keeper of Japanese Pottery from 1892 until his death. He also assembled an encyclopedic collection of ethnological materials for the Peabody Museum of Salem, of which he was director from 1880 until 1916. Morse spent many a long day with the Havemeyer tea jars, ferreting out the enigma of province, clay, kiln, and maker, copying the marks and seals, and leaving a trail of cigar ashes. Mr. Havemeyer could not comprehend why the professor spent more time studying the bottom of each jar than admiring the top. When he and Mrs.

Havemeyer went to see the Morse collection in Boston, Mr. Havemeyer's reaction was very telling—he was annoyed that more care had not been taken in creating an aesthetic arrangement![13]

William Sturgis Bigelow (1850–1926) was a wealthy bachelor who followed Morse and Fenollosa to Japan in 1882 and remained there for seven years—like Fenollosa, an earnest convert to Buddhism and a discriminating collector. In 1911 he officially presented the Museum of Fine Arts in Boston, of which he was a trustee, with a gift of 15,000 Chinese and Japanese works of art (of which 3,600 were paintings), as well as some 40,000 ukiyo-e prints.

Ernest F. Fenollosa (1853–1908) went to Japan in 1878 with an introduction from Morse to teach philosophy at Tokyo University. He stayed for twelve years, becoming a passionate collector of the traditional arts of Japan, and from 1890 through 1895 he was the first curator of the Japanese department of the Museum of Fine Arts in Boston, where his own collection was housed. Subsequently he lectured widely and wrote on the arts of China and Japan. His first lectures in New York were at the Metropolitan Museum in 1896, and it is likely that Louisine Havemeyer was in the audience. "Excitement ran high among the little New York group who had listened to Fenollosa tell them of Japan's marvelous civilization," she recalled in her memoirs.[14] Fenollosa, esteemed in his day as the preeminent authority on Asian art, became the personal adviser to Detroit businessman Charles Lang Freer (1854–1919), whose world-famous collection was bequeathed to the Smithsonian Institution in Washington, D.C. Freer's first trip to Japan was a four-month stay in 1895 as a serious tourist (fig. 21). Once he had committed himself to collecting, he made many more pilgrimages to both Japan and China.

The Havemeyers had known Freer for fifteen years or more (they often competed at auctions in New York) but not at all well until September 1906, when they spent two days with him in Detroit viewing his collection from early morning until ten at night. "I think it will make H.O.H.'s few hairs stand up, to see it!" gloated Fenollosa when he heard of the impending visit.[15] "They were both completely overwhelmed by the things they saw," Freer reported afterward to Fenollosa. "Naturally, I showed them only the cream of the collection, which included all of the better screens and kakemono [hanging scrolls] and about twenty-five per-cent of the potteries. The few pieces of lacquer and bronzes were also shown, and a few of the Whistlers. They certainly were tremendously impressed by the finer Japanese and Chinese paintings, and frankly said that they had never before seen so many things of Oriental production for which they cared so much. The Koyetsu screens and the early Buddhistic and Chinese paintings really staggered Mr. Havemeyer."[16] A year later Harry Havemeyer was dead; his exposure to the Freer collection came too late to influence his patterns of acquisition. Years later, when Freer was in failing health and came to New York to be near his physician, he and Louisine Havemeyer renewed their warm friendship:

> Day after day, month after month, Mr. Freer and I would spend hours together looking over my collection, applying the acid test of knowledge to the purchases made during our years of inexperience, and we would laugh together over the mistakes *we* had made and, what was worse, over the deliberate mistakes that had been "put over" on us.

"Why, I wont have any paintings left," I said one day, when the discards lay in a heap upon the floor and the "chosen few" made a pitifully small showing.

"Oh, wait until you have seen my graveyard!" Mr. Freer answered encouragingly. "I have culled hundreds to your tens." It was cold comfort, but I had to be content.[17]

The Havemeyers, of course, had access to the same dealers and auction houses in New York, Boston, and Paris as Freer. They loved the excitement and publicity of the auction room, and it was Thomas Ellis Kirby, founder of the American Art Association (later Parke Bernet and now the New York branch of Sotheby's) on Madison Square in 1885, who "knocked the art of Japan into the very hearts of the American people," to quote Mrs. Havemeyer.[18] Kirby managed elite sales for most of the local Oriental art dealers. The largest and most influential of these was Yamanaka and Co., an international art firm with headquarters in Osaka and branches in Paris, London, Boston, Chicago, New York, and the Boardwalk in Atlantic City. Yamanaka Sadajirō (1866–1936) was regarded by Freer as "the most experienced critic of Japanese art in this country" after Fenollosa.[19] Encouraged by Morse, Bigelow, and Fenollosa, he opened a shop in New York at 4 West 27th Street in 1894. Sadajirō opened the first official branch of Yamanaka and Co. at 20 West 27th Street, near Broadway, in 1895 and relocated to 254 Fifth Avenue by 1899. Yamanaka and Co. sold everything from the finest archaic bronzes to cut-velvet framed pictures of tigers.

Matsuki Bunkio (1867–1912) was a small, independent dealer in Boston. Thanks to an introduction from Morse, he had graduated from high school in Salem, Massachusetts, in 1892; he subsequently took an American wife and opened a gallery on Boylston Street. From 1898 the "clever little Matsuki,"[20] as Mrs. Havemeyer called him, began to stage auctions of Japanese art in Boston, New York, and Philadelphia. The Havemeyers purchased an intriguing group of Japanese embossed leather panels, possibly intended for book covers, at Matsuki's 1903 auction at the American Art Association.[21] Other local dealers of Asian art patronized by the Havemeyers were Kano Oshima and Dikran Kelekian (1868–1951), both on Fifth Avenue, and Moore and Curtis, partners in an art-import firm on Broadway. They were probably clients of Kobayashi Bunshichi (1861–1923), a Tokyo print dealer with a

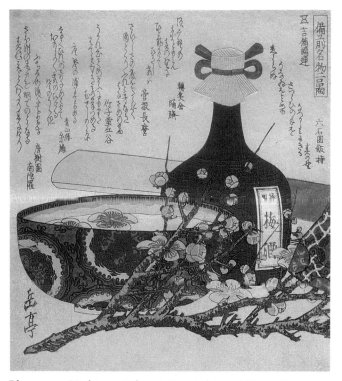

Plate 120. Kubo Shunman. *Hare and Dandelion (New Year's Card for the Hare Year)*, Japan, Edo period, probably 1819. Color woodblock print, *surimono*, 7⅞ x 7 in. (20 x 17.8 cm). H. O. Havemeyer Collection, Bequest of Mrs. H. O. Havemeyer, 1929 (JP 1951)

Plate 121. Yashima Gakutei. *Specialties of Bizen Province*, Japan, Edo period, ca. 1825. Color woodblock print, *surimono*, 8 1/16 x 7 3/16 in. (20.4 x 18.3 cm). H. O. Havemeyer Collection, Bequest of Mrs. H. O. Havemeyer, 1929 (JP 2115)

gallery on Boylston Street in Boston, of Shugio Hiromichi (1853–1927), the manager of The First Japanese Manufacturing and Trading Co. on Broadway (Shugio and H. O. Havemeyer were both members of the Grolier Club), and of Tozo Takayanagi, an importer on Fifth Avenue whose letterhead advertised "High Class Japanese Art Objects and Choice collection of Bric-a-Brac." Siegfried Bing (1838–1905), the most influential Parisian dealer in Oriental art (he knew everyone, according to Freer) and a major patron of the Art Nouveau movement, was well known to the Havemeyers; he visited their new home soon after it was completed. Bing had turned toward the profitable American market as early as 1887, when he sold Chinese and Japanese bronzes, porcelains, jade, and crystal through Moore's Art Galleries on Fifth Avenue, and he began to sell both decorative arts and prints through the American Art Association by 1894.[22]

Japanese color woodblock prints represent the best of the Havemeyer Asian collection. There are about 324 prints and a set of three albums containing 492 *surimono*, the small, limited-edition and privately commissioned prints issued as collectors' items by amateur poetry clubs for New Year celebrations.[23] Con-

Figure 22. Hayashi Tadamasa, 1896

sidered the jewels of the Japanese printmaking tradition, *surimono* are printed with the finest and most costly pigments (see pls. 120, 121). Nearly fifty artists are represented in the Havemeyer albums, and many of the prints not only are rare but also are known by only one extant impression. The albums contain what may be the best and largest collection in the world (172 examples) by Kubo Shunman (1757–1820).

The individual responsible for assembling these albums was the remarkable Japanese art dealer Hayashi Tadamasa (1853–1906) (fig. 22). In his handwritten inscription in the last album, dated April 1, 1889, he states that he began collecting *surimono* while living in Paris and that he acquired one large album of *surimono* from Mr. Yamanaka (of Yamanaka and Co.) in Osaka the preceding year. Hayashi added 150 prints to the Yamanaka group and arranged them in three albums

with two or three prints to a page, carefully composed with an eye for design, color, and subject matter.

Hayashi had arrived in Paris in 1878 as a foreign-language interpreter for the Japanese corporation charged with managing Japan's participation in the Paris Exposition Universelle that year. He stayed on, working for several Japanese trading companies, and in 1884 went into partnership with Wakai Kenzaburō (1834–1908), who was trained in the antiques trade. During the next few years Hayashi traveled widely in China, Europe, and America, cultivating clients for Chinese porcelains as well as for Japanese lacquer, bronzes, and prints. From about 1889, when he established himself in sole proprietorship as a merchant of prints in Paris, until 1900, when he ceased his commercial activities (his collection was sold at auction in Paris in 1902), he imported 160,000 prints and nearly 10,000 illustrated printed books."[1]

The round red seal bearing Hayashi's name appears on fine prints in many Western collections and is still regarded as a sign of quality and authenticity, although it was often forged after his death. One cannot be certain that the Havemeyers met Hayashi, although it is possible that they were led to his apartment on the rue de la Victoire by Mary Cassatt sometime during the 1890s. The Hayashi seal is found on only a very few of their prints, notably three of the great examples by Kitagawa Utamaro (1753–1806) (pls. 118, 122, 123). One of these (pl. 122) has the even more desirable seal of Wakai in addition to the Hayashi seal. (Mrs. Havemeyer inscribed the HOH monogram in pencil in the lower corner of a great many of the prints, presumably the ones she liked best, a highly unusual custom for a serious print collector.)

Prints are not mentioned by Mrs. Havemeyer in her memoirs, but two eighteenth-century pillar prints (narrow and vertical and similar to pl. 124) were incorporated into the Tiffany-Colman decor of her bedroom, where they framed the fireplace mantel (fig. 37). It is well known that the French Impressionists favored by the Havemeyers were themselves serious collectors of ukiyo-e prints. Cassatt and Degas, for example, made purchases at the great exhibition and sale of seven hundred prints Bing organized at the Ecole des Beaux-Arts in 1890. The next year Cassatt designed a series of ten color etchings that are strongly indebted to Utamaro in their composition and color tones (see pl. 147, fig. 23). Her own collection of Utamaro hung

Plate 122. Kitagawa Utamaro. *Beauty*, Japan, Edo period, ca. 1795–96. Color woodblock print, 14 1/16 x 9 3/4 in. (35.7 x 24.8 cm). H. O. Havemeyer Collection, Bequest of Mrs. H. O. Havemeyer, 1929 (JP 1663)

on the glass-covered veranda of her château near Beauvais.[25] The colors used in eighteenth-century prints are light-sensitive, fugitive vegetable dyes; by exposing her prints to daylight, Cassatt inadvertently (we hope) hastened the process of fading. It seems that French collectors actually preferred the soft colors of toned and faded prints. Out of ignorance, some Europeans were prone to suspect forgery if the colors were fresh. Around the turn of the century some Japanese dealers did, in fact, begin to make new color blocks to brighten faded prints. Hayashi has been accused of bleaching prints in the sun in order to make them more attractive to his European clients.[26]

The Havemeyers' prints reflect French taste (or Cassatt taste) and practice insofar as they are often faded and toned, as well as trimmed. It is also typical of French taste that eighteenth-century figure prints predominate in their collection, which has only a modest

Plate 125 (right). Katsushika Hokusai. *The Great Wave at Kanagawa*, Japan, Edo period, ca. 1831. Color woodblock print, 10⅛ x 14¹⁵⁄₁₆ in. (25.7 x 37.9 cm). H. O. Havemeyer Collection, Bequest of Mrs. H. O. Havemeyer, 1929 (JP 1847)

Plate 124. Koikawa Harumasa. *Umegawa and Chūbei*, Japan, Edo period, ca. 1800. Color woodblock pillar print, 23½ x 4⁹⁄₁₆ in. (59.7 x 24.3 cm). H. O. Havemeyer Collection, Bequest of Mrs. H. O. Havemeyer, 1929 (JP 1827)

Plate 123. Kitagawa Utamaro. *In the Kitchen*, Japan, Edo period, ca. 1795. Right side of a diptych, color woodblock print, 14¾ x 9¾ in. (37.5 x 24.8 cm). H. O. Havemeyer Collection, Bequest of Mrs. H. O. Havemeyer, 1929 (JP 1675)

group of landscapes and seascapes, seventeen by Hokusai and twenty-five by Hiroshige. Admittedly, the latter include a wonderful early impression of Hokusai's *Great Wave at Kanagawa* (pl. 125) and two of Hiroshige's most famous triptychs, *Rapids at Naruto* (pl. 126), and the *Panorama of the Eight Views of Kanazawa Under a Full Moon* (pl. 127). The print collection formed by Harry Havemeyer's contemporary New York lawyer Howard Mansfield (1849–1938) is more representative of American taste. Among the approximately three hundred outstanding ukiyo-e prints that he assembled (and which are now in the Metropolitan Museum), there are ninety-six examples by Hiroshige. Mansfield, a trustee and treasurer of the Metropolitan

Plate 126 (center). Utagawa Hiroshige. *Rapids at Naruto*, Japan, Edo period, 1857. Triptych, color woodblock prints, each 14½ x 9¹¹⁄₁₆ in. (36.8 x 24.7 cm). H. O. Havemeyer Collection, Bequest of Mrs. H. O. Havemeyer, 1929 (JP 1892)

Plate 127 (bottom). Utagawa Hiroshige. *Panorama of the Eight Views of Kanazawa Under a Full Moon*, Japan, Edo period, 1857. Triptych, color woodblock prints, each 14⅝ x 9¹⁵⁄₁₆ in. (37.2 x 25.3 cm). H. O. Havemeyer Collection, Bequest of Mrs. H. O. Havemeyer, 1929 (JP 1893)

Plate 128. Kitagawa Utamaro. *The Bridge*, Japan, Edo period, ca. 1795. Hexaptych, color woodblock prints. Top: overall 14⅝ x 30 in. (37.2 x 76.2 cm); bottom: overall 15 x 29¾ in. (38.1 x 75.6 cm). H. O. Havemeyer Collection, Bequest of Mrs. H. O. Havemeyer, 1929 (JP 1686,03)

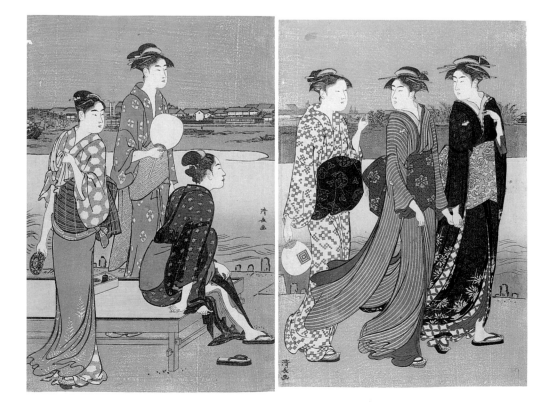

Plate 129. Torii Kiyonaga. *Cooling Off on the Banks of the Okawa River*, Japan, Edo period, ca. 1785. Diptych, color woodblock prints, a.: 15 x 10 in. (38.1 x 25.4 cm); b.: 14⅝ x 9¹⁵⁄₁₆ in. (37.2 x 25.2 cm). H. O. Havemeyer Collection, Gift of Mrs. H. O. Havemeyer, 1929 (JP 1734a,b)

Plate 130. *Sword guard (tsuba)*, Japan, Edo period, 19th century. Lacquered copper and abalone shell, diam. 2⅞ in. (7.3 cm). H. O. Havemeyer Collection, Bequest of Mrs. H. O. Havemeyer, 1929 (29.100.1062)

Plate 131. *Sword guard (tsuba)*, Japan, Edo period, 17th century. *Shakudō*, gold, silver, and copper, diam. 3⅛ in. (7.9 cm). H. O. Havemeyer Collection, Bequest of Mrs. H. O. Havemeyer, 1929 (29.100.967)

Museum, was conscientious about quality and condition. He was also selective, selling a print for every new one he acquired. New York painter Francis Lathrop (1849–1909) represents the opposite extreme—the indiscriminate, compulsive accumulator: during the last fifteen years of his life he amassed twelve thousand woodblock prints, including four thousand by Hokusai alone. A small number of these were later purchased by the Metropolitan from his estate.[27]

Among the Havemeyer prints (excluding *surimono*), works by Utamaro, Cassatt's favorite, predominate; there are thirty-nine examples, some of which are actually diptychs and triptychs, and they include a very high percentage of first-rate and rare masterpieces. The rare double triptych of *The Bridge* is one such print (pl. 128). In terms of quantity Suzuki Harunobu is next, with thirty-three examples, followed by Torii Kiyonaga, with twenty-four. One Kiyonaga diptych (pl. 129) has been cited as the best impression of the subject in the world. Many of the Harunobu, by contrast, are either physical wrecks or outright fakes.

The Havemeyer prints, incidentally, include a good many prurient *abuna-e* (literally, "dangerous pictures") featuring seminudity, reflecting an undercurrent of naughty Victorian taste.

A welcome surprise in the Havemeyer collection is the high quality of the sword fittings. Sword guards (*tsuba*) (see pls. 130, 131), hilt ornaments (*fuchigashira*), and knife handles (*kozuka*) were very popular among Western collectors, including the Havemeyers, at the turn of the century. Mrs. Havemeyer was up-to-date when she took twelve *kozuka* and had them made into fish forks.[28] Like *inrō* (lacquer medicine containers) and accompanying netsuke (toggles for suspending *inrō*) also favored by Mr. and Mrs. Havemeyer, they were small, inexpensive (a sword guard could be had for about one hundred dollars), technically complex (they dazzle the eye with their craftsmanship), and available in unlimited quantity and hence ideal for filling a display cabinet and impressing one's friends. The Havemeyers' predilection for such small objects—the collection originally included 316 *inrō* and more than 200 *kozuka* (not to mention the hundreds of ceramic tea caddies)—typified contemporary taste: the Victorians were passionate for small, finely crafted things they could touch and feel.

Samurai were abolished as a class after the Meiji Restoration of 1868, and the wearing of swords was proscribed in 1876. Discarded swords and mounts flooded the market and were eagerly snapped up by the Victorians. It is said that five million sword guards had been sent to Europe by the turn of the century. Westerners insisted on signed pieces, however, and crafts-men were kept busy at the wharf in Yokohama adding signatures to netsuke and sword guards. Tokyo-based British journalist and collector-dealer Frank Brinkley (1841–1912) described the demise of sword fittings after 1876 in his *Japan: Its History, Arts, and Literature*, published in 1902. When swords were banned,

> purchasers of their furniture were at once reduced from hundreds of thousands of *samurai* and privileged persons, to a few scores of foreign curio collectors. Thousands of grand specimens found their way at once to the melting-pot for the sake of the modicum of precious metal that could be extracted from them, and in an incredibly short time the multitude of master-pieces that must have existed in 1876 disappeared almost completely. . . . Incredible though the fact may seem, it is nevertheless a fact that when, about the year 1880, United States' collectors began to interest themselves keenly in Japanese sword-mounts, and to acquire them in the resolute manner of New York and Chicago, the supply of genuine specimens could not meet this fitful and comparatively paltry demand, and the forger drove a brisk trade for a season, casting where he could not chisel, and substituting flash and profusion of ornament for force and delicacy of sculpture.[29]

There are a few of these recently signed pieces in the Havemeyer collection, and a few blatant forgeries, as is to be expected. A dagger (*tantō*) with solid-gold fittings attributed to Kano Natsuo (1828–1898), a renowned Meiji-era metalworker, was given a full page of illustrations in the 1930 Havemeyer exhibition catalogue, for example, but is now judged by Japanese experts to be a high-quality forgery made during Natsuo's lifetime (MMA 29.100.1375). Overall, however, the mounts—primarily from the eighteenth and nineteenth centuries—seem to have been carefully chosen and include many excellent and rare pieces. One of the finest Havemeyer daggers in the Museum's collection (pl. 148, top), has solid-gold fittings with floral designs by the mid-nineteenth-century master Masaharu. The scabbard is lacquered black with gold cherry blossoms. It was no doubt the decorative pictorial qualities and fine craftsmanship of the metal mounts and lacquer-work that appealed to the Havemeyers rather than the dagger's superb blade, dated 1330, a rare work signed by Kagemasa (fl. 1320–40), a master of the Osafune school of swordsmiths in Bizen, and son of the famous Nagamitsu.

The Japanese paintings (hanging scrolls) are for the most part predictably competent but dull, in sadly worn condition. Figural examples predominate, with more than a dozen Buddhist images and another dozen ukiyo-e subjects—courtesans of the "floating world." The remainder are decorative bird and flower paintings. The pair of fourteenth-century hanging scrolls depicting legends from the life of Shōtoku Taishi stands apart as an exceptional work of fine quality, if not a masterpiece (pl. 151). Mrs. Havemeyer faithfully recorded the artist and date of each work as given by the vendor. A typical example is a heavily restored painting of a peacock, which we would now place in the eighteenth century (MMA 29.100.474). It was purchased as the work of the famous Momoyama-period artist Kano Eitoku (1543–1590) and precisely dated to 1573.

We marvel at the audacity of dealers who regularly assigned not only artists but also the exact year of production for undated (and unsigned) paintings! On the other hand, scholars have been changing their minds about many of these paintings ever since they were given their original attributions and dates. A frontal standing figure of the Bodhisattva Ksitigarbha (pl. 152) was purchased as thirteenth-century Tibetan, according to a Havemeyer label pasted on the box. In recent years it has been reattributed as nineteenth-century Japanese, fifteenth-century Japanese, fifteenth-century Chinese, and, now, fourteenth-century Korean. We can hardly blame the Havemeyers for not knowing what they had; Japanese art scholarship was truly in its infancy at the turn of the century, and misattribution to famous names going back into hoary antiquity was quite common. Blame, however, can be placed squarely on the shoulders of Matsuki and Yamanaka: a perusal of their sales catalogues from the years around 1900, for example, reveals frequent attributions to the late ninth-century artist Kose Kanaoka, none of whose paintings are now thought to survive.

The Havemeyers did not collect Western religious art, yet Buddhist paintings are prominent in their Asian collection.[30] In the Meiji era, when the Japanese were discarding Buddhist art as old-fashioned, these would have been inexpensive—and thus appealing to the frugal Mrs. Havemeyer. There was the lure of the exotic, as well; a Buddhist deity was palpable evidence of the unknown, mysterious, and romantic Orient, which many nineteenth-century Westerners, disillusioned by the industrial revolution, found so appealing. Closed to the outside world for two and a half centuries until the arrival of Commodore Perry in 1853, Japan was still perceived as a primitive country in which childlike people lived in perfect harmony with nature. "Le Japon, pour nous, est né d'hier," wrote one collector in 1889.[31] Those who found solace in the Orient and for whom it exerted a spiritual as well as a psychological attraction, include—to name only two of the most obvious—Vincent van Gogh and Frank Lloyd Wright (1867–1959). In his own home Wright always grouped Buddhist painting and sculpture close to the hearth, the symbolic household altar.[32]

Louisine Havemeyer's bedroom (fig. 37), the innermost sanctum of her home, is just as revealing. Japanese paintings were hung on either side of the bed—a bird and flower painting to the right and a Buddhist scroll to the left. The latter depicts the Eleven Headed Kannon, Bodhisattva of Mercy, descending on a cloud from the deity's island paradise, which is suggested by a background of waves (pl. 132).[33] In Japan such paintings, associated with the Pure Land sect of Buddhism, were displayed in temples or at the bedside of a devotee who was on the verge of expiring. The deity, emitting golden rays of light, descends to earth to welcome the deceased and escort him or her to paradise. The image is clearly not appropriate in the bedroom, except as glittering exotica (the Havemeyers obviously had no understanding of Buddhist iconography), but the sentiment (and naïveté) its placement conveys is rather touching.

There are more than twenty Japanese screens in the collection. One charming six-panel screen (pl. 133), half of a pair, features bands of autumn flowers on a gold ground. The other half was given by Mrs. Havemeyer to Cassatt and later found its way into the Philadelphia Museum of Art, a gift of Cassatt's brother, J. Gardner Cassatt. These screens are eighteenth-century paintings in Tosa style but were thought at the time of their acquisition by the Havemeyers to be the work of Oguri Sotan (1413–1481) and were carefully dated (on one of Mrs. Havemeyer's labels) to 1429.[34]

Interior views of the Havemeyer home show only one screen in use. This stood on the floor of the music room and was a small painting of a dancer holding a fan, mounted in a lavish nineteenth-century gold lacquer stand (pl. 134, fig. 32). Close study of this decorative object reveals that it is a pastiche: the heavily repainted

late seventeenth-century figure of a courtesan, originally mounted as a hanging scroll modeled on the type known as Kambun Beauty, has been patched in and dark ink contour lines cover the patching.

Oriental textiles fascinated the Havemeyers, as we know from the amazing collage of Chinese and Japanese brocades and embroideries covering the walls of the music and reception rooms and the ceiling of the library. (In 1896 the Havemeyers gave the Metropolitan a total of over two thousand fragments of Japanese textiles of the eighteenth and nineteenth centuries purchased en masse from Bing [see pl. 136].[35] It is probably no coincidence that they acquired numerous screens —two singles and two pairs—of the type known as *ta-*

Plate 132. *Eleven-Headed Kannon, Bodhisattva of Mercy*, Japan, Muromachi period, 14th–16th century. Hanging scroll, ink, gold, and colors on silk, 36 ½ x 15 ½ in. (92.7 x 39.4 cm). H. O. Havemeyer Collection, Bequest of Mrs. J. Watson Webb, 1930 (30.72.3)

Plate 133. *Autumn Grasses*, Japan, Edo period, 18th century. Six-panel folding screen, ink, colors, and gold leaf on paper, overall 67⅞ x 144 in. (172.4 x 365.7 cm). H. O. Havemeyer Collection, Bequest of Mrs. H. O. Havemeyer, 1929 (29.100.490)

Plate 134. *Dancer with Fan*, Japan, Edo period, late 17th century. Painting, ink, colors, and silver leaf on paper, 20 x 17 in. (58.8 x 43.2 cm). Mounted on portable standing screen, Japan, Edo period, 19th century. Lacquer. H. O. Havemeyer Collection, Bequest of Mrs. H. O. Havemeyer, 1929 (29.100.520)

gasode ("Whose Sleeves?"), featuring robes hung from lacquer clothing racks (see pl. 135). The motif of circular family crests decorating some of these robes is reminiscent of the design on a fine eighteenth-century white satin Nō robe in the Havemeyer collection (pl. 137).

Most of the Havemeyer screens are decorative and in poor condition; it is not uncommon to find examples that have been almost totally repainted. Quite a few have a dollar sign on the vendor's inventory tag pasted on the back; clearly, they represent what was available locally. Some were purchased in Paris, however, and not necessarily at bargain prices. An eighteenth-century six-panel landscape screen with flowers, trees, and a river, originally from Hayashi, was offered in the sale of the Gillot estate in Paris in February 1904 as a work by Ogata Kenzan (1663–1743) (fig. 24).[36] The printer and connoisseur Charles Gillot had been accumulating Japanese art since the 1870s and was a regular at Bing's ukiyo-e print dinners attended by Raymond Koechlin, Henri Vever, Whistler, Albert Besnard, Edmond de Goncourt, Alexis Rouart, and other Japanophiles. Freer was an unsuccessful contender for the screen. On February 18 he wrote Bing, who had presumably bid for him: "I am quite astonished at the price fetched for No. 2060, the Low Screen, attributed to Kenzan. Who bought it? And was the buyer sober at the time?"[37] He passed Bing's response on to his trusted adviser,

Plate 135. *Whose Sleeves? (Tagasode)*, Japan, Momoyama period, early 17th century. One of a pair of six-panel folding screens, ink, colors, and gold leaf on paper, overall 65 x 141 in. (165.1 x 358.1 cm). H. O. Havemeyer Collection, Bequest of Mrs. H. O. Havemeyer, 1929 (29.100.494)

Fenollosa, in New York: "Full reports of the Gillot Sale have at last reached me. . . . The low, six-fold screen attributed to Kenzan, which you thought might be by Koyetsu, fetched fifty thousand francs. Bids for it on my account were made up to sixty-five hundred francs. I am told the extraordinary price was brought about by competition between the Berlin Museum, who bid up to forty-five thousand francs, and Mr. H. O. Havemeyer, whose final bid, through Mr. Yamanaka, was fifty thousand francs. Please consider this . . . confidential."[38] Fifty thousand francs at the time was the equivalent of about one hundred and eighty thousand dollars today.

There is a real mystery surrounding this screen. Lot 2060 as described and illustrated in the Gillot catalogue is the left-hand screen of a pair and depicts autumn. The screen that entered the Museum with the Havemeyer collection (pl. 153), however is the right-hand screen, depicting spring. The screen illustrated in the Gillot sale was acquired by the Metropolitan Museum not from the Havemeyers but from Yamanaka and Co. in New York for eleven thousand dollars in 1915, one of the first purchases of S. C. Bosch Reitz (1860–1938), a Dutch painter and connoisseur of Chinese ceramics who had been appointed the new Curator of Far Eastern art that same year. This was certainly the first screen of real quality to enter the Museum's collection. It had been published by Fenollosa in his 1912

Plate 136. *Textile fragments*, Japan, Edo period, 18th–19th century. Silk brocade, mounted on mat board. Board: 25 x 19 ¼ in. (63.5 x 48.9 cm). H. O. Havemeyer Collection, Bequest of H. O. Havemeyer, 1896 (96.14.207-14)

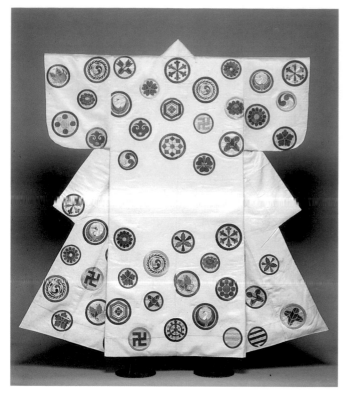

Plate 137. *Nō robe*, Japan, Edo period, 18th century. Colored silk embroidery and gold leaf on white satin, l. 53½ in (135.9 cm). H. O. Havemeyer Collection, Bequest of Mrs. H. O. Havemeyer, 1929 (29.100.541)

Epochs of Chinese and Japanese Art as "one of the finest existing screens" by Hon'ami Kōetsu (1558–1637).[39] He makes no mention of the Havemeyer (spring) screen, which he may not have seen at the time his manuscript was completed in 1906, but does confirm that Yamanaka bought the autumn screen at the Gillot sale. Over the years many scholars have noted a dramatic difference between the right (spring) and left (autumn) halves of the screen, which are now reunited in the Metropolitan Museum. Some have gone so far as to suggest that they were painted by different artists. The discrepancies are caused by the heavy repainting and damage that mar and blur the details of the right-hand (Havemeyer) screen, notably the water and pine tree, which have been ineptly retouched.

If Harry Havemeyer purchased the autumn screen in 1904, how could it have been sold to the Metropolitan by Yamanaka in 1915? Perhaps a pair was miscatalogued as a single in the Gillot sale, and Yamanaka, although acting as Havemeyer's agent, kept one half. Even so, the successful bidder should have insisted on taking the half (the much better half!) that was illustrated. Perhaps Bing gave Freer misinformation; he

may not have wanted to admit that Yamanaka, his rival, could outbid Freer (and Bing himself) by such an enormous sum. At the time Bosch Reitz made his purchase he was well aware that Mrs. Havemeyer owned the spring screen—he referred to it in his recommendation for purchase to the director of the Metropolitan. Perhaps Mrs. Havemeyer could have supplied the answer to this mystery, but she remained discreetly tight-lipped. "Gillot was a Parisian and an early patron of Oriental art, and had exquisite taste," she wrote in the memoirs. "When after his death his collection was sold, every piece was disputed, disputed hotly as is sometimes the case at an auction, and thereby hangs a tale—an interesting one about a pair of screens, one of which belongs to me and the other, the one from the Gillot sale, is in the Metropolitan Museum. No more digressions however! I can tell you nothing about it at present."[40]

The attribution to Kōetsu is interesting. Kōetsu was among the first in a line of artists who worked with sumptuous materials to create colorful, decorative, boldly stylized designs drawn from nature or based on classical literary themes. They are referred to as the Rimpa school, the *rim* derived from *rin* in the name of Ogata Kōrin (1658–1716), and the *pa* meaning "school." Tawaraya Sotatsu (d. ca. 1643), Kōetsu, Kōrin, his brother Kenzan, all active in Kyoto, and Sakai Hōitsu (1761–1828), active in Edo (Tokyo), were adherents of this style. The French were mad for Rimpa artists, whose names were applied all too freely to any decorative painting, lacquer, or ceramic from Japan. The sensuous beauty and curvilinear rhythm of Rimpa-style designs were influential in shaping the Art Nouveau movement. In 1883 Louis Gonse wrote in *L'Art Japonais*, the first serious history of Japanese art, that Kōrin was "le plus original et le plus personnel des peintres du Nippon, le plus Japonais des Japonais."[41] Thanks to modern scholarship, we now know that Kōetsu was not a painter nor even a lacquer artist, as was thought to be the case at the turn of the century. A sword appraiser by profession, he was a master calligrapher and an amateur potter and provided ideas for professional lacquer craftsmen.

Freer was the first American champion of Kōetsu as painter and lacquer artist. Art dealers (notably Yamanaka), as well as collectors and scholars, followed suit. Fenollosa described Kōetsu as "by far the greatest artist of the Tokugawa days—in fact, one of the greatest art-

Plate 138. *Inrō with ojime and netsuke*, Japan, late Edo or early Meiji period, late 19th century. *Inrō*: lacquer, pewter, shell, amber, h. 3 ½ in. (8.9 cm). Signed: *Ya Chohei*. *Ojime*: lacquer; netsuke: carved ivory. H. O. Havemeyer Collection, Bequest of Mrs. H. O. Havemeyer, 1929 (29.100.788)

Plate 139. *Inrō with ojime and netsuke*, Japan, Edo period, late 18th century. Design probably taken from Wen Cheng Ming (1558) by Kano Jukyoku. *Inrō*: wood, h. 4 ½ in. (11.4 cm). *Ojime*: carved nut. H. O. Havemeyer Collection, Bequest of Mrs. H. O. Havemeyer, 1929 (29.100.820). Netsuke: red lacquer. Gift of Mrs. Russell Sage, 1910 (10.211.2073)

ists of any race."[42] Today the many Kōetsu in the Freer collection (as well as the above-mentioned spring and autumn screens) have been reattributed to "Anonymous."

When the manager of Yamanaka's New York office, Daijirō Ushikubo, published his *Life of Koyetsu* in 1926, he dedicated it to his two best customers, Louisine Havemeyer and Charles Freer.[43] There was a cult of Rimpa style in Japan itself right up to the later nineteenth century, but the Rimpa revival in the Meiji era was probably spurred largely by foreign demand. The Havemeyer collection has its share of Rimpa-style items made for the tourist trade: there is a chunky, ostentatiously sculpted pink-and-green-glazed tea ceremony water container attributed to Kōetsu (MMA 29.100.615), as well as two crudely potted ceramic writing boxes with rough, bubble-gum pink glaze signed "Kenzan"(MMA 29.100.669,670). These are Meiji export pieces and

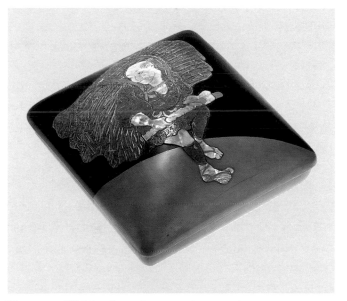

Plate 140. *Writing box*, Japan, Edo period, 19th century. Lacquer with pewter, mother-of-pearl, and gold, 9 ⅜ x 9 x 3 ¾ in. (23.9 x 22.9 x 9.5 cm). H. O. Havemeyer Collection, Bequest of Mrs. H. O. Havemeyer, 1929 (29.100.689)

were probably produced in a pottery studio in Tokyo. They are late interpretations but are of interest nonetheless to historians tracking the evolution of the Kenzan style. The art name Kenzan was passed on to generations of amateur potters; the style became a stock one for the Kyoto stoneware industry and was transmitted to Edo by the mid-eighteenth century. Westerners were first exposed to so-called Kenzan wares at the Philadelphia Centennial Exhibition.[44] Similarly, among the many Havemeyer lacquers that once bore attributions to Kōrin (three acquired in the Gillot sale), there are no fewer than three handsome nineteenth-century writing boxes with nearly identical designs of a mountain woodcutter on the lid inlaid with shell (see pl. 140). (One example was illustrated in Gonse's 1883 *L'Art Japonais*.[45]) These dramatic images are a type now associated with Kōetsu; they hark back to an original seventeenth-century design on a box with a high domed lid now in the MOA Museum of Art in Atami.

The lacquer artist most in demand in the late nineteenth century was Ogawa Haritsu, or Ritsuō (1663–1747), who specialized in intricately crafted works combining various materials for an exotic, decorative effect. He was featured in an 1889 issue of Bing's influential monthly publication, *Le Japon Artistique*.[46] The Havemeyers had no fewer than twenty works attributed to him, including several bird and flower paintings, seven *inrō*, a large cabinet, three writing boxes (see pl. 140), and several large vertical panels.[47] Most are Meiji revival pieces. The versatile Ritsuō, who was both painter and lacquer artist (and was perceived by Europeans as potter and sculptor as well), fit the idealized model of the artist-craftsman celebrated in the Arts and Crafts movement, a late nineteenth-century reaction against industrialization. The multifaceted Rimpa artists were appreciated for the same reasons.

Colman chose an olive green Ritsuō panel as the inspiration for the color he used in staining the woodwork and molding in the Havemeyer library (fig. 30).[48] He also based his decoration of the furniture in the music room on a carved ivory *inrō*. The collection of *inrō* (pls. 138, 139) and lacquer was displayed in a large glass cabinet that was the focal point of the music room. It amused Mrs. Havemeyer to show her guests the *inrō* that had served as Colman's model.[49] Probably owing to prolonged exposure to air and light in this cabinet, many of the Havemeyer lacquers, which are almost

exclusively eighteenth and nineteenth century in date, have acquired a dull finish, and the color of exposed portions has lightened considerably.

The Havemeyer holdings in Chinese art were less extensive than their Japanese collection, but their taste was consistent and fairly conventional in both. One of their two Chinese limestone Buddhist sculptures is an obvious forgery, but the presence of a fake in a collection of Chinese art is not unusual for the time. Freer, for example, purchased a number of fake stone steles in Shanghai between about 1913 and 1915. The Havemeyers did not do well with their Chinese paintings, which are primarily figural (and include Buddhist subjects) or decorative blue-and-green landscapes. Most are now regarded as late interpretations, and almost all were blithely attributed to the usual famous early names (the eighth-century Wu Daozi, for example). Westerners were not being offered ink paintings in the literati tradition of the sort we value today.

There are only three Chinese lacquers (one of which was purchased as Japanese) in the Havemeyer holdings. Most likely they were acquired from Japanese dealers: the pieces are small and appropriate for tea ceremony use (MMA 29.100.680,704, pl. 159). Hardly any Westerners were collecting Chinese lacquer in the late nineteenth century; the few pieces on the market came from Japan, where they were highly valued. The handful of Chinese bronzes that remain in the collection are late (late Ming or Qing dynasty, sixteenth to nineteenth century), with one exception—a magnificent and very important Zhou dynasty bronze *hu* with copper inlay dating from the fifth century B.C. (pl. 160). The mate to this bronze was purchased by Lucy Maud Buckingham from Yamanaka prior to 1928, when it was given to The Art Institute of Chicago.[50] The Havemeyers may not have known they had a great treasure; the 1930 exhibition catalogue dates the *hu* to the Han dynasty.

Bronzes were the special love of Harry Havemeyer: they lined the fireplace mantels (fig. 30) in his library and his wife's bedroom (fig. 37), among other places. When the director of the Metropolitan Museum invited Havemeyer to lend them for exhibition in 1894, he refused. "My Bronzes have been collected as ornaments for my house," he replied, "and are so distributed through the house that it would be impossible for me to remove them without damage to the surroundings."[51] As Aline Saarinen noted, Havemeyer had a discriminating eye for three-dimensional objects. Like

Plate 141. *Six objects for a writing table*, China, Qing dynasty, Kangxi marks, late Kangxi period, ca. 1700–22. Porcelain with peachbloom glazes. Clockwise from l.: brush washer: diam 4½ in. (11.4 cm); water coupe: diam. 3⅞ in. (9.8 cm); "beehive" water coupe: h. 3½ in. (8.9 cm); brush washer: diam. 4½ in. (11.4 cm); seal color box: diam. 2¾ in. (7 cm); seal color box: diam. 2¾ in. (7 cm). H. O. Havemeyer Collection, Bequest of Mrs. H. O. Havemeyer, 1929 (29.100.352, 331, 334, 349, 362a,b, 358)

Benjamin Altman, J. P. Morgan, William Walters, and so many other business tycoons, "he responded particularly to craftsmanship and form. He kept two handsome Greek fourth-century helmets in his library. He caressed them frequently, like a blind man experiencing their shape."[52] Ironically, almost all of these prized bronzes (82 Chinese lots and 153 Japanese lots) were sold in the 1930 Havemeyer auction; taste had changed and they were no longer perceived as vital to the collection. Most are, indeed, archaizing rather than genuinely archaic, but they are typical of late nineteenth-century taste both in the West and in China. The great archaic bronzes that grace the collections of Freer and of New Yorker Grenville Winthrop (1864–1943), for example, did not begin to emerge from excavations in China until somewhat later. It is worth remarking, however, that Louisine Havemeyer was still buying Chinese bronzes in the 1920s from Chinese dealers.[53] Might she have purchased the *hu*? The later, archaizing bronzes (for which there is a renewed appreciation today) fell out of favor in the 1920s, when early works became more readily available. At this time there was also a new generation of young Western scholars trained in China who were less sympathetic to the dec-

orative arts. In 1928, for example, Alan Priest (1898–1969), a Harvard-trained student of Chinese art who had spent four years in Beijing, replaced Bosch Reitz as Curator of Far Eastern art at the Metropolitan. By his day Chinese painting and sculpture were valued as the highest art forms.

The Havemeyers were certainly in the mainstream with their large assemblage of Qing dynasty (1644–1912) monochrome cabinet pieces, including a staggering total of thirty-six peachbloom glazes (see pl. 141). An imperial ware, peachbloom was highly prized both by Chinese and Western connoisseurs. It was accessible as well as beautiful, with an infinite variety of subtle color nuances ranging from pink to red to grayish green—mottled effects that were the result of very complicated technological advances. Peachbloom fever was at a peak in 1886, when the American Art Association claimed to have sold one small vase to William Walters for a record price of eighteen thousand dollars.[54] Mr. Havemeyer's first purchase for his new home was an exceptionally fine red-glazed Lang-yao vase (pl. 142). It was given pride of place at the center of the case for Japanese lacquer and is just barely visible at the far right edge of the 1891 interior view of the music

Plate 142. *Vase*, China, Qing dynasty, Kangxi period, late
17th–early 18th century. Porcelain with sang de boeuf
glaze, h. 17½ in. (44.5 cm). H. O. Havemeyer Collection,
Bequest of Mrs. H. O. Havemeyer, 1929 (29.100.317)

Plate 143. *Jar*, China, Han dynasty, 206 B.C.–A.D. 220.
Earthenware with relief decoration under green iridescent
glaze, h. 16¼ in. (41.3 cm). H. O. Havemeyer Collection,
Bequest of Mrs. H. O. Havemeyer, 1929 (29.100.170)

room (fig. 32). With some hyperbole Mrs. Havemeyer
claimed that it was "the best-known piece of *sang de
boeuf* in America."⁵⁵ Today we could point to nearly
identical pieces collected by contemporaries such as
Altman, Walters, Morgan, and Joseph E. Widener.

The Havemeyers' seventeen lead-glazed earthenware
Han tomb vessels (see pl. 143), on the other hand, represent a departure from the prevailing preference for
late monochromes and decorative enameled wares;
there was no interest in archaeological wares until
Western railroad engineers began unearthing Chinese
tombs at the end of the nineteenth century. No invoices
are extant for the objects in the Havemeyer Asian collection, but it seems likely that the Han vessels were
purchased around the turn of the century. As with
Roman glass, burial has enhanced some glazes with a

shimmering yellow-white iridescence; this effect may
have had special appeal for a couple so devoted to Tiffany glass.

Asian art was more than a peripheral interest for the
Havemeyers; they acquired in substantial numbers and
placed many of the decorative pieces on permanent display in their home. Screens and scrolls, on the other
hand, were difficult to display, and most of them were
shut away in storerooms. They did not have the sophisticated understanding of Freer or Bigelow, nor did they
really feel the need to immerse themselves in the study
of Asian culture. They relied heavily on local Japanese
art dealers who—then as now—were adept at catering
to the particular needs and level of connoisseurship of
each client. George Walter Vincent Smith, for example,
would leave Yamanaka and Co. with a snuff bottle,

Harry Havemeyer with a *temmoku* tea bowl, and Freer with a rare Korean inlaid celadon vase. Caught up in the wave of enthusiasm for Asian art, the Havemeyers accumulated what pleased them. They looked for themselves rather than merely following popular trends, and this accounts for the diversity of their collection. Their story is typical of a fascinating era in the history of Japonism in America.

The author is grateful for advice and assistance generously provided by the staff of The Metropolitan Museum of Art, most especially Martin Fleischer, James C. Y. Watt, Suzanne G. Valenstein, Maxwell K. Hearn, Angela Howard, and many others in the Department of Asian Art; Jeanie M. James in Archives; Patrick F. Coman, Ayako Y. Nakada, and Katria Czerwoniak in the Thomas J. Watson Library; Stuart W. Pyhrr, Donald J. LaRocca, Morihiro Ogawa, and Ann Willard in Arms and Armor; and Alice Cooney Frelinghuysen, American Decorative Arts. Thanks are also due to James Lally; to Thomas Lawton, Louise A. Cort, and Colleen Hennessey at the Freer Gallery of Art and the Arthur M. Sackler Gallery, Smithsonian Institution, Washington D.C.; to Robert D. Mowry, Arthur M. Sackler Museum, Harvard University, Cambridge, Massachusetts; to Hiram W. Woodward, Jr., The Walters Art Gallery, Baltimore; to Lisa Phillips and Emiko Mikisch, the Philadelphia Museum of Art; to Sebastian Izzard, Christie's, New York; to Robert Haynes, Seattle; Robert Buraway, Paris; and to Emil G. Schnorr, The George Walter Vincent Smith Art Museum, Springfield, Massachusetts.

1. Havemeyer 1961, p. 79.
2. There were 1,486 lots of Asian art in the 1930 sale, but some lots had up to 6 pieces. (See *The Estate of Mrs. H.O. Havemeyer, Part III: Japanese and Chinese Art*, sale cat., American Art Association, New York, April 14–19, 1930.) Gifts to the Museum by Horace Havemeyer, Mrs. J. Watson Webb, and other family members who inherited from Louisine Havemeyer are included in this essay under the blanket term "Havemeyer collection." Of the 324 Havemeyer prints, for example, 9 were a gift of Mrs. Webb in 1930. Asian art originally from the Havemeyer collection can also be found in the Shelburne Museum, Shelburne, Vermont, and in The Brooklyn Museum.
3. Havemeyer 1961, p. 73.
4. In her memoirs Mrs. Havemeyer credits Ushikubo of the Yamanaka Co. in New York as the source of their first tea jars (ibid., p. 70). These objects were evidently much in demand. We can, for example, point to the 1892 sale of nearly seven hundred tea caddies from the estate of R. Austin Robertson, a former partner in the American Art Association in New York. Individual lots contained up to fifty caddies. *Catalogue of The Collections of the American Art Association — The estate of R. Austin Robertson*, sale cat., New York, April 1892.
5. Havemeyer 1961, p. 18.
6. Havemeyer "Notes" [1974], p. 1.
7. Havemeyer 1961, pp. 81–82. The two *temmoku* bowls in question are MMA 29.100.221,220.
8. Ibid., p. 16.
9. *Catalogue of the valuable art collection of Samuel Colman . . . of Chinese and Japanese pottery and porcelain . . . ukiyoe prints, fine old lacquer, bronzes and other rare objects*, sale cat., American Art Galleries, New York, March 19–22, 1902; Japanese prints were also included in the 1927 sale of his estate: *The Art Collections of the late Samuel Colman*, sale cat., Anderson Galleries, New York, April 19–20, 1927.
10. Havemeyer 1961, p. 205.
11. Hiram W. Woodward, Jr., "An Overview of Asian Art at the Walters Art Gallery," *Orientations* 22 (April 1991), pp. 32–37; Kathleen Emerson-Dell, "Beyond the Exotic: Reflections on Later Japanese Decorative Arts in the Walters Art Gallery" in ibid., pp. 43–50.
12. For Dresser's trip to Japan, see Widar Halen, "Japan Mania," *Andon* 7 (1987), pp. 112–23. For the best overview of the cult of Japan, see William Hosley, *The Japan Idea: Art and Life in Victorian America*, exh. cat., Wadsworth Atheneum, Hartford, 1990.
13. Havemeyer 1961, pp. 75–76. For more discussion of Japonism in America and the early American collectors, see Julia Meech and Gabriel Weisberg, *Japonisme Comes to America: The Japanese Impact on the Graphic Arts 1876–1925*, New York, 1990.
14. Havemeyer 1961, p. 63; "Lectures at the Metropolitan Museum," *The Lotos*, no. 9 (1896), pp. 731–33.
15. Ernest Fenollosa to CLF, 9/25/06, Charles Lang Freer Papers, Freer Gallery of Art/Arthur M. Sackler Gallery Archives, Smithsonian Institution, Washington, D.C. For a discussion of Freer and Fenollosa, see Warren I. Cohen, *East Asian Art and American Culture*, New York, 1992, pp. 53–54.
16. CLF to Ernest Fenollosa, 9/27/06, Charles Lang Freer Papers, Freer Gallery of Art/Arthur M. Sackler Gallery Archives, Smithsonian Institution, Washington, D.C.
17. Louisine Havemeyer, "The Freer Museum of Oriental Art," *Scribner's Magazine* 73 (May 1923), p. 532.
18. Havemeyer 1961, p. 76. Kirby was at the American Art Association from 1885 until 1923.
19. CLF to Halsey C. Ives, 4/2/04, Charles Lang Freer Papers, Freer Gallery of Art/Arthur M. Sackler Gallery Archives, Smithsonian Institution, Washington, D.C.
20. Havemeyer 1961, p. 70.
21. Leather panels in the Havemeyer collection at the Metropolitan Museum that can be identified with the 1903 Matsuki sale are MMA 29.100.482–87. For more about Matsuki, see Lee Bruschke-Johnson, "Studies in Provenance: Japanese Wood Carvings and Sculptures from the Matsuki Sale of 1906," *Orientations* 22 (April 1991), pp. 38–42.
22. Meech and Weisberg, pp. 23–31; Gabriel Weisberg, *Art Nouveau Bing: Paris Style 1900*, New York, 1986, p. 34.
23. Joan B. Mirviss, "Jewels of *Ukiyo-e*: Hayashi's *Spring Rain Collection of Surimono* Albums," *Orientations* 20 (February 1989), pp. 26–37; Leslie Richardson, "The Spring Rain Collection of Japanese Surimono in the H. O. Havemeyer Collection," *Bulletin of The Metropolitan Museum of Art* 26 (July 1931), pp. 171–74.
24. *Collection T. Hayashi*, vol. 1, *Objets d'Art du Japon et de la Chine*, sale cat., Galerie Durand-Ruel, Paris, 1902; vol. 2, *Collection Hayashi: Estampes, Dessins, Livres illustrés*, sale cat., Hôtel Drouot, Paris, 1903. The Hayashi sales included Buddhist sculptures—generally late and often obvious fakes—later lacquer, especially *inrō*, Chinese and Japanese ceramics, Chinese and Japanese bronzes, Japanese sword fittings, prints, and printed books. Bing was the expert in charge of these sales. For Hayashi, see Julia Meech-Pekarik, "Early Collectors of Japanese Prints and The Metropolitan Museum of Art," *Metropolitan Museum Journal* 17 (1982), pp. 96–97; Peter van Dam, "Wakai Kenzaburo, the connoisseur," *Andon* 5 (1985), pp. 35–41.
25. George Biddle, "Some Memories of Mary Cassatt," *The Arts* 10 (August 1926), p. 108; S. Bing, *Exposition de la gravure japonais*, exh. cat., Paris, 1890.
26. Harry G. C. Packard, "Nihon bijutsu shushuki," *Geijutsu shincho* 27 (February 1976), p. 140.

27. For more about the Metropolitan Museum and print collectors, see Meech-Pekarik, "Early Collectors."

28. Havemeyer "Notes" [1974], p. 9. For fish forks, see Weitzenhoffer 1986, pl. 27, far right.

29. Frank Brinkley, *Japan: Its History, Arts, and Literature*, vol. 7, Boston and Tokyo, 1902, pp. 297–98.

30. In addition to the Buddhist paintings still in the collection at the Metropolitan Museum, there were another seven in the 1930 Havemeyer sale.

31. Ernest Hart, "Ritsuō et son Ecole," *Le Japon Artistique* 11 (1889), p. 147.

32. Julia Meech-Pekarik, "Frank Lloyd Wright's Other Passion," in *The Nature of Frank Lloyd Wright*, ed. Carol R. Bolon, Robert S. Nelson, and Linda Seidel, Chicago, 1988, pp. 125–53.

33. The painting, a rather dull and lifeless copy of an earlier model, is on coarse silk and in poor condition, with many cracks and considerable pigment loss. It is modeled on an image such as the *Descent of the Eleven-Headed Kannon* in the Matsunoo-dera in Nara. See Jōji Okazaki, *Pure Land Buddhist Painting*, trans. and adap. Elizabeth ten Grotenhuis, Tokyo, 1977, fig. 159.

34. "A Japanese Screen Attributed to Oguri Sotan," *The Pennsylvania Museum Bulletin* 12 (June 1927), pp. 400–404. The screen was given to the Philadelphia Museum of Art by J. Gardner Cassatt in 1946; it had been on loan for many years prior to that. A label on the back of the Metropolitan Museum screen records that "Miss Cassatt has the mate to this." At the time Mrs. Havemeyer wrote her little black book of notes to her children, she referred to the Cassatt screen: "If Miss Cassatt leaves me a screen it is a fine Yeitoku [*sic*] we gave her and may be a mate to one I have designated for someone" (Havemeyer "Notes" [1974], p. 4). She has confused Sotan with Kano Eitoku, active in the late sixteenth century. Eitoku is one of those famous names that all collectors would have known; any number of late screens in the Havemeyer collection were in fact misattributed to Eitoku.

35. The textile fragments, a treasure house of motifs and techniques, are mounted in portfolio style, sometimes as many as fifteen to a panel. According to records in the Museum Archives, Bing had been commissioned by an English gentleman to make a collection of such pieces for the Kensington Museum school of design in London (now the Victoria and Albert Museum). He did so and also made a duplicate set for himself, which he sold to the Havemeyers. In 1896 Bing offered the Metropolitan Museum a third collection of fragments for two thousand dollars. This group of 1,187 fragments apparently had been on loan to the Museum in 1894. Samuel Avery recommended to the director that it would be most sensible to ask Mr. Havemeyer to purchase the group for the Museum. Havemeyer willingly acceded to this request.

36. *Collection Ch. Gillot: Objets d'Art et Peintures d'extrême-Orient*, sale cat., Galerie Durand-Ruel, Paris, 1904. The Hayashi provenance is given by S. C. Bosch Reitz, "The Magnolia Screen by Koyetsu," *Bulletin of The Metropolitan Museum of Art* 11 (January 1916), pp. 10–11.

37. CLF to S. Bing, 2/18/04, Charles Lang Freer Papers, Freer Gallery of Art/Arthur M. Sackler Gallery Archives, Smithsonian Institution, Washington, D.C.

38. CLF to Ernest Fenollosa, 2/29/04, Charles Lang Freer Papers, Freer Gallery of Art/Arthur M. Sackler Gallery Archives, Smithsonian Institution, Washington, D.C.

39. Ernest F. Fenollosa, *Epochs of Chinese and Japanese Art*, vol. 2, London, 1912, pp. 133–34.

40. Havemeyer 1961, p. 13. There are at least six lots of paintings, ceramics, and lacquer in the Gillot sale (280, 282, 287, 831, 870, 2078) that were acquired by the Havemeyers and are now in the Metropolitan Museum.

41. Louis Gonse, *L'Art Japonais*, vol. 1, Paris, 1883, p. 231.

42. Fenollosa, *Epochs*, p. 127.

43. Perpetuating the prevailing mythology, he writes: "The paintings of Koyetsu and his intimate friend Sotatsu, be it minute or coarse, resemble each other so closely that it is sometimes almost impossible even for veteran connoisseurs to make clear distinction at a glance." He goes on to point out that "no irony would be more cynical than the naked fact that the true estimation of Koyetsu had not been discovered by a native, but, funny to say, by an American who was no other than the well-known art-collector, the late Mr. Charles L. Freer of Detroit. His attachment for Koyetsu was so intense that it was absolutely beyond words. In truth, it was he who unearthed the tomb of Koyetsu in Takagamine" (Daijirō Ushikubo, *Life of Koyetsu*, Kyoto, 1926, pp. 23–25). For a superb lacquer box in the style of Kōetsu acquired by Freer in 1904, see *The Freer Gallery of Art*, 2, *Japan*, compiled by The Freer Gallery of Art, Tokyo, 1972, pl. 112.

   For a recent overview of Rimpa, see Richard L. Wilson, "Aspects of Rimpa Design," *Orientations* 21 (December 1990), pp. 28–35.

44. See Richard Wilson, *The Art of Ogata Kenzan*, New York and Tokyo, 1991, p. 186.

45. Gonse, p. 231.

46. The article was written by the English collector Ernest Hart. Hart, "Ritsuō," pp. 147–54. Bing's monthly journal was published simultaneously in English and German as well as French.

47. A Ritsuō painting of ducks (sold in the 1930 Havemeyer sale) hung over the piano in Mrs. Havemeyer's house at the time she wrote her "Notes to Her Children" (Havemeyer "Notes" [1974], p.11). Two narrow panels (probably MMA 29.100.69,70) hung in the breakfast room. (ibid., p. 30).

48. Havemeyer 1961, p. 18. The green Ritsuō panel was to hang over the sofa in Louisine Havemeyer's breakfast room. (See Havemeyer "Notes" [1974] p. 39.) This object has not been located among the works now in the Metropolitan Museum.

49. Havemeyer 1961, pp. 11–12. There are two carved ivory *inrō* in the Havemeyer collection at the Metropolitan Museum: MMA 29.100.819,821.

50. Thomas W. Chase, *Ancient Chinese Bronze Art: Casting the Precious Sacral Vessel*, exh. cat., China Institute in America, New York, 1991, no. 29, pp. 66–67. The author is indebted to Thomas Lawton for identifying the Yamanaka provenance.

51. HOH to L. P. Di Cesnola, Director of The Metropolitan Museum of Art, 7/30/9[4], MMA Archives.

52. Aline B. Saarinen, "The Proud Possessors," *Vogue* 132 (October 1, 1958), p. 148; Havemeyer 1961, p. 21.

53. Havemeyer "Notes" [1974], p. 29.

54. For the scandal and confusion concerning this sale, see Michael Forrest, "The Peach Blow Affair," *The Antique Collector* 57 (January 1986), pp. 85–87; Hiram W. Woodward, Jr., *Asian Art in the Walters Art Gallery: A Selection*, Baltimore, 1991, p. 62.

55. Havemeyer 1961, pp. 12–13.

JAPANESE AND CHINESE TEA CERAMICS

The implements used in the ritual preparation of tea in Japan have been treasured since the Muromachi period (1392–1568), when the practice and its utensils were codified by the connoisseurs who served the Ashikaga shoguns. Among the most important items used in *Chanoyu*, as the tea ritual is called, are the ceramic tea jar for powdered tea, employed in the formal service of thick tea, and the tea bowl in which the powder is mixed with a bamboo whisk into hot water by the host and presented to his guest. The Havemeyers' acquaintance with this practice probably came secondhand from Japanese dealers, along with the several hundred such objects they eventually acquired, beginning one day probably in 1884, when Mr. Havemeyer announced to his wife that a case of tea jars was on its way: "Well, I don't know much about them myself. They are little brown jars that hold tea. I guess that covers it, but they are very beautiful, so soft you want to hold them in your hand, and so lovely in color you cannot but admire them; just sober dark brown."[1] Mrs. Havemeyer related:

I opened the case and was surprised to find it contained innumerable small boxes. I opened these small boxes and found they contained each another box inside. Upon opening the second box I found it had a silk bag and upon undoing the silk bag my little "brownie" revealed himself to me. Like a child with a toy I soon had rows of brownies about me, while the little boxes were in a heap upon the floor beside me. . . . I cannot tell you of all their dainty forms or solemn tones; rows of tiny jars as varied as the smile of as many lips, or varied as the twinkle of as many eyes. Never shall I forget that morning with my tea jars, those little jars which were taken from their many wrappings upon some grand occasion when princes knelt before them, when they crawled into the sequestered room and joined in the solemn tea ceremony.[2]

Mrs. Havemeyer's delight must have been renewed many times over the years as she and her husband competed with other Western collectors for these accoutrements of the tea ceremony.

Today, among sixty-five ceramic objects from the Havemeyer holdings in the Japanese collection at the Metropolitan Museum there are twenty-three tea jars (*chaire*) and twelve tea bowls (*chawan*). Like the most treasured implements of their kind in Japan, these are influenced by Chinese and Korean forms that were imported together with the practice of drinking tea. Whether or not the Havemeyers knew of the famous episode in 1569 in which two prized Chinese Song-period tea jars

Plate 144. *Tea jars*, Japan, Edo period, 18th century; l.: Takatori-ware pottery, brown clay with blackish glaze and olive brown overglaze, h. 2 ½ in. (6.4 cm); r.: ca. 1850, Bizen-ware pottery, dark reddish-brown clay with very dark olive glaze and splashes of olive brown, h. 3 ¼ in. (8.3 cm). H. O. Havemeyer Collection, Bequest of Mrs. H. O. Havemeyer, 1929 (29.100.648,664)

Plate 145. *Tea bowls.* l.: Japan, Edo period, 18th century. Karatsu-ware pottery, brown clay with light brown crackled and pitted glaze with six spur marks on bottom interior, diam. 6⅞ in. (17.5 cm); r.: China, Song dynasty, 960–1279. Jian-ware stoneware with hare's-fur glaze, iridescent black with brown streaks and gold rim, diam. 4¾ in. (12.1 cm). H. O. Havemeyer Collection, Bequest of Mrs. H. O. Havemeyer, 1929 (29.100.636, 239)

Plate 146. *Tea bowl*, Japan (Kyoto), Edo period, ca. 1825. Kyoto-ware pottery, white clay with white crackled glaze painted in red, gold, green, and black enamel, diam. 4⅞ in. (12.4 cm). Stamped near foot: *Eiraku*. H. O. Havemeyer Collection, Bequest of Mrs. H. O. Havemeyer, 1929 (29.100.635)

were presented to Nobunaga as victor's booty when he entered Kyoto to take control of that long-contested capital, they seemed as avid as any Japanese daimyo in their collecting of such ceramics; they were equally passionate in their enjoyment of the subtle charms of these small, easily handled objects with their varieties of natural glazes. The Havemeyers were able to acquire a number of Chinese Jian ware bowls of the Song period, the type of utensils prized by Japanese collectors in the Muromachi period (pl. 145, right). Most of their tea ceramics, however, are Japanese examples made during the Edo period, when the practice of *Chanoyu* spread throughout all classes of Japanese society.

An eighteenth-century Japanese tea jar (pl. 144, left), a globular type known as *bunrin* (apple-shaped), was used in the most formal style of *Chanoyu*. Its dark brown glaze mottled with olive tones is characteristic of the Takatori kiln, one of several kilns in Kyushu that has produced tea wares to the specifications of tea masters since the late sixteenth century. This piece has a slight indentation on its side, a consciously made refinement that facilitates handling by providing a place for the thumb when the jar is held.

Another prevalent shape for the tea jar is the taller, round-shouldered form of the Bizen example (pl. 144, right). The metallic, almost iridescent surface results from the high reduction firing of the reddish clay of the Bizen area. A dramatic splash of ash glaze that settled on the piece during the firing to form a thick rivulet of molten glaze that hardened to a blackish olive streak at the center of a field of warm brown mottling marks the "front" of the vessel. Such accidental or induced effects were the subject of keen aesthetic interest among connoisseurs.

The importance and sophistication of the tea jar, once a humble utilitarian vessel, is indicated by the gold-lined ivory lid with which it is provided in Japan. Moreover, jars of the most formal shapes, such as those discussed above, are customarily set on trays of Chinese carved lacquer and carefully stored in bags of rare Chinese brocade, damask, or striped silk when not in use. Some famous examples in Japan have three, four, and even eight silk bags that are used on particular occasions. Mrs. Havemeyer, in fact, took great pains to dispel the rumor that she had used some of the bags that came with her tea jars to decorate the ceiling of her library, which was actually covered with Japanese silks bought at the Philadelphia Centennial Exhibition of 1876. She defended herself to Mr. Ushikubo of Yamanaka and Co., who was afraid that she no longer had them, by counting 475 tea-jar covers that she had kept.[3] Unfortunately, none of the Havemeyer pieces now in the Museum still have their covers or original boxes.

At the end of the sixteenth century the Japanese preference for Chinese utensils gave way to a taste on the part of the Momoyama tea masters for the rustic charm of Korean wares. In fact, starting in the late fifteenth century, when tea masters began to develop the aesthetic known as *wabi*, the cultivation of simple rusticity based on ideals of Zen Buddhism, natural effects were contrived by potters patronized by the feudal daimyo. During Hideyoshi's campaigns in Korea in 1593, potters and their families were resettled in Kyushu, where, at several rural kilns, they produced variations of the Korean wares that so well suited the tastes of the Momoyama tea masters. The Karatsu bowl (pl. 145, left) is an eighteenth-century Japanese example in the Korean rustic tradition. The slightly distorted circular shape as well as the marks left by the spatula and by the artisan's fingers where he held the bowl while he coated the reddish clay with white slip prior to glazing (a technique called *kohiki*) are highly appreciated as traces of the potter's lack of artifice. They contribute as well to the intimate, natural feel of the bowl in the hand, which is also prized. The soft creamy glaze, with its fine crackle and spotting where the iron of the clay fired through the slip, is characteristic of a type of ware first imported from Korea and subsequently made by the descendants of the resettled Korean potters. Both the *kohiki* technique, involving traces of the spatula and fingers of the potter, and the wreath of unglazed spurs left when the bowl was fired in a stack are characteristic of Karatsu ware, a kind of pottery that is admired above all for the mellow quality of its glaze.

An entirely different aesthetic, that rooted in ancient Japanese court culture, reemerged in the seventeenth century and developed throughout the Edo period, giving rise to the production of refined decorated wares such as the Kyoto ware bowl (pl. 146). This bowl's hard white clay body is covered with a creamy white glaze and embellished with autumn grasses—the maidenflower and purple trousers—in gold, green, and black set against a huge reddish moon. These are familiar motifs in Japanese poetry, and the brilliant colored enamels with gold accents underscore their courtly associations. A fine sprinkling of gold powder along the rim of the bowl intensifies the gorgeous effect when it is taken in hand for drinking the bright frothy green tea. Stamped near the foot is the round mark, reading *Eiraku*, of the Kyoto potter Eiraku Hozen, who was active in the first half of the nineteenth century.

BBF

1. Havemeyer 1961, pp. 73–74.
2. Ibid., p. 74.
3. Ibid., p. 70.

Plate 147
Kitagawa Utamaro

A MOTHER BATHING HER SON

Japan, Edo period, 18th century
Color woodblock print, 14¾ x 9⅞ in.
(37.5 x 25.1 cm)
H. O. Havemeyer Collection, Bequest of
Mrs. H. O. Havemeyer, 1929
JP1661

The Havemeyer ukiyo-e collection is distinguished not only by the great number of its prints, which total nearly one thousand, but also by its variety and comprehensiveness. The inclusion of all ukiyo-e types and subjects and the balanced representation of artists and schools that exemplify the major stages in the development of ukiyo-e prints indicate the Havemeyers' appreciation of this beguiling art. In terms of both quality and quantity, the high point of the collection is undoubtedly the prints of Utamaro (1753–1806).

The mother and child theme is integral, if not central, to the mature stage of this art form. The subject testifies to the newfound interest in the activities of common people that marked eighteenth-century Japanese art and at the same time provides a clever guise for a displaced expression of eroticism. Utamaro's treatment is more poignant than that of other ukiyo-e artists, perhaps because his mothers are often depicted with a seductive sexuality. Here, a mother is performing one of her daily tasks, bathing her son, as she awkwardly (or coquettishly) hunches over the child and the bucket in which he sits. To enhance the visual excitement, Utamaro crops the bucket, the woman's leg, and the child's kimono. This type of print may well have been the inspiration for the first series of prints made by Cassatt (see fig. 23).

HO

Figure 23. Mary Cassatt. *The Bath*, 1891. Color print with drypoint and softground, 17 x 11¹³⁄₁₆ in. (43.2 x 30 cm). Gift of Paul J. Sachs, 1917 (16.2.7). Location of Havemeyer impression unknown

JAPANESE SWORDS AND SWORD FITTINGS

The Havemeyer bequest to the Metropolitan Museum included twenty Japanese short swords (*wakizashi*) and daggers (*tantō*) and more than two hundred and fifty sword fittings. Another forty swords and sixty fittings were sold at auction in 1930, and still others were given to family members, so that the total number suggests a substantial accumulation in this specialized area of collecting. A review of the holdings suggests that the Havemeyers, like so many collectors of their day, acquired swords and fittings as small-scale decorative objects to be admired for their exquisite metalworking techniques, the picturesque qualities of their design, and the aspects of Japanese history, mythology, and poetry evoked by their ornament. That the Havemeyers sought small-scale weapons is evidenced in the collection's notable lack of full-length swords, *katana* or *tachi*, whose blades measure longer than sixty centimeters.

The mounted weapons were no doubt acquired for the attractiveness of their lacquered scabbards and ornamental soft metal fittings, with little concern for the blades they contained. Indeed, the blades are of

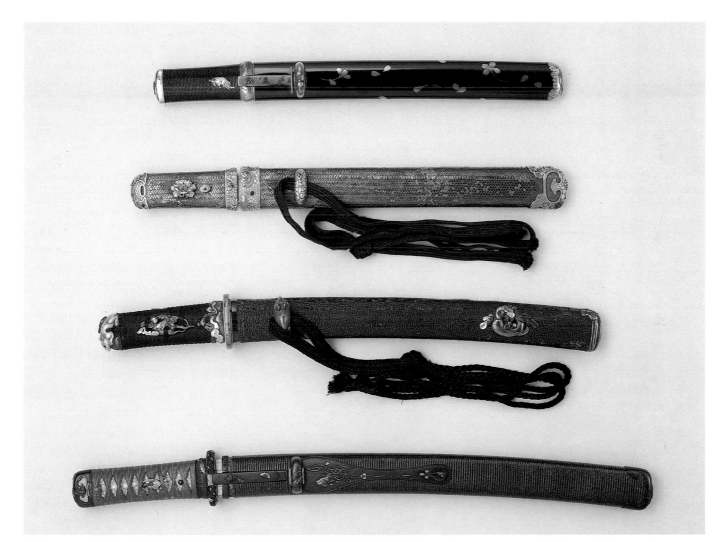

Plate 148. *Sword and dagger mountings.* Japan. Top: blade for a dagger (*tantō*). Late Kamakura period, dated 1330. Steel, l. 10 ⅛ in. (25.7 cm). Signed and dated: *Kage[masa], 1330.* Mounting: Edo period, 19th century. Fittings by Masaharu. Gold, lacquered wood, silver, and whalebone, l. 14 ¼ in. (36.1 cm). Gift of J. Watson Webb, Jr., 1972 (1972.12). Second from top: mounting for a dagger (*tantō*). Edo period, 18th–19th century. Fittings (except *menuki*) by Ohara Kyūtei, 18th century; *menuki* by Iamoto Kansai, 19th century. Silver, gold, *shakudō*, silk, and wood, l. 15 ⅝ in. (39.7 cm). Second from bottom: blade for a short sword (*wakizashi*). Momoyama period, late 16th–early 17th century. Attributed to Yasutsugu. Steel, l. 12 ⅜ in. (31.5 cm). Mounting: Edo period, dated 1828. Fittings by Nakamura Kazuyuki. *Shakudō*, gold, silver, copper, lacquered leather, ray skin, and wood, l. 18 ¼ in. (46.3 cm). Bottom: mounting for a short sword (*wakizashi*). Edo period, 19th century. Fittings by Nakagawa Ishō and Itō Masanaga. *Shakudō*, gold, *shibuichi*, silver, lacquer, wood, ray skin, and leather, l. 20 ⅞ in. (53 cm). H. O. Havemeyer Collection, Bequest of Mrs. H. O. Havemeyer, 1929 (29.100.1376a,b, 1370a–c, 1379a–d)

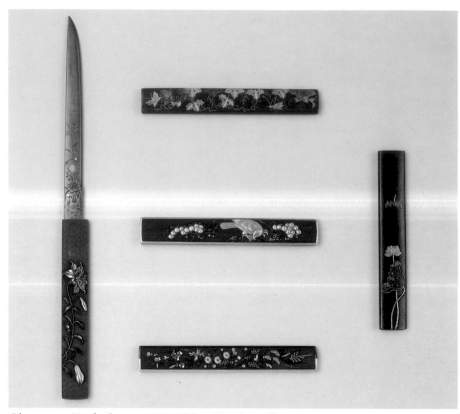

Plate 149. *Knife (kogatana) and handles (kozuka)*, Japan, Edo period; l. (koga-tana): 19th century. By Juō Masayoshi. Steel, *shakudō*, *shibuichi*, and gold, l. 8 ¼ in. (21 cm); c. top (kozuka): 18th century. Kaga Zōgan school. *Shakudō*, gold, and silver, l. 3 ¾ in. (9.5 cm).; c. (kozuka): late 18th–early 19th century. By Ishiguro Masayoshi. *Shakudō* and gold, l. 3 ¾ in. (9.5 cm); c. bottom (kozuka): late 17th–early 18th century. By Goto Mitsunobu. *Shakudō*, gold, and silver, 3 ¾ in. (9.5 cm); r. (kozuka): late 18th–early 19th century. Attributed to the Hirata school. *Shakudō*, gold, and cloisonné enamel, l. 3 ¾ in. (9.5 cm). H. O. Havemeyer Collection, Bequest of Mrs. H. O. Havemeyer, 1929 (29.100.1196, 1150, 1195, 1117, 1297)

Plate 150. *Sword guards (tsuba)*, Japan, Edo period; u.l.: dated 1762. By Ōmori Terumasa. *Shakudō*, gold, *shibuichi*, copper, and silver, l. 3 in. (7.6 cm); u.r.: late 18th century. By Bairyūken Kiyotatsu. Iron, gold, silver, and *shakudō*, l. 3 ¼ in. (8.3 cm); l.l.: late 18th–early 19th century. By Nakanori. Brass, *sha-kudō*, gold, and copper, l. 3 ½ in. (8.9 cm); l.r.: 19th century. By Toshiyoshi. Copper, *shibuichi*, *shakudō*, gold, and silver, l. 2 ¾ in. (7 cm). H. O. Havemeyer Collection, Bequest of Mrs. H. O. Havemeyer, 1929 (29.100.1010, 1045, 959, 1011)

mediocre quality with the notable exception of that by Kagemasa dated 1330 (pl. 148, top), which is one of the finest in the Museum's collection. Not surprisingly, this superb blade is encased in a black lacquered scabbard ornamented in gold with cherry blossoms and has exquisitely engraved and silver-inlaid gold mounts signed by the nineteenth-century master Masaharu.

The sword mountings in the collection encompass sword guards (*tsuba*)(see pl. 150), grip ornaments (*menuki*), hilt washers and pommels (*fuchigashira*), knife handles (*kozuka*)(see pl. 149), and skewerlike hairdressing tools (*kogai*), the latter two being contained in recesses within the scabbard. The majority of the Havemeyer fittings date from the mid-eighteenth century or nineteenth century and most are of soft metal—gold, silver, brass, copper, and the uniquely Japanese *shakudō* (a blue-black alloy of copper and gold) and *shibuichi* (a dark gray alloy of copper and silver). The combinations of these varicolored metals seem endless. Among the finest of the 150 Havemeyer *tsuba* is that signed by Ōmori Terumasa and dated 1762 (pl. 150, upper left), which is decorated with three powerful Chinese lions rendered in high relief in *shibuichi*, copper, gold, and silver on a stippled *shakudō* ground. Iron *tsuba* are less common in the collection; without doubt the finest of them is an openwork example by Bairyūken Kiyotatsu in the form of a folding screen decorated with chrysanthemums in flush gold and silver inlays (pl. 150, upper right). No doubt the Havemeyers found in the charming designs and colorful metalwork of these fittings a sense of the essence and spirit of the Japanese.

MO

Plate 151
THE LIFE OF PRINCE SHŌTOKU

Japan, Kamakura period, 14th century
Hanging scroll diptych, ink and colors on
silk, l.: 67 ⅝ x 33 ⅜ in. (171.8 x 84.8 cm);
r.: 67 ⅝ x 33 ¼ in. (171.8 x 84.5 cm)
H. O. Havemeyer Collection, Bequest of
Mrs. H. O. Havemeyer, 1929
29.100.470,471

East Asian religious narrative paintings such as the present diptych
pose challenging problems of interpretation to the modern viewer.
These works normally contain small-
scale scenes laid out over a broad
surface. Sometimes the monumental
format used is a mural or large hanging scroll; at other times the composition and meaning are rendered far
more complex because the narrative
is depicted on several large scrolls
that hang together or is painted on
all four walls of a room. Whatever
the format, the artist's task was to
organize these small scenes and their
separate meanings into an order that
would convey an integrated message
to the viewer.

The early Japanese response to
this problem is intriguing precisely
because it was not the pat solution
of a diachronic sequence. Scenes of
the Buddha's deeds and miracles, for
example, were scattered in a seemingly random manner over the picture surface, creating a mystic whole
by ignoring the actual sequence of
life. Such imaginative reorderings of
religious experience were encouraged by the monks' use of these narrative paintings in their preaching.

With the monks providing the verbal logic needed to explain shifts of scene, the artists could allow viewers' eyes and minds to travel freely through the paintings, confident that the integral place and hidden meaning of each element in Buddhist fable and faith would be apparent and comprehensible.

The Life of Prince Shōtoku is a particularly interesting example of this genre of Buddhist narrative art. It commemorates the life of a seventh-century Japanese ruler long venerated for his espousal of Buddhism and his establishment of high cultural standards. Painted in the early fourteenth century, at the very time the tradition of nondiachronic schemes was falling out of favor, it seems at first glance to present the legendary events of the prince's life in a rational, chronological order. However, the artist does not, in fact, adhere to the simple pattern of diachronic presentation common to most extant works of the time. The first scroll for the most part appears to depict the first half of Shōtoku's life, and the second scroll the second half, yet there are many exceptions to this division. Furthermore, in each scroll scenes of feats and miracles from both halves of his life are scattered randomly and freely interwoven.

The artist draws on the full hagiographical painting tradition surrounding this icon of sacred kingship and Buddhist sainthood, which dates from as early as the eighth century. Thus a sense of grandiose myth rather than realistic narrative is created. As is often the case in mythological discourse, temporal links between the scenes readily give way to topographical ones. Events of varying date believed to have occurred at the same site, for example, the imperial palace, are depicted alongside one another. Similarly, scenes from the prince's childhood that may have been set in different locales are placed within the same house, allowing the viewer to perceive them in a single glance and creating a sense of the miraculous nature of this man's birth and growth.

Scholars have speculated about the possibility of a direct link between the present work and the few other surviving examples of the early nonchronological narrative tradition, especially a diptych at Daizoji temple in Nara. Detailed comparison of the images and brushwork, however, reveals the Daizoji work to be much later than the Havemeyer. Although the artistic lineage is unclear, the Havemeyer diptych presumably shares a direct common ancestor with another unidentified scroll, which is, in turn, the direct source for a six-scroll work in Shitennoji, in Osaka, a temple founded by Prince Shōtoku. The direct predecessor of the Shitennoji painting, one assumes, is also the direct source for the Daizoji work. Less involved is the speculation that the Havemeyer and Shitennoji scrolls were painted in the same workshop and that the Havemeyer diptych was hung for ceremonial occasions on the side walls of a hall in a temple affiliated with Shitennoji, the center of the cult of Prince Shōtoku.

HO

Plate 152
THE BODHISATTVA KSITIGARBHA (CHIJANG POSAL)

Korea, 1st half of 14th century
Hanging scroll, colors and gold on silk,
41 ⅛ x 18 ⅜ in. (104.1 x 46.7 cm)
H. O. Havemeyer Collection, Gift of Horace Havemeyer, 1929
29.160.32

Bodhisattva Ksitigarbha (Chijang Posal in Korean) is the Bodhisattva of the Underworld, whose role it is to release deceased souls from the endless cycle of suffering, or, in Buddhist terms, the Six Paths of Transmigration. The cult of Ksitigarbha, closely related to the Pure Land sect of Buddhism, was introduced to Korea by the mid-eighth century, during the Unified Silla period (668–918). In paintings of the Koryo dynasty (918–1392) Ksitigarbha is represented either as the principal deity or as the attendant Bodhisattva of Amitabha or the companion Bodhisattva of Avalokitesvara. As the principal deity he is represented as a single figure or attended by the Ten Kings of Hell or other Buddhist divinities.

The Metropolitan's Ksitigarbha is depicted as a monk with shaved head and carrying his usual attributes: a six-ringed staff in his right hand and a round transparent *cintamani* (magic jewel) in his half-raised left hand. In other Koryo

158

paintings the magic jewel is more frequently held in the right hand and the staff in the left. Standing on lotus petals, this figure is slightly turned to the right with head and torso facing frontally as if pausing momentarily before taking a step forward. The halo is outlined in gold, providing a divine aura.

Much of the beauty of this scroll lies in the exquisitely ornamented garment of the Bodhisattva. Both the transparent shawl and the red robe are decorated with a variety of patterns, such as spiral roundels, diamond-shaped peony medallions, scroll borders, cloud scrolls, and wave patterns, all of which are drawn in gold. There is a close correspondence between these textile patterns and motifs found on contemporaneous ceramics and lacquerware. The lavish use of gold and the opulence of the textile reflect the taste of the Koryo royal family and the aristocrats who were the principal patrons of richly decorated Buddhist paintings.

Symmetrical elements dominate in the face of the deity: the hairline frames the forehead in balanced curves, and the full rotundity of the face is echoed in the evenly arched brows. Facial details are drawn in thin red lines softened by subtle shading, and the proportionately small lips resemble those of a child. Solemnity coexists with gentleness of expression in a face that typifies the ideal Koryo image of the divinity.

To judge from the facial features and the details of the decorative patterns—such as the supple and naturalistic lotus-head scrolls along the border of the undergarment—which here are not yet stylized into linear abstraction, the Metropolitan Ksitigarbha can be dated to the first half of the fourteenth century. The scroll is one of the few known extant Koryo paintings of a single standing image of Chijang.

HMC

159

Figure 24. *Autumn*, Japan, Edo period, Rimpa school, 17th century. One of a pair of six-fold screens, colors and silver foil on paper, overall 48 x 123 in. (121.9 x 312.4 cm). Rogers Fund, 1915 (15.127)

SPRING, A JAPANESE SCREEN

The delicate beauty of springtime is captured in the carefully orchestrated array of trees and flowers depicted on this screen (pl. 153). The trees and flowers are set within a space defined by an undulating stream that meanders from the upper right across the entire six panels. A clump of red azalea provides the single and effective accent for white blossoms that predominate, in subtle contrast to the deep greens and browns of pine and rocks, whose boldly abstracted forms act as foils for the carefully observed naturalism of the flowering plants. The white azalea in the second panel from the right draws one's gaze into the landscape. At the upper right, lilies peek from behind rocks; in the third panel a clump of tiny green leaves of lespedeza, or bush clover (*hagi*), appears

as new growth at the base of last year's withered stalks. The eye is led farther left, toward red and white azalea beneath a profusely blossoming cherry tree; at the upper left a stand of kerria (*yamabuki*) borders the stream, and emerging from the lower left are the top branches of a flowering pear and magnolia. All of these elements are ranged on a ground scattered with small squares of cut silver. Age has darkened the silver and deepened the creamy tone of the paper ground to wonderful effect.

This screen, with its springtime symphony of flowering trees and plants, forms a pair with another in the Metropolitan's collection (fig. 24), where the stream continues leftward behind autumnal flora. In the autumn half of the composition,

dramatic closeup views of vividly colored flowering plants and trees convey the stronger impact of nature's final efflorescence. Dominating the right is a towering chestnut, its huge leaves already a warm brown, framed by golden stalks of miscanthus grass and dense clumps of white chrysanthemums. A single blossom of wild pink stands out against the flowering bush clover and valerian that fill the opposite bank of the stream. In the two panels at the extreme left, late afternoon light seems to dance on the ginkgo leaves, painted in varied hues of brilliant yellow and set against the red and white leaves of a maple: an ensemble that presents a grand finale to the progress of the seasons.

The autumn screen was bought by the Metropolitan Museum in 1915

Plate 153. *Spring*, Japan, Edo period, Rimpa school, 17th century. One of a pair of six-fold screens, colors and silver foil on paper, overall 48 x 123 in. (121.9 x 312.4 cm). H. O. Havemeyer Collection, Gift of Horace Havemeyer, 1949 (49.35.2)

from the Japanese dealer Yamanaka, from whom the Havemeyers also obtained many of their Asian objects.[1] Sigisbert Chretien Bosch Reitz, the Dutch expert on Chinese ceramics who headed the Metropolitan's newly formed department of Far Eastern art, reported that this early acquisition was one of a pair—the other half of which belonged to H. O. Havemeyer—that had been brought to Europe from the Kōrin Tea House in Tokyo. According to Bosch Reitz, in Tokyo it had been attributed to Ogata Kenzan, the younger brother of Ogata Kōrin by "Mr. Hayashi."[2] Mr. Hayashi is presumably Hayashi Tadamasa, a dealer active in Paris.

In a rapturous appreciation in his *Epochs of Chinese and Japanese Art* (1912), Ernest Fenollosa judged the autumn screen a supreme example of Japanese "impressionism" attributable to no less a hand than that of Hon'ami Kōetsu, the progenitor of the renaissance of classic Japanese art that came to be named Rimpa, after his artistic heir, Kōrin.

Today, for lack of evidence, scholars refrain from ascribing paintings to Kōetsu, and this pair of screens, bearing neither seal nor signature, is judged from its combination of abstract forms of rock, stream, and pines with the carefully observed naturalism of the flowers, including the unconventional magnolia and ginkgo, to be an anonymous work done in the second half of the seventeenth century. Technical details such as the darkened silver lines of the flowing water and the decorative technique of scattered silver, as well as the rich profusion of flora, are antique elements that link this work to fifteenth- and sixteenth-century screens in the *yamato-e* tradition. These screens, with their bold decorative treatment of Japan's landscape, embody the rebirth of the *yamato-e* tradition in the Edo period.

BBF

1. See Julia Meech, "The Other Havemeyer Passion: Collecting Asian Art," this catalogue. Meech dates the screen to the eighteenth century.
2. S. C. B[osch] R[eitz], "The Magnolia Screen," *Bulletin of The Metropolitan Museum of Art* 11 (January 1916), pp. 10–12.

JAPANESE LACQUERS

Japanese lacquerware has dazzled and delighted Westerners ever since it was introduced to Europe in the late sixteenth century. By the nineteenth century intricate lacquer pieces, usually done in various techniques of *maki-e*, or sprinkled gold or silver decoration, were proudly displayed in American parlors as well as in European castles. The Havemeyer home was no exception as a showcase for Japanese arts; indeed it was perhaps one of the most lavish settings for a huge collection of lacquer items, including many *inrō*, the small, tiered medicine containers worn suspended from the waist, which had been an important part of the traditional Japanese wardrobe. When Western dress was adopted in the late nineteenth century, these exquisite creations of the

Edo lacquerers' craft were eagerly collected in great number by admiring Westerners. The Museum received 190 *inrō* and some 60 other lacquer objects in the Havemeyer bequest, a group that included nearly every technique and style of the lacquer craft. These pieces must have provided countless hours of fascinating viewing for the Havemeyers and visitors to their music room, where many were displayed. Most of the Havemeyer lacquerware collection is of nineteenth-century date and reflects the taste of the time for exquisite gold lacquer boxes with conventional designs.

The rectangular box with rounded inset corners (pl. 154) is a type that was used to store incense and the various implements employed in the refined pastime of comparing fragrances, although it does not contain the tray and matching set of utensils for the incense ceremony. Appropriate to this aristocratic pastime is its minutely

detailed decoration, which depicts a classic literary image: the cherry blossoms in the mountains of Yoshino south of Nara, here rendered in various types and tones of sprinkled gold alloys. The lid presents a distant view of the Yoshino range, which is nearly synonymous with its mountain cherries in full bloom. The range also is the fabled place of refuge for Japan's most romantic hero, the twelfth-century warrior Yoshitsune, and the locus of the southern court established in the fourteenth century by Emperor Daigo in a failed attempt to restore the supremacy of the imperial court over its daimyo protectors. The poignance surrounding these tragic historical figures is evoked in the landscape on the front of the box. In this scene, blossoms at their peak of beauty will soon fall, to be carried away by the swiftly flowing mountain stream.

Equally precious in its execution but reflecting the innovations in

Plate 154. *Box*, Japan, Tokugawa period, 19th century. Gold lacquer decorated with sprinkled and inlaid gold, 4 x 8 ½ x 7 ⅜ in. (10.2 x 21.6 x 18.7 cm). H. O. Havemeyer Collection, Bequest of Mrs. H. O. Havemeyer, 1929 (29.100.687)

Plate 155. *Box*, Japan, Tokugawa period, 19th century. Black lacquer decorated with sprinkled gold and silver and inlaid gold and mother-of-pearl, 2 x 4 ⅛ x 3 ⅞ in. (5.1 x 10.5 x 9.8 cm). H. O. Havemeyer Collection, Bequest of Mrs. H. O. Havemeyer, 1929 (29.100.685)

shape that characterize late nineteenth-century works is a small box (pl. 155) that takes its complex form from that of two confronted butterflies. The gossamer wings of the butterflies are rendered in intricately sprinkled gold and silver with subtle iridescent inlay. The lobed sides of the box carry a decoration of a field of wild pinks, an image with erotic associations of youthful beauty.

An entirely different kind of lacquerware eagerly sought by the Havemeyers and their circle is that executed in the style of Ritsuō, one of the few Japanese artists singled out in the journal *Le Japon Artistique*. This miscellany of connoisseurs' reports of varying veracity, published in French, English, and German by the Parisian dealer Siegfried Bing from 1888 to 1891, exerted a profound influence on contemporary collectors as well as forgers. Ritsuō was the studio name of Ogawa Haritsu (1663–1747), an innovative artist who began his career as a haiku poet and later developed an eccentric style of lacquer decoration that made use of ceramic and other kinds of inlays. His new approach to lacquer involved subject matter as well as technique: like his fellow haiku poets he had turned away from the restricted, elegant vocabulary of court poetry to express emotion and experience through uncommon juxtapositions of new images of everyday life, and he drew upon these themes for his visual art as well.

The renewed vogue for Ritsuō's work in the late nineteenth century, particularly in the West, inspired many inferior imitations, some of which were acquired by the Havemeyers. A superior example, one of the few works in Western collections that are now accepted as genuine eighteenth-century examples of Ritsuō lacquer, is a writing box decorated with mice chewing a fan (pl. 156) that stands out for its technique and subtle humor. The charms

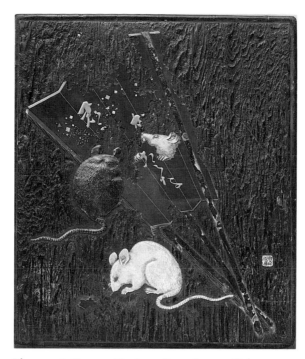

Plate 156. Ogawa Haritsu. *Box*, Japan, Tokugawa period, 17th–18th century. Wood with polychrome lacquer and inlaid ceramic, 10 ⅛ x 8 ⅛ x 1 ¾ in. (25.7 x 20.6 x 4.5 cm). Seal on top of cover: *Kan*. H. O. Havemeyer Collection, Bequest of Mrs. H. O. Havemeyer, 1929 (29.100.703)

Plate 157. Zōkoku. *Pipe case with pipe*, Japan, Tokugawa period, 19th century. Carved black and red lacquer with silver fittings, 11 x 1 ½ in. (27.9 x 3.8 cm). Seal near base: *Zōkoku*. H. O. Havemeyer Collection, Bequest of Mrs. H. O. Havemeyer, 1929 (29.100.722)

of this box emerge gradually, as one comes to notice that the long-used appearance of the ostensibly simple wooden box has been achieved by craftsmanship and finish as meticulous as that lavished on the pristine and gorgeous boxes that are intricately decorated in sprinkled gold lacquer. This artifice reflects an appreciation of the natural processes of decline and decay, an aesthetic that is particularly important in haiku poetry. The box opens to reveal on the underside of the cover the rear view of one of the white mice pictured on the exterior; the mouse thus is seen to have gnawed through the box to ravage the fan and the poem written on it—a humorous twist akin to the fresh insights prized in haiku. The contrived

affectation of simplicity and wear reflects the sophisticated taste of the eighteenth-century literati, among whom Haritsu was honored as both poet and inventive craftsman.

Eighteenth-century literati taste also fostered Japanese versions of Chinese-style carved lacquer, a fine example of which is the pipe case with a mark of Zōkoku (1805–1869) (pl. 157), the lacquerer most renowned for such work. On its rounded sides lotus and chrysanthemums are carved through thick layers of black lacquer down to a base layer of red lacquer intricately carved in a stylized wave pattern. The upper portion of the case is decorated with a floral scroll, and stylized butterflies are curled over the ends of the pipe sheath.   BBF

Plate 158
DRAGONS AND LANDSCAPE

China, late Song or early Yuan dynasty, late
13th century
Handscroll, ink on paper, 17 5/8 x 75 1/8 in.
(44.8 x 190.7 cm)
H. O. Havemeyer Collection, Bequest of
Mrs. H. O. Havemeyer, 1929
29.100.531

The earliest and most important
of the Chinese paintings in the
Havemeyer collection is this short
handscroll showing two dragons in
a windswept landscape. Dragons, as
symbols of nature's elemental forces,
have been depicted in Chinese art
from time immemorial. A special
genre, dragon paintings were given
powerful treatment by such Southern Song masters as the Daoist
scholar-painter Chen Rong (fl. ca.
1235–62) and the Chan (Zen) Buddhist artist Muqi (fl. ca. 1240–75).

This scroll, which formerly was attributed to Chen Rong, presents a
view of undulating ocean billows
and a jagged, rocky shoreline where
several gnarled trees, their branches
bent over by the force of a powerful
storm, cling to the bare cliff. To the

left of the trees two dragons appear
amid the clouds and inky darkness.
The dragons' writhing bodies and
hooked claws contrast with the angular planes of the rock faces and
echo the twisted trunks and cling-
ing roots of the trees. One dragon
seems to emerge from the rock itself, while the other is depicted play-
fully, stretched belly up across a
rocky incline.

The short, abruptly cropped composition of the Havemeyer painting
indicates that it was originally part
of a much longer handscroll, other
fragments from which are now the
property of the Agency for Cultural
Affairs in Japan[1] and in the collection of the Museum of Fine Arts in
Boston.[2] A later, more complete version of the original handscroll in
The Art Museum, Princeton University, confirms the compositional in-
terrelationship of these fragments.[3]

Stylistically, the fragments do not
appear very distant in date from
Chen Rong's single surviving masterpiece, the *Nine Dragons* handscroll
of 1244.[4] The brushwork of the
Havemeyer painting exhibits the

same boldness found in the Chen
Rong but is much coarser. In spite
of their roughness, however, the
brushstrokes of the present painting
remain descriptive in intent, without
any trace of the self-consciously calligraphic stylizations seen in later
works, such as a Yuan dynasty
dragon painting in the Metropolitan
done by Zhang Yucai, the thirty-
eighth Daoist pope (r. 1295–1316).[5]
In Zhang's painting, forms are
defined by emphatically calligraphic
outlines rather than through illu-
sionistically descriptive texturing
and ink washes. The spontaneous
brushwork of the Havemeyer painting recalls the exuberant ink-wash
style employed by Chan Buddhist
painters of the late thirteenth century. Most likely the Havemeyer
dragon painting was made by a
close follower of Chen Rong working under the aegis of the Buddhist
or Daoist church.

The fragments of the original
scroll were furnished with spurious
artists' signatures and collectors'
seals in recent times, probably when
the work was cut apart. The

Havemeyer painting bears a three-character seal-script signature on one of the vertical tree trunks: *painted by Souweng [Chen Rong]*. Five spurious seals of the Qianlong emperor (r. 1736–95) have also been affixed to the painting, and in 1891 the calligrapher Xu Fu (1836–after 1891) added a label strip attributing the scroll to Chen Rong.

MKH

1. Kojiro Tomita, *Portfolio of Chinese Paintings in the Museum (Han to Sung Periods)*, Cambridge, Mass., 1933, pls. 134, 135.
2. Seiichi Taki, "Ga ryû setsu" (On the painting of dragons), *Kokka*, no. 550 (September 1936), pp. 251–56, pls. 1, 2.
3. George Rowley, *Principles of Chinese Painting, with Illustrations from the Du Bois Schanck Morris Collection*, Princeton, N.J., 1947, pls. 47, 48.
4. Tomita, pls. 127–33.
5. Wen Fong and Maxwell K. Hearn, "Silent Poetry: Chinese Paintings in The Douglas Dillon Galleries," *The Metropolitan Museum of Art Bulletin* 39 (Winter 1981/82), figs. 20, 21.

Plate 159
INCENSE BOX

China, Yuan period, 14th century
Carved black and red lacquer (*tixi*), diam. 5 in. (12.7 cm)
H. O. Havemeyer Collection, Bequest of Mrs. H. O. Havemeyer, 1929
29.100.713

Lacquerware, produced by the application of the sap of the lac tree (*rhus verniciflua*) on a substrate of wood or almost any other material, has been used in China since prehistoric times. It can be decorated by painting, carving, or inlay. Carving is possible when a thick layer of lacquer is built up by successive applications of as many as two hundred thin coats of lacquer. As each coating is allowed some forty-eight hours to harden before the next one is applied, the production of a thick layer of lacquer is a laborious process. However, the solid substance thus produced possesses a soft texture and a warm luster that is very attractive. The finest carved lacquer, in terms of both quality of material and artistry of carving, was made in the late Song through the Yuan to early Ming period—corresponding to the thirteenth to fourteenth century. Carved lacquer of these periods was made both for the domestic market and for export to other Asian countries.

There are several types of carved lacquer. The incense box from the Havemeyer collection is a good example of the type known as *t'i-hsi*, which was popular in the Yuan period (1279–1368). The thick layer of red lacquer (colored by the addition of cinnabar) is built up on a wooden core and interspersed with two relatively thin layers of black lacquer (colored by carbon or an iron compound). It is carved in a sword pommel pattern, so called because the shape of the scroll forms is similar to that of the pommel of the Chinese sword. *T'i-hsi* lacquer, especially in the form of boxes and dishes suitable for use in tea ceremonies, was a popular item of export to Japan, where it is known as *guri*—a term that refers to the shape of the pommel scrolls. *T'i-hsi* and other categories of Chinese carved lacquer inspired a type of Japanese lacquer known as *Kamakurabori*, first produced in Kamakura in the fifteenth century. In simulation of carved lacquer, *Kamakurabori* was made by first carving the wood core and subsequently coating it with lacquer. Most lacquer of this type is in the form of incense boxes like the present one, which was bought by the Havemeyers as *Kamakurabori*. Recently, however, it was recatalogued as Chinese *t'i-hsi* of the Yuan period.

JCYW

Plate 160
RITUAL WINE VESSEL (*HU*)

China, Eastern Zhou dynasty, late Spring and Autumn–early Warring States period, 5th century B.C.
Bronze inlaid with copper, h. 17½ in. (44.5 cm)
H. O. Havemeyer Collection, Bequest of Mrs. H. O. Havemeyer, 1929
29.100.545

This ceremonial wine vessel, or *hu*, belongs to a group of inlaid bronze objects from the late Zhou period that are closely related to one another by their distinctive design and style as well as by their innovative technique of manufacture.[1] A number of containers in the group are in other museum collections, and many additional examples have been excavated in China in recent years. The decoration on these vessels, many of which are *hu*, consists of copper inlays representing birds, felines, deer, animal-face patterns, fire motifs, and paired isosceles triangles.[2] Although some of the inlays are clearly based on the dense, linear spirals seen on earlier Shang and Zhou vessels, those found on the Havemeyer vessel and related objects in other collections are distinguished by their broad, open design. Typically, the extended portions of an inlay, such as an animal's tail, horns, and hind feet, are connected to one another or to the beast's body by small bridges of the inlay metal; the coils of spirals within bird motifs or animal face patterns are similarly interconnected. It would seem that the bridges were designed to support and maintain the shapes of elements that were once freestanding pieces of metal.

Careful examination of the interior and exterior surfaces of the vessels and X-ray radiography of the walls (see fig. 25) indicate this supposition to be correct and reveal the unusual method of manufacture employed. Initially, each motif was cut from a sheet of nearly pure copper approximately one millimeter thick. Small bronze coupons of about the same thickness and of roughly square cross section were then affixed to the back of each motif with a solder of lead-based alloy to yield an assemblage of platforms, each of which had the intended thickness of the

Figure 25. Radiograph of portion of *hu* wall showing inlay-chaplet assemblages

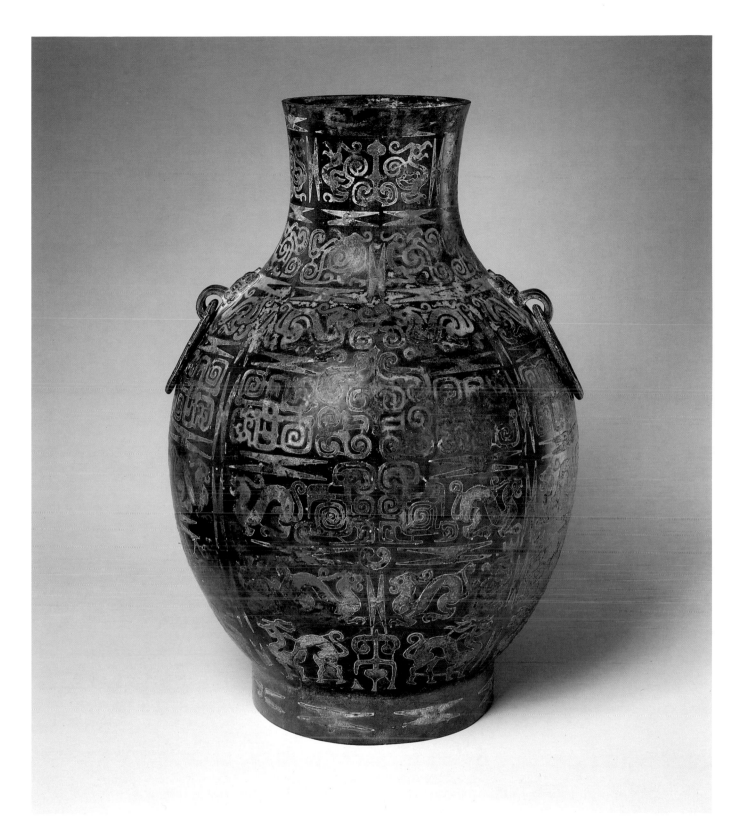

finished vessel wall. These platforms were subsequently distributed over the surface of a prepared clay core in the shape of the vessel interior so that they function as core spacers, or chaplets, during the casting process. The inlay-chaplets maintained the proper registration of core and outer investment and became an in-

tegral part of the finished work when the molten alloy of the vessel matrix solidified. We may conjecture that the outer investment was a clay piece-mold similar to those used in earlier times and was assembled around the inlays that served as chaplets.

JHF

1. C. D. Weber, *Chinese Pictorial Bronze Vessels of the Late Chou Period*, Ascona, 1968.
2. A. Le Bas, N. Kennon, R. Smith, and N. Barnard, "Bronze Vessels with Copper Inlaid Decor and Pseudo-Copper Inlay of Ch'un-Ch'iu and Chan-Kuo Times," preprint no. 16, Kioloa Conference, N.S.W., *Ancient Chinese and Southeast Asian Bronze Cultures*, February 8–12, 1988.

a

b

c

d

Plate 161
A GROUP OF INCENSE BURNERS

China, Ming period, late 16th to 1st half of 17th century
a. bronze, h. 2⅞ in. (7.3 cm); b. bronze, h. 3⅞ in. (9.8 cm); c. bronze with gold splashes, h. 3 in. (7.6 cm); d. bronze with gold and silver inlay, h. 4 in. (10.2 cm)
H. O. Havemeyer Collection, Bequest of Mrs. H. O. Havemeyer, 1929
29.100.547,548,550,549

Delectation of the olfactory sense by burning incense was a fashionable pastime in the prosperous cities of southeastern China in the late sixteenth to early seventeenth century. The active sea trade conducted from the ports of coastal China resulted in the ready availability of a wide variety of incense and aromatics. Precious materials such as aromatics and ivory were exchanged for Chinese manufactured goods such as silk and porcelain. The resultant prosperity also generated a lively home market for fine articles for daily use like bronze incense burners. Made for a sophisticated clientele, the incense burners were modeled after archaic bronzes (d) and antique porcelain, especially the classical celadon wares of the twelfth and thirteenth centuries (a, b). Others were miniaturized versions of large storage jars for water that stood in the grounds of temples and palatial buildings (c). Great skills were employed to give them various "antique" patinations, ranging from rich reddish browns (a) to dark tea greens (b). As if to balance their austere shapes, some bronzes were decorated with splashes of gold (c)—using the fire-gilding method, whereby gold in the form of a gold-mercury amalgam is applied to the vessel, which subsequently is heated to drive off the mercury. The makers of these objects traded on the legend of the fabulous ritual bronzes manufactured for the imperial court in the reign of Xuande (1426–35): most of the incense burners carried the mark of the Xuande reign, as exemplified by three of the Havemeyer pieces shown here (a, b, c).

Many of these "Xuande" incense burners survived in southern households until the turn of the twentieth century, when social turmoil and the rapidly declining economy caused them to be handed over to the antiques market. Some of these attractive bronzes, divorced from their original function and setting, were among the earliest Chinese works of art to decorate mantelpieces in Manhattan homes.

JCYW

Plate 162
COVERED EWER

China, Qing dynasty, Qianlong mark and
period, 1736–95
Porcelain painted in underglaze red,
h. 5 ¾ in. (14.6 cm)
H. O. Havemeyer Collection, Bequest of
Mrs. H. O. Havemeyer, 1929
29.100.314

Both the shape and decorative vocabulary of this splendid little eighteenth-century red-and-white ewer
pay homage to celebrated Chinese
porcelains produced during the
Ming dynasty, in the early part of
the fifteenth century. This archaism
no doubt reflects the passion for antiquities of the Qianlong emperor,
for whom the object undoubtedly
was produced.

It is believed that the prototype
for this ewer, known as a *sengmao
hu* (monk's-cap jug) because of a resemblance to the caps worn by Bud
dhist monks in winter, was first
produced during the reign of the
Ming Yongle emperor (1403–24).
These imperial porcelain *sengmao
hu* are thought to have been based
on similar metal vessels used in ritu-
als of the Tibetan sect of Buddhism,
to which the emperor was devoted.
One of the principal Tibetan lamas
of the time, Halima, as he was
called by the Chinese, was the fifth
incarnation in the Black Hat lineage
of the Karma-pa sect of Tibetan Buddhism. In 1406, at the invitation of
the Yongle emperor, Halima went
to China, where he presided at religious services for the emperor's deceased parents. Historical accounts
show that he was treated royally
and was showered with many magnificent gifts. Among them may have
been white-glazed porcelain *sengmao
hu* that were manufactured by imperial command for the occasion.

The lotus scrolls, cloud collar
points, lotus petal panels, and thun-
der pattern that are so deftly
painted on this ewer clearly parallel
incised or painted motifs that deco-

rate early fifteenth-century Ming
wares. Also from that period comes
the faint "orange peel" effect seen in
the lustrous glaze. The eighteenth-
century potter further extended his
tribute to the past in the way he
shaded his outline drawing with
small dots. This recalls the uninten-
tional "heaped and piled" effect,
which was probably due to the
presence of iron oxide in the cobalt
pigment, visible in early Ming blue-
and-white porcelains.

There is, however, one distinctly
Qing characteristic that can be seen
here: unlike his Ming predecessors,
who never fully mastered the control of copper oxide in producing
underglaze-red painted designs, the

Qing potter exhibited a truly remarkable control of this most difficult
painting medium.

The ewer is one of the finest of
the approximately 170 Chinese ceramics in the Havemeyer bequest,
which encompasses examples from a
broad time span: pieces from the
Han, Tang, Song, and Yuan as well
as Qing dynasties are included. The
majority are porcelains dating to
the Qing dynasty: underglaze blue-
painted pieces, as well as objects
with tea dust, white, *sang de boeuf*,
and peachbloom monochrome glazes
typical of the Chinese ceramics favored by American collectors of the
late nineteenth and early twentieth
centuries.   SGV

House and Furnishings

THE HAVEMEYER HOUSE

ALICE COONEY FRELINGHUYSEN

 Louisine and Henry Osborne Havemeyer lavished as much attention on the interior decoration of their mansion at 1 East 66th Street as they did on each aspect of their collecting endeavors. This exceptional house is important in a number of respects. For one, it epitomizes decorating principles current in the late nineteenth century, including the juxtaposition of many different flat patterns, the use of a wide variety of wall coverings—in this case mosaic, fabric, stenciled and painted, and carved—a predilection for a subdued palette, and a concern for the display of art objects. Further, it highlights the special relationship between two great art patrons of the late nineteenth and early twentieth centuries and the two men of enormous talent who designed the interiors of their home—Louis Comfort Tiffany (1848–1933) and Samuel Colman (1832–1920). The Havemeyer house presents an unusual opportunity to examine in depth what is arguably Tiffany's most extraordinary interior: although the building was demolished in 1930, unlike most homes with Tiffany interiors, it was well documented photographically soon after it was completed,[1] a number of the original architectural details and Tiffany-designed furnishings still survive, and the client—Louisine Havemeyer—left behind detailed accounts of the design process in her memoirs. In addition, the house represents a summation of many of the design tenets that Tiffany valued and pursued throughout his career.

The Havemeyers' first residence, purchased in 1884 prior to the birth of their first child, Adaline, was a modest brownstone town house at 34 East 36th Street, across the street from affluent neighbor J. Pierpont Morgan. Unfortunately, no photographs or other documents of the interior of this house survive. Horace, their second child, was born in 1886 and a third child, Electra, arrived in August of 1888; by the end of the latter year the combination of a growing family and a significant increase in Mr. and Mrs. Havemeyer's collecting activities compelled them to begin thinking

about a larger house. During the 1870s and 1880s fashionable New Yorkers were moving north on Fifth and Madison avenues, and the Havemeyers would decide to live farther uptown, one block from equally well-to-do Mrs. William Astor.

In 1889 the Havemeyers purchased land on the northeast corner of Fifth Avenue and 66th Street on which to build their new residence. Mr. and Mrs. Havemeyer chose as their architect Charles Coolidge Haight (1841–1917), who was socially well connected but not particularly inspired. Haight had built few houses of note, and the Havemeyers' reason for selecting him is not known. They may have been influenced by Tiffany, who had worked with Haight on the Leonard Jerome house at Madison Avenue and 26th Street in 1884, when it was renovated and adapted for use by the Manhattan Club. In about 1888, at the time the Havemeyers approached him to create the interiors of their home, Tiffany was producing windows for Christ Episcopal Church, at 71st Street and Broadway, which Haight was designing.

Like Tiffany's own residence at 72nd Street and Madison Avenue, designed by Stanford White and built about 1885, the Havemeyer house, which was begun by 1890, was built in the Romanesque Revival style (fig. 26). Characteristic features of this style, which had been in vogue in America for over a decade, were the exterior material—granite cut in quarry-faced random ashlar—the large round turreted bay that bulged out at the Fifth Avenue corner, and the round-arched openings of the three ground-floor windows and the door.[2] Also typical of this mode was the four-story mansion's effect of massiveness and severity achieved by Haight's minimal use of ornament. The entrance, rather than giving directly onto Fifth Avenue, was placed discreetly on the side street.

If the house was conspicuously conservative on the outside, its internal spaces would depart substantially from the norm, for the Havemeyers were impatient with the repetitive interior treatments in the homes of their

Figure 26. The
H. O. Havemeyer
house, Charles
Coolidge Haight,
architect, 1 East
66th Street, New
York, ca. 1920s

peers and neighbors, families like the Goulds, the Vanderbilts, or the Astors. Mrs. Havemeyer recalled saying to her husband on a particularly tiring day of visiting: "I felt dizzy and confused as I was ushered into one room after another, for they were all alike. The popular decorator of the day had done them all with impartial similarity."[3] The latter sentiment was underlined by a contemporary architect, who remarked, "My patrons all want Louis Fourteenth 'street' apartments."[4]

The Havemeyers, by virtue not only of their wealth but also of their temperaments, were equipped to experiment in the realm of interior decoration. Unlike their society neighbors, who clung to imported or imitation European furnishings and hangings, they had the courage to move away from traditional, conservative taste and to embrace creative, original—and American—solutions. To accomplish a dramatic break with the prevailing decorating idiom, the Havemeyers entrusted the interiors of their new residence to Tiffany and Colman.[5]

Tiffany began his career in interior decoration in 1878, when he designed his own home on the top floor of the Bella Apartments on East 26th Street. Here he utilized a wide range of designs and motifs borrowed from exotic cultures, including Japan, India, and the world of Islam, combining disparate elements in re-

freshing relationships. The impression conveyed was unusual to say the least, original yet harmonious. Even this, his earliest project, reveals the underlying principle of Tiffany's artistic philosophy, that aesthetic effect is the primary justification of decoration—an essential tenet of the American Aesthetic movement of the mid-1870s to the mid-1880s.

In 1879 Tiffany formed an interior design firm called Louis C. Tiffany and Associated Artists with Colman, Lockwood de Forest, and Candace Wheeler. Each of the four artists involved in this collaborative effort would bring to bear on the firm's commissions his or her special talents and interests. De Forest's forte was the design of carved woodwork and furniture, for which he established a shop in Ahmadabad, India, in 1881. Colman's main responsibility was the design of and color choice for fabrics, wall and ceiling papers, and painted or stenciled patterns. Wheeler was a specialist in textile design and art embroidery. The rooms created by the firm incorporate a profusion of pattern on floors, walls, and ceilings; all manifest a feeling for textures and unusual materials, a concern for the display of collections, particularly of pottery and porcelains, and a preference for motifs and designs of an exotic nature, especially those with an Indian, Islamic, or Japanese flavor.

Associated Artists experienced meteoric success,

Plate 163. Tiffany Glass and Decorating Co., New York. *Entrance hall doors, exterior*, 1891. Wood, copper, beach stones, and favrile glass, 100 1/16 x 36 3/16 x 3 15/16 in. (254.2 x 91.9 x 9.9 cm). The University of Michigan School of Art and College of Architecture and Urban Planning, on extended loan to the University of Michigan Museum of Art, Ann Arbor (1986.146.3a,b)

Plate 164. Tiffany Glass and Decorating Co., New York. *Entrance hall doors, interior*, 1891 (see plate 163)

Figure 27. Interior view of entrance hall doors

which was in large part due to Tiffany's social connections. During its short life the company created designs for some of New York's most successful business magnates, for the Veterans' Room of the Seventh Regiment Armory in New York,[6] and the White House, as well as for America's most famous author, Mark Twain. Despite its achievements, the partnership of Tiffany, Colman, de Forest, and Wheeler dissolved in 1883, after only four years of collaboration.

After the demise of Associated Artists, Tiffany continued to design interiors on his own. By 1885, together with Stanford White, he built a massive residence for his father at Madison Avenue and 72nd Street. In the apartment he designed for himself on the top two floors of this house, Tiffany incorporated objects from diverse cultures as an integral part of the interior scheme and in particular demonstrated his debt to Near Eastern art and architecture. The Havemeyer house would be his next important project.

Although there is no record of when the Havemeyers first met Tiffany, it can be presumed that Colman introduced them. Clearly Colman and Harry Havemeyer were acquainted by 1875 or 1876, as they often attended exhibitions together; in 1876, for example, Colman accompanied Havemeyer to the Centennial Exhibition in Philadelphia, where both men became intensely interested in the displays from the Far East, especially those of Japan. Mrs. Havemeyer recounted that "my husband bought many beautiful objects of art and a collection of Japanese textiles, a wonderful lot of brocades of lustrous gold and silver, and rich blues, reds and greens [from this exhibition]. Never did more splendid fabrics come out of the East."[7] In fact, it was on the occasion of their visit to the Philadelphia Centennial that Colman suggested a novel way of decorating Mr. Havemeyer's rooms, an idea that was to be realized fourteen years later.

The interiors of Colman's own Newport house, although far more modest than the Havemeyer rooms, may have influenced the scheme at 1 East 66th Street. In particular, Colman's quiet color harmonies, wall patternings, and displays of Chinese and Japanese ceramics and bronzes as well as Near Eastern works of art find echoes in the Havemeyer home. Undoubtedly, the concern for such features that both Colman and Tiffany revealed in their work inspired the Havemeyers to entrust the decoration of their house to the two artists.

Tiffany was engaged to design the interiors of the Havemeyer house with the assistance of Colman by 1888; although the construction of the building was completed in spring 1890, the interiors, which were well under way by late 1891, were not finished until spring 1892. The Havemeyer commission afforded an unusual opportunity for Tiffany and Colman, who were often restrained by their wealthy clients, to work with both artistic and financial freedom. Thoroughly confident that Tiffany and Colman would invent decorative schemes hospitable to their diverse collections, Mr. and Mrs. Havemeyer gave the two designers full rein to develop their ideas, with little attention to the substantial costs involved.[8] For their part, Tiffany and Colman were familiar with the Havemeyers' possessions and at ease with their taste, so similar to their own.

All of Tiffany's interiors, and those of the Havemeyer house in particular, are characterized by a close and ultimately homogeneous accord among their many disparate decorative elements. Each room of the Havemeyer residence had its own theme and unity and, in turn, worked with the adjoining spaces to create a larger, harmonious whole. As Siegfried Bing, the Parisian dealer who played a key role in defining and developing international Art Nouveau, observed about the Havemeyer interiors, "Art objects of the most far-flung origins are placed side by side, but the ingenious eclecticism responsible for these interiors has so skillfully combined disparate elements, integrating them so artfully, that we are left with an impression of perfect harmony."[9]

The ingenious eclecticism Bing perceived epitomized the prevailing historicism of late nineteenth-century taste and allowed Tiffany to assemble a remarkable amalgam of non-Western and Western elements—Japanese, Chinese, Islamic, Byzantine, Celtic, and Viking—which he wove into a gleaming, integrated setting for the Havemeyers' collection. "The whole house is a background for the objects it contains,"[10] said another visitor, aptly expressing Louisine's own sentiments. However, the house was far more than a background; it also stood alone, with a character and unity related to yet independent from the collections it embraced. Tiffany was able to achieve harmonious and unified effects in the Havemeyer house, as well as in his other projects of the period, through his sensitive arrangement of elements and because the many materials he

Figure 28. Main entrance hall

used were fabricated in his own studios—the Tiffany Glass and Decorating Co.—in the era of the Havemeyer commission. Thus the various branches of the industrial arts were brought together, as craftsmen skilled in the techniques of metal, wood, glass, and paper worked with a single vision, making lighting fixtures, fabrics, hand-blocked wallpapers, rugs, glass mosaics, and cast ornamental bronze objects. (Teakwood carvings were executed in India from Tiffany and Colman's designs.)

In the Havemeyer rooms, above all in its glass, Tiffany revealed his genius as a colorist and a luminist. He called himself "a humble believer in Color"[11] and valued color above form and line, much like the French Impressionists, whose work was to be displayed in the house. Again like the Impressionists, he loved light, which, in the context of his work in glass, was as essential to him as color. As Tiffany utilized glass "in any

place that could provide a rationale for its sparkle,"[12] its role in his interiors, especially in the Havemeyer house, was paramount, whether in the form of leaded-glass windows, mosaics, lighting fixtures, cabochons, hanging chains, or balustrades. Also paramount, therefore, was the role of light—light as it filtered through the colored shapes of a leaded-glass window or illuminated a lamp or chandelier or gave life in the form of sparkling reflections on a mosaic or a melting glow on an iridescent vase. Perhaps it was in terms of their shared feeling for color and light that the sensibilities of the Havemeyers—the great patrons of Impressionism—and Tiffany were most closely attuned.

The first thing a visitor saw upon entering the house was an extraordinary pair of doors, which are unique in Tiffany's oeuvre in terms of use and combination of materials. Appropriately, the patinated bronze frame and large applied bronze studs of the exterior of the

Plate 165. Tiffany Glass and Decorating Co., New York. *Peacock mosaic overmantel from entrance hall*, 1891. Favrile glass, pottery, and plaster, 52 x 64 in. (132.1 x 162.6 cm). The University of Michigan School of Art and College of Architecture and Urban Planning, on extended loan to the University of Michigan Museum of Art, Ann Arbor (1986.146.9)

Plate 167. Tiffany Glass and Decorating Co., New York. *Fire screen from entrance hall*, 1891. Gilt metal and favrile glass, 39⁷⁄₁₆ x 42⁷⁄₈ in. (100.2 x 108.9 cm). The University of Michigan School of Art and College of Architecture and Urban Planning, on extended loan to the University of Michigan Museum of Art, Ann Arbor (1986.146.10)

178

Plate 166. Tiffany Glass and Decorating Co., New York. *Two mosaic frieze panels from entrance hall*, 1891. Favrile glass and plaster, each 33 ¹¹/₁₆ x 21 ¹³/₁₆ (85.6 x 55.4 cm). The University of Michigan School of Art and College of Architecture and Urban Planning, on extended loan to the University of Michigan Museum of Art, Ann Arbor (1986.146.8a,b)

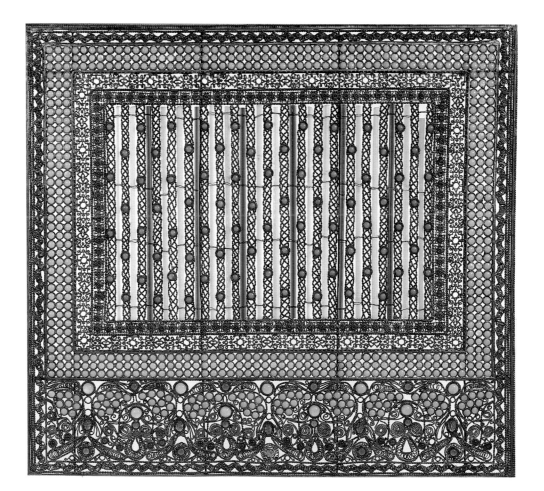

doors (pl. 163) linked them to the medieval fortress aspect presented by the facade. However, the doors are faced with marbleized opalescent glass from Tiffany's glass furnaces, offering a hint of and a transition to the luminescent, jewellike rooms within. The doors opened onto a large main entrance hall, where their appearance was transformed: intricately coiled lead came embedded with large, beach-worn quartz stones frames the interior surface and gives the marbleized panes of glass added definition and significance (pl. 164, fig. 27).

The hall was one of the most important rooms of any Victorian home. This area had a public, almost ceremonial function and suggested the character of the adjoining rooms; it was meant to be a grand space, for it provided visiting social peers with their first impression of the resident. Thus, the Havemeyers' main entrance hall (fig. 28) was one of Tiffany's most sumptuous schemes. Although sparsely furnished, it had an air of gleaming opulence, with literally every inch of surface utilized for decorative effect. The floor was embedded with over one million Hispano-Moresque tiles and the walls were completely covered in glass mosaic ornament. The late 1880s had seen a resurgence in the use of mosaics,[13] and between 1889 and 1893 Tiffany employed them extensively in his interiors, especially in churches. However, this luxurious medium was well suited to the decoration of entrance halls in homes, and Tiffany occasionally used it in the most elegant private houses, adapting the intense palette of his ecclesiastical designs to the subtler harmonies appropriate to domestic settings like the Havemeyers' hall. As Bing recalled of rooms epitomized by the Havemeyer interior, "From the walls of spacious entrance halls, gleamed a rich variety of subtle shadings, sober, chalky whites surmounted by polychromed friezes, diapered with the thousand details of woven cashmere."[14]

The particular frieze to which Bing referred encircled the Havemeyers' entrance hall and was composed of individual mosaic panels that repeated a motif of Islamic character (pl. 166). The most dazzling focal point of the glittering hall was an overmantel glass mosaic in fabulous colors showing two peacocks framed by golden scrolls (pl. 165). The opulently hued and patterned peacock was especially appropriate to the mosaic medium and was a favorite motif of late nineteenth-century artists because of its potent, many-leveled symbolism; with its admirable replication of the oily iridescence of the birds' feathers, this is perhaps the most successful of Tiffany's many renditions of the subject. That Tiffany was particularly satisfied with this piece is clear, because just two years after its completion, he duplicated the motif almost exactly in the mosaic panel that formed the reredos in his famous chapel at the 1893 World's Columbian Exposition in Chicago.[15] In the Chicago Exposition version the size of the panel is doubled and jewellike heavens are added, but the peacock design remains unchanged.

The glass mosaic faced staircase in the hall was modeled after that of the Doges' Palace in Venice, a conscious allusion to the exalted status of the inhabitants. The center of the hall was dominated by a great table and a state chair, so called for its thronelike size, and to the side of the desk stood a reversible settee derived from Indian prototypes; all were inlaid with mosaic.[16] An elaborate fire screen (pl. 167) provided additional embellishment in the dazzling entryway. Composed of delicate cast and twisted metalwork, which was originally gilt, it is reminiscent of intricate handmade Indian jewelry. The entire surface is encrusted with a variety of opalescent and amber glass jewels; amethyst glass rods contribute to the decorative effect as well as to the screen's vertical support.

In its bejeweled splendor the Havemeyer entry hall represents one of Tiffany's crowning achievements in the use of glass to create a unified decorative whole. Bing noted that "no other part of the house surpasses this room, and the other sections are grouped around it in so felicitous a manner, that it is a joy to proceed through the vast ensemble. No interior doors encumber circulation. Large archways, artistically draped, lead from one room to another."[17] Indeed, only the door to the exterior closed, and the five doorways in the hall were hung with heavy Asian portieres.

After guests had taken in the splendors of the great hall, they were led into a small reception room (fig. 29) to be greeted by their host and hostess. This room featured elegantly carved maple furniture in the Chinese taste, which was most apparent in the delicate spindles of the settee and chair backs. The set was upholstered in black velvet. The walls were covered with Chinese embroidered silk hangings. The smaller details, integral parts of the general scheme, were considered in relation to the larger objects and motifs, so that all was stylistically en suite. To this end the andirons, fire tools, and lighting fixtures above the mantel were all designed by Tiffany.

Figure 29. Reception room

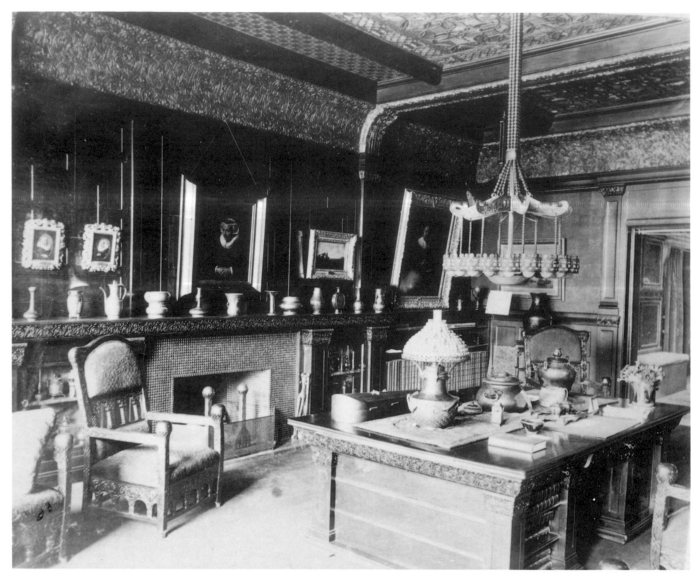

Figure 30. Rembrandt Room/library

In the library (fig. 30), also called the Rembrandt Room because it was intended to house the Havemeyers' Dutch pictures, the goal of unifying a multiplicity of diverse elements was perhaps most fully realized. The scroll motif in the carved details of the mantel was repeated throughout the room, in the architectural woodwork as well as in the furnishings. The interlaced Celtic strapwork found consistent use as a carved coved frieze, a stenciled wall pattern, carved detailing on the seating furniture, and as a design in the quilted upholstery. Although he does not identify it, Bing must have been describing this room in his essay on the industrial arts in America when he wrote: "The walls, hung with Dutch paintings, are separated from a Japanese ceiling by a frieze based upon Scandinavian designs; the lighting fixtures reveal a Byzantine influence and the furnishings, although obviously reflecting indi-

vidual taste, suggest the severe forms of our beautiful Louis XIII lines. Yet, in spite of this amalgam, the visitor is struck, from the moment he enters, by the charming atmosphere of calm and repose."[18]

Colman, who worked closely with Tiffany on this room, is credited with the design of its furniture (see pl. 168). He worked out the designs, the patterns of which were influenced by Norwegian Viking and Celtic prototypes, on wax models; the final forms, which were appropriately masculine and massive in scale, were carved in oak. Mrs. Havemeyer described the finishing process, whereby many coats of varnish were applied and buffed laboriously to create an effect akin to Japanese lacquerwork.[19] The furniture was covered in deep amber and olive silk velvet with a Celtic design quilted with colored silks that corresponded to the carving of the chairs and the woodwork; the lustrous sheen of the upholstery harmonized with the elaborate silk ceiling. Again, in the interest of unity, Tiffany designed the andirons and fireplace tools (pl. 170)—the latter with finials embellished with blue-black glass orbs—to match the furniture.

The lighting in the library is of particular interest and significance. Tiffany, deeply and consistently involved with glass and light throughout his career, designed and fabricated special-order lighting fixtures for his clients from the time of his initial interior decorating activity, but his lamps were not made available to the public at large until 1896. The fixture that hung over the desk in the library was installed in 1891 and is perhaps the earliest extant Tiffany chandelier (pl. 169). Composed of wrought metal, square, emeraldlike opalescent glass jewels, and small beach-worn stones in patterns that clearly recall medieval sources, it conceals a circle of tiny light bulbs. These bulbs illuminated the silk panels

Plate 169. Tiffany Glass and Decorating Co., New York. *Chandelier from Rembrandt Room/library*, 1891–92. Favrile glass, beach stones, and bronze, h. 70 in. (177.8 cm). The University of Michigan School of Art and College of Architecture and Urban Planning, on extended loan to the University of Michigan Museum of Art, Ann Arbor (1986.146.4)

Plate 168. Samuel Colman and Louis Comfort Tiffany, New York. Detail, *Armchair*, 1891–92. Oak and quilted silk velvet, h. 45 in. (114.3 cm). Purchase, Harry W. Havemeyer and Frelinghuysen Foundation Gifts, in memory of H. O. Havemeyer, 1992 (1992.125)

Plate 170. Tiffany Glass and Decorating Co., New York. *Pair of andirons and set of fire tools from Rembrandt Room/library*, 1891–92. Bronze and favrile glass, h. 23 ½ in. (59.5 cm). Private collection

Figure 31. Library in Samuel Colman's house, Newport, Rhode Island. Published in *Artistic Houses, Being a Series of Interior Views of a Number of the Most Beautiful and Celebrated Homes in the United States*, New York, 1883–84, vol. 1, pt. 2, opp. p. 70

of the ceiling in such a way that those who sat at the desk were conscious only of the reflected glow from above. This was Tiffany's first use in a lighting device of beach stones, whose manner of transmitting light is totally different from that of glass. Here, as in the front entrance-hall doors, he revealed his predilection for combining natural found materials with glass and metal.[20] Although Tiffany produced pioneering work in electric lighting for the Havemeyers, it is interesting to note that the library table lamp, whose shade features the same square mosaiclike glass jewels that appear in the chandelier, was without doubt lit with kerosene.

The mosaic theme of the adjoining entrance hall was reinforced in the library ceiling, where textiles rather than glass created the effect. The ceiling was composed of the lustrous Japanese silk brocades that Colman and Mr. Havemeyer had purchased at the 1876 Philadelphia Centennial Exhibition and designed by Colman based on the concept of his own library in Newport, which was completed by 1883 (fig. 31). In Newport he

had pieced together a number of different Japanese silks, described by a contemporary as "varied and deeply lustrous surfaces, simple and embroidered,"[21] and overlaid them with a network of ebony in a Persian star pattern. Colman transported the Havemeyer fabrics to his studio in his Newport home, where he arranged them in panels and outlined individual pieces with heavy braid. Once installed in the ceiling in New York, the panels were set off by richly carved moldings with patterns similar to those of the silks and burnished with gold. Mrs. Havemeyer, enraptured by the luminescence of the ceiling, admiringly remarked, "It glowed like the rich mosaic of the East, like Saint Sophia and the splendid tombs of Constantinople, like the Palatine Chapel of Palermo, the pride of Roger of Sicily. Like them our ceiling recalled the art of the East both in color and in design. . . . Many and many a time have I been questioned about this ceiling which was so full of beauty and brilliancy, so rich and yet so subdued."[22]

Fig. 32. Music room

Plate 171. Tiffany Glass and Decorating Co., New York. *Table from music room*, 1891–92. Ash, h. 27 in. (68.6 cm). Shelburne Museum, Shelburne, Vermont (3.6–104)

Plate 172. Tiffany Glass and Decorating Co., New York. *Chair from music room*, 1891–92. Ash, h. 33 ½ in. (85.1 cm). Shelburne Museum, Shelburne, Vermont (3.3–328a)

The large scale of the library's furnishings, the Celtic allusions in its design, its dark and subdued colors, and somewhat severe architectural treatment—most notable in the stark rectilinear fireplace facing composed of a small mosaic grid that is echoed in the mosaic hearth and the fire screen—as well as the function of the area as a place of work all contributed to the room's gender specificity. In every sense it was a masculine space. Without doubt it was H. O. Havemeyer's room. He personally saw to the purchase of the old master paintings, which were acquired specifically with this room in mind, and he placed his prized Stradivarius violin prominently on his massive desk. In his wife's words, "Mr. Havemeyer's library was indeed his castle."[23]

Designers and artists of the late nineteenth century were profoundly influenced by exotic cultures, particularly those of the Near and Far East—Tiffany and Colman's affinity for such sources has already been mentioned in the contexts of the Bella Apartments and the Associated Artists firm. In the Havemeyer house this taste was especially evident in Tiffany and Colman's designs for the music room (fig. 32), where an eclectic array of exotica was assembled. The walls were hung with Asian textiles, the gilded cornice and ceiling resembled Japanese bamboo, and a large cabinet at one end of the room housed the Havemeyers' collection of Japanese lacquerwork and other objects of art. According to Louisine Havemeyer, one of the carved ivory *inrō* in that cabinet "suggested the carving of the furniture."[24] However, both in style and workmanship, the furniture also appears to relate closely to Near Eastern sources (pls. 171, 172). A large suite of furniture (including at least three settees, some half-dozen armchairs and side chairs, and tables of various sizes and shapes) was designed and probably made at the Tiffany Studios. These pieces are remarkably consistent: they exhibit delicately reeded legs, each finished off with a brass claw clasping a glass ball,[25] and the crest rails of the chairs and settees as well as the skirts of the tables all show patterns dominated by intertwined naturalistic plant and flower forms in shallow relief recalling Indian carving. Although the style of this suite is anything but Art Nouveau, its decorative details and exotic references reveal parallels to Art furniture. The music room furnishings, like those of the library, were painstakingly finished: gold leaf was applied to the carved areas and then carefully rubbed to leave the details in high relief almost bare.[26] The technique created a soft,

aged appearance, suggesting that the wood had been handled for many years, and, at the same time, gave definition to the carving.

An extraordinary chandelier that defied stylistic characterization and three Tiffany-designed window panels added a flourish to the music room's decor. The inspiration for the ingenious ceiling fixture was a source in nature, the wildflower Queen Anne's lace, as a delighted Mrs. Havemeyer recognized when she exclaimed to Tiffany, "Queen Anne's Lace! . . . How well you have adapted it. Even the stems twine themselves together and disappear into the ceiling as if you had but just gathered them."[27] In fact, the dainty appearance of the flowers was closely approximated: each of hundreds of small opalescent blown-glass balls—the petals—fit into a delicate wire stem, which in turn was connected to one of two or three rings that made up a flower, into whose center a bulb was inserted; each cluster of bulbs was supported by a sinuous wire arm that radiated from a central vertical member. The lacy, realistic effect was enhanced by the slender, gently swaying chains on which the chandelier hung; one

Plate 173. Attributed to Tiffany Glass and Decorating Co., New York. *Frame*, 1892–93. Gilded wood, 43 x 50 x 4 in. (109.2 x 127 x 10.2 cm). Alexandre-Gabriel Decamps. *The Good Samaritan*, ca. 1853. Oil on canvas, 36 5/8 x 29 1/8 in. (93 x 74 cm). H. O. Havemeyer Collection, Bequest of Mrs. H. O. Havemeyer, 1929 (29.160.36) A185

Figure 33. Dining room

could imagine them to be stems moving in a slight breeze. With its long arms from which elements were suspended, the object must almost have seemed to be a giant mobile. Despite its delicacy, the scale of the fixture, which filled almost the entire room, was vast. Tiffany explained to Mrs. Havemeyer: "It [the concept] gave me an opportunity to make the chandelier as large as I pleased . . . and to diffuse the light for the musicians' needs. I put but one light in those bays over there, so those who listen will not be disturbed by any glare."[28] Tiffany's consideration must have been appreciated, for the Havemeyers took music seriously, and the musicales held in the room were important events in their social life.

Society manifested an overriding concern with material goods at the end of the nineteenth century. Thorstein Veblen, the astute commentator on the Gilded Age, perceived that in this era it was only through possessions that individuals could be judged by their peers and by the world at large.[29] Thus the display of collections became a primary concern in the decoration of the period. The popular decorating magazines of the day were filled with pronouncements on the importance of art objects in the home and with advice about how they should be shown. In this context, we can see clearly why one of Tiffany's central responsibilities was the presentation of the Havemeyers' immense and important collections. He may even have designed frames for two of their paintings (see pl. 173). Surviving records indicate that Durand-Ruel supplied most of the Havemeyers' frames; however, the frames for two works, Courbet's *Torso of a Woman* (pl. 194) and Decamps's *Good Samaritan* (pl.173), differ markedly from any others in the Havemeyer holdings, resembling neither standard European nor American examples of the period.[30] On the other hand, in their

Plate 174. Tiffany Glass and Decorating Co., New York. *Window*, 1891–92. Leaded favrile glass and wood, 28 x 47 13/16 in. (71.1 x 121.4 cm). The University of Michigan School of Art and College of Architecture and Urban Planning, on extended loan to the University of Michigan Museum of Art, Ann Arbor (1986.146.2)

Plate 175. Tiffany Glass and Decorating Co., New York. *Table from breakfast room*, 1891–92. Cherry and ebonized cherry, h. 30 in. (76.2 cm). Christian Havemeyer

Figure 34. Second-floor paintings gallery with "flying" staircase

profiles they recall frames Stanford White designed for Thomas Wilmer Dewing and other artists, and their motifs of organic curls and circles correspond closely to decorative themes in Tiffany's metalwork and his glass mosaics for the Havemeyer entrance hall.

Tiffany's most important task in terms of the Havemeyers' possessions, of course, was the design not of frames but of sympathetic environments in which to display a wide range of objects and paintings. This he did throughout the house, devoting particular rooms to specific types of material—Dutch painting in the library and Asian art in the music room, as we have seen. In the same way he made the dining room (fig. 33) the setting for the display of the Havemeyers' Hispano-Moresque lusterware and Islamic pottery, which hung on the walls or rested on the ledge at the top of the wainscoting. These pieces formed a decorative frieze

that encircled the room, much as similar objects did in Tiffany's own dining room only a few blocks away.[31] The dining room also housed the Havemeyers' collection of Barye bronzes, which were arranged in a decorative manner, with the large animals on a shelf above the mantel and the smaller ones on the mantelpiece itself and two others perched on the andirons (fig. 6).[32]

Amid this array a focal point was provided by a three-part chandelier of oxidized bronze and opalescent glass prisms suspended from the ceiling on twisted wires. Additional elements of decor were three sets of wall sconces that repeated the chandelier's components, a bay window with two Tiffany leaded-glass windows surmounted by three leaded-glass panels, a deeply coffered ceiling, and elaborately carved woodwork whose motifs were carried through in the carved oak furniture covered in blue silk. The slightly bowed profile of a sur-

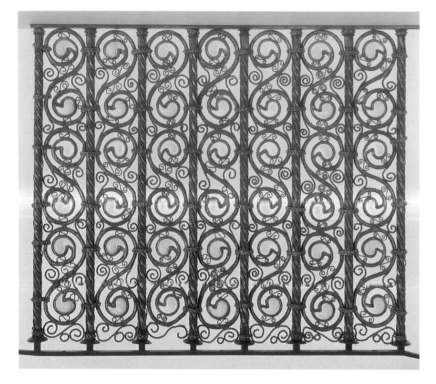

Plate 176. Tiffany Glass and Decorating Co., New York. *Partial balustrade*, 1891. Gold-plated metal and favrile glass, 31 ¹¹⁄₁₆ x 41 ⅝ in. (80.5 x 105.7 cm). The University of Michigan School of Art and College of Architecture and Urban Planning, on extended loan to the University of Michigan Museum of Art, Ann Arbor (1986.146.6)

Figure 35. Balconies surrounding the two-story picture gallery

viving leaded-glass window (pl. 174) suggests that it probably was installed in the transom of the bay in this room or in the music room. Its fluid lead lines and stylized foliage are rooted in the Art Nouveau style and reflect Tiffany's preoccupation with nature.

The adjoining breakfast room was furnished with an unusual table that can be expanded by unfolding panels on its top (pl. 175). The table's carved central medallion relates to Japanese motifs, and its ebonized legs and carved fretwork skirt also carry Asian overtones.

The single most spectacular and innovative element in the house was the second-floor gallery's golden or "flying" staircase (fig. 34), "stripped of all supporting masonry, suspended from the topmost ceiling by elegant shafts or graceful chains, sparkling with ornaments"[33]—to quote Bing. Aline Saarinen has provided the most vivid description of this extraordinary structure:

A narrow balcony with an alcove ran around the second story of the picture gallery. The spectacular staircase was suspended, like a necklace, from one side of the balcony to the other. A curved piece of cast iron formed the spine to which, without intermediate supports, the stair treads were attached. The sides of this astonishing construction, as well as the balcony railing, were a spider web of gold filigree dotted with small crystal balls [pl. 176]. The concept of a construction in space was revolutionary indeed for 1890, and its daring was dramatized by a crystal fringe on the center landing which tinkled from the slight motion when the staircase was used.[34]

The glitter of the ornaments adorning the chains and the pearliness of the opalescent glass jewels that encrusted the gilt-metal balustrade and stair risers were accentuated by the natural light that filtered through the Tiffany leaded-glass suspended ceiling above the staircase.

The balconies (fig. 35) surrounding the two-story

Figure 36. Gallery ceiling light fixtures

191

Figure 37. Louisine Havemeyer's bedroom

picture gallery were lined with display cases that held much of the Havemeyers' collection of Asian ceramics. The gallery itself, one of the more public areas in the house, was not a unique feature, for in the nineteenth century a tradition of incorporating separate semipublic museum spaces in private homes had developed. As early as 1832 Luman Reed had a private gallery for his collection of American paintings in his New York house. During the 1870s and 1880s private galleries became increasingly popular as the numbers of monied collectors who were building grand residences swelled. In fact, *Artistic Houses*, a sumptuous folio of 1883–84 devoted to the most notable contemporary houses in the United States, published discussions and photographs of no fewer than eight individual galleries. This was, after all, an era in which private individuals assembled collections that rivaled those of the newly

formed public museums and frequently set aside times for artists and other interested parties to study their holdings.[35]

The lighting of these picture galleries presented difficult problems. In the late 1870s and 1880s it was standard practice to rely on natural illumination from a leaded-glass skylight supplemented by unsightly gas jets on a central rectangular frame suspended from the ceiling. In one instance an even more infelicitous solution was devised—bare electric light bulbs projected from the walls.[36] As might be expected, Tiffany was able to achieve far more pleasing results in the Havemeyer gallery—augmenting natural illumination with artificial light provided by filigree ceiling fixtures suspended on long, heavily worked chains (fig. 36).

The furniture Tiffany designed for the gallery, of plain ivory-painted wood embellished only by uphol

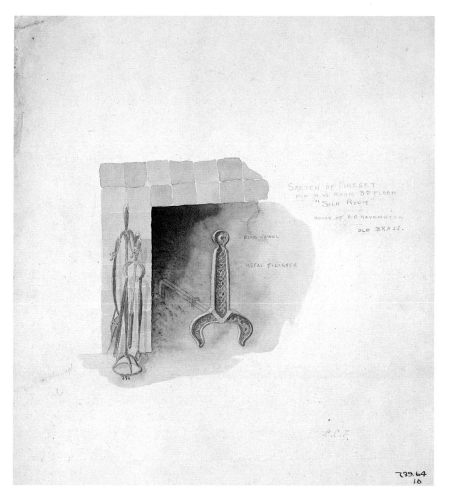

Figure 38. Louis Comfort Tiffany. *Drawing of fireset for third-floor silk room*, ca. 1891. Watercolor and pencil on paper, 14 x 11 ¹⁄₁₆ in. (35.6 x 28.1 cm). Purchase, Walter Hoving and Julia T. Weld Gifts and Dodge Fund, 1967 (67.654.405)

stery of patterned velour, stands in sharp contrast to the ornate ensembles in most of the house. It resembles the furniture Tiffany made for Laurelton Hall, his own grand summer house in Cold Spring Harbor, New York, especially that in the dining room;[37] he doubtless did not wish the furnishings to conflict or compete with the two spectacular attractions of the Havemeyer gallery—the paintings and the suspended staircase.

Tiffany borrowed concepts—in the form of motifs, colors, designs, the flavor of foreign climates—throughout the Havemeyer house, but he apparently borrowed an actual object from another country for Louisine Havemeyer's second-floor bedroom overlooking Fifth Avenue (fig. 37): what seem to be two long printing blocks, possibly Indian and perhaps for textiles, adorn the headboard and footboard of the bed. The use of this kind of found element was not unprec-

edented in Tiffany's oeuvre; in 1879–80 in the Veterans' Room of the Seventh Regiment Armory in New York, he had employed printing rolls as the legs of the massive center table and printing blocks as applied decoration on the crest rails of the large armchairs.

On the third floor, directly over Mr. and Mrs. Havemeyer's bedrooms, were two guest rooms, one of which presumably was called the silk room. Although no photographs or contemporary descriptions of these rooms survive, it can be assumed that their treatment was consistent with that of the rest of the house. A watercolor depicts one andiron and some fireplace tools for the silk room (fig. 38). The only extant known Tiffany design sketch for the Havemeyer commission, it is signed *Louis Comfort Tiffany* and inscribed *Sketch of Fireset/for N.W. Room 3d floor "Silk Room"/ House of H. O. Havemeyer* and indicates that the andiron is

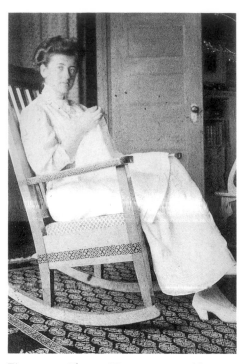

Plate 177. Tiffany Glass and Decorating Co., New York. *Dressing table, possibly from the second-floor bedroom of one of the Havemeyer children*, 1891–92. Maple, h. 31¾ in. (80.7 cm). Adaline Havemeyer

Figure 39. Electra Havemeyer Webb seated in a painted and stenciled rocking chair by Louis Comfort Tiffany or Samuel Colman, ca. 1908

meant to be old brass with an interlaced metal filigree pattern and a finial ornamented with one glass jewel. Unfortunately, this design was never executed, as the notation *not ordered* in the lower left-hand corner of the watercolor reveals.

Although the furnishings of the three children's bedrooms on the second floor, and probably of the servants' quarters as well, were simple, they showed Tiffany and Colman's distinctive touch in the form of

decorative accents. A desk or dressing table, for example, might be embellished with delicate reeded legs or one or more carved rosettes in the Japanese taste or with a bit of ornamental hardware (see pl. 177), a plain bed and dresser with carved reeding on the finials. Even an ordinary painted wood rocker bore around its seat rail a stenciled design distinctly reminiscent of Tiffany's mosaics and Colman's wall decorations (fig. 39).

The Havemeyers patronized Tiffany and Colman not

Figure 40. Architectural drawing of Hilltop, Palmer Hill, Greenwich, Connecticut, Peabody and Stearns, architects

Figure 41. The Havemeyers' villa at Bayberry Point

only for the initial decoration of 1 East 66th Street but also for the interiors of their country home and for an addition to their New York house. They engaged Peabody and Stearns of Boston to design the exterior of their country house, Hilltop (fig. 51), located on top of Palmer Hill in Greenwich, Connecticut, but entrusted at least some of the furnishings to Colman and Tiffany. Hilltop, which was completed by 1890, no longer stands, but the original architects' drawings (see fig. 40) reveal that it was a sprawling shingle-style building with weathered shingle siding, eyebrow windows, extensive porches, and broad double gables. The various rooms featured delicate Tiffany- and Colman-designed furniture and walls covered with Japanese papers in subdued colors.[38]

About 1896 Harry Havemeyer purchased one hundred acres of land at Bayberry Point, in Islip, on the south shore of Long Island, with the intention of developing the property as a modern Venice. His plan was to build a series of twelve relatively low-cost stucco villas of Venetian design on one-and-a-half-acre plots along a grand canal—the Great South Bay.[39] Ten of these houses, one of which was for the Havemeyer family (fig. 41), were completed in 1901. With their white stucco facades and projecting porticos and patios, they had an exotic look that was almost shocking

in comparison with the typical architecture of the day; they might have seemed more at home on the Dalmatian coast or in Morocco than on the shores of the Great South Bay. In fact, upon receiving a photograph of the Havemeyers' new house at Bayberry Point, Mary Cassatt exclaimed that "it is oriental, and Adaline on the balcony looks Eastern enough for Algiers or Egypt."[40] Although Grosvenor Atterbury was the architect of record for the Bayberry Point villas, Tiffany suggested their Moorish-inspired design.[41] That Tiffany greatly admired the architecture he saw in North Africa and painted views of Moorish cities with structures that bear a striking resemblance to the houses of Bayberry Point gives credence to this assumption.

A few years after the modern Venice development was built, in 1903, Tiffany was called back to 1 East 66th Street to create a large paintings gallery in a rear courtyard; the gallery was connected to the house by a corridor that displayed sculpture and led to the first-floor entrance hall. The peacock motif of the hall's overmantel mosaic was reiterated in the new corridor, where ten polygonal glass mosaic columns that rested on black marble bases were finely inlaid in a design simulating peacock feathers.[42] Leaded-glass windows (see pl. 178) that may have served as a frieze in the new corridor show a stylized geometric design that recalls

Plate 178. Tiffany Studios, New York. *Window from corridor leading to gallery*, ca. 1903–4. Leaded favrile glass and wood, 25¾ x 54 in. (65.4 x 137.2 cm). The University of Michigan School of Art and College of Architecture and Urban Planning, on extended loan to the University of Michigan Museum of Art, Ann Arbor (1986.146.1a)

the patterns of Islamic carpets. Sadly, no photographs survive of this renovation. It was probably at the same time the corridor was constructed that Tiffany made alterations to the entrance hall, placing at its center a "mosaic fountain with stained glass panel; circular bowl; and octagonal base"[43] that, as Mrs. Havemeyer explained, "was allowed to splash but a few drops at a time."[44] (This new fountain may have been the inspi-

ration for the fountain court at Tiffany's own Laurelton Hall [fig. 42], which was completed about 1905.)

Over the years the extraordinary collections and interiors of the Havemeyer house attracted many members of the international art world. Louisine recalled that "our house had a far greater reputation abroad than here, and strangers were deeply impressed by the work of Mr. Colman and Mr. Tiffany."[45] Bing toured

Figure 42. Possibly by David Aronow. *Hall at Laurelton Hall*, ca. 1920s. Gelatin silver print, 8 1/16 x 10 in. (20.5 x 25.4 cm). Part of the gift of Robert Koch to The Metropolitan Museum of Art, Department of Prints and Photographs, 1978 and 1981 (1978.646.18)

the premises shortly after the interiors were completed. He was to write about it in the most positive terms and in great detail, although he never identified the object of his praise as the Havemeyer residence. Another early and admiring visitor was the artist Jean-François Raffaëlli, who came to see the house when he lectured in New York in 1895. In his critique of the Tiffany and Colman designs for "Mr. Havemeyer's palace in New York," first published in late August of that year, he remarked:

> There the furniture also has been considered and has its individual form. Taken altogether it forms an abode in the most perfect taste, doing honor to the owner and to the artist[s] who created these things. It will certainly be imitated and perhaps will be the starting point for a decorative style in which our own individuality will have a part, instead of manifesting itself, as is the case with us here, by the owners going so far as to prefer the Louis XVI style to the Louis XIV for his bedroom, or the Louis XIII, to the Henry II for his dining room.[46]

The house continued to receive international exposure later in the decade: numerous photographs of the primary rooms and of details such as doors and particular pieces of furniture were published in two articles on Tiffany, the first in *L'Art Décoratif* of December 1898, the second in an issue of *Dekorative Kunst* of the following year.[47] Yet it was not universally praised—for example, Cassatt confided to her close friend Louisine that "much as I admire Tiffany glass, I don't like his furniture."[48] And Mary Berenson, the wife of Bernard Berenson, with whom the Havemeyers were not on particularly good terms, dismissed it as the Havemeyers' "awful Tiffany house."[49]

Miss Cassatt's and Mrs. Berenson's opinions notwithstanding, it was truly the Havemeyers' dream house, where "the mysterious gleam of a luminous wall emerge[d] from the shadows, magical in its harmonies and whose appearance, stimulating the imagination, transport[ed] it to enchanted dreams."[50] H. O. Havemeyer died in 1907, Louisine Havemeyer in 1929. Their house was demolished in 1930, after it had been stripped of every accessible decorative feature[51]—by this time, at the beginning of the Depression, Tiffany was well out of favor and the Havemeyer children were settled in their own homes.

The destruction of the Havemeyer house was an incredible loss for the history of decoration, for it was one of Tiffany's crowning achievements in functional ornamental design. The interiors were a testament to the originality and creative genius of both Colman and Tiffany as well as to the skill of the craftsmen who executed their designs. In their historicism and their attention to surface pattern, these interiors were products of their time, rooted in the traditions of art and ornament of the 1870s and 1880s. Yet in certain of their elements—the simple, geometric, light-colored painted furniture of the two-story gallery and the kinetic chandelier of the music room, for example—they presaged art movements to come. They combined many arts in ingenious, novel, and often whimsical ways; they wholeheartedly embraced lushness, naturalism, exoticism, and both technical and imaginative virtuosity, and they were one of the most important venues for the works of art produced in Tiffany's studios.

I am grateful to Adaline Havemeyer Rand, George G. Frelinghuysen, and J. Watson Webb, Jr., all grandchildren of Louisine and H. O. Havemeyer, for their clear recollections of 1 East 66th Street.

1. Views of seven room interiors in the Havemeyer house were first published in "Modern American Residences," *Architectural Record* 1 (January–March 1892), n.p.
2. For a contemporary discussion of buildings in this style, including the Havemeyer house, see Montgomery Schuyler, "The Romanesque Revival in New York," *Architectural Record* 1 (July–September 1891), pp. 34–36.
3. Havemeyer 1961, p. 12.
4. Ibid.
5. For detailed information on Tiffany, see Hugh McKean, *The*

"Lost" Treasures of Louis Comfort Tiffany, New York, 1980, and Alastair Duncan, Martin Eidelberg, and Neil Harris, *Masterworks of Louis Comfort Tiffany*, London and New York, 1989. For Colman, see Wayne Craven, "Samuel Colman 1832–1920: Rediscovered Painter of Far-Away Places," *American Art Journal* 8 (May 1976), pp. 16–37.
6. The Veterans' Room is one of the few surviving nonecclesiastical Tiffany interiors. For a discussion of this room, see Marilynn Johnson, "The Artful Interior," in Doreen Bolger Burke et al., *In Pursuit of Beauty: Americans and the Aesthetic Movement*, exh. cat., MMA, New York, 1986, pp. 126–27.
7. Havemeyer 1961, p. 16.
8. The conservative published estimate for the cost of the Havemeyer house was more than $250,000. (See "Decorating

the Havemeyer House," *New York Times*, November 8, 1891, p. 16.) However, the actual costs undoubtedly far exceeded the estimate.

9. S. Bing, "Artistic America," trans. of the 1895 French version, "La Culture artistique en Amérique," by Benita Eisler, in *Artistic America, Tiffany Glass, and Art Nouveau*, intro. Robert Koch, Cambridge, Mass., and London, 1970, p. 130.

10. Havemeyer 1961, p. 19.

11. Louis C. Tiffany, "Color and Its Kinship to Sound [Address before the Rembrandt Club of Brooklyn]," *Art World* 2 (May 1917), p. 143.

12. Bing, "Artistic America," p. 141.

13. "Mosaics in Interior Decoration," *Art Amateur* 22 (April 1890), pp. 104–5.

14. Bing, "Artistic America," p. 141.

15. See McKean, *"Lost" Treasures*, fig. 134.

16. None of the furniture from this room survives, and it is impossible to tell from the existing photographs whether the inlaid mosaic of the chair, table, and settee is glass. Tiffany was known to have employed a micromosaic composed of brass and various colorful exotic woods as well as glass mosaic.

17. Bing, "Artistic America," p. 107.

18. Ibid., p. 130, n. 1.

19. Havemeyer 1961, p. 18.

20. This chandelier and the front entrance-hall doors may represent Tiffany's first experiments with the particular combination of glass, metal, and beach stones. He used these three materials again in 1893 in his chapel at the World's Columbian Exposition in Chicago and in table lamps he designed between 1896 and about 1900. (See Horace Townsend, "American and French Applied Art at the Grafton Galleries," *The Studio and Illustrated Magazine of Fine and Applied Art* 8 [1899], p. 43.)

21. *Artistic Houses, Being a Series of Interior Views of a Number of the Most Beautiful and Celebrated Homes in the United States*, New York, 1883–84, vol. 2, pt. 1, p. 73.

22. Havemeyer 1961, p. 16.

23. Ibid., p. 24.

24. Ibid., p. 11.

25. A small number of late nineteenth-century pieces of furniture have been attributed to Tiffany on the basis of their similar reeded legs ending in brass claws and glass balls (for example, MMA 64.202.1,2). However, it is possible that other cabinetmakers as well as Tiffany used these features.

26. Havemeyer 1961, p. 11.

27. Ibid., p. 10.

28. Ibid.

29. Thorstein Veblen, *The Theory of the Leisure Class: An Economic Study of Institutions*, 1899, reprint, New York, 1953, p. 7.

30. I am grateful to Eli Wilner and Carrie Rebora for sharing their knowledge of nineteenth-century American frames with me.

31. Charles De Kay, "A Western Setting for the Beauty of the Ori-

ent: Studio Home of L. C. Tiffany, Painter, Craftsman and Collector," *Arts and Decoration* 1 (October 1911), pp. 471–72.

32. See Clare Vincent, "The Havemeyers and Antoine-Louis Barye," this catalogue.

33. Bing, "Artistic America," p. 107.

34. Aline B. Saarinen, *The Proud Possessors*, New York, 1958, p. 157.

35. Specially printed invitations were sent to art lovers to view the paintings collection in the grand gallery of the William H. Vanderbilt house, completed in 1882. Visitors were admitted through a special entrance on Thursdays between 11:00 A.M. and 4:00 P.M. from 1882 to 1884, when Vanderbilt discontinued the practice. (See Arnold Lewis, James Turner, and Steven McQuillin, *The Opulent Interiors of the Gilded Age*, New York, 1987, p. 119.)

36. For descriptions of the galleries of Mrs. A. T. Stewart, W. H. Vanderbilt, and Mrs. Robert L. Stuart, see *Artistic Houses*, vol. 1, pt. 1, pp. 10–17; vol. 1, pt. 2, pp. 118–24; vol. 2, pt. 1, pp. 87–89.

37. McKean, *"Lost" Treasures*, fig. 119.

38. Weitzenhoffer 1986, p. 52.

39. "Henry Havemeyer's Venice," *New York Times Magazine*, May 23, 1897, p. 14.

40. MC to LWH, 8/9/01, Havemeyer correspondence.

41. The title page of the real estate prospectus produced for the development, *Moorish Houses at Bayberry Point, Islip, L.I., Built by Mr. H. O. Havemeyer*, n.d., lists Atterbury as architect, "from suggestions by L. C. Tiffany."

42. *Furnishings and Decorations from the Estate of Mrs. H. O. Havemeyer*, on the premises, 1 East 66th Street, sale cat., American Art Association, Anderson Galleries, New York, April 22, 1930, p. 14.

43. Ibid., p. 16.

44. Havemeyer 1961, p. 13.

45. Ibid., p. 51.

46. [Interview] *Sun*, August 21, 1895, reprinted as "Raffaëlli on American Art," *Collector* 6 (September 1, 1895), pp. 294–95.

47. M. G., "M. Louis C. Tiffany," *L'Art Décoratif* (December 1898), pp. 105–6, 116–28; "Louis Comfort Tiffany," *Dekorative Kunst* 2 (1899), pp. 98–99, 108–20.

48. MC to LWH, 3/12/13, Havemeyer correspondence.

49. Mary Berenson in David A. Brown, *Berenson and the Connoisseurship of Italian Painting: A Handbook to the Exhibition*, exh. cat., National Gallery of Art, Washington, D.C., 1979, p. 17.

50. Bing, "Artistic America," p. 183.

51. "Havemeyer Mansion to Be Razed," *Sun*, July 30, 1930. After the house was torn down, the site remained empty for nearly two decades before a high-rise apartment building was erected in its place. (See "5th Ave. Sites of Old Havemeyer Houses Bought by Builders for Modern Apartments," *New York Times*, August 1, 1947, p. 5.)

Chronology

SUSAN ALYSON STEIN

1847

October 18 Henry Osborne Havemeyer (always known as Harry or H. O.) is born. He is the eighth of ten children of Sarah Louise Henderson (1812–1851) and Frederick Christian Havemeyer, Jr. (1807–1891). The family lives at 323 West 14th Street, New York. The sugar-refining firm of W. and F. C. Havemeyer, established in 1807, is the family business.

Havemeyer 1944, p. 67.

Figure 43. Label for sugar packaged by Havemeyers and Elder

1851

January 7 Harry's mother dies. The three-year-old is raised by his eldest sister, Mary (Mary O. Havemeyer, 1834–1865), who, on January 13, 1858, marries J. Lawrence Elder (1832–1868). Elder is the uncle of Louisine Elder, whom Harry will marry. After age fifteen, Harry is cared for by Louisine's parents and grows up in the same household as his future wife.

Havemeyer 1944, pp. 48, 67; Weitzenhoffer 1986, p. 29.

1855

July 28 Louisine Waldron Elder, the second of four children in the family, is born to Mathilda Adelaide Waldron (1834–1907) and George William Elder (1831–1873), a merchant, of 114 West 22nd Street, New York. Her two sisters are Anne (1853–1917) and Adaline (1857–1943), her brother is George (1860–1916). By 1869 the family moves to 127 West 21st Street.

Weitzenhoffer 1982, p. 28, n. 3; Weitzenhoffer 1986, pp. 19, 29–30.

1861

November 27 Harry's brother George (b. 1837) dies in an accident at the Havemeyers' sugar refinery in the Williamsburg section of Brooklyn.

Havemeyer 1944, pp. 47, 49.

1863

February 2 With the signing of a new partnership agreement between Frederick C. Havemeyer, Jr., Theodore A. Havemeyer, Harry's older brother, and J. Lawrence Elder, the family sugar-refining firm, which had operated under various names for over five decades, becomes Havemeyers and Elder.

Havemeyer 1944, pp. 110–12.

1869

February 1 Harry is admitted to partnership in Havemeyers and Elder, where he had earlier apprenticed in various aspects of the business: first in the refineries, then as assistant sales agent, and subsequently as head of the merchandising department.

Havemeyer 1944, p. 47; see Weitzenhoffer 1986, p. 30.

Figure 44. Harry, 1871, age twenty-four

1870

March 1 Harry Havemeyer marries Mary Louise Elder (1847–1897), Louisine's aunt. The couple lives at 10 West 45th Street. They have no children and are eventually divorced.

Havemeyer 1944, p. 70; Weitzenhoffer 1986, pp. 29, 260, chap. 2, n. 2.

I would like to acknowledge the enormous contribution that Frances Weitzenhoffer's scholarship has made to this chronology. My work is in large part indebted to her studies (Weitzenhoffer 1982 and Weitzenhoffer 1986) and to the extensive unpublished archives (Weitzenhoffer files) that she generously placed at the disposal of the Metropolitan Museum for the preparation of the present catalogue. I am also grateful to Rebecca A. Rabinow for her invaluable research assistance.

1873

March 25 Louisine's father dies.

Weitzenhoffer 1982, pp. 12, 28, n. 4.

Figure 45. The Elder sisters, ca. 1872. L. to r.: Louisine, age seventeen; Anne, age nineteen; Adaline, age fifteen

1874

February Mrs. Elder and her three daughters leave for Europe, arriving in Paris by the end of the month. Louisine and Adaline stay at 88, boulevard de Courcelles with the Del Sartre family. Anne and her mother stay on nearby avenue de Friedland. The girls are enrolled in Mme Del Sartre's fashionable boarding school.

Weitzenhoffer 1982, p. 12; Weitzenhoffer 1986, pp. 19–20.

February 28 Louisine and her cousin Sophie Mapes Tolles attend a musical soirée at Mme Leonard's, where they "heard some very distinguished musicians play." Louisine studies singing with Mme Leonard.

See Weitzenhoffer 1986, p. 20, with date derived from letter cited p. 259, n. 1.

March 7 The Elders attend the theater in Paris; they are joined by Emily Sartain, a thirty-three-year-old art student from Philadelphia and fellow boarder at the Del Sartre pensionnat, who had worked with Mary Cassatt in Parma in the winter of 1871–72. She accompanies the family on various excursions, including one to Fontainebleau on April 25, as well as to the theater, opera, and other events.

Weitzenhoffer 1986, pp. 20, 259, n. 1. with date of Fontainebleau excursion derived from letter cited p. 259, n. 2.

June Cassatt arrives in Paris to look for a studio. At Mme Del Sartre's she is introduced by Sartain to Louisine, on whom she makes a great impression, both in terms of her love for the art of the old masters and for her adventurous travels to Spain "in the days of the Carlista wars, or to

Italy before the bandits were controlled." Cassatt retreats for the summer to a studio in the countryside. Upon her return to Paris, she rents a studio at 19, rue de Laval.

Weitzenhoffer 1986, pp. 20, 259, n. 3.

Before October 13 The Elders sail for America.

Weitzenhoffer 1986, pp. 21, 259, n. 5.

1875

June 30 The Elders are scheduled to arrive in Paris, via the *Russia*, a "very expensive vessel." Louisine boards at Del Sartre's until the end of October.

Weitzenhoffer 1986, pp. 21, 259, n. 6.

December Harry probably meets Samuel Colman, who had "just returned from a lengthened visit to Europe," at an exhibition of the artist's works on view at "the new and well-lighted Snedecor Gallery," New York.

"Mr. Samuel Colman's Paintings," *New York Times*, December 19, 1875, p. 6, col. 7; for the probable meeting, see Weitzenhoffer 1986, p. 32.

1876

May 10–November 10 The Centennial Exhibition is held in Philadelphia (fig. 18). Harry visits the exhibition with Colman and purchases, in quantity, Japanese decorative arts, including textiles, lacquer boxes, sword guards, and dozens of lacquer *inros*.

Weitzenhoffer 1986, pp. 32–33; see also Weitzenhoffer 1982, p. 40.

Figure 46. Mary Cassatt, ca. 1872, age twenty-eight

1877

February 21 From M. Knoedler and Co., New York, Harry purchases four watercolors by Louis Rossi (A466) ($250), Vibert (A505) ($205), Earp (A276) ($10), and E. Klimsch (A337) ($60).

Knoedler sales book no. 3, p. 155, no stock nos.

Plate 179. Jean-Jacques Henner. *Louisine W. Elder, Later Mrs. H. O. Havemeyer (1855–1929)*, 1877. Oil on canvas, 25 x 19 in. (63.5 x 48.3 cm). Private collection. A323

During the year Louisine and her mother have their portraits (A323, pl. 179; A324) painted by the fashionable Salon artist Henner; they are delighted with the results.

It is probably during this visit to Paris that Cassatt takes Louisine to a color shop, likely Julien Tanguy's at 14, rue Clauzel, to see one of Degas's pastels. On Cassatt's advice Louisine buys Degas's *Ballet Rehearsal* (A215, pl. 2), for Fr 500. Her purchase of Monet's *Drawbridge* (A395, pl. 3) for Fr 300 may also date to this time. With these acquisitions Louisine becomes one of the first American collectors to own works by Degas and Monet.

Weitzenhoffer assigned both purchases to 1875 (1986, p. 21). An 1875 purchase date for the Degas no longer seems tenable, since it is unlikely that the work was executed before 1876, as Michael Pantazzi convincingly argued in Boggs et al. 1988, p. 258. According to Louisine's account in her memoirs, the Degas was her first acquisition and she "still wanted a Monet and a Pissarro" (Havemeyer 1961, pp. 249–50).

1878

February 3–March 3 Under the name G. N. Elder, Louisine lends two works to the *Eleventh Annual Exhibition of the American Water Color Society*, National Academy of Design, New York. Her Degas *Ballet Rehearsal*, as "A Ballet," is shown in the West Room along with her *Reverie* by Tofano (A490).

Shown as nos. 233, 252.

1879

October 14 Harry purchases Firmin Girard's *Ladies Caught in the Rain* (A289) from M. Knoedler and Co.,

New York, for $750; the gallery had just acquired this painting from the artist for Fr 2,000.

Knoedler sales book no. 4, stock no. 1989.

This is the probable year of Louisine's purchases of a Pissarro fan painting, *The Cabbage Gatherers* (A427, pl. 4), and a small gouache by Cassatt, a *Self Portrait* of 1878 (A49, pl. 180).

1880

February Louisine, under the name Mrs. A.S.W. Elder, lends "A Study" by Cassatt and "Jean Valjean" by Raffaëlli to the *Thirteenth Annual Exhibition of the American Water Color Society*, National Academy of Design, New York.

The Cassatt, shown as no. 628, must be the artist's *Self-Portrait* of 1878 (A49), as Weitzenhoffer first proposed (1986, p. 26). The Raffaëlli, no. 747, is presumably his *Winter Landscape with the Figure of Jean Valjean* (A439), dated 1879. The loan of the Raffaëlli was overlooked by Weitzenhoffer, who proposed that this picture was bought from Day et Cie, Paris, in 1895 (1982, p. 250, n. 53); it should, however, be considered one of Louisine's earliest purchases, acquired from that gallery in 1879.

November 18 Cassatt writes her brother Alexander: "I sent home a Diaz [de la Peña (A268)] to the Elders, for Mr. Havemeyer, they are polite enough to say they were pleased, I hope they were."

Mathews 1984, p. 152; see also Weitzenhoffer 1986, pp. 22, 260, n. 8.

Plate 180. Mary Cassatt. *Self-Portrait*, 1878. Gouache on wove paper laid down on buff-colored wood-pulp paper, 23 ½ x 17 ½ in. (59.7 x 44.5 cm). Bequest of Edith H. Proskauer, 1975 (1975.319.1) A49

1881

May Louisine is in Paris and makes several visits to the Salon, where Manet's *Portrait of M. Henri Rochefort* (Rouart and Wildenstein 1975, I, no. 366) and *Portrait of M. Pertuiset, the Lion Hunter* (Rouart and Wildenstein 1975, I, no. 365) elicit much "tittering, elbow nudging, and shoulder shrugging . . . laughter and vociferous exclamations" from the crowd.

Shown as nos. 1516, 1517; Havemeyer 1961, pp. 217–18.

June In the company of Cassatt, whose passion for Courbet is infectious, Louisine sees the small and "scantily attended" Courbet exhibition held in the foyer of the Théâtre de la Gaîté, Paris (opened June 4).

Havemeyer 1961, p. 190; opening date per *Chronique des Arts et de la curiosité*, no. 23 (June 11, 1881), p. 184.

Summer In London Louisine, her mother, and a friend of her mother's visit the *V Summer Exhibition*, Grosvenor Gallery, May 2–July 31, where they see Whistler's *Portrait of Cicely Alexander* (Young et al. 1980, no. 129), a work that "appealed to [Louisine] very much." A few days later they pay a visit to Whistler at his Tite Street studio, where Louisine buys five pastels, which the artist chooses, for a total of £30: *Campo S. Marta: Winter Evening* (A511), *Nocturne: San Giorgio* (A516), *The Steps* (A517), *Sunset in Red and Brown* (A519), *Winter Evening* (A520). Afterward Whistler delivers the framed pastels "as gaily and cheerily as any troubadour" to Louisine at her hotel in Jermyn Street, where "he touched upon every subject of interest in London at the time, artistic, theatrical, and literary," between 11:00 P.M. and 2:00 A.M. On September 21 he pens Louisine a bon voyage note and presents her with a copy of his pamphlet *Art & Art Critics* (fig. 47).

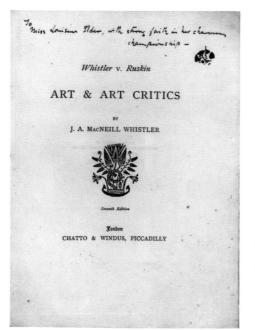

Figure 47. Cover of Whistler's *Art & Art Critics*, inscribed by the author, 1881

Sequence of events as recalled by Louisine in Havemeyer 1961, pp. 205–11, but dated on the basis of the availability of the pastels, the date Whistler's portrait of Cicely Alexander was on view in London, and the fact that he had just moved into his studio at 13 Tite Street (which he had leased on March 22). His recent occupancy of the studio would explain why Louisine did "not recall any furniture in the room, not even chairs." Nor did she remember that Whistler had exhibited any other portraits or Nocturnes in the Grosvenor exhibition —not surprisingly, since the portrait of Cicely Alexander was the only Whistler included in the show. Weitzenhoffer was the first to propose an 1881 date for the acquisition of the pastels, since they were part of the unsold surplus from Whistler's exhibition of fifty-three Venice pastels that opened on January 29, 1881, at the Fine Art Society, London (as nos. 18, 23, 25, 50, 51) (1982, pp. 17, 23, 25, n. 19; 1986, pp. 22 23, 25, n. 14). See Young et al. 1980, pp. lviii, 78–79, nos. 129. In an article she wrote on the Freer collection, Louisine noted that the letter, "which was to say 'Bon Voyage'. . . and to express the wish that I would soon return to England," was dated to the "very time he selected for me the pastels" that she later gave to the Freer Gallery of Art ("The Freer Museum of Oriental Art, with Personal Recollections of the Donor," *Scribner's Magazine* 73 [May 1923], p. 534).

September 29 Harry purchases three Barbizon paintings from M. Knoedler and Co., New York: two by Diaz de la Peña, *Children Playing with a Lizard* (A266) ($12,500) and *Forest* (A267) ($2,500), and "Roche de Berri" by Corot (possibly A112, 118, 119, 120, or 121) ($2,000). He also buys Henner's *Woman Lying on the Grass* (A325) ($3,000).

Knoedler sales book no. 4, stock nos. 3428, 3431, 2802, 3511; see note on Corot, Appendix.

Plate 181. J.-F. Millet. *Mother and Child (Les Errants)*, 1848/49. Oil on canvas, 20 x 16 in. (50.8 x 40.6 cm). The Denver Art Museum, Gift of Horace Havemeyer in memory of William D. Lippitt (1934.14) A375

November 28 Harry acquires Millet's *Mother and Child (Les Errants)* (A375, pl. 181) for $3,800 and a landscape by Rousseau, possibly *Farm in Sologne* (A468), for $2,200, from M. Knoedler and Co., New York.

Knoedler sales book no. 5, Millet, stock no. 3388; Rousseau, stock no. 3311, as "Paysage, arbres et cabanes"; see also Weitzenhoffer 1982, pp. 41, 49, n. 19; Weitzenhoffer 1986, p. 33.

1882

January 8 Fire completely destroys the twenty-five-year-old Williamsburg plant of Havemeyers and Elder; it is subsequently rebuilt into the largest and most modern sugar refinery in the world.

Havemeyer 1944, p. 67; see *Harper's Weekly* 26 (January 21, 1882), p. 36.

April 1 Harry acquires Ziem's *Venice* (A525) for $875 and R. Ribera's *Concert* (A465) for $875 from M. Knoedler and Co., New York.

Knoedler sales book no. 5, stock nos. 2559, 2864.

September 4 Harry purchases Delacroix's *Arab Rider* (A262) for $7,000 from M. Knoedler and Co., New York, but returns it to the gallery for a $7,000 credit in December.

Knoedler sales book no. 5, stock no. 4065.

Late December Louisine is in Paris. She spends time with Cassatt on December 22 and again on the day before Christmas, when they attend at the "American chapel . . . a very original service . . . a sort of Methodist performance with the Apostles Creed."

Quote from Lois Cassatt's diary entries of December 22, 24, in Frederick A. Sweet, *Miss Mary Cassatt, Impressionist from Pennsylvania*, Norman, Okla., 1966, p. 73.

Figure 48. Louisine, ca. 1882

1883

August 22 Louisine Waldron Elder and Henry Osborne Havemeyer marry in Greenwich, Connecticut. They move into a brownstone in New York at 34 East 36th Street.

Weitzenhoffer 1986, p. 29.

December The Havemeyers visit the *Pedestal Fund Art Loan Exhibition*, National Academy of Design, New York.

Weitzenhoffer 1986, p. 35.

1884

July 11 Louisine and Harry's first child, Adaline, is born at 34 East 36th Street.

Havemeyer 1944, p. 70.

Plate 182. Six of the Havemeyers' Japanese tea jars

During the year Louisine makes her first acquaintance with Japanese tea jars (see pls. 144, 182), these "pretty, dainty things" that Harry—who would eventually amass some 475 examples—"began collecting . . . in his usual way," in "grand style."

Havemeyer 1961, pp. 73–74. For futher information on tea jars, see Julia Meech, "The Other Havemeyer Passion: Collecting Asian Art," and Barbara B. Ford, "Japanese and Chinese Tea Ceramics," this catalogue.

1885

Spring Harry is among the initial subscribers to the American Art Association's *Prize Fund Exhibition*, American Art Galleries, New York, April 20–fall.

Weitzenhoffer 1982, p. 57.

Figure 49. Marcelin Desboutin. *Portrait of Paul Durand-Ruel*, 1882. Drypoint, plate: 7¾ x 5¾ in. (19.7 x 14.7 cm). Durand-Ruel Archives

Fall Paul Durand-Ruel is in New York and possibly calls on the Havemeyers.

Weitzenhoffer 1986, p. 40. After 1889 the Havemeyers bought the vast majority of their pictures through the Durand-Ruel galleries in New York and Paris. At this time the Paris establishment, at 16, rue Laffitte and 11, rue Le Peletier, was directed by Paul Durand-Ruel (1831–1922), a pioneering dealer of Impressionist works; the New York branch, which opened in 1887, was managed on a rotating basis by Paul's sons Charles (1865–1892), Joseph (1862–1928), and George (1866–1931).

October 23 Harry purchases Daubigny's "Evening on the Marne" (probably A175) for $2,675; the painting had been consigned to M. Knoedler and Co., New York, since 1882.

Knoedler sales book no. 5, no stock no.; gallery records indicate the seller's name as J. E. Chase.

1886

March 5 From the American Art Association sale of the *Art Collection formed by the Late Mrs. Mary J. Morgan*, Chickering Hall, New York, March 3–5, Harry purchases Decamps's *Christ at Emmaus* (A187) for $3,100.

Lot no. 225.

Plate 183. Rembrandt Harmensz. van Rijn. *Christ and His Parents Returning from the Temple*. Etching and drypoint, sheet: 3¾ x 5¾ in. (9.5 x 14.6 cm), cut to plate. H. O. Havemeyer Collection, Bequest of Mrs. H. O. Havemeyer, 1929 (29.107.7)

March 15 Harry acquires at least four prints from the continuation of the Morgan estate sale, *The Collection of Engravings and Etchings*: Rembrandt's *Christ and His Parents Returning from the Temple* (MMA 29.107.7, pl. 183) and *Landscape with Trees, Farm Buildings and a Tower* (MMA 29.107.34), Claude Lorrain's *Harbor with Large Tower at Left* (MMA 29.107.43), and Meryon's *Pump at Notre Dame* (MMA 29.107.105).

Rembrandts, lot nos. 2042, 2096; Lorrain, lot no. 1769 or 1770; Meryon, lot no. 2323. The Havemeyers would eventually acquire another Rembrandt included in this sale, *Portrait of Rembrandt with Plumed Cap* (MMA 29.107.25), lot no. 2026.

March 19 Louisine and Harry's second child, Horace, is born at 34 East 36th Street.

Havemeyer 1944, p. 72.

April 10 *Works in Oil and Pastel by the Impressionists of Paris*, organized by Durand-Ruel, opens at the galleries of the American Art Association, New York; the exhibition re-opens on May 25 at the National Academy of Design, New York, with the addition of twenty-one Impressionist paintings, thirteen privately owned. The latter include the Havemeyer loans of Pissarro's "Peasant Girls at Normandy" (A427, *The Cabbage Gatherers*, pl. 4) and Monet's "View in Holland" (A395, *The Drawbridge*, pl. 3). Harry, who visits the show in the company of Colman, purchases Manet's "Still Life" (A350, *The Salmon*, pl. 5) for Fr 11,000 for Louisine. He declines to buy for $2,500 Manet's *Boy with a Sword* (MMA 89.21.2, fig. 1), lent by Erwin Davis, as "it was too much for me."

Havemeyer loans, nos. 307, 308, Manets, nos. 23, 303; regarding purchases made and considered and prices, see Weitzenhoffer 1982, pp. 65, 74, n. 46, p. 76, n. 2; Havemeyer 1961, pp. 220–21. The Manet (A350) is referred to in "The Impressionists, II," *New York Mail and Express* (April 21, 1886), p. 3: "The finest work of Manet in this room, from a technical point of view, is (No. 23) Nature Morte—a salmon with culinary accessories, which is simply the perfection of still-life painting."

Spring Harry contributes to the American Art Association's second *Prize Fund Exhibition*, as he had to the first. By 1888 he is no longer listed among the subscribers to the fund.

Weitzenhoffer 1986, p. 39.

December 7 Harry returns Ribera's *Concert* (A465) to M. Knoedler and Co., New York, for a credit of $850 ($25 less than he had paid for it in 1882). He uses this credit for the $850 purchase of Clays's *On the Sheldt* (A82).

Knoedler sales book no. 6, stock nos. 5495, 5336.

1887

January 18 From M. Knoedler and Co., New York, Harry acquires Corot's "Study of Trees" (possibly A112, 118, 119, 120, or 121) for $400 plus the exchange of Firmin Girard's *Ladies Caught in the Rain* (A289).

Knoedler sales book no. 6, Corot, stock no. 5351; Firmin Girard, stock no. 5545 when returned; the latter picture was sold to Thomas P. Salter of Portsmouth, New Hampshire, on April 30, 1887; see note on Corot, Appendix.

February 23 Harry purchases four watercolors by Barye from M. Knoedler and Co., New York, for $2,000.

Knoedler sales book no. 6, no titles or stock nos., but an annotation indicates that the works were "left with Montaignac in Paris"; see note on Barye, Appendix.

December Sugar Refineries Co., the second trust in America, is formed through the merger of seventeen plants in Boston, New York, Philadelphia, and New Orleans. (Standard Oil, established by the Rockefellers in 1870 and organized as a trust in 1882, was the first American trust.) The Sugar Trust earned profits of $25,000,000 during its first two-and-one-half years of existence.

Havemeyer 1944, p. 68.

During the year Durand-Ruel opens its New York branch in modest quarters, an apartment at 297 Fifth Avenue.

1888

May Harry makes his first gift to the Metropolitan Museum: the portrait *George Washington* by Gilbert Stuart (A484).

MMA Registrar's records indicate the gift was received by the Museum on May 21.

Figure 50. The Havemeyer family, 1888. l. to r.: Horace, Louisine, Electra, Harry, Adaline

August 16 Electra, the Havemeyers' third child, is born in Babylon, Long Island.

Havemeyer 1944, p. 71.

October The Attorney General of New York objects to the Sugar Trust's attempt to absorb the North River Refining Co. and starts proceedings to annul the charter of Havemeyers and Elder Sugar Refining Co.

See Weitzenhoffer 1986, pp. 68–69; *New York Tribune*, October 9, 1888, p. 1.

Fall Plans are under way for the construction of a new residence for the Havemeyers at 1 East 66th Street, with interiors designed by Tiffany and Colman. Charles Haight is hired as architect. Construction is finished in spring 1890, but the interiors are not completed until two years later.

Weitzenhoffer 1986, pp. 49–51. For further information concerning the house, see Alice Cooney Frelinghuysen, "The Havemeyer House," this catalogue.

December 6 Harry returns Henner's *Woman Lying on the Grass* (A325) to M. Knoedler and Co., New York, for a credit of $1,750 ($1,250 less than he had paid for the painting in 1881). He applies this credit toward the $2,000 purchase of Corot's "Landscape with Pond (Le Côteau)" (possibly A122).

Knoedler sales book no. 6, stock nos. 6222, 6120.

December 8 Harry acquires from Cottier and Co., New York, Rembrandt's *Portrait of a Man* (A445, pl. 61) and *Portrait of a Woman* (A446, pl. 62) for the then staggering sum of $60,000, and Delacroix's *Expulsion of Adam and Eve* (A265, now considered Studio of Delacroix) for about $10,000. He begins collecting paintings on a grand scale. The Rembrandts and the *Expulsion* are placed on loan to the Metropolitan Museum on December 18.

See Weitzenhoffer 1982, pp. 94–95, nn. 16, 18; original bill, MMA Department of European Paintings Archives; date of loan per MMA Registrar's loan receipt book no. 4 [5], no. 21.

1889

March 2 The *22nd Annual Exhibition of the American Water Color Society*, National Academy of Design, New York, closes. From this show the Havemeyers purchase watercolors by contemporary Americans: Wiggins's *Landscape* (A522) ($35) and *Near Fontainebleau* (A523) ($200); Tryon's *Country Landscape* (A495) ($100); Ranger's *Autumn* (A441) and *Evening at Lydd* (A442) ($125 each).

Probably shown as no. 293 and nos. 333, 372, 390, 458.

March 7 Harry acquires Rembrandt's portrait *Herman Doomer* (A449, pl. 63) from William Schaus, a prominent New York art dealer, reputedly for between $70,000 and $100,000. He immediately places it on loan to the Metropolitan, where his two other Rembrandts had been on view for several months.

See Weitzenhoffer 1982, pp. 99, 117, n. 6. Schaus to HOH, 3/7/89, indicating that the Rembrandt was on loan to the Museum by this date; purchase date recorded from a lost letter from Schaus to HOH, MMA Department of European Paintings Archives.

March 19–20 Harry attends the Orties and Co. sale of *The Erwin Davis Collection of Modern Paintings*, Chickering Hall, New York. He may have bought one of the 145 paintings auctioned: *The Haymakers* (A418) by the Hungarian realist Munkácsy for $2,000.

Lot no. 103; acquisition noted in Weitzenhoffer 1982, p. 100, but seemingly refuted in Weitzenhoffer 1986, p. 54.

Plate 184. James Abbott McNeill Whistler, *The Greek Slave Girl*, ca. 1870. Pastel on brown paper, 10¼ x 7⅛ in. (26 x 18.1 cm). Shelburne Museum, Shelburne, Vermont (27.3.1–40) A512

March From an exhibition of sixty-two works by Whistler, *Notes—Harmonies—Nocturnes*, H. Wunderlich and Co., New York, Harry purchases three watercolors, *Grey and Green* (A513), *Grey and Silver* (A514), *Marine* (A515), and one pastel, *The Greek Slave Girl* (A512, pl. 184). Soon thereafter he buys from the same gallery Whistler's *First Venice Set* (Kennedy 1910, nos. 183–89, 191–95), a suite of twelve etchings that had been published by the London Fine Art Society in 1880.

Watercolors shown as nos. 36, 8, 24, pastel, no. 46; Weitzenhoffer 1982, pp. 101, 118, n. 10.

April Harry presents to the Metropolitan Museum Schrader's *Baron Alexander von Humboldt (1769–1859)* (A475), a portrait that had been commissioned by a Havemeyer relative in Berlin in 1859.

Weitzenhoffer 1986, p. 55.

Figure 51. Hilltop, the Havemeyers' Connecticut residence

May Colman is placed in charge of the decor for Hilltop, the Havemeyers' new Connecticut residence located on a ninety-acre site (subsequently expanded) in Greenwich (figs. 40, 51). Tiffany would collaborate on the interiors. The house is perched on the highest point of Palmer Hill.

Weitzenhoffer 1986, p. 51. For further information, see Alice Cooney Frelinghuysen, "The Havemeyer House," this catalogue.

June The Havemeyer family sails for France, arriving during the last week in the month.

June 21–August *Claude Monet, A. Rodin* is held at Galerie Georges Petit, Paris. Louisine probably visits this large exhibition of paintings by Monet and sculpture by Rodin.

Weitzenhoffer 1986, p. 60.

June 29–30 At the preauction display of the *Collection de M. E. Secrétan*, Galerie Charles Sedelmeyer, Paris, July 1–7, Harry is "too excited over the other [old master] pictures in the exhibition, many of which he intended to buy," to give ample attention to Courbet's *Landscape with Deer* (fig. 52), a picture Louisine thinks is "splendid" and wants to acquire. Though not "favorably impressed" at first, by July 1 Harry—who had left Paris for a business trip—cables "Buy the Courbet." Despite his quick turnaround, it is too late: on July 1, the picture is sold to the Louvre for Fr 76,000. Regretting the loss of this Courbet, "he immediately told Durand-Ruel to try to get him one as fine."

Lot no. 6; Havemeyer 1961, p. 191; see also Weitzenhoffer 1982, p. 107.

Figure 52. Gustave Courbet. *Landscape with Deer*, 1866. Oil on canvas, 68½ x 82¼ in. (174 x 208.9 cm). Musée d'Orsay, Paris (RF 583)

July 1 On the first night of the Secrétan sale, Durand-Ruel obtains the following oils for the Havemeyers: Decamps's *Experts* (A183, pl. 8) (Fr 70,000); Delacroix's *Desdemona Cursed by Her Father* (A264, now Attributed to Delacroix) (Fr 15,000); Gericault's *Riderless Racers at Rome* (A284, pl. 185) (Fr 9,200); Rousseau's *Hamlet in Normandy* (A469) (Fr 22,000); Ziem's *Canal in Holland* (A524) (Fr 20,500). He also secures for them a gouache by Decamps, *Christ with the Doctors* (A188) (Fr 28,500), and Millet's pastel *Peasant Watering His Cows on the Banks of the Allier River, Dusk* (A379, pl. 186) (Fr 26,000). The collectors would later return the Gericault and the Rousseau.

Plate 185. Théodore Gericault. *Riderless Racers at Rome*, 1817. Oil on paper mounted on canvas, 17 ½ x 23 ⅜ in. (44.5 x 59.4 cm). Walters Art Gallery, Baltimore (37.189) A284

Plate 187. Pieter de Hooch. *The Visit*, ca. 1657. Oil on wood, 26¾ x 23 in. (68 x 58.4 cm). H. O. Havemeyer Collection, Bequest of Mrs. H. O. Havemeyer, 1929 (29.100.7) A326

Plate 186. J.-F. Millet. *Peasant Watering His Cows on the Banks of the Allier River, Dusk*, ca. 1868. Pastel on paper, 28 ¼ x 37 in. (71.8 x 94 cm). Yale University Art Gallery, New Haven, Gift of J. Watson Webb, B.A., 1907, and Electra Havemeyer Webb (1942.299) A379

August 1 The Havemeyers purchase from Durand-Ruel, Paris, a group of old master paintings from the collection of Edouard Warneck—van der Neer's *Landscape at Sunset* (A419), Teniers's *Inn—Drinkers and Smokers* (A486), Metsu's *Fish Seller* (A372), a portrait of a man by Gainsborough (A282), and a picture by van Ostade (probably A422 or A423)—for a total of Fr 72,000. They also buy a de Hooch (A328) and a van der Cappelle *Seascape* (A47) for Fr 15,000; and Corot's *Destruction of Sodom* (A100, pl. 14), formerly in the Camondo collection, for Fr 125,000. The Havemeyers will later return the Teniers and the van de Cappelle to the gallery.

Durand-Ruel Archives, which indicate that these works were paid for on August 1, the same day as the pictures acquired for the Havemeyers from the Secrétan sale. The total paid on this date was Fr 822,200.

Plate 188. Etching after Gustave Courbet. *Landscape with Cattle*, 1859. Oil on canvas, 27 ½ x 35 ⅜ in. (69.9 x 89.9 cm). Location unknown

Lot nos. 11, 18, 35, 72, 83, 84, 100; Durand-Ruel Archives confirm that these works were purchased for the Havemeyers on the first day of the sale and were paid for on August 1. There has been confusion about the Havemeyers' acquisitions from the Secrétan sale because a contemporary art critic, writing under the pseudonym Montezuma, erroneously reported that Theodore Havemeyer (Harry's brother) bought the Decamps gouache (A188, lot no. 84) and that H. O. Havemeyer purchased Diaz's *Descent of the Gypsies* (lot no. 20) and Delacroix's *Christopher Columbus* (lot no. 16), which "proved too large to be seen to advantage in his house, and I understand that Durand-Ruel, through whom he bought it, will take it off his hands" ("My Note Book," *Art Amateur* 21 [November 1889], p. 115). Durand-Ruel Archives indicate that the Delacroix was purchased by Boussod, Valadon et Cie, Paris, for Fr 36,000, but have no information about the buyer of the Diaz.

July 2 On the second day of the Secrétan sale, Durand-Ruel obtains the old master pictures Harry wanted: Codde's *Dutch Family* (A85) (Fr 11,000); Cuyp's *Cuyp Designing After Nature* (A172) (Fr 41,000); a pair of small panel portraits by Hals, *Petrus Scriverius* (A320, pl. 64) and *Anna van der Aar* (A319, pl. 65) (Fr 45,500 each); and de Hooch's *Visit* (A326, pl. 187) (Fr 276,000).

Lot nos. 105, 107, 124, 125, 128; Durand-Ruel Archives indicate that these works were purchased for the Havemeyers and paid for on August 1.

August 17 Louisine and Harry buy their first Courbet, *Landscape with Cattle* (A130, pl. 188) for Fr 20,000. Though the collectors had wanted a picture similar in quality to the one they lost at the Secrétan sale, Paul Durand-Ruel had been able to locate for them only this "fine, but not remarkable Courbet."

Havemeyer 1961, p. 191; see also Weitzenhoffer 1986, pp. 58, 80; purchase date and price of *Landscape with Cattle*, stock no. 2440, as "Vaches," per Durand-Ruel Archives.

August 21 From Durand-Ruel, Paris, the Havemeyers buy their second landscape by Courbet, *The Source of the Loue* (A140), for Fr 15,000, and a Decamps, *The Good Samaritan* (A185, pl. 173), for Fr 55,000.

Late August Harry and the children meet Cassatt for the first time, at the artist's apartment at 10, rue de Marignan; she had broken her leg in a riding accident and was confined to bed. It is possibly during this visit that Cassatt presents Louisine with a monotype by Degas of a nude girl putting on her stocking (pl. 80). From this point on, Cassatt is on the "lookout" for new acquisitions for the Havemeyers.

Cassatt's accident is described in an undated letter from Degas to Henri Rouart; on the basis of the other events discussed, this letter can be firmly assigned to August 1889 (see *Lettres de Degas*, ed. Marcel Guérin, Paris, 1931, no. LXXX, pp. 118–19, erroneously dated [1888]). Louisine recalled that the meeting took place in the summer of 1889, after they bought "one of [Courbet's] landscapes" (unpublished chapter on Cassatt not included in Havemeyer 1961, MMA Archives). See also Weitzenhoffer 1982, p. 280, n. 21; Weitzenhoffer 1986, pp. 60, 116, 262, n. 13.

Summer The Havemeyers make several visits to the Exposition Universelle, or World's Fair, in Paris. The many attractions of the fair include the newly erected Eiffel Tower and La Galerie des Machines, but the Havemeyers are especially drawn to the *Exposition Centennale des Beaux-Arts* in the palace of the Champs de Mars. Here they see for the first time two paintings they would later own, Courbet's *Woman with a Parrot* (A145, pl. 19) and Manet's *Boating* (A358, pl. 31). However, what interests Harry at this date is an oil by Fromentin, *The Arrival of Calife*, which he tries to purchase from the lender, M. Van den Eynde, but it is not for sale. The following summer Paul Durand-Ruel advises Harry that the Fromentin may now be available for "the price formerly refused," but it is not acquired.

Courbet shown as no. 210, Manet, no. 498, Fromentin, no. 353; PD-R to HOH, 7/90, also recommending a watercolor concert given by monkeys and a "superb" painting illustrating the fable *La Mort et le bûcheron* by Decamps, neither of which is acquired, correspondence, Weitzenhoffer files.

September 9 The Havemeyers acquire from Durand-Ruel, Paris, their only painting by Boudin, *Washerwomen near a Bridge on the Touques River* (A44); they would return this small oil panel to the dealer ten years later.

October 10 Harry and Louisine purchase Courbet's *Hunter in the Snow* (A155) from Durand-Ruel, Paris, for Fr 7,000.

October 21 Corot's *Young Women of Sparta* (A111, pl. 189) is acquired by the Havemeyers from Durand-Ruel, Paris, for Fr 8,400.

Durand-Ruel Archives.

Plate 189. Camille Corot. *Young Women of Sparta*, 1868–70. Oil on canvas, 16½ x 29½ in. (41.9 x 74.9 cm). The Brooklyn Museum, Gift of Mrs. Horace Havemeyer (42.195) A111

October 30 From Galerie Durand-Ruel, Paris, the Havemeyers purchase Puvis de Chavannes's *Allegory of the Sorbonne* (A438), which they lend to the Metropolitan Museum from November 1890 to April 1891. This fall they also buy Millet's pastel *Temptation of Saint Hilarion* (A385) from the gallery.

MMA Department of European Paintings Archives; see also Weitzenhoffer 1982, pp. 132, 143, n. 21.

Late October Durand-Ruel sells Renoir's *Young Woman Reading*, 1889 (A461), to the Havemeyers for Fr 1,500; the gallery had just bought this pastel from the artist for Fr 500. Louisine would return it to Durand-Ruel in 1908.

See Weitzenhoffer 1982, p. 113.

Before November 27 The Havemeyers, who had planned to stay longer in Paris, return home, as one of their children had fallen "ill with mucous fever." Their premature departure prevents them from seeing etchings by Pissarro about which they had inquired.

MC to Camille Pissarro, 11/27/89, cited in Weitzenhoffer 1986, p. 61.

During the year The Havemeyers purchase from Cottier and Co., New York, a *Still Life* by William Kalf (A336) and *The Domestic* by Mettling (A373).

In his Newport studio, Colman designs the Havemeyer library ceiling panels from Japanese textiles Harry had purchased at the Philadelphia Centennial of 1876.

Harry joins the Grolier Club of New York.

Weitzenhoffer 1986, pp. 51–52.

December 1889–January 1890 The Havemeyers visit the *Barye Monument Fund Exhibition*, American Art Galleries, New York, November 15, 1889–January 15, 1890, which includes over five hundred works by Barye and over one hundred works by his contemporaries. The show encourages Harry (who already owned several Barye watercolors) to buy from Durand-Ruel Barye sculpture for his dining room—bronzes for the mantelpiece and a pair of andirons in the form of a lion and lioness (see fig. 6).

See Weitzenhoffer 1982, p. 113; Weitzenhoffer 1986, p. 59. For further information, see Clare Vincent, "The Havemeyers and Antoine-Louis Barye," this catalogue.

1890

January 2 The Havemeyers return to Durand-Ruel, New York, Teniers's *Inn—Drinkers and Smokers* (A486) for a credit of $6,000; they purchase de Hooch's *Concert* (A327) for the same amount.

Durand-Ruel Archives.

April 3 An exhibition of Whistler's drawings, watercolors, and pastels, to which Harry lends a selection of drawings, opens at the Grolier Club, New York.

Unpublished Weitzenhoffer notes from *New York Daily Tribune*, April 6, 1890; April 12, 1890.

April 9 Louisine and Harry purchase Daumier's watercolor *Man Reading in a Garden* (A178, pl. 76) for $240 from Durand-Ruel, New York. The "hastily washed-in portrait sketch . . . owned by Mr. Durand-Ruel" was included in the "collection of water-colors that accompanied the [April] exhibition of artistic glass at the Union League Club." Since "a large urn belonging to Mr. Havemeyer" was among the pieces of Roman glass on view, the collectors no doubt saw the watercolor and bought it from the dealer before the show closed.

Purchase date per Durand-Ruel Archives; quote from Montezuma, "My Note Book," *Art Amateur* 22 (May 1890), p. 112.

June The Havemeyers' Connecticut residence is ready for occupancy.

Weitzenhoffer files.

November 29 On Cassatt's recommendation, Harry purchases *Masquerade* by Watteau (A508, now considered Style of Watteau) from Durand-Ruel for $8,000. It is likely that this picture is one of three works— "a Terborg, a Watteau and a Van der Meer"—that Joseph Durand-Ruel had called to Harry's attention in July of this year. During November Harry also buys Rembrandt's *Portrait of a Man— The Treasurer* (A456, now considered Style of Rembrandt) from Durand-Ruel.

JD-R to HOH, 7/18/90, correspondence, Weitzenhoffer files, partially cited in Weitzenhoffer 1982, p. 141, n. 8, and Weitzenhoffer 1986, p.

64. Durand-Ruel Archives indicate that the Parisian collector Warneck had deposited the Watteau with Durand-Ruel in June and sold it to the gallery in October.

November 1890–April 1891 H. O. Havemeyer lends fourteen pictures to the Metropolitan Museum's *Loan Collection of Paintings*, held in the Old Eastern Gallery.

The Metropolitan Museum of Art Hand-Book No. 6, New York, n.d., pp. 15–16, nos. 1–14.

During the year The New York branch of Durand-Ruel moves to a new location, 315 Fifth Avenue.

1891

January 10 Over twenty refineries are incorporated in New Jersey as the American Sugar Refining Co. subsequent to the reorganization of the Sugar Trust by the Havemeyers and their associates "due to questions regarding its legality." Harry serves as President and Chief Executive Officer of the company until his death in 1907.

Havemeyer 1944, p. 68.

February 1 In the article "Corot as Figure Painter" in the *Collector*, Corot's *Portrait of a Child* (A98, pl. 15) is referred to as belonging to the Havemeyers, the source of this acquisition is unknown.

Vol. 2 (February 1, 1891), p. 77, cited in Weitzenhoffer 1982, p. 143, n. 19.

February 3 Harry purchases Rembrandt's *Portrait of an Old Woman* (A11, now considered Style of Backer) from Durand-Ruel, New York, for $50,000. He seems to have taken on approval but decided not to keep Rembrandt's *David Playing Before Saul* (Bredius/Gerson 1969, no. 526), a much-acclaimed work. Despite Durand-Ruel's urgings, he also declines to acquire Ter Borch's *Glass of Lemonade* (Gudlaugsson 1960, no. 192c), a painting originally offered to him in July 1890.

See Weitzenhoffer 1982, p. 126; Weitzenhoffer 1986, p. 64. For Harry's brief ownership or possession on approval of Rembrandt's *David Playing Before Saul*, see A. B. de Vries et al., *Rembrandt in the Mauritshuis*, The Hague, 1978, p. 164, n. 11. Notes on the reverse of the photograph of the picture in the Photo Archives, Frick Art Reference Library, New York, record H. O. Havemeyer as a former owner and indicate that it came from and was returned to Durand-Ruel, Paris.

February 13 On the third day of the sale of the *George I. Seney Collection*, Assembly Room, Madison Square Garden Building, New York, February 11–13, Charles Durand-Ruel purchases Troyon's *Landscape at Sunset* (A491) for the Havemeyers for $2,900.

Weitzenhoffer 1982, pp. 130, 142, n. 15.

Plate 190. Alexandre-Gabriel Decamps. *The Oak and the Reed*, 1842. Location unknown. A194

February 18 From Durand-Ruel Harry buys Decamps's *Eastern Farm* (A190), *Eastern Travellers* (A191), and *The Oak and the Reed* (A194, pl. 190). The last, purchased for $8,000, would be sold back to the gallery in 1909.

Durand-Ruel Archives; Weitzenhoffer 1982, pp. 130, 142, n. 14. It was reported that *Le Chêne et le Roseau* (*The Oak and the Reed*) "est exposé dans les galeries Durand-Ruel" ("Courrier d'Amérique," *L'Art dans les Deux Mondes*, February 17, 1891, p. 148).

March 21 Harry testifies in New York before the Senate Committee on General Laws, whose investigation of the affairs of the Sugar Trust, in particular the reasons for its reorganization in New Jersey, had commenced several weeks earlier. Harry's brother Theodore testifies on March 23.

New York Tribune, March 22, 1891, p. 3, col. 3; March 24, 1891, p. 3.

March Harry's Oriental and Greek objects are mentioned in "Notes for Collectors" in the *Art Courier*.

Vol. 24 (March 1891), p. 2.

April From Durand-Ruel Harry buys Dupré's *Forest* (A270) and *The Woodcutter* (A272), the latter for $13,000. However, by 1898 he is disenchanted with these acquisitions: he sells back *The Forest* in March and tries to dispose of *The Woodcutter* in December, the same month he and Louisine purchase major works by Manet and Courbet.

Purchase price and early consignment dates for *The Woodcutter* per GD-R to LWH, 11/3/09, correspondence, Weitzenhoffer files.

The Havemeyers are in Paris. Presumably during this trip, Louisine and Harry visit Degas's studio in the company of Cassatt and buy his *Collector of Prints* (A197, pl. 44) for Fr 3,000 or Fr 5,000. Degas retains the oil to "add a few touches" and does not release it to the Havemeyers for three years. This month Cassatt has her first solo show, *Exposition de tableaux, pastels, et gravures par Mlle Mary Cassatt*, at Durand-Ruel, Paris.

Weitzenhoffer 1982, p. 164; Weitzenhoffer 1986, p. 81. Other visits to Degas's studio by the Havemeyers also resulted in acquisitions. On one occasion, for example, they left his studio with three drawings of ballet dancers on pink paper (A206, 208, 221), which Louisine kept in a portfolio under the sofa in her upstairs sitting room (Havemeyer 1961, pp. 251–52).

May–November H. O. Havemeyer lends twelve pictures to the Metropolitan Museum's *Loan Collection of Paintings* held in the Old Eastern Gallery.

The Metropolitan Museum of Art Hand Book No. 6, Part 2, Loan Collections, New York, n.d., pp. 15–16, nos. 1–12.

June 18 On the last day of the sale of *The Collection of Prints and Drawings formed by Francis Seymour Haden, Esq.*, Sotheby, Wilkinson & Hodge, London, June 15–18, Durand-Ruel purchases eight Rembrandt drawings (A447, 448, 450, pl. 66, A451–54, and A335, now considered Hans Jordaens III) for the Havemeyers.

Lot nos. 582, 584, 587, 590, 573, 586, 577, 589.

June 23 Joseph Durand-Ruel asks Harry if he wishes the gallery to pursue "one or several" Troyons from the collection of "Mr. Miéville of London." On July 11 he suggests that Harry offer Fr 400,000 for three of the paintings. No sale is consummated.

For correspondence pertaining to this offer, see Weitzenhoffer 1982, pp. 142–43, n. 17. Four paintings by Troyon were sold from the *Highly Important Collection of Ancient and Modern Pictures formed by Jean Louis Miéville, Esq. deceased . . .*, Christie, Manson & Woods, London, April 29, 1899, lot nos. 44–47 (*illus.*).

July 28 Harry's father dies.

Havemeyer 1944, p. 48.

Plate 191. Mary Cassatt. *The Coiffure*, 1891. Color print with drypoint, soft-ground etching, and aquatint, 14 ¼ x 10 ½ in. (36.2 x 26.7 cm). Shelburne Museum, Shelburne, Vermont (27.6.8–18)

August As soon as the works arrive in New York, the Havemeyers buy from Durand-Ruel a complete set of ten colored aquatints by Cassatt (Breeskin 1948, nos. 143–52; see fig. 23, pl. 191); these prints had formed the core of Cassatt's show at Durand-Ruel, Paris, in April.

See Weitzenhoffer 1982, pp. 156–57, 167, n. 20.

Figure 53. The Havemeyer house at Fifth Avenue and 66th Street, ca. 1901

November 8 The *New York Times* reports that "decorators have been at work for eighteen months in the interior of Henry O. Havemeyer's house, 1 East 66th Street, and will not finish before Spring. . . . Meanwhile the family occupy only a part of the house."

P. 16.

1892

January Harry advises Durand-Ruel that a syndicate of New York collectors, of which he is a member, is willing to offer Fr 8,500,000 to buy the celebrated collection of nearly four thousand medieval and Renaissance objects amassed by the late Fréderic Spitzer of Paris. The bid is too low and presumably is not raised. Consequently, the Spitzer collection—which the syndicate had hoped to preserve intact for an American museum—is disseminated when it is sold at auction the following year.

Weitzenhoffer 1982, pp. 202–6.

January–March The *Architectural Record* devotes its "Modern American Residences" section to the Havemeyer home at 1 East 66th Street, publishing seven photographs of the interior (see figs. 28, 29, 30, 32, 34, 35).

Vol. 1 (January–March 1892), n.p.; *Architectural Record* 1 (April–June 1892), n.p., illustrates the Havemeyer Building, at Church, Cortlandt, and Dey streets, designed by George B. Post.

February 1 A brief article on the Havemeyers' collection of old masters appears in the *Collector*; the anonymous au-

thor remarks "that they are, with scarcely an exception, in magnificent condition and of the finest representative quality, in only a few instances having even been touched with the impudent brush of the restorer."

"The World of Collectorship," *Collector* 3 (February 1, 1892), pp. 97–98.

February 28 Harry purchases a Barye watercolor, "Panther and Serpent," from M. Knoedler and Co., New York, for $950.

Knoedler sales book no. 6, no stock no.; see note on Barye, Appendix.

March 10 Harry buys Corot's "Meadow" (possibly A112, 118, 119, 120, or 121) from M. Knoedler and Co., New York, for $2,500.

Knoedler sales book no. 6, stock no. 7110; see note on Corot, Appendix.

Plate 192. Style of Rembrandt. *Portrait of a Man with a Breastplate and Plumed Hat*. Oil on canvas, 47¾ x 38¾ in. (121.3 x 98.4 cm). H. O. Havemeyer Collection, Bequest of Mrs. H. O. Havemeyer, 1929 (29.100.102) A457

Plate 193. Style of Rembrandt. *Portrait of a Woman*. Oil on canvas, 47⅝ x 38⅝ in. (121 x 98.1 cm). H. O. Havemeyer Collection, Bequest of Mrs. H. O. Havemeyer, 1929 (29.100.103) A458

June In Trouville Charles Durand-Ruel, acting on Harry's behalf, arranges to purchase from the Princesse de Sagan her pair of Rembrandt portraits of a man and a woman (A457, 458, now considered Style of Rembrandt, pls. 192, 193). Cassatt sees the works on view at Durand-Ruel, Paris, in early July, before they are shipped to the New York branch and acquired by the Havemeyers on September 7. Shortly thereafter, Harry buys from the princess Rembrandt's *Portrait of a Young Man in a Broad-Brimmed Hat* (A459, now considered Style of Rembrandt). This would be Harry's last Rembrandt acquisition, since he feels that his library, the Rembrandt Room (fig. 30), is complete now that it houses eight portraits by the master.

Weitzenhoffer 1982, p. 129; Weitzenhoffer 1986, p. 65; purchase date per MMA Department of European Paintings Archives.

June 2–3 At the sale of the *Collection de M. Barbedienne*, Durand-Ruel, Paris, the gallery purchases a large Decamps pastel, *The Battle of Jericho* (A189), for Fr 52,600 and two Barye paintings, *Lion Resting* (A29) and *Tiger Lying Down* (A38), for Fr 9,400 and Fr 7,100, respectively. On June 17 the three works are sold to Harry, the Decamps for the same amount, but the Baryes with a 5-percent commission added to the purchase price.

Lot nos. 120, 1, 5; Durand-Ruel Archives.

July 15 Joseph Durand-Ruel recommends Courbet's *Hunting Dogs* (A128) to Harry, with an asking price of Fr 35,000; by August 19 arrangements are made for its shipment from Paris to New York. At about this time the Havemeyers pass up opportunities to buy Delacroix's *Ophelia* (Johnson 1986, no. 282) for Fr 75,000 and Daumier's *Third-Class Carriage* (A177, pl. 261) for Fr 45,000. Louisine would, however, purchase the Daumier in 1913.

Weitzenhoffer 1982, pp. 163–64, 168–69, nn. 35–37; Weitzenhoffer 1986, p. 209; prices per JD-R to HOH, 7/15/92, correspondence, Weitzenhoffer files.

Plate 194. Gustave Courbet. *Torso of a Woman*, 1863. Oil on canvas, 29 1/2 x 24 in. (74.9 x 61 cm). H. O. Havemeyer Collection, Bequest of Mrs. H. O. Havemeyer, 1929 (29.100.60) A137

October 19 The Havemeyers acquire their first nude by Courbet when Harry purchases for Louisine the artist's *Torso of a Woman* (A137, pl. 194) from Durand-Ruel, New York, for $1,800. Despite Harry's initial disapproval of the painting, it soon becomes—he would often maintain—"next to the Rembrandts—my favorite!"

Quote from Havemeyer 1961, p. 193.

November 9 H. O. Havemeyer's donation of $10,000 to help keep the Metropolitan open on Sundays (a practice initiated on May 31, 1891) is reported to the Museum's Board of Trustees.

MMA Archives.

December 3 The American Fine Arts Society's Vanderbilt Gallery opens on West 57th Street. Harry, who had

pledged $5,000, was among the original contributors to the building campaign.

Weitzenhoffer 1986, p. 68.

1893

January Harry buys two bronzes and a watercolor by Barye from Durand-Ruel.

Weitzenhoffer 1982, p. 199; see note on Barye, Appendix.

January 30 Louisine convinces her husband to purchase their second nude by Courbet, *The Woman in the Waves* (A148, pl. 20), from Durand-Ruel, New York, for $5,000.

February 8 Harry acquires from Durand-Ruel Dupré's *Pasture* (A271) for Fr 100,000 (about $20,000) and Troyon's *Return from Market* (A493), valued at $45,000. The Dupré would be sold back in five years.

For the dollar valuations, see Weitzenhoffer 1982, p. 199.

February 13–March 31 The Havemeyers lend two Rembrandt portraits (A449, pl. 63, and A11, now considered Style of Backer) and "An Interior" by de Hooch (probably A326, pl. 187) to a special *Loan Exhibition* at the Fine Arts Society Building, New York. Harry had served on the organizing committee for the show, which was selected largely from the collections of its trustees and others affiliated with the society.

Shown as nos. 15–17.

Plate 195. Samuel Colman. *Spanish Peaks, Southern Colorado, Late Afternoon*, 1887. Oil on canvas, 31 1/8 x 72 1/4 in. (79.1 x 183.5 cm). Gift of H. O. Havemeyer, 1893 (93.21) A87

March 29 Harry attends the sale *Paintings in Oil and Water-Color by Samuel Colman*, Fifth Avenue Art Galleries, New York, with Henry Marquand, President of the Metropolitan Museum. He purchases Colman's *Spanish Peaks, Southern Colorado, Late Afternoon* (A87, pl. 195) for $700 in order to present it to the Museum.

Lot no. 51. The price paid was the second highest of the auction. It was reported in the *Art Amateur*—perhaps erroneously, since there is no supporting documentation—that "the highest price given at the sale was $1,000 for a Venetian 'Moonrise—Early Evening,' which was bought by Mr. H. O. Havemeyer" (28 [May 1893], p. 155). MMA Registrar's loan receipt book no. 4 [5], no. 117, indicates that the gift was received by the Museum on April 1.

March 31 The Havemeyers acquire from Durand-Ruel, New York, Millet's pastel *Peasant Children at Goose Pond* (A377, pl. 9) for $7,000 and charcoal drawing *Girl with Sheep* (A382) for $3,000.

Durand-Ruel Archives.

April 17–June 16 From the enormous, long-running sale *Objets d'Art et de Haute Curiosité du Moyen Age et de la Renaissance composant l'important et précieuse collection Spitzer*, held at the Spitzer family's mansion in Paris, Harry apparently buys "some delightful terra-cotta Asia Minor groups." Curiously, however, despite Paul Durand-Ruel's urgings, he does not place bids on any of the furnishings, glass, or small fifteenth-century Belgian tapestries, in which he had expressed interest the previous year.

Quote from Montague Mark, "My Note Book," *Art Amateur* 29 (September 1893), p. 80; see Weitzenhoffer 1982, pp. 206–9, 218, n. 18.

May 1 The World's Columbian Exposition opens in Chicago and features the loan exhibition *Foreign Masterpieces Owned in the United States* (through October 30). The show of 126 works was organized by Sara Hallowell, who by January 6 of this year had persuaded her friends the Havemeyers to lend Corot's *Destruction of Sodom* (A100, pl. 14) and Courbet's *Hunting Dogs* (A128).

Shown as nos. 2886, 2898; see Weitzenhoffer 1982, pp. 187–88.

The New York branch of Durand-Ruel purchases Corot's *Eel Gatherers* (A109) from Erwin Davis for $10,000 and sells it to the Havemeyers the same day for $12,000.

May 26 Harry buys Louisine a $100,000 five-strand pearl necklace with diamond clasp that had been displayed by the Parisian jeweler Vever at the World's Columbian Exposition in Chicago. The day before he had bought from the same jeweler three rings for a total of $18,300.

Photocopy of bill of sale from Vever (19, rue de la Paix, Paris) preserved in Weitzenhoffer files.

October 20 The Havemeyers purchase Decamps's *Smyrna Harbor* (A182) for $2,800 from Durand-Ruel, New York. Louisine would try to sell this picture back to the gallery in 1908.

Durand-Ruel Archives; see Weitzenhoffer 1982, p. 217, n. 3.

Plate 196. Edouard Manet. *Ball at the Opera*, 1873. Oil on canvas, 23 ¼ x 28 ½ in. (59.1 x 72.4 cm). National Gallery of Art, Washington, D.C., Gift of Mrs. Horace Havemeyer in memory of her mother-in-law, Louisine W. Havemeyer (1982.75.1) A357

1894

January 16 Louisine and Harry acquire five Impressionist paintings from Durand-Ruel, New York: Manet's *Ball at the Opera* (A357, pl. 196), a picture that Count Isaac de Camondo had wanted to buy; Sisley's *Banks of the Seine, near the Island of Saint-Denis* (A477); Monet's *Customs House at Varengeville* (A401), *Morning on the Seine* (A410), and *Haystacks (Effect of Snow and Sun)* (A406), the first three oils by the artist they purchase jointly; a color print by Cassatt, *The Banjo Lesson* (Breeskin 1948, no. 156); and three works on paper by Degas—two landscape pastels over monotype (one of which is A248) and one drawing of dancers (possibly *Two Dancers* [A229]). In addition they buy Delacroix's *Christ Asleep During the Tempest* (A261, pl. 197) and Corot's *Albanian Woman*

Plate 197. Eugène Delacroix. *Christ Asleep During the Tempest*, 1853. Oil on canvas, 20 x 24 in. (50.8 x 61 cm). H. O. Havemeyer Collection, Bequest of Mrs. H. O. Havemeyer, 1929 (29.100.131) A261

(A117) but return to the gallery a Courbet still life with apples (A153).

Regarding Camondo's interest in the Manet, see Havemeyer 1961, pp. 219–20. Durand-Ruel Archives indicate that the Degas landscapes were stock nos. P2761/NY1101 and P2752/NY1102. The latter, which was returned on February 13, 1894, can be identified as *Landscape* (A248). The Havemeyers bought three more monotypes in February, one in March, and another the following September. All seven (A245–51) were purchased from the artist on June 2, 1893, for Fr 1,000 each and sold to the Havemeyers as "Paysage, pastel" for $460 each (or Fr 2,000). Only P2752/NY1102 can be identified, since its return distinguishes it from the other six, which are identical, save for their stock numbers, in the gallery records.

Plate 198. Edgar Degas. *Landscape with Cows*, ca. 1888–92. Pastel over monotype on off-white laid paper, 10 ¼ x 13 ⅞ in. (26 x 35.2 cm). Private collection. A245

February 13 The Havemeyers purchase three more pastel over monotype landscapes by Degas from Durand-Ruel, New York, for $460 each (see A245, pl. 198, A246, 247, 249–51). However, they return one of the landscapes (A248) they had selected on January 16.

Durand-Ruel Archives, stock nos. P2758/NY1138, P2753/NY1140, P2775/NY1137; see January 16, 1894, n.

February 16 Louisine and Harry are sleigh riding when a "runaway horse" collides with their cutter and throws the couple "heavily to the frozen ground." The accident, which Harry survives "without a scratch" and in which Louisine sustains "an ugly scalp wound, as well as some bruises," is described two days later as "a narrow escape from death."

New York Times, February 18, 1894, p. 9, col. 5; see also Weitzenhoffer 1982, pp. 224–25, 244, n. 5.

March 1 The Havemeyers buy another pastel over monotype landscape by Degas from Durand-Ruel, New York, for $460 (see A245–47, 249–51).

Durand-Ruel Archives, stock no. P2762/NY1103; see January 16, 1894, n.

June 12 Accused of lobbying on behalf of his interests through substantial campaign contributions in 1892–93, Harry testifies before the United States Senate Sugar Investigating Committee in Washington, D.C. He "declares . . . he made no threats and demanded no favors because of campaign contributions." The case is sent to the Grand Jury of the Criminal Court of the District of Columbia after Harry declines, upon the advice of counsel on June 13, to furnish data on these contributions.

Quote from *New York Tribune*, June 13, 1894, p. 4, col. 1; see also Weitzenhoffer 1982, pp. 223, 244, n. 4.

June The Havemeyers purchase from Durand-Ruel, New York, Cassatt's *Family* (A50, pl. 199), a painting that Alfred Pope had returned to the gallery on May 24.

Weitzenhoffer 1982, p. 211.

October 1 The Grand Jury of the Criminal Court of the District of Columbia issues an indictment against Henry O. Havemeyer, President, and John E. Searles, Secretary, of the Sugar Trust, for influencing legislation through campaign contributions.

See Weitzenhoffer 1982, pp. 223–24, 244, nn. 3, 4.

October 24 Cassatt, interceding for Galerie Durand-Ruel, tries to persuade Degas to release *The Collector of Prints* (A197, pl. 44) to the Havemeyers, as three years have passed since its purchase; on December 13 the gallery is finally able to send the long-awaited picture to New York; it arrives on February 12, 1895.

MMA Department of European Paintings Archives.

November 14 Corot's *Italian Woman* (A116) is acquired from Durand-Ruel, New York, by the Havemeyers.

November Durand-Ruel's new gallery (figs. 54, 55), located in a building owned by H. O. Havemeyer—the former Lorillard mansion at 389 Fifth Avenue, on the corner of East 36th Street—holds its inaugural exhibition.

Plate 199. Mary Cassatt. *The Family*, ca. 1892. Oil on canvas, 32 ¼ x 26 ⅛ in. (81.9 x 66.4 cm). The Chrysler Museum, Norfolk, Virginia, Gift of Walter P. Chrysler, Jr. (71.498) A50

Figure 54. Facade, Durand-Ruel gallery, Fifth Avenue at 36th Street, New York, 1894–1904. Durand-Ruel Archives

Figure 55. Interior, Durand-Ruel gallery, New York, December 1894. Durand-Ruel Archives

Weitzenhoffer, 1986, pp. 94–95.

December 18 The Havemeyers purchase Degas's *Woman Ironing* (A205, pl. 87) for Fr 2,500 from Durand-Ruel, New York.

1895

January 12 On the opening day of an exhibition of forty landscapes by Monet at Durand-Ruel, New York (through January 27), the Havemeyers purchase the artist's *Poplars* (A407, pl. 35) and *Haystacks in the Snow* (A405, pl. 200); the latter was lent to the exhibition by Pope.

Shown as nos. 14, 16.

February Raffaëlli, who is in New York prior to the opening of his retrospective exhibition at the American Art Galleries, late February–March 16, visits the Havemeyers and finds their "abode in the most perfect taste, doing honor to the owner and to the artist[s] [Tiffany and Colman] who created these things."

Quote from interview in the *Sun*, August 21, 1895; reprinted in "Raffaëlli on American Art," *Collector* 6 (September 1, 1895), pp. 294–95. Raffaëlli's presence in New York by mid-February can be established from an entry dated 2/14/95 in Theodore Robinson's diary: "to Weir for dinner to meet Raffaëlli," Weitzenhoffer files.

By March 12–30 The Havemeyers anonymously lend Manet's *Salmon* (A350, pl. 5) and *Ball at the Opera* (A357, pl. 196) to the artist's first one-man exhibition in America, *Paintings by Edouard Manet*, Durand-Ruel, New York.

Dates and title of show per review, *New York Times*, March 12, 1895, p. 4, col. 7.

March 13 The Havemeyers consign for sale to Durand-Ruel, New York, a Barye bronze, *Lion and Serpent*, and van Ostade's *People Playing Bowls* (A422); on March 20 they consign Metsu's *Fish Seller* (A372) to the gallery.

Unpublished Weitzenhoffer notes from Durand-Ruel American stock book, 1894–1905.

March 30 Harry purchases a Degas pastel, *Racehorses in Training* (A255, pl. 46), from the New York branch of Durand-Ruel.

April 8 One week after the Manet exhibition at Durand-Ruel, New York, closes, the Havemeyers buy two more works by the artist: *The Grand Canal, Venice (Blue Venice)* (A359, pl. 30) for $12,000 and *Luncheon in the Studio*

Plate 200. Claude Monet. *Haystacks in the Snow*, 1891. Oil on canvas, 23 x 39 in. (58.4 x 99.1 cm). Shelburne Museum, Shelburne, Vermont (27.1.2–106) A405

Plate 201. Edouard Manet. *Luncheon in the Studio*, 1868. Oil on canvas, 46⅝ x 60⅝ in. (118.4 x 154 cm). Neue Pinakothek, Munich (inv. 8638) A349

(A349, pl. 201) for $7,000. The former had been admired by Cassatt and especially by the press, but the latter was not so well received; in fact, Harry did not particularly like it and would return it in October. Also on April 8, in advance of the opening of the show of sixty-four works by Cassatt at the same gallery (April 16–30), they acquire Cassatt's *Mother and Child* (A52) and *Baby's First Caress* (A53) for $2,000 and $6,000, respectively. For a Fr 5,000 (about $1,000) credit, they return to Durand-Ruel a seascape by van de Cappelle (A47), which would be sold to John G. Johnson on April 22 for $1,000.

Transaction dates and prices per Durand-Ruel Archives; see also Weitzenhoffer 1982, pp. 237, 246–47, nn. 29, 31; Weitzenhoffer 1986, p. 102. The Havemeyers would eventually acquire three other paintings shown in the Manet exhibition: *Gare Saint-Lazare* (A356), *A Matador* (A348), *The Dead Christ and the Angels* (A346).

April 25   On the first day of the liquidation sale *The Artistic Property Belonging to the American Art Association*, Chickering Hall, New York, April 25–27, 29–30, the Havemeyers purchase Monet's *View of Rouen* (A393) and *Floating Ice* (A398, pl. 36) for $2,600 and $4,250, respectively.

Lot nos. 146, 163.

May 8   The Havemeyers consign van Marcke's *Milking* (A368) to Durand-Ruel, New York; it is bought by the gallery two years later.

Unpublished Weitzenhoffer notes from Durand-Ruel American stock book, 1894–1905.

June 6   The Havemeyer family sails to London on the *Teutonic* with Adaline and Samuel Peters, Louisine's sister and brother-in-law. They are in London through mid-July.

Per D-R to MC, 6/7/95; GD-R to MC, 7/13/95, correspondence, Weitzenhoffer files.

June 15   At the important sale *Modern Pictures Chiefly of the Early English School, James Price, Esq. Deceased*, Christie's, London, Thomas Agnew bids unsuccessfully for Harry Havemeyer on Gainsborough's *Portrait of Lady Mulgrave* (Waterhouse 1958, p. 79, version 1). It is sold for £10,500 (£500 more than the limit Harry had set) to a Mr. Campbell, presumably as agent for Cornelius Vanderbilt. Angered by his loss, Harry would avoid further dealings with Agnew's firm.

Lot no. 70; Weitzenhoffer 1982, p. 238; more obtusely in Weitzenhoffer 1986, p. 104.

July 14   The Havemeyers arrive in Paris, where they spend a few days and see objects of interest in Emile Gavet's collection: a large tapestry, a case with Italian faience, a case with medallions, a piece of Italian ebony furniture, a por-

trait of François I, and a marble by Mino da Fiesole. Negotiations are left to Paul Durand-Ruel, and on July 31 Harry purchases Mino's *Virgin and Child* (MMA 29.100.25, pl. 202) for the asking price of Fr 120,000; it is shipped to New York on November 30.

Dates in Paris per GD-R to MC, 7/13/95, correspondence, Weitzenhoffer files; see Weitzenhoffer 1982, pp. 239, 249, n. 46; Weitzenhoffer 1986, pp. 104–5; purchase price and acquisition and shipping dates per Durand-Ruel book no. 2, 1892–1897, pp. 198–99, Weitzenhoffer files; for an indication of works in the Gavet collection that the Havemeyers must have seen, see *Objets d'Art et de Haute Curiosité de la Renaissance, Tableaux, Tapisseries composant la Collection de M. Emile Gavet*, Galerie Georges Petit, Paris, May 31–June 9, 1897, which includes a sixteenth-century Italian-school portrait of François I, lot no. 763.

Plate 202. Mino da Fiesole. *Virgin and Child*, ca. 1465–70. Carrara marble, 37 ¼ x 23 in. (94.6 x 58.4 cm). H. O. Havemeyer Collection, Bequest of Mrs. H. O. Havemeyer, 1929 (29.100.25)

July 18   The Havemeyers are in Basel at the Hôtel des Trois Rois. By this date Paul Durand-Ruel has succeeded in acquiring for them—"at a 1,000 franc reduction"—the Millet watercolor of interest, *Girl Burning Weeds* (A381), for Fr 7,000.

PD-R to HOH, 7/18/95, correspondence, Weitzenhoffer files; Weitzenhoffer 1982, pp. 239, 249, n. 47; Weitzenhoffer 1986, p. 105.

August   The Havemeyer family visits Cassatt at her country residence, the Château de Beaufresne, at Mesnil-Théribus, some fifty miles northwest of Paris. Louisine and her children may have enjoyed an extended stay while Harry was elsewhere on business. The occasion no doubt gives rise to Cassatt's pastel portraits of Louisine and Electra (A55, pl. 83) and of Adaline (A54, pl. 84).

Weitzenhoffer 1982, pp. 240, 250, nn. 48, 49; Weitzenhoffer 1986, p. 105. For more on this subject, see H. Barbara Weinberg, "Four Cassatt Pastels of Havemeyer Women," this catalogue.

August 27 In Paris the Havemeyers buy Manet's *Copy after Delacroix's "Bark of Dante"* (A343) for Fr 400 from Paul Durand-Ruel, who had just acquired it from the dealer Ambroise Vollard.

September 19 The Havemeyers purchase eleven pictures from Durand-Ruel, Paris. Six are by Degas: *The Bath* (A260) (Fr 600); *Fan Mount: The Ballet* (A224) (Fr 1,500); a landscape pastel over monotype (see A245, pl. 198, A246, 247, 249–51) (Fr 2,000); three pastels from the dealer's private collection, *Waiting* (A237) (Fr 15,000), *Dancer in Green* (A230) (Fr 5,500), *Dancer in Yellow*

Plate 203. Camille Corot. *Greek Girl—Mlle Dobigny*, ca. 1868–70. Oil on canvas, 32¾ x 21½ in. (83.2 x 54.6 cm). Shelburne Museum, Shelburne, Vermont (27.1.1-149) A113

(A219) (Fr 3,500). The others are a Millet pastel, *The Shepherdess* (A383) (Fr 7,000); Daumier's wash drawing *The Connoisseur* (A179, pl. 75) (Fr 8,000); and three major paintings, Manet's *Boating* (A358, pl. 31) (Fr 55,000), Courbet's *Deer* (A144) (Fr 7,000), and Corot's *Greek Girl—Mlle Dobigny* (A113, pl. 203) (Fr 25,000).

Partially recorded in Weitzenhoffer 1986, p. 107; Durand-Ruel Archives indicate that the Degas monotype was stock no. 2273; see January 16, 1894, n.

October 28 Galerie Durand-Ruel buys back from the Havemeyers for Fr 35,000 Manet's *Luncheon in the Studio* (A349, pl. 201).

Durand-Ruel Archives.

November The Havemeyers consign to Durand-Ruel, New York, van Marcke's *Return to the Farm* (A369), Dupré's "Paysage Route et fôret" (presumably *The Forest* [A270]), Clays's *Seascape* (see A83), and three pictures by Rousseau—two landscapes (see A469), one of which is bought back by the gallery before the end of the following year, and *Farm in Sologne* (A468), which is returned to the collectors in January. The other works would not be purchased by Durand-Ruel until 1898.

Unpublished Weitzenhoffer notes from Durand-Ruel American stock book, 1894–1905.

1896

January 6 Dupré's *Pasture* (A271) is consigned to Durand-Ruel, New York, by the Havemeyers; it, too, would not be sold until 1898.

Unpublished Weitzenhoffer notes from Durand-Ruel American stock book, 1894–1905.

Spring While Louisine is in France, Cassatt begins a pastel portrait of her, which she completes from a photograph (A56, pl. 85).

Weitzenhoffer 1986, p. 113.

Plate 204. Jan Cornelisz. Vermeyen. *Jean de Carondelet (1469–1545)*, ca. 1537–40. Oil on wood, 30¾ x 24½ in. (78.1 x 62.2 cm). The Brooklyn Museum, Gift of Mr. Horace Havemeyer (47.76) A502

Plate 205. Edgar Degas. *Dancer Onstage with a Bouquet*, ca. 1876. Pastel over monotype on laid paper, 10⅝ x 14⅞ in. (27 x 37.8 cm). Private collection. A214

August 13 Hallowell, who had moved to France in 1894, follows up on her initial communication of August 3 and advises the Havemeyers that the Duc de la Trémoïlle in Paris is willing to part with his "famous portrait by Holbein," *Jean de Carondelet* (A502, now considered Vermeyen, pl. 204), for Fr 110,000 inclusive. She also informs them that the dealer Alphonse Portier has a "charming little pastel by Degas [of] a dancer who holds a bouquet as she salutes her audience" for Fr 4,000. The Havemeyers will subsequently buy the portrait and the Degas, *Dancer Onstage with a Bouquet* (A214, pl. 205).

Quote from Sara Hallowell to HOH, 8/13/96, correspondence, Weitzenhoffer files; see also Weitzenhoffer 1986, pp. 116, 265, chap. 10, n. 16. In her memoirs Louisine recorded other purchases made through Portier—whom she called Pottier—which presumably also date to this period, 1896 until the dealer's death in 1902. According to her account, she and Harry bought a Degas pastel of *Two Dancers* (A227) for the asking price of Fr 10,000 from the noted collection of Parisian dentist Georges Viau, to whose home Portier and Cassatt escorted them; later that afternoon they went with their guides to an "attractive house" in a "distant part of Paris" and purchased Manet's *George Moore* (A360) for the same amount (Havemeyer 1961, pp. 233–35). Louisine also related that on another visit arranged by Portier and Cassatt, the Havemeyers acquired, for the asking price of $2,000, their "Taigny portrait," namely Degas's *Artist's Cousin* (A204), from the collector Edmond Taigny at 41, avenue Montaigne (Havemeyer 1961, pp. 260–61); see also Weitzenhoffer 1982, p. 259; Taigny is listed in *Répertoire Général des Collectionneurs de la France, des ses colonies et de l'Alsace-Lorraine*, Paris, 1908, p. 149, no. 4327.

August Harry begins to take an active role in extending the art collection of his neighbor Colonel Oliver Payne, by recommending works for acquisition, by engaging the services of the Durand-Ruels and Hallowell, and, later, by making purchases on his behalf.

See Weitzenhoffer 1982, pp. 286, 311, n. 1; Weitzenhoffer 1986, pp. 123–25.

Plate 206. Edouard Manet. *Georges Clemenceau (1841–1929)*, 1879–80. Oil on canvas, 37 x 29¼ in. (94 x 74.3 cm). Musée d'Orsay, Paris (RF 2641) A363

Fall The Havemeyers, accompanied by Cassatt, visit Georges Clemenceau, who lives in "a pretty villa out of the whirl of Paris." They purchase the portrait Manet had painted of him in 1879–80 (A363, pl. 206) for Fr 10,000 and "a woman's portrait in oil by Manet." Shortly afterward the Havemeyers depart for home.

Havemeyer 1961, pp. 229–31. The woman's portrait Louisine described in her memoirs—"It is not quite life-size, her hair is undone, and she leans her cheek upon her hand and looks directly at you"—is the *Portrait of Marguerite de Conflans* (A355), which was not purchased from Clemenceau but from Paul Rosenberg in 1903. The picture bought from Clemenceau is perhaps *Young Woman with Loosened Hair* (A354). No doubt she confused the two Manet portraits when she recalled the purchase years after it was made.

October 26 The Havemeyers' gift to the Metropolitan Museum of over 2,000 fragments of Japanese silks and brocades (MMA 96.14.1–.2138, see pl. 136) is accepted by the Executive Committee of the Board of Trustees. Two years earlier the Museum had expressed interest in exhibiting these textiles, which were then in the collection of S. Bing, who sent them to New York so they could be shown at the Metropolitan. Though no exhibition of the textiles seems to have taken place, their shipment was fortunate: eventually Metropolitan Trustee Samuel P. Avery persuaded Harry to buy the entire collection and donate it to the Museum.

MMA Archives indicate that the offer of the gift was presented to the Board in two separate groups. The first group of Japanese textiles (101 mats with 942 patterns) was presented on May 20; a second group of Japanese silks, called the Bing Collection (167 mats with 1,187 patterns), was presented on June 3. Some of the original accession numbers were subsequently reassigned as the collection was catalogued. For more on this subject, see Gabriel P. Weisberg, *Art Nouveau Bing, Paris Style 1900*, New York, 1986, p. 34.

December 8 Harry offers the Metropolitan his collection of Tiffany favrile glass. In January this group of fifty-six objects dating from 1893 to 1896 (MMA 96.17.1–56ab) is delivered to the Museum.

Weitzenhoffer 1986, p. 118. For further information on this subject, see Alice Cooney Frelinghuysen, "Favrile Glass," this catalogue.

December 15 The New York branch of Durand-Ruel purchases from the Havemeyers a Barye watercolor, *Lion* (A27), and a Rousseau landscape (see A469), which would be sold to Avery in 1899. Louisine buys Degas's *Sulking* (A201, pl. 45) from the same gallery for $4,500.

Unpublished Weitzenhoffer notes from Durand-Ruel American stock book, 1894–1905; MMA Department of European Paintings Archives.

Figure 56. Jean-Baptiste-Camille Corot. *The Golden Age*, ca. 1855–60. Oil on canvas, 21⅝ x 37⅜ in. (55 x 95 cm). Location unknown

1897

January 7 Galerie Durand-Ruel secures for a German client three Corots owned by Emile Dekens, a Belgian collector. However, once the dealers learn from Hallowell that Harry, who had passed on these pictures in March 1896, wishes to obtain them for Payne, the transaction is canceled and the pictures are sold to H. O. Havemeyer on January 9 for Fr 125,000 ($25,000). Thus, thanks to Harry's intervention, Payne acquires Corot's *Golden Age* (fig. 56) and *Woman and Cupid* (Robaut 1905, no. 1998); by March Payne decides not to buy the third painting, *Portrait of Mlle de Foudras* (Robaut 1905, no. 2133).

Weitzenhoffer 1986, pp. 125–26; see also Weitzenhoffer 1982, p. 290; additional information from D-R to HOH, cable, n.d. [ca. 1/7–1/9/97]; JD-R to HOH, 1/18/97; D-R to Sara Hallowell, 3/25/97, correspondence, Weitzenhoffer files; and unpublished Weitzenhoffer notes from Durand-Ruel stock books. These documents record the gallery's purchase of the works on January 7, 1897, and their sale to H. O. Havemeyer on January 9, 1897. JD R to HOH, 1/18/97, acknowledges payment in full for the three works.

Plate 207. Camille Corot. *Bacchante by the Sea*, 1865. Oil on wood, 15 ¼ x 23 ⅜ in. (38.7 x 59.4 cm). H. O. Havemeyer Collection, Bequest of Mrs. H. O. Havemeyer, 1929 (29.100.19) A106

February 2 Durand-Ruel purchases Corot's *Bacchante by the Sea* (A106, pl. 207) for Fr 30,750 from the Henri Vever sale, *Collection H. V.*, Galerie Georges Petit, Paris. He sells it the next day to the Havemeyers for Fr 31,500.

February 3 The Havemeyers purchase from Durand-Ruel and I. Montaignac, Monet's *Ice Floes* (A408), a painting the dealers had bought jointly from the artist for Fr 11,400. Louisine and Harry consign Pourbus's *Portrait of a Woman* (A433) to Durand-Ruel, New York.

In January Joseph Durand-Ruel had informed Harry that he was still negotiating a price for the picture with Monet (JD-R to HOH, 1/18/97, correspondence, Weitzenhoffer files).

February 6 Harry appears before a special New York State legislative committee, chaired by Senator Lexow from Nyack, that is investigating the affairs of the American Sugar Refining Co.

See Weitzenhoffer 1986, p. 118.

February 12 Harry's first wife, Mary Louise Havemeyer, dies shortly after midnight, from a heart ailment, at age fifty, at her residence in Stamford, Connecticut.

Obituary, *New York Times*, February 12, 1897.

April 26 Harry's older brother Theodore dies, after developing a severe cold, at the age of fifty-eight, at his home in New York.

Havemeyer 1944, p. 54.

May 23 The *New York Times* announces H. O. Havemeyer's plans for the construction of a dozen moderately priced Venetian-style villas—"a modern Venice"—along the beachfront property that he had recently acquired at Bayberry Point, on Long Island's south shore. Harry chooses the extreme southwest corner of the site for his own $11,000 house. By 1901, when the Havemeyers vaca-

tion here, only ten "Moorish Houses" designed by architect Grosvenor Atterbury with the advice of Tiffany have been built.

Weitzenhoffer 1986, pp. 121, 144, 148, 265, chap. 10, n. 29, chap. 12, n. 18.

Figure 57. Cover of the prospectus for the Bayberry Point development, Islip, Long Island

May 25–27 Some two and a half years after his indictment for contempt of court for refusing to provide the U.S. Senate Sugar Investigating Committee with information concerning campaign contributions, Harry is brought to trial at the Criminal Court of the City Hall, Washington, D.C. Successfully defended by a team of lawyers headed by the country's leading corporate attorney, John G. Johnson of Philadelphia, he is found not guilty and the indictment is dismissed. (Johnson is said to have asked for $3,000 and a picture from the Havemeyer collection for his services; however, Harry insists on paying him $100,000 instead.)

Weitzenhoffer 1986, p. 120; see also B. F. Winkelman, *John G. Johnson, Lawyer and Art Collector, 1841–1917*, Philadelphia, 1942, p. 297.

Plate 208. Claude Monet. *Ice Floes, Bennecourt*, 1893. Oil on canvas, 25 ½ x 39 ⅜ in. (64.8 x 100 cm). Private collection. A409

September 23 The Havemeyers, who must just have arrived in Paris from London, purchase Monet's *Ice Floes, Bennecourt* (A409, pl. 208) from the dealer Montaignac.

Figure 58. Cartoon depicting the Arbuckle-Havemeyer coffee-sugar war, 1900

A letter cited in Weitzenhoffer 1986, p. 117, indicates that the Havemeyers were in London the previous day.

September 27 Louisine and Harry buy a version of Monet's *La Grenouillère* (A389, pl. 33) from the Galerie Durand-Ruel, Paris, for Fr 12,500.

September 28 Paul Durand-Ruel brings Goya's *Bartolomé Sureda y Miserol* (A291, pl. 10) and *Thérèse Louise de Sureda* (A292, pl. 11) to the Havemeyers' attention. They buy the portraits the same day, for "less than fifty thousand [pesetas]." This acquisition marks the beginning of Louisine and Harry's interest in Spanish painting.

Weitzenhoffer 1982, p. 265; for purchase price, see Havemeyer 1961, p. 136.

By mid-October The Havemeyers return to New York.

October 15 Paul Durand-Ruel, who had learned on September 22 that Harry wished to acquire Courbet's *The Stream* (A126), obtains the picture from Haro père et fils, Paris. The Chicago collector Charles Tyson Yerkes had also wanted the painting; however, the dealer sells it instead to Harry for Fr 66,950 ($13,390) on October 19.

See Weitzenhoffer 1986, p. 117.

October 25 Harry is "taken ill at his residence." Stock prices fall until he is diagnosed and undergoes surgery for appendicitis on November 1. He returns to his office at 98 Wall Street just before the end of the year.

New York Times, November 5, 1897, p. 5; *New York Tribune*, December 30, 1897, p. 7.

During the year H. O. Havemeyer takes over several coffee-roasting plants in response to the Arbuckles' challenge to the Sugar Trust. The Arbuckles, who control world trade in packaged coffee, had extended their interests to include the refining and packaging of sugar.

See Weitzenhoffer 1986, p. 138.

1898

January 4 Cassatt, who had been abroad for two decades, returns to America for a visit, arriving in New York aboard the *Bretagne*. After spending the first two weeks of her stay in her hometown of Philadelphia, she visits the Havemeyers in New York. The artist returns to France in the spring.

See Weitzenhoffer 1986, pp. 127–28.

January 20 In Cassatt's company, Louisine purchases Manet's *Port of Calais* (A353) from the New York branch of Durand-Ruel for $3,500. The gallery buys back van Marcke's *Return to the Farm* (A369), which the Havemeyers had consigned for sale two years earlier.

The Manet purchase is described in Havemeyer 1961, pp. 222–23; date of van Marcke sale per unpublished Weitzenhoffer notes from Durand-Ruel American stock book, 1894–1905.

February 14 The Havemeyers acquire Degas's *Ballet from "Robert le Diable"* (A202, pl. 7) from Durand-Ruel, New York, for $4,000. They sell the gallery Pourbus's *Portrait of a Woman* (A433), which had been on consignment for a year.

Boggs et al. 1988, no. 103; the sale per unpublished Weitzenhoffer notes from Durand-Ruel American stock book, 1894–1905.

Figure 59. Edgar Degas. *The Dance Class*, 1874. Oil on canvas, 32¾ x 30¼ in. (83.2 x 76.8 cm). Bequest of Mrs. Harry Payne Bingham, 1986 (1987.47.1)

February 19 Paul Durand-Ruel acquires Degas's *Dance Class* (MMA 1987.47.1, fig. 59) from Jean-Baptiste Faure and recommends it to the Havemeyers. According to Louisine, Harry, in a spirit of great generosity, "relinquished" the picture to Payne, who acquires it from the gallery's New York branch on April 4 for $25,000 (Fr 125,000).

Havemeyer 1961, p. 263; see Weitzenhoffer 1986, p. 126; Boggs et al. 1988, no. 130.

February 28 An exhibition of Cassatt's paintings, pastels, and etchings opens at Durand-Ruel, New York; the Havemeyers lend at least three works: *Mother and Child* (A52) —which is featured on the cover of the May issue of the *Art Amateur*—*Baby's First Caress* (A53), and their portrait *Adaline Havemeyer* (A54, pl. 84).

See Weitzenhoffer 1986, pp. 129–30, where the portrait of Adaline is erroneously identified as *Adaline Havemeyer in a White Hat* (fig. 8). According to a contemporary account, the portrait of "Miss Havemeyer" exhibited was "done in browns" ("The Week in the Art World," *New York Times Saturday Review of Books and Art*, March 5, 1898). *Art Amateur* 38 (May 1898) reproduces *Baby's First Caress* on p. 131, as well as *Mother and Child* on the cover.

March 11 The New York branch of Durand-Ruel purchases six works from the Havemeyers that had been consigned to the gallery for some time: a Delacroix pastel, *Tiger* (A263), van Marcke's *Milking* (A368), a landscape by Rousseau (see A469), a seascape by Clays (see A82), and Dupré's *Forest* (A270) and *The Pasture* (A271). The gallery sells a *Madonna and Child* by Martin Schoen (Schongauer) (A285, now considered unknown German painter) to the Havemeyers for $4,000.

Unpublished Weitzenhoffer notes from Durand-Ruel American stock book, 1894–1905, without indication of consignment date for the Delacroix (dates of consignment for the other pictures are cited above); Durand-Ruel Archives.

March 30 At the auction of the Gustave Goupy collection, *Collection de M. G. G. . . .,* Hôtel Drouot, Paris, Durand-Ruel purchases for the Havemeyers Manet's *Kearsarge at Boulogne* (A347, pl. 209) for Fr 4,000 and *In the Garden* (A351, pl. 28) for Fr 22,000. Harry acknowledges his receipt of the paintings in a letter of April 27 to Durand-Ruel, in which he expresses his interest in acquiring additional marines by Manet.

Lot nos. 20, 21; see MMA 1983, nos. 122, 133; HOH to D-R, 4/27/98, correspondence, Weitzenhoffer files; see also Weitzenhoffer 1986, p. 129.

April 15 The Havemeyers purchase Monet's *Snow at Argenteuil* (A397) for Fr 1,864 ($358) from Boussod, Valadon et Cie, Paris, the gallery that had sold them Degas's pastel *Dancer Tying Her Slipper* (A233, pl. 41).

The Dieterle Archives, Getty Center, Malibu.

Plate 209. Edouard Manet. *The Kearsarge at Boulogne*, 1864. Oil on canvas, 32 x 39 ¼ in. (81.3 x 99.7 cm). Private collection. A347

April 30 Louisine convinces Harry to purchase Courbet's *Woman with a Parrot* (A145, pl. 19) for $12,000 from Durand-Ruel, New York, just before it is to be sent back to Paris. Though she acknowledged that the work was too provocative to hang in their gallery—"lest the anti-nudists should declare a revolution"—she "begged" her husband to buy it because she felt it important "to keep it in America . . . for future generations."

Havemeyer 1961, p. 196.

May 14 The Havemeyers acquire Bronzino's *Portrait of a Young Man* (A45, pl. 58) from Durand-Ruel, New York, for $40,000.

MMA Department of European Paintings Archives.

Plate 210. Claude Monet. *The Green Wave*, 1865. Oil on canvas, 19 ⅛ x 25 ½ in. (48.6 x 64.8 cm). H. O. Havemeyer Collection, Bequest of Mrs. H. O. Havemeyer, 1929 (29.100.111) A387

July 1 Louisine and Harry buy Monet's *Green Wave* (A387, pl. 210) from Durand-Ruel, New York, for $1,000.

The picture had been sold back to the gallery for $1,000 by J. Gardner Cassatt, who had acquired it through his sister, Mary, in 1883.

August 18 Paul Durand-Ruel solicits Cassatt's advice about whether to secure Courbet's *Portrait of Jo (La Belle Irlandaise)* (A147, pl. 211) for the Havemeyers before he purchases it from the Paris dealer Brame on September 9.

Plate 211. Gustave Courbet. *Portrait of Jo (La Belle Irlandaise)*, 1866. Oil on canvas, 22 x 26 in. (55.9 x 66 cm). H. O. Havemeyer Collection, Bequest of Mrs. H. O. Havemeyer, 1929 (29.100.63) A147

The painting is sent to Durand-Ruel, New York, exhibited in *Old and Modern Paintings* at the Union League Club of New York in November, and sold to the Havemeyers at the end of the year.

Weitzenhoffer 1986, p. 136; MMA Department of European Paintings Archives; Durand-Ruel Archives.

Plate 212. Edouard Manet. *A Matador*, 1866 or 1867. Oil on canvas, 67⅜ x 44½ in. (171.1 x 113 cm). H. O. Havemeyer Collection, Bequest of Mrs. H. O. Havemeyer, 1929 (29.100.52) A348

Plate 213. Edgar Degas. *The Dance Lesson*, ca. 1879. Pastel and black chalk on three pieces of wove paper joined together, 25⅜ x 22⅛ in. (64.5 x 56.2 cm). H. O. Havemeyer Collection, Anonymous Gift, 1971 (1971.185) A226

Figure 60. Edgar Degas. *The Pedicure*, 1873. Essence on paper mounted on canvas, 24 x 18⅛ in. (61 x 46 cm). Musée d'Orsay, Paris (RF 1986)

December 31 Louisine prevails over her husband's objections to Manet's large-scale works: the Havemeyers acquire from Durand-Ruel, New York, the artist's *Mlle V . . . in the Costume of an Espada* (A344, pl. 25) for $15,000, *A Matador* (A348, pl. 212) for $8,000, and *Gare Saint-Lazare* (A356, pl. 29) for $15,000; on the same day they buy Courbet's *Portrait of Jo (La Belle Irlandaise)* for $2,800. This month Harry consigns to the gallery Dupré's *Woodcutter* (A272), asking $13,000, the price he paid for it in 1891, but it is returned to him unsold in May.

Durand-Ruel Archives; consignment of the Dupré per GD-R to LWH, 11/3/09, correspondence, Weitzenhoffer files.

1899

January 3 H. O. Havemeyer informs Paul Durand-Ruel that he and Louisine are pleased with their new Degas pastels, *The Dance Lesson* (A226, pl. 213), which had belonged to Caillebotte and then Renoir, and *The Dance Examination* (A228). Harry also expresses their interest in acquiring Degas's *Pedicure* (fig. 60), albeit for a price lower than the Fr 62,500 ($12,500) that purportedly had been set by its owner, the Englishman James Burke. However, on January 13 the dealer advises the Havemeyers that *The Pedicure* had already been sold for its asking price to Camondo. This causes some friction between the Havemeyers and Durand-Ruel.

See Weitzenhoffer 1982, pp. 301–2, 315–16, nn. 37–40. Contrary to what Durand-Ruel told the Havemeyers, the gallery had purchased *The Pedicure* from Burke on December 27, 1898, for Fr 27,000 and had sold it to Camondo on January 11, 1899, for Fr 60,000; see Boggs et al. 1988, no. 120.

Plate 214. Edgar Degas. *Rehearsal in the Studio*, ca. 1874. Oil and tempera on canvas, 17 ¼ x 23 in. (43.8 x 58.4 cm). Shelburne Museum, Shelburne, Vermont (27.3.1–35a). A210

January 13 Paul Durand-Ruel urges the Havemeyers to authorize his New York gallery to purchase for them for Fr 125,000 ($25,000) two pictures by Degas that had been bought in at the Ernest May auction in 1890: a painting, *Rehearsal in the Studio* (A210, pl. 214), and a pastel, *The Rehearsal on the Stage* (A211). On January 25 Harry agrees to the acquisition, provided the price does not exceed Fr 125,000; on February 17 the Havemeyers acquire the two works, paying Fr 48,197 for the pastel.

See Weitzenhoffer 1982, pp. 304, 317, nn. 43, 44; Boggs et al. 1988, no. 125.

January 24 The Havemeyers purchase Degas's *At the Milliner's* (A236, pl. 47) from the New York branch of Durand-Ruel.

January 27 From the American Art Association sale *Valuable Modern Paintings . . . Collected by Mr. Walter Richmond*, Chickering Hall, New York, Durand-Ruel acquires Courbet's *Valley in Franche-Comté, near Ornans* (A162) for the Havemeyers for $1,900. The collectors consign Corot's *Evening* (A119) to Durand-Ruel, New York.

Lot no. 38; consignment per unpublished Weitzenhoffer notes from Durand-Ruel American stock book, 1894–1905.

February 3 Paul Durand-Ruel recommends to the Havemeyers a Degas painting that Cassatt greatly admires "of two dancers, one of whom sits on a piano" and Manet's "Femme à la guitare" (*Street Singer*, fig. 61). On February 20 Harry purchases the Degas, *Dancers at Rest* (A209, pl. 215), although he "considered the price extreme"; on the same day he informs the dealer that he is not interested in

Plate 215. Edgar Degas. *Dancers at Rest*, 1874. Oil and gouache on paper laid down on canvas, 18 ⅛ x 12 ¾ in. (46 x 32.4 cm). Private collection. A209

Figure 61. Edouard Manet. *Street Singer*, ca. 1862. Oil on canvas, 67 ⅜ x 41 ⅝ in. (171.3 x 105.8 cm). Museum of Fine Arts, Boston, Bequest of Sarah Choate Sears in Memory of her husband, Joshua Montgomery Sears (66.304)

the Manet, which "although a superb painting has the great drawback of having the visage obscured by her hand."

PD-R to HOH, 2/3/99; HOH to PD-R, 2/20/99, correspondence, Weitzenhoffer files; see also Weitzenhoffer 1982, p. 304 ; Weitzenhoffer 1986, p. 135. The *Street Singer* was subsequently sold by Durand-Ruel for Fr 70,000 (about $14,000) to the Boston collector Sarah Choate Sears, who bequeathed it to the Museum of Fine Arts, Boston.

February 4 Durand-Ruel, New York, buys from the Havemeyers Diaz de la Peña's *Children Playing with a Lizard* (A266), one of Harry's early acquisitions from Knoedler's, Corot's *Evening* (A119), and a seascape by Clays (see A82). The day before, February 3, the collectors had sold to Durand-Ruel Gericault's *Riderless Racers at Rome* (A284, pl. 185), and a week later, on February 11, they would sell the same gallery Maris's *Dutch Town on a River* (A370).

Unpublished Weitzenhoffer notes from Durand-Ruel American stock book, 1894–1905.

February 17 The Metropolitan Museum acquires Inness's *Delaware Valley* (MMA 99.27) from the sale of the *Private Collection of Thoms B. Clarke*, American Art Association, New York, for $8,100. H. O. Havemeyer was among the subscribers to a fund that made the acquisition possible.

Lot no. 365; see Spassky 1985, pp. 247–50.

Plate 216. Mary Cassatt. *Family Group Reading*, ca. 1898. Oil on canvas, 22 ¼ x 44 ⅜ in. (56.5 x 112.7 cm). Philadelphia Museum of Art, Gift of Mr. and Mrs. J. Watson Webb (42-102-1) A57

February 20 Harry advises Paul Durand-Ruel that he has purchased Cassatt's *Family Group Reading* (A57, pl. 216), which had been sent on approval from Paris to New York.

Weitzenhoffer 1982, pp. 308, 318, n. 50.

February 24 The Havemeyers buy Manet's *Young Man in the Costume of a Majo* (A345) from Durand-Ruel, New York, for $10,000.

MMA 1983, no. 72.

Plate 217. Claude Monet. *Chrysanthemums*, 1882. Oil on canvas, 39 ½ x 32 ¼ in. (100.3 x 81.9 cm). H. O. Havemeyer Collection, Bequest of Mrs. H. O. Havemeyer, 1929 (29.100.106) A400

March 10 The Havemeyers purchase three pictures from Durand-Ruel, New York, that had been returned to the gallery this year by Catholina Lambert, an American collector who had owned them since 1892. Two, Monet's *Bouquet of Sunflowers* (A399, pl. 38) and *Chrysanthemums* (A400, pl. 217), had been in the collection of Alden Wyman Kingman, another American, between 1886 and 1892. The third, Renoir's *By the Seashore* (A460, pl. 6), bought for $4,000, was an acquisition Louisine would always regret and the only painting by the artist to enter the Havemeyer collection. Louisine and Harry sell their Boudin, *Washerwomen near a Bridge on the Touques River* (A44), back to Durand-Ruel, New York.

Weitzenhoffer 1986, p. 135; unpublished Weitzenhoffer notes from Durand-Ruel American stock book, 1894–1905.

April 6 Louisine and Harry buy Corot's *Muse: History* (A104) from Durand-Ruel, New York; the painting had been secured from the Paris branch on March 8.

May 1 The New York branch of Durand-Ruel purchases from the Havemeyers two Barye watercolors, *Tiger Devouring Antelope* (A36) and *Lion* (A26).

Unpublished Weitzenhoffer notes from Durand-Ruel American stock book, 1894-1905.

June 14 H. O. Havemeyer appears before the Industrial Commission in Washington, D.C., in connection with its investigation of trusts. His "testimony related almost wholly to the sugar industry, and he opened with a vigorous attack upon the customs tariff."

Plate 218. Mary Cassatt. *Mother and Child*, ca. 1899. Oil on canvas, 32 ⅛ x 25 ⅞ in. (81.6 x 65.7 cm). H. O. Havemeyer Collection, Bequest of Mrs. H. O. Havemeyer, 1929 (29.100.47) A58

New York Times, June 15, 1899, p. 1, col. 2, under the headlines: "Mr. Havemeyer on Trusts. Tells the Industrial Commission the Tariff is Responsible. Discriminates Against Sugar. He Asserts that the Day of the Individual Is Past and Business Combinations Are Necessary." According to Louisine, Harry designated the customs tariff "the mother of all trusts," a phrase that became a free-trade slogan (Havemeyer 1961, pp. 27–28).

July 7 The Havemeyers advise Paul Durand-Ruel that, on the basis of a photograph they had been sent in June, they have decided to buy Cassatt's *Mother and Child* (A58, pl. 218) for $2,000; the transaction is finalized on July 25.

Weitzenhoffer 1982, pp. 308–9.

July 24 Louisine and Harry decline to purchase Degas's *False Start* and *The Dance Class* (Lemoisne 1946, nos. 258, 341), which Galerie Durand-Ruel had offered to them —by letter with photographs enclosed—on July 7 for $10,000 and $16,000, respectively. Though they often bought pictures on the basis of photographs, they were "embarrassed" to do so in this case, especially given the "high" prices. Paul Durand-Ruel, who had felt obliged to offer *The False Start* to the Havemeyers, was pleased to be able to retain the painting for his personal collection.

Weitzenhoffer 1982, pp. 300–301; Weitzenhoffer 1986, pp. 130–33.

August 31 The Havemeyers purchase Corot's *Woman in Thought* (A99) for Fr 25,000 ($5,000) from Durand-Ruel.

1900

April 10 At the sale of the *Private Collection of Mr. Frederic Bonner with additions by the American Art Association*, Chickering Hall, New York, Durand-Ruel purchases for the Havemeyers Monet's paintings *Old Church at Vernon* (A411) for $3,100 and *Haystacks at Giverny* (A402) for $2,300.

Lot nos. 63, 66.

December 14 Through Durand-Ruel, New York, the Havemeyers dispose of six animal-subject watercolors by Barye (A42) and two pastels by Millet, *Sunset over a Plain* (A384) and *Alley of Chestnut Trees* (A380).

Unpublished Weitzenhoffer notes from Durand-Ruel American stock book, 1894–1905.

1901

Early January After three years of fierce and costly competition in the sugar and coffee industries, John Arbuckle and H. O. Havemeyer agree to reduce their involvement in each other's trades.

Weitzenhoffer 1986, p. 138.

Plate 219. Claude Monet. *Bridge over a Pool of Water Lilies*, 1899. Oil on canvas, 36 ½ x 29 in. (92.7 x 73.7 cm). H. O. Havemeyer Collection, Bequest of Mrs. H. O. Havemeyer, 1929 (29.100.113) A414

Plate 220. Claude Monet. *Water Lilies and Japanese Bridge*, 1899. Oil on canvas, 35 ⅜ x 35 ⅜ in. (89.9 x 89.9 cm). The Art Museum, Princeton University, Princeton, New Jersey, from the Collection of William Church Osborn, gift of his family (72–15) A413

January 22 The Havemeyers purchase D'Espagnat's *Sailboats on the River* (A174) from Durand-Ruel, New York.

January 26 Before leaving for Europe, the Havemeyers buy from Durand-Ruel, New York, *Bridge over a Pool of Water Lilies* (A414, pl. 219), one of two paintings by Monet of this subject they acquire in January. The other, *Water Lilies and Japanese Bridge* (A413, pl. 220), they would return to Durand-Ruel in 1902.

MMA Department of European Paintings Archives and Weitzenhoffer 1986, p. 143.

January 30 The Havemeyers, in the company of Louisine's older sister, Anne Munn, sail on the *Kaiserin Augusta Victoria* for Madeira, Gibraltar, Algiers, and Genoa.

Weitzenhoffer 1986, p. 138; Havemeyer 1961, p. 85.

Figure 62. Titian (Tiziano Vecellio). *Danaë and Cupid*, 1545–46. Oil on canvas, 47 ¼ x 67 ¾ in. (120 x 172 cm). Gallerie Nazionali di Capodimonte, Naples

Mid-February Cassatt joins the Havemeyers and Anne in Genoa; they tour the city together and then depart for Turin, where Harry is eager to see an Egyptian statue, "the black Ramses." At Cassatt's urging they go to Milan—to "see the Luinis, the Veroneses and the Moronis." Here they visit a number of dealers and find "one fairly good Moroni, the portrait of a man in a green coat and dark hat," but do not purchase it, as "Cassatt convinced Mr. Havemeyer it was not up to his standard." The party then "sped rapidly southward" to Naples, where Louisine is disappointed to find that the museum—in which she had first seen Titian's *Danaë and Cupid* (fig. 62) as a young girl—is closed for alterations.

Havemeyer 1961, pp. 86–90.

February 24 The Havemeyer family, having "traveled very fast, until now one day for each city," is about to leave Naples for Sicily and then spend a few days in Rome. Harry "wants to go to Constantinople via Venice and Vienna and then to Paris before proceeding to Spain." He is interested in acquiring a Velázquez.

MC to D-R, 2/24/01, from Hotel Bristol, Naples, correspondence, Weitzenhoffer files, cited in Weitzenhoffer 1986, p. 138.

Late February–mid-March The party "hastened on to Sicily," stopping in Reggio and Messina before arriving in "beautiful Taormina." From there they travel "to Syracuse, which was rather depressing," as the "dirty activity of a seaport town was not suggestive of Grecian splendor." They proceed "between the mountain heights to Girgenti," where they "see those marvelous temples on the borders of the sea," and visit, in Palermo, the Palantine chapel. They spend a few days in Rome, touring its many sites and mu-

seums; here another dealer offers Louisine and Harry the Moroni they had refused in Milan. They stop briefly in Bologna and then move on to Ravenna—where, as Louisine notes, "Louis Tiffany found his inspiration for our white mosaic hall and the ten pillars at the entrance of our gallery." From here they proceed to Venice (probably arriving on Saturday, March 9, at the Hotel Danieli, where they stay a few days). Their next stops are Ferrara, which "had little to interest us," Mantua, where "an air of comfortable luxury pervaded the place," Padua, whose interest "centered in the church of Saint Anthony and in Donatello," and Florence, in the "cold, snow, frost, ice and wind" of that "wintry March."

Havemeyer 1961, pp. 86–90, 94–107.

Mid–late March In Florence Cassatt introduces the Havemeyers to A. E. Harnisch, whose services they engage to ferret out unknown treasures in Italian private collections. Harnisch arranges for several adventurous outings, including a visit to the palazzo of an impoverished Italian noble —from whom they buy "a marble 'Madonna and the Infant Christ' by Mino da Fiesole [now considered Master of the Marble Madonnas, pl. 221] . . . a more realistic work than the one we bought in Paris from Gavet [pl. 202]"— and another to the home of Countess Fossi to see a "robust Veronese" (A417, now considered Montemezzano), which they would later acquire.

Havemeyer 1961, pp. 110–13, 124–29; see also Weitzenhoffer 1986, p. 139. The marble, purchased through Harnisch from the Bombici collection, was described as a "bas relief" and valued at 50,000 (lire?) when it was taxed "as marble pure and simple" upon shipment to New York in August. In October Cassatt, who hoped that Harnisch had been in touch about a frame, was eager to know "if the Mina [*sic*] looks well" (MC to LWH, 8/9/[01], 10/1/[01], Havemeyer correspondence).

Plate 221. Master of the Marble Madonnas. *Virgin and Child*, late 15th century. Carrara marble, 33 x 24 ¾ in. (83.8 x 62.9 cm). H. O. Havemeyer Collection, Bequest of Mrs. H. O. Havemeyer, 1929 (29.100.26)

The party travels from Florence to Milan; from Milan they make an excursion with Harnisch to a villa in Brescia to see Veronese's *Boy with a Greyhound* (A503, pl. 57), a picture they would secure a few years later for L 25,000. Their last visit in Italy is to Bergamo, "in a fruitless hunt for a Moroni."

Havemeyer 1961, pp. 124–29.

Late March The Havemeyers stop briefly in Paris, where they deposit Anne at Cassatt's apartment, and then proceed to Spain. Upon their arrival in Madrid, they immediately go to the Prado with Cassatt; Louisine and Harry find the museum a "revelation of art" and return "many times" to see the "irresistible" works of El Greco and Goya. While in Madrid, they pay a visit to the El Greco scholar Manuel B. Cossío and the same morning they see Goya's portraits of Antonio Zárate (Gassier and Wilson 1971, nos. 892, 893) belonging to the sitter's descendant Adelaida Gil y Zárate. The owner refuses the Havemeyers' offer of Pts 20,000 for the pair and counters with an asking price of Pts 100,000, which the collectors do not seriously entertain. Later that day Cassatt discovers a small canvas by El Greco, *Christ Carrying the Cross* (A305, now considered Copy after El Greco), hanging in a doorway of an antique shop; Louisine buys it, framed, for Pts 1,500. The same dealer shows them a *Saint Peter* by El Greco (Wethey 1962, no. x-440) "in a brilliant green robe, holding the keys upon his arm," which as Louisine notes, "eight years afterwards, when we were again traveling in Spain, my daughter Electra bought . . . in Vitoria."

Havemeyer 1961, pp. 130–37. The Saint Peter, "a much repainted and somewhat saccharine replica"(Wethey 1962, p. 255) was included in the 1930 Havemeyer sale, no. 98.

Early April Cassatt stays in Madrid while the Havemeyers sightsee in the south of Spain. Cassatt makes contact with Joseph Wicht. He is well acquainted with members of the Spanish aristocracy and arranges for her to see El Grecos and Goyas that belong to noble families—several of which the Havemeyers would later acquire. Among the El Grecos Cassatt sees in Wicht's company are *Portrait of a Cardinal* (A304, pl. 59), *View of Toledo* (A303, pl. 60), and the *Assumption of the Virgin* (fig. 66); she also goes with him to see the dozen or so Goyas then in the Palace of the Boadilla del Monte (none of which are purchased by the Havemeyers) and *Majas on a Balcony* (A296, pl. 13).

In Toledo Harry is overwhelmed by El Greco's *Burial of the Conde de Orgaz* (Capilla de Santo Tomé). Louisine and Harry continue southward to Seville, Cadiz, and Córdoba. Their last stop is Granada, where they purchase—from an antique shop for several thousand dollars—what they believe are original "Moorish tiles from the villa of Charles V at Guadix." Upon delivery of the tiles in 250 cases two years later, the Havemeyers would

discover them to be made-to-order copies. Some would be used in an addition built to their summer home; the rest would be stored in their stable.

Havemeyer 1961, pp. 147–56; see also Weitzenhoffer 1986, pp. 141, 190.

Mid-April The Havemeyers rejoin Cassatt in Madrid. In her company Louisine purchases from a Señor Moreno a "Madonna" altarpiece by Patinir (A279, *The Rest on the Flight into Egypt*, now considered unknown early 16th-century Flemish painter) for Pts 20,000. Wicht takes the collectors to see the Duchess of Villahermosa's full-length portraits by Velázquez (Lopez-Rey 1963, nos. 236, 506, and 494 or 580). One of these (no. 494 or 580) is for sale, but they do "not admire it sufficiently to buy it." Thanks to Wicht, just before they depart Madrid for Paris, the Havemeyers buy two Hispano-Moresque plates, "one with a copper and the other with a moonlight luster," from an "owner [who] had taken them from off his walls."

Havemeyer 1961, pp. 153–56, 160, 179; see Weitzenhoffer 1986, pp. 141, 190; MC to LWH, 6/16/[01], mentioning her visit to the customhouse for the Patinir, Havemeyer correspondence.

Plate 222. Claude Monet. *Petit Gennevilliers*, 1874. Oil on canvas, 21 ½ x 29 in. (54.6 x 73.7 cm). Private collection. A396

April 19 From the Galerie Durand-Ruel, Paris, the Havemeyers acquire *The Garden* (A9) and *Seamstresses* (A10) by the contemporary French artist André. They also purchase Monet's *Petit Gennevilliers* (A396, pl. 222) from Boussod, Valadon et Cie, Paris, for Fr 20,000 ($3,846).

The Andrés were paid for upon their arrival in New York on July 12. Durand-Ruel Archives; The Dieterle Archives, Getty Center, Malibu.

April 22 The Havemeyers enlarge their collection with several pictures from Galerie Durand-Ruel, Paris: Millet's *Spring* (A376)—which would later be returned—Corot's *Mlle Dobigny—The Red Dress* (A110, pl. 16), Manet's pastel portrait *Mlle Isabelle Lemonnier* (A362), Degas's

Plate 223. Edgar Degas. *Woman with a Towel*, 1894. Pastel on cream-colored wove paper with red and blue fibers throughout, 37¾ x 30 in. (95.9 x 76.2 cm). H. O. Havemeyer Collection, Bequest of Mrs. H. O. Havemeyer, 1929 (29.100.37) A257

Woman with a Towel (A257, pl. 223), and Monet's *River Zaan at Zaandam* (A390). The following day they acquire Cassatt's *Young Mother Sewing* (A59, pl. 86) from the same gallery.

These works were paid for upon their arrival in New York: the Millet on June 17, the others on July 12.

April On their first visit together to Vollard's gallery on the rue Laffitte, the Havemeyers probably select two Cézanne still lifes with flowers (A69, pl. 224, A73) and per-

Plate 224. Paul Cézanne. *Flowers in a Glass Vase*, 1872–73. Oil on canvas, 16⅜ x 13⅛ in. (41.6 x 33.3 cm). The Putnam Foundation/Timken Museum of Art, San Diego. A69

haps also an Auvers landscape (A70). Harry advances Vollard a large sum of money on account, which "saved [the dealer's] financial life in 1901."

Weitzenhoffer 1986, pp. 142–43, where it is proposed that Vollard may also have encouraged the Havemeyers to acquire Cézanne's *Still Life with a Ginger Jar and Eggplants* (A78) and *Mont Sainte-Victoire and the Viaduct of the Arc River Valley* (A74). Quote from MC to LWH, 7/16/[13], Havemeyer correspondence.

April 29 The Havemeyers are in Brussels. Harry advises Galerie Durand-Ruel: "Please cancel my order to buy the nude Courbet, of two figures. It is too similar to the one I possess to interest me." Presumably Harry withdraws his bid on Courbet's *Le Réveil* (fig. 63)—a picture close in composition and imagery to the Havemeyers' Courbet *Woman with a Parrot* (A145, pl. 19)—which is coming up for sale on May 7 in the *Collection M. Z. . . ,* Galerie Georges Petit, Paris.

Lot no. 4; HOH to D-R, 4/29/[01], correspondence, Weitzenhoffer files.

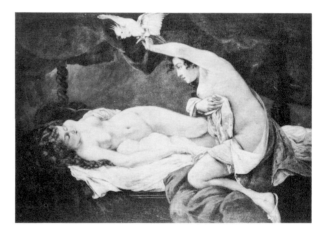

Figure 63. Gustave Courbet. *Le Réveil*, 1864. Oil on canvas, 57⅞ x 75⅝ in. (147 x 192 cm). Private collection

May 9 After a three-month sojourn in Europe, the Havemeyers return home.

Weitzenhoffer files.

Plate 225. Claude Monet. *Barges at Asnières*, 1873. Oil on canvas, 22 x 29½ in. (55.9 x 74.9 cm). Private collection. A394

May 24 From the New York branch of Durand-Ruel, the Havemeyers purchase Corot's *Bacchante in a Landscape* (A107, pl. 17) for $6,000. They also acquire Monet's *Barges at Asnières* (A394, pl. 225) from Boussod, Valadon et Cie, Paris, for Fr 20,000 ($3,846).

Durand-Ruel Archives; The Dieterle Archives, Getty Center, Malibu.

Early June Cassatt makes a one-day trip to Madrid and then proceeds to Italy to view pictures for the Havemeyers.

Weitzenhoffer 1986, p. 144.

Figure 65. Harry at Bayberry Point, ca. 1903

Figure 64. Édouard Manet. *The Port of Bordeaux*, 1871. Oil on canvas, 25⅝ x 39⅜ in. (65 x 100 cm). Private collection, Switzerland

June 17 Durand-Ruel advises H. O. Havemeyer that Manet's *Port of Bordeaux* (fig. 64) is available for sale from the Faure collection for Fr 70,000–75,000, and that he must act quickly, since Camondo is interested in buying it. On July 5 Harry rejects the picture as "not the sort of sea view that I care to acquire."

D-R to HOH, 6/17/01; HOH to D-R, 7/5/01, correspondence, Weitzenhoffer files.

July 4–Labor Day The Havemeyer family spends the summer sailing, swimming, and horseback riding at their new Venetian-style villa at Bayberry Point, Long Island.

Weitzenhoffer 1986, p. 144.

July Through Harnisch the Havemeyers secure the "robust Veronese" they had seen in March in Florence. The picture, *Portrait of a Woman* (A417, now considered Montemezzano), which was purportedly en route to New York by late this month and for which a new frame was found by December 1901, seems not to have been shipped from Europe until July 1905.

AEH to MC, 7/8/01, 8/5/01; MC to LWH, 10/1/[01]; AEH to MC, 12/20/01; AEH to HOH, 2/16/05, 7/6/05, Havemeyer correspondence. The picture is referred to as "Venice" or "Venetia" in correspondence. In her memoirs Louisine noted the use of the code name "Venice" and recounted that "it required two years of 'pazienza' before we owned that picture" (Havemeyer 1961, pp. 110–12).

August 5 Harnisch asks Cassatt to authorize the purchase for the Havemeyers of a del Sarto for which he has offered L 75,000 and has already secured with a down payment of L 1,000. In forwarding this offer to Louisine, Cassatt writes, "[Harnisch] seems to think I would buy a picture for Mr. Havemeyer on my very own judgment without consulting Mr. Havemeyer. . . . Mr. Havemeyer must decide as to whether he will risk it." The decision is positive: the Havemeyers acquire *Madonna and Child with Saint John* (A474, now Attributed to del Sarto).

AEH to MC, 8/5/01; MC to LWH, 8/9/[01], Havemeyer correspondence; see also Havemeyer 1961, pp. 113, 115.

First week of August Cassatt writes the Havemeyers, "Wellington is yours at 17,975 fcs. As you left it to my discretion I bought it on the principal [sic] I have always seen you follow of getting a fine thing when it comes your way." On August 9 Goya's *Duke of Wellington* (A302, now considered Workshop of Goya, pl. 226), which Cassatt had secured through Wicht, is in Paris for repacking and shipping.

Plate 226. Workshop of Francisco de Goya y Lucientes. *The Duke of Wellington*, ca. 1812. Oil on canvas, 41½ x 33 in. (105.4 x 83.8 cm). National Gallery of Art, Washington, D.C., Gift of Mrs. P.H.B. Frelinghuysen (1963.4.1) A302

Quote from MC to HOH, n.d. [ca. 8/5–8/9/[01], Havemeyer correspondence. The portrait is also mentioned in MC to LWH, 8/9/[01], and Joseph Wicht to MC, 7/8/[01], sent by Cassatt to the Havemeyers and annotated: "The Wellington is interesting from every point of view, perhaps Colonel Paine [sic] might fancy it. It is intact, has not been retouched. . . . [but] I did not see the picture down, it was [hanging] in the hall," Havemeyer correspondence.

August 9 Durand-Ruel advises the Havemeyers that Manet's "La Buveur d'eau" (Rouart and Wildenstein, 1975, I, no. 43) is now available from the collection of Mr. Dreyfus-Gonzales for $5,500. The work is not acquired.

D-R to HOH, 8/9/01, correspondence, Weitzenhoffer files.

October 1 Cassatt informs the Havemeyers that Harnisch has secured two small portraits, one of a man, the other of a woman, then thought to be by Holbein (A287, 286, now considered unknown 16th-century German painter). Harnisch had discovered these pictures in July but relied on Cassatt—who felt "it would be a pity to miss two Holbein portraits at 18,000 lire"—to intervene with the Havemeyers.

AEH to MC, 7/8/01; MC to LWH, 8/9/[01], including quote, 10/1/[01], Havemeyer correspondence.

October The town boards of Islip and Babylon sue Harry to recover title, which he had received from New York State in 1894, to land under the waters of the bay in front of his "modern Venice" development.

Weitzenhoffer 1986, p. 145.

1902

January Harry places Dupré's *Woodcutter* (A272) on consignment with Durand-Ruel, New York, through March, asking $20,000 for it ($7,000 more than the 1891 purchase price and the 1898 asking price). The gallery would not find a buyer for the painting until 1912—after Louisine had tried to dispose of it for three years.

Consignment per GD-R to LWH, 11/3/09, correspondence, Weitzenhoffer files.

February 7 The Havemeyers purchase Degas's *Rehearsal of the Ballet Onstage* (A212, pl. 227) from Boussod, Valadon et Cie, Paris, for Fr 82,845.

Boggs et al. 1988, no. 124.

February 14 At the American Art Association sale of *Mr. E. F. Milliken's Private Collection of Valuable Paintings*, Mendelssohn Hall, New York, Durand-Ruel purchases

Plate 227. Edgar Degas. *The Rehearsal of the Ballet Onstage*, 1874? Oil colors freely mixed with turpentine, with traces of watercolor and pastel over pen-and-ink drawing on cream-colored wove paper, laid on bristol board and mounted on canvas, 21 3/8 x 28 3/4 in. (54.3 x 73 cm). H. O. Havemeyer Collection, Gift of Horace Havemeyer, 1929 (29.160.26) A212

Degas's *Dancers in the Rehearsal Room, with a Double Bass* (A238) for the Havemeyers for $6,100.

Lot no. 11

March 22 Harry, who had already financed the construction of a $200,000 school in Greenwich, Connecticut, now gives seven acres of land to the town's South Beach school district. He donates 2,000 books to the school's library in April.

"Mr. Havemeyer's Gift Accepted," *New York Times*, March 25, 1902, p. 2, col. 4; "H. O. Havemeyer Gives Library to School," *New York Times*, May 1, 1902, p. 1, col. 6.

May 1 Harry testifies before a Senate committee in Washington, D.C., providing a "distinct and emphatic contradiction of the oft-repeated statement that practically all the sugar in Cuba is owned by the American Sugar Refining Company."

"Senate Committee Hears Mr. Havemeyer," *New York Times*, May 2, 1902, pp. 1–2.

1903

By January 12 Paul Durand-Ruel, who had learned from Cassatt that Louisine is interested in "la petite tête" by Degas, sends a photograph of the work to the Havemeyers for their review. This portrait, *Joseph-Henri Altès* (A199, pl. 228), priced at Fr 10,000, is transferred to Durand-Ruel, New York, in February and sold to the Havemeyers on March 4.

MC to PD-R, n.d. [before 1/12/03]; PD-R to MC, 1/12/03, correspondence, Weitzenhoffer files; MC to LWH, 1/26/03, Havemeyer correspondence.

Plate 228. Edgar Degas. *Joseph-Henri Altès (1826–1895)*, 1868. Oil on canvas, 10 ⅝ x 8 ½ in. (27 x 21.6 cm). H. O. Havemeyer Collection, Bequest of Mrs. H. O. Havemeyer, 1929 (29.100.181) A199

January 15 Harnisch advises the Havemeyers that "a very beautifully painted 'Danae & the shower of gold' by Titian" is available from a private collection in Florence for L 120,000. Louisine convinces Harry that he should not buy the picture (possibly Wethey 1975, III, no. 5, under copies, no. 12), since she is certain it is a copy—the original (fig. 62) had made a "great impression" on her when she saw it in Naples as a young girl.

MC to LWH, 1/5/[03]; AEH to HOH, 1/15/03; MC to HOH, 2/3/[03]; AEH to MC, 2/4/03, Havemeyer correspondence; Havemeyer 1961, pp. 89–90.

January 17 Isabella Stewart Gardner visits Louisine, eager to compare her collection at Fenway Court in Boston to the collection housed in the Havemeyers' Tiffany-designed home. Louisine had granted Gardner's request for a Saturday visit, albeit reluctantly, as Saturday mornings were generally reserved for cleaning. Cassatt subsequently writes to Louisine, "of course Mrs Jack Gardner did not like to see the riches in your house, & her pictures must have increased in number if she has the 'best collection of Old Masters in America!'" When the time comes for a reciprocal visit, Mrs. Gardner gives "some feeble excuse in order a competitor should not see her works of art"; this makes Louisine "very angry."

MC to LWH, 2/2/[03], replying to Louisine's letter of Sunday, 1/18/03, Havemeyer correspondence; Havemeyer 1961, p. 24.

January 27 The Havemeyers purchase Monet's *Thames at Charing Cross Bridge* (A415, pl. 37) from Durand-Ruel, New York.

February 2 Paul Durand-Ruel is in Madrid to see paintings of interest to the Havemeyers: El Greco's *Portrait of a Cardinal* (A304, pl. 59) and Goya's *Doña Narcisa Barañana de Goicoechea* (A294, pl. 233). He also sees El

Greco's monumental *Assumption of the Virgin* (fig. 66), which he prefers to the *Cardinal*. Over the next year the dealer's estimation of the *Assumption* wavers little, but his efforts to convince the Havemeyers to acquire this thirteen-foot-high altarpiece are in vain. In a letter to Harry written on April 1, 1904, Durand-Ruel relents on the subject of the "great Greco that Miss Cassatt would [also] like to have seen bought by you or by an American Museum. This painting is a masterpiece, but I certainly understand that its size is an insurmountable obstacle for you." The dealer steadfastly pursues the acquisition, however, and by the end of 1904, thanks to Harry's financial backing, is able to

Fig. 66. El Greco (Domenikos Theotokopoulos). *Assumption of the Virgin*, 1577. Oil on canvas, 158 ⅛ x 90 in. (401.4 x 228.7 cm). The Art Institute of Chicago, Gift of Nancy Atwood Sprague in memory of Albert Arnold Sprague (1906.99)

secure the *Assumption of the Virgin*. Thereafter, it becomes a matter of placing the masterpiece in an American museum.

MC to LWH, 2/2/[03]; MC to HOH, 2/3/03, 2/10/[03], Havemeyer correspondence; D-R to HOH, 4/1/04, correspondence, Weitzenhoffer files.

February 4 The Havemeyers sell Millet's *Spring* (A376) back to Durand-Ruel for $21,500. They had informed the gallery of their wish to return the picture in March 1902, after owning it for less than a year.

Date of return per Durand-Ruel Archives; intent to return per HOH to D-R, 3/24/02, correspondence, Weitzenhoffer files.

February 7 The Havemeyers purchase Corot's *Sibylle* (A114, pl. 18) and *Reverie* (A102, pl. 229) for $6,000 and $8,000, respectively, from Durand-Ruel, New York. From

Plate 229. Camille Corot. *Reverie*, ca. 1860–65. Oil on wood, 19⅝ x 14⅜ in. (49.9 x 36.5 cm). H. O. Havemeyer Collection, Bequest of Mrs. H. O. Havemeyer, 1929 (29.100.563) A102

Durand-Ruel they also buy Manet's *Dead Christ and the Angels* (A346, pl. 32) for $17,000, but they find it "impossible to live with that mighty picture. Consequently, they put the Manet in storage, where it remains for years— until it is placed on extended loan at the Metropolitan Museum.

Quote from Havemeyer 1961, pp. 236–37.

February 12–14 The Havemeyers acquire a group of Japanese embossed leather panels (including MMA 29.100.482–87) from the American Art Association's sale of Bunkio Matsuki's *Rare Objects in Brass, Leathers and Wood illustrating the Art of Old Japan*, American Art Galleries, New York.

February 16 H. O. Havemeyer is one of several candidates nominated by the Metropolitan Museum's Board of Trustees to fill two existing vacancies on the board. At the May 18 meeting ballots are cast and George A. Hearn and Daniel Chester French are elected. The following year, at the February 15, 1904, meeting of the Board of Trustees, Harry is again among the nominees proposed for two recent vacancies on the board, but when ballots are cast on May 16, Charles F. McKim and William Church Osborn are elected trustees.

MMA Archives. Weitzenhoffer maintained that Harry was earlier turned down as a trustee on the basis of the following statement in a letter of June 23, 1891, from Henry Marquand to Louis P. di Cesnola: "Havemeyer is a hard man to *get along* with—though very knowing —I fear he won't do" (1986, p. 66). However, the statement is wrongly attributed to Marquand, who was, in fact, commenting on a remark made by Colman. Moreover the letter does not indicate that Havemeyer "won't do" as a trustee, only that he "won't do." Although an undated archival notation accompanying the letter questions whether the text might mean that H. O. Havemeyer wouldn't do as a trustee, there is no documentation in the MMA Archives to substantiate Weitzenhoffer's contention.

February 25 The Havemeyers consign Decamps's *Tobias and the Angel* (A186) to Durand-Ruel, New York; it is purchased by the gallery the following year.

Unpublished Weitzenhoffer notes from Durand-Ruel American stock book, 1894–1905.

March The Havemeyers board the *Oceanic* for Europe. They "pass a day in London" before arriving in Paris to pick up Cassatt, who had planned to join them on their trip through northern Italy, but does not because she has her "hands full & cannot possibly leave just at present."

MC to Theodate Pope, n.d. [3/03], indicating that Cassatt expects the Havemeyers "tomorrow," correspondence, Weitzenhoffer files.

March 23 Harnisch reports his discovery of a Filippo Lippi that he and friends, disguised as "artists with paint box[es]," were fortunate enough to see after a long trek to

Plate 230. Follower of Fra Filippo Lippi. *Madonna and Child with Two Angels*, 15th century. Tempera on wood, 39¼ x 28 in. (99.7 x 71.1 cm). H. O. Havemeyer Collection, Bequest of Mrs. H. O. Havemeyer, 1929 (29.100.17) A340

a remote "little chapel . . . up in the mountains beyond Cortona." The asking price for this "exquisite Madonna" is L 115,000. Shortly after the find is reported, the Havemeyers, escorted by Harnisch, make the same journey from Florence—"partly by train, partly by *vettura*, partly by foot"—masquerading as wine merchants. By July Harnisch finds a "fine old frame" for the picture, *Madonna and Child with Two Angels* (A340, now considered Follower of Lippi, pl. 230).

AEH to MC, 3/23/03, reporting contents of lost letter AEH to HOH, ca. 3/20/03, 7/14/03, both including quotes, Havemeyer correspondence; quote re second journey, Havemeyer 1961, pp. 115–23.

March 25 From the American Art Association's sale of *Paintings and Water Colors by and Belonging to Samuel Colman, N.A. Together with his private collection of pic-*

234

tures by artists of the Barbizon School and others, American Art Galleries, New York, the Havemeyers acquire, presumably through an agent who bids on their behalf, Sartain's *Head of an Italian Girl* (A473) for $240.

Lot no. 76.

April The Havemeyers are in Paris and purchase from Vollard Cézanne's *Abduction* (A67) for Fr 6,000 and *Gustave Boyer in a Straw Hat* (A68, pl. 231) for Fr 1,500. From Paul Rosenberg they purchase Puvis de Chavannes's

Plate 231. Paul Cézanne. *Gustave Boyer in a Straw Hat*, ca. 1871. Oil on canvas, 21 ⅝ x 15 ¼ in. (54.9 x 38.7 cm). H. O. Havemeyer Collection, Bequest of Mrs. H. O. Havemeyer, 1929 (29.100.65) A68

Plate 232. Edouard Manet. *Portrait of Marguerite de Conflans*, 1873. Oil on canvas, 21 x 17 ½ in. (53.3 x 44.5 cm). Smith College Museum of Art, Northampton, Massachusetts, Purchased, Drayton Hillyer Fund, 1945 (1945.6) A355

Tamaris (A437) (Fr 10,000), Degas's "La Toilette" (probably A225, *Three Dancers Preparing for Class*) (Fr 10,000), and Manet's *Constantin Guys* (A365) (Fr 22,000) and *Marguerite de Conflans* (A355, pl. 232) (Fr 28,000). These works are shipped to the Havemeyers by Durand-Ruel on May 7, along with thirty-four pieces of "poteries anciennes."

Figure 67. 1919 photograph of *The Little Fourteen-Year-Old Dancer*, 1879–81. Durand Ruel Archives. Sculpture: wax with cotton skirt and satin hair ribbon, h. 37 ½ in. (95.2 cm). Collection of Mr. and Mrs. Paul Mellon, Upperville, Virginia

Durand-Ruel Archives, which indicate that Galerie Durand-Ruel made arrangements for the photographing, from April 27 to 29, and shipping of the pictures but was not involved with any financial transactions. The precise purchase date of the Puvis was April 21 (MMA Department of European Paintings Archives).

Louisine goes to Degas's studio with Cassatt and sees the original wax version of *The Little Fourteen-Year-Old Dancer* (fig. 67) "in pieces" in a "little vitrine." The visit sparks Louisine's "great desire to possess" the wax, and she asks Durand-Ruel "to interview Degas and find out if the statue could not be put together again" for her. Thanks to the persuasions of Durand-Ruel and Cassatt, the artist does not dismiss the idea: in the fall he addresses the challenge of restoring the piece, but he ultimately abandons it. Late in the year Louisine rejects Degas's offer of a replica in bronze or plaster coated with wax—she wants the original, even in its blackened state.

Boggs et al. 1988, pp. 343–44; quote from Havemeyer 1961, p. 255. Louisine would attempt to obtain the original from Degas's heirs in 1918–19.

In an article titled "Captains of Industry" in *Cosmopolitan*, Robert N. Burnett profiles "Henry Osborne Havemeyer . . . [who] in business circles . . . is regarded as one of the most brilliant men of this generation"; he is considered a shrewd businessman, whose success is attributed to his great "capacity for producing results."

Vol. 34 (April 1903), pp. 701–4.

April 13 The New York branch of Durand-Ruel purchases Decamps's *Ferme du verrier* (A192) from the Havemeyers.

Unpublished Weitzenhoffer notes from Durand-Ruel American stock book, 1894–1905.

April 24 The Havemeyers sail for America aboard the *Deutschland*; Cassatt sees them off.

MC to Mrs. Whittemore, 4/25/03, correspondence, Weitzenhoffer files.

April 30 From Durand-Ruel the Havemeyers buy Goya's *Doña Narcisa Barañana de Goicoechea* (A294, pl. 233). Paul Durand-Ruel, who, like Cassatt, had hoped that his February trip to Madrid was not "for nothing," succeeded in acquiring the portrait from Don Felipe Modet of that city on April 4.

MC to HOH, 2/3/03, Havemeyer correspondence; Durand-Ruel Archives.

May Lacking sufficient exhibition space, the Havemeyers begin construction of a gallery on the main floor of their home, in the area of a rear courtyard. The gallery, which is meant to house their new El Grecos and Goyas (both

Plate 233. Francisco de Goya y Lucientes. *Doña Narcisa Barañana de Goicoechea*, ca. 1805. Oil on canvas, 44¼ x 30¾ in. (112.4 x 78.1 cm). H. O. Havemeyer Collection, Bequest of Mrs. H. O. Havemeyer, 1929 (29.100.180) A294

recent and anticipated acquisitions), is completed in November.

Weitzenhoffer 1986, pp. 47–48, 72.

Plate 234. Unknown Flemish painter. *Portrait of a Woman with a Lapdog*, ca. 1620. Oil on canvas, 43 x 33¼ in. (109.2 x 84.5 cm). Location unknown. A280

July 31 After "voluminous correspondence" on the subject, Harry informs Durand-Ruel that he will buy the "Coello" that Theodore Davis has also expressed interest in acquiring. The next day the Havemeyers purchase the *Portrait of a Woman with a Lapdog*, thought to be by

Coello but sold to them as Dutch school (A280, pl. 234, now considered unknown Flemish painter). Cassatt is not entirely sanguine about the acquisition: though she imagines that the picture will be greatly admired in the Havemeyers' home, she "puts it far below other things, especially the Goya woman," and asserts that it is not "frankly enough painted to suit my taste."

HOH to D-R, 7/31/03; D-R to MC, 7/13/03, 7/16/03, correspondence, Weitzenhoffer files. MC to LWH, 8/30/[03], including quote, Havemeyer correspondence. The work had been attributed to Coello when it was exhibited in 1901; however, unpublished Weitzenhoffer notes from Durand-Ruel Archives indicate that it was sold to the Havemeyers as a Dutch school *Portrait d'une dame*.

October Horace enters the family business; he apprentices in all divisions of the Brooklyn refinery for the next year and a half

Havemeyer 1944, p. 72.

November 28 A court ruling grants the Havemeyers "undisputed title [under the name of the Alaska Copper Co.] to rich bonanza copper mines located 160 miles from Valdez, on the Chittyna, a branch of the Copper River." Plans for the immediate development of the enormous property in Alaska include the construction of a railroad from Valdez to Bonanza.

New York Times, November 30, 1903, p. 10, col. 2.

December 29 Paul Durand-Ruel, trying to soften the blow that the owner of El Greco's *Portrait of a Cardinal* (A304, pl. 59) will not sell, even for the Fr 100,000 Harry has offered, advises the Havemeyers that another El Greco, a "portrait of a monk" (*Fray Hortensio Félix Paravicino* [fig. 4]), is available. Harry rejects the painting on principle: "Why buy a monk when you [can] have a cardinal." The following spring—two months after the Museum of Fine Arts, Boston, secures the monk—Harry finally succeeds in obtaining the *Cardinal*.

D-R to MC, 12/29/03; D-R to HOH, 4/1/04, indicating regret that Harry did not pursue the portrait of a monk, which had just been sold to the Museum of Fine Arts in Boston, correspondence, Weitzenhoffer files; quote from Havemeyer 1961, p. 156. The Havemeyers had already declined to buy the painting of the monk when Sargent described it as "one of the best El Grecos I ever saw" and brought it to the attention of Edward Robinson, who would acquire it for the

Plate 235. *Jar in the form of a cone-shaped basket*, Japan (Kaga province), Edo period ca. 1800. Glazed Ōhi-ware pottery with lacquer cover, h. 7⅜ in. (18.7 cm). H. O. Havemeyer Collection, Bequest of Mrs. H. O. Havemeyer, 1929 (29.100.622)

Boston museum for $17,000. See W. M. Whitehall, *Museum of Fine Arts, Boston: A Centennial History*, Cambridge, Mass., 1970, vol. 1, pp. 191–93.

1904

February 8–13   The Havemeyers acquire "several" items from the estate sale of the Parisian collector Charles Gillot, "an early patron of Oriental art [who] had exquisite taste." Their purchases from the *Collection Ch. Gillot, Objets d'Art et Peinture d'Extrême-Orient*, Durand-Ruel, Paris, include two Japanese lacquer boxes—one showing a peasant carrying faggots down a hill (MMA 29.100.689, pl. 140, 29.100.690, or 29.100.691), the other in the shape of a baby crane (MMA 29.100.712)—and two Japanese vases—a basket-weave Ōhi ware (MMA 29.100.622, pl. 235) and a bamboo vase (MMA 29.100.616).

Quote from Havemeyer 1961, p. 13, which also refers to "a pair of screens, one of which belongs to me and the other, the one from the Gillot sale [which] is in the Metropolitan Museum." On the screens, see Julia Meech, "The Other Havemeyer Passion: Collecting Asian Art," this catalogue.

February 23   The *Memorial Exhibition of the Works of Mr. J. McNeill Whistler* opens at Copley Hall, Boston. Harry, who had served on the show's honorary committee, lends two pastels, *White and Pink (The Palace)* (A518) and *The Greek Slave Girl* (A512, pl. 184).

Shown as nos. 123, 124.

March 3   Bernard and Mary Berenson visit the Havemeyers' "awful Tiffany house" and find their collection of "Rembrandts, Monets, Degases ad infinitum" of "no real taste."

Mary Berenson, in David A. Brown, *Berenson and the Connoisseurship of Italian Painting: A Handbook to the Exhibition*, exh. cat., National Gallery of Art, Washington, D.C., 1979, p. 17.

April 12–15   Paul Durand-Ruel is in Madrid to negotiate the purchase of Goya's *Marquesa of Pontejos* (Gassier and Wilson 1971, no. 221) on behalf of the Havemeyers. He is authorized to offer up to Fr 125,000 ($25,000) to the owner, the Marquesa de Martorell. Though Harry reiterates that he is still interested in pursuing the acquisition in May, it is never realized—possibly because Louisine does not care for the picture. She later confesses: "For some reason, 'La Marquesa de Pontejos,' with her *bouffant* skirts, her quaint attitude and her shepherd style of Louis XVI, did not interest me."

Weitzenhoffer 1986, pp. 152–55; quote from Havemeyer 1961, p. 167.

April 26   On the first day of the sale of *La Collection Mame*, Galerie Georges Petit, Paris (April 26–29), Paul Durand-Ruel purchases for the Havemeyers a portrait of a

man by Antonello da Messina (A290, now considered van der Goes, pl. 55) for Fr 50,000 and a portrait of a woman by Clouet for Fr 30,000 (A96, *Anne de Pisseleu (1508–1576), duchesse d'Etampes*, now Attributed to Corneille de Lyon). Durand-Ruel thought that a Corot, a Delacroix, and two Millets in the sale were also worthy of consideration, but the Havemeyers had solicited Cassatt's opinion only on the Corot (Robaut 1905, no. 1370), which must have been unfavorable, and on the works actually purchased. The two portraits are received by the Havemeyers in an October shipment that includes El Greco's *Cardinal*.

Works acquired, lot nos. 1, 8; Corot, lot no. 72; Delacroix, lot no. 74; Millets, lot nos. 107, 108; D-R to HOH, 4/1/04; HOH to D-R, 4/11/04, 4/27/04, correspondence, Weitzenhoffer files.

May 6   In response to a letter of April 28 from Paul Durand-Ruel, Harry cables the dealer to buy El Greco's *Portrait of a Cardinal* (A304) from the Conde de Paredes de Nava for Fr 225,000. (A condition of sale is that the picture must be copied prior to its release.) The painting arrives at the gallery "in perfect condition" on May 30 and is sold to the Havemeyers the next day.

Weitzenhoffer 1986, pp. 153–54; HOH to D-R, 5/6/04, correspondence, Weitzenhoffer files.

May 9–June 4   *Claude Monet: Vues de la Tamise à Londres* is held at Galerie Durand-Ruel, Paris. During the run of this show, an enthusiastic Paul Durand-Ruel repeatedly tries to persuade Harry to consider buying at least one example from the series of Monet's views of the Thames on display. The collector is recalcitrant; he wants to acquire Goyas, not more Monets.

D-R to HOH, 5/10/04; HOH to D-R, 5/19/04; D-R to HOH, 5/20/04, 5/31/04, correspondence, Weitzenhoffer files.

Mid-May   Paul Durand-Ruel goes to Brussels to see four paintings—portraits by Veronese, El Greco, Guido Reni, and a Venus and Cupid by Cranach the Elder—that will be included in the sale of the *Collections de Somzée*, 22, rue de Palais, Brussels, May 24–30. He finds nothing of merit for the Havemeyers.

Lot nos. 326, 475, 511, 624; PD-R to HOH, 5/10/04; HOH to PD-R, 5/19/04, correspondence, Weitzenhoffer files.

May 20   Paul Durand-Ruel advises the Havemeyers of good quality works by Decamps coming up for sale in the *Collection Emile Gaillard*, Galerie Georges Petit, Paris, on June 7. Of the twelve paintings and six drawings by Decamps included, he recommends in particular *Le Boucher turc* (Mosby 1977, no. 392). The Havemeyers ignore this opportunity.

PD-R to HOH, 5/20/04; GD-R to HOH, 5/21/04, enclosing a catalogue and remarking that HOH saw the collection at the Place Malserbes, Paris, correspondence, Weitzenhoffer files.

June Paul Durand-Ruel goes to Madrid to negotiate the purchase of Goya's *Majas on a Balcony* (A296, now Attributed to Goya, pl. 13) and El Greco's *Assumption of the Virgin* (fig. 66), owned by the same Spanish family. Harry had cabled Fr 250,000 toward the purchase of the Goya for his own collection and had also "offered to advance" Fr 100,000 toward the dealer's purchase of the El Greco. The Fr 100,000 had been offered to Durand-Ruel "as an act of friendship"; Harry made it clear that he "was not [to] participate in the venture—any profit that might arise would be solely for your account." This trip is not successful.

Weitzenhoffer 1986, pp. 154–55; quote from HOH to PD-R, 7/25/04, correspondence, Weitzenhoffer files.

July 5 Carl Snyder wants to include the Havemeyers among fifty collectors who will be featured in the projected fifteen-volume series *Concerning Noteworthy Paintings in American Private Collections* and asks Cassatt to intercede with Harry on his behalf. This luxury publication is being prepared by Snyder's employer, August F. Jaccaci, with John LaFarge. Since only the first two volumes are realized, the Havemeyer collection, which would have been represented by six pictures, by artists ranging from Hals to Manet, is not featured.

Weitzenhoffer 1986, pp. 158, 266, chap. 13, n. 5.

September 27 Though the Havemeyers had expressed interest in a work by Ingres, they reject—on the basis of a photograph they "received and carefully scrutinized"—the picture proposed by Paul and Joseph Durand-Ruel: a portrait of a young woman painted in Rome in 1811, probably *Mme Panckoucke* (Wildenstein 1954, no. 77). Louisine feels "the face lacks charm, being rather sweet and insipid," and Harry objects to the price of Fr 150,000 (about $30,000). They would, however, be willing to reconsider the portrait at a "much lower price."

Weitzenhoffer 1986, p. 155.

October 9 Paul Durand-Ruel returns to Madrid, where he succeeds in securing Goya's *Majas on a Balcony* (A296, now Attributed to Goya, pl. 13) from the first Duke of Marchena's heirs. It is sold to the Havemeyers exactly one month later. As of October 22, however, Durand-Ruel is still pursuing El Greco's *Assumption of the Virgin* (fig. 66) with the four "héritiers" but he expects to close the deal on the twenty-fourth. By November he finally acquires the El Greco. In the weeks that follow, Louisine tries to convince the Metropolitan Museum to purchase the large-scale painting (Harry thinks the effort is futile). Trustee Avery declines the picture at the price paid for it (Fr 100,000), since the Museum is in the process of buying a "finer" El Greco, *Adoration of the Shepherds* (MMA 05.42). After November 21, when J. Pierpont Morgan becomes President of the

Metropolitan's Board of Trustees, Paul Durand-Ruel, at Cassatt's behest, offers Morgan the *Assumption* for the Museum's collection. By mid-December the dealer is discouraged with prospects at the Metropolitan and he and Cassatt turn their attention to The Art Institute of Chicago, where they ultimately meet with success: in 1906 the Art Institute acquires the *Assumption* with funds provided by Mrs. Albert Sprague.

Weitzenhoffer 1986, pp. 154–57; Havemeyer 1961, pp. 155–56; D-R to HOH, 10/4/04; GD-R to MC, 10/04, 10/22/04, correspondence, Weitzenhoffer files.

October 10 Harry, his son, Horace, and business associates arrive in Denver. They depart the next day for a two-day inspection tour of the beet sugar plants of the Great Western Sugar Co. in Fort Collins, Greeley, Eaton, Windsor, Longmont, and other points in Colorado. They return to Denver on October 13 and leave for Salt Lake City the following day. A spokesman for the Sugar King reports that "the purpose of this trip was to let Mr. Havemeyer see for himself the great continental divide" and to determine "what the prospects are for the extension of the sugar beet industry of the state."

"Sugar King is in Denver," *Denver Post*, October 10, 1904, p. 5; "Sugar King Inspects Northern Factories," *Denver Post*, October 11, 1904, p. 8; quote from "String of Sugar Plants," *Denver Post*, October 13, 1904, p. 2.

Figure 68. Harry in Denver. From *Denver Post*, October 11, 1904

October 28 Durand-Ruel, New York, purchases Decamps's *Tobias and the Angel* (A186) from the Havemeyers.

Unpublished Weitzenhoffer notes from Durand-Ruel American stock book, 1894–1905.

Plate 236. Paul Cézanne. *Self-Portrait with a Cap*, ca. 1875. Oil on canvas, 20⅞ x 15 in. (53 x 38.1 cm). Hermitage State Museum, St. Petersburg. A71

Plate 237. Gustave Courbet. *Portrait of a Man*, 1865. Oil on canvas, 16¼ x 13⅛ in. (41.3 x 33.3 cm). H. O. Havemeyer Collection, Bequest of Mrs. H. O. Havemeyer, 1929 (29.100.201) A143

December 23 Goya's newly relined *Majas on a Balcony* is delivered to Galerie Durand-Ruel, Paris; it is shipped to the Havemeyers six days later with Cézanne's *Self-Portrait with a Cap* (A71, pl. 236), which Cassatt had asked Vollard to deliver to Durand-Ruel in time to pack with the Goya.

Weitzenhoffer 1986, p. 156; D-R to MC, 12/23/04, correspondence, Weitzenhoffer files.

During the year The New York branch of Durand-Ruel relocates to 5 West 36th Street, its address until 1913.

1905

January 9 Joseph Durand-Ruel has received five of Monet's views of London (selected by his father and the artist), which he would like the Havemeyers to see at the New York gallery.

JD-R to HOH, 1/9/05, correspondence, Weitzenhoffer files.

March 28–29 Vollard purchases Courbet's *Portrait of a Man* (A143, pl. 237) from the estate sale *Tableaux Modernes . . . de M. Félix Gerard père*, Hôtel Drouot, Paris. Cassatt subsequently sees the portrait at Vollard's and by September buys it for the Havemeyers.

Lot no. 40; MC to LWH, 9/[05], indicating that Cassatt prefers the "Courbet head" she bought for Harry to Manet's *Bon Bock* and that she is glad the sale of the Faure Manets, which included *Bon Bock*, fell through, unpublished chapter on Cassatt from Louisine Havemeyer's memoirs, MMA Archives.

March 29 Harry informs Paul Durand-Ruel that he is not interested in Manet's *Bon Bock* (fig. 69), *The Virgin with the Rabbit*, and *Springtime* (Rouart and Wildenstein 1975, I, nos. 5, 372) from the Faure collection at the "preposterous" sum of Fr 300,000. Louisine, however, is willing to pay half that amount—$30,000. Over the next weeks the dealer is unable to negotiate a lower price with Faure or to convince the Havemeyers or Cassatt that the pictures are worth the amount asked. On August 1 Harry reconsiders and offers Durand-Ruel Fr 250,000 (about $50,000) for the three works plus another Manet, the *Port of Bordeaux* (fig. 64), the same seascape he had rejected four years earlier. Harry angrily revokes the offer on August 21, after Durand-Ruel urges him to entertain a purchase price of Fr 300,000.

Weitzenhoffer 1986, pp. 159–61.

March 31 Durand-Ruel informs Harry: "Following your orders, we sent to Agnew of London the Reynolds which you had deposited with us; it has been received."

D-R to HOH, 3/31/05, correspondence, Weitzenhoffer files. This reference does not confirm that the Havemeyers owned the Reynolds; it is possible that Harry was handling these arrangements for Payne.

May 11 Paul Durand-Ruel advises the Havemeyers that *La Baigneuse* and *La Petite gardeuse d'oies*, the Millets

Figure 69. Edouard Manet. *Le Bon Bock*, 1873. Oil on canvas, 37 x 32⅝ in. (94 x 83 cm). Philadelphia Museum of Art, Mr. and Mrs. Carroll S. Tyson Collection (63.116.9)

Figure 70. Adaline at her graduation from Bryn Mawr College, 1905

Figure 71. The Havemeyers out West, 1905. Louisine is second from left with Harry behind her; Electra is fourth from right

they are considering in the May 26 sale of the *Collection de M. Henri Heugel*, Galerie Georges Petit, Paris, are not of first quality; he recommends instead Delacroix's *Lion Hunt* (Johnson 1986, no. 199), priced at Fr 80,000– 100,000, and a small, exquisite Corot, *Paysage de l'Artois*, which Cassatt also admires. On May 24 Joseph Durand-Ruel reiterates his father's opinions, emphasizing that the Delacroix is "positively superb"; neither the Delacroix nor the Corot is purchased, however.

Millets, lot nos. 12, 13; Delacroix, lot no. 5; Corot, lot no. 3; PD-R to HOH, 5/11/05; JD-R to HOH, 5/24/05, also enclosing catalogues for the upcoming auctions of the Warneck collection, Hôtel Drouot, Paris, June 13–16, and the Rey collection, Galerie Georges Petit, Paris, June 2–3, correspondence, Weitzenhoffer files.

June Horace, age nineteen, is appointed sales manager for all the offices of the American Sugar Refining Co.; his principal duty is to increase corporate sales. Adaline graduates from Bryn Mawr.

Havemeyer 1944, p. 72; Bryn Mawr College Archives.

Late September The Havemeyer family and their business associates the W. B. Thomas family commence a train journey aboard the private cars *Edgemore* and *Carrizo* to inspect their beet sugar factories and mining properties out West. Their first stop, on September 27, is Niagara Falls; on October 1 they pass through Denver, en route to Colorado Springs.

"Trust May Buy Control of Independent Sugar Factories," *Denver Post*, October 2, 1905, p. 3.

October 4 The Havemeyers survive a potentially fatal mining disaster when a dynamite explosion occurs some five feet from where their party is inspecting the rock crevices of the great Portland Mine at Cripple Creek; the most

seriously injured of the group is W. B. Thomas. They return to Colorado Springs in the evening. The incident is reported on the front page of the *New York Times*.

"Havemeyer Family in Mine Explosion," *New York Times*, October 5, 1905, p. 1, col. 5.

Early October The Havemeyers continue their western journey, visiting the Grand Canyon before traveling along the coast of California from Los Angeles to San Francisco. By mid-October they embark on their return trip to the East via Salt Lake City.

October 18 Louisine and Harry attend a concert in Denver to celebrate his fifty-eighth birthday; the family leaves for New York on October 21.

Plate 238. Claude Monet. *The Houses of Parliament, Sea Gulls*, 1903. Oil on canvas, 31⅞ x 36¼ in. (81 x 92.1 cm). The Art Museum, Princeton University, Princeton, New Jersey, Bequest of Mrs. Vanderbilt Webb, 1979 (79–54) A416

Figure 72. Harry at the mortuary temple of
Ramesses III, Medinet Habu, Egypt, 1906

Figure 73. Harry in Egypt, 1906

"Havemeyer Having a Birthday," *Denver Post*, October 18, 1905,
p. 14; "Sugar Trust will Invest No More Money in State Unless Tariff
is Retained," *Denver Post*, October 19, 1905, p. 1.

November 21 After securing the twenty-four Manets in
the Faure collection for Fr 800,000, Galerie Durand-Ruel
offers Louisine and Harry a final chance to buy the four
Manets they were considering in August; the purchase
price is still Fr 300,000, and the Havemeyers decline again.

GD-R to HOH, 11/21/05, correspondence, Weitzenhoffer files; Weitzenhoffer 1986, p. 181.

Late November Harry is ill with pneumonia.

Weitzenhoffer files.

1906

January 10 The United States Department of State issues
the Havemeyers the necessary documents for a trip to
Egypt and Greece.

Weitzenhoffer 1986, p. 164.

January 26 The Durand-Ruels, who for nearly two years
had tried to interest the Havemeyers in at least one of
Monet's views of the Thames, sell them the artist's *Houses
of Parliament, Sea Gulls* (A416, pl. 238). Their ownership
of this picture is short-lived; it is returned to the gallery
two years later.

February Harry, Louisine, and Electra spend most of the
month in Egypt, visiting the Great Pyramids of Giza and
the tombs at Luxor.

Figure 74. Louisine in Delphi, Greece, 1906

Weitzenhoffer indicated that only Adaline chose to stay at home
(1986, p. 164); however, according to Harry Havemeyer, Horace's
son, it is unlikely that Horace, then sales manager of the American
Sugar Refining Co., went on the trip (Harry Havemeyer to Susan
Alyson Stein, 9/4/1992, correspondence).

March The Havemeyers are in Greece.

AEH to MC, 3/27/06, reporting that he has just received a letter from
Athens from H. O. Havemeyer, who said the family had traveled from
New York to Egypt and will proceed to Vienna after Athens, Have-
meyer correspondence.

April 6 The Havemeyers leave Constantinople.

Per travel document stamped with this date preserved in Weitzen-hoffer files.

Weitzenhoffer 1986, p. 166.

Mid-April The Havemeyers are in Vienna, where they attend the opera, visit palaces and museums, and enjoy dining out. They spend the next three weeks in Paris.

MC to her niece Minnie Cassatt, 4/12/06, correspondence, Weitzen-hoffer files.

Late April–early May Cassatt arranges for the Havemeyers to see, at her Paris apartment, Courbet's *Woman in a Riding Habit* (A127, pl. 24), which belongs to the critic and collector Théodore Duret. Louisine and Harry, who share Cassatt's enthusiasm for the picture, buy it for Fr 15,000, and ask that she "tell Duret to have it packed and shipped. But this was not to be for a long time . . . for Miss Cassatt said she would like to make a study of it," and hence "the portrait remained some time in France."

Havemeyer 1961, pp. 201–2; Weitzenhoffer 1986, p. 164. The picture may not have been shipped for nearly a decade: MMA Department of European Paintings Archives indicate that the work was acquired "??January 17, 1916."

Harry acquires fifty-seven pieces of Near Eastern glazed earthenware, including jugs, jars, plates, bowls, and vases, as well as seven Islamic bronzes from the dealer Dikran Kelekian in Paris (2, place Vendôme); from Kelekian he has been purchasing the "choicest examples" of decorative arts, both Near Eastern and European, since 1889. From Bing, another dealer with whom the Havemeyers had a long association, they buy two Chinese vases with iridescent green glaze and a Japanese black lacquer writing box. In October Cassatt oversees the shipment to the Havemeyers of a terracotta statue and an urn purchased from Kelekian. From now until 1919, through her letters Cassatt would keep Louisine informed of Kelekian's holdings and acquisitions.

Weitzenhoffer 1986, p. 165; for quote and description of Harry's purchases from Kelekian since 1889, see T[homas] B. C[larke], "Letter to the Editor," *American Art News* 6 (December 21, 1907), p. 4; October shipment per MC to LWH, 10/12/[06], 10/29/[06], Havemeyer correspondence.

May 4 The Havemeyers purchase Goya's *Young Lady Wearing a Mantilla and a Basquiña* (A293) from Galerie Durand-Ruel, Paris, for Fr 90,000. On May 8, just before their departure from Europe, they buy Manet's pastel *Mlle Suzette Lemaire* (A364) from the same gallery for Fr 15,000.

Durand-Ruel Archives; JD-R to HOH, 5/8/06, indicating the purchase of the Manet on this date and its addition "to the shipment we make this week of the Goya, Chinese ware, Chinese box, catalogues, etc. . . . belonging to you," correspondence, Weitzenhoffer files.

May 9 The Havemeyers sail home aboard the *Kaiser Wilhelm II.*

June 2 Cassatt writes the Havemeyers that Vollard is reserving drawings by Degas for them, including *Russian Dancer* (A258, pl. 239) and probably *Dancer with a Fan* (A254)—two works they would own. She notes that the former drawing was of interest "to a member of the buying committee for the Lyons Musée," who "asked Vollard to keep it," but instead Louisine and Harry are "to have first call." In the same letter Cassatt notes that she intends to see a "Courbet of a girl in a black hat and feathers" (presumably Fernier 1977–78, no. 358)—a picture that is not acquired. She also reports that she went to Durand-Ruel's gallery at the dealer's request to see Goya's *Portrait*

Plate 239. Edgar Degas. *Russian Dancer*, 1899. Pastel over charcoal on tracing paper, 24 3/8 x 18 in. (61.9 x 45.7 cm). H. O. Havemeyer Collection, Bequest of Mrs. H. O. Havemeyer, 1929 (29.100.556) A258

Plate 240. Agustin Esteve. *Portrait of a Lady with a Guitar.* Oil on canvas, 65 5/8 x 46 in. (166.7 x 116.8 cm). The John and Mable Ringling Museum of Art, Sarasota, Bequest of John Ringling, 1936 (SN358, as *Portrait of the Duchess of Alba*) A277

of a Lady with a Guitar (A277, now considered Esteve, pl. 240), which she found "very charming" and apt to "please most people more than Goyas usually do," even though it is "*Inferior in Art* qualities" to the "Little Lady" (A294, pl. 233) and the "Balcon" (A296, pl. 13). The Havemeyers buy the portrait; by December they have received their new acquisition and are pleased with it.

Quote from MC to LWH, 6/2/[06]; MC to LWH, 12/18/[06], Havemeyer correspondence.

Late spring–summer   The Havemeyers reside at their home on Bayberry Point, Long Island.

Weitzenhoffer 1986, p. 167.

July 19   Cassatt advises the Havemeyers about a Chardin portrait, "really *the best* woman's portrait of the 18th century exclusive of the pastels," that she thinks the owner will sell for Fr 150,000. Before the end of the month she learns that Harry is interested in the picture—probably *Portrait of a Woman with a Fan* (A80, now Attributed to Chardin)—which is subsequently acquired by the Havemeyers from the collection of Henri Michel-Levy, Paris.

MC to LWH, 7/19/[06], 7/19/[06], including Roger Marx's reservations about the portrait, 7/27/[06], Havemeyer correspondence.

July 27   Cassatt informs Louisine and Harry that Vollard is sending them a photograph of "the Greco in Paris belonging to the Russian"—presumably the collector Ivan Shchukin—and "some photos of Cezannes which he says he can get." It is likely that the Cézannes include two landscapes, one of which is probably *The Banks of the Marne* (A77), and *Still Life: Flowers in a Vase* (A76, pl. 50).

MC to LWH, 7/27/[06], Havemeyer correspondence, partially recorded in Weitzenhoffer 1986, p. 167. According to Manuel B. Cossío, Shchukin (Stchoukine) lived at 91, avenue de Wagram, in Paris and owned nine El Grecos at this time (*El Greco*, Madrid, 1908, pp. 601–2, nos. 314–22). For identification of the Cézannes, see Weitzenhoffer 1986, p. 167.

Figure 75. Harry and his associates. From *Denver Post*, October 2, 1906

Late September   Louisine and her sister Anne accompany Harry on a business trip to Denver; the first stop on the way is Detroit, where, from September 24 to 26, they stay at the home of Charles Lang Freer. The Havemeyers are charmed by their host and overwhelmed by his extensive collection of Asian art. (This fall Freer will arrange to have his sixteen Ririomin portraits of Buddhist saints sent from the Lincoln Warehouse, where they are being photographed, to the Havemeyers' home for a private viewing.) After departing Detroit, they visit The Art Institute of Chicago especially to see El Greco's *Assumption of the Virgin* (fig. 66) in its new home.

Weitzenhoffer 1986, pp. 169–70.

October 2   Harry, his business associates, Louisine, and Anne leave Denver on the "sugar special" for a three- to four-day tour of their Colorado factories and to attend a conference in Fort Collins, Colorado. They return to New York by mid-October.

"Sugar King Inspecting Beet Land," *Denver Post*, October 2, 1906, pp. 1, 3; for return date, see Weitzenhoffer 1986, p. 170; also per MC to LWH, 10/12/[06], Havemeyer correspondence.

November 8   The engagement of Adaline Havemeyer to Peter Hood Ballantine Frelinghuysen is announced in the evening *Herald*. Louisine is busy with wedding preparations and celebratory luncheons, teas, dinners, and dances through February 7, 1907, the date set for the marriage.

Newspaper clipping preserved in Weitzenhoffer files; Weitzenhoffer 1986, p. 174.

November 15   Durand-Ruel is eager to have Cassatt's opinion regarding the suitability for the Havemeyers of Manet's *Portrait of Mme Michel Levy* (Rouart and Wildenstein 1975, II, no. 71), which the gallery has just received. Louisine and Harry do not acquire the pastel.

D-R to MC, 11/15/06, correspondence, Weitzenhoffer files.

November 30   Cassatt encourages the Havemeyers to pursue Ingres's *Turkish Bath* (fig. 76), since "it is so rare a thing" and may be available owing to the financial straits of its owner, Prince Amédée de Broglie. (She had sent a photograph of the painting to Louisine earlier in the month.) Louisine responds positively to the picture; however, Cassatt notes that "it remains to be seen what Mr. Havemeyer thinks," though she is "sure the oriental feeling will appeal to him." Harry's opinion is still unclear by mid-December, and it seems to Cassatt that Louisine—busy with her social activities as mother of the bride-to-be—"were flying from me and I were trying my best to catch hold of [her] skirt." The Ingres is not acquired because Harry does not care for it or Louisine is too preoccupied

Figure 76. J.-A.-D. Ingres. *The Turkish Bath*, 1859/63. Oil on canvas, diam. 42 ½ in. (108 cm). Musée du Louvre, Paris (RF 1934)

or Cassatt failed to inquire discreetly about the situation in early January—as she had planned to do. On May 1, 1911, *The Turkish Bath* is purchased by the Société des amis du Louvre.

MC to LWH, 11/23/[06], 11/30/[06], including quote, 12/18/[06], including quote, 12/27/[06], 1/5/[07], Havemeyer correspondence; see also Weitzenhoffer 1986, p. 175.

December 9   Cassatt informs the Havemeyers that Paul Durand-Ruel would have bought El Greco's "St Martin dividing his cloak with a poor man" and the "Assumption

Figure 77. El Greco (Domenikos Theotokopoulos). *Saint Martin and the Beggar*, 1597–99. Oil on canvas, 76 ⅛ x 40 ½ in. (193.5 x 103 cm). National Gallery of Art, Washington, D.C., Widener Collection (1942.9.25.[621])

which it seems hangs opposite it in the same church" had he not been encumbered by tapestries he was bringing back to Paris from Spain. Now, however, "it is too late," perhaps because Joseph Widener had already secured or at least reserved the paintings (fig. 77 and Wethey 1962, no. 17) from the Church of Saint Joseph of Toledo. (These works had been sought not only by the Havemeyers but also by the Prince de Wagram, who had offered Pts 200,000 for the Saint Martin, and by Trotti et Cie, Paris, which would have paid as much as Pts 400,000 for one or both.) On December 21 Cassatt reports that "as for Spain they have not yet got the St. Martin out and won't for some time," evidence that the paintings could not have been in Widener's possession by the end of 1906, as is generally held. Indeed, he seems not to have obtained the El Grecos until two and one half years later.

MC to LWH, 12/9/[06], 12/21/[06], Havemeyer correspondence. In her memoirs Louisine wrote that she and Harry were considering these pictures just before Mr. Havemeyer died. She said they were offered to her after his death, but, "feeling little interest in art," she refused them and "they passed into the collection of Mr. Widener of Philadelphia" (Havemeyer 1961, p. 167).

1907

January 1   Horace is admitted to partnership in Havemeyers and Elder.

Havemeyer 1944, p. 116.

Harnisch sends Cassatt sketches and a thorough description of two pictures in Florence. By January 5 he is convinced they are by Poussin and advises the Havemeyers that the asking price for the pair is L 15,000. After they are cleaned, *Orpheus and Eurydice* (A434, now considered Style of Poussin, pl. 241) and "Orpheus Asking the Way to Hades" (A374, now considered Francisque Millet, *Mercury and Battus*, pl. 242), are shipped to the Havemeyers from Leghorn aboard the SS *Calabria* on July 13.

AEH to MC, 1/1/07; AEH to HOH, 1/5/07, annotated by Louisine, "our Poussins"; AEH to MC, 1/3/07; AEH to HOH, 7/10/07, Havemeyer correspondence. Weitzenhoffer maintained that the works were secured in Italy in April 1907 (1986, p. 178).

January   The Havemeyers host a cotillion for Electra in their main-floor gallery and a dinner for two hundred guests, followed by another cotillion and supper at Sherry's restaurant. During the course of the month Louisine holds a series of Sunday afternoon chamber music recitals at home; seventy-five to one hundred guests are invited to each musicale.

Weitzenhoffer 1986, pp. 175–76.

Plate 241. Style of Nicolas Poussin. *Orpheus and Eurydice*, 3rd quarter of 17th century. Oil on canvas, 47½ x 70¾ in. (120.7 x 179.7 cm). H. O. Havemeyer Collection, Bequest of Mrs. H. O. Havemeyer, 1929 (29.100.20) A434

Plate 242. Francisque Millet. *Mercury and Battus*, 17th century. Oil on canvas, 40 x 70 in. (119.4 x 177.8 cm). H. O. Havemeyer Collection, Bequest of Mrs. H. O. Havemeyer, 1929 (29.100.21) A374

Figure 78. Electra, ca. 1906

Figure 79. Adaline in her wedding gown, 1907

February 7   Adaline weds Peter Hood Ballantine Frelinghuysen at Saint Thomas's Church on Madison Avenue; a reception for 350 guests is held at 1 East 66th Street.

Weitzenhoffer 1986, p. 177.

February 19   Paul Durand-Ruel unsuccessfully tries to persuade the Havemeyers to purchase pictures—by Cézanne (Venturi 1936, no. 341), Daumier (Maison 1968, no. 1-142), Renoir (Daulte 1971, no. 225), Degas (Lemoisne 1946, no. 971), and Manet (Rouart and Wildenstein 1975, II, no. 36)—before they come up for auction in the sale *Collection de M. George Viau* at his Paris gallery on March 4.

Lot nos. 13, 14, 61, 81, 87; D-R to HOH, 2/19/07, identifying the works by lot no., subject, and artist, correspondence, Weitzenhoffer files.

February 26   Adaline and Peter Frelinghuysen leave for an extended honeymoon in Europe. The Havemeyers had intended to go away at the same time as the newlyweds but cancel their plans to travel in Spain with Cassatt, as "Mr. Havemeyer is too busy repulsing the attacks on the Sugar Trust to leave home."

Weitzenhoffer 1986, p. 177, with quote from MC to Minnie Cassatt, 2/26/07, cited.

March 19   Louisine and Harry give Holbein's portrait of *Jean de Carondelet* (A502, now considered Vermeyen, pl. 204) to Horace for his twenty-first birthday.

Unpublished Weitzenhoffer notes from an interview with George G. Frelinghuysen.

March A $30,000,000 suit is filed by the Pennsylvania Sugar Refining Co. against H. O. Havemeyer's American Sugar Refining Co. for restraint of trade under the Sherman Antitrust Act. Harry engages a team of lawyers, headed by John G. Johnson, which prepares for the trial over the next few months.

Weitzenhoffer 1986, pp. 177–78.

April The Havemeyers take a hasty trip to Europe and spend the month in Italy and France. Through Cassatt they purchase two landscapes, a still life, and a woman's portrait by Courbet, two studies of dancers by Degas, one of which may be his pastel *Dancers at the Bar* (A218), a Cézanne still life (probably A72 or A78, pl. 243), and a portrait of a woman by an unknown artist. This group of pictures "belonging to Mr. H. O. Havemeyer" is deposited by Cassatt with Galerie Durand-Ruel on May 7 and shipped to the collectors on May 11.

For the trip, see Weitzenhoffer 1986, p. 178; date per MC to Minnie Cassatt, 3/5/08, recalling the Havemeyers' visit "last April," correspondence, Weitzenhoffer files. The acquisitions, first cited by Weitzenhoffer, who erroneously identified them as purchased from Durand-Ruel (1986, p. 178), correspond to a list of paintings that Cassatt deposited with Durand-Ruel on May 7 for shipment to the Havemeyers. Durand-Ruel Archives record the works as D11178–85; they are listed on a consular invoice of May 8 as Courbet, "Le puits noir," "Nature morte," "Paysage," and "Portrait de femme"; two Degases, both "Etude de danseuse"; Cézanne, "Fruits"; and "*Inconnu*. Portrait de femme."

Plate 243. Paul Cézanne. *Still Life with a Ginger Jar and Eggplants*, ca. 1890. Oil on canvas, 28½ x 36 in. (72.4 x 91.4 cm). Bequest of Stephen C. Clark, 1960 (61.101.4) A78

Late April Just before their departure for New York, the Havemeyers seem to have made a one-day trip to Brussels in the company of Cassatt and Duret to see Courbet's portrait of *Mme de Brayer* (A129, pl. 244), which they acquire. Presumably this is the "fine woman's portrait" that Cassatt advised her friends in June 1906 is "in Belgium" and that "Duret hopes to be able to get"; no doubt it is

Plate 244. Gustave Courbet. *Mme de Brayer*, 1858. Oil on canvas, 36 x 28⅝ in. (91.4 x 72.7 cm). H. O. Havemeyer Collection, Bequest of Mrs. H. O. Havemeyer, 1929 (29.100.118) A129

the Courbet portrait included in the group of works the Havemeyers bought through Cassatt this month.

Weitzenhoffer 1986, pp. 178–79; MC to LWH, 6/2/[06], Havemeyer correspondence.

May 6–12 Some 2,000 foreign-born workers stage a wage strike at the Havemeyers and Elder refinery in Williamsburg. The company's compromise offer of a 1½-cent-an-hour increase is accepted on May 12.

New York Times, May 13, 1907, p. 2.

June 29 Paul Durand-Ruel solicits Cassatt's opinion about two paintings by El Greco he has just received from Madrid —a "Tête de philosophe ou d'apôtre" and "une vue de Toledo." By August 8 he advises the Havemeyers that the painting of interest—El Greco's *View of Toledo* (A303, pl. 60)—is available for $16,000, inclusive of delivery; the collectors do not buy the picture. However, Louisine would acquire it in 1909, after Harry's death.

D-R to MC, 6/29/07, 8/8/07, reporting the contents of a cable he has sent to HOH, correspondence, Weitzenhoffer files. Unpublished Weitzenhoffer notes indicate that the El Greco head was sold to Mrs. Huntington in 1909.

October–December Louisine cares for her sick mother and attends to her daughter Adaline, whose pregnancy confines her to bed at 1 East 66th Street.

Weitzenhoffer 1986, p. 180.

November 19 The suit filed by the Pennsylvania Sugar Refining Co. against the Havemeyers' American Sugar Refining Co. is brought to trial in the United States Circuit Court in Philadelphia. However, after the jury is selected, the trial is postponed so that the complaint can be amended.

New York Times, November 20, 1907, p. 16, col. 3.

November 20 During a raid on the Brooklyn docks of the American Sugar Refining Co., a special agent of the Treasury Department discovers that the scales used to weigh and assess raw sugar have been tampered with. The United States Attorney, now armed with concrete evidence, is able to bring a charge of systematic fraud against the company.

Weitzenhoffer 1986, p. 180.

Figure 82. Electra and Louisine in mourning, December 1907

Figure 83. Horace, ca. 1907

Figure 80. Harry on horseback, Commack, Long Island, 1907

November 28 After Thanksgiving dinner Harry and Horace set out to hunt game birds at Merrivale, the Havemeyers' three-hundred-acre wooded retreat in Commack, Long Island; Harry is stricken with severe abdominal pains.

Obituary, *New York Times*, December 5, 1907, p. 3, col. 1; Havemeyer 1944, p. 70.

November 29 Cassatt tells Louisine that the portrait by David (*La Vestale*, fig. 81), a photograph of which she has sent to the Havemeyers, is not too expensive, considering its charm, and is a fine work "but it isn't the Ingres." She also says Duret strongly advises the Havemeyers to buy it and that he has reproached her for "being impervious to charm." Harry's state of health precludes consideration of the David and of the "two very good pictures" by Corot

Figure 81. Jacques-Louis David. *La Vestale*, ca. 1784–87. Oil on canvas, 31 ⅞ x 25 ⅝ in. (81 x 65 cm). Private collection

(Robaut 1905, nos. 1332, 2004) that George Durand-Ruel had recommended on November 25 from the upcoming Paris sale of the *Collection de M. Alfred Robaut*, Hôtel Drouot, Paris, December 18, 1907.

MC to LWH, 11/29/[07], including description that allows identification of the portrait as *La Vestale*, which Duret owned by 1909, Havemeyer correspondence; GD-R to HOH, 11/25/07, indicating Corot recommendations—lot nos. 3, 4—and enclosing a catalogue of the Robaut sale, correspondence, Weitzenhoffer files.

December 4 Harry Havemeyer dies in Commack, Long Island, at 3:00 P.M. at age sixty from acute nephritis with uremia.

Weitzenhoffer 1986, p. 181; obituary, *New York Times*, December 5, 1907, p. 3, col. 1; Havemeyer 1944, p. 70.

December 6 Harry's funeral is held and Louisine's mother dies.

Weitzenhoffer 1986, p. 181; obituary, *New York Times*, December 7, 1907, p. 9, col. 5.

December 31 Adaline gives birth to twin girls, who die within a few days.

Decimal Record of the Class of 1905 in Bryn Mawr College, Bryn Mawr, n.d., p. 47.

1908

January Horace becomes Director of the American Sugar Refining Co. and President of the firm of Havemeyers and Elder.

Havemeyer 1944, p. 72.

March Louisine, accompanied by her daughter Electra, who had taken charge of the travel arrangements, and by her sister Anne, sail for Europe aboard the *Kaiser Wilhelm*.

Cassatt meets them when they arrive on March 10. They are back in New York by May.

Weitzenhoffer 1986, p. 183.

October 15 Cassatt writes to Electra that "it is just as well that [she] did not buy" the "large Goya" that the Havemeyer children had intended to present to the Metropolitan in memory of their father. (The gift would have seemed fitting, since Goyas "were [among] the last pictures [her] father saw intending to buy.")

MC to EH, 10/15/[08], including quote, n.d. [ca. 9 or 10/08], correspondence, Weitzenhoffer files; see also Weitzenhoffer 1986, p. 184. The subject of the intended gift is not revealed in the correspondence. However, among the Goyas that Harry had wanted to acquire prior to his death was a "Queen on Horseback" (presumably a copy after Gassier and Wilson 1971, no. 777), a painting that Cassatt and the children were unable to convince Louisine to buy at this time (MC to EH, 5/27/[08], 10/15/[08], correspondence, Weitzenhoffer files).

November Cassatt books passage to New York so that she can be with Louisine on the first anniversary of Harry's death.

Weitzenhoffer 1986, p. 183.

November 25 Louisine decides to dispose of a group of pictures in order to buy El Greco's "St. Martin" with the proceeds from their sale. The Durand-Ruels will try to find buyers for these works in Paris. However, in late March 1909 Cassatt breaks the disappointing news to Louisine—and to Electra and Horace, who are equally enthusiastic about the acquisition—that the "St. Martin" is no longer available, since the dealer Boussod had "found an amateur in America for the two Grecos . . . and that the affair, while *not absolutely* fixed . . . will be concluded in June." (The dealer had wanted to sell the two pictures together; Louisine had been interested only in the "St. Martin," for which she was willing to spend $60,000.)

JD-R to LWH, 11/25/08; MC to EH, 3/21/[09], Monday, n.d. [probably 3/22/09], correspondence, Weitzenhoffer files. Though neither the American collector's name nor the subject of the other El Greco is revealed in these letters, it is likely that the reference is to Widener's acquisition of the two paintings from the Church of Saint Joseph of Toledo (Wethey 1962, no. 17 and fig. 77), about which Cassatt had written the Havemeyers in December 1906.

November 30 Durand-Ruel, New York, receives ten pictures consigned for sale by Louisine: a seascape by Clays (A83); Decamps's *Smyrna Harbor* (A182), *The Oak and the Reed* (A194, pl. 190), and *The Battle of Jericho* (A189); Monet's *Houses of Parliament, Sea Gulls* (A416, pl. 238) and *Bridge over a Pool of Water Lilies* (A414, pl. 219); *Episode from the Acts of the Apostles* and *The Road to Golgotha* by Vasari (A332, 333, both now considered unknown 16th-century Italian [Ferrarese] painter); a Spanish school "Buste de femme" (A424, now Attributed to

Pantoja de la Cruz); and a School of Lippi, *Madonna and Child, with Bishop Adoring* (A341, now considered Imitator of Lippi). Only three are sold: the gallery buys back Monet's *Houses of Parliament* before the end of the year and the *Madonna and Child* and Decamps's *Oak and the Reed* in February. In the summer of 1909 Louisine decides to keep the Clays and Monet's *Bridge over a Pool of Water Lilies*; the remaining works are returned to her in May 1910. Decamps's *Smyrna Harbor* is not reconsigned after this date, but the four other paintings are consigned to the gallery each year through May 1914 in the hope, which proves vain, that buyers would be found.

Unpublished Weitzenhoffer notes from Durand-Ruel Stock et Depot, 1904–1924–25; JD-R to LWH, 11/30/08, 12/16/08, 12/31/08, correspondence, Weitzenhoffer files, supplemented and confirmed by Durand-Ruel Archives; see also Weitzenhoffer 1982, p. 217, n. 3; for subsequent consignment dates for A189, 332, 333, 424, see Appendix.

December 3 At a preliminary hearing of the United States government's suit against the American Sugar Refining Co., Treasury Agent Richard Parr testifies that "fraudulent scales were in use at the company's piers in Brooklyn, where the raw sugar was weighed before being assessed for duty." Photographs of the scales are introduced as evidence.

New York Times, December 4, 1908, p. 1, col. 1.

December 9 Cassatt arrives in New York; she stays at the Havemeyer residence through the "last of next week." Her brief visit to the States includes holidays spent with her family in Philadelphia and an overnight stay with Louisine at Hill-Stead—the Connecticut home of their friends Mr. and Mrs. Alfred Pope and their daughter Theodate.

Date per MC to Minnie Cassatt, 12/10/08, written from 1 East 66th Street, indicating that she "got here yesterday" and is "well enough now" to enjoy "any number of engagements," correspondence, Weitzenhoffer files; see also Weitzenhoffer 1986, p. 186.

December 16 Louisine, no doubt in Cassatt's company, must have admired a figure painting by Corot at Durand-Ruel, New York, because Joseph Durand-Ruel informs her that he will "faciliter l'entrée dans votre collection de notre belle figure de Corot," not by sale but by exchange. (Feeling financially insecure as a new widow, Louisine for the moment seems to prefer acquiring by exchange.) The dealer, taking into account the pictures Louisine had consigned to the gallery two weeks earlier, proposes four options for an exchange: "Le nymphéas de Monet" and "le Cazin" (A414, 66); "le Clays," "le Cazin," and "le petit pastel de Renoir" (A83, 66, 461); "le parlement de Monet" and "le Clays" (A416, 83); or, should she decide to sell it, Renoir's "femme au bord de la mer" (A460, *By the Seashore*, pl. 6). Though Louisine seems not to have acquired the Corot through exchange at this time, she does dispose of the Cazin (A66) and Renoir's pastel *Young Woman Reading* (A461) through Durand-Ruel. Both are sold to the gallery this month, the Renoir on December 31 for $500, the same day she sells back Monet's *Houses of Parliament, Sea Gulls* (A416, pl. 238) for $5,000.

MC to Minnie Cassatt, 12/10/08, indicating that Cassatt had planned a luncheon at Louisine's house on December 16, which suggests that they may have gone to the gallery together; JD-R to LWH, 12/16/08, 12/31/08, correspondence, Weitzenhoffer files. Though there is no evidence that Louisine acquired the "belle figure" in question, the possibility remains that she bought it at this date or later, since acquisition dates for three paintings of single figures by Corot in the Havemeyer collection are still unknown (see A101, 105, 108).

1909

Early January Cassatt returns to France; she is in Paris by January 14 after her "stormy passage" aboard the *America*.

MC to LWH, 1/14/[09], Havemeyer correspondence; see also Weitzenhoffer 1986, p. 186.

January 27 Louisine purchases Cassatt's *Mother and Child* (A61) from Durand-Ruel, New York, for $2,500. This painting is among the handful of works she lends to the Cassatt exhibition at the St. Botolph Club, Boston, February 8–22, 1909.

February 1 Durand-Ruel, New York, buys Louisine's School of Lippi *Madonna and Child, with Bishop Adoring* (A341, now considered Imitator of Lippi) for $6,500; it is sold the same day to Mrs. Collis P. Huntington for $8,000. Prior to this sale, the picture had been seriously considered by the Worcester Art Museum, which had requested "it on approval during January so that the board of directors may examine it."

JD-R to LWH, 12/31/08, including quote, correspondence, Weitzenhoffer files. Weitzenhoffer described this picture as having been sold in Italy (1986, p. 184); Durand-Ruel Archives indicate that it was purchased in Italy.

February 9–10 The United States government's suit against the American Sugar Refining Co. for customs fraud is tried in a United States district court. Federal authorities seek penalties amounting to $1,250,000. In March the government obtains a verdict penalizing the defendant $134,000. In addition, on April 29, the Attorney General and the Secretary of the Treasury accept the sugar company's offer of restitution, totaling $2,239,000 in back duties. Criminal charges may still be filed, however, by the Department of Justice.

New York Times, February 10, 1909, p. 6, cols. 3, 4; February 11, 1909, p. 12, col. 1; April 30, 1909, p. 2, col. 5.

Early February Seeking respite from unfavorable press coverage of the Sugar Trust scandal, Louisine, her sister Anne, and Electra sail for Europe on the *Kaiser Wilhelm*.

En route Louisine tries to throw herself overboard but is saved by Electra.

Weitzenhoffer 1986, p. 188.

February 16 Joseph Durand-Ruel sends Horace a check for $12,000 for Decamps's *Oak and the Reed* (A194, pl. 190), which the New York gallery had sold on Louisine's behalf to James J. Hill on February 5 for $13,500.

JD-R to HH, 2/16/09, correspondence, Weitzenhoffer files; purchase date and prices confirmed by Durand-Ruel Archives. This is the painting Weitzenhoffer identified as the Decamps consigned in November "with the asking price of $11,000" (1986, p. 184).

Early–mid-February Louisine is quite ill upon her arrival in Brussels, apparently suffering from a "nervous breakdown." Louisine, Anne, and Electra spend a day in Bruges and Ghent. Cassatt expects them in Paris about February 17 or 18. After depositing Anne in Paris, Louisine and Electra proceed to Italy.

Weitzenhoffer 1986, p. 188; MC to EH, Sunday evening, n.d. [2/09], Thursday, n.d. [2/09], correspondence, Weitzenhoffer files.

End of February–mid-March Louisine and Electra sail to Sicily with a stopover in Tunis. They spend the first three weeks of March in Italy. Along the "wonderful route from Pisa to Genoa," they stop in Florence, visiting the Uffizi and several private collections in the company of Harnisch. Louisine later pursues a number of works they see with Harnisch, including two in the Martelli family collection, a so-called Veronese *Portrait of a Lady* (A278, now Attributed to Fasolo, pl. 247) shown "high up on the wall & [in] miserable light," which she ultimately acquires, and a marble bust of Saint John the Baptist (fig. 92).

MC to EH, 3/21/[09], correspondence, Weitzenhoffer files; Uffizi visit per AEH to LWH, 3/5/13; Martelli visit per AEH to LWH, 7/30/09, 7/18/13, Havemeyer correspondence. Weitzenhoffer dated the departure for Sicily to February 29 (1986, p. 188); however, 1909 was not a leap year.

Plate 245. J.-A.-D. Ingres. *Maria Luigi Carlo Zenobia Salvatore Cherubini (1760–1842)*, 1841. Oil on canvas, 32 ¼ x 28 in. (81.9 x 71.1 cm). Cincinnati Art Museum, Bequest of Mary M. Emery (1927.386) A331

March 10 Horace arranges for Ingres's *Maria Luigi Carlo Zenobia Salvatore Cherubini* (A331, pl. 245) to be delivered to Durand-Ruel, New York, so that it can be shown to "a few amateurs who will be in town for the coming auction sales." Before she left for Europe, Louisine had told Joseph Durand-Ruel that the portrait was to be left at his "disposition in case [he] had a chance to dispose of it": the asking price is $10,000. The work is returned to Louisine on May 11, 1910, but is eventually sold; by 1922 it appears on the art market.

JD-R to HH, 3/8/09, including quote, 3/12/09, correspondence, Weitzenhoffer files; date of return per unpublished Weitzenhoffer notes from Durand-Ruel Stock et Depot, 1904–1924–25.

March 19–22 Louisine and Electra travel by car "across the mountains" to Nice and then to Pau. They plan to be in Spain by March 24.

MC to EH, 3/19/[09], n.d. [probably 3/22/09], correspondence, Weitzenhoffer files.

Figure 84. Attributed to Francisco de Goya y Lucientes. *Portrait of a Little Girl*. Oil on canvas, 32¾ x 23 in. (83.2 x 58.4 cm). Private collection

Late March–late April Louisine and Electra visit Seville en route to Madrid. Ricardo de Madrazo shows them "nearly all the great Goyas in Madrid." He secures Goya's *Doña Maria Teresa de Borbón y Vallabriga, Condesa de Chinchón* (A295, now Attributed to Goya, pl. 12) for Louisine and handles the negotiations involved in Electra's purchase of the artist's *Portrait of a Little Girl* (now Attributed to Goya, fig. 84) for Pts 70,000 on April 20. Though the two works are to be sent to New York on May 22, their shipment is delayed until October owing to problems with customs documents.

Weitzenhoffer 1986, pp. 188–89, 195, repr. of Electra's receipt; MC to EH, 3/21/[09], 4/13/[09], correspondence, Weitzenhoffer files; RdM to LWH, 5/22/09; RdM to EH, 6/2/09, RdM to LWH, 10/3/09, 10/7/09, 10/16/09; MC to LWH, 2/22/[10], indicating that she thought Electra's purchase and the way it was handled by Madrazo were ill-advised, Havemeyer correspondence; quote from Havemeyer 1961, p. 166. The Goyas they saw with Madrazo included Gassier and Wilson 1971, nos. 341, 793, 807, 808, 828, and possibly nos. 221, 805. With Madrazo they also visited the collections of the Duke of Alba and his grandmother (Havemeyer 1961, pp. 166–74).

Mid-April At Cassatt's suggestion, Louisine and Electra drive from Madrid to the nearby town of Illescas to see El Greco's *Saint Ildefonso* (Wethey 1962, no. 23). From May through September Madrazo explores whether it may be possible for Louisine to acquire the painting, though he feels "that [it] will never leave the Church" because of impending legislation that will "prevent objects of art from leaving Spain"; by September 3 he believes "there is no hope."

MC to EH, 3/19/[09], 4/2/[09], correspondence, Weitzenhoffer files; RdM to LWH, 5/22/09, including quote; RdM to EH, 6/2/09, 6/14/09, RdM to LWH, 9/3/09, including quote, Havemeyer correspondence.

April 25 Louisine and Electra arrive in Paris. The next day Louisine purchases Rubens's *Saint Cecilia* (A471, now considered Workshop of Rubens) from Trotti et Cie, Paris. Cassatt, who had reserved the work for Louisine, arranges for its shipment to New York. In October Cassatt laments that the picture—which had been delayed owing to problems with a consular invoice and affidavits—"surely . . . must be free by this time." Louisine receives the work by December.

MC to EH, 3/21/[09], 4/2/[09], correspondence, Weitzenhoffer files; MC to LWH, 10/17/[09], including quote, 12/28/[09], Havemeyer correspondence; acquisition date per MMA Department of European Paintings Archives. Louisine had been interested in acquiring a Rubens just before Harry's death (MC to D-R, 9/15/07, correspondence, Weitzenhoffer files).

April 29 Louisine buys El Greco's *View of Toledo* (A303, pl. 60) from Galerie Durand-Ruel, Paris, for Fr 70,000.

May 1 Louisine and Electra visit the Paris home of Mme Cassin, "the wealthiest courtisane in France," and see her "marvellous collection of pictures."

Weitzenhoffer 1986, pp. 190, 267, n. 18.

May 5 Louisine and Cassatt spot Courbet's *Mme Auguste Cuoq* (A133, pl. 246) "amid the most dreadful lot of trash" at the presale viewing of the collection of *Mme de V.* [Mme de Vermeulen de Villiers], Galerie Georges Petit, Paris. On May 6 Paul Durand-Ruel acquires it for Louisine with a bid of Fr 50,000. The painting is shipped to Louisine in early September, along with El Greco's *View of Toledo* and a drypoint by Cassatt.

Lot no. 38; quote from Havemeyer 1961, p. 200; D-R to LWH, 8/20/09, 9/17/09, correspondence, Weitzenhoffer files. The shipment, which arrived in New York on October 13, also included works for Payne: Courbet's *Young Ladies from the Village* (MMA 40.175), Degas's "une répétition de danse" (Lemoisne 1946, no. 362) and Manet's *Springtime* (Rouart and Wildenstein 1975, I, no. 372), the last a picture "to try out," which he decided to acquire this year.

Mid-May Louisine and Electra are in London.

Weitzenhoffer files.

Plate 246. Gustave Courbet. *Mme Auguste Cuoq (Mathilde Desportes, 1828–1910)*, 1857. Oil on canvas, 69½ x 42½ in. (176.5 x 108 cm). H. O. Havemeyer Collection, Bequest of Mrs. H. O. Havemeyer, 1929 (29.100.130) A133

Plate 247. Attributed to Giovanni Antonio Fasolo. *Portrait of a Lady*. Oil on canvas, 70⅛ x 45⁹⁄₁₆ in. (178.1 x 115.7 cm). The Art Institute of Chicago, Gift of Chester Dale (1946.382) A278

May 20 Louisine and Electra are returning to New York on board the *Mauretania*.

RdM to EH, 6/2/09, Havemeyer correspondence.

May 25 On Cassatt's recommendation, Louisine consigns Cézanne's *Self-Portrait with a Cap* (A71, pl. 236) and *The Banks of the Marne* (A77) to Joseph Durand-Ruel. Because the market is stronger abroad, they are sent to the Paris gallery in early June, a fact bemoaned by the art critic for the New York *Sun* on June 11. On August 20 Durand-Ruel, Paris, advises Louisine that the gallery has found a buyer for the pictures and that she will realize a profit of more than $3,000. The Cézannes are sold to the Russian collector Ivan Morosof on September 14 for Fr 30,000 ($6,000).

Weitzenhoffer 1986, pp. 191, 267, n. 19; unpublished Weitzenhoffer notes from Durand-Ruel Stock et Depot, 1904–1924–25; D-R to LWH, 8/20/09, correspondence, Weitzenhoffer files. Durand-Ruel Archives record that the Cézannes were purchased from Louisine on August 31 for Fr 15,000 and sold to Morozov on September 14 for Fr 30,000.

June 8 After two weeks of litigation, the Pennsylvania Sugar Refining Co. agrees to an out-of-court settlement: the American Sugar Refining Co. must make combined payments of $10,250,000.

New York Times, June 9, 1909, p. 1, col. 7.

By July 30 Harnisch, who in early May had told Louisine that he hoped she would not "lose" the Veronese they had seen together in Florence, examines the picture in better light and finds "no retouchings." He sends Cassatt complete documentation on the painting, *Portrait of a Lady* (A278, pl. 247, now Attributed to Fasolo), in order to spare her a hot summer trip to Italy. Louisine remits L 70,000 for the purchase of the picture in August; however, it requires another year and an additional payment of

L 40,000 in August 1910 before Harnisch is able to conclude his difficult negotiations with the owners, the three Martelli brothers. (Despite equally strenuous efforts, Morgan had earlier failed to acquire four Donatellos from the Martellis.) Though the portrait is "with" Harnisch by early September 1910, Louisine does not receive it for another year and a half for various reasons, including the quarantine of steamers during a cholera epidemic in the fall of 1910, the illness of an elderly restorer throughout "the frightful 3-month long rainy season," problems with customs duties and export taxes, and a "dreadful mishap" to the SS *Princesse Irene*, aboard which the portrait had been shipped from Genoa to New York in April 1911.

Also by July 30 Harnisch has secured for L 3,000, plus 5 percent commission, Kobell's *Landscape with Figures* (A338) and *The Storm* (A339), which Louisine intends "as a surprise for Electra." Since he planned to send the Kobells along with the so-called Veronese, he ultimately keeps them for some time, until April 1911—nine months after he expected to ship the three pictures to Louisine by American Express care of Cassatt in Paris.

AEH to LWH, 5/5/09, including quote; AEH to MC, 7/30/09, including quote; AEH to LWH, 7/30/09, 8/31/09, 12/9/09; MC to LWH, 2/4/[10]; AEH to LWH, 3/12/10, 7/16/10, 8/15/10; LWH to AEH, 8/15/10; AEH to LWH, 9/5/10, including quote, 1/18/11, including quote, 2/28/11, 3/20/11, 4/20/11, 4/29/11, including quote, 2/4/12, indicating the price paid for the Veronese as L 115,500 inclusive and that of its frame as L 5,250 inclusive and the price of the Kobells as L 3,150 inclusive, Havemeyer correspondence. In the correspondence the code names "Paul," "Paula," and "Paolo" were used for the so-called Paolo Veronese, a necessary precaution, as the Italian government was closely monitoring the export of works of art.

August 7 Adaline and Peter Frelinghuysen's first child to survive, Frederica Louisine, is born in Morristown, New Jersey.

Havemeyer 1944, p. 70.

August 20 Monet's *Bridge over a Pool of Water Lilies* (A414, pl. 219) and Clays's seascape (A83), which had been consigned for sale to Durand-Ruel, New York, since early last winter, are returned to Louisine at her request. At the end of the month Louisine advises Paul Durand-Ruel that she has decided to keep these pictures because they please Adaline, who is building a house in Morristown, and that she would prefer "to sell the largest paintings, such as the Decamps and the Dupré." Presumably Louisine still wishes to dispose of Decamps's *Battle of Jericho* (A189) and/or *Smyrna Harbor* (A182), which are already with the gallery, and Dupré's *Woodcutter* (A272), which she places on consignment in the fall.

D-R to LWH, 8/20/09; LWH to PD-R, 8/31/09, correspondence, Weitzenhoffer files.

September 14 At Louisine's request, Cassatt asks Durand-Ruel if a certain portrait by Hals from the Maurice Kann collection is for sale, as Horace has "a great desire for a Hals." Of the six Hals paintings in the collection, Durand-Ruel singles out three on September 18, noting that the largest and most important male portrait is available for £45,000. This work, *Portrait of a Man* (Slive 1974, no. 67), would be purchased by Frick in 1910.

MC to D-R, 9/14/09; D-R to MC, 9/18/09, correspondence, Weitzenhoffer files. The Frick portrait was described in the same terms used by the dealer and illustrated in two 1909 articles on the Kann collection: Louis Gillet, *Revue de l'Art* 26 (November 1909); A. Marguillier, "Collection de Feu M. Maurice Kann," *Les Arts* 8 (April 1909), no. 88, pp. 17, 18. The latter may have triggered Horace's interest.

September 20–November 30 Louisine lends three Dutch paintings (A11, 326, pl. 187, A449, pl. 63) to *The Hudson-Fulton Celebration* at the Metropolitan Museum.

Shown as nos. 89, 53, 88.

Plate 248. *Angel*, French, 13th-century style. Limestone, originally polychromed, h. 26 ½ in. (67.3 cm). H. O. Havemeyer Collection, Bequest of Mrs. H. O. Havemeyer, 1929 (29.100.27)

October 6 Cassatt discovers a statue of an angel priced at Fr 25,000 at Trotti et Cie, Paris; in early December she urges Louisine to acquire this "guardian angel," possibly as a wedding gift for Electra. Louisine sees the statue

(*Angel*, now considered French 13th-century style, pl. 248), which Cassatt thinks "goes with the Rubens & all [Louisine's] best" before the end of December and acquires it before the end of the following year.

This sculpture was "recorded as of doubtful authenticity" by the Executive Committee of the Metropolitan Museum on May 15, 1933, as were two other Gothic statues, *Saint John the Evangelist as a Youth* and the *Foolish Virgin* (MMA 29.100.31), which Louisine later acquired through Cassatt. The three pieces were published as forgeries in James J. Rorimer, "Forgeries of Medieval Stone Sculpture," *Gazette des Beaux-Arts* 26 (July–December 1944), pp. 195–210.

October 17 Cassatt writes Louisine that "the Courbet flowers [Fernier 1977–78, no. 182 or 361] . . . were sold [by the Bernheims] in Germany either to Berlin or Hamburg Museum, so there is no chance of your getting it now." Louisine later laments that "Les Pivoines," which is "now I am told in a German Museum," was lost "through my own stupidity."

MC to LWH, 10/17/[09], Havemeyer correspondence; Havemeyer 1961, p. 195. Cassirer Archives indicate that Bernheim-Jeune sold Fernier 1977–78, nos. 182 and 361, to the German dealer Paul Cassirer on June 9, 1909; that month Cassirer sold the former to the Kunsthalle Hamburg for DM 28,000 and the latter to the Kunsthalle Bremen for DM 20,000. Walter Feilchenfeldt kindly provided this information.

November 3 Durand-Ruel, New York, collects Dupré's *Woodcutter* (A272) and "the Italian school pictures" from 1 East 66th Street. George Durand-Ruel reminds Louisine that Harry had tried to sell the Dupré years ago and asks what the lowest acceptable price would be.

GD-R to LWH, 11/3/09, correspondence, Weitzenhoffer files; Weitzenhoffer notes from Durand-Ruel Stock et Depot, 1904–1924–25, which indicates that Dupré's "Le bûcheron" and a Piazzetta *Madonna* (A425) were consigned on this date.

November 16–25 While Louisine is at Hilltop, three prominent art-world figures visit the Havemeyer collection at 1 East 66th Street: August F. Jaccaci and Max Friedländer, escorted by George Durand-Ruel, and Ludwig Justi, the new director of the Nationalgalerie, Berlin. Justi is "deeply impressed" by the collection and calls it "a monument to American artistic taste"; he praises the "perfectly ideal way" the pictures are installed "by a woman of real art understanding."

GD-R to LWH, 11/17/09, correspondence, Weitzenhoffer files; see also Weitzenhoffer 1986, p. 197, with quote from an interview with Justi in the *New York Times*, January 23, 1910, part 5, p. 2.

December 3 Madrazo offers Louisine the opportunity to buy Goya's portrait of a "little child [from] the Duke of Sexto . . . with the big hat and the music sheet" (Gassier and Wilson 1971, no. 1553) as well as a pair of portraits, Goya's *Don Ignacio Garcini y Queralt, Brigadier of Engineers* and *Doña Josefa Castilla Portugal de Garcini* (figs. 85, 86), available for Fr 150,000 from Vincente Garcini, a

Figure 85. Francisco de Goya y Lucientes. *Don Ignacio Garcini y Queralt, Brigadier of Engineers*, 1804. Oil on canvas, 41 x 32¾ in. (104.1 x 83.2 cm). Bequest of Harry Payne Bingham, 1955 (55.145.1)

Figure 86. Francisco de Goya y Lucientes. *Doña Josefa Castilla Portugal de Garcini*, 1804. Oil on canvas, 41 x 32⅜ in. (104.1 x 82.2 cm). Bequest of Harry Payne Bingham, 1955 (55.145.2)

descendant of the sitters. Louisine does not pursue the child's portrait, and, rather than acquiring the Garcini pictures for her own collection, she arranges for their sale for Fr 165,000 inclusive to Payne, to whom they are sent on February 12, 1910. The paintings arrive in New York by April 3 and are thought to be "beautiful" by Louisine when she sees them the following week. In this transaction Louisine ignores Cassatt's admonition that "buying Goyas through Madrazo [presents too great] a risk."

RdM to LWH, 12/3/09, including quote, 12/4/09, 2/14/10, 4/22/10, including quote; MC to LWH, 2/22/10, including quote, Havemeyer correspondence. MC to EH, 3/7/[09], indicates that Gassier and Wilson 1971, no. 1553, was one of two children's portraits by Goya known to Cassatt—she liked the picture but recalled that Harry and Louisine did not care for it when it was offered to them for Fr 80,000, correspondence, Weitzenhoffer files.

December 12 Electra's engagement to James Watson Webb is formally announced.

Weitzenhoffer 1986, p. 193.

December 24 The Metropolitan's Board of Trustees approves Louisine's offer to lend the Museum Courbet's *Woman with a Parrot* (A145, pl. 19), and Assistant Director Edward Robinson sends her an official loan request.

MMA Archives.

During the year Kelekian publishes *The Potteries of Persia: Being a Brief History of the Art of Ceramics in the Near East*, in which he illustrates a Persian bowl (MMA 45.153.4) and a Persian vase (pl. 99) in the Havemeyer collection. The latter is described as "the finest dark blue specimen I know in the very choice collection of potteries made during the last few years of his life by the late Mr. H. O. Havemeyer of New York." A "fine red bottle" in the Havemeyer collection is singled out as one of the "few handsome specimens [of Persian lusterware] in ruby red."

Dikran Khan Kelekian, *The Potteries of Persia: Being a Brief History of the Art of Ceramics in the Near East*, Paris, 1909, pp. 25, 34, figs. 2, 17.

1910

February 8 The wedding of Electra and James Watson Webb takes place at Saint Bartholomew's Church on Park Avenue, and a small family reception follows at 1 East 66th Street. On the next day the Webbs leave for their honeymoon in Europe; they spend three weeks in England and a week in Holland and visit with Cassatt while in Paris in April. The couple returns to the States in early May.

Weitzenhoffer 1986, pp. 212–13; MC to LWH, 4/8/[10], 4/20/[10], 4/25/[10], 5/10/[10], Havemeyer correspondence.

Figure 87. Electra and James Watson Webb, winter 1909–10

February 18 Louisine receives a letter from the Black Hand, a Sicilian gang active in Italy and the United States, threatening to "blow up house destroy everybody, kill with revolver or with dagger or send in poinsend food for you" if she does not pay $2,500. She meets with detectives and arranges a plan for entrapping the extortionists, which she implements on February 24 by dropping off a tin filled with green paper and marked bills at a designated spot, the East 66th–67th Street entrance to Central Park. Two teenage members of the gang fall victim to the trap and are arrested at about nine that evening.

Evening World, February 25, 1910, p. 2.

March 10 At the posthumous sale of *The James S. Inglis Collection*, American Art Association, New York, Durand-

Plate 249. Julian Alden Weir. *Fruit*, ca. 1888. Oil on canvas, 21⅛ x 17⅛ in. (53.7 x 43.5 cm). Purchase, Gift of Robert E. Tod, by exchange, 1980 (1980.219) A5091

Ruel purchases for Louisine Degas's *Woman Drying Her Arm* (A243) for $2,500, Rousseau's *Landscape Sketch* (A470) for $500, and Weir's *Fruit* (A509, pl. 249) for $325.

Lot nos. 63, 99, 101.

March 12 Harnisch informs Louisine that the Amerighi family is now willing to sell the "lovely terracotta Madonna" by Donatello for L 120,000. He resumes discussion of the sculpture in spring 1912, advising her that Morgan is not interested in it. When Louisine and Harry had first seen the piece in Italy the owners did not intend to sell it; therefore, as Harnisch remarks in September, "no price was to my knowledge offered by Mr. Havemeyer." Harnisch attempts to obtain a reduction in price and export permission, and in February 1913 he tells Louisine that "with ready money" the Donatello can be acquired for L 100,000. Whether she purchases this sculpture is not known.

AEH to LWH, 3/12/10, including quote, 3/14/12, 5/11/12, 7/16/12, 9/17/12, including quote, 2/3/13, including quote, 2/5/13, Havemeyer correspondence. Although the correspondence does not confirm that Louisine bought the piece in question, the Havemeyer collection included a terracotta *Virgin and Child* (MMA 29.100.145) that was "wrongly attributed to Donatello" at the time of her bequest to the Metropolitan. The erroneous attribution of a nonetheless "attractive and important piece" was noted by Joseph Breck, Curator, Department of Decorative Arts, in a letter of 4/5/29 to Edward Robinson, Director, MMA Archives. The terracotta, which Breck thought was late 16th–early 17th-century French, is now ascribed to Biardeau.

March 19 Louisine celebrates Horace's twenty-fourth birthday with a dinner and theater party, where he meets his future wife, Doris Anna Dick.

Weitzenhoffer 1986, p. 200.

April 5 At the posthumous sale of *The Charles T. Yerkes Collection of Very Valuable Paintings, Ancient Oriental Rugs and Beautiful Old Tapestries*, Mendelssohn Hall, New York, Durand-Ruel buys Courbet's *Silent River* (A141) for Louisine for $3,100.

Lot no. 29.

April 20 Louisine, who had conveyed to George Durand-Ruel and Cassatt her interest in acquiring a Manet pastel from the Auguste Pellerin collection, learns that the picture has already been sold.

GD-R to LWH, 4/19/10, 4/20/10, correspondence, Weitzenhoffer files. It is impossible to identify the work in question, since Pellerin owned seventeen Manet pastels, and at least ten (Rouart and Wildenstein 1975, II, nos. 22, 23, 31, 34, 37–39, 55, 69, 76) were sold, mostly by Bernheim-Jeune, in 1910.

April 22 Madrazo advises Louisine that Goya's *Portrait of a Boy, Manuel Cantin y Lucientes* (A297, now Attributed to Goya, pl. 250) is available from the sitter's descendants for Pts 30,000; he had first offered it to her in May 1909 for Pts 40,000. She does not ignore the offer as she had done the year before but insists on an even lower price. By June 2 the dealer receives her payment of Pts 27,500 (inclusive of 5 percent commission). Not until October 15, however—after the close of the exhibition in Barcelona to which the picture had been lent and after the summer, when "one can do nothing"—is Madrazo able to retrieve the portrait from its owner. Thanks to Madrazo's persistence, it is finally sent to Louisine on October 19.

RdM to LWH, 5/5/09, 5/6/09, 5/22/09, 4/22/10, 6/1/10, 6/2/10, 6/8/10, 10/16/10, 10/21/10, 11/15/10, Havemeyer correspondence. The portrait is probably the "little boy" mentioned in MC to LWH, 4/4/[10], Havemeyer correspondence.

Plate 250. Attributed to Francisco de Goya y Lucientes. *Portrait of a Boy, Manuel Cantin y Lucientes*. Oil on wood, 21½ x 16¾ in. (54.6 x 42.6 cm). Location unknown. A297

Figure 88. Francisco de Goya y Lucientes. *La Tirana*, 1794. Oil on canvas, 44⅛ x 31⅛ in. (112 x 79 cm). Private collection, Spain

April 24 Madrazo asks Louisine if she would like him to pursue a version of Goya's *La Tirana* (fig. 88), owned by the Countess Villagonzagalo. On May 12 he informs her that the portrait "has not been offered to anyone thanks to [his] perseverance." It seems that Louisine makes an offer on May 26 that is lower than the asking price of Fr 200,000 despite Madrazo's efforts to convince her that the picture is worth more. The owner refuses Fr 200,000 from a German dealer in November 1910 and Fr 350,000 from another dealer in October 1912; she sets what Madrazo deems a "fantastic price" on the portrait in June 1914, casting doubt on the sincerity of her desire to sell.

RdM to LWH, 4/24/10, 5/8/10, 5/12/10, 5/15/10, 6/1/10, 6/8/10, 11/15/10, 3/22/12, 4/13/12, 6/1/14, Havemeyer correspondence. Madrazo had written in his first letters that he hoped that if Louisine was not interested in the work, she would advise Henry Clay Frick, who was looking for an important Goya portrait when he was in Madrid in 1909. In her memoirs Louisine recalls offering this work to Frick, who "unfortunately . . . was negotiating for a Velazquez at the time and felt poor" (Havemeyer 1961, p. 136).

June Louisine is in Chicago.

Weitzenhoffer files.

September 5 At Kelekian's gallery in Paris, Cassatt—who is "crazy about these statues"—sees a "lovely Saint," which Berenson thinks is "the finest he had ever seen" and for which the dealer Demotte has a client willing to offer Fr 50,000. On Cassatt's recommendation alone, Louisine is ready to buy the piece in September, but Cassatt prefers to have it sent to her on approval. On December 3, after Louisine returns to New York from Chicago, she cables Cassatt that she will purchase the statue (*Saint John the Evangelist as a Youth*, now considered French 14th–15th-century style, pl. 251), presumably for Fr 50,000 since Cassatt "could not get Kelekian to come down."

MC to LWH, 9/7/[10], 9/28/[10], 10/3/[10], 10/11/[10], 10/18/[10], 10/20/[10], 11/13/[10], 11/25/[10], 12/5/[10], 1/4/11, Havemeyer correspondence. The sculpture has since been published as a forgery; see October 6, 1909, n.

Figure 89. Louisine with her granddaughter Electra Webb, 1910

By September 7 Louisine is in Chicago to attend to the birth of Electra and J. Watson Webb's first child, Electra, who is born on November 3. She returns to New York by December 3.

Dates of stay per MC to LWH, 9/7/[10], 10/3/[10], 10/18/[10], 11/4/[10], 11/7/[10], 11/25/[10], 12/5/[10], Havemeyer correspondence; date of birth per Havemeyer 1944, p. 71.

September 10 Walter P. Fearon, President of Cottier and Co., New York, congratulates Louisine on her acquisition of Courbet's *After the Hunt* (A131, pl. 252) and thanks her for "the consideration [she] showed at the time of the transaction."

Walter P. Fearon to LWH, 9/10/10, correspondence, Weitzenhoffer files.

Plate 252. Gustave Courbet. *After the Hunt*, 1863. Oil on canvas, 93 x 73 ¼ in. (236.2 x 186.1 cm). H. O. Havemeyer Collection, Bequest of Mrs. H. O. Havemeyer, 1929 (29.100.61) A131

Plate 251. *Saint John the Evangelist as a Youth*, French, 14th–15th century style. Stone, painted in tempera, h. 42 ¾ in. (108.6 cm). H. O. Havemeyer Collection, Bequest of Mrs. H. O. Havemeyer, 1929 (29.100.30)

November 17 A front-page headline in the *New York Times* announces Horace Havemeyer's intention to resign from the Board of Directors of the American Sugar Refining Co.: "Last Havemeyer Out of Sugar Trust. The Family Owns Little of the Stock Now, but is in Beet Sugar Companies. Sold Out Very Long Ago." The family still retains substantial interests in independent, rival companies, most notably 95,000 shares of common stock in the National Sugar Refining Co. worth $10,000,000. These shares would be the subject of months of litigation; in August 1912 they would be invalidated by court decree.

New York Times, November 17, 1910, p. 1; August 4, 1912, p. 9, col. 6; see Weitzenhoffer 1986, p. 201.

November 21 Madrazo advises Louisine that a Madrid collector is willing to sell for Fr 60,000 a "very beautiful" *Saint Martin* by El Greco (Wethey 1962, no. X-402) that differs only in "some small details" from the artist's original composition for the Church of Saint Joseph of Toledo (fig. 77). He asks if Payne might be interested in it. Presumably both collectors decide not to buy the picture, which would be offered to Louisine again in 1912, after it is acquired by Durand-Ruel.

RdM to LWH, 11/21/10, Havemeyer correspondence; Durand-Ruel's acquisition of the picture per MC to LWH, 2/25/12, n.d. [after 3/16/12]; RdM to LWH, 4/13/12, Havemeyer correspondence. Identification based on Madrazo's description, including measurements and presence of a signature, and its subsequent history of ownership. For later provenance, see late March 1912, n.

December 31 Horace resigns from the American Sugar Refining Co.; after 1912 he will devote himself to the development of the beet sugar industry in the United States and the cane sugar industry in the Caribbean.

Havemeyer 1944, p. 72.

During the year Louisine resumes her Sunday afternoon musicales and becomes concerned with woman suffrage.

Weitzenhoffer 1986, pp. 205, 268, chap. 17, n. 16.

1911

January 4 The engagement of Horace Havemeyer and Doris Anna Dick is formally announced.

New York Times, January 4, 1911.

January 17 Louisine purchases Monet's *In the Garden* (A392, pl. 34) from Durand-Ruel.

February 17 Joseph Durand-Ruel advises Louisine that he has several fine works by Pissarro that he would like her to see at the New York gallery.

Figure 90. Wedding photograph of Horace and Doris Havemeyer, 1911

JD-R to LWH, 2/17/11, correspondence, Weitzenhoffer files.

February 28 Horace Havemeyer and Doris Anna Dick are married at the Church of the Incarnation; a reception follows at the bride's parents' home at 20 East 53rd Street. The couple will live at 1 East 66th Street.

Weitzenhoffer 1986, p. 200.

April 20 Harnisch informs Louisine that he has just returned from "up in the Lucca country," where he has purchased "the Siena Madonna"—*Madonna and Child with Saint John* (A436, now considered Pseudo Pier Francesco Fiorentino, pl. 253)—for her for L 15,000. She pays Harnisch for the painting in May and is, therefore, angry that she has neither heard from him nor received the work by January 1912: "You know the only time I can enjoy my pictures is in the winter when I am at home." Harnisch replies that a Fra Angelico "Madonna della Stella" had been stolen from the San Marco gallery that fall and that he could not ship her Madonna until that "mystery" was resolved (lest her painting be mistaken for the Fra Angelico) and the work recovered; moreover, he explains, he had been ill subsequent to the theft. On April 18, 1912, the picture is finally shipped from Genoa to New York aboard the *Prince Albert.*

Plate 253. Pseudo Pier Francesco Fiorentino. *Madonna and Child with Saint John,* late 15th century. Tempera and gold on wood, 33 x 22½ in. (83.8 x 57.2 cm). Location unknown. A436

AEH to LWH, 1/18/11, 2/28/11, 4/20/11, 4/29/11, 5/27/11; LWH to AEH, 1/15/12; AEH to LWH, 2/4/12, indicating the purchase price as L 15,000 plus a 5 percent commission, L 750, 3/19/12, 4/23/12, noting details of iconography and condition, Havemeyer correspondence. The picture is referred to as "Siena Madonna" and "gem" in the letters.

May 6 The Durand-Ruels are apprised of Louisine's wishes concerning the sale of the *Collection de Feu M. Alexis Rouart*, Hôtel Drouot, Paris, May 8–10: they are to purchase Degas's *Little Milliners* (A235) and, if this cannot be obtained, Degas's "fan" (Lemoisne 1946, no. 613). On May 9 Durand-Ruel acquires the *Little Milliners* for her for Fr 51,000.

Lot nos. 214, 218; JD-R to LWH, 5/6/11, 5/9/11, 5/22/11, 5/23/11, acknowledging receipt of her check for $10,814.46 inclusive, correspondence, Weitzenhoffer files.

May 30 The sale of *La Collection de Feu M.-J.R.P.C.H. de Kuyper de la Haye* takes place at Galeries Frederik Muller et Cie, Amsterdam. Louisine had considered bidding on the Courbets and Millets and had sought Paul Durand-Ruel's opinion of them. However, he is not able to inform her that he thinks they are of relatively inferior quality and condition until three days after the sale.

PD-R to LWH, 6/2/11, correspondence, Weitzenhoffer files. The sale included two Courbets, lot nos. 22, 23, and four Millets, lot nos. 85–88.

June 20–21 Horace Havemeyer appears in "defense of his father's good name" before a nine-member House committee, headed by Thomas Hardwick of Georgia, in Washington, D.C. The committee is investigating whether the American Sugar Refining Co. had been "doing business in violation of the anti-trust law and of the Customs Acts, and whether the trust has crushed out competition among refining companies and so increased the price of sugar over the price that prevails in other countries." Horace, who welcomes the opportunity to publicly respond to repeated attacks on his father's reputation, "forcibly and effectively" defends the late Sugar King against charges such as customs fraud and at the same time proves himself a "virile successor of the founder of the trust." He testifies about a number of matters concerning the past, present, and future of the sugar industry. He emphasizes his independence from the Sugar Trust and his plans to do business as its competitor now that "the day of monopolistic combination is past. The country, the public and the great industrial enterprises themselves demand competition."

"Young Havemeyer Foe of Sugar Trust," *New York Times*, June 21, 1911, p. 3; Weitzenhoffer 1986, pp. 202–3. Horace testified that H. O. Havemeyer could not have had any knowledge of the light weighing of raw sugar because he had not been to the sugar refinery since 1903, when he took Horace there to work. For discussion of the unfair charges of fraud that were brought against H. O. Havemeyer posthumously, see Havemeyer 1944, p. 70.

July 25 George Griswold, Adaline and Peter Frelinghuysen's second child, is born in Morristown, New Jersey.

Havemeyer 1944, p. 71.

Figure 91. Mary Cassatt and Mme Joseph Durand-Ruel at the Château de Beaufresne, Mesnil-Théribus, ca. 1910

August–September 22 Louisine visits Cassatt at her country home at Mesnil-Théribus; she offers care and consolation to the artist, who is in poor health and is grieving for her brother Gardner, who had died that April. In mid-August Louisine takes a trip to Paris.

Weitzenhoffer 1986, p. 204; RdM to LWH, 8/20/11, Havemeyer correspondence.

September 22 Louisine's train from Mesnil-Théribus is scheduled to arrive in Paris at 11:15 A.M. She had hoped that Paul Durand-Ruel could arrange for her "to see the Dollfus pictures [which would be sold at auction on March 2, 1912] once more" that afternoon or the following morning. During her stay in Paris Louisine reestablishes contact with Duret, through whom she wishes to acquire works by Courbet. On September 26 and 27 Duret wants to show her a Courbet nude of 1868 from a Parisian collection (possibly *Woman with a Dog* [A149]). Louisine embarks on her journey home before the end of the month.

LWH to PD-R, 9/18/11, from Mesnil-Théribus, correspondence, Weitzenhoffer files; TD to LWH, 9/26/11, 9/27/11 (at Hotel Crillon), Havemeyer correspondence.

November 16 Duret advises Louisine that he has secured Courbet's *Lone Rock* (A136, pl. 254) for her and is send-

Plate 254. Gustave Courbet. *The Lone Rock*, 1874. Oil on canvas, 25 9/16 x 31 15/16 in. (64.9 x 81.1 cm). The Brooklyn Museum, Gift of Mrs. Horace Havemeyer (41.1258) A136

ing it to New York on November 18 aboard the *Savoie*. He believes that this seascape "will make an excellent pendant to the marine [*The Calm Sea* (A151)] [she] recently received." He also informs her that the Bernheims still have Ingres's *Portrait of M. Devillers* (Wildenstein 1954, no. 79), which she saw in Paris; he thinks she "will in the end make them an offer, for want of any others and a portrait by David being unobtainable."

TD to LWH, 11/16/11, Havemeyer correspondence. In her memoirs Louisine erroneously recalls buying the two Courbet seascapes on the same day (Havemeyer 1961, p. 186).

December 14 Cassatt, who liked the piece "so much," advises Louisine that she has sent her the stone "Virgin of the Annunciation" from Demotte. She has one reservation, apparently of no concern to Louisine—that it "would be hard to place," as "the back is flat." Later in December Cassatt tells Louisine that she has instructed Kelekian, who was "going to send the fine Babylonian bottle & the Persian bowl home . . . to send two . . . fine Alabaster vases with them." She says "he lit a match & put it in, oh such color." This month Cassatt also keeps Louisine abreast of other objects she may want to acquire through Kelekian: a "Greek boy head," a "little wooden statue of which the hand is restored," and an Egyptian "Royal Scribe."

MC to LWH, n.d. [before 12/14/11], 12/14/11, n.d. [after 12/14/11], Havemeyer correspondence.

During the year Duret sells Louisine Courbet's *Spring Flowers* (A164, now considered Copy after Courbet).

1912

January 2 Duret informs Louisine that he has negotiated a price of Fr 18,000 for Courbet's *Russet Wood* (A161, pl. 255). The picture, which Cassatt is certain Louisine will like—"it is different from anything of his you have, and so strong"—was first offered to James Stillman, who "did not buy it because [he felt] it is too like an American landscape." The work is secured for Louisine by early April.

TD to LWH, 1/2/[12]; MC to LWH, 1/9/[12], 2/18/[12], including quote, n.d. [after 3/16/12]; TD to LWH, 4/3/12, Havemeyer correspondence.

January 24 Durand-Ruel purchases for Louisine from the sale of *Important Paintings Belonging to the Estates of the Late George Crocker, Alice Newcomb, Emily H. Moir, Frederic Bonner*, Grand Ballroom, Plaza Hotel, New York, Monet's *Garden of the Princess, Louvre* (A388) for $4,100. The gallery acknowledges its receipt of Louisine's check in this amount on January 31.

Lot no. 36; D-R to LWH, 1/31/12, correspondence, Weitzenhoffer files.

January 28 The *New York Times* reports the arrest of three "hoboes" who had spent the last month living in a vacant bungalow on the Havemeyer estate on Palmer Hill in Greenwich, Connecticut.

P. 6, col. 1.

January Cassatt's portrait *Adaline Havemeyer in a White Hat* (fig. 8) has arrived safely. The artist had kept the pastel for over twelve years but has now sent it to Adaline for her daughter Frederica's nursery. Cassatt confesses to Louisine that "it is like Adaline & between you and me it may be the F[relinghuysen]'s like it better than a stronger thing."

MC to LWH, n.d. [after 12/14/11], including quote, 2/4/[12], Havemeyer correspondence.

February 12 Harnisch offers Louisine the opportunity to buy Ribera's "Martyrdom of Saint Peter" and "Flaying of Saint Bartholomew." In April he informs her that these two lifesize pictures are available from the Spapotelli collection for L 60,000. Though Louisine considers the acquisition, she seems to have reservations about the subjects, for on September 17 Harnisch replies to a communication from her: "I admit what you say about the subjects, but, the manner in which they are painted make them desirable founts from which young artists can draw strength to carry out their thoughts & inspirations." Apparently he does not convince her of their value—either for her collection or for "students, who hadn't the opportunity to study abroad"—as she does not acquire them.

AEH to LWH, 2/4/12, 3/10/12, 4/23/12, 5/11/12, 9/17/12, Havemeyer correspondence.

Plate 255. Gustave Courbet. *The Russet Wood*. Oil on canvas, 46 x 35 ½ in. (116.8 x 90.2 cm). Richard Shelton, San Francisco. A161

February 22   Electra and J. Watson Webb's second child, Samuel Blatchley, is born in New York.

Havemeyer 1944, p. 71.

February 27   Louisine purchases Cassatt's *Girl Reading* (A62) from Durand-Ruel, New York.

GD-R to LWH, 2/28/12, correspondence, Weitzenhoffer files.

March 2   From the estate sale of the *Collections de M. Jean Dollfus*, Galerie Georges Petit, Paris, Joseph Durand-Ruel secures Courbet's *Wave* (A150) for Louisine with a bid of Fr 16,000. Though she had been willing to pay as much as Fr 200,000 for Corot's *Woman with the Pearl* (Robaut 1905, no. 1507), the Louvre, by arrangement with the Dollfus heirs, obtains the picture for Fr 150,000.

Courbet, lot no. 24; Corot, lot no. 6; GD-R to LWH, 1/31/12, indicating that the catalogue was sent to her; MC to D-R, n.d. [2/12]; GD-R to LWH, 2/14/12; JD R to MC, 2/27/12, correspondence, Weitzenhoffer files; MC to LWH, 2/25/[12], 3/13/[12], n.d. [after 3/16/12]; TD to LWH, 7/2/12, Havemeyer correspondence.

March 10   Harnisch informs Louisine that the Martellis have finally reached an agreement with the Italian government regarding the expropriation and sale of sculpture from their collection. in exchange for donating their Donatello *Saint John the Baptist* to the R. R. Galerie e Musei di Firenze (for the Bargello collection, Florence), they are now at liberty to sell and to export their statue *David* and their marble bust *Young Saint John the Baptist* (fig. 92). Louisine has wanted the bust ever since she saw it in Florence in the spring of 1909. The Martellis reject Trotti and Joseph Duveen's offer of $250,000 for the two pieces, as they would rather sell through Harnisch, to whom they have given first preference. By March 14 the price for the marble bust is set at L 800,000 (about $160,000). Because of the high price or the frustration involved in dealing with the "half-cracked" Martellis, Louisine does not acquire the piece.

Figure 92. Antonio Rossellino. *Young Saint John the Baptist*, ca. 1455. Marble, h. 15 ½ in. (39.7 cm). National Gallery of Art, Washington, D.C., Widener Collection (1942.9.142)

AEH to MC, 7/30/09; AEH to LWH, 2/4/12, 3/10/12, 3/14/12, including quote, Havemeyer correspondence. *David* and *Young Saint John the Baptist* (now National Gallery of Art, Washington, D.C., Widener Collection) were acquired by Widener in 1916 through Giuseppe Salvadori, an agent for P. W. French and Co., New York, for L 1,300,000. (See Alessandra Civai, *Dipinti e sculture in casa Martelli, Storia di una collezione patrizia fiorentina dal Quattrocento all'Ottocento*, Florence, 1990, p. 114, and figs. 3, 4, 98.)

March 16   Horace and Doris Havemeyer's first child, Doris, is born at 1 East 66th Street.

Havemeyer 1944, p. 74.

Figure 93. Francisco de Goya y Lucientes. *Portrait of General José Manuel Romero*, ca. 1810. Oil on canvas, 41 ⅜ x 33 ⅛ in. (105.2 x 84.1 cm). The Art Institute of Chicago, Gift of Mr. and Mrs. Charles Deering McCormick (1970.1036)

Late March   Cassatt advises Louisine that she has seen at Galerie Durand-Ruel, Paris, "the fine *small* St. Martin by Greco," which "is really beautiful in [her] opinion," and also a "fine man's portrait by Goya with a wonderful uniform, & gold embroideries." Despite Cassatt's recommendations, Louisine declines to buy both the Goya (*Portrait of General José Manuel Romero*, fig. 93) and the El Greco (Wethey 1962, X-402). She had once before passed up the El Greco, when Madrazo offered it to her in November 1910.

MC to LWH, n.d. [after 3/16/12], Havemeyer correspondence; RdM to LWH, 4/13/12, indicating that both pictures were acquired by Galerie Durand-Ruel and confirming that the El Greco is the same picture offered to Louisine in 1910, Havemeyer correspondence. (Presumably Louisine had received photographs of these works earlier in the year: GD-R to LWH, 1/31/12, enclosing photographs of a Goya and an El Greco that had just arrived at Durand-Ruel, Paris, correspondence, Weitzenhoffer files.) Identification of the Goya per Durand-Ruel Archives, which indicate that it was purchased jointly with M. Knoedler on December 29, 1911 (stock no. 9838). Knoedler sales books indicate that the Goya arrived in New York in July 1912 and was sold to Charles Deering in October 1912 (stock no. 12895). This same month Knoedler's also purchased a half-share in the El Greco from Durand-Ruel, Paris, and sold it to Deering (stock no. 12971). Both pictures were subsequently given by Deering's descendants to The Art Institute of Chicago.

April 2–20   *Paintings by El Greco and Goya*, a small benefit exhibition in support of woman suffrage, is held at M. Knoedler and Co., New York. Except for two paintings lent by Electra, all the works are drawn from Louisine's collection. Louisine is involved in the design of the poster, for which she adopts the "party's colors, the purple, white, and green," and in the hanging of the show.

Weitzenhoffer 1986, pp. 206–7, 268, nn. 13, 15; on this subject, see Rebecca A. Rabinow, "The Suffrage Exhibition of 1915," n. 6, this catalogue.

April 5 The New York branch of Durand-Ruel purchases Dupré's *Woodcutter* (A272) from Louisine for $15,000. She is sent a check in this amount on April 13.

Unpublished Weitzenhoffer notes from Durand-Ruel Stock et Depot, 1904–1924–25; GD-R to LWH, 4/13/12, enclosing check, correspondence, Weitzenhoffer files.

April 13 Madrazo thinks that the Duke of Valencia may be willing to sell Goya's portrait of his grandmother, *Marquesa de Espeja* (not in Gassier and Wilson 1971) for Fr 150,000. Louisine makes an offer—which does not meet the asking price—immediately upon her receipt of a photograph of the painting on April 25. Madrazo, however, is unable to negotiate a lower price and the work is not acquired. The portrait is no longer considered to be by Goya.

See August L. Mayer, *Francisco de Goya*, London and Toronto, 1924, p. 154, no. 253 (207); A. de Beruete y Moret, *Goya as Portrait Painter*, New York and Boston, 1922, pp. 64, 211, no. 186; RdM to LWH, 4/13/12, 5/8/12, 5/18/12, Havemeyer correspondence.

September 6 Cassatt urges Louisine to sell a selection of her Cézannes to Bernheim-Jeune, Paris, from whom she could "get good prices & put [her] money into something really fine in the Rouart sale." Louisine, despite a similar suggestion by Cassatt in October, ignores her friend's advice.

Weitzenhoffer 1986, pp. 207–8, 268, nn. 19, 20.

September 12 Harnisch tells Louisine that he is now convinced that the "fine portrait" of a man—*Portrait of a Man, Said to Be the Painter Vicente Lopez* (A301, now consid-

Plate 256. Style of Francisco de Goya y Lucientes. *Portrait of a Man, Said to Be the Painter Vicente Lopez (1772–1850).* Oil on canvas, 22 x 17½ in. (55.9 x 44.5 cm). H. O. Havemeyer Collection, Bequest of Mrs. H. O. Havemeyer, 1929 (29.100.179) A301

ered Style of Goya, pl. 256)—is by Goya, though he was dubious of its authenticity at first; he reports that it is available for L 50,000. On December 8 Louisine's offer of L 30,000 is accepted and she acquires the work. It is shipped to her from Genoa aboard the SS *Mendoza* on January 17, 1913. The frame, which had been repaired in December, arrives damaged, presumably "from clumsy handling at [the] Custom House."

AEH to LWH, 9/12/12, including quote, 12/2/12, 12/8/[12]; LWH to AEH, 12/8/[12]; AEH to LWH, 12/7/12, 2/3/13, enclosing the opinion of art critic August L. Mayer, 2/5/13, 3/5/13, including quote, Havemeyer correspondence.

November 10 Louisine rejects the two Courbets, pendants of hunting dogs (not in Fernier 1977–78), that Duret had first offered to her in July for Fr 30,000.

TD to LWH, 7/2/12, 9/4/12, 10/29/12, annotated by Louisine, "dogs ans refused nov. 10," Havemeyer correspondence. According to Duret, the pictures had never been shown commercially or published.

November 18 Louisine buys Goya's *City on a Rock* (A300, now considered Style of Goya) for $8,000 from Cottier and Co., New York.

December 9 Joseph Durand-Ruel reports to Louisine that, despite the bids she placed with his gallery's Paris branch, nothing has been purchased for her on the first day of the sale *Tableaux Anciens . . . et des Tableaux Modernes . . . composant la collection de feu M. Henri Rouart*, Galerie Manzi-Joyant, Paris, December 9–11. Two works of interest to her, a Manet nude (*Brunette with Bare Breasts* [Rouart and Wildenstein 1975, I, no. 176]) and Degas's *Rape of the Sabines* (Lemoisne 1946, no. 273), were bought by the Rouart family for very high prices.

JD-R to LWH, 12/9/12, correspondence, Weitzenhoffer files. Manet, lot no. 236, for Fr 106,700; Degas, lot no. 180, for Fr 60,000.

December 10 On the second day of the Rouart sale, Paul Durand-Ruel obtains Degas's *Dancers Practicing at the Bar* (A216, pl. 40) for an anonymous client, who is Louisine, for the record price of Fr 478,500 (about $95,700). This is the highest price paid to date for a work by a living artist and perhaps the most expensive acquisition ever made by Harry or Louisine. (It is rivaled only by the price of $70,000–$100,000 reputedly paid for Rembrandt's *Herman Doomer* [A449, pl. 63]). The buyer's identity is kept in the strictest confidence and there is much speculation about it, not only in the press but also among Louisine's closest friends—Cassatt included. (Cassatt does not learn that Louisine bought the Degas until about two weeks after the sale; she congratulates her on Christmas Day, having just received Louisine's letter "with the news.") Louisine had also been interested in Delacroix's *Coin d'atelier: le poêle* (Johnson 1986, no. R44, under doubtful works), but it is acquired by the amis du Louvre for Fr 33,000.

Degas, lot no. 177; Delacroix, lot no. 189; discretion and bids per JD-R to LWH, 11/18/12, 12/7/12, 12/9/12, 12/11/12; HH to D-R, 12/13/12, enclosing draft for Fr 478,500 inclusive for this purchase, correspondence, Weitzenhoffer files; MC to LWH, 12/18/[12], noting that Harry had wanted to buy the Degas from Rouart and musing about who bought it, 12/25/[12], Havemeyer correspondence. The purchase was announced in the *New York Times*, December 12, 1912, p. 4, under the headline: "The $87,000 Degas Coming to America. Monsieur Durand-Ruel Bought It for a Customer Here—The Name Not Stated." The $87,000 figure quoted by the *Times* is based on the hammer price of Fr 435,000.

Plate 257. Gustave Courbet. *Marine: The Waterspout*, 1870. Oil on canvas, 27 1/8 x 39 1/4 in. (68.9 x 99.7 cm). H. O. Havemeyer Collection, Gift of Horace Havemeyer, 1929 (29.160.35) A152

By December 12 Acting on Louisine's request for an important stormy seascape by Courbet, Duret locates the artist's *Marine: The Waterspout* (A152, pl. 257) and convinces the owners to sell it for Fr 16,000, 20 percent less than their asking price. Louisine remits this amount on December 22, and the painting is sent to her aboard the *Lorraine* on January 11, 1913.

TD to LWH, 12/12/12, annotated by Louisine, "Tempête G. Courbet 1870. I bought it," 1/9/13, 2/12/13, Havemeyer correspondence.

Plate 258. Gustave Courbet. *Still Life—Fruit*, 1871. Oil on canvas, 23 1/8 x 28 1/4 in. (58.7 x 71.8 cm). Shelburne Museum, Shelburne, Vermont (27.1.3–23) A154

December 13 At the auction of the collection of *Isidore vanden Eynde*, Galerie Le Roy Frères, Brussels, Louisine is underbidder to Rosenberg, who acquires Courbet's *Still Life—Fruit* (A154, pl. 258) for Fr 28,300. The loss is particularly disappointing to her because she lacks a fruit painting by Courbet. A week later she learns that Rosenberg will not sell the picture for less than $10,000 (Fr 50,000), which Paul Durand-Ruel believes is twice its value. Therefore, on December 22 Louisine sets Duret to the task of filling this gap in her collection. Ironically, on January 9 Duret proposes the very same picture from Rosenberg for Fr 50,000, unaware that she had just lost it to him. In February Louisine declines to buy *Still Life—Fruit* at a reduced price of Fr 42,500, and it is subsequently sold to an Austrian collector, with whom it remains until she acquires it, through Rosenberg, eight years later—for considerably more money.

Lot no. 2; JD-R to LWH, 12/16/12, 12/20/12, 12/31/12; PR to TD, 2/11/13, correspondence, Weitzenhoffer files; TD to LWH, 1/9/13, indicating contents of LWH to TD, 12/22/12, 1/9/13, 2/12/13, Havemeyer correspondence; see also Weitzenhoffer 1986, p. 239.

December 16 At the second part of the Rouart sale, *Dessins et Pastels anciens et modernes . . . composant la collection de feu M. Henri Rouart*, Galerie Manzi-Joyant, Paris, December 16–18, Durand-Ruel secures Degas's pastel *The Song of the Dog* (A217) for Louisine for Fr 55,100 inclusive.

Lot no. 71; JD-R to LWH, 12/17/12; JD-R to HH, 12/17/12; HH to D-R, 12/18/12, enclosing Fr 55,100, correspondence, Weitzenhoffer files.

1913

January 8 On the first night of the American Art Association sale of the *Collection of the Late Tadamasa Hayashi of Tokyo, Japan*, American Art Galleries, New York, January 8–9, Joseph Durand-Ruel purchases for Louisine a Degas pastel, *Woman Stepping into a Tub* (A253), and two Guys drawings, *Driving in the Bois de Boulogne* (A308) and *Two Fat Peasant Women* (A312), for $3,100, $52.50, and $25, respectively. From the same auction he buys another Guys drawing, *Sailors and Women* (A311), for $27 and immediately sells it to Louisine.

Degas, lot no. 85; Guys, lot nos. 35, 36, 33, as "unknown" artist; JD-R to LWH, 1/9/13, indicating that he purchased "for [her] account yesterday the Degas 'nude' for $3,100 and also the two Guys for $52.50 and $25," with no mention of the third Guys, correspondence, Weitzenhoffer files.

January 9 On the second night of the Hayashi sale, Grand Ballroom, Plaza Hotel, New York, Joseph Durand-Ruel purchases for Louisine Sisley's *Allée of Chestnut Trees* (A478, pl. 53) ($2,100), Pissarro's *Bather in the Woods* (A432, pl. 259) ($4,200) and *Haymakers Resting* (A431)

Plate 259. Camille Pissarro. *Bather in the Woods*, 1895. Oil on canvas, 23¾ x 28¾ in. (60.3 x 73 cm). H. O. Havemeyer Collection, Bequest of Mrs. H. O. Havemeyer, 1929 (29.100.126) A432

Plate 260. Claude Monet. *Germaine Hoschedé in the Garden at Giverny*, 1888. Oil on canvas, 28¼ x 36 in. (71.8 x 91.4 cm). Private collection. A404

($2,800), and Monet's *Germaine Hoschedé in the Garden at Giverny* (A404, pl. 260) ($3,100).

Lot nos. 138, 146, 157, 160.

January 10 Louisine acquires Pissarro's *Potato Gatherers* (A428) from Durand-Ruel, New York, for $3,000; Erwin Davis had sold the picture back to the gallery for one-tenth this amount in 1901.

Mid-January The Marquis de la Vega Inclan calls on Louisine in New York and is impressed by her Goyas—which include the *Condesa de Chinchón* (A295, pl. 12), formerly in his collection.

RdM to LWH, 2/7/13, 2/17/13, both referring to the visit, about which Louisine had written to Madrazo on January 24, Havemeyer correspondence.

January 31 The Parisian collector Carlos de Beistegui purchases Goya's *Portrait of Marquesa de la Solana* (Gassier and Wilson 1971, no. 341) from the Marquis de Socorro for Fr 600,000. Madrazo and Louisine had been trying to secure this painting for Frick since October 1912.

RdM to LWH, 10/7/12, 1/24/13, 2/7/13, 6/1/14, enclosing presentation card that will enable her and Cassatt to visit Beistegui in Paris and see the portrait, 6/8/16, Havemeyer correspondence.

February 3 Harnisch recommends a van Dyck portrait of "two young and beautiful princes" (possibly Larsen 1988, no. A255/1) to Louisine. On March 22 he tells her that the picture cannot be sent to Paris for Cassatt's opinion, as the owners, the Corsini family, will not allow it to leave Rome. Cassatt does not feel strong enough to travel to Italy in April to see the picture and does not receive a photograph—Harnisch had sent it to an incorrect address. Lacking Cassatt's opinion, Louisine rejects the offer. By May 30, when the sale of the work to another collector is imminent, Harnisch cables Louisine "nothing against Mary sorry lose fine work."

AEH to LWH, 2/3/13, listing measurements (145 × 142 cm) and describing the picture as "two German princes," 2/5/13, 3/19/13, 3/22/13, 3/23/13, annotated by Louisine, "Boys/Van Dyke/I refuse"; MC to LWH, 4/4/[13]; AEH to LWH, 5/30/13, Havemeyer correspondence.

February 7 Madrazo offers Louisine Velázquez's *Portrait of the Poet, Francisco de Rioja* (Lopez-Rey 1963, no. 483), which is available for only Fr 150,000 because of its poor condition. Louisine rejects it, presumably on the basis of the photograph sent.

RdM to LWH, 2/7/13, Havemeyer correspondence.

February 11 Louisine consigns her supposed Veronese *Portrait of a Woman* (A504) to Durand-Ruel, New York, through May; at the end of the year she again places it on consignment with the gallery, where it remains until May 1914, when it is returned to her along with other unsold pictures.

Durand-Ruel Archives.

February 13–14 At the American Art Association sale of *Notable Paintings Collected by the Late M.C.D. Borden*,

Plate 261. Honoré Daumier. *The Third-Class Carriage*, 1863–65. Oil on canvas, 25¾ x 35½ in. (65.4 x 90.2 cm). H. O. Havemeyer Collection, Bequest of Mrs. H. O. Havemeyer, 1929 (29.100.129) A177

Esq., Grand Ballroom, Plaza Hotel, New York, Joseph Durand-Ruel obtains for Louisine Daumier's *Third-Class Carriage* (A177, pl. 261) at the record-breaking price of $40,000. Durand-Ruel had offered the picture to the Havemeyers in 1892, four years before he sold it to Matthew Borden, for one-fifth this amount.

Lot no. 76. Though Joseph Durand-Ruel secured the Daumier for Louisine, he had wanted it to go to railway magnate James J. Hill. The dealer urged Hill to bid on the picture ten days before the sale and in May advised him, "I can purchase back Daumier which brought $40,000" (see Sheila Ffolliott, "James J. Hill as Art Collector, A Documentary View," in *Homecoming: The Art Collection of James J. Hill*, St. Paul, 1991, pp. 36–37, 109–10, n. 86).

February 14 Joseph Durand-Ruel advises Louisine that he has received the Delacroix about which they had spoken, and he would be happy to show it to her together with a "remarkable group of small paintings by Renoir," which will be placed on view at the New York gallery the following day.

JD-R to HH, 2/7/13, including quote and opening date; JD-R to LWH, 2/14/13, mentioning the Delacroix and the Renoirs, correspondence, Weitzenhoffer files.

February 17 Madrazo advises Louisine that a lifesize painting of Saint Peter by Ribera is available from a Madrid nobleman. She ignores the offer.

RdM to LWH, 2/17/13, Havemeyer correspondence.

February 17–March 15 The *International Exhibition of Modern Art*, better known as the Armory Show, is held at the Armory of the Sixty-ninth Regiment in New York. Louisine no doubt attends but is not a lender.

May 2 Horace and Doris Havemeyer's second child, Adaline, is born at 1 East 66th Street.

Havemeyer 1944, p. 74.

May 3 Louisine marches up Fifth Avenue in the largest parade for the woman suffrage movement ever held in New York.

May 16 Madrazo advises Louisine that Carreño's portrait of the Marquesa de Santa Cruz is available from the sitter's descendants. The offer seems to have been ignored.

RdM to LWH, 5/16/13, referring to A. de Beruete y Moret, *The School of Madrid*, London and New York, 1909, p. 203, Havemeyer correspondence.

July 5 Electra and J. Watson Webb's third child, Lila Vanderbilt, is born in Westbury, Long Island.

Havemeyer 1944, p. 71.

Figure 94. Suffrage parade on Fifth Avenue, New York, May 1913

July 18 Harnisch offers Louisine a small oval portrait by Goya of a man "with a large wig" for L 22,000, which she rejects. He also informs her that the Martellis have finally settled their "statue business with the [Italian] Government" and are now fully at liberty to dispose of their pictures as well as their sculpture. On September 16 Harnisch makes his last offer to Louisine: Mulich's *Pancratus von Freyburg and His Wife Maria von Kitscher*, a pair of portraits available from a member of the royal family in Florence for L 150,000. Harnisch's wife dies four days later, and his correspondence with Louisine ceases; neither the Martelli pictures nor the Mulich portraits are pursued.

AEH to LWH, 7/18/13, annotated by Louisine, "Goya/Maus portrait/I did not like it," 9/16/13, 9/20/13, Havemeyer correspondence. For paintings in the Martelli collection, see Alessandra Civai, *Dipinti e sculture in casa Martelli, Storia di una collezione patrizia fiorentina dal Quattrocento all'Ottocento*, Florence, 1990.

August Louisine spends time in Islip, Long Island, and Cooperstown, New York.

Weitzenhoffer files; MC to LWH, 8/28/[13], Havemeyer correspondence.

October Louisine accompanies her son and daughter-in-law, Horace and Doris, on a business trip to Denver.

Weitzenhoffer files.

November 12 Madrazo offers Louisine a pair of van Dycks representing scenes from the life of Saint Francis de Paul for Fr 80,000; he sends photographs and dimensions the following week. The paintings are not acquired.

RdM to LWH, 11/12/13, 11/18/13, Havemeyer correspondence.

November 18 Madrazo offers Louisine or "some collector friend who wishes a Goya" a "very fine" Goya portrait available for Fr 110,000 from the widow Silvela. He mistakenly identifies the sitter as Leandro Fernández de Moratín; the picture is actually Goya's *Portrait of Manuel Silvela* (Gassier and Wilson 1971, no. 891). Louisine rejects it, presumably on the basis of the photograph sent.

According to Beruete y Moret, the two portraits owned by the widow of D. Francisco Silvela, Marquesa de Silvela—one of Manuel Silvela, the other of Leandro Fernández de Moratín (Gassier and Wilson 1971, no. 1661)—were confused with each other in the Goya exhibition of 1900 in Madrid (*Goya as Portrait Painter*, Boston and New York, 1922, p. 181). RdM to LWH, 11/18/13, describing the Moratín portrait as measuring 95 × 68 cm, the precise dimensions of the Silvela portrait, which is now in the Museo del Prado, Madrid, Havemeyer correspondence.

November 28–December 13 Paintings by Edouard Manet, the inaugural exhibition at Durand-Ruel's new premises in New York at 12 East 57th Street, is held; Louisine is the anonymous lender of nearly half the pictures included. (The gallery would remain at this address until 1948.)

During the year Louisine, together with Lila Vanderbilt Webb (Electra's mother-in-law) and Tiffany, helps decorate Woodbury House, Electra's new fifty-two-room gabled English Tudor mansion, built by Cross and Cross on 222 acres of land near Syosset, Long Island. (Since the decor does not reflect the taste of Electra and J. Watson Webb, the house and its contents would be sold at auction within seven years.) Watson's parents give 1,000 acres and a small brick house on their estate in Shelburne, Vermont, to the couple. Electra and her husband furnish the Vermont house to their own taste, with Americana.

Weitzenhoffer 1986, pp. 212–14.

1914

January 16 George Durand-Ruel advises Louisine that Dr. and Mrs. Albert C. Barnes, accompanied by the American artist Glackens, wish to visit her.

GD-R to LWH, 1/16/14, correspondence, Weitzenhoffer files.

January Louisine buys Cranach's *Portrait of a Man with a Rosary* (A168, pl. 56) through Cottier and Co., New York.

MMA Department of European Paintings Archives.

February 28 Encouraged by Harriot Stanton Blatch, President of the Women's Political Union, Louisine begins to take a more active role in the woman suffrage campaign: she speaks publicly for the first time when she introduces Helen Todd of California at a meeting at 1 East 66th Street in support of the state-by-state referendum for equal rights.

Weitzenhoffer 1986, p. 221.

Plate 262. Mary Cassatt. *Mother and Sleeping Child*, 1914. Pastel on paper mounted on canvas, 26⅝ x 22½ in. (67.6 x 57.2 cm). H. O. Havemeyer Collection, Bequest of Mrs. H. O. Havemeyer, 1929 (29.100.50) A65

March 20 Louisine arrives in Genoa but departs immediately for the south of France. The next day she reaches Grasse, where she spends some time at Cassatt's rented house, the Villa Angeletto. During her stay Cassatt works on a pastel, *Mother and Sleeping Child* (A65, pl. 262), which Louisine buys from Durand-Ruel, Paris, in late May.

Weitzenhoffer 1986, p. 214.

Early April Louisine makes a "little tour of Provence and Italy"; she visits Arles and Florence, among other places, before returning to Grasse.

LWH to D-R, 3/25/14 (from Grasse); MC to D-R, n.d. [early April]; LWH to D-R, 4/17/14 (upon return to Grasse), including quote, correspondence, Weitzenhoffer files.

April 18 Louisine travels from Grasse to Montreux by way of Grenoble to see her sister-in-law, Emilie de Loosey Havemeyer, who is ill. She remains in Montreux until at least April 24 but has left for Germany by April 27.

Weitzenhoffer 1986, p. 217; LWH to D-R, 4/24/14, correspondence, Weitzenhoffer files.

April 28 On the second day of the sale *Estampes Modernes Composant la Collection Roger Marx*, Hôtel Drouot, Paris, April 27–May 2, Durand-Ruel purchases for Louisine the Cassatt prints of interest: *Feeding the Ducks* (two proofs, one in color) for Fr 320 (MMA 29.107.99 and pl. 263) and *The Bare-Footed Child* (two proofs, one in color) for Fr 310 (MMA 29.107.95, 98). The Degas self-portrait etching (pl. 43) she asked the gallery to bid on is sold to a Mr. Strölin for Fr 2,500; however, Durand-Ruel acquires it for her immediately after the sale for Fr 4,000.

Cassatts, lot nos. 249, 250 bis; Degas, lot no. 389; results of sale per JD-R to LWH, 4/30/14, 5/13/14, correspondence, Weitzenhoffer files. The auction prices do not include a 10 percent commission. Louisine eventually acquires two other Cassatt prints that were in this sale, *Peasant Mother and Child* (MMA 29.107.97) and *Under the Horse Chestnut Tree* (MMA 29.107.96).

Plate 263. Mary Cassatt. *Feeding the Ducks*, ca. 1895. Color print with drypoint over soft-ground etching and aquatint, fourth state, plate: 11 5/8 x 15 3/4 in. (29.5 x 40 cm); sheet: 14 1/2 x 20 in. (36.8 x 50.8 cm). H. O. Havemeyer Collection, Bequest of Mrs. H. O. Havemeyer, 1929 (29.107.100)

Louisine is in Munich; on April 30 she attends the opera in Nuremberg. Her next destination is Dresden, where she sees Oscar Schmitz's art collection and reencounters, at the Gemäldegalerie, Courbet's *Stone Breakers* (Fernier 1977–78, no. 101), a painting she had "lost" during the period "after Mr. Havemeyer's death [when she] did not buy pictures"; she spends the evenings of May 2 and 3 at the opera.

Weitzenhoffer 1986, p. 230; specific dates per opera programs, Weitzenhoffer files, and LWH to JD-R, 4/28/14; JD-R to LWH, 4/30/14; LWH to JD-R, 5/2/14, correspondence, Weitzenhoffer files; quote from Havemeyer 1961, p. 193.

May 4 Louisine is in Berlin, where she visits galleries, museums, and private collections, including that of Eduard Arnhold, owner of Manet's *Bon Bock* (fig. 69)—which the Havemeyers had declined to buy in 1905. In Berlin she learns of the death, on May 3, of Emilie Havemeyer in Montreux.

Weitzenhoffer 1986, p. 217; LWH to JD-R, 4/24/14; JD-R to LWH, 4/27/14; LWH to JD-R, 5/2/14; D-R to LWH, 5/4/14; MC to D-R, 5/7/14, correspondence, Weitzenhoffer files.

By May 7 Louisine returns to Montreux to pay her respects and pick up Emilie Havemeyer's grandson, who had been visiting. Louisine and the boy, who is her grandnephew and Harry's namesake, depart Montreux for Paris, presumably early Sunday morning, May 10, "in order to make the run to Paris in a day and be there for the [Roger Marx] auction the next morning." Louisine arranges for his return to America but stays on in Paris at the Hotel Crillon through at least the end of the month.

Quote from Havemeyer 1961, p. 262, in which Louisine (writing only a few years after the event) vividly recalled not only the hurried Sunday afternoon car ride through wartime Germany and France but also her presence in Paris at the time of the sale on May 12. LWH to JD-R, 5/2/14; MC to D-R, 5/7/14, correspondence, Weitzenhoffer files, indicate that Louisine had planned to arrive in Paris by May 9 or 10 but thought she might be delayed by her unexpected trip to Montreux. Her presence in Paris at the Hotel Crillon by May 13 can be established

by D-R to LWH, 5/13/14, correspondence, Weitzenhoffer files; her memoirs indicate she was there by May 12. Weitzenhoffer, however, contended that she missed the sale and dated her arrival in Paris to May 13 (1986, p. 218).

May 12 On the second day of the sale of *Tableaux, Pastels, Dessins, Aquarelles . . . Faisant partie de la collection Roger Marx*, Galerie Manzi-Joyant, Paris, May 11–12, Joseph Durand-Ruel acquires Cassatt's *Mother and Child* (A60) for Fr 15,500 and Degas's *Woman Having Her Hair Combed* (A242, pl. 48) for Fr 101,000 for Louisine, in accordance with her wishes. Louisine, who very much wanted the Degas nude "because Mr. Havemeyer had admired it," purportedly "entered the auction room just in time to see the picture knocked down to [her]."

Cassatt, lot no. 15; Degas, lot no. 125; LWH to JD-R, 4/17/14, including first quote, 4/24/14, 5/2/14; D-R to LWH, 5/13/14, D-R to MC 5/13/14, correspondence, Weitzenhoffer files; second quote from Havemeyer 1961, p. 262. The prices do not include 10 percent commission.

May 13 Cassatt is back in Paris. Sometime during the next two weeks or so, Louisine convinces the artist to rummage "through all the store closets in her apartment and into the big chest in the corridor" to see if she has enough works on hand for a Degas-Cassatt exhibition Louisine is planning in support of woman suffrage. Hence Cassatt uncovers her early portrait of Mrs. Robert Moore Riddle, *Lady at the Tea Table* (fig. 95); thanks to Louisine's encouragement, she exhibits the picture to great acclaim in *Tableaux, pastels, dessins, et pointes-seches par Mary Cassatt* at Durand-Ruel, Paris, June 8–27.

Figure 95. Mary Cassatt. *Lady at the Tea Table*, 1883–85. Oil on canvas, 29 x 24 in. (73.7 x 61 cm). Gift of the artist, 1923 (23.101)

Quote from Louisine Havemeyer, "Mary Cassatt," *Pennsylvania Museum Bulletin* 22 (May 1927), pp. 381–82, cited in Weitzenhoffer 1986, p. 219; Cassatt's presence in Paris by this date per D-R to MC, 5/13/14, correspondence, Weitzenhoffer files. The painting was placed on deposit with Durand-Ruel, Paris, on June 3.

Mid–late May Louisine purchases from Gimpel and Wildenstein, Paris, David's *Portrait of a Young Woman in White* (A180, now considered Follower of David) and from Paul Rosenberg, Paris, Courbet's *Alphonse Promayet* (A124, pl. 23). She also acquires, probably from Trotti et Cie, Paris, a Rubens portrait, *Ladislas Sigismund IV* (A472, now considered Workshop of Rubens), and a thirteenth-century Gothic sculpture of a king's head (MMA 29.100.28 or 29).

Rubens per MC to LWH, 11/24/[14], 8/24/20, Havemeyer correspondence; king's head per MC to LWH, 5/7/15, 12/8/19, indicating its purchase by Louisine in Paris in 1914, Havemeyer correspondence.

May 28 Louisine buys Cassatt's *Mother and Sleeping Child* (A65, pl. 262), which she had admired while it was in progress in Grasse, and *Young Mother, Daughter, and Baby* (A63) from Durand-Ruel, Paris, for Fr 8,000 and Fr 15,000, respectively. These pastels "were to have been shipped the week preceding the outbreak of war" but are not sent until later in the year. They arrive in New York on December 30, along with a watercolor by Madrazo (a copy after one of Velázquez's portraits of Balthasar Carlos for Electra) that the Paris gallery had been instructed to send her.

Purchase per LWH to D-R, 5/28/14; D-R to LWH, 5/29/14; shipment per D-R to LWH, 9/4/14, including quote, 12/30/14, correspondence, Weitzenhoffer files; RdM to LWH, 6/1/14, indicating subject of watercolor, that it is a gift Madrazo had long ago promised for Electra, and that he expects it to arrive at Louisine's hotel, the Crillon, on June 7.

May 29 Decamps's *Battle of Jericho* (A189), the two supposed Vasaris (A332, 333), a presumed Veronese *Portrait of a Woman* (A504), and the Spanish school "Buste de femme" now Attributed to Pantoja de la Cruz (A424), which have been placed on consignment with Durand-Ruel intermittently since 1908 are returned to Louisine for the last time.

Durand-Ruel Archives, unpublished Weitzenhoffer notes from Durand-Ruel Stock et Depot, 1904–1924–25.

June Louisine returns to New York.

Weitzenhoffer 1986, p. 220.

July 14 Horace and Doris Havemeyer's third child, Horace Jr., is born at Islip, Long Island.

Havemeyer 1944, p. 74.

Figure 96. Horace and Doris's family, 1914. L. to r.: Little Doris, Doris, Horace Jr., Horace, Adaline

After mid-August With the outbreak of World War I on the western front, Cassatt flees Grasse for Dinard, where Louisine sends her money to help support Belgian refugees. The artist returns to Grasse in late November.

Early November Louisine delivers a ten-minute address in Greenwich, Connecticut, in support of woman suffrage.

Weitzenhoffer 1986, p. 221.

November 14 Cassatt sees Trotti, who is eager to sell back to Louisine the Veronese portrait of a woman that his gallery has "from [her] in exchange"; she had "left the portrait there . . . at 50,000 francs." Duret thinks she should buy it back now that it has been restored. If Louisine recovers the picture, she does not do so until after October 1917, when, "according to their agreement," Trotti et Cie, Paris, is "still keeping it" for her but is willing, "since the falling off of the exchange has brought a considerable loss in value of the franc," to sell it for Fr 40,000.

MC to LWH, 11/11/[14], 11/15/[14], 6/19/[15], 7/31/[16]; TD to LWH, 9/18/17, including quotes; MC to LWH, 10/2/[17], Havemeyer correspondence. The portrait possibly is one of three once considered a Veronese: A278, now Attributed to Fasolo; A417, now Attributed to Montemezzano; A504, now considered Style of Veronese; if it is not, the picture was not returned to Louisine.

November 15 Cassatt recommends to Louisine Courbet's *La Vigneronne de Montreux* (fig. 97)—a "good picture" in "excellent condition" available for Fr 30,000. At Cassatt's instigation Duret takes up the subject again in June 1915: "It is, as I have told you, the only figure by Courbet which exists that one may have at the old price. This sort of subject is lacking in your collection and would more than complete it. After all you have done to have an unrivaled collection of Courbet works, it seems to me that it might suit you to add this one." Evidently Louisine does not care for the picture: she does not buy it even though

Figure 97. Gustave Courbet. *La Vigneronne de Montreux*, 1874. Oil on canvas, 39 ⅜ x 31 ⅞ in. (100 x 81 cm). Collection Musée Cantonal des Beaux-Arts, Lausanne

Duret has arranged matters so that she can acquire it for Fr 25,000, with half to be paid immediately and half to be paid when convenient, even after the war.

MC to LWH, 11/15/[14], including quote, 12/28/[14]; TD to LWH, 6/21/15, including quote, Havemeyer correspondence.

December 29 Louisine writes to Roland Knoedler, thanking him for agreeing to mount *Masterpieces by Old and Modern Painters*, her proposed benefit exhibition in support of woman suffrage, at M. Knoedler and Co., New York, in April. She had originally planned the event as a Degas exhibition to be held at Durand-Ruel, New York, but later extended its scope to include Cassatts and old masters; its venue is changed to Knoedler's.

Weitzenhoffer 1986, p. 222.

1915

January 12–23 Louisine lends four works (A294, 299, 303, 304) to *Paintings by El Greco and Goya*, a loan exhibition for the "Benefit of the American Women War Relief Fund and the Belgian Relief Fund" at M. Knoedler and Co., New York.

Shown as nos. 14, 13, 3, 2.

January 21 Louisine speaks on behalf of woman suffrage in Waterbury, Connecticut. This is the first of many speeches she delivers in 1915 in the tri-state area to rally support for the cause.

Louisine's notes, Weitzenhoffer files, summarily list some of her subsequent speaking engagements in 1915: February 23 (5 minutes), March 20, April 3, May 10 (Fifth Avenue, New York), June 8 (Bayshore), July 9 (Easthampton), July 10, August 7, September 30 (Hackensack), October 30 (Hotel Astor, New York, 10 minutes). The notes also indicate one date in 1916: May 15.

February 1 Cassatt rejects Louisine's idea of raffling off pictures from the suffrage exhibition at Knoedler's to raise money for the movement.

MC to LWH, 2/1/15, Havemeyer correspondence.

Early February Louisine is interested in purchasing Cassatt's *Lady at the Tea Table* (fig. 95), which the artist "would give . . . to [her] at once (of course to be left to a Museum) only [she has] more than half promised it to the Petit Palais." She does not acquire the portrait but keeps it for Cassatt, administering loan requests and tending to framing and the like, from April 26, 1915, after the close of the suffrage exhibition, in which it is included, until March 11, 1918, when it is lent to the Metropolitan. (The picture remains on loan to the Museum until April 7, 1923, when it enters the collection as a gift of the artist.)

MC to LWH, 2/4/[15], including quote, 12/12/[17], 3/3/[18], 8/24/[18], Havemeyer correspondence; see also Spassky 1985, pp. 638–42; dates of loan and transfer to gift per MMA Registrar's loan cards.

February 20–December 4 Louisine lends four pen-and-ink drawings by Abbey (A2, 4–6) to the *Panama Pacific International Exposition* at the Fine Arts Palace in San Francisco.

Shown as nos. 2655, 2648, 2656, 2658.

February 28 Cassatt sends Louisine letters that she has written to Mrs. Alfred Pope and to Payne, from whom Louisine had tried to secure loans for the suffrage exhibition. Cassatt's attempt to convince them to lend proves futile as well. Other collectors, however, are more cooperative.

Weitzenhoffer 1986, pp. 222–23.

April 6–24 Louisine's suffrage exhibition, *Masterpieces by Old and Modern Painters*, is held at M. Knoedler and Co., New York. Over two dozen works by Degas and at least nineteen by Cassatt are displayed in the ground-floor gallery; two smaller galleries are devoted to eighteen old master paintings. Nearly half the pictures included come from the Havemeyer collection. At 5:00 P.M. on the exhibition's opening day, Louisine delivers a one-hour talk, "Remarks on Edgar Degas and Mary Cassatt." It is warmly received by the approximately eighty people in the audience and praised by the press; the publicity gives Louisine a platform for furthering woman suffrage and helps to popularize the show. Joseph Durand-Ruel has an abridged version of the talk printed; copies are sent to European clients and are sold to benefit suffrage. The admission fee likewise generates revenue for the cause.

Weitzenhoffer 1986, pp. 222–23. See Rebecca A. Rabinow, "The Suffrage Exhibition of 1915," this catalogue.

April 9 Durand-Ruel, New York, delivers to Louisine three Cassatt drypoints that she had bought recently.

D-R to LWH, 4/9/15, correspondence, Weitzenhoffer files.

Plate 264. Mary Cassatt. *Mother and Child*, ca. 1913. Pastel on paper mounted on canvas, 32 x 25 ⅝ in. (81.3 x 65.1 cm). H. O. Havemeyer Collection, Bequest of Mrs. H. O. Havemeyer, 1929 (29.100.49) A64

April 13 Louisine purchases Cassatt's *Mother and Child* (A64, pl. 264), a pastel done especially for the suffrage exhibition. In February the artist had told Louisine she could have the picture, which she referred to as "the pastel of the boy standing," but cautioned her to "just be sure it is better or as good as what you have got [and] wait until after the exhibition & see then what you think." Louisine, it seems, buys the work directly from Cassatt, or somehow sidesteps the Durand-Ruels in the negotiations, because years later the artist would write about the dealers to her friend, "Oh! how they behaved about the pastel you bought."

Shown as no. 54; MC to LWH, 2/28/[15], 3/22/20, both including quotes, the latter also recalling that Durand-Ruel "never got over" a direct sale she made in 1915 to Harris Whittemore of a tondo (Breeskin 1970, no. 472), no. 42 in the suffrage exhibition, Havemeyer correspondence.

April 21 Durand-Ruel, New York, advises Louisine that the gallery has just received three Manet pastels from the Pellerin collection. These works, which Louisine does not acquire, possibly are *Portrait of Mlle Claire Campbell* (Rouart and Wildenstein 1975, II, no. 69), sold to Ralph King of Cleveland in 1916, and two portraits (ibid., nos. 31, 34) sold by 1918 to the Boston collector Joseph Flanagan.

D-R to LWH, 4/21/15, correspondence, Weitzenhoffer files; identification of works proposed on the basis of provenance information in Rouart and Wildenstein 1975, II.

April Barnes praises the Havemeyer collection as "the best and wisest collection in America" in his article "How to Judge a Painting" in *Arts and Decoration*.

Vol. 5 (April 1915), pp. 246, 249, cited in Weitzenhoffer 1986, p. 226.

June Louisine campaigns for woman suffrage on a tenday tour of New York State, where, from Manhattan to Buffalo, she delivers an average of seven speeches a day and carries the party's symbolic Torch of Liberty.

New York Times, August 8, 1915, II, p. 13, col. 5, indicates that the tour began at Montauk Point, Long Island, in early June.

July 5 Cassatt advises Louisine that she has told Trotti that "the one thing" Louisine is interested in is the Titian but the dealer "didn't think Cook would give it up." She also mentions that she "saw a fair Kings head at Kelekians, 13th Century from Rheims, different from yours but very fine."

MC to LWH, 7/5/15, Havemeyer correspondence, cited in Mathews 1984, pp. 324–25; see Wethey 1971, nos. 24, 31, or X-95, for works then attributed to Titian that were in the collection of Herbert L. Cook, Richmond, England, at this time.

Figure 98. Louisine speaking at a suffrage rally, New York, 1915. From Louisine W. Havemeyer, "The Suffrage Torch: Memories of a Militant," *Scribner's Magazine* 71 (May 1922), p. 534

Figure 99. Louisine passing the Torch of Liberty to the New Jersey branch of the Woman's Political Union. From Louisine W. Havemeyer, "The Suffrage Torch, Memories of a Militant," *Scribner's Magazine* 71 (May 1922), p. 537

By July 22 Duret learns from Cassatt that Louisine wants to acquire Courbet's *Source* (fig. 5), a picture that "had not been for sale at any price" when Harry had wanted to buy it from the artist's daughter, now deceased. In September Louisine confirms to George Durand-Ruel that she is "interested in *La Source* . . . but on account of the unusual financial conditions due to the war, I can say nothing definitely until I know the price." Over the next months the price set by the new owner, Mme de Tastes, fluctuates between Fr 200,000 and Fr 400,000, and her desire to sell the painting seems less than sincere. Hence by January 1917 Cassatt, Duret, and Durand-Ruel suspend their efforts to obtain *La Source* on Louisine's behalf. (Ironically, in March 1916 Louisine is willing to pay as much as Fr 150,000, precisely the amount for which the Louvre would acquire the picture at auction in 1919.)

TD to LWH, 7/22/15, 12/29/15, 2/9/16, 5/4/16, 6/29/16; MC to LWH, 8/30/[16]; TD to LWH, 10/12/16, 1/17/17, 1/21/17, Havemeyer correspondence; GD-R to LWH, 9/3/15, regarding Harry's interest in the picture and including quote; LWH to GD-R, 9/15, including quote; GD-R to LWH, 1/26/16, 2/19/16, 3/15/16, correspondence, Weitzenhoffer files.

July 28 Louisine celebrates her sixtieth birthday. This summer she begins writing *Sixteen to Sixty: Memoirs of a Collector*, which she continues to work on for the next few years. The text, published posthumously in 1930 and reprinted with minor changes in 1961, is more or less complete by the summer of 1917. She does not finish her chapter on Cassatt, which is not published, until early 1922.

The text can be dated on the basis of events and acquisitions recorded and dates included by Louisine. In the first chapter she noted, "This very day there lies upon my writing table a letter from Spain begging me to send a photograph of the Duke's portrait [Goya's *Duke of Wellington* (A302)] to Señor Beruete of Madrid, in order that he may put it in the work he is now writing on Goya [*Goya: Pintor de Retratos*, Madrid, 1916, with preface dated October 1915]" (Havemeyer 1961, p. 7). Correspondence on this subject dates to the summer of 1915: RdM to LWH, 6/18/15, 7/28/15, asking Louisine on behalf of his friend Aureliano Beruete y Moret to send a photograph of the Goya; LWH to Beruete y Moret, 8/15/15, enclosing photographs and a list of "all my canvases by Goya," Havemeyer correspondence. Louisine was writing chapter 4 in spring 1916 (p. 35, indicating that the text dates to the time of James J. Hill's death, May 29, 1916); chapter 11, on Courbet, is dated 1917 (p. 180), and her final chapter, 14, on Degas, was completed just prior to the artist's death on September 27, 1917 (p. 267). With one possible exception (p. 195), noting a Courbet that she managed to obtain at a very high price (presumably A154), her activities as a collector are chronicled only through 1917. There are a handful of other entries that date to the early 1920s. Neither the 1930 nor the 1961 edition includes Louisine's later chapter on Cassatt, which the family felt did not meet the same standard as the rest of the text.

August 7 Representing the New York branch of the Women's Political Union, Louisine stands in a tugboat on the Hudson River and passes the Torch of Liberty to a member of the New Jersey chapter who is aboard another tug; she "stepped up from the ranks" to make the presentation speech in this ceremony of solidarity, substituting for

Figure 100. Louisine's Ship of State

Harriot Stanton Blatch, who had returned to England owing to the death of her husband.

See Weitzenhoffer 1986, pp. 227, 229; *New York Times*, August 8, 1915, II, p. 13, col. 5.

August 9 Louisine campaigns for suffrage in New Jersey, carrying the symbolic torch to Long Branch and Asbury Park.

New York Times, August 8, 1915, II, p. 13, col. 5.

Late summer or early fall Louisine devises a new symbol to represent the enlightened future for voting women: a battery-powered Ship of State, modeled on the *Mayflower* and illuminated by thirty-three light bulbs (fig. 100).

Weitzenhoffer 1986, p. 228.

October 29 Madrazo informs Louisine that Goya's portrait of his grandson (Gassier and Wilson 1971, no. 885) is available for sale in Madrid; the owner, D. Enrique Crooke, has not yet set a price but knows the value of the work and has already refused Fr 100,000 for it.

RdM to LWH, 10/29/15, including description that accords with Gassier and Wilson 1971, no. 885, except that the boy is said to be holding a string attached to a "little owl" (*chouette*) rather than a "little cart" (*charrette*), presumably due to an error in transcription when the letter was typed, 6/8/16, Havemeyer correspondence. For identification of the owner, see A. Beruete y Moret, *Goya as Portrait Painter*, New York and Boston, 1922, p. 116.

October 30 Louisine delivers a short speech at the Astor Hotel, New York, at a luncheon celebrating the centennial of Elizabeth Cady Stanton's birth.

According to Harriot Stanton Blatch and Alma Lutz, the luncheon was scheduled so that it would occur before election day, November 2, and hence took place prior to Stanton's actual birthday, November 12 (*Challenging Years: The Memoirs of Harriot Stanton Blatch*, New York, 1940, p. 237). Speech per Louisine's notes, Weitzenhoffer files.

November 2 Louisine is crushed by the defeat today of the woman suffrage referendum in New York State.

See Weitzenhoffer 1986, p. 229.

November 12 In Seneca Falls, New York, on the centennial of Stanton's birth, Louisine speaks on the suffrage movement, tracing its origins back to the first enlightened conversation between Lucretia Mott and Stanton on "one hot Sunday morning in July . . . about seventy years ago in a little town near Seneca Falls."

Havemeyer 1922a, p. 531.

November 22 George Durand-Ruel would like to show Louisine several paintings the New York gallery has received from Paris. He especially notes Manet's *Virgin with the Rabbit* (Rouart and Wildenstein 1975, I, no. 5), which she "always liked so much." Louisine passes up the Manet, which she and Harry had turned down when it was offered to them ten years earlier.

GD-R to LWH, 11/22/15, correspondence, Weitzenhoffer files.

December 29 Duret offers Louisine what he thinks may be "a last chance to have a large Courbet painting at a reasonable price": *La Pointe de Vallières* (A160) for Fr 15,000. Louisine seizes the opportunity and sends him a check in this amount on January 14. Though the picture is with the packer by February 9, the war delays its arrival in New York until late April.

TD to LWH, 12/29/15, including quote, 2/9/16, acknowledging Louisine's "letter of January 14 with the check of 15,000 fcs, in payment for Courbet's painting *La Pointe de Vallières*" and indicating that it is with the packer, 5/4/16, indicating that Louisine has received the picture and is pleased with it, sheet dated 1916, possibly the second page or an enclosure from a Duret letter, describing the picture and annotated by Louisine, "For Adaline," "Love to Adaline 1916," Havemeyer correspondence.

1916

January 9 Electra and J. Watson Webb's fourth child, James Watson, Jr., is born in Syosset, Long Island.

Havemeyer 1944, p. 71.

January 17 Twin boys, Henry O. H. and Peter H. B., Jr., are born to Adaline and Peter Frelinghuysen at the Ritz Hotel, New York.

Havemeyer 1944, p. 71.

January 18 From the American Art Association sale of *The Private Collection of the Late Hugo Reisinger of New York City*, Grand Ballroom, Plaza Hotel, New York, January 18–20, Durand-Ruel purchases Pissarro's *Girl with a Goat* (A429, pl. 265) for Louisine for $5,100.

Lot no. 74.

Plate 265. Camille Pissarro. *Girl with a Goat*, 1881. Oil on canvas, 32½ x 25½ in. (82.6 x 64.8 cm). Private collection. A429

March 6–October 15 Louisine lends a statuette, three vases, two jars, and five bowls to the Metropolitan's *Exhibition of Early Chinese Pottery and Sculpture* (see fig. 101). The Museum had planned this exhibition, hoping "with the generous help of some of our most zealous collectors, to bring together, a comparatively small but choice group" that would "explain the great interest taken nowadays in early Chinese ceramics by showing what they are at their best."

Quote from *Bulletin of The Metropolitan Museum of Art* 11 (February 1916), pp. 49–50. MMA Registrar's special exhibition loan book no. 3, receipt no. 265, 1–11, indicates that the loans were received by the Museum on January 25.

Figure 101. Installation view, *Exhibition of Early Chinese Pottery and Sculpture*, The Metropolitan Museum of Art, 1916

March 11 Louisine purchases Courbet's *Source* (A135, pl. 21), an earlier and smaller version of the picture owned by Mme de Tastes, for Fr 50,000 from Durand-Ruel, New York.

Plate 266. Gustave Courbet. *The Knife Grinders*, ca. 1848–50. Oil on canvas, 34¾ x 40⅞ in. (88.3 x 103.8 cm). Columbus Museum of Art, Ohio, Museum Purchase, Howald Fund (54.5) A123

May 19 Duret believes that Courbet's *Knife Grinders* (A123, pl. 266) will add a "new note" to Louisine's collection and recommends it to her for Fr 22,000. By June 26 Cassatt has "climbed Duret's stairs" to see the painting and reports to Louisine, "Duret leaned on the historical interest of the picture . . . &, I told him you did not care for that you looked at the value of the picture as a work of Art." Louisine cables Cassatt on July 1 that she will buy *The Knife Grinders* for Fr 12,000 ($3,389.87), the figure Cassatt has mistakenly quoted. Since the reduced price is actually Fr 20,000, the acquisition is not finalized until the end of the summer.

TD to LWH, 5/19/16, including quote; MC to LWH, n.d. [ca. 5/19–6/26/16], 6/26/[16], including quote; TD to LWH, 6/29/16; LWH to MC, 7/1/16; TD to LWH, 7/2/16, noting that the "'Remouleurs' is about the size of 'Chasseur à cheval retrouvant la piste' [A138] which you have as a result of my enterprise and for which you paid Fr 30,000 before the war"; MC to LWH, 7/7/[16], 8/30/[16]; TD to LWH, 10/12/16, Havemeyer correspondence.

May–June Louisine considers but does not purchase from Durand-Ruel, New York, Courbet's *Choir Boys* (Fernier 1977–78, no. 183), "which Miss Cassatt mistakenly thinks is a study for the Enterrement d'Ornans." The painting is sold in November to Bernheim-Jeune, Paris.

JD-R to MC, 5/18/16; GD-R to LWH, 6/14/16, including quote, correspondence, Weitzenhoffer files.

June 1 Louisine's younger brother, George Waldron Elder, dies.

Weitzenhoffer files.

June 26 Cassatt advises Louisine about works by Degas available from the collection of the late Michel Manzi; she has met with his widow, Charlotte, who "has two paintings both fine & six pastels." Over the next few months Cassatt negotiates the acquisition for Louisine of Degas's *Mme Théodore Gobillard* (A200) and *The Dancing Class* (A203, pl. 267) as well as a bonus: not only do the heirs agree to "come down in price" for the "two paintings" but they also "have brought something that they will add to the bargain," an oil sketch on pink paper, Degas's *Woman on a Sofa* (A213, pl. 268). The transaction is completed on December 5, 1916, and the three pictures are shipped to Louisine in April 1917.

Plate 267. Edgar Degas. *The Dancing Class*, 1871. Oil on wood, 7¾ x 10⅝ in. (19.7 x 27 cm). H. O. Havemeyer Collection, Bequest of Mrs. H. O. Havemeyer, 1929 (29.100.184) A203

Plate 268. Edgar Degas. *Woman on a Sofa*, 1875. Oil on pink paper, 19⅛ x 16¾ in. (48.6 x 42.6 cm). H. O. Havemeyer Collection, Bequest of Mrs. H. O. Havemeyer, 1929 (29.100.185) A213

MC to LWH, 6/26/[16], including first quote, 7/31/[16], 7/12/[17], inquiring "Have you Charlotte's receipt?," Havemeyer correspondence; second quote from Havemeyer 1961, pp. 264–65. The existence of a receipt for the works, signed by Charlotte Manzi, is noted in MMA Department of European Paintings Archives. The date of this receipt is transcribed in the Archives as December 5, 1915, which precedes by six months Cassatt's mention of the works to Louisine in her letter dated 6/26. Though no year is noted on this letter, it can be dated firmly to 1916 on the basis of internal evidence. Presumably, therefore, the last digit of the date on the receipt was mistranscribed or misread.

July 31 Cassatt recommends to Louisine Courbet's oil study (Fernier 1977–78, no. 207) for one of the women in his *Demoiselles des bords de la Seine*, which is available from Bernheim-Jeune, Paris, for Fr 70,000. Duret fails to convince the gallery to lower its price in August, yet Cassatt continues to pursue the subject through the fall. The high price deters Louisine from seriously considering the purchase, just as it had Kelekian, who had hoped to buy the painting for half the amount asked. On January 16 Duret informs Louisine that Bernheim-Jeune has sold the work but that Courbet's second sketch for the *Demoiselles* (Fernier 1977–78, no. 206) is now for sale at Fr 125,000. Duret and Cassatt are unable to convince Louisine that "Courbets are going up in price" and that "the old prices are finished."

MC to LWH, 7/31/[16], including quote, 8/30/[16], 9/30/[16]; TD to LWH, 10/12/16, including quote, 1/16/17, Havemeyer correspondence.

November 4 The *New York Herald* reports "the discovery today that the country homes of Mrs. H. O. Havemeyer and Julius H. Seymour on Palmer's Hill had been robbed." The paper notes that family members will arrive today to draw up lists of missing items and that other summer residents will return to see if they also have been robbed.

Newspaper clipping, Weitzenhoffer files.

During the year Louisine serves on the Advisory Council of the National Woman's Party, working for the enfranchisement of women.

Weitzenhoffer 1986, p. 232.

1917

January 8 Louisine purchases Degas's pastel *Before the Entrance Onstage* (A232) from Durand-Ruel, New York, for $30,000.

January 16–21 Duret urges Louisine to advance him Fr 60,000 so that he can negotiate the purchase of a Courbet painting of a lifesize bather set against a landscape background. Three years later, on February 10, 1920, Louisine receives *The Young Bather* (A146, pl. 269), about which Cassatt comments: "It is splendid to think you have the Bruxelles nude it was not dear. It is so fine."

Plate 269. Gustave Courbet. *The Young Bather*, 1866. Oil on canvas, 51¼ x 38¼ in. (130.2 x 97.2 cm). H. O. Havemeyer Collection, Bequest of Mrs. H. O. Havemeyer, 1929 (29.100.124) A146

TD to LWH, 1/16/17, annotated by Louisine, "Nude recd Feb. 10," 1/21/17; MC to LWH, 2/7/[20], including quote, 2/14/20, Havemeyer correspondence.

January Louisine gives the five Whistler pastels (A511, 516, 517, 519, 520) she purchased from the artist in 1881 to Freer for the museum he intends to establish. After Freer dies in 1919, these works are transferred to the Smithsonian Institution, Washington, D.C., for the Freer Gallery of Art.

Charles Lang Freer Papers, Freer Gallery of Art, Arthur M. Sackler Gallery Archives, Smithsonian Institution, Washington, D.C.

May 15 Louisine's older sister, Anne, suffers a fatal heart attack.

Weitzenhoffer 1986, p. 231.

June Louisine delivers a speech on recruiting for the Red Cross.

Louisine's notes, Weitzenhoffer files.

July 2 Louisine speaks on "War Dangers and Food Conservation" to a large audience in High School Hall in Pittsfield, Massachusetts.

"Society Notes, The Berkshires," *New York Herald*, July 2, 1917, p. 8.

July 31 Louisine draws up her will.

See Weitzenhoffer 1986, pp. 254–57.

August 11 Justin Godart, Ministère de la Guerre, Cabinet du Sous-secrétaire d'Etat, of France, acknowledges Louisine's "genérosité et l'actif dévouement . . . en faveur des malades et blessés de nos armées." This recognizes her service during World War I when she "spoke continuously . . . on Liberty Loans, land army food conservation, economy and relief, and conducted a 'jam campaign,' in which the women of several counties . . . made and shipped, the first year of [the] war, thirty thousand pounds of jam to the wounded soldiers at the front, and the second year increased it to forty thousand pounds." These activities earned Louisine the nickname "Jam Queen."

Quotes from unpublished Weitzenhoffer notes from Justin Godart to LWH, 8/11/17, folder, National Gallery of Art, Washington, D.C., and Havemeyer 1922a, p. 528; for the nickname, see F.W.G., "Women to Use Vote to Gain Equality," *Washington Herald*, February 17, 1921, p. 4, col. 3.

August 26(?) Madrazo dies.

October 3 Louisine addresses a meeting of 150 suffragists in Baltimore, where she remarks on the hypocrisy of working for the Liberty Loan when those "who demand true democracy are thrown into jails for doing so." The next day the *New York Herald* misrepresents Louisine's position with an article headlined "Suffrage Boycott on Loan Is Urged by Mrs. Havemeyer." On October 5 the paper prints two corrections: Louisine's letter to the editor and a short article entitled "Mrs. H. O. Havemeyer Not Against Loan."

New York Herald, October 4, 1917, p. 9; October 5, 1917, pp. 8, 12.

October 3–November 7 Louisine places three six-fold Japanese screens, *Hotei and Children* (MMA 29.100.498), *Fans and Waves* (MMA 29.100.499), and *No Rules* (MMA 29.100.500), on loan to the Metropolitan. They are included in the Museum's *Loan Exhibition of Japanese Screens and Paintings of the Korin School* (September 27–October 28).

Dates of loan per MMA Registrar's loan cards, L 1704.1 -.3.

October 13–14 Louisine visits Freer at his country house in Great Barrington, Massachusetts, to "enjoy the beauty and quiet" of the Berkshires in autumn. (Freer had been her guest at Hilltop that summer.) This fall plans are under way for the construction of the Freer Gallery of Art in Washington, D.C., where, toward the end of the year, Louisine sees "'the first floor' of the future home of so many things [they] mutually love."

LWH to CLF, 10/9/17; CLF to LWH, 10/11/17, including first quote; 7/12/17, indicating summer visit; 12/25/17, regarding Washington visit, including second quote, correspondence, Weitzenhoffer files.

December 25 Freer writes to Louisine: "Interesting news comes regularly from China and young Mr. Wong is now en route to New York bringing he says a number of fine

things.—Hold on to your purse until he arrives." Freer is in New York in mid-January, at which time it seems he arranges for Louisine to see this shipment: on January 18 he sends her "Mr. Wong's receipt for the seven thousand dollar check" for an unknown purchase. The following spring Freer would inform Louisine of offerings through the dealer Yue and would also tell her to expect "another lot from Wong."

CLF to LWH, 12/25/17, 1/18/18, enclosing receipt, 4/24/19, all including quotes, correspondence, Weitzenhoffer files.

December 28 Cassatt offers Louisine Degas's *Woman Bathing in a Shallow Tub* (A239, pl. 271), *Portrait of a Young Woman* (A240), and *Fan Mount: Ballet Girls* (A223, pl. 270) for $20,000. In February, after Vollard takes the works from the walls of Cassatt's apartment, she

Plate 270. Edgar Degas. *Fan Mount: Ballet Girls*, 1879. Watercolor, silver, and gold on silk, 7½ x 22¾ in. (19.1 x 57.8 cm). H. O. Havemeyer Collection, Bequest of Mrs. H. O. Havemeyer, 1929 (29.100.555) A223

Plate 271. Edgar Degas. *Woman Bathing in a Shallow Tub*, 1885. Charcoal and pastel on light green wove paper, now discolored to warm gray, adhered to silk bolting in 1951, 32 x 22⅛ in. (81.3 x 56.2 cm). H. O. Havemeyer Collection, Bequest of Mrs. H. O. Havemeyer, 1929 (29.100.41) A239

asks the Durand-Ruels to safeguard them during the war. They remain on deposit with Durand-Ruel, Paris, from March 8, 1918, until May 9, 1919, when they are shipped to New York. Louisine is advised of their arrival on June 12, 1919. Years earlier Cassatt had written to Louisine about the bather, "I cannot believe that many would care for the nude I have. Those things are for painters and connoisseurs."

MC to LWH, 12/28/[17], Havemeyer correspondence, cited in Mathews 1984, p. 330; JD-R to MC, 2/18/18; MC to D-R, 2/21/18; D-R to MC, 12/26/18, all discussing wartime storage; GD-R to MC, 5/13/19, indicating shipping date; D-R to LWH, 6/12/19, indicating arrival in New York, correspondence, Weitzenhoffer files; MC to LWH, n.d. [4/13], including quote, Havemeyer correspondence; see also Boggs et al. 1988, nos. 209, 269.

1918

March 26 At the posthumous sale of the *Collection Edgar Degas*, Galerie Georges Petit, Paris, March 26–27, Joseph Durand-Ruel obtains Cassatt's *Girl Arranging Her Hair* (A51, pl. 272) for Louisine with a bid of Fr 21,000. This painting had occupied a place of honor in Degas's sitting room for many years. He had acquired it from Cassatt in exchange for his *Woman Bathing in a Shallow Tub* after the close of the 1886 Impressionist exhibition in Paris, in which the two works were shown. Louisine now owned both pictures (see December 28, 1917).

Lot no. 8; D-R to LWH, 4/4/18, acknowledging receipt of Fr 23,000 inclusive, correspondence, Weitzenhoffer files.

Plate 272. Mary Cassatt. *Girl Arranging Her Hair*, 1886. Oil on canvas, 29⅝ x 24⅝ in. (75.3 x 62.6 cm). National Gallery of Art, Washington, D.C., Chester Dale Collection (1963.10.97) A51

June 1 Duret tells Louisine that the man's portrait by Prud'hon about which Cassatt had commented favorably last November is available for Fr 30,000. Louisine is interested but seems to abandon consideration of the acquisition by the end of the summer, after failing to negotiate a lower price.

TD to LWH, 6/1/18, noting that he was responsible for two earlier acquisitions, an Ingres portrait (A330) and a Courbet (A127); MC to LWH, 11/27/17, 9/11/18, replying to Louisine's letter of the "20th" that she "thought [Duret] would come down" in price for this portrait and criticizing his prices and commissions in general, Havemeyer correspondence.

By December 7 Kelekian reproaches Cassatt for letting Louisine pay too much for the Foolish Virgin (*Bust of a Foolish Virgin*, now considered late 13th–early 14th century style [MMA 29.100.31]), a statue she had recently bought from Demotte.

MC to LWH, 12/7/[18], 12/28/[18?], describing the piece as "not nearly as fine as the little Saint [MMA 29.100.30], what ever Demotte may say," Havemeyer correspondence; Havemeyer 1931, p. 218, ill. The sculpture has since been published as a forgery; see October 6, 1909, n.

1919

February 9 At the behest of Alice Paul, head of the National Woman's Party, Louisine leads a demonstration by one hundred women in Washington, D.C., the day before the Senate vote on the federal suffrage amendment. She is arrested with thirty-nine other demonstrators after they burn an effigy of President Wilson in front of the White House, events reported on the front page of the *New York Times*. Louisine is given a choice of a "five dollars fine, or five days in jail" and is released on February 12, after spending three nights, much to her family's horror, "in a dirty, discarded prison . . . unfit to hold a human being." While she is in jail, the amendment is defeated by one vote.

New York Times, February 10, 1919, p. 1, col. 5; February 12, 1919, p. 1, col. 2; see Inez Haynes Irwin, *Up Hill with Banners Flying*, Penobscot, Me., 1964, p. 417 (originally published as *The Story of the Woman's Party*, 1921); quote from Havemeyer 1922b, pp. 669–71.

February 15 Louisine returns to Washington, D.C., where, with over two dozen other suffragists who had also been incarcerated, she boards the "Prison Special" train for a three-week transcontinental tour to garner support for woman suffrage. Louisine is "usually placed on the programme as the first speaker" at their stops. The itinerary includes "South Carolina, Florida, Tennessee, Louisiana, Texas, etc., and on to San Francisco, returning by Colorado, Wisconsin, Illinois, Michigan, New York, Massachusetts, Connecticut, and disbanding in New York City." From the "opening night in Charleston, South Carolina,

Figure 102. Louisine Havemeyer shaking hands with the captain of the Detroit traffic police, 1919. From Louisine W. Havemeyer, "The Prison Special, Memories of a Militant," *Scribner's Magazine* 71 (June 1922), p. 672

Figure 103. Installation view of *Loan Exhibition of the Works of Gustave Courbet*, The Metropolitan Museum of Art, 1919

when the opera-house was packed from floor to dome . . . to our great final mass-meeting in Carnegie Hall, we had immense audiences who evinced for us large sympathy and keen interest."

New York Times, February 12, 1919, p. 7, col. 2; March 11, 1919, p. 10, col. 8; quote from Havemeyer 1922b, pp. 675–76.

March 10 In New York, the last stop of the "Prison Special," Louisine addresses a reception attended by 3,500 women at Carnegie Hall. Her speech begins, "The militants are here and we haven't broken anything, not even broken down."

New York Times, March 11, 1919, p. 10, col. 8; see also Weitzenhoffer 1986, pp. 236, 269, n. 9.

April 7–June 1 Louisine anonymously lends sixteen paintings to the centennial *Loan Exhibition of the Works of Gustave Courbet* at the Metropolitan Museum (see fig. 103). (She had helped Curator Bryson Burroughs plan the show and related events.) Louisine's participation as a lender—her works constituted nearly half of the exhibition—must have been extremely gratifying to Cassatt, who had written to her in November 1912: "There is one thing I have always wished to ask you to do before I die. To lend all your Courbets for a short time to the Metropolitan. Only you can show what Courbet is, what influence he had. I am sure it would help the young painters it might make an artist. Can you do this?"

The exhibition was scheduled to run through May 18 but was extended until June 1; MMA Registrar's special exhibition loan book, book no. 4, receipt no. 644, 1–14, indicates that the pictures were borrowed from Louisine on March 18 and returned to her on June 2; MC to LWH, 11/30/12, Havemeyer correspondence.

April 10 Angele L. de Calle, Madrazo's widow, corresponds with Louisine about Goya's *Marquesa de Santa Cruz* (fig. 104), which her husband "absolutely wanted [her] to acquire by his mediation"; it was impossible when he pursued it, however, since the owner proved unwilling to cede his painting "at any price." Now, she says, the deceased owner's sons might accept a "high sum" but are not really inclined to sell or to give her preference as Madrazo's client. Indeed, they have already refused Fr 1,000,000. When Madrazo had first written Louisine about this portrait in March 1912, he remarked incredulously that the owner "didn't want to sell" for Fr 700,000 and "you will see how soon they will offer *one million* and who knows then."

Angele L. de Calle to LWH, 4/10/19, also indicating that Louisine had been in correspondence with Madrazo about this picture when he died in 1917, 7/10/18; RdM to LWH, 3/22/12, also indicating that Louisine had seen the portrait with him, Havemeyer correspondence. In her memoirs Louisine referred to the portrait as "one of the most

Figure 104. Francisco de Goya y Lucientes. *Marquesa de Santa Cruz*, 1805. Oil on canvas, 49 ¼ x 81 ¾ in. (125.1 x 207.6 cm). Museo del Prado, Madrid (7070)

beautiful [by Goya] I ever saw" (Havemeyer 1961, pp. 171–72). This may be the picture about which Louisine and Madrazo corresponded in 1916: RdM to LWH, 6/8/16, 6/9/16; LWH to RdM, n.d., n.d. [two cables, received 6/16], all indicating that both parties were pursuing seriously a work for which Louisine was willing to pay Fr 412,000 but which Madrazo thought he could obtain for her only at the nonnegotiable price of Pts 800,000, Havemeyer correspondence.

May 21 The woman suffrage amendment is passed by the House of Representatives; on June 4 it is passed by the Senate. Louisine continues to campaign for the enfranchisement of women—traveling widely, giving speeches, and lobbying special committees—to rally support for ratification of the amendment by thirty-six state legislatures, which is necessary if it is to become part of the Constitution.

Weitzenhoffer 1986, p. 236.

May 24 In reply to Louisine's plea for counsel regarding the works of art she should leave to the Metropolitan Museum, Cassatt responds: "I wish I could advise you as to what would be the best for a Museum in your collection. Almost everything would be fine. In the French school I would begin with Poussin & then skip to the 19th Century your Courbets, an Ingres & then Corot Degas Manet Monet. You certainly have a choice. If only we could talk it over!"

MC to LWH, 5/24/19, Havemeyer correspondence.

July 24 Louisine writes the first codicil to her will, selecting 113 works to be bequeathed to the Metropolitan Museum: 62 old master and modern pictures, 13 sculptures from different periods, 3 Japanese lacquer pieces, and a quantity of European decorative objects—25 pieces of Cyprian glass, 4 of Italian faience, 6 Hispano-Moresque plates or plaques to be chosen by Horace. Her selection of pictures reflects Cassatt's advice to some extent; however, she adds Cézanne to the roster of artists but, curiously, neglects Monet.

For the codicil, see Weitzenhoffer 1986, pp. 254–56; for the pictures named, see works marked with * in Appendix.

September 24 Durand-Ruel, New York, collects Louisine's "little Decamps" (A184) from the Metropolitan Museum, although "the repairing of [it] is not yet finished." Four years later Joseph Durand-Ruel would advise Louisine that "the restoration on her little Decamps was well done but the value of the painting is now very small." The picture remains on deposit with the gallery until 1928.

D-R to LWH, 9/24/19; JD-R to LWH, 6/6/23, correspondence, Weitzenhoffer files. Durand-Ruel Archives indicate that the gallery received Decamps's "Little Traveller (Landscape)" from Louisine on this date.

September 25 Freer dies at his apartment in the Hotel Gotham, New York. He had moved to New York earlier in the year to "be near his physician." During the spring and summer of 1919 Freer and Louisine "saw each other constantly" either at her home, "looking over the accumulations of the preceding years," or at "his hotel to see some new consignment from China."

Obituary, *New York Times*, September 26, 1919; quote from Louisine Havemeyer, "The Freer Museum of Oriental Art, with Personal Recollections of the Donor," *Scribner's Magazine* 73 (May 1923), pp. 530–31.

December 8–15 Louisine makes a trip to the Midwest, probably to marshal support for suffrage. Her hectic schedule includes engagements in Chicago, Detroit, Milwaukee, and St. Paul.

Itinerary, Weitzenhoffer files.

December 14 Cassatt informs Louisine that Kelekian has received her cable concerning the "fine" king's head, which will be auctioned the following day at the estate sale *Sculptures. . .Tableaux, Tapisseries . . . Composant La Collection de Feu M. Manzi*, Galerie Manzi, Joyant et Cie, Paris, December 15–16, but that she "wont get" the piece, presumably because her bid is too low. Cassatt—who had joined Kelekian in "strongly" advising the acquisition earlier in the month—endeavors to soften the blow by reminding Louisine, "You are rich in 13th century you can console yourself for the loss of the head."

Presumably lot 99; MC to LWH, 12/4/19, 12/8/[19], 12/14/[19], including quote, 12/17/[19], 12/31/[19], both regarding Duveen's interest in the piece and Demotte's apparent purchase of it, Havemeyer correspondence.

Late December After pursuing the acquisition for a year and a half, Louisine finally abandons the idea of purchasing Degas's wax statue *The Little Fourteen-Year-Old Dancer* (fig. 67) from the artist's heirs. On December 9 the heirs, who had equivocated about whether to sell the piece and for what sum, set a price of Fr 500,000 on it and, as Cassatt informs Louisine, "Now they give you a month to get an answer to me, & then if you do not accept the statue will be cast not in bronze but in something as much like the original wax as possible." On December 31 Cassatt acknowledges Louisine's "cable refusing the 'danseuse' . . . Of course I knew you would not accept such a preposterous price." When Louisine had originally attempted to buy the sculpture from Degas, he had told Vollard he was finishing it for her for Fr 40,000.

MC to LWH, 12/8/[19] (with addition of 12/10/[19]), including quote, 12/31/[19], including quote; 8/4/18 (with addition of 8/5/18), regarding Vollard information, Havemeyer correspondence. On this subject, see Boggs et al. 1988, no. 227.

1920

Mid–late April Louisine pays $100 for a "unique etching" by Degas, "un essai wet grain" done under Braquemond's guidance. This etching, *Head of a Woman in Profile* (pl. 273), was among the approximately one hundred items Cassatt had sold to Durand-Ruel, Paris, before she departed Paris for Grasse in late December; the other works included "all [she] had left of [her] drypoints & a lot of pastel drawings."

MC to LWH, 3/22/20, 4/10/[20], annotated by Louisine, "Unique proof by Degas/pd $100 for it Apl 1920," 5/18/20, Havemeyer correspondence; dates of Cassatt's departure for and arrival in Grasse, per MC to LWH, 12/17/[19], 12/31/19, Havemeyer correspondence.

Plate 273. Edgar Degas. *Head of a Woman in Profile*, 1879. Soft-ground etching, aquatint, and drypoint on laid paper, plate: 4 ½ x 4 ⁷⁄₁₆ in. (11.5 x 11.3 cm); sheet: 7 ⅝ x 10 ¼ in. (19.4 x 26 cm). Inscribed in pencil, bottom of sheet: *essaie de grain liquide epreuve unique par M. Degas/Mary Cassatt.* H. O. Havemeyer Collection, Bequest of Mrs. H. O. Havemeyer, 1929 (29.107.52)

April 17–May 9 Louisine anonymously lends two Cassatt paintings (A51, 59) to *Exhibition of Paintings and Drawings by Representative Modern Masters* at the Pennsylvania Academy of the Fine Arts, Philadelphia. She visits the show before May 2 especially to see the room devoted to Cassatt's works; the artist's own family in Philadelphia does not bother to come.

Shown as nos. 7, 9; MC to LWH, 5/18/20, Havemeyer correspondence.

April 20 Louisine delivers a moving speech on Cassatt, touching on her increasing frailty, to the National Association of Women Painters and Sculptors at the Fine Arts Building, New York, on the occasion of the group's twenty-ninth exhibition.

Weitzenhoffer 1986, pp. 240, 267, chap. 15, n. 7.

May 7–October 31 To the Metropolitan Museum's *Fiftieth Anniversary Exhibition* Louisine anonymously lends two Poussins (A434, 374, now considered Style of Poussin and Francisque Millet, pls. 241, 242), El Greco's *View of Toledo* (A303, pl. 60), and Corot's *Reverie* (A102, pl. 229).

June 8–9 Louisine pickets the Republican National Convention in Chicago, carrying a banner that reads "Theodore Roosevelt Advocated Woman Suffrage. Has the Republican Party Forgotten the Principles of Theodore Roosevelt?"

Inez Haynes Irwin, *Up Hill with Banners Flying*, Penobscot, Me., 1964, pp. 459–60.

June 11 In response to the artist Sheeler's request to photograph the work, Louisine informs Director Robinson of the Metropolitan Museum that she objects "to anyone's having a photograph of El Greco's *Toledo*."

Weitzenhoffer 1986, p. 245.

June 20 Durand-Ruel, New York, acting on instructions from the Paris gallery, is to deliver Cassatt's painting "Femme et enfant vu de dos" (fig. 105) to Louisine. No doubt this is the painting that Cassatt had sent to New York for the 1915 suffrage exhibition at Knoedler's and that Durand-Ruel, New York, had kept on deposit until now. From March through May of this year Cassatt had fretted that her "only remaining picture" was on deposit with Durand Ruel, since "if I sell it when in [their] hands . . . they will want the largest part of the price!" Doubting that she could obtain the $3,000 she wanted for the picture from the dealer, in April she contemplated sending it to her nephew Gardner or giving "it to [Louisine] until I can dispose of it." In October Louisine offers to sell the picture, now in her care, for Cassatt, but the artist replies, "I dont want it sold, only for you to have it." Louisine does not keep the painting; eventually it would go to Cassatt's family.

D-R to LWH, 6/20/20, correspondence, Weitzenhoffer files; MC to LWH, 3/22/20, 4/9/20, 4/10/[20], including quote; 4/18/20, including quote, 4/28/20, 5/18/20, 11/9/[20], in reply to Louisine's letter of 10/24/20 and including quote, Havemeyer correspondence. The picture was no. 43, lent by Cassatt, in the suffrage exhibition.

Figure 105. Mary Cassatt. *Mother in Large Hat Holding Her Nude Baby Seen in Back View*. Oil on canvas, 32 x 26 in. (81 x 66.2 cm). Location unknown

July 21 Louisine and fellow suffragists meet with members of the Republican National Committee and secure their party's endorsement of the ratification of the suffrage amendment by the Tennessee legislature. The following day Senator Warren Harding is notified that he has been nominated for the presidency and two hundred members of the National Woman's Party march through Marion, Ohio, to the lawn of his home. Louisine is among those who appeal to the candidate for his support of a solid Republican vote in Tennessee. On August 26, when the Tennessee legislature provides the final ratification necessary, the Nineteenth Amendment becomes part of the United States Constitution.

Inez Haynes Irwin, *Up Hill with Banners Flying*, Penobscot, Me., 1964, pp. 465–66. A photograph of Louisine and Harding captioned "Senator Harding listened attentively while Mrs. Havemeyer made her appeal for a solid Republican vote in Tennessee" appears in Havemeyer 1922b, p. 671.

October 2 Rosenberg offers Louisine Courbet's *Still Life —Fruit* (A154, pl. 258), a painting she had lost to him at auction in December 1912. By November 2 Louisine decides to purchase the picture for Fr 205,000; it is delivered to her on February 1 and paid for during the same month.

Paul Rosenberg to LWH, 10/2/20, 11/2/20, 11/26/20, 12/9/20; Wildenstein and Co. to LWH, 2/1/21; Paul Rosenberg to LWH, 2/13/21, acknowledging payment, correspondence, Weitzenhoffer files.

Plate 274. Edgar Degas. *Dancer at the Bar*, ca. 1889. Pastel on paper, 26¼ x 18½ in. (66.7 x 47 cm). Shelburne Museum, Shelburne, Vermont (27.3.1–34) A244

1921

January 28 From Durand-Ruel, New York, Louisine purchases Degas's painting *A Woman Seated Beside a Vase of Flowers (Mme Paul Valpinçon?)* (A196, pl. 39) for $30,000 and pastel *Dancer at the Bar* (A244, pl. 274) for

$10,000. The painting was one of two works by Degas from the Boivin collection that were first offered to her in June 1920; the other, "a pastel *nude*" (Lemoisne 1946, no. 883), was not acquired.

GD-R to LWH, 6/11/20, correspondence, Weitzenhoffer files.

January 28–February 26 Louisine lends eleven prints to the *Exhibition of Etchings by Mary Cassatt* at the Grolier Club, New York; the show travels to The Art Institute of Chicago.

February 12 On Ladies Day at the Grolier Club, New York, Louisine gives a talk, "Recollections of Miss Cassatt and Her Work," before 307 people, the largest audience ever to have attended an event at the club.

Weitzenhoffer 1986, p. 240.

February 16 In Washington, D.C., Louisine presents to Charles D. Walcott of the Smithsonian Institution "as a permanent suffrage memorial exhibit from the National Woman's party the 'Ship of State,' the suffrage torch, the pen used in signing the ratification of the suffrage amendment by the governor of Pennsylvania." The next day an interview with Louisine appears in the *Washington Herald*, in which she asserts that "there is no position in the United States today which a woman could not fill," including "the nation's Chief Executive." Though "the time is not ripe yet," she believes that "there is no question but that we shall soon have women in Congress, in both the Senate and the House. It will take time."

F.W.G., "Women to Use Vote to Gain Equality," *Washington Herald*, February 17, 1921, p. 4, col. 3.

May 3–September 15 Louisine anonymously lends Courbet's *Mme de Brayer* (A129, pl. 244) and Degas's *Woman Bathing in a Shallow Tub* (A239, pl. 271) to the Metropolitan Museum's *Loan Exhibition of Impressionist and Post-Impressionist Paintings*.

Shown as nos. 25 and 32.

May 17–September 15 To an exhibition of modern French prints at the Metropolitan Museum Louisine anonymously lends ten lithographs—five by Gericault, four by Gavarni, and Manet's "Polichinelle"—as well as four watercolor drawings by Guys (A306, 315, 317, 318).

Loans per MMA Department of Prints Archives.

Probably August 24 Louisine arrives in France aboard the *Paris*.

GD-R to MC, 8/25/21, indicating that he has seen "dans les journaux ce matin que Mme Havemeyer est arrivée en France sur le Paris," correspondence, Weitzenhoffer files.

Late August Shortly after she arrives in Paris, Louisine purchases a set (series A) of bronzes by Degas (MMA 29.100.371–438, see pl. 79) cast posthumously at the foundry of Adrien A. Hébrard and exhibited at his gallery from May to June 1921. The following year she buys a posthumous bronze cast of Degas's *Little Fourteen-Year-Old Dancer* (MMA 29.100.370, pl. 78).

For further information about the bronzes, see Clare Vincent, "The Havemeyers and the Degas Bronzes," this catalogue.

Late summer–early fall Louisine remains in France, dividing her time between Paris and Cassatt's country house in Mesnil-Théribus.

Weitzenhoffer 1986, p. 241.

Early fall From Duret in Paris Louisine buys four Courbet paintings, including *Portrait of a Woman, called Héloïse Abélard* (A166, now considered Style of Courbet); through Duret she also acquires Guys's *Lady with a Veil* (A307) and *Portrait of a Lady* (A310), watercolors that had been included in the sale *Dessins, Pastels, Aquarelles Modernes . . . Composant la Collection de M.A. Beurdeley*, June 3, 1920, Galerie Georges Petit, Paris.

Weitzenhoffer 1986, p. 241; MMA Department of European Paintings Archives; Guys, lot nos. 189, 199.

1922

January 7 Electra and J. Watson Webb's fifth child, Harry Havemeyer, is born in New York.

Havemeyer 1944, p. 71.

January 21 The Grolier Club, New York, holds its press preview of *Prints, Drawings and Bronzes by Degas*, to which Louisine anonymously lends her set of bronzes as well as seventeen drawings and pastels, two fan mounts, and four prints. The show, originally scheduled to run from January 26 to February 28, is extended through the week of March 18, owing to its popularity. Through the exhibition Louisine comes to know William M. Ivins, Jr., the Metropolitan Museum's Curator of Prints.

See Weitzenhoffer 1986, p. 242.

February 5 Louisine's friend and dealer Paul Durand-Ruel dies.

April Louisine intends to go to New Orleans to "free the vote from all the impediments . . . imposed on it."

LWH to TD, 1/10/22, cited in Weitzenhoffer 1986, p. 242.

May 8 Pursuant to a decree of April 18, France decorates Louisine with the Cross of the Knight of the Legion of Honor.

Original documents preserved in Weitzenhoffer files.

May Louisine's "Suffrage Torch: Memories of a Militant" is published in *Scribner's Magazine*.

Vol. 71 (May 1922), pp. 528–39.

June "The Prison Special: Memories of a Militant" by Louisine is published in *Scribner's Magazine*.

Vol. 71 (June 1922), pp. 661–76.

June 26 Louisine writes a second codicil to her will, enlarging her intended bequest to the Metropolitan Museum by twenty-nine pictures, of which six are old masters and twenty-three are nineteenth-century French works, including eight Monets and Renoir's *By the Seashore* (A460, pl. 6), a painting Barnes had tried to purchase from her this year for $10,000.

For the codicil, see Weitzenhoffer 1986, pp. 256–57; for Barnes's offer, see Aline B. Saarinen, *The Proud Possessors*, New York, 1958, p. 221; for the pictures named, see works marked with ** in Appendix.

August 1 Duret acknowledges payment from Louisine for her latest Guys acquired through Galerie Druet, Paris, and advises her that the same source has a "very important" work by the artist, "deux Grisettes, in color." She subsequently acquires Guys's *Two Grisettes* (A314, pl. 275)—

Plate 275. Constantin Guys. *Two Grisettes*. Pen and brown ink, watercolor, and gouache, over traces of graphite on wove paper, 9 3/16 x 7 1/4 in. (23.3 x 18.4 cm). H. O. Havemeyer Collection, Bequest of Mrs. H. O. Havemeyer, 1929 (29.100.601) A314

exactly the kind of work she had wanted—directly from Galerie Druet.

TD to LWH, 8/1/22, Havemeyer correspondence.

August 18 In the third codicil to her will, Louisine empowers Horace to give the Metropolitan Museum "all such other pictures, paintings, engravings, statuary and works of art" not previously specified, as he might "appoint to it." Hence the bequest, to be known as the H. O. Havemeyer Collection, would involve Louisine's children's participation and reflects her faith in their largess.

See Weitzenhoffer 1986, p. 257.

During the year Louisine purchases several paintings, which she would later describe as the "Flotsam and Jetsam of War results," through M. J. Rougeron, a New York art dealer and restorer. These pictures—all secured by Rougeron from the daughter of the late "Mr. Harrington of Boston" —include Titian's *Saint Cecilia* (A489, now considered Style of Titian) and *Doge Girolamo Priuli* (A488, now considered Workshop of Tintoretto), Rembrandt's *Portrait of Rembrandt in a Cap and a Polish Jacket* (A455, now considered Copy after Rembrandt), Moro's *Portrait of a Man of the Elrington Family* (A322, now considered Lucas de Heere), and Goya's *Portrait of an Officer on Horseback* (A298, now Attributed to Goya) and *Portrait of Ferdinand VII* (A463, now Attributed to Ribelles). Rougeron had originally been contacted by the Harrington heirs to restore a "large altarpiece"; Louisine also buys through him this "injured work," namely Francia's *Madonna and Child with Saints John the Baptist, Stephen, and Lawrence* (A7, now considered Follower of Albertinelli, pl. 276).

Havemeyer "Notes" [1974], pp. 12–14, 33–34. M. J. Rougeron is listed in the 1922 *American Art Annual* index of art dealers as located at 94 Park Avenue, New York, with a studio for the restoration of paintings that was founded in 1840 and established in New York in 1907.

1923

January 16 From Durand-Ruel, New York, Louisine purchases Degas's *Mlle Marie Dihau* (A198, pl. 277).

Plate 277. Edgar Degas. *Mlle Marie Dihau (1843–1935)*, 1867–68. Oil on canvas, 8¾ x 10¾ in. (22.2 x 27.3 cm). H. O. Havemeyer Collection, Bequest of Mrs. H. O. Havemeyer, 1929 (29.100.182) A198

February 15 Louisine anonymously lends twelve Degas bronzes from her collection (MMA 29.100.370–438) to the Metropolitan Museum for an extended period; they are returned to her on January 10, 1925.

MMA Registrar's loan cards; *Bulletin of The Metropolitan Museum of Art* 18 (March 1923), pp. 59, 79.

February Louisine is guest speaker at breakfast, lunch, tea, and dinner receptions in her honor at the headquarters of the National Woman's Party in Chicago.

Weitzenhoffer 1986, p. 246.

May 28 The Metropolitan Museum's Board of Trustees accepts Tiepolo's *Glorification of Francesco Barbaro* (A487, pl. 278), a ceiling decoration painted for the Palazzo Barbaro, Venice, as an anonymous gift from Louisine in memory of Oliver H. Payne, who had died in 1917.

MMA Archives, which indicate that the work was presented to Curator of Paintings Burroughs on April 30 and that he recommended that the Museum accept it on May 2. After her death Louisine was revealed as the donor of this gift in the *Bulletin of The Metropolitan Museum of Art* 24 (February 1929), p. 38.

May Louisine publishes a tribute to her late friend Charles Freer—"an intrepid discoverer, a sagacious collector, and a munificent donor"—"The Freer Museum of Oriental Art, with Personal Recollections of the Donor" in *Scribner's Magazine*.

Vol. 73 (May 1923), pp. 529–40.

Plate 276. Follower of Mariotto Albertinelli. *Madonna and Child with Saints John the Baptist, Stephen, and Lawrence.* Oil on wood, 79 x 58 in. (200.7 x 147.3 cm). Location unknown. A7

Plate 278. Giovanni Battista Tiepolo. *The Glorification of Francesco Barbaro*, ca. 1745–50. Oil on canvas, 96 x 183¾ in. (243.8 x 466.7 cm). Anonymous Gift, in memory of Oliver H. Payne, 1923 (23.128) A487

1924

March 1 Joseph Durand-Ruel is informed by Cassatt that she "has broken off completely" with Louisine; this follows a bitter dispute that had begun with the discovery by Cassatt's maid in October 1923 of twenty-five of the artist's old copper drypoint plates. Cassatt, whose failing eyesight led her to believe assurances by the maid and by her printer, Delâtre, that the plates had never been used, had the printer pull proofs from them. In an attempt to preserve Cassatt's reputation, Louisine, who had been told by Metropolitan Curator Ivins that the proofs were pulled from worn out plates, advises the artist not to present the prints as new. Cassatt is indignant, outraged, and eventually vindictive, and a long, close friendship ends.

Weitzenhoffer 1986, pp. 246–47.

March 17–April 20 Louisine anonymously lends her still life entitled *Fruit* (A509, pl. 249) to the Metropolitan Museum's *Memorial Exhibition of the Works of Julian Alden Weir.*

Shown as no. 18.

April 1 George Durand-Ruel informs Louisine that his brother Joseph is able to obtain a plaster *Ratapoil* by Daumier and asks if she is interested in it.

GD-R to LWH, 4/1/24, correspondence, Weitzenhoffer files.

Before June 1 Duret takes advantage of Louisine's trust when he sells her a *Portrait of a Woman in Black* (A167, now considered Style of Courbet) as a genuine Courbet, without furnishing information on the sitter or the work's provenance. "He would never write me who she was— I repeatedly asked him," she later records.

Weitzenhoffer 1986, p. 247; quote from Havemeyer "Notes" [1974], p. 16.

December 15 Louisine is elected a Benefactor of the Metropolitan Museum at the meeting of the Museum's Board of Trustees; she is advised of this by letter on December 17.

MMA Archives.

During the year Through Rougeron, Louisine purchases a "war picture by Goya" (A342, *Scene from the War of Independence*, now considered Lucas y Padilla), and at about this time she buys from the same dealer a van Dyck (A482, *Saint Francis in Ecstasy*, now considered unknown 16th-century Spanish painter). Rougeron had secured both works from the widow of an ambassador to Spain. Also to this year or to 1923 dates Louisine's purchase of a supposed Velázquez (A497, *Philip IV [1605–1665], King of Spain*, now considered Copy after Velázquez, pl. 279)

Plate 279. Copy after Diego Velázquez. *Philip IV (1605–1665), King of Spain*. Oil on canvas, 21 x 17 in. (53.3 x 43.2 cm). Location unknown. A497

from the Muñoz family in Valencia. The painting had first been offered to her as Velázquez's "Portrait of the Cardinal Infante Don Fernando of Austria" in July 1918 by Angele L. de Calle.

Havemeyer "Notes" [1974], pp. 12–13, 24, 34; Angele L. de Calle to LWH, 7/10/18, Havemeyer correspondence.

1925

January 28 Joseph Durand-Ruel advises Louisine that the New York gallery has taken back Harris Whittemore's Degas pastel *La Femme au tub* (Lemoisne 1946, no. 1097) and offers it to her for $5,600. It is sold to another collector on March 13.

JD-R to LWH, 1/28/25, correspondence, Weitzenhoffer files; date of purchase per Durand-Ruel stock books, which indicate that the buyer was Nicola.

February Louisine anonymously lends to the Metropolitan eleven Degas bronzes from her collection (MMA 29.100.370–438) and a pair of bronzes by Girardon, *The Tiber* and *The Nile* (MMA 29.100.148,149, now considered late 17th-century French). The Degases remain on view for nearly three years; the "Girardons" are at the Museum for almost two years.

MMA Registrar's loan cards indicate that the Degas bronzes were received on January 22, 1925, and returned to Louisine on December 8, 1927, and that the "Girardons" were returned in January 1927. The loans are noted in the *Bulletin of The Metropolitan Museum of Art* 20 (February 1925), pp. 58, 61. The "Girardons" are listed among acquisitions made between 1922 and 1925 in Havemeyer "Notes" [1974], p. 34.

July 28 Louisine celebrates her seventieth birthday with her family at Hilltop in Connecticut.

Weitzenhoffer 1986, p. 247.

August Louisine is "ill with fever," having suffered a "relapse" brought on by nervous exhaustion. As she is infirm through the fall, Marthe Giannoni, the French governess for the Webb children, moves into 1 East 66th Street to care for her. By December Louisine seems to have "completely regained her health . . . she is simply very tired."

MC to D-R, n.d. [8/25], n.d. [8/25], both including quotes; JD-R to MC, 12/17/25, including quote, correspondence, Weitzenhoffer files. Weitzenhoffer suggested that Louisine may have fallen (1986, p. 248), an assumption presumably based on MC to D-R, n.d. [8/25], n.d. [ca. 12/25], indicating that she had a "nouveau tombé" [*sic*] and a "rechute," correspondence, Weitzenhoffer files.

During the year Louisine begins cataloguing her immense art collection; she tags the works with collector labels that she has annotated with identifications, earmarking pieces

destined for the Metropolitan with the letter Z. She writes "Notes to Her Children," with detailed instructions as to her wishes, in terms of both her bequest to the Museum and her legacies to individual family members.

1926

June 14 Cassatt dies at Mesnil-Théribus.

October 11–January 1, 1927 Louisine and Horace are among the lenders to a *Special Persian Exhibition*, devoted to Persian art from the ninth to the eighteenth century organized by Arthur Upham Pope, at the Pennsylvania Museum of Art in Philadelphia. Loans from the Havemeyer collection include three pieces of pottery (pl. 108, MMA 29.160.10,12) and a rug (MMA 41.165.47).

Pennsylvania Museum Bulletin 22 (October 1926), p. 234; (November 1926), p. 245; (December 1926), p. 276. The private viewing was held on October 11; the exhibition was to close at Thanksgiving but was extended to January 1, 1927.

During the year Daijiro Ushikubo, the manager of Yamanaka's New York office, publishes *Life of Koyetsu* and dedicates it to Louisine and Freer, his two best clients. It was Ushikubo who long ago had sold the Havemeyers their first tea jars.

For tea jars, see Havemeyer 1961, p. 70.

1927

April 30–May 30 Louisine lends several pictures (A49–52, 58, 61, and possibly A62) to the *Memorial Exhibition of the Work of Mary Cassatt* at the Pennsylvania Museum of Art, Philadelphia.

May Louisine contributes to the *Pennsylvania Museum Bulletin* "an interpretation of the work of Mary Cassatt" excerpted from the talk she gave at the opening of the 1915 suffrage exhibition, as well as "a more personal word," recently written at the museum's request, in which she endeavored "to crowd in a few lines the recollections of a friendship that has lasted a lifetime."

Vol. 22 (May 1927), pp. 373, 377–82.

July 4 Louisine presents Manet's portrait *Georges Clemenceau* (A363, pl. 206) to the Musée du Louvre, Paris.

November 30 Because of her poor health, Louisine—who had suffered a mild stroke this year—is unable to attend the ceremony dedicating the town hall of Shelburne, Vermont, which Electra has donated to the community in Harry's memory.

Weitzenhoffer 1986, p. 250.

1928

Early in the year The German art historian and critic Julius Meier-Graefe visits Louisine and views her collection.

Weitzenhoffer 1986, p. 251.

February 7 Several dealers, including Carroll Carstairs and Etienne Bignou, and the collector Robert Sterling Clark, who is accompanied by George Davey of Knoedler's, visit Louisine's house. Clark admires portraits by Rembrandt and Hals and the "fine Pieter de Hoogh," as well as the Spanish pictures—from the "fine Goya portraits & the marvellous 'Balcony'" to the "superb Greco of the Cardinal & the Toledo." Among the modern school, he notes "several fine Courbets, a fine Manet still life, 2 good Cezannes . . . [and] several fine Corot figures." He dismisses a "Rubens portrait [of] doubtful authenticity, several rotten Veronese . . . [and] a vile Titian." He meets Mrs. Havemeyer, a "wonderful old lady, full [of] life & no frills, bright as a button, small, sharp featured, full of talk." On May 9 Clark, together with his wife, Francine, again visits 1 East 66th Street, where he sees Mrs. Havemeyer and finds that "the Degas, the Manets, the Courbets, the Grecos, the Goyas, Corot figure pieces are probably finer & more representative than in any other collection." In April 1943 Clark would purchase for $12,000 one of Louisine's Manets, *Manet's Family at Home in Arcachon* (A352, pl. 27), which Electra had inherited and consigned to Knoedler's.

Quotes from Clark's unpublished diaries, entries of 2/7/28, pp. 1–5, and 5/9/28, pp. 1–8; intent to buy the Manet noted under 4/7/43, 4/10/43, purchase recorded under 4/12/43. Information courtesy of David Brooke, Director, Sterling and Francine Clark Art Institute, Williamstown, Massachusetts.

February 9 George Durand-Ruel informs Louisine that the New York gallery has on deposit from her Real del Sarte's "La révérence" (A444), Stalk's "Fan shape" (A483), and Decamps's "Little Traveller (landscape)" (A184). The first two, he maintains, "have no market value." The Decamps is returned to her the following day, but the others are not retrieved by Louisine. In February 1932 the gallery would write to Horace about the works by Real del Sarte and Stalk "that your mother consigned to us in 1907; she told us many times to destroy them, as they have absolutely no value and are rather cumbersome and ugly. Kindly let us know what we are to do with these pictures, as we are very anxious to dispose of them."

GD-R to LWH, 2/9/28; D-R to HH, 2/19/32, correspondence, Weitzenhoffer files.

February 17–April 15 Louisine anonymously lends her Pantoja de la Cruz *Portrait of a Young Woman* (A424, now Attributed to Pantoja de la Cruz) to *Spanish Paintings from El Greco to Goya* at the Metropolitan Museum. The show, originally scheduled to close on April 1, "proved so popular" that it was extended for two weeks; its attendance, in fact, "exceeded that of any previous exhibition—94,742 in the fifty-nine days it was on view."

Shown as no. 49; of the sixty-seven works listed in the catalogue, this was the only anonymous loan; quote from the *Bulletin of The Metropolitan Museum of Art* 23 (April 1928), p. 100.

February 28 George Durand-Ruel informs Louisine that he has "just received a cable from Paris saying it is impossible to certify that the Guys is the same one which [she] saw formerly in Mr. Duret's house" but "the picture is genuine and their estimate is eight thousand francs."

GD-R to LWH, 2/28/28, correspondence, Weitzenhoffer files.

March 5 Pursuant to a decree of March 1, the government of France promotes Louisine to the rank of Officer of the Legion of Honor.

Original documents preserved in Weitzenhoffer files.

March 20–April 14 Louisine lends at least six works to the *Loan Exhibition of French Masterpieces of the Late XIX Century* at Durand-Ruel, New York. The show is extended four days beyond its scheduled closing.

Extension per GD-R to LWH, 4/3/28, correspondence, Weitzenhoffer files.

After May 21 Louisine departs for Paris, accompanied by her nurse, Giannoni. She visits Cassatt's burial place, the family vault at Mesnil-Théribus, and leaves rambler roses on her tomb.

Weitzenhoffer 1986, p. 251.

Mid-November Louisine is confined to bed with advanced arteriosclerosis; her condition worsens progressively after Thanksgiving.

Date per copy of death certificate, indicating that she had been attended by her doctor from November 15, preserved in Weitzenhoffer files; failing health per obituary, *New York Times*, January 7, 1929, p. 29.

1929

January 2–5 Louisine develops bronchopneumonia.

Weitzenhoffer 1986, p. 251.

January 6 Louisine, age seventy-three, dies at 4:15 P.M. in the company of her three children. The cause of death is arteriosclerosis, from which she had suffered for three years, complicated by bronchopneumonia.

Copy of death certificate, preserved in Weitzenhoffer files.

January 9 Funeral services for Louisine are held at Saint Bartholomew's Church, Park Avenue and 51st Street, at 10:30 A.M.; she is buried next to Harry in the Havemeyer family vault in Greenwood Cemetery, Brooklyn.

Weitzenhoffer 1986, p. 251.

January 29 The Metropolitan Museum's Board of Trustees unanimously votes to accept the "munificent bequest of Mrs. H. O. Havemeyer" under the terms of her will. "The only stipulations made in the will were that all objects received under it should 'be known as the H. O. Havemeyer Collection,' and that they should be on 'permanent exhibition.' It was her intention, however, and in this the family entirely concurred, that the collection should not be kept segregated, but that the objects should be distributed among the departments to which they properly belong, and there displayed in the galleries devoted to work of a similar kind." Approved on this date are the 142 works specifically listed in the first two codicils of Louisine's will. The third codicil, leaving further gifts to the discretion of her son, is subsequently implemented by Horace and his sisters in consultation with Metropolitan curators; the three children ensure that all works earmarked for the Museum's collection or of interest to the institution, including pieces from their own inheritances, are donated. According to Robinson, the bequest ultimately totals 1,967 objects.

Bulletin of The Metropolitan Museum of Art 24 (February 1929), p. 38; (March 1930), p. 54; Edward Robinson, "Introduction: The H. O. Havemeyer Collection," in Havemeyer 1930, p. x. Weitzenhoffer gave a figure of 1,972 objects (1986, p. 252). Some of the 142 works originally bequeathed to the Museum would be withdrawn (see below). The first codicil included MMA 29.100.1–101, 180; the second codicil, MMA 29.100.102–128. The order in which the works are listed in the codicils would determine their present accession numbers. They are consecutive with two exceptions: one Degas is out of sequence, and a Goya, MMA 29.100.180, was held out for cleaning and hence assigned a higher number.

April 15 The members of the Metropolitan Museum's Board of Trustees meet and resolve to express "their sincere appreciation" to Horace and his sisters; to appoint a special committee, consisting of the President and three other trustees appointed by him, to handle questions that "may arise in connection with the selection and installation of the objects" in the Havemeyer bequest; and to plan, if the family approves, an exhibition of "these distinguished collections."

V. Everit Macy, Chairman of the Board, to Edward Robinson, Director, 5/10/29, transcribing contents of a letter to HH of the same date, MMA Archives.

April 16 Curator of Paintings Burroughs draws up a list of five paintings that the Metropolitan wants to withdraw from the Havemeyer bequest and compiles a prioritized list of eleven possible substitutions for Director Robinson. On April 25 Curator of Decorative Arts Breck advises Horace that two pieces of sculpture and a majolica plate promised to the Museum are unsuitable for permanent exhibition. Horace, aware that the Museum does "not feel that these works of art are of the high standard set by the rest of the Havemeyer bequest," requests a formal statement from the trustees on May 1 so that "I can deed to the Museum under the power granted me by the third codicil of my Mother's will five other pictures on the list which Mr. Burroughs sent to me some time ago and perhaps some other works which will be more than the artistic equivalent of those which are not accepted." He also asks that the trustees confirm "that they do not care to accept for permanent exhibition . . . the marble bas-relief, the statue and the Italian plate about which Mr. Breck has written to me."

Bryson Burroughs to Edward Robinson, 4/16/29; Joseph Breck to HH, 4/25/29; HH to Edward Robinson, 5/1/29, MMA Archives.

May 8 The Special Committee on the Havemeyer Bequest —consisting of the President of the Museum, Robert W. de Forest, and three trustees, Chairman V. Everit Macy, Howard Mansfield, and William Sloan Coffin—view "some of the paintings and other objects" included in the bequest and "favor the withdrawal" of five pictures and three objects listed in the first two codicils of Louisine's will. These eight works are officially declined by the Museum on May 20. Of the rejected works, Electra keeps Goya's *Condesa de Chinchón* (A295, now Attributed to Goya) and two sculptures, a "Foolish Virgin" and a "Madonna and Child," wrongly attributed to Desiderio da Settignano, and Adaline retains Corot's *Mother, Nurse and Child* (A115). The remaining four, two Veronese portraits (A278, now Attributed to Fasolo, and A504, now Style of Veronese), del Sarto's *Madonna and Child with Saint John* (A474, now Attributed to del Sarto), and a majolica dish, would be sold at auction in April 1930.

V. Everit Macy to HH, 5/10/29; minutes of the May 20 Board of Trustees meeting, MMA Archives.

May 15 Robinson meets with Horace, from whom he secures a "definite offer" of five substitute paintings for the pictures declined by the Museum. The works offered are the first five on the list of pictures "arranged according to their desirability" that Burroughs had prepared: Daumier's *Third-Class Carriage* (A177), Courbet's *Mme Auguste Cuoq* (A133), Delacroix's *Christ Asleep During the Tempest* (A261), Courbet's *Alphonse Promayet* (A124), and

Goya's *Portrait of a Man, Said to Be the Painter Vicente Lopez* (A301, now considered Style of Goya). On May 20 the Board of Trustees accepts these as substitutes for the works withdrawn.

Edward Robinson to V. Everit Macy, 5/15/29, regarding his meeting with Horace Havemeyer; HH to V. Everit Macy, 5/20/29, agreeing "to deed to the Museum . . . five pictures from the list," MMA Archives. The paintings following the five selected from Burroughs's list are, in order of choice: Corot's *Reverie* (A102), *Girl Weaving a Garland* as "Lady with Violets (unfinished)" (A105), and *The Muse: History* (A104) and three old master portraits, one by Carreño (A48), the others presumed at the time to be by Moro (A322, now considered Lucas de Heere) and Pourbus (A275, now considered 16th-century Dutch or Flemish). The first three were subsequently added to the bequest, the last three, auctioned at the 1930 Havemeyer sale. The paintings approved on May 15 are MMA 29.100.129–32,179; the latter was held out for cleaning, hence its high number.

June 10 The Board of Trustees accepts forty-three additional objects presented by Horace under the third codicil of his mother's will and approves the withdrawal of five objects bequeathed in the first codicil. The works added are a dozen Hispano-Moresque plates (MMA 29.100.133–44), three French sculptures (MMA 29.100.145,148,149), a Venetian glass tazza (MMA 29.100.146), a fifteenth-century blue velvet cope (MMA 29.100.147), two Egyptian sculptures (MMA 29.100.150,151), six Chinese silk wall hangings (MMA 29.100.152–57), a Chinese rug (MMA 29.100.158), and seventeen Han dynasty ceramics (MMA 29.100.159–75); those withdrawn are a stucco "Madonna and Child" wrongly attributed to Donatello, a "Greco-Roman" marble head of a dying man, and three pieces of "Cyprian glass." Three limestone Gothic columns and bases (MMA 29.100.176–78) are also accepted on this date.

The identification of additions to the bequest approved by the Board of Trustees on this date and on December 16, 1929, and January 20, 1930, is based on descriptions of the works in documents preserved in the MMA Archives; these identifications have been confirmed by or deduced from the sequence of accession numbers assigned to works added at a given date. The documents include minutes of the meetings of the Special Committee and of the trustees, offer of gift forms, memoranda, and lists of works submitted by curators to the director or reported to the trustees. The Gothic columns and bases are recorded, but apparently were not counted among the forty-three objects added to the bequest on June 10; possibly they came into the Museum as pedestals for sculpture.

October 21 The Metropolitan Museum's Board of Trustees elects Horace an Honorary Fellow for Life.

Bulletin of The Metropolitan Museum of Art 24 (November 1929), p. 304.

October 28 Horace's secretary telephones Burroughs and asks him "to stop at the late Mrs. H. O. Havemeyer's house to examine a group of drawings and paintings from the Havemeyer collection and to report [to Horace his] opinion as to their desirability as Museum acquisitions." Bur-

roughs replies "that they [are] all exceedingly desirable." Hence, on October 31 Horace decides to add twenty-two pictures to the bequest: eleven Degas paintings and pastels (A198, 199, 203, 207, 212 [owned by Horace], 213, 229, 231, 240, 253, 260), two Ingres drawings (A281, now considered unknown French artist, A329), two Daumier watercolors (A178, 179), one Renoir pastel (A462), and one painting each by Cézanne (A79), Corot (A104), Courbet (A143), Corneille de Lyon (A96), Decamps (A183), and van Ostade (A423). These are accepted by the Special Committee on the Havemeyer Bequest on December 3 and approved by the Board of Trustees on December 16.

Bryson Burroughs to Edward Robinson, 11/4/29, including quote and enclosing a list dated 11/1/29 of the pictures offered by Horace, MMA Archives. The list's order would determine the accession numbers assigned to the works, MMA 29.100.181–201. These are consecutive, except that the fifth item, Horace's Degas, like all his gifts to the Museum, was given a number beginning with the digits 29.160, in this case 29.160.26.

November 18 Horace is elected Benefactor of the Metropolitan Museum by the Board of Trustees in recognition of his gift of Degas's *Rehearsal of the Ballet Onstage* (A212). Horace believes that this painting will make "a desirable addition to the H. O. Havemeyer collection," since his mother had already bequeathed to the Museum a work "of the same subject executed in pastel" (A211).

Minutes of the Board of Trustees meeting of November 18, 1929, MMA Archives. Quote from Bryson Burroughs to Edward Robinson, 11/4/29, MMA Archives.

November 30 Harry Waldron, Horace and Doris Havemeyer's fourth child, is born at 853 Fifth Avenue, New York.

Havemeyer 1944, p. 74.

November Metropolitan curators propose works to be added to the H. O. Havemeyer Collection at the Museum. On December 13 the Special Committee on the Havemeyer Bequest accepts these recommendations and on December 16 the Board of Trustees confirms them. Additions to the bequest are single items of special interest—a Degas print, *Head of a Woman in Profile* (MMA 29.107.52), recommended by Ivins, and a Greek bronze helmet (MMA 29.100.488), recommended by Gisela Richter—as well as more sizable numbers of works suggested by other curators: 364 Japanese swords and sword furnishings dating from the seventeenth to the nineteenth century (included among MMA 29.100.946–1396) for the department of arms and armor; 69 Degas bronzes (MMA 29.100.370–438) for the department of decorative arts; 49 Chinese and Japanese paintings and Japanese lacquered leather panels (MMA 29.100.439–87), and 168 pieces of Far Eastern pottery and porcelain (MMA 29.100.202–369), largely Chinese with a small number of Japanese and Korean examples, for the department of Asian art. Also accepted on this date are Horace's gifts of Near Eastern pottery and miniatures (MMA 29.160.1–25) and the 22 pictures he had offered to the Museum in late October. One of the 6 Hispano-Moresque plates accepted under the terms of the first codicil (MMA 29.100.98) is officially withdrawn by the board pursuant to curatorial and Special Committee recommendations of December 3 and 13, respectively. The board approves Horace's agreement to exempt certain objects from the terms of Louisine's will with regard to permanent exhibition.

Documents including HH to Edward Robinson, 12/11/29, granting exemption to the permanent exhibition clause in his mother's will, MMA Archives.

1930

January 7 Curators' recommendations for further additions to the Havemeyer collection are accepted by the Special Committee on the Havemeyer Bequest. On January 20 the Board of Trustees approves the following additions for the Western collections: 17 paintings and pastels, including works by Degas (A202, 223–25, 243, 254, 258), Corot (A98, 102, 105, 107, 114), Courbet (A151), Manet (A361), Millet (A383), and old masters then attributed to Patinir (A279) and Jusepe Leonardo (A481); 61 watercolors and drawings, including examples by Abbey (A1–6), Barye (A12–25, 28, 30–35, 37, 39–41), Guys (A306–18), Degas (A206, 208, 221), Rembrandt (A335, now considered Jordaens III, and A447, 448, 450–54), Cuyp (A173), Dupré (A269), Gavarni (A283), Millet (A381), van de Velde (A498), and a false Beardsley (A43); 211 European and American prints, including 34 Rembrandt etchings (MMA 29.107.1–51,53–184); and a piece of Russian gold brocade (MMA 29.100.489). In the area of Far Eastern art the following additions are approved: 328 Japanese prints (MMA JP 1584–1860, 1862–99), 11 Japanese illustrated books (MMA 29.100.1398–1402, MMA JP 1900–2391, and MMA Japanese illustrated books 77, 78), 55 Japanese screens, Chinese and Japanese paintings and textiles (MMA 29.100.490–544, 945), 7 Chinese bronzes (MMA 29.100.545–51), 63 Japanese ceramics (MMA 29.100.608–70), 53 Japanese and 2 Chinese lacquers, including 43 Japanese boxes, 2 of which were accessioned as Chinese (MMA 29.100.671–725), and 197 Japanese *inro* and netsuke (MMA 29.100.726–921). For the department of arms and armor the following Japanese arms are approved: 42 sword guards, 2 sets of *fuchigashira*, 22 sword fittings, and 17 *kozuka* (included among MMA 29.100.946–1396). The board also approves Horace's gift of 6 Japanese and Chinese paintings (MMA 29.160.27–32), Courbet's *Marine: The Waterspout* (A152) and *The Deer* (A144), Decamps's *Good Samaritan* (A185), and Corot's *Letter* (A108), as well as Adaline's gift of Corot's *Mother and Child* (A103) and Electra's gift of Puvis de Chavannes's *Tamaris* (A437).

Figure 106. Installation view, *The H. O. Havemeyer Collection*, The Metropolitan Museum of Art, 1930

MMA Archives. The pictures identified by Appendix numbers above are MMA 29.100.552–607, 923–44, 29.160.33–36, 30.13, 30.20. The number of American and European prints added to the collection on this date is accurate, since MMA 29.107.79 is a bound volume of 29 lithographs, each of which was counted, and MMA 29.107.185 was later transferred to the collection from the paintings department. Individual Japanese prints as well as diptychs and triptychs were assigned single accession numbers. The number of Japanese prints does not include the Spring Rain collection volumes containing 492 *surimono*, which were accessioned among the Japanese illustrated books. Additional prints, including *surimono*, were donated to the collection by Electra in 1930 and designated MMA JP 2392–2402.

February 17 Horace is elected Trustee of The Metropolitan Museum of Art.

Bulletin of The Metropolitan Museum of Art 25 (March 1930), p. 78.

March 10–November 2 The entire Havemeyer Bequest is presented at the Metropolitan Museum in the exhibition *The H. O. Havemeyer Collection*. The scope, size, and "remarkable character" of the collection dictated that "six galleries, emptied of their regular contents for the time being, were set aside . . . for this temporary grouping." The much-publicized exhibition draws over 25,000 visitors in its first week and a total attendance of nearly 100,000. After it closes, the 1,967 objects in the bequest are distributed to the appropriate departments in the Museum, enriching the Metropolitan's holdings in nearly all areas of the decorative arts and, most significantly, extending the institution's collections of European painting, of old master and modern prints, and of the arts of China and Japan.

Quote from *Metropolitan Museum of Art, Sixty-first Annual Report of The Trustees 1930*, New York, 1931, p. 7; attendance figures per MMA Archives.

Before April The Havemeyer children select what they want from the portion of their parents' collection that was

Figure 107. Installation view, *The H. O. Havemeyer Collection*, The Metropolitan Museum of Art, 1930

not given to the Metropolitan and from the contents of 1 East 66th Street; the remaining artworks and objects will be sold in a five-part auction held over a twelve-day period.

April 10 A standing-room-only crowd attends Part I of the American Art Association sale of *The Estate of Mrs. H. O. Havemeyer: Oil Paintings* at the Anderson Galleries, New York. The auction of 119 pictures (which are primarily oils but also include watercolors, pastels, gouaches, and drawings), 3 rare violins, and a cello brings $241,315. Chester Dale is a principal buyer; he purchases 10 pictures —including a Monet, a Delacroix, and 3 Cassatts—and pays the highest prices of the evening: $26,000 for David's *Portrait of a Young Woman in White* (A180, now considered Follower of David) and $24,000 for Cézanne's *Abduction* (A67).

For buyers and prices, see *American Art Annual* 28, 1930, pp. 468–72; see also Weitzenhoffer 1986, p. 258. Dale purchases, lot nos. 40, 46, 54, 71, 75, 79–83.

April 10–12 Part II of the American Art Association sale of *The Estate of Mrs. H. O. Havemeyer: Roman, Syrian & Egyptian Glass, Hispano-Moresque Lustre Ware Mohammedan Pottery and Italian Majolica Fine Rugs* is held at Anderson Galleries, New York. The three sessions include 626 lots and yield $55,384.25.

Per annotated sale catalogue, Thomas J. Watson Library, MMA.

April 14–19 Part III of the American Art Association sale of *The Estate of Mrs. H. O. Havemeyer: Japanese & Chinese Art* is held in six sessions at the Anderson Galleries, New York. The 1,486 lots bring $58,391.50.

Per annotated sale catalogue, Thomas J. Watson Library, MMA; *American Art Annual* 28, 1930, p. 472.

April 16–17 The American Art Association sale of *Etchings, Sporting & Color Prints and a Fine Group of Rowlandson Drawings, Property of The Estate of Mrs. H. O. Havemeyer . . . The Estate of Charles A. Gould . . . And of The Estate of the Late Th. Berg . . . with additions from other private sources* is held in two sessions at the Anderson Galleries, New York. Of the 347 lots sold, 51 are identified as coming from the Havemeyer collection; all the Havemeyer works are sold on the second day. The majority are by contemporary artists but also included are old master prints—among them etchings by van Dyck and Dürer—as well as examples by Goya, Fortuny, Cassatt, and others.

Havemeyer works, lot nos. 192, 194–211, 218–20, 224–33, 235–42, 245, 247, 248, 250, 251, 269, 271, 293–95, 297.

April 22 The sale of *Furnishings & Decorations From the Estate of Mrs. H. O. Havemeyer* takes place at 1 East 66th Street. All lots, "including fixtures, architectural details, paneling, mosaic work, etc.," are sold on the premises and removed at the risk and expense of the buyers. The 259 lots yield $12,345.50.

Lots and prices per annotated sale catalogue, Thomas J. Watson Library, MMA, noting that 72 lots were added to the 187 lots listed. These numbers are misleading, since individual lots generally represented groups of related objects, such as suites of furniture, collections of ornamental panels, and assorted glassware, rather than single items.

July 30 The *New York Times* announces that the former home of the Sugar King and adjoining residences owned by Electra and Horace will be demolished to make way for an apartment house.

"Havemeyer Home on Fifth Avenue to Go," *New York Times*, July 30, 1930. The property, which was to be "improved at once with a cooperative apartment house," was leased to a syndicate organized by Douglas L. Elliman and Co.; projected building costs were estimated in excess of $25,000,000. The Havemeyer house was torn down, but the lot remained vacant until after World War II, when the apartment house that stands today was constructed.

Appendix

GRETCHEN WOLD

This checklist includes only European and American paintings, watercolors, and drawings collected by Mr. and Mrs. H. O. Havemeyer. Information about each work has been provided to the extent possible. Titles and attributions are those used by the current owner, when known, or those that appear in a catalogue raisonné or the latest reference. Earlier titles, when differing substantially from the current ones, and attributions are included under the relevant reference, exhibition, or sale. For the most part titles have been translated into English; in a few instances both an English and a French title are given, since the latter reflects the official title used by a museum. The exhibition listings end in 1928.

All works with MMA numbers with the prefix 29.100 are H. O. Havemeyer Collection, Bequest of Mrs. H. O. Havemeyer, 1929. Works marked with an asterisk (*) were specifically bequeathed to The Metropolitan Museum of Art by Mrs. Havemeyer in the first codicil of her will, dated July 24, 1919. Works marked with two asterisks (**) were so bequeathed in the second codicil, dated June 26, 1922. Five paintings in these codicils were declined by the Museum. Works marked with three asterisks (***) are not included in the 1931 catalogue of the Havemeyer collection (Havemeyer 1931).

1
Edwin Austin Abbey
American, 1852–1911
IN A TAVERN
Pen and ink on cardboard, 11 ¼ x 17 ⅞ in.
(28.6 x 45.4 cm)
Signed and dated l.r.: *E.A. Abbey / 1886*
PROVENANCE: Mrs. H. O. Havemeyer,
New York, d. 1929; MMA 29.100.928.
REFERENCES: Havemeyer 1931, p. 192;
Havemeyer 1958, p. 3, no. 3.

3
Edwin Austin Abbey
HAYMAKERS RESTING
Pen and ink on paper, 11 x 17 ½ in.
(27.9 x 44.5 cm)
Signed and dated l.r.: *E.A. Abbey / Nov.
1887*
PROVENANCE: Mrs. H. O. Havemeyer,
New York, d. 1929; MMA 29.100.926.
REFERENCES: Havemeyer 1931, p. 192;
Havemeyer 1958, p. 3, no. 1.

5
Edwin Austin Abbey
QUINCE
Pen and ink on cardboard, 17 ⅞ x 13 ⅛ in.
(45.4 x 33.3 cm)
Signed and dated l.r.: *E.A. Abbey / 1888*
PROVENANCE: Mrs. H. O. Havemeyer,
New York, by 1915–29; MMA 29.100.924.
EXHIBITION: 1915 San Francisco,
no. 2656.
REFERENCES: Havemeyer 1931, p. 192;
Havemeyer 1958, p. 4, no. 5.

2
Edwin Austin Abbey
A LOVE SONG
Pen and ink on cardboard, 19 ¾ x 15 in.
(49.2 x 38.1 cm)
Signed and dated l.r.: *E.A. Abbey / 1887*
PROVENANCE: Mrs. H. O. Havemeyer,
New York, by 1915–29; MMA 29.100.927.
EXHIBITION: 1915 San Francisco,
no. 2655.
REFERENCES: Havemeyer 1931, p. 192;
Havemeyer 1958, p. 3, no. 4.

4
Edwin Austin Abbey
IN THE LIBRARY
Pen and ink on cardboard, 17 ¾ x 11 ¼ in.
(45.1 x 28.6 cm)
Signed and dated l.r.: *E.A. Abbey 1888*
PROVENANCE: Mrs. H. O. Havemeyer,
New York, by 1915–29; MMA 29.100.925.
EXHIBITION: 1915 San Francisco,
no. 2648.
REFERENCES: Havemeyer 1931, p. 192;
Havemeyer 1958, p. 3, no. 2.

6
Edwin Austin Abbey
SALLY IN OUR ALLEY
Pen and ink on cardboard, 17 ⅜ x 12 ⅜ in.
(44.1 x 31.4 cm)
PROVENANCE: Mrs. Abbey, the artist's
widow, in 1912; Mrs. H. O. Havemeyer,
New York, by 1915–29; MMA 29.100.923.
EXHIBITIONS: 1912 London, no. 302;
1915 San Francisco, no. 2658.
REFERENCES: Havemeyer 1931, p. 192;
Havemeyer 1958, p. 4, no. 6.

7

Mariotto Albertinelli, Follower of
Italian (Florentine), 1474–1515
MADONNA AND CHILD WITH
SAINTS JOHN THE BAPTIST,
STEPHEN, AND LAWRENCE
Oil on wood, 79 x 58 in.
(200.7 x 147.3 cm)
Inscribed on plinth: *F. Francia*
PROVENANCE: S.A.R. la Duchesse de Berri,
Venice; Harrington, Boston; M. J. Rougeron,
New York, bought from Harrington's
daughter; Mrs. H. O. Havemeyer, New
York, bought from Rougeron as by
Francia, in 1922–29; her sale, American
Art Association, New York, Apr. 10, 1930,
no. 101, as by Francia; bought at sale by
Metropolitan Galleries for $1,700.
Note: The current attribution was supplied
by Everett Fahy.
REFERENCE: Havemeyer 1931, p. 494, as
by Francia.

8

American Painter, Unknown
JONQUILS
Pastel, 21 x 17 in. (53.3 x 43.2 cm)
PROVENANCE: Mrs. H. O. Havemeyer,
New York, d. 1929; her sale, American Art
Association, New York, Apr. 10, 1930,
no. 30.
REFERENCE: Havemeyer 1931, p. 511.

9

Albert André
French, 1869–1954
THE GARDEN
Oil on wood, 25½ x 31½ in.
(64.8 x 80 cm)
Signed l.r.: *A. André*
PROVENANCE: Durand-Ruel, Paris, bought
from the artist, Apr. 17, 1901 (stock no.
6290); Mr. and Mrs. H. O. Havemeyer,
New York, bought from Durand-Ruel, Apr.
19, 1901 (New York stock book says July
12); until 1907; Mrs. H. O. Havemeyer,
New York, 1907–29; her daughter Adaline
Havemeyer Frelinghuysen, Morristown,
N.J., 1929–63; private collection.
REFERENCE: Havemeyer 1931, p. 328.

9

10

Albert André
SEAMSTRESSES
Oil on canvas transferred to wood,
22 x 26½ in. (55.9 x 67.3 cm)
Signed l.r.: *A. André*
PROVENANCE: Durand-Ruel, Paris, bought
from the artist, Apr. 17, 1901, for Fr 500
(stock no. 6295); Mr. and Mrs. H. O.
Havemeyer, New York, bought from
Durand-Ruel, Apr. 19, 1901 (New York
stock book says July 12); until 1907; Mrs.
H. O. Havemeyer, New York, 1907–29;
her sale, American Art Association, New
York, Apr. 10, 1930, no. 59; bought at sale
by R. D. Smith for $300.
REFERENCE: Havemeyer 1931, p. 501, as
Interior—Women Sewing.

11

Jacob Adriaensz. Backer, Style of
Dutch, 2nd quarter 17th century
PORTRAIT OF AN OLD WOMAN*

Oil on wood, 28 x 24 in. (71.1 x 61 cm)
Inscribed and dated l.r.: *Rembrandt / f.
1640*; inscribed u.l.: *Æ T • SVÆ • 87 •*
PROVENANCE: Gerrit Muller, Amsterdam;
his sale, at his residence, Heerengracht, Am-
sterdam, Apr. 2, 1827, no. 57; probably
bought at sale by Lelie(?) for G 2,005;
Comte de Robiano, Brussels; his sale,
Hôtel du Defunt, Brussels, May 1, 1837,
no. 543, as *Portrait d'une femme de grand
âge*, by Rembrandt; D. Nieuwenhuys, Brus-
sels; Prince Demidoff, Paris, until 1868;
M. B. Narischkine, Paris, bought from
Demidoff in 1868 for Fr 55,000; his sale,
Galerie Georges Petit, Paris, Apr. 5, 1883,
no. 29, as *Portrait d'une vieille femme*, by
Rembrandt, for Fr 51,000; Baron de
Beurnonville, Paris, by 1884–85; Durand-
Ruel, New York, from Nov. 1890
(stock no. 1063); Mr. and Mrs. H. O.
Havemeyer, New York, bought from
Durand-Ruel, Feb. 3, 1891, for $50,000;
until 1907; Mrs. H. O. Havemeyer, New
York, 1907–29; MMA 29.100.2.
EXHIBITIONS: 1891 New York; 1891 New
York Metropolitan, no. 12; 1893 New
York, no. 17, as *Old Woman*; 1909 New
York Metropolitan, no. 89; 1915 New
York Masterpieces, no. 8, as by Rembrandt.
REFERENCES: Havemeyer 1931, pp. 26f.,
ill., as by Rembrandt; Havemeyer 1958,
p. 8, no. 29, as 18th- or 19th-century copy
after Rembrandt; Havemeyer 1961, p. 19;
Weitzenhoffer 1982, pp. 125–28, 132,
138, 149, 155, 166, n. 7, fig. 25; Sumow-
ski 1983, I, no. 61, as by Backer;
Weitzenhoffer 1986, pp. 64, 66, 68, 254,
pl. 20, ill. pp. 74, 224.

12

Antoine-Louis Barye
French, 1795–1875
On Feb. 23, 1887, the Havemeyers bought
four Barye watercolors from M. Knoedler
and Co. for $2,000. This transaction is an-
notated in the Knoedler stock book with
the words "left with Montaignac in Paris."
On Feb. 28, 1892, the Havemeyers bought
a Barye watercolor of a panther and serpent from Knoedler for $950. Knoedler
has no stock numbers for any of these five
works, and it is impossible to identify them
definitely with any of the Barye watercolors included in the checklist. Likewise, a
Barye watercolor that the Havemeyers
bought from Durand-Ruel in January 1893
(see Weitzenhoffer 1982, p. 199) is also impossible to identify.
BEAR KILLING BULL
Watercolor on wove paper, 8⅜ x 13⅜ in.
(21.3 x 34 cm)
Signed u.l.: *BARYE*
PROVENANCE: Charles Binder, Paris, by
1860; his sale, Hôtel Drouot, Paris, Apr. 8,

12

15

18

13

16

19

14

17

20

1873, no. 14, for Fr 1,505; Mrs. H. O. Havemeyer, New York, d. 1929; MMA 29.100.591.
EXHIBITION: 1860 Paris, no. 6.
REFERENCES: Havemeyer 1931, p. 181; Zieseniss 1953, no. H3; Havemeyer 1958, p. 10, no. 37.

13
Antoine-Louis Barye
BEAR KILLING BULL
Watercolor on wove paper, lined,
8 7/16 x 13 3/8 in. (21.4 x 34 cm)
Signed u.r.: *BARYE.*
PROVENANCE: Baron Papeleu; his sale, Hôtel Drouot, Paris, Feb. 17, 1859, no. 1, for Fr 265; Charles Binder, Paris, by 1889; sale, American Art Association, New York, Apr. 7–8, 11–27, 1892, no. 45, for $800; Mrs. H. O. Havemeyer, New York, d. 1929; MMA 29.100.578.
EXHIBITION: 1889 Paris, no. 681.
REFERENCES: Havemeyer 1931, pp. 181, 183, ill.; Zieseniss 1953, no. H4; Havemeyer 1958, p. 10, no. 36.

14
Antoine-Louis Barye
BISON LYING DOWN
Watercolor on laid paper, 4 5/8 x 6 13/16 in. (11.8 x 17.3 cm)
Signed u.l.: *BARYE*
PROVENANCE: Mrs. H. O. Havemeyer, New York, d. 1929; MMA 29.100.581.
REFERENCES: Havemeyer 1931, p. 181; Zieseniss 1953, no. J3; Havemeyer 1958, p. 10, no. 38.

15
Antoine-Louis Barye
DEAD HORSES
Watercolor on wove paper, lined,
9 3/4 x 13 1/4 in. (24.8 x 33.7 cm)
Signed l.r.: *BARYE*
PROVENANCE: Antoine-Louis Barye, d. 1875; his sale, Hôtel Drouot, Paris, Feb. 7–12, 1876, no. 121, for Fr 180; Ducasse; Guyotin, in 1889; Cottier and Co., New York; Mrs. H. O. Havemeyer, New York, bought from Cottier; d. 1929; MMA 29.100.590.

EXHIBITIONS: 1875 Paris, no. 468; 1889 Paris, no. 711.
REFERENCES: Havemeyer 1931, p. 181; Zieseniss 1953, no. I4; Havemeyer 1958, p. 10, no. 39.

16
Antoine-Louis Barye
DEER AND TREE AGAINST SUNSET
Watercolor on wove paper, lined,
10 5/8 x 15 1/8 in. (27 x 38.4 cm)
Signed lower center: *BARYE*
PROVENANCE: Antoine-Louis Barye, d. 1875; his sale, Hôtel Drouot, Paris, Feb. 7–12, 1876, no. 160, for Fr 275; Ferdinand Barbedienne; his sale, Durand-Ruel, Paris, June 2–3, 1892, no. 108, for Fr 2,600; Samuel P. Avery, New York; Mrs. H. O. Havemeyer, New York, bought from Avery; d. 1929; MMA 29.100.594.
EXHIBITIONS: 1875 Paris, no. 461; 1889 Paris, no. 724.
REFERENCES: Havemeyer 1931, pp. 181, 183, ill.; Zieseniss 1953, no. D28; Havemeyer 1958, p. 10, no. 41.

17
Antoine-Louis Barye
DEER IN LANDSCAPE
Watercolor on wove paper, 7 ½ x 9 ⅜ in.
(19.1 x 23.9 cm)
Signed twice l.r.: *BARYE*
PROVENANCE: Goupil, Paris; Mrs. H. O.
Havemeyer, New York, bought from
Goupil; d. 1929; MMA 29.100.584.
REFERENCES: Havemeyer 1931, p. 181;
Zieseniss 1953, no. D23; Havemeyer 1958,
p. 10, no. 40.

18
Antoine-Louis Barye
DYING ELEPHANT
Watercolor on wove paper, 9 ¹³⁄₁₆ x 11 ¾ in.
(24.9 x 29.9 cm)
Signed l.l.: *BARYE*
PROVENANCE: Théodore Rousseau, possi-
bly bought from the artist for Fr 300;
d. 1867; his sale, Hôtel Drouot, Paris, Apr.
27–May 2, 1868, no. 528; bought at sale
by Durand-Ruel, Paris, for Fr 1,500;
Durand-Ruel, from 1868; Mme Millet;
Charles Tillot; his sale, Hôtel Drouot,
Paris, May 14, 1887, no. 2, for Fr 970;
Philippe Burty, Paris, in 1889; Cottier and
Co., New York; Mrs. H. O. Havemeyer,
New York, bought from Cottier; d. 1929;
MMA 29.100.582.
EXHIBITION: 1889 Paris Universelle, no. 4.
REFERENCES: Havemeyer 1931, p. 181;
Zieseniss 1953, no. E1; Havemeyer 1958,
p. 11, no. 42.

19
Antoine-Louis Barye
ELEPHANTS BY A POOL
Watercolor on wove paper, 13 x 19 ⅝ in.
(33 x 49.9 cm)
PROVENANCE: Charles Noel, by 1889; his
sale, Hôtel Drouot, Paris, Feb. 23, 1891,
no. 53, for Fr 6,100; Goupil, Paris; Mrs.
H. O. Havemeyer, New York, bought
from Goupil; d. 1929; MMA 29.100.593.
EXHIBITION: 1889 Paris, no. 704.
REFERENCES: Havemeyer 1931, p. 181;
Zieseniss 1953, no. E8; Havemeyer 1958,
p. 11, no. 43.

20
Antoine-Louis Barye
GROUP OF BISON
Watercolor on laid paper, 6 ¾ x 13 ¹⁵⁄₁₆ in.
(17.2 x 35.4 cm)
Signed l.r.: *BARYE*
PROVENANCE: Antoine-Louis Barye,
d. 1875; his sale, Hôtel Drouot, Paris, Feb.
7–12, 1876, no. 120, for Fr 305; Hecht;
Hayem; Durand-Ruel (stock no. 2527);
Mrs. H. O. Havemeyer, New York, bought
from Durand-Ruel; d. 1929; MMA
29.100.595.
EXHIBITION: 1889 Paris Universelle, no. 8.
REFERENCES: Havemeyer 1931, p. 181;
Zieseniss 1953, no. J5; Havemeyer 1958,
p. 11, no. 44.

21
Antoine-Louis Barye
HERON IN LANDSCAPE
Watercolor on wove paper, 6 ¼ x 8 ¾ in.
(15.9 x 22.2 cm)
Signed l.r.: *Barye*
PROVENANCE: Samuel P. Avery, New York;
Mrs. H. O. Havemeyer, New York, bought
from Avery; d. 1929; MMA 29.100.573.
REFERENCES: Havemeyer 1931, p. 181;
Zieseniss 1953, no. G7; Havemeyer 1958,
p. 11, no. 45.

22
Antoine-Louis Barye
IZARDS IN THE GLACIERS
Watercolor on wove paper, 7 ¾ x 10 in.
(19.7 x 25.4 cm)
Signed l.r.: *BARYE*
PROVENANCE: Georges Petit, Paris; Hector
Brame, Paris; Philippe Burty, Paris, in
1889; Goupil, Paris; Mrs. H. O. Have-
meyer, New York, bought from Goupil; d.
1929; MMA 29.100.592.
EXHIBITION: 1889 Paris, no. 710.
REFERENCES: Havemeyer 1931, p. 181;
Zieseniss 1953, no. D31; Havemeyer 1958,
p. 11, no. 46.

23
Antoine-Louis Barye
LEOPARD AND SERPENT
Watercolor on laid paper, lined,

29

31

33

30

32

34

6 ¹¹⁄₁₆ x 9 ⅞ in. (17 x 25.1 cm)
Signed: r.: *BARYE*
PROVENANCE: Durand-Ruel; Mrs. H. O.
Havemeyer, New York, bought from
Durand-Ruel; d. 1929; MMA 29.100.579.
REFERENCES: Havemeyer 1931, p. 181;
Zieseniss 1953, no. C19; Havemeyer 1958,
p. 11, no. 48.

24
Antoine-Louis Barye
LEOPARD LYING DOWN
Watercolor on wove paper, 6 ⁵⁄₁₆ x 8 ⅞ in.
(16 x 22.5 cm)
Signed u.l.: *BARYE*
PROVENANCE: Mrs. H. O. Havemeyer,
New York, possibly bought from Samuel P.
Avery; d. 1929; MMA 29.100.575.
REFERENCES: Havemeyer 1931, p. 182;
Zieseniss 1953, no. C2; Havemeyer 1958,
p. 11, no. 47.

25
Antoine-Louis Barye
LEOPARD WATCHING SERPENT
Watercolor on wove paper, 6 ⁹⁄₁₆ x 9 ¹³⁄₁₆ in.
(16.7 x 24.9 cm)
Signed r.: *BARYE*
PROVENANCE: Mrs. H. O. Havemeyer,
New York, d. 1929; MMA 29.100.588.
REFERENCES: Havemeyer 1931, pp. 182f.,
ill.; Zieseniss 1953, no. C18; Havemeyer
1958, p. 11, no. 49.

26
Antoine-Louis Barye
LION***
Watercolor
PROVENANCE: Mr. and Mrs. H. O.
Havemeyer, New York, until 1899;
Durand-Ruel, New York, bought from
Havemeyer, May 1, 1899.

27
Antoine-Louis Barye
LION***
Watercolor
PROVENANCE: Mr. and Mrs. H. O.
Havemeyer, New York, until 1896;
Durand-Ruel, New York, bought from
Havemeyer, Dec. 15, 1896.

28
Antoine-Louis Barye
LION DEVOURING PREY
Watercolor on wove paper, lined,
10 ⁷⁄₁₆ x 14 ½ in. (26.5 x 36.8 cm)
Signed l.r.: *BARYE*
PROVENANCE: Cottier and Co., New York;
Mrs. H. O. Havemeyer, New York, bought
from Cottier; d. 1929; MMA 29.100.583.
REFERENCES: Havemeyer 1931, p. 182;
Zieseniss 1953, no. A40; Havemeyer 1958,
p. 11, no. 50.

29
Antoine-Louis Barye
LION RESTING***

Oil on canvas, 9 ⅝ x 13 in. (24.5 x 33 cm)
Signed l.r.: *BARYE*
PROVENANCE: Ferdinand Barbedienne, by
1889; his sale, Durand-Ruel, Paris, June 2–
3, 1892, no. 1; bought at sale by Durand-
Ruel for Fr 9,400; Durand-Ruel, Paris,
1889 (stock no. 2285); Mr. and Mrs.
H. O. Havemeyer, New York, bought
from Durand-Ruel, June 17, 1892, for
Fr 9,870.
EXHIBITIONS: 1875 Paris, no. 354; 1889
Paris, no. 748; 1909 New York, no. 107(?).
REFERENCES: Weitzenhoffer 1982, pp. 131,
143, n. 18, p. 168, n. 33; Weitzenhoffer
1986, p. 65.

30
Antoine-Louis Barye
LION RESTING
Watercolor on wove paper, lined,
5 ¾ x 9 ³⁄₁₆ in. (14.6 x 23.3 cm)
Signed l.r.: *Barye*
PROVENANCE: Durand-Ruel; Mrs. H. O.
Havemeyer, New York, bought from
Durand-Ruel; d. 1929; MMA 29.100.580.
REFERENCES: Havemeyer 1931, pp. 182f.,
ill.; Zieseniss 1953, no. A6; Havemeyer
1958, p. 11, no. 51.

31
Antoine-Louis Barye
LION SLEEPING
Watercolor on wove paper, lined,
9 ³⁄₁₆ x 11 ⅝ in. (23.3 x 29.5 cm)
Signed l.l.: *BARYE*

35

38

40

37

39

41

PROVENANCE: Charles Binder, Paris, by 1860; his sale, Hôtel Drouot, Paris, Apr. 8, 1873, no. 9, for Fr 1,805; Cottier and Co., New York; Mrs. H. O. Havemeyer, New York, bought from Cottier; d. 1929; MMA 29.100.585.
EXHIBITION: 1860 Paris, no. 7.
REFERENCES: Havemeyer 1931, p. 182; Zieseniss 1953, no. A5; Havemeyer 1958, p. 11, no. 52.

32
Antoine-Louis Barye
LYNX AND HERON
Watercolor on wove paper, 8 ½ x 11 ⅝ in. (21.6 x 29.5 cm)
Signed l.l.: *BARYE*
PROVENANCE: Antoine-Louis Barye, d. 1875; his sale, Hôtel Drouot, Paris, Feb. 7–12, 1876, no. 126, for Fr 220; Beugnet; Cottier and Co., New York; Mrs. H. O. Havemeyer, New York, bought from Cottier; d. 1929; MMA 29.100.587.
EXHIBITION: 1875 Paris, no. 481.
REFERENCES: Havemeyer 1931, p. 182; Zieseniss 1953, no. C24; Havemeyer 1958, p. 12, no. 53.

33
Antoine-Louis Barye
TIGER
Watercolor on lined paper, 4 ¹¹⁄₁₆ x 6 ¹⁵⁄₁₆ in. (11.9 x 17.6 cm)
Signed l.r.: *BARYE*
PROVENANCE: Reichart and Co.; Mrs.

H. O. Havemeyer, New York, bought from Reichart; d. 1929; MMA 29.100.577.
REFERENCES: Havemeyer 1931, p. 182; Zieseniss 1953, no. B28; Havemeyer 1958, p. 12, no. 55.

34
Antoine-Louis Barye
TIGER
Watercolor on heavy wove paper, lined, 6 ⅝ x 10 ¹⁄₁₆ in. (16.8 x 25.6 cm)
Signed l.r.: *BARYE*
PROVENANCE: Samuel P. Avery, New York; Mrs. H. O. Havemeyer, New York, bought from Avery; d. 1929; MMA 29.100.576.
REFERENCES: Havemeyer 1931, p. 182; Zieseniss 1953, no. B11; Havemeyer 1958, p. 12, no. 54.

35
Antoine-Louis Barye
TIGER APPROACHING POOL
Watercolor on wove paper, lined, 10 ¹¹⁄₁₆ x 15 ⅛ in. (27.2 x 38.4 cm)
Signed l.l.: *BARYE*
PROVENANCE: Charles Noel, by 1889; his sale, Hôtel Drouot, Paris, Feb. 23, 1891, no. 52, for Fr 4,800; Mrs. H. O. Havemeyer, New York, d. 1929; MMA 29.100.597.
EXHIBITION: 1889 Paris, no. 705.
REFERENCES: Havemeyer 1931, p. 182; Zieseniss 1953, no. B40; Havemeyer 1958, p. 12, no. 56.

36
Antoine-Louis Barye
TIGER DEVOURING ANTELOPE***
Watercolor
PROVENANCE: Mr. and Mrs. H. O. Havemeyer, New York, until 1899; Durand-Ruel, New York, bought from Havemeyer, May 1, 1899.

37
Antoine-Louis Barye
TIGER IN LANDSCAPE
Watercolor on paper, 9 ¾ x 13 in. (24.8 x 33 cm)
Signed l.: *BARYE*
PROVENANCE: Charles Binder, Paris, by 1860; his sale, Hôtel Drouot, Paris, Apr. 8, 1873, no. 3, for Fr 1,505; Samuel P. Avery, New York; Mrs. H. O. Havemeyer, New York, bought from Avery; d. 1929; MMA 29.100.589.
EXHIBITION: 1860 Paris, no. 5.
REFERENCES: Havemeyer 1931, p. 182; Zieseniss 1953, no. B26; Havemeyer 1958, p. 12, no. 57.

38
Antoine-Louis Barye
TIGER LYING DOWN***
Oil on canvas, 9 ⅞ x 13 in. (25.1 x 33 cm)
Signed l.l.: *BARYE*
PROVENANCE: Ferdinand Barbedienne, by 1889; his sale, Durand-Ruel, Paris, June 2–3, 1892, no. 5; bought at sale by Durand-Ruel for Fr 7,100; Durand-Ruel, Paris,

1889 (stock no. 2286); Mr. and Mrs.
H. O. Havemeyer, New York, bought
from Durand-Ruel, June 17, 1892, for
Fr 7,455.
EXHIBITIONS: 1875 Paris, no. 356; 1889
Paris, no. 750; 1909 New York, no. 109(?).
REFERENCES: Weitzenhoffer 1982, pp. 131,
143, n. 18, p. 168, n. 33; Weitzenhoffer
1986, p. 65.

39
Antoine-Louis Barye
TIGER ROLLING ON ITS BACK
Watercolor on heavy wove paper,
9 ⅛ x 11 ⁹⁄₁₆ in. (23.2 x 29.4 cm)
Signed l.r.: *BARYE*
PROVENANCE: Charles Binder, Paris, by
1860; his sale, Hôtel Drouot, Paris, Apr. 8,
1873, no. 8, for Fr 2,120; Cottier and Co.,
New York; Mrs. H. O. Havemeyer, New
York, bought from Cottier; d. 1929; MMA
29.100.586.
EXHIBITION: 1860 Paris, no. 8.
REFERENCES: Havemeyer 1931, p. 182;
Zieseniss 1953, no. B19; Havemeyer 1958,
p. 12, no. 58.

40
Antoine-Louis Barye
VULTURE
Watercolor on laid paper, 2 ¹⁵⁄₁₆ x 4 ⅜ in.
(7.5 x 11.1 cm)
Signed lower center: *BARYE*
PROVENANCE: Mrs. H. O. Havemeyer,
New York, d. 1929; MMA 29.100.574.
REFERENCES: Havemeyer 1931, p. 182;
Zieseniss 1953, no. G2; Havemeyer 1958,
p. 12, no. 59.

41
Antoine-Louis Barye
VULTURES ON A TREE
Watercolor on wove paper,
10 ¹¹⁄₁₆ x 15 ⅛ in. (27.2 x 38.4 cm)
Signed bottom, l. c.: *BARYE*
PROVENANCE: Mr. and Mrs. H. O.
Havemeyer, New York, until 1907; Mrs.
H. O. Havemeyer, New York, 1907–29;
MMA 29.100.596.
Note: Unpublished notes by Mrs. Have-
meyer indicate that this was the first Barye
work her husband bought.
REFERENCES: Havemeyer 1931, p. 182;
Zieseniss 1953, no. G3; Havemeyer 1958,
p. 12, no. 60.

42a–f
Antoine-Louis Barye
SIX ANIMAL SUBJECTS***
Watercolor
PROVENANCE: Mr. and Mrs. H. O.
Havemeyer, New York, until 1900;
Durand-Ruel, New York, bought from
Havemeyer, Dec. 14, 1900.

43
Aubrey Beardsley, Imitator of
British, 20th century
MAN WITH A MASK
Pen and black ink on wove paper,
13 ¾ x 10 ⁹⁄₁₆ in. (34.9 x 26.8 cm)
Inscribed l.l.: *AUBREY / BEARDSLEY*
PROVENANCE: Mrs. H. O. Havemeyer,
New York, d. 1929; MMA 29.100.929.
REFERENCES: Havemeyer 1931, p. 192, as
by Beardsley; Havemeyer 1958, p. 4,
no. 11, as by Beardsley.

44
Eugène Boudin
French, 1824–1898
WASHERWOMEN NEAR A BRIDGE
ON THE TOUQUES RIVER***
Oil on wood, 6 ¼ x 8 ¼ in. (15.9 x 21 cm)
Signed l.l.: *E. Boudin*
PROVENANCE: Durand-Ruel, Paris, bought
from the artist, Sept. 9, 1889; Mr. and
Mrs. H. O. Havemeyer, New York, bought
from Durand-Ruel, Sept. 9, 1889; until
1899; Durand-Ruel, New York, bought
from Havemeyer, Mar. 10, 1899, as
Washerwomen at Honfleur; Joseph
Stransky, New York, bought from Durand-
Ruel, Apr. 1917; Galerie J. Allard, Paris,
until 1929; Esther Slater Kerrigan, New
York, bought from Allard in 1929; her
sale, Parke-Bernet, New York, Jan. 8–10,
1942, no. 57; bought at sale by Weinzerg
for $475; private collection.
EXHIBITION: 1889 Paris Boudin, no. 82.
REFERENCES: Schmit 1973, no. 1784;
Weitzenhoffer 1982, p. 142, n. 13, p. 198,
n. 45.

45
Bronzino (Agnolo di Cosimo di Mariano)
Italian (Florentine), 1503–1572
PORTRAIT OF A YOUNG MAN*
Oil on wood, 37 ⅝ x 29 ½ in.
(95.5 x 74.9 cm)
PROVENANCE: Lucien Bonaparte, prince of
Canino, Rome, by 1808; sale, London,
Stanley, May 14–16, 1816, no. 163, as by
Sebastiano del Piombo; Charles J. Nieuwen-
huys, London, from 1816; Alexandre, comte
de Pourtalès-Gorgier, Paris, by 1841; his
collection cat., 1841, no. 49, as by Sebasti-

45

ano del Piombo, or, more likely, Andrea
del Sarto; sale, Paris, Mar. 27–Apr. 1,
1865, no. 114, as the figure of a young
man believed to be a Duke of Urbino, by
Sebastiano del Piombo; Baron Achille
Seillière, Paris and Château de Mello,
1865–73; Jeanne Marguerite Seillière,
Princesse de Sagan, later Duchesse de
Talleyrand-Perigord, Paris, from 1873;
M. Bourdariat, Paris, until 1898; Durand-
Ruel, Paris, bought from Bourdariat, Apr.
8, 1898, for Fr 140,000 (stock no. 4618);
Durand-Ruel, New York, bought from
Durand-Ruel, Paris, May 23, 1898 (stock
no. 1996); Mr. and Mrs. H. O. Havemeyer, New York, bought from Durand-
Ruel, May 14, 1898, for $40,000; until
1907; Mrs. H. O. Havemeyer, New York,
1907–29; MMA 29.100.16.
EXHIBITIONS: 1874 Paris, no. 19; 1915
New York Masterpieces, no. 1, as *Portrait
of the Duke of Urbino*.
REFERENCES: Havemeyer 1931, pp. 4f.,
ill.; Wehle 1940, pp. 68f., ill.; Havemeyer
1958, p. 33, no. 184, ill.; Havemeyer
1961, pp. 20, 111; Zeri and Gardner
1971, pp. 201f., ill.; Baccheschi 1973,
no. 25; Weitzenhoffer 1982, p. 166, n. 7;
Weitzenhoffer 1986, pp. 176, 254.

46
Vincent Canadè
American, 1877–1961
HEAD OF A YOUNG GIRL
Oil on wood, 10 x 8 in. (25.4 x 20.3 cm)
Signed l.l.: *Vince Canadè*

PROVENANCE: Mrs. H. O. Havemeyer, New York, d. 1929; her sale, American Art Association, New York, Apr. 10, 1930, no. 1; bought at sale by Pauline Haggarty for $50.

REFERENCE: Havemeyer 1931, p. 507.

47
Jan van de Cappelle
Dutch, 1624/26–1679
SEASCAPE***
Oil
PROVENANCE: Charles Sedelmeyer, Paris, until 1889; Durand-Ruel, Paris, bought from Sedelmeyer, Aug. 1, 1889, for Fr 5,000 (stock no. 2408, as *Marine*); Mr. and Mrs. H. O. Havemeyer, New York, bought from Durand-Ruel, Aug. 1, 1889, for Fr 15,000 with a de Hooch (A328); Durand-Ruel, New York, bought back from Havemeyer, Apr. 8, 1895, for $3,000 or Fr 5,000 (stock no. 1397, as *Marine*); John G. Johnson, Philadelphia, bought from Durand-Ruel, Apr. 22, 1895, for $1,000.

48
Juan Carreño de Miranda
Spanish, 1614–1685
CARLOS II, KING OF SPAIN
Oil on canvas, 21¾ x 17 in.
(55.3 x 43.2 cm)
PROVENANCE: Mrs. H. O. Havemeyer, New York, d. 1929; her sale, American Art Association, New York, Apr. 10, 1930, no. 95; bought at sale by F. Kouchakji for $700.

REFERENCE: Havemeyer 1931, p. 499.

49
Mary Cassatt
American, 1844–1926
SELF-PORTRAIT
Gouache on wove paper, laid down on buff-colored wood pulp paper, 23½ x 17½ in. (59.7 x 44.5 cm)
Signed l.l.: *Mary Cassatt*
PROVENANCE: Mary Cassatt, Paris; Mrs. H. O. Havemeyer, New York, probably acquired in Paris in 1879; d. 1929; her sale, American Art Association, New York, Apr.

10, 1930, no. 74; bought at sale by Jonas for $4,300; Edouard Jonas, Paris; Mr. and Mrs. Richman Proskauer, Larchmont, N.Y., by 1932; MMA (Bequest of Edith H. Proskauer, 1975), 1975.319.1.

EXHIBITIONS: 1880 New York, no. 628(?), as *A Study*, lent by Mrs. A.S.W. Elder; 1895 New York Cassatt, no. 35; 1926–27 Chicago, no. 33, as *Woman Leaning on Her Right Hand*; 1927 Philadelphia, no. 23, as *Portrait of the Artist*; 1928 Pittsburgh, no. 28.

REFERENCES: Havemeyer 1931, p. 508; Breeskin 1970, no. 55; Weitzenhoffer 1982, pp. 15, 19, 29, n. 13, pp. 45, 64, fig. 3; Weitzenhoffer 1986, pp. 22, 26, 34, 41, colorpl. 3.

50
Mary Cassatt
THE FAMILY
Oil on canvas, 32¼ x 26⅛ in.
(81.9 x 66.4 cm)
Signed l.r.: *Mary Cassatt*
PROVENANCE: Durand-Ruel, Paris, bought from the artist, Nov. 24, 1893 (stock no. 2860); Durand-Ruel, New York, bought from Durand-Ruel, Paris, Feb. 7, 1894 (stock no. 1726); Alfred Atmore Pope, Cleveland, bought from Durand-Ruel, Feb. 28, 1894; Durand-Ruel, New York, bought back from Pope, May 24, 1894; Mr. and Mrs. H. O. Havemeyer, New York, bought from Durand-Ruel, June 1894; until 1907; Mrs. H. O. Havemeyer, New York, 1907–29; her sale, American Art Association, New York, Apr. 10, 1930, no. 78; bought at sale by R. D. Smith for $5,500; Durand-Ruel, New York; F. Dupré, Paris; Marlborough Fine Art, London, until 1954; Trafo, Zurich, sold Mar. 23, 1954; Walter P. Chrysler, Jr., New York, by 1960; Chrysler Art Museum of Provincetown, by 1962; The Chrysler Museum, Norfolk, Va., from 1971 (Gift of Walter P. Chrysler, Jr.), 71.498.

EXHIBITIONS: 1886 New York, no. 27; 1887 Pittsburgh; 1893 Paris, no. 3; 1895 New York Cassatt, no. 36; 1911 New York; 1927 Philadelphia, no. 6, as *Family Group*; 1928 Pittsburgh, no. 5.

REFERENCES: Havemeyer 1931, p. 507; Breeskin 1970, no. 145; Weitzenhoffer 1982, pp. 211, 219, n. 28, p. 226, fig. 64; Weitzenhoffer 1986, pp. 94, 98, pl. 48.

51
Mary Cassatt
GIRL ARRANGING HER HAIR
Oil on canvas, 29⅝ x 24⅝ in.
(75.3 x 62.6 cm)
PROVENANCE: Edgar Degas, Paris, 1886–17; deposited with Durand-Ruel, Oct. 30–Dec. 2, 1908 (deposit no. L11369); his sale, Galerie Georges Petit, Paris, Mar. 26–

27, 1918, no. 8; bought at sale by Durand-Ruel for Havemeyer for Fr 21,000; Mrs. H. O. Havemeyer, New York, 1918–29; her sale, American Art Association, New York, Apr. 10, 1930, no. 75; bought at sale by Dale for $4,600; Chester Dale, New York, 1930–62; National Gallery of Art, Washington, D.C. (Chester Dale Collection), 1963.10.97.

EXHIBITIONS: 1886 Paris, no. 9, as *Etude*; 1893 Paris, no. 17; 1908 Paris, no. 1, as *La Toilette*, lent by M.E.D. . . .; 1920 Philadelphia, no. 7, as *Filet de Coiffant* [sic], lent anonymously; 1926–27 Chicago, no. 4, as *Girl Combing Her Hair*; 1927 Philadelphia, no. 7, as *Girl Arranging Her Hair, 1886*; 1928 Pittsburgh, no. 9, as *Girl Twisting Her Hair*.

REFERENCES: Havemeyer 1931, p. 507; Breeskin 1970, no. 146; Weitzenhoffer 1986, p. 238, colorpl. 159.

52
Mary Cassatt
MOTHER AND CHILD
Oil on canvas, 18¼ x 15⅝ in.
(46.4 x 39.7 cm)
Signed l.r.: *Mary Cassatt*
PROVENANCE: Durand-Ruel, Paris, bought from the artist, Oct. 31, 1890 (stock no. 730); Durand-Ruel, New York, bought from Durand-Ruel, Paris, Mar. 13, 1895 (stock no. 1390, as *Mère et enfant*); Mr. and Mrs. H. O. Havemeyer, New York, bought from Durand-Ruel, Apr. 8, 1895, for $2,000; until 1907; Mrs. H. O. Havemeyer, New York, 1907–29; deposited with Durand-Ruel, Jan. 25–Mar. 2, 1909 (deposit no. 7521); her daughter Electra Havemeyer Webb, New York, from 1929; destroyed in a fire.

EXHIBITIONS: 1891 Paris Cassatt, no. 1; 1893 Paris, no. 11; 1895 New York Cassatt(?); 1898 New York; 1909 Boston, no. 3; 1915 New York Masterpieces, no. 48; 1926–27 Chicago, probably one of nos. 13–18, all as *Mother and Child*; 1927 Philadelphia, probably one of nos. 15–21, all as *Mother and Child*.

REFERENCES: Havemeyer 1931, pp. 434f., ill.; Breeskin 1970, no. 151, as *The Quiet Time*; Weitzenhoffer 1982, pp. 236f., 298, fig. 68; Weitzenhoffer 1986, pp. 104, 130, ill. p. 225, pl. 54.

53
Mary Cassatt
BABY'S FIRST CARESS
Pastel on paper, 30 x 24 in. (76.2 x 61 cm)
Signed u.l.: *Mary Cassatt*
PROVENANCE: Durand-Ruel, Paris, bought from the artist, Dec. 22, 1890, for Fr 500 (stock no. 805, as *Jeune mère enfant*); Durand-Ruel, New York, bought from Durand-Ruel, Paris, Mar. 13, 1895 (Paris

stock book), or Apr. 8, 1895 (New York stock book, no. 1391, as *La première caresse*); Mr. and Mrs. H. O. Havemeyer, New York, bought from Durand-Ruel, Apr. 8, 1895, for $1,000; until 1907; Mrs. H. O. Havemeyer, New York, 1907–29; her daughter Electra Havemeyer Webb, New York, from 1929; her daughter Electra Webb Bostwick, New York, until 1948; Macbeth Gallery, New York, bought from Bostwick, Jan. 17, 1948; Alex W. Stanley, New Britain, Conn., bought from Macbeth, Jan. 21, 1948; New Britain Museum of American Art, New Britain, Conn., received from Stanley, Dec. 31, 1948 (Harriet Russell Stanley Fund, Permanent Collection), 1948.14.

EXHIBITIONS: 1891 Paris Cassatt, no. 2; 1893 Paris, no. 25; 1895 New York Cassatt, no. 26; 1898 New York; 1915 New York Masterpieces, no. 58, as *Maternal Love*; 1924 Paris, no. 30; 1928 New York, no. 1, as *Mère et enfant*, lent anonymously.

REFERENCES: Havemeyer 1931, pp. 436f., ill., as *The First Caress*; Breeskin 1970, no. 189, as *Baby's First Caress*; Weitzenhoffer 1982, pp. 236f., 298, fig. 69; Weitzenhoffer 1986, pp. 104, 130.

54

Mary Cassatt
ADALINE HAVEMEYER (1884–1963)
Pastel on wove paper, 28⅞ x 23¾ in.
(73.3 x 60.3 cm)
Signed and dated u.r.: *Mary Cassatt / 95*
PROVENANCE: Mr. and Mrs. H. O. Havemeyer, New York, until 1907; Mrs. H. O. Havemeyer, New York, 1907–29; her daughter, the sitter, Adaline Havemeyer Frelinghuysen, Morristown, N.J., from 1929; private collection.
EXHIBITION: 1898 New York.
REFERENCES: Havemeyer 1931, p. 432; Breeskin 1970, no. 256; Weitzenhoffer 1982, pp. 240, 250, n. 49, p. 298, fig. 73; Weitzenhoffer 1986, pp. 105f., colorpl. 57.

55

Mary Cassatt
LOUISINE HAVEMEYER AND HER DAUGHTER ELECTRA
Pastel on wove paper, 24 x 30½ in.
(61 x 77.5 cm)
Signed and dated u.r.: *Mary Cassatt / 95 / Mary*
PROVENANCE: Mr. and Mrs. H. O. Havemeyer, New York, 1895–1907; Mrs. H. O. Havemeyer, New York, 1907–29; her daughter Electra Havemeyer Webb, New York, 1929–60; her daughter Electra Webb Bostwick, New York, 1960–82; her daughter Electra Bostwick McDowell, New York, 1982–89; private collection.
EXHIBITION: 1895 New York Cassatt, no. 31, as *Portraits*.

49

53

50

54

51

55

52

56

57

60

58

59

61

REFERENCES: Havemeyer 1931, p. 432; Breeskin 1970, no. 248; Weitzenhoffer 1982, pp. 240, 250, n. 48; Weitzenhoffer 1986, p. 105, colorpl. 56.

56
Mary Cassatt
LOUISINE HAVEMEYER (1855–1929)
Pastel on wove paper, 29 x 24 in.
(73.7 x 61 cm)
PROVENANCE: Mr. and Mrs. H. O. Havemeyer, New York, until 1907; Mrs. H. O. Havemeyer, New York, 1907–29; her daughter Electra Havemeyer Webb, New York, 1929–60; her son J. Watson Webb, Jr., Shelburne, Vt., 1960–73; Shelburne Museum, Shelburne, Vt. (Gift of J. Watson Webb, Jr., 1973), 27.3.1–19.
REFERENCES: Havemeyer 1931, p. 432; Breeskin 1970, no. 255; Weitzenhoffer 1986, pp. 113, 216f., pl. 67.

57
Mary Cassatt
FAMILY GROUP READING
Oil on canvas, 22¼ x 44⅜ in.
(56.5 x 112.7 cm)
Signed l.l.: *Mary Cassatt*
PROVENANCE: Durand-Ruel, Paris, bought from the artist, Nov. 24, 1898 (stock no. 4817); Durand-Ruel, New York, bought from Durand-Ruel, Paris, Jan. 24, 1899; Mr. and Mrs. H. O. Havemeyer, New York, bought from Durand-Ruel by Feb.

20, 1899; until 1907; Mrs. H. O. Havemeyer, New York, 1907–29; her daughter Electra Havemeyer Webb, New York, 1929–42; Philadelphia Museum of Art (Gift of Mr. and Mrs. J. Watson Webb), 42–102–1.
REFERENCES: Havemeyer 1931, p. 433; Breeskin 1970, no. 343, as *The Garden Lecture*; Weitzenhoffer 1982, pp. 308, 318, n. 50, fig. 122; Weitzenhoffer 1986, p. 136, pl. 100, as *Landscape with Three Figures (Family Group Reading)*.

58
Mary Cassatt
MOTHER AND CHILD*
Oil on canvas, 32⅛ x 25⅞ in.
(81.6 x 65.7 cm)
Signed l.l.: *Mary Cassatt*
PROVENANCE: Durand-Ruel, Paris, bought from the artist, Apr. 21, 1899 (stock no. 5155); Durand-Ruel, New York, bought from Durand-Ruel, Paris, July 4, 1899 (stock no. 2257); Mr. and Mrs. H. O. Havemeyer, New York, bought from Durand-Ruel, July 25, 1899, for $2,000; until 1907; Mrs. H. O. Havemeyer, New York, 1907–29; deposited with Durand-Ruel, New York, Jan. 25–Mar. 2, 1909 (deposit no. 7522), and again May 25–28, 1909 (deposit no. 7553); MMA 29.100.47.
EXHIBITIONS: 1909 Boston, no. 17; 1915 New York Masterpieces, no. 46, as *Mother and Son with Mirror*; 1926–27 Chicago,

no. 31 or 32, both as *Woman and Child*; 1927 Philadelphia, no. 20, as *Mother and Child*.
REFERENCES: Havemeyer 1931, pp. 172f., ill.; Havemeyer 1958, p. 4, no. 7; Breeskin 1970, no. 338, as *The Oval Mirror*; Weitzenhoffer 1982, pp. 308f., fig. 123; Spassky et al. 1985, pp. 646–48, ill.; Weitzenhoffer 1986, pp. 136, 255, pl. 101, ill. p. 225, as *The Oval Mirror*.

59
Mary Cassatt
YOUNG MOTHER SEWING*
Oil on canvas, 36⅜ x 29 in.
(92.4 x 73.7 cm)
Signed l.r.: *Mary Cassatt*
PROVENANCE: Durand-Ruel, Paris, bought from the artist, Jan. 3, 1901 (stock no. 6188); Mr. and Mrs. H. O. Havemeyer, New York, bought from Durand-Ruel, Apr. 23, 1901 (Durand-Ruel, New York, stock book no. 2628 states that it bought the picture from Durand-Ruel, Paris, on July 2 and sold it to Havemeyer on July 12); until 1907; Mrs. H. O. Havemeyer, New York, 1907–29; deposited with Durand-Ruel, New York, Jan. 25–Mar. 2, 1909 (deposit no. 7523); MMA 29.100.48.
EXHIBITIONS: 1909 Boston, no. 13; 1915 New York Masterpieces, no. 47, as *Little Girl Leaning upon Her Mother's Knee*; 1920 Philadelphia, no. 9, as *Young Mother*, lent anonymously.

62

64

63

65

REFERENCES: Havemeyer 1931, p. 507, as *Jeune femme allaitant son enfant*; Breeskin 1970, no. 504; Weitzenhoffer 1986, ill. p. 225.

62
Mary Cassatt
GIRL READING
Oil on canvas, 28 ¼ x 23 in.
(71.8 x 58.4 cm)
Signed l.r.: *Mary Cassatt*
PROVENANCE: Durand-Ruel, Paris, bought from the artist, Aug. 9, 1909 (stock no. 9131); Durand-Ruel, New York, bought from Durand-Ruel, Paris, Dec. 1, 1910; Mrs. H. O. Havemeyer, New York, bought from Durand-Ruel, Feb. 27, 1912; d. 1929; her daughter Adaline Havemeyer Frelinghuysen, Morristown, N.J., from 1929; private collection.
EXHIBITIONS: 1926–27 Chicago, no. 7; 1927 Philadelphia(?); 1928 Pittsburgh, no. 38.
REFERENCES: Havemeyer 1931, pp. 430f., ill; Breeskin 1970, no. 535.

63
Mary Cassatt
YOUNG MOTHER, DAUGHTER, AND BABY
Pastel on paper, 43 ¼ x 33 ¼ in.
(109.9 x 84.5 cm)
Signed l.r.: *Mary Cassatt*
PROVENANCE: Durand-Ruel, Paris, bought from the artist, Nov. 5, 1913 (stock no. 10435); Mrs. H. O. Havemeyer, New York, bought from Durand-Ruel, May 28, 1914, for Fr 15,000; d. 1929; her sale, American Art Association, New York, Apr. 10, 1930, no. 86, as *Jeune mère, fillette et fils*, for $1,800; Mrs. Albert Kahn, Detroit, until 1946; Wildenstein, New York, bought from Kahn in 1946; A. Schneider, bought from Wildenstein, Jan. 1952; Walter P. Chrysler, Jr., New York; Caesar R. Diorio, New York, 1959; Memorial Art Gallery of the University of Rochester (Marion Stratton Gould Fund, 1959), 59.16.
EXHIBITIONS: 1914 Paris, no. 17; 1915 New York Masterpieces, no. 56, as *Family Group*.
REFERENCES: Havemeyer 1931, p. 508, as *Family Group*; Breeskin 1970, no. 597.

64
Mary Cassatt
MOTHER AND CHILD*
Pastel on paper mounted on canvas,
32 x 25 ⅝ in. (81.3 x 65.1 cm)
Signed l.r.: *Mary Cassatt*
PROVENANCE: Mary Cassatt, Paris, deposited with Durand-Ruel, Paris and New

REFERENCES: Havemeyer 1931, pp. 172f., ill.; Havemeyer 1958, p. 4, no. 8; Breeskin 1970, no. 415; Spassky et al. 1985, pp. 648–51, ill.; Weitzenhoffer 1986, pp. 143, 255, pl. 110, ill. p. 225.

60
Mary Cassatt
MOTHER AND CHILD
Oil on canvas, 36 ¼ x 29 in.
(92.1 x 73.7 cm)
Signed l.r.: *Mary Cassatt*
PROVENANCE: Claude Roger-Marx, Paris, on deposit with Durand-Ruel, Oct. 30–Dec. 2, 1908 (deposit no. 11393); d. 1913; his sale, Galerie Manzi-Joyant, Paris, May 11–12, 1914, no. 15; bought at sale by Durand-Ruel for Havemeyer for Fr 15,500; Mrs. H. O. Havemeyer, New York, 1914–29; her sale, American Art Association, New York, Apr. 10, 1930, no. 82, as *La Femme au tournesol*; bought at sale by Dale for $8,500; Chester Dale, New York, 1930–62; National Gallery of Art, Washington, D.C. (Chester Dale Collection), 1963.10.98.
EXHIBITIONS: 1908 Paris, no. 6, as *Le Miroir*, lent by M.R.M. . . . ; 1915 New York Masterpieces, no. 50, as *Mother with Baby Reflected in Mirror*; 1928 Pittsburgh, no. 3, as *Child Looking into Mirror*.
REFERENCES: Havemeyer 1931, p. 507, as *La Femme au tournesol*; Breeskin 1970,

no. 473, as *Mother Wearing a Sunflower on Her Dress*; Weitzenhoffer 1986, pp. 217f., ill. p. 225, pl. 151.

61
Mary Cassatt
MOTHER AND CHILD
Oil on canvas, 39 ⅝ x 32 ⅛ in.
(100.7 x 81.6 cm)
Signed l.l.: *Mary Cassatt*
PROVENANCE: Durand-Ruel, Paris, bought from the artist, Oct. 15, 1908, for Fr 6,000 (stock no. 8856, as *Jeune femme allaitant son enfant*); Durand-Ruel, New York, bought from Durand-Ruel, Paris, Dec. 17, 1908 (stock no. 3296); Mrs. H. O. Havemeyer, New York, bought from Durand-Ruel, Jan. 27, 1909, for $2,500; d. 1929; her sale, American Art Association, New York, Apr. 10, 1930, no. 83, as *Jeune femme allaitant son enfant*; bought at sale by Dale for $4,800; Chester Dale, New York, from 1930; Art Institute of Chicago (Gift of Alexander Stewart), 1956.760.
EXHIBITIONS: 1908 Paris, no. 22, as *Jeune femme allaitant son enfant*; 1909 Boston, no. 8; 1915 New York Masterpieces, no. 49, as *Mother and Baby in Pink and Lilac*; 1926–27 Chicago, possibly one of nos. 13–18, all as *Mother and Child*; 1927 Philadelphia, possibly one of nos. 15–21, all as *Mother and Child*; 1928 Pittsburgh; Dallas Art Association(?), listed in Mrs. Havemeyer's 1930 sale cat.

York, 1913–14 (deposit no. 11686); Mrs. H. O. Havemeyer, New York, bought Apr. 13, 1915, probably from the artist; d. 1929; MMA 29.100.49.
EXHIBITION: 1915 New York Masterpieces, no. 54, as *Mère et enfant*.
REFERENCES: Havemeyer 1931, p. 175; Havemeyer 1958, p. 4, no. 9; Breeskin 1970, no. 600; Weitzenhoffer 1986, p. 255, ill. p. 225.

65
Mary Cassatt
MOTHER AND SLEEPING CHILD*
Pastel on paper mounted on canvas, 26⅝ x 22½ in. (67.6 x 57.2 cm)
Signed l.l.: *Mary Cassatt*
PROVENANCE: Durand-Ruel, Paris, bought from the artist, May 25, 1914 (stock no. 10570); Mrs. H. O. Havemeyer, New York, bought from Durand-Ruel, May 28, 1914, for Fr 8,000; d. 1929; MMA 29.100.50.
EXHIBITION: 1915 New York Masterpieces, no. 57, as *Child Asleep on Mother's Shoulder*
REFERENCES: Havemeyer 1931, pp. 174f., ill.; Havemeyer 1958, p. 4, no. 10; Breeskin 1970, no. 599; Weitzenhoffer 1986, pp. 216, 219, 255, pl. 150.

66
Jean-Charles Cazin
French, 1841–1901
PAINTING***
Oil on canvas
PROVENANCE: Mr. and Mrs. H. O. Havemeyer, New York, until 1907; Mrs. H. O. Havemeyer, New York, 1907–8; Durand-Ruel, New York, bought from Havemeyer, Dec. 1908.
REFERENCE: Weitzenhoffer 1986, p. 184.

67
Paul Cézanne
French, 1839–1906
THE ABDUCTION
Oil on canvas, 35½ x 46 in. (90.2 x 116.8 cm)
Signed and dated l.l.: *67 Cezanne*
PROVENANCE: Emile Zola, Paris, d. 1902; his sale, Mar. 9–13, 1903, no. 115; bought at sale by Vollard; Ambroise Vollard, Paris, 1903; Mr. and Mrs. H. O. Havemeyer, New York, bought from Vollard for Fr 6,000 and shipped to them by Durand-Ruel, May 7, 1903; until 1907; Mrs. H. O. Havemeyer, New York, 1907–29; her sale, American Art Association, New York, Apr. 10, 1930, no. 80; bought at sale by Dale for $24,000; Chester Dale, New York, from 1930; Galerie F. Bignou, Paris; Société de la Peinture Contemporaine, Lu-

cerne; its sale, Galerie Charpentier, Paris, June 26, 1934, no. 4; Wildenstein, London, until 1935; J. Maynard Keynes, London, bought from Wildenstein, 1935–46; The Provost and Fellows of King's College, Cambridge University (Keynes Collection), on loan to the Fitzwilliam Museum, Cambridge.
EXHIBITION: 1917 New York.
REFERENCES: Havemeyer 1931, p. 501, as *Academic—Landscape with Nude Figures*; Venturi 1936, no. 101; Weitzenhoffer 1986, pp. 147, 258, colorpl. 116.

68
Paul Cézanne
GUSTAVE BOYER IN A STRAW HAT*
Oil on canvas, 21⅝ x 15¼ in. (54.9 x 38.7 cm)
Signed l.r.: *P. Cezanne*
PROVENANCE: Ambroise Vollard, Paris, until 1903; Mr. and Mrs. H. O. Havemeyer, New York, bought from Vollard for Fr 1,500 and shipped to them by Durand-Ruel, May 7, 1903; until 1907; Mrs. H. O. Havemeyer, New York, 1907–29; MMA 29.100.65.
REFERENCES: Havemeyer 1931, pp. 58f., ill., as *Portrait—Man with a Straw Hat*; Venturi 1936, no. 131; Havemeyer 1958, p. 13, no. 63; Sterling and Salinger 1967, pp. 97f., ill.; Weitzenhoffer 1986, pp. 147, 256, pl. 117.

69
Paul Cézanne
FLOWERS IN A GLASS VASE
Oil on canvas, 16⅜ x 13⅛ in. (41.6 x 33.3 cm)
PROVENANCE: Mr. and Mrs. H. O. Havemeyer, New York, probably bought from Vollard in 1901; until 1907; Mrs. H. O. Havemeyer, New York, 1907–29; her son, Horace Havemeyer, New York, 1929–34; deposited with Durand-Ruel, New York, in 1931 (deposit no. 8472); The Denver Art Museum, given anonymously by Havemeyer in 1934; deaccessioned and sold, May 14, 1949; M. Knoedler and Co., New York, received on consignment from Denver, June 1949 (stock no. CA 3310); Dr. and Mrs. David M. Levy, New York, bought from Knoedler, June 1949; Adele R. Levy Fund, Inc., New York, until 1962; The Putnam Foundation/Timken Museum of Art, San Diego (given by the Levy Fund in 1962).
REFERENCES: Havemeyer 1931, p. 330; Venturi 1936, no. 184; Weitzenhoffer 1986, p. 142, pl. 105.

70
Paul Cézanne
WINTER LANDSCAPE OF AUVERS
Oil on canvas, 23½ x 19¼ in.

(59.7 x 48.9 cm)
Signed l.l.: *P.Cezanne*
PROVENANCE: Mr. and Mrs. H. O. Havemeyer, New York, possibly bought from Vollard in 1901; until 1907; Mrs. H. O. Havemeyer, New York, 1907–29; her son, Horace Havemeyer, New York, 1929–56; his widow, Doris Dick Havemeyer, New York, 1956–82; her sale, Sotheby's, New York, May 18, 1983, no. 7, as *La Route tournante à Auvers*, mistakenly sold for $467,500; sale canceled; her son Horace Havemeyer, Jr., New York, 1983–90; sale, Sotheby's, New York, May 17, 1990, no. 10, as *La Route tournante à Auvers*; bought at sale by Muira for $1,760,000.
REFERENCES: Havemeyer 1931, p. 328; Venturi 1936, p. 348, no no. Weitzenhoffer 1986, p. 142, colorpl. 106.

71
Paul Cézanne
SELF-PORTRAIT WITH A CAP***
Oil on canvas, 20⅞ x 15 in. (53 x 38.1 cm)
PROVENANCE: Ambroise Vollard, Paris, until 1904; Mr. and Mrs. H. O. Havemeyer, New York, bought from Vollard, shipped by Durand-Ruel via Mr. Huss, Dec. 29, 1904; until 1907; Mrs. H. O. Havemeyer, New York, 1907–9; consigned to Durand-Ruel, New York, May 25, 1909 (deposit no. 7551); delivered to Durand-Ruel, Paris, June 1909 (deposit no. 11445); Durand-Ruel, Paris, bought from Havemeyer, Aug. 31, 1909, for Fr 7,500 (stock no. 9147); Ivan Abramovich Morozov, Moscow, bought from Durand-Ruel, Sept. 14, 1909, for Fr 30,000 with *The Banks of the Marne* (A77); Museum of Modern Western Art, Moscow, from 1918; museum collection cat., 1928, no. 555; Hermitage State Museum, St. Petersburg, from 1930.
REFERENCES: Venturi 1936, no. 289; Havemeyer 1961, p. 8; Weitzenhoffer 1986, pp. 156, 191, pl. 124.

72
Paul Cézanne
STILL LIFE WITH JAR, CUP, AND APPLES*
Oil on canvas, 23⅞ x 29 in. (60.6 x 73.7 cm)
PROVENANCE: Mr. and Mrs. H. O. Havemeyer, New York, until 1907; Mrs. H. O. Havemeyer, New York, 1907–29; MMA 29.100.66.
Note: On May 11, 1907, Durand-Ruel, Paris, shipped a Cézanne "Fruits" (deposit no. 11185), along with several other works, to Havemeyer. It can probably be identified either as this picture or as A78.
REFERENCES: Havemeyer 1931, pp. 58f., ill.; Venturi 1936, no. 213; Havemeyer 1958, p. 13, no. 65; Sterling and Salinger 1967, pp. 98f., ill.; Weitzenhoffer 1986, p. 256.

68

72

76

69

73

77

70

74

78

71

75

79

73
Paul Cézanne
FLOWERS
Oil on canvas, 21¾ x 16¾ in.
(55.3 x 42.6 cm)
PROVENANCE: Mr. and Mrs. H. O. Have-meyer, New York, probably bought from Vollard in 1901; until 1907; Mrs. H. O. Havemeyer, New York, 1907–29; her son, Horace Havemeyer, 1929–42; The Brooklyn Museum (Gift of Mrs. Horace Havemeyer, 1942), 42.197; Wildenstein and Co., New York, bought from The Brooklyn Museum, June 15, 1966; Paul Mellon, Upperville, Va., bought from Wildenstein, Nov. 1967; his sale, Christie's, New York, Nov. 15, 1983, no. 11; bought at sale by a private collector, Switzerland, for $286,000; Galerie Schmit, Paris, bought from the Swiss collector; private collection, Paris, bought from Schmit about 1986.
REFERENCES: Havemeyer 1931, p. 329; Venturi 1936, p. 348, no no.; Weitzen-hoffer 1986, p. 142, colorpl. 104, as in the collection of Franz Heinz, Munich.

74
Paul Cézanne
MONT SAINTE-VICTOIRE AND THE VIADUCT OF THE ARC RIVER VALLEY*
Oil on canvas, 25¾ x 32⅛ in.
(65.4 x 81.6 cm)
PROVENANCE: Ambroise Vollard, Paris; Mr. and Mrs. H. O. Havemeyer, New York, bought from Vollard for Fr 15,000; until 1907; Mrs. H. O. Havemeyer, New York, 1907–29; MMA 29.100.64.
REFERENCES: Havemeyer 1931, pp. 56f., ill., as *Landscape—Paysage du Midi*; Venturi 1936, no. 452; Havemeyer 1958, p. 13, no. 62, ill.; Sterling and Salinger 1967, pp. 107f., ill.; Weitzenhoffer 1986, pp. 142f., 256, pl. 108.

75
Paul Cézanne
THE GULF OF MARSEILLES SEEN FROM L'ESTAQUE*
Oil on canvas, 28¾ x 39½ in.
(73 x 100.3 cm)
PROVENANCE: Mr. and Mrs. H. O. Have-meyer, New York, possibly bought through Vollard; until 1907; Mrs. H. O. Havemeyer, New York, 1907–29; MMA 29.100.67.
REFERENCES: Havemeyer 1931, pp. 56f., ill., as *Landscape—L'Estaque*; Venturi 1936, no. 429; Havemeyer 1958, p. 12, no. 61; Sterling and Salinger 1967, pp. 105f., ill.; Weitzenhoffer 1986, p. 256.

76
Paul Cézanne
STILL LIFE: FLOWERS IN A VASE
Oil on canvas, 18¼ x 21⅞ in.
(46.4 x 55.6 cm)

PROVENANCE: Mr. and Mrs. H. O. Have-meyer, New York, possibly bought from Vollard in 1906; until 1907; Mrs. H. O. Havemeyer, New York, 1907–29; her son, Horace Havemeyer, New York, 1929–56; his widow, Doris Dick Havemeyer, New York, 1956–82; her sale, Sotheby's, New York, May 18, 1983, no. 10; bought at sale by a private collector for $2,090,000; private collection.
REFERENCES: Havemeyer 1931, p. 329; Venturi 1936, p. 348, no no.; Weitzen-hoffer 1986, p. 167, colorpl. 131.

77
Paul Cézanne
THE BANKS OF THE MARNE***
Oil on canvas, 25½ x 31⅞ in.
(64.8 x 81 cm)
PROVENANCE: Mr. and Mrs. H. O. Have-meyer, New York, possibly bought from Vollard in 1906; until 1907; Mrs. H. O. Havemeyer, New York, 1907–9; consigned to Durand-Ruel, New York, May 25, 1909 (deposit no. 7552, as *Castle on a Lake*); delivered to Durand-Ruel, Paris, June 1909 (deposit no. 11446); Durand-Ruel, Paris, bought from Havemeyer, Aug. 31, 1909, for Fr 7,500 (stock no. 9148); Ivan Abramovich Morozov, Moscow, bought from Durand-Ruel, Sept. 14, 1909, for Fr 30,000 with *Self-Portrait with a Cap* (A71); Museum of Modern Western Art, Moscow, from 1918; museum collection cat., 1928, no. 559; Hermitage State Museum, St. Petersburg, from 1930.
REFERENCES: Venturi 1936, no. 630; Havemeyer 1961, p. 8; Weitzenhoffer 1986, pp. 167, 191, pl. 130.

78
Paul Cézanne
STILL LIFE WITH A GINGER JAR AND EGGPLANTS
Oil on canvas, 28½ x 36 in.
(72.4 x 91.4 cm)
PROVENANCE: Ambroise Vollard, Paris, in 1899–1900; Mr. and Mrs. H. O. Have-meyer, New York, until 1907; Mrs. H. O. Havemeyer, New York, 1907–29; her son, Horace Havemeyer, New York, 1929–48; M. Knoedler and Co., New York, on consignment from Havemeyer from Sept. 1948 (stock no. CA 3141); Stephen C. Clark, New York, bought from Knoedler, Nov. 1948–60; MMA (Bequest of Stephen C. Clark, 1960), 61.101.4.
Note: On May 11, 1907, Durand-Ruel, Paris shipped a Cézanne *Fruits* (dep. no. 11185), along with several other works, to Havemeyer. It can probably be identified either as this picture or as A72.
EXHIBITION: 1928 New York, no. 4.
REFERENCES: Havemeyer 1931, p. 329; Venturi 1936, no. 597; Sterling and Salin-

ger 1967, pp. 111f., ill.; Weitzenhoffer 1986, p. 142, pl. 107.

79
Paul Cézanne
ROCKS IN THE FOREST
Oil on canvas, 28⅞ x 36⅜ in.
(73.3 x 92.4 cm)
PROVENANCE: Ambroise Vollard, Paris, in 1899–1900; Durand-Ruel, Paris; Mr. and Mrs. H. O. Havemeyer, New York, until 1907; Mrs. H. O. Havemeyer, New York, 1907–29; MMA 29.100.194.
REFERENCES: Havemeyer 1931, p. 37, as *Landscape—Forest of Fontainebleau*; Venturi 1936, no. 673; Havemeyer 1958, p. 13, no. 64; Sterling and Salinger 1967, p. 117, ill.

80
Jean Siméon Chardin, Attributed to
French, 1699–1779
PORTRAIT OF A WOMAN WITH A FAN
Oil on canvas, 39 x 32½ in.
(99.1 x 82.6 cm)
PROVENANCE: Henri Michel-Lévy, Paris; Mr. and Mrs. H. O. Havemeyer, New York, possibly bought through Cassatt, summer 1906; until 1907; Mrs. H. O. Havemeyer, New York, 1907–29; her daughter Adaline Havemeyer Freling-huysen, Morristown, N.J., from 1929.
REFERENCES: Guiffrey [1907], no. 162, as Attributed to Chardin, in the collection of M. Léon Michel-Lévy [sic]; Havemeyer 1931, p. 330, as *Portrait of a Woman*; Wildenstein 1933, no. 544, as possibly by Jacques-André-Joseph Aved (1702–1766).

81
William Merritt Chase
American, 1849–1916
AZALEAS (VASE OF FLOWERS)
Oil on canvas, 31 x 37 in. (78.7 x 94 cm)
Signed u.r.: *W. M. Chase*
PROVENANCE: Mr. and Mrs. H. O. Have-meyer, New York, bought from the artist; Mrs. H. O. Havemeyer, New York, 1907–29; her sale, American Art Association, New York, Apr. 10, 1930, no. 42, as

Vase of Flowers; bought at sale by A. R. Black or A. D. Whiteside for $1,500; Berry-Hill Galleries, New York, until 1965; Lawrence A. Fleischman, Detroit; Kennedy Galleries, New York, 1966; Mr. and Mrs. Aaron J. Boggs, Washington, D.C., 1966–86; Hirschl and Adler Galleries, New York, 1986; private collection, from 1986.
EXHIBITION: 1892 New York.
REFERENCE: Havemeyer 1931, p. 508, as *Still Life—Flowers*.

82
Paul Jean Clays
Belgian, 1819–1900
ON THE SHELDT***
PROVENANCE: E. LeRoy et Cie, Paris, until 1886; M. Knoedler and Co., New York, bought from LeRoy, Sept. 18, 1886, for Fr 2,400, as *Cabane* (stock no. 5336); Mr. and Mrs. H. O. Havemeyer, New York, bought from Knoedler, Dec. 7, 1886, for $850, as *On the Sheldt*.
Note: This work can probably be identified as one of two seascapes by Clays sold by the Havemeyers to Durand-Ruel: one consigned to Durand-Ruel, Nov. 1895, and bought by the gallery, Mar. 11, 1898, and the other bought by Durand-Ruel, Feb. 4, 1899.

83
Paul Jean Clays
SEASCAPE
Oil on canvas, 28¾ x 43 in.
(73 x 109.2 cm)
Signed: *P. J. Clays*
PROVENANCE: Mrs. H. O. Havemeyer, New York, consigned to Durand-Ruel, Nov. 30, 1908–Aug. 20, 1909, as *Marine*; d. 1929; her daughter Adaline Havemeyer Frelinghuysen, Morristown, N.J., from 1929.
REFERENCES: Havemeyer 1931, p. 331; Weitzenhoffer 1986, p. 184.

84
François Clouet, Attributed to
French, fl. by 1536; d. 1572
PORTRAIT OF A MAN
Oil on wood, 15½ x 10¾ in.
(39.4 x 27.3 cm)

PROVENANCE: Mrs. H. O. Havemeyer, New York, d. 1929; her sale, American Art Association, New York, Apr. 10, 1930, no. 121, as *Portrait of a Gentleman with Fur Collar*, by a follower of Bartholomeus Bruyn (Dutch, 16th century); bought at sale by F. Kouchakji for $525.
REFERENCES: Havemeyer 1931, p. 501; Weitzenhoffer 1986, pp. 257f., erroneously identified.

85
Pieter Jacobs Codde
Dutch, 1599–1678
A DUTCH FAMILY
Oil on wood, 15 x 20 in. (38.1 x 50.8 cm)
Dated l.l.: *1672*
PROVENANCE: Baron E. de Beurnonville, Paris; his sale, 3, rue Chastal, Paris, May 9–16, 1881, no. 236, for Fr 7,000; E. Secrétan, Paris; his sale, Galerie Charles

Sedelmeyer, Paris, July 1–7, 1889, no. 105; bought at sale by Durand-Ruel for Havemeyer for Fr 11,000 (stock no. 2400); Mr. and Mrs. H. O. Havemeyer, New York, 1889–1907; Mrs. H. O. Havemeyer, New York, 1907–29; her sale, American Art Association, New York, Apr. 10, 1930, no. 94; bought at sale by William Brown for $2,200.
REFERENCES: Havemeyer 1931, p. 497, as *Interior with Figures—A Dutch Family*; Weitzenhoffer 1982, pp. 109, 119, n. 24, p. 127; Weitzenhoffer 1986, p. 64.

86
Samuel Colman
American, 1832–1920
VENICE: THE DOGE'S PALACE AND CAMPANILE
Watercolor, 39½ x 26½ in.
(100.3 x 67.3 cm)
Signed and dated l.l.: *Saml. Colman 1880*
PROVENANCE: Mrs. H. O. Havemeyer, New York, d. 1929; her sale, American Art Association, New York, Apr. 10, 1930, no. 27, for $70.
REFERENCES: Havemeyer 1931, p. 509; Weitzenhoffer 1982, p. 49, n. 14.

87
Samuel Colman
SPANISH PEAKS, SOUTHERN COLORADO, LATE AFTERNOON***

Oil on canvas, 31⅛ x 72¼ in.
(79.1 x 183.5 cm)
Signed and dated l.r.: *Samuel Colman 1887*
PROVENANCE: Samuel Colman, New York, until 1893; his sale, Fifth Avenue Art Galleries, New York, Mar. 29, 1893, no. 51; bought at sale by Havemeyer for $700; H. O. Havemeyer, New York, 1893; MMA (Gift of H. O. Havemeyer, 1893), 93.21.
EXHIBITIONS: 1890 New York, no. 4; 1896 New York, no. 268.
REFERENCES: Weitzenhoffer 1982, pp. 268, 281f., n. 33, fig. 95; Spassky et al. 1985, pp. 354f., ill.; Weitzenhoffer 1986, p. 118.

88
Samuel Colman
AUTUMN TWILIGHT: FARMINGTON, CONNECTICUT
Watercolor, 10 x 17 in. (25.4 x 43.2 cm)
Signed and dated l.l.: *Saml. Colman 1888*
PROVENANCE: Mrs. H. O. Havemeyer, New York, d. 1929; her sale, American Art Association, New York, Apr. 10, 1930, no. 25, bought at sale by W. Willett for $70.
REFERENCES: Havemeyer 1931, p. 508; Weitzenhoffer 1982, p. 49, n. 14.

89
Samuel Colman
MT. HOOD, COLUMBIA RIVER
Watercolor, 9 x 21½ in. (22.9 x 54.6 cm)
Signed and dated l.r.: *Saml. Colman 1888*
PROVENANCE: Goupil, New York, sold to Havemeyer; Mrs. H. O. Havemeyer, New York, d. 1929; her sale, American Art Association, New York, Apr. 10, 1930, no. 16, for $60.
REFERENCES: Havemeyer 1931, p. 508; Weitzenhoffer 1982, p. 49, n. 14.

90
Samuel Colman
MOJAVE DESERT, CALIFORNIA
Watercolor, 9 x 20 in. (22.9 x 50.8 cm)
Signed and dated l.r.: *Saml. Colman 1888*
PROVENANCE: Mrs. H. O. Havemeyer, New York, d. 1929; her sale, American Art Association, New York, Apr. 10, 1930, no. 17; bought at sale by J. W. Spencer for $60.
REFERENCES: Havemeyer 1931, p. 508; Weitzenhoffer 1982, p. 49, n. 14.

91
Samuel Colman
DUTCH LANDSCAPE
Oil on canvas, 9 x 12½ in. (22.9 x 31.8 cm)

Signed l.r.: *Saml. Colman*
PROVENANCE: Mrs. H. O. Havemeyer, New York, d. 1929; her sale, American Art Association, New York, Apr. 10, 1930, no. 7, as *Dutch Canal with Windmills*; bought at sale by Meade for $80.
REFERENCES: Havemeyer 1931, p. 508; Weitzenhoffer 1982, p. 49, n. 14.

92
Samuel Colman
EARLY EVENING: OSSIPEE, NEW HAMPSHIRE
Watercolor, 8½ x 12½ in. (21.6 x 31.8 cm)
Signed l.l.: *Saml. Colman*
PROVENANCE: Mrs. H. O. Havemeyer, New York, d. 1929; her sale, American Art Association, New York, Apr. 10, 1930, no. 4, for $40.
REFERENCES: Havemeyer 1931, p. 508; Weitzenhoffer 1982, p. 49, n. 14.

93
Samuel Colman
LAKESIDE LANDSCAPE WITH FIGURE AND CATTLE
Watercolor, 9½ x 20 in. (24.1 x 50.8 cm)
Signed l.r.: *Saml. Colman*
PROVENANCE: Mrs. H. O. Havemeyer, New York, d. 1929; her sale, American Art Association, New York, Apr. 10, 1930, no. 13; bought at sale by M. Tannenbaum for $50.
REFERENCES: Havemeyer 1931, p. 508; Weitzenhoffer 1982, p. 49, n. 14.

94
Samuel Colman
VIEW OF AMSTERDAM MARKET
Oil on canvas, 8½ x 11 in.
(21.6 x 27.9 cm)
Signed l.l.: *Saml. Colman*
PROVENANCE: Mrs. H. O. Havemeyer, New York, d. 1929; her sale, American Art Association, New York, Apr. 10, 1930, no. 5, as *Marche Neuf: Amsterdam*; bought at sale by Charles Henry for $55.
REFERENCES: Havemeyer 1931, p. 508; Weitzenhoffer 1982, p. 49, n. 14.

95
John Constable
British, 1776–1837
LANDSCAPE***
PROVENANCE: Mr. and Mrs. H. O. Havemeyer, New York, consigned to Durand-Ruel, New York, Jan. 27–Mar. 31, 1899.

96
Corneille de Lyon, Attributed to
Dutch, fl. by 1533; d. 1575
ANNE DE PISSELEU (1508–1576), DUCHESSE D'ETAMPES

96

Oil on wood, 7 x 5⅝ in. (17.8 x 14.3 cm)
PROVENANCE: James Alexandre, comte de Pourtalès-Gorgier, d. 1855; sale, Pillet, Paris, Mar. 27–Apr. 4, 1865, no. 234, as by Clouet; Alfred Mame, Tours, 1865–93; his son, Paul Mame, Tours, from 1893; his sale, Galerie Georges Petit, Paris, Apr. 26–29, 1904, no. 8, as by Clouet; bought at sale by Durand-Ruel for Havemeyer for Fr 30,000; Mr. and Mrs. H. O. Havemeyer, New York, 1904–7; Mrs. H. O. Havemeyer, New York, 1907–29; MMA 29.100.197.
EXHIBITIONS: 1890 Tours, pl. VI of the Album de l'exposition rétrospective, as *Portrait de Claude de France*, probably by Jean Clouet, lent by Alfred Mame; 1904 Paris, no. 175.
REFERENCES: Havemeyer 1931, pp. 60f., ill., as *Portrait of a Lady*, by Corneille de Lyon, attributed also to Jean Clouet; Sterling 1955, pp. 34f., ill.; Havemeyer 1958, p. 13, no. 66; Weitzenhoffer 1986, p. 155.

97
Corneille de Lyon, Attributed to
PORTRAIT OF A MAN*
Oil on wood, 6⅞ x 6⅛ in.
(17.5 x 15.6 cm)
PROVENANCE: Mr. and Mrs. H. O. Havemeyer, New York, bought from Durand-Ruel, Paris, in 1889; until 1907; Mrs. H. O. Havemeyer, New York, 1907–29; MMA 29.100.22.
REFERENCES: Havemeyer 1931, pp. 60f., ill., as by Corneille de Lyon, formerly at-

tributed to François Clouet, dit Janet; Sterling 1955, p. 36, ill.; Havemeyer 1958, p. 13, no. 67; Weitzenhoffer 1986, p. 255, as by Clouet.

98
Jean-Baptiste-Camille Corot
French, 1796–1875
The following information concerns three Corot landscapes bought from M. Knoedler and Co. that may correspond to A112, 118, 119, 120, or 121:
PROVENANCE: Baguet et Cie, Paris, until 1880; M. Knoedler and Co., New York, bought from Baguet, Sept. 1, 1880, for Fr 6,500, as *Roches en Berri* (stock no. 2802); H. O. Havemeyer, New York, bought from Knoedler, Sept. 29, 1881, for $2,000, as *Roche de Berri*.
REFERENCES: Weitzenhoffer 1982, pp. 41, 49, n. 19; Weitzenhoffer 1986, p. 33.
PROVENANCE: F. Simonson, Paris, until 1886; M. Knoedler and Co., New York, bought from Simonson, Sept. 11, 1886, for Fr 1,000, as *Paysage* (stock no. 5351); Mr. and Mrs. H. O. Havemeyer, New York, bought from Knoedler, Jan. 18, 1887, for $400 plus the return of Girard's *Ladies Caught in the Rain* (A289), as *Study of Trees*.
PROVENANCE: William Schaus, New York; his sale, Fifth Avenue Art Galleries, New York, Mar. 8, 1892, no. 52, as *The Meadow*, 16½ x 12 in.; bought at sale by Knoedler for $2,100; M. Knoedler and Co., New York, 1892 (stock no. 7110); Mr. and Mrs. H. O. Havemeyer, New York, bought from Knoedler, Mar. 10, 1892, for $2,500, as *The Meadow*.

PORTRAIT OF A CHILD
Oil on wood, 12⅝ x 9¼ in.
(32.1 x 23.5 cm)
Signed l.l.: *COROT*
PROVENANCE: Mr. and Mrs. H. O. Havemeyer, New York, by 1891–1907; Mrs. H. O. Havemeyer, New York, 1907–29; MMA 29.100.564.
REFERENCES: Havemeyer 1931, p. 68, as *Portrait of Rosa Bonheur*; Havemeyer 1958, p. 15, no. 75; Sterling and Salinger 1966, pp. 47f., ill.; Weitzenhoffer 1982, p. 143, n. 19.

99
Jean-Baptiste-Camille Corot
WOMAN IN THOUGHT
Oil on canvas, 19 x 16 in. (48.3 x 40.6 cm)
Signed l.l.: *COROT*
PROVENANCE: Alfred Robaut, bought from the artist in 1858; Mr. and Mrs. H. O. Havemeyer, New York, bought from Durand-Ruel, Aug. 31, 1899, for $5,000 or Fr 25,000; until 1907; Mrs. H. O. Have-

98

100

99

101

102

meyer, New York, 1907–29; her son, Horace Havemeyer, New York, 1929–34; The Denver Art Museum (Gift of Horace Havemeyer in memory of William D. Lippitt), 1934.13.
REFERENCES: Robaut 1905, no. 1041, as *La femme à la pensée*; Havemeyer 1931, pp. 340f., ill.

100
Jean-Baptiste-Camille Corot
THE DESTRUCTION OF SODOM*
Oil on canvas, 36⅜ x 71⅜ in.
(92.4 x 181.3 cm)
Signed l.r.: COROT.
PROVENANCE: Durand-Ruel, Paris, 1868–73; Count Abram de Camondo, Paris, bought from Durand-Ruel in 1873 for Fr 20,000; d. 1889; his son, Count Isaac de Camondo, Paris, 1889; Durand-Ruel, Paris, bought from Camondo in 1889 for Fr 100,000 (stock no. 2409); Mr. and Mrs. H. O. Havemeyer, New York, bought from Durand-Ruel, Aug. 1, 1889, for Fr 125,000; until 1907; Mrs. H. O. Havemeyer, New York, 1907–29; MMA 29.100.18.
EXHIBITIONS: 1844 Paris, no. 399; 1857 Paris, no. 593; 1865 Toulouse(?); 1875 Paris Corot, no. 209; 1890–91 New York,

no. 6; 1893 Chicago, no. 2886, as *The Flight from Sodom*, lent by Mr. Henry O. Havemeyer, New York.
REFERENCES: Robaut 1905, nos. 460, 1097; Havemeyer 1931, pp. 72f., ill.; Havemeyer 1958, p. 14, no. 78; Sterling and Salinger 1966, pp. 52–54, ill.; Weitzenhoffer 1982, pp. 112, 115, 131f., 187f., fig. 20; Weitzenhoffer 1986, pp. 60, 66, 89, 255, pl. 18.

101
Jean-Baptiste-Camille Corot
WOMAN AT A FOUNTAIN
Oil on canvas, 24¼ x 17 in.
(62.9 x 43.2 cm)
Signed l.r.: COROT
PROVENANCE: Possibly Ernest Hoschedé, Paris; his sale, Paris, Apr. 20, 1875, no. 16, for Fr 2,350; private collection; sale, Paris, Mar. 4, 1878, for Fr 2,500; Paul Michel-Lévy; his sale, Paris, Oct. 16, 1889, for Fr 5,500; bought at sale by Durand-Ruel; Camentron, until 1898; Durand-Ruel, Paris, bought from Camentron, Jan. 18, 1898, for Fr 16,500 (stock no. 4530); Mrs. H. O. Havemeyer, New York, d. 1929; her daughter Adaline Havemeyer Freling-

huysen, Morristown, N.J., 1929–63; private collection.
REFERENCES: Robaut 1905, no. 1342, as *La Rêveuse à la fontaine*; Havemeyer 1931, p. 334.

102
Jean-Baptiste-Camille Corot
REVERIE
Oil on wood, 19⅝ x 14⅜ in.
(49.9 x 36.5 cm)
Signed l.l.: COROT
PROVENANCE: Hadengue-Sandras, Paris; sale, Hôtel Drouot, Paris, Feb. 2–3, 1880, no. 17, for Fr 1,305; Brame, Paris, until 1897; Durand-Ruel, Paris, bought from Brame père, Apr. 22, 1897, for Fr 11,000 (stock no. 4180, as *Figure de femme, rêverie*); Durand-Ruel, New York, received on deposit from Durand-Ruel, Paris, Mar. 7, 1899 (deposit no. 5824, as *Rêverie*); bought from Paris, Aug. 31, 1899 (Paris stock book), or Mar. 28, 1899 (New York stock book, no. 2169, as *Rêverie*); Mr. and Mrs. H. O. Havemeyer, New York, bought from Durand-Ruel, Feb. 7, 1903, for $8,000; until 1907; Mrs. H. O. Havemeyer, New York, 1907–29; MMA 29.100.563.

103

105

107

104

106

108

EXHIBITION: 1920 New York.
REFERENCES: Robaut 1905, no. 1422, as *Bohémienne Rêveuse*; Havemeyer 1931, pp. 64f., ill.; Havemeyer 1958, p. 15, no. 76, ill.; Sterling and Salinger 1966, pp. 54f., ill.; Weitzenhoffer 1982, p. 312, n. 9, with erroneous acquisition date; Weitzenhoffer 1986, p. 245.

103
Jean-Baptiste-Camille Corot
MOTHER AND CHILD
Oil on wood, 12¾ x 8⅞ in.
(32.4 x 22.5 cm)
Signed l.r.: *COROT*

PROVENANCE: Cléophas, Paris, ceded to him by the artist in 1873/74; Jules Paros Paton, Paris; his sale, Hôtel Drouot, Paris, Apr. 24, 1883, no. 40; bought at sale by Doria for Fr 1,400; Count Armand Doria, Paris, from 1883; Mrs. H. O. Havemeyer, New York, probably by 1913; d. 1929; her daughter Adaline Havemeyer Frelinghuysen, Morristown, N.J., 1929–30; MMA (H. O. Havemeyer Collection, Gift of Mrs. P.H.B. Frelinghuysen, 1930), 30.13.
REFERENCES: Robaut 1905, no. 1380; Havemeyer 1931, pp. 66f., ill.; Havemeyer 1958, p. 14, no. 73; Sterling and Salinger 1966, p. 56, ill.

104
Jean-Baptiste-Camille Corot
THE MUSE: HISTORY
Oil on canvas, 18⅛ x 13⅞ in.
(46 x 35.2 cm)
Signed l.l.: *COROT*

PROVENANCE: Corot, Paris, d. 1875; his sale, Hôtel Drouot, Paris, May 26–28, 1875, no. 176, for Fr 1,005; Léon Michel-Lévy, Paris, from 1875; Durand-Ruel, Paris, bought from Michel-Lévy through Brame fils,* Jan. 25, 1899, for Fr 9,000 (stock no. 4995); Durand-Ruel, New York, bought from Durand-Ruel, Paris, June 7, 1899 (stock no. 2162); Mr. and Mrs. H. O. Havemeyer, New York, bought from Durand-Ruel, Mar. 8, 1899 (according to Paris stock book), or Apr. 6, 1899 (according to New York stock book); until 1907; Mrs. H. O. Havemeyer, New York, 1907–29; MMA 29.100.193.
*According to Brame letter of Jan. 23, 1992, Brame bought from Michel-Lévy, Jan. 26, 1899, and sold to Durand-Ruel, Jan. 28, 1899, for Fr 20,500.
EXHIBITIONS: 1871 Pau; 1895 Paris, no. 109.
REFERENCES: Robaut 1905, no. 1388, as *La Comédie*; Havemeyer 1931, pp. 62f., ill., as *Figure Piece—La Muse, Comédie*;

Havemeyer 1958, p. 15, no. 74, ill.; Sterling and Salinger 1966, pp. 56f., ill.; Weitzenhoffer 1982, p. 312, n. 9.

105
Jean-Baptiste-Camille Corot
GIRL WEAVING A GARLAND
Oil on canvas, 16½ x 11¾ in.
(41.9 x 29.9 cm)
Stamped l.r.: *VENTE / COROT*

PROVENANCE: Corot, Paris, d. 1875; his sale, Hôtel Drouot, Paris, May 29–30, 1875, no. 435; bought at sale by Doria for Fr 380; Count Armand Doria, Paris, from 1875; Mrs. H. O. Havemeyer, New York, d. 1929; MMA 29.100.562.
REFERENCES: Robaut 1905, no. 1337; Havemeyer 1931, p. 68; Havemeyer 1958, p. 14, no. 71; Sterling and Salinger 1966, pp. 57f., ill.

106
Jean-Baptiste-Camille Corot
BACCHANTE BY THE SEA*
Oil on wood, 15¼ x 23⅜ in.
(38.7 x 59.4 cm)
Signed and dated l.r.: *COROT 1865*
PROVENANCE: Possibly Count de

109

113

110

111

114

Camondo, Paris; Henri Vever, Paris, by 1895; his sale, Galerie Georges Petit, Paris, Feb. 2, 1897, no. 23; bought at sale by Durand-Ruel for Fr 30,750 (stock no. 4037, as *Nymphe couchée au bord de la mer*); Mr. and Mrs. H. O. Havemeyer, New York, bought from Durand-Ruel, Feb. 3, 1897, for Fr 31,500; consigned to Durand-Ruel, New York, Jan. 19–Feb. 14, 1898 (deposit no. 5657); until 1907; Mrs. H. O. Havemeyer, New York, 1907–29; MMA 29.100.19.
EXHIBITION: 1895 Paris, no. 139.
REFERENCES: Robaut 1905, no. 1376; Havemeyer 1931, pp. 70f., ill.; Havemeyer 1958, p. 14, no. 69; Sterling and Salinger 1966, p. 59, ill.; Weitzenhoffer 1982, p. 291, fig. 99; Weitzenhoffer 1986, pp. 126, 176, 255, pl. 78.

107
Jean-Baptiste-Camille Corot
BACCHANTE IN A LANDSCAPE
Oil on canvas, 12 ⅛ x 24 ¼ in.
(30.8 x 61.6 cm)
Signed l.l.: *COROT*
PROVENANCE: Jaquette; Bernheim-Jeune, Paris, until 1900; Durand-Ruel, Paris, bought from Bernheim-Jeune, Jan. 20,

1900, for Fr 12,000 (stock no. 5618, as *Femme nue couchée*); Durand-Ruel, New York, bought from Durand-Ruel, Paris, Feb. 20, 1901 (stock no. 2493); Mr. and Mrs. H. O. Havemeyer, New York, bought from Durand-Ruel, May 24, 1901, for $6,000; until 1907; Mrs. H. O. Havemeyer, New York, 1907–29; MMA 29.100.598.
REFERENCES: Robaut 1905, no. 1377; Havemeyer 1931, p. 69, ill.; Havemeyer 1958, p. 14, no. 68; Sterling and Salinger 1966, pp. 59f., ill.; Weitzenhoffer 1986, p. 176, pl. 134.

108
Jean-Baptiste-Camille Corot
THE LETTER
Oil on wood, 21 ½ x 14 ¼ in.
(54.6 x 36.2 cm)
Signed l.l.: *COROT*
PROVENANCE: Gustave Arosa, Paris; his sale, Hôtel Drouot, Paris, Feb. 25, 1878, no. 13; bought at sale by Pinart for Fr 3,300; Mrs. H. O. Havemeyer, New York, d. 1929; her son, Horace Havemeyer, New York, 1929; MMA (H. O. Havemeyer Collection, Gift of Horace Havemeyer, 1929), 29.160.33.
REFERENCES: Robaut 1905, no. 1426;

Havemeyer 1931, pp. 66f., ill.; Havemeyer 1958, p. 14, no. 72; Sterling and Salinger 1966, pp. 60f., ill.

109
Jean-Baptiste-Camille Corot
THE EEL GATHERERS
Oil on canvas, 23 ¾ x 32 in.
(60.3 x 81.3 cm)
Signed l.r.: *COROT*
PROVENANCE: Alfred de Knyff, Paris, in 1878; Erwin Davis, New York, until 1893; Durand-Ruel, New York, bought from Davis, May 1, 1893, for $10,000 (stock no. 1070, as *Les pêcheurs d'anguilles*); Mr. and Mrs. H. O. Havemeyer, New York, bought from Durand-Ruel, May 1, 1893, for $12,000; until 1907; Mrs. H. O. Havemeyer, New York, 1907–29; her daughter Adaline Havemeyer Frelinghuysen, Morristown, N.J., 1929–43; National Gallery of Art, Washington, D.C. (Gift of Mr. and Mrs. P.H.B. Frelinghuysen in memory of her father and mother, Mr. and Mrs. H. O. Havemeyer), 1943.15.1.
EXHIBITION: 1878 Paris, no. 204, lent by M. de Knyff.
REFERENCES: Robaut 1905, no. 1532 bis, as *La Rive verte*; Havemeyer 1931, p. 332; Weitzenhoffer 1982, pp. 199, 217, n. 3.

115

117

121

116

118

122

110

Jean-Baptiste-Camille Corot
MLLE DOBIGNY—THE RED DRESS
Oil on wood, 30¾ x 18½ in.
(78.1 x 47 cm)
Signed l.r.: *COROT*
PROVENANCE: Benoist; sale, Paris, Mar. 9,
1883, no. 9, for Fr 3,280; Bessonneau, An-
gers, in 1900; Bernheim-Jeune, Paris, until
1901; Durand-Ruel, Paris, bought from
Bernheim-Jeune, Mar. 29, 1901, for
Fr 555,000 (stock no. 6261); Mr. and Mrs.
H. O. Havemeyer, New York, bought from
Durand-Ruel, Apr. 22, 1901 (New York
stock book says July 12, 1901); until 1907;
Mrs. H. O. Havemeyer, New York, 1907–
29; her daughter Electra Havemeyer Webb,
New York, 1929–60; Shelburne Museum,
Shelburne, Vt., from 1960, 27.1.1–154.
EXHIBITION: 1900 Paris, no. 119.
REFERENCES: Robaut 1905, no. 1573, as
Orientale rêveuse; Havemeyer 1931,
pp. 336f., ill.; Weitzenhoffer 1986, p. 143,
colorpl. 109.

111

Jean-Baptiste-Camille Corot
YOUNG WOMEN OF SPARTA
Oil on canvas, 16½ x 29½ in.
(41.9 x 74.9 cm)
Signed l.l.: *COROT*
PROVENANCE: Michel-Lévy; his widow's

sale, Paris, Mar. 17, 1876, for Fr 1,700;
Paul Michel-Lévy; his sale, Hôtel Drouot,
Paris, Oct. 16, 1889, no. 2; bought at sale
by Durand-Ruel for Fr 8,000 (stock no.
2536, as *Jeune femme au repos*); Mr. and
Mrs. H. O. Havemeyer, New York, bought
from Durand-Ruel, Oct. 21, 1889, for
Fr 8,400; until 1907; Mrs. H. O. Have-
meyer, New York, 1907–29; her son, Hor-
ace Havemeyer, New York, 1929–42; The
Brooklyn Museum (Gift of Mrs. Horace
Havemeyer), 42.195.
REFERENCES: Robaut 1905, no. 1575, as
Jeunes filles de Sparte; Havemeyer 1931,
p. 345, as *Figure Piece—Gypsy Reclining*;
Weitzenhoffer 1982, p. 120, n. 33.

112

Jean-Baptiste-Camille Corot
LANDSCAPE
Oil on wood, 14 x 24⅞ in.
(35.6 x 63.2 cm)
Signed l.r.: *COROT*
PROVENANCE: Dr. Seymour or M. Stumpf,
in 1875; Mrs. H.O. Havemeyer, New
York, d. 1929; her daughter Adaline
Havemeyer Frelinghuysen, Morristown,
N.J., from 1929.
EXHIBITION: 1875 Paris Corot, no. 174 or
208.
REFERENCES: Robaut 1905, no. 1804(?);
Havemeyer 1931, p. 333.

113

Jean-Baptiste-Camille Corot
GREEK GIRL—MLLE DOBIGNY
Oil on canvas, 32¾ x 21½ in.
(83.2 x 54.6 cm)
Signed l.r.: *COROT*
PROVENANCE: John Saulnier, Bordeaux;
his sale, Hôtel Drouot, Paris, June 5, 1886,
no. 17, bought in for Fr 1,100; his sale,
Galerie Charles Sedelmeyer, Paris, Mar. 25,
1892, no. 3; bought at sale by Durand-
Ruel for Fr 4,500; Bernheim-Jeune, Paris,
from 1892 (stock no. 6.164, as *Jeune fille à
la grecque*); Durand-Ruel, Paris, bought
from Bernheim-Jeune, May 28, 1895, for
Fr 10,000 (stock no. 3315); Mr. and Mrs.
H. O. Havemeyer, New York, bought
from Durand-Ruel, Sept. 19, 1895, for
Fr 25,000; until 1907; Mrs. H. O. Havemeyer, New York, 1907–29; her daughter
Electra Havemeyer Webb, New York,
1929–60; Shelburne Museum, Shelburne,
Vt., from 1960, 27.1.1–149.
EXHIBITION: 1886 Paris Bayard, no. 48.
REFERENCES: Robaut 1905, no. 1995, as
La Jeune grecque; Havemeyer 1931,
pp. 338f., ill.; Weitzenhoffer 1982,
pp. 241f., fig. 80; Weitzenhoffer 1986,
p. 107, pl. 62.

114

Jean-Baptiste-Camille Corot
SIBYLLE

Oil on canvas, 32¼ x 25½ in.
(81.9 x 64.8 cm)
PROVENANCE: Alfred Robaut, Paris, until
1899; Durand-Ruel, Paris, bought from
Robaut, Feb. 21, 1899, for Fr 6,000 (stock
no. 5026, as *Italienne*); Durand-Ruel, New
York, bought from Durand-Ruel, Paris,
Jan. 25, 1900 (Paris stock book), or Dec.
8, 1899 (New York stock book, no. 2286);
Mr. and Mrs. H. O. Havemeyer, New
York, bought from Durand-Ruel, Feb. 7,
1903, for $6,000; until 1907; Mrs. H. O.
Havemeyer, New York, 1907–29; MMA
29.100.565.
REFERENCES: Robaut 1905, no. 2130;
Havemeyer 1931, pp. 64f., ill.; Havemeyer
1958, p. 15, no. 77, ill.; Sterling and Salinger
1966, pp. 65–67, ill.

115
Jean-Baptiste-Camille Corot
MOTHER, NURSE AND CHILD*
Oil on canvas, 24¼ x 19¾ in.
(61 6 x 50.2 cm)
Signed l.r.: *COROT*
PROVENANCE: sale, Hôtel Drouot, Paris,
Dec. 14, 1883, no. 13, for Fr 9,000; Mrs.
H. O. Havemeyer, New York, d. 1929; her
daughter Adaline Havemeyer Frelinghuysen, Morristown, N.J., 1929–63; private collection.
REFERENCES: Robaut 1905, no. 2143, as
Deux femmes jouant avec un enfant;
Havemeyer 1931, p. 335; Weitzenhoffer
1986, p. 255.

116
Jean-Baptiste-Camille Corot
THE ITALIAN WOMAN
Oil on canvas, 17½ x 14 in.
(44.5 x 35.6 cm)
Signed l.r.: *COROT*
PROVENANCE: M. Edwards, Paris, by
1878; his sale, Hôtel Drouot, Paris, Feb.
24, 1881, no. 9, for Fr 5,420; Adolphe
Tavernier, Paris; his sale, Galerie Georges
Petit, Paris, June 11, 1894, no. 2, as
Italienne assise, for Fr 4,950; Durand-Ruel,
New York, 1894; Mr. and Mrs. H. O. Havemeyer, New York, bought from Durand-
Ruel, Nov. 14, 1894; until 1907; Mrs.
H. O. Havemeyer, New York, 1907–29;
her son, Horace Havemeyer, New York,
1929–56; his widow, Doris Dick
Havemeyer, New York, 1956–82; her sale,
Sotheby's, New York, May 18, 1983, no.
4; bought at sale by Cherry for $715,000;
Wendell Cherry, Louisville and New York,
from 1983.
EXHIBITION: 1878 Paris Durand-Ruel,
no. 60.
REFERENCES: Robaut 1905, no. 2144, as
Juive d'Alger; Havemeyer 1931, p. 344;
Weitzenhoffer 1986, p. 147, pl. 119, with
erroneous acquisition date.

117
Jean-Baptiste-Camille Corot
THE ALBANIAN WOMAN
Oil on canvas, 29⅛ x 26 in. (74 x 66 cm)
PROVENANCE: Corot, d. 1875; his sale,
Hôtel Drouot, Paris, May 26–28, 1875,
no. 189; bought at sale by M. Detrimont
for Fr 2,150; Henri Vever, Paris, until
1893; Durand-Ruel, Paris, bought from
Vever, Oct. 24, 1893, for Fr 25,000 (stock
no. 2853, as *Italienne*); Durand-Ruel, New
York, bought from Durand-Ruel, Paris,
Nov. 16, 1893 (Paris stock book), or Dec.
5, 1893 (New York stock book, no. 1099,
as *Italienne*); Mr. and Mrs. H. O. Havemeyer, New York, bought from Durand-
Ruel, Jan. 16, 1894, for $7,000; until
1907; Mrs. H. O. Havemeyer, New York,
1907–29; her son, Horace Havemeyer,
New York, 1929–42; The Brooklyn Museum (Gift of Mrs. Horace Havemeyer),
42.196.
REFERENCES: Robaut 1905, no. 2147, as
L'Albanaise; Havemeyer 1931, pp. 342f.,
ill., as *Figure Piece—Italienne*; Weitzenhoffer 1982, pp. 225f., fig. 63; Weitzenhoffer 1986, p. 98.

118
Jean-Baptiste-Camille Corot
ARLEUX SEEN FROM THE PALLUEL
MARSHES
Oil on canvas, 12⅝ x 17 in.
(32.1 x 43.2 cm)
Signed l.l.: *COROT*
PROVENANCE: Mr. and Mrs. H. O. Havemeyer, New York, until 1907; Mrs. H. O.
Havemeyer, New York, from 1907; deposited with Durand-Ruel, June 12, 1908 (deposit no. 7482, as *Paysage et rivière*); her
daughter Adaline Havemeyer Frelinghuysen, Morristown, N.J.; returned to her
by Durand-Ruel, June 20, 1908.
REFERENCES: Robaut 1905, no. 2181, as
Arleux vu des marais de Palluel; Havemeyer 1931, p. 332, as *Landscape*.

119
Jean-Baptiste-Camille Corot
EVENING***
PROVENANCE: Mr. and Mrs. H. O. Havemeyer, New York; consigned to Durand-
Ruel, New York, Jan. 27, 1899; bought by
Durand-Ruel, Feb. 4, 1899.

120
Jean-Baptiste-Camille Corot
LANDSCAPE
Oil on wood, 11⅝ x 18¾ in.
(29.5 x 47.6 cm)
PROVENANCE: Mrs. H. O. Havemeyer,
New York, d. 1929; her daughter Adaline

Havemeyer Frelinghuysen, Morristown,
N.J., from 1929.
REFERENCE: Havemeyer 1931, p. 331.

121
Jean-Baptiste-Camille Corot
LANDSCAPE
Oil on canvas, 14½ x 19¼ in.
(36.8 x 48.9 cm)
Signed l.r.: *COROT*
PROVENANCE: Mrs. H. O. Havemeyer,
New York, d. 1929; her daughter Adaline
Havemeyer Frelinghuysen, Morristown,
N.J., 1929–63; private collection.
REFERENCE: Havemeyer 1931, p. 333.

122
Jean-Baptiste-Camille Corot
LANDSCAPE
Oil on canvas, 15½ x 21¼ in.
(39.4 x 54 cm)
Signed l.r.: *COROT*
PROVENANCE: Goupil, New York; Mrs.
H. O. Havemeyer, New York, d. 1929; her
sale, American Art Association, New York,
Apr. 10, 1930, no. 70, as *Paysage au bord
d'un lac*; bought at sale by O. B. Carrott
for $3,500.
Note: This picture may be the one bought
by the Havemeyers in 1888 as *Landscape
with Pond*, which has the following provenance: Max Kleber, Paris, until 1888;
Boussod, Valadon et Cie, Paris, bought
from Kleber, Sept. 5, 1888, for Fr 3,000
(stock no. 19452, as *Le Coteau*); M.
Knoedler and Co., New York, bought from
Boussod, Valadon, Sept. 5, 1888 (Boussod,
Valadon stock book), or Sept. 24, 1888
(Knoedler stock book, no. 6120, as *Le
Coteau*), for Fr 4,500; Mr. and Mrs. H. O.
Havemeyer, New York, bought from
Knoedler, Dec. 6, 1888, for $2,000, as
Landscape with Pond.
REFERENCE: Havemeyer 1931, p. 501.

123
Gustave Courbet
French, 1819–1877
THE KNIFE GRINDERS
Oil on canvas, 34¾ x 40⅞ in.
(88.3 x 103.8 cm)
Signed l.l.: *G. Courbet*
PROVENANCE: the artist's sister, Juliette
Courbet; Mrs. H. O. Havemeyer, New
York, bought through Théodore Duret, for
Fr 20,000, summer 1916–29; her sale,
American Art Association, New York, Apr.
10, 1930, no. 84; bought at sale by Scott
and Fowles for $3,100; Scott and Fowles,
New York; their sale, Parke-Bernet, New
York, Mar. 28, 1946, no. 54; bought at
sale by Nicholas de Koenigsberg (Le Passe

Ltd.); Le Passe, Ltd., New York, 1946–54; sale, Parke-Bernet, New York, Feb. 24, 1954, no. 87; bought at sale by Columbus Museum of Art for $1,300; Columbus Museum of Art, Ohio (Museum Purchase, Howald Fund), 54.5.
Note: While the provenance of this work is sound, the attribution to Courbet is currently being reevaluated by the Columbus Museum of Art.
EXHIBITION: 1919 New York, no. 3.
REFERENCES: Havemeyer 1931, p. 502, as *Les Remouleurs*; Havemeyer 1961, pp. 193f.; Fernier 1977–78, no. 25; Weitzenhoffer 1986, p. 230, pl. 155.

124
Gustave Courbet
ALPHONSE PROMAYET (1822–1872)
Oil on canvas, 42 ⅛ x 27 ⅝ in.
(107 x 70.2 cm)
Inscribed l.r., in another hand: *G. Courbet*
PROVENANCE: Alphonse Promayet, Paris, in 1855; Courbet, 1873; Romanoff family, St. Petersburg, from 1873(?); Nicolai Dmitrivitch Romanoff, St. Petersburg, until 1913/14; Paul Rosenberg, Paris, until 1914; Mrs. H. O. Havemeyer, New York, bought from Rosenberg, May 1914; d. 1929; MMA 29.100.132.
EXHIBITIONS: 1855 Paris Courbet, no. 6; 1857 Paris, no. 625; 1867 Paris, no. 74; 1912 St. Petersburg, no. 343; 1919 New York, no. 5.
REFERENCES: Havemeyer 1931, pp. 96f., ill.; Havemeyer 1958, p. 16, no. 79; Havemeyer 1961, p. 199; Sterling and Salinger 1966, pp. 110f., ill.; Fernier 1977–78, no. 128; Weitzenhoffer 1986, pp. 219, 258.

125
Gustave Courbet
WOMAN PAINTED AT PALAVAS
Oil on canvas, 23 ¼ x 19 in.
(59.1 x 48.3 cm)
Signed l.l.: *G. Courbet*
PROVENANCE: Lefevre, London, before 1926; Mrs. H. O. Havemeyer, New York, d. 1929; her sale, American Art Association, New York, Apr. 10, 1930, no. 58, as *Femme peinte à Calavas* [sic]; bought at sale by M. Knoedler and Co., probably as agent, for $900; Alex Reid and Lefevre, London, until 1956; Art Gallery of Ontario, Toronto, bought from Reid and Lefevre (Gift of Reuben Wells Leonard Estate, 1956), 56/13.
REFERENCES: Havemeyer 1931, p. 502, as *Portrait of a Peasant Woman*; Fernier 1977–78, no. 162.

126
Gustave Courbet
THE STREAM
Oil on canvas, 41 x 54 in.
(104.1 x 137.2 cm)
Signed and dated l.l.: *G. Courbet 55*.
PROVENANCE: M. Vauthrin, 1855 until at least 1867; Laurent-Richard; his sale, Hôtel Drouot, Paris, May 23–25, 1878, no. 6, for Fr 13,000; M. X, in 1882; Haro père et fils, Paris, by 1885; their sale, Galerie Charles Sedelmeyer, Paris, May 30–31, 1892, no. 69, for Fr 39,000, bought in(?); Durand-Ruel, Paris, bought from Haro, Oct. 15, 1897, for Fr 40,000 (stock no. 4447); Mr. and Mrs. H. O. Havemeyer, New York, bought from Durand-Ruel, Oct. 19, 1897, for Fr 66,950; until 1907; Mrs. H. O. Havemeyer, New York, 1907–29; her daughter Adaline Havemeyer Frelinghuysen, Morristown, N.J., 1929–43; National Gallery of Art, Washington, D.C. (Gift of Mr. and Mrs. P.H.B. Frelinghuysen in memory of her father and mother, Mr. and Mrs. H. O. Havemeyer), 1943.15.2.
EXHIBITIONS: 1855 Paris, no. 2810, lent by M. Vauthrin; 1858 Bordeaux; 1858 Le Havre; 1858 Dijon, no. 192; 1858 Besançon; 1866 Lille, no. 385; 1867 Paris, no. 20, lent by M. Vauthrin; 1882 Paris, no. 56, lent by M. X; 1885 Paris Louvre, no. 81, lent by Haro et fils.
REFERENCES: Havemeyer 1931, pp. 346f., ill., as *Landscape—Le ruisseau du puits noir*; Havemeyer 1961, p. 194; Fernier 1977–78, no. 174; Weitzenhoffer 1982, pp. 261f., fig. 87; Weitzenhoffer 1986, p. 117.

127
Gustave Courbet
WOMAN IN A RIDING HABIT*
Oil on canvas, 45 ½ x 35 ⅛ in.
(115.6 x 89.2 cm)
Signed l.l.: *G. Courbet*.
PROVENANCE: Théodore Duret, Paris, until 1906; Mr. and Mrs. H. O. Havemeyer, New York, bought from Duret, spring 1906, for Fr 15,000; until 1907; Mrs. H. O. Havemeyer, New York, 1907–29; MMA 29.100.59.
EXHIBITION: 1919 New York, no. 6.
REFERENCES: Havemeyer 1931, p. 93, ill., as *Portrait of Louise Colet—L'Amazone*; Havemeyer 1958, p. 16, no. 80; Havemeyer 1961, pp. 188f., 201–3; Sterling and Salinger 1966, pp. 113–15, ill.; Fernier 1977–78, no. 202; Weitzenhoffer 1986, pp. 164f., 180, 256, pl. 127.

128
Gustave Courbet
HUNTING DOGS

Oil on canvas, 36 ½ x 58 ½ in.
(92.7 x 148.6 cm)
Signed l.r.: *G. Courbet*.
PROVENANCE: Brame, Paris; Durand-Ruel, Paris, bought from Brame, June 23, 1892, for Fr 12,000 (stock no. 2334); Durand-Ruel, New York, bought from Durand-Ruel, Paris, Sept. 26, 1892, for Fr 40,000; Mr. and Mrs. H. O. Havemeyer, New York, bought from Durand-Ruel in 1892; until 1907; Mrs. H. O. Havemeyer, New York, 1907–29; her son, Horace Havemeyer, New York, 1929–33; MMA (H. O. Havemeyer Collection, Gift of Horace Havemeyer, 1933), 33.77.
EXHIBITIONS: 1867 Paris Universelle, no. 171; 1878 Brussels; 1893 Chicago, no. 2898, as *Dogs and Hare*, lent by Henry O. Havemeyer, New York; 1919 New York, no. 7.
REFERENCES: Havemeyer 1931, pp. 352f., ill.; Havemeyer 1961, p. 194; Sterling and Salinger 1966, pp. 116f., ill.; Fernier 1977–78, no. 620, as *Le Lièvre forcé*; Weitzenhoffer 1982, pp. 163, 187f., 198, n. 45, fig. 47; Weitzenhoffer 1986, pp. 80, 89, pl. 31.

129
Gustave Courbet
MME DE BRAYER**
Oil on canvas, 36 x 28 ⅝ in.
(91.4 x 72.7 cm)
Signed and dated l.r.: *G. Courbet . .58*
PROVENANCE: family of the sitter, Brussels, until 1907; Mr. and Mrs. H. O. Havemeyer, New York, bought through Théodore Duret, spring 1907; shipped to them by Durand-Ruel, May 11, 1907 (deposit no. 11181, as *Portrait de femme*); Mrs. H. O. Havemeyer, New York, 1907–29; MMA 29.100.118.
EXHIBITIONS: 1878 Brussels; 1889 Brussels, no. 51; 1921 New York, no. 25.
REFERENCES: Havemeyer 1931, pp. 90f., ill.; Havemeyer 1958, p. 17, no. 84, ill.; Havemeyer 1961, p. 188; Sterling and Salinger 1966, pp. 118f., ill.; Fernier 1977–78, no. 232; Weitzenhoffer 1986, pp. 178, 180, 245, 257, pl. 137.

130
Gustave Courbet
LANDSCAPE WITH CATTLE
Oil on canvas, 27 ¾ x 36 in.
(70.5 x 91.4 cm)
Signed: *G. Courbet*
PROVENANCE: sale, Hôtel Drouot, Paris, May 31, 1872, no. 10, and May 8, 1873, no. 24; Ernest Hoschedé; sale, Hôtel Drouot, Paris, Apr. 20, 1875, no. 28, for Fr 1,600; M. M***; sale, Hôtel Drouot, Paris, Apr. 14, 1876, no. 15; sale, Hôtel Drouot, Paris, May 17, 1879, no. 11, for

123

127

131

124

128

132

125

133

126

129

134

136

138

135

137

140

Fr 2,600; Durand-Ruel, Paris, 1889 (stock no. 2440, as *Vaches*); Mr. and Mrs. H. O. Havemeyer, New York, bought from Durand-Ruel, Aug. 17, 1889, for Fr 20,000; until 1907; Mrs. H. O. Havemeyer, New York, 1907–29; her son, Horace Havemeyer, New York, 1929–34; The Denver Art Museum, 1934–47 (William D. Lippitt Memorial Collection, anonymous gift of Horace Havemeyer); deaccessioned Apr. 21, 1947, and sent to New York.
REFERENCES: Havemeyer 1931, p. 356; Havemeyer 1961, p. 191; Fernier 1977–78, no. 245, as *Le dormoir au bord de la mer*; Weitzenhoffer 1982, pp. 109, 111, 198, n. 45, fig. 19; Weitzenhoffer 1986, pp. 58, 60, pl. 17.

131
Gustave Courbet
AFTER THE HUNT*
Oil on canvas, 93 x 73 ¼ in.
(236.2 x 186.1 cm)
Signed l.l.: *G. Courbet*.
PROVENANCE: Mrs. H. O. Havemeyer, New York, possibly bought from Cottier and Co., New York, Sept. 1910; d. 1929; MMA 29.100.61.
EXHIBITION: 1919 New York, no. 14.
REFERENCES: Havemeyer 1931, pp. 84f.,

ill.; Havemeyer 1958, p. 15, no. 78; Havemeyer 1961, p. 194; Sterling and Salinger 1966, pp. 117f., ill.; Fernier 1977–78, no. 342; Weitzenhoffer 1986, p. 256.

132
Gustave Courbet
M. SUISSE**
Oil on canvas, 23 ¼ x 19 ⅜ in. (59.1 x 49.2 cm)
Signed l., along edge: *G. Courbet*.
PROVENANCE: Brivet, in 1867; Félix Courbet, Paris; his sale, Hôtel Drouot, Paris, Dec. 21, 1882, no. 18, for Fr 1,080; Durand-Ruel, Paris, received on deposit from Mr. Gadala, Dec. 28, 1894 (deposit no. 8595, as *Portrait de Mr. Suisse*); Mr. and Mrs. H. O. Havemeyer, New York, possibly from about 1895–96; until 1907; Mrs. H. O. Havemeyer, New York, 1907–29; MMA 29.100.120.
EXHIBITIONS: 1867 Paris, no. 72; 1882 Paris, no. 43.
REFERENCES: Havemeyer 1931, pp. 98f., ill.; Havemeyer 1958, p. 18, no. 91; Havemeyer 1961, p. 199; Sterling and Salinger 1966, p. 119, ill.; Fernier 1977–78, no. 295; Weitzenhoffer 1982, pp. 263f., fig. 89; Weitzenhoffer 1986, pp. 113, 257, pl. 66.

133
Gustave Courbet
MME AUGUSTE CUOQ (MATHILDE DESPORTES, 1828–1910)
Oil on canvas, 69 ½ x 42 ½ in.
(176.5 x 108 cm)
Signed l.r.: *G. Courbet*.
PROVENANCE: Gustave Courbet, d. 1877; his studio sale, Hôtel Drouot, Paris, June 28, 1882, no. 17, as *Portrait of Mme XXX*, 174 x 108 cm, signed at right (probably this picture); bought at sale by Hecht for Fr 1,210; reportedly sold in Brussels, 1891; Mme de Vermeulen de Villiers, by 1907; her sale, Galerie Georges Petit, Paris, May 6, 1909, no. 38; bought at sale by Durand-Ruel for Havemeyer for Fr 50,000; Mrs. H. O. Havemeyer, New York, 1909–29; MMA 29.100.130.
EXHIBITIONS: 1867 Paris, no. 87; 1873 Vienna; 1882 Paris, no. 163; 1907 Paris, no. 63, as *Portrait de Marie Crocq* [sic] *dit "La femme aux gants,"* lent by Mme Vermeulen de Villiers; 1919 New York, no. 9.
REFERENCES: Havemeyer 1931, pp. 94f., ill.; Havemeyer 1958, p. 17, no. 85; Havemeyer 1961, pp. 200f.; Sterling and Salinger 1966, pp. 115f., ill.; Fernier 1977–78, no. 223; Weitzenhoffer 1986, pp. 190f., 258, pl. 142.

134
Gustave Courbet
LANDSCAPE WITH WATER
Oil on canvas, 25 x 31¼ in.
(63.5 x 79.4 cm)
Signed and dated(?) l.l.: 62 *Gustave
Courbet*
PROVENANCE: possibly Mrs. H. O. Have-
meyer, New York, d. 1929; her son, Hor-
ace Havemeyer, New York, by 1931–34;
The Denver Art Museum, 1934–47 (Gift
of Horace Havemeyer), A34–297; de-
accessioned Apr. 21, 1947, and sent to
New York.
EXHIBITIONS: 1867 Paris(?); 1882 Paris.
REFERENCES: Havemeyer 1931, p. 356, as
Landscape—Bords de la Charente; Fernier
1977–78, no. 323(?).

135
Gustave Courbet
THE SOURCE*
Oil on canvas, 47¼ x 29¼ in.
(120 x 74.3 cm)
Signed l.r.: *G. Courbet.*
PROVENANCE: Bernheim-Jeune, Paris; pri-
vate collection, Bordeaux, until 1916;
Durand-Ruel, Paris, bought from the pri-
vate collection in 1916; Durand-Ruel, New
York, bought from Durand-Ruel, Paris,
Apr. 11, 1916 (stock no. 3954); Mrs.
H. O. Havemeyer, New York, bought from
Durand-Ruel, Mar. 11, 1916, for
Fr 50,000; d. 1929; MMA 29.100.58.
EXHIBITION: 1919 New York, no. 13.
REFERENCES: Havemeyer 1931, pp. 80f.,
ill.; Havemeyer 1958, p. 17, no. 88, ill.;
Havemeyer 1961, pp. 185, 197f.; Sterling
and Salinger 1966, pp. 121f., ill.; Fernier
1977–78, no. 328; Weitzenhoffer 1986,
pp. 230, 256, pl. 154.

136
Gustave Courbet
THE LONE ROCK
Oil on canvas, 25⁹⁄₁₆ x 31¹⁵⁄₁₆ in.
(64.9 x 81.1 cm)
Signed l.l.: *G. Courbet*
PROVENANCE: Mrs. H. O. Havemeyer,
New York, bought through Théodore
Duret, fall 1911, and shipped to her, Nov.
18, 1911; d. 1929; her son, Horace Have-
meyer, New York, 1929–41; The Brooklyn
Museum (Gift of Mrs. Horace Have-
meyer), 41.1258.
EXHIBITIONS: 1863 Saintes, no. 99, as
Rochers de Vallières; 1867 Paris, one of
nos. 57–66; 1919 New York, no. 22.
REFERENCES: Havemeyer 1931, p. 357;
Havemeyer 1961, p. 186; Fernier 1977–
78, no. 332.

137
Gustave Courbet
TORSO OF A WOMAN*
Oil on canvas, 29½ x 24 in. (74.9 x 61 cm)
Signed l.r.: *G. Courbet*
PROVENANCE: Jean-Paul Mazaroz and
Ribalier, Paris; their sale, Hôtel Drouot,
Paris, May 13–14, 1890, no. 2, as *Le
Printemps*; Lambert, Paris, 1890; Durand-
Ruel, Paris, bought from Lambert, June 7,
1890, for Fr 1,800 (stock no. 475, as
Femme nue, étude); Lerolle, bought from
Durand-Ruel, July 28, 1891, for Fr 3,000;
Durand-Ruel, Paris, bought back from
Lerolle, Sept. 30, 1891, for Fr 4,000 (stock
no. 1841, as *Femme nue*); Durand-Ruel,
New York, bought from Durand-Ruel,
Paris, Mar. 9, 1892, for Fr 4,500 (stock
no. 916, as *Torse de femme*); Mr. and Mrs.
H. O. Havemeyer, New York, bought
from Durand-Ruel, Oct. 19, 1892, for
$1,800; until 1907; Mrs. H. O. Have-
meyer, New York, 1907–29; MMA
29.100.60.
EXHIBITION: 1919 New York, no. 15.
REFERENCES: Havemeyer 1931, pp. 80f.,
ill., as *Nude—La Branche de Cerisier*;
Havemeyer 1958, p. 18, no. 92; Havemeyer 1961, pp. 190–93, 196; Sterling and
Salinger 1966, pp. 120f., ill.; Fernier 1977–
78, no. 336; Weitzenhoffer 1982,
pp. 161f., 168, ns. 28, 31, p. 198, n. 45,
p. 262, fig. 46; Weitzenhoffer 1986,
pp. 79f., 112, 256, pl. 33.

138
Gustave Courbet
HUNTER ON HORSEBACK
Oil on canvas, 46¹³⁄₁₆ x 38 in.
(118.9 x 96.5 cm)
PROVENANCE: Gustave Courbet, d. 1877;
his studio sale, Hôtel Drouot, Paris, June
28, 1882, no. 5; bought at sale by Bern-
heim for Fr 1,600; Mrs. H. O. Havemeyer,
New York, bought through Théodore
Duret for Fr 30,000, before 1914–29; her
daughter Electra Havemeyer Webb, New
York, 1929–42; Yale University Art Gal-
lery, New Haven (Gift of J. Watson Webb,
B.A. 1907, and Electra Havemeyer Webb),
1942.301.
EXHIBITIONS: 1867 Paris, no. 98; 1882
Paris, no. 151; 1919 New York, no. 26.
REFERENCES: Havemeyer 1931, pp. 350f.,
ill.; Havemeyer 1961, p. 195; Fernier
1977–78, no. 375, as *Chasseur à cheval
retrouvant la piste*.

139
Gustave Courbet
LANDSCAPE—NEAR ORNANS
Oil on canvas, 25⅜ x 31½ in.
(64.5 x 80 cm)
Signed: *G. Courbet*

PROVENANCE: Mrs. H. O. Havemeyer,
New York, d. 1929; her daughter Adaline
Havemeyer Frelinghuysen, Morristown,
N.J., from 1929.
REFERENCES: Havemeyer 1931, p. 348;
Fernier 1977–78, no. 378(?).

140
Gustave Courbet
THE SOURCE OF THE LOUE**
Oil on canvas, 39¼ x 56 in.
(99.7 x 142.2 cm)
Signed b.c.: *G. Courbet*
PROVENANCE: Félix Gérard père, Paris; M.
Darlu, Paris, until 1889; Durand-Ruel,
Paris, received on deposit from Darlu, May
16, 1889 (deposit no. 6746, as *Rochers*);
bought from him, Aug. 21, 1889, for
Fr 7,000 (stock no. 2448, as *La Loue*);
Mr. and Mrs. H. O. Havemeyer, New
York, bought from Durand-Ruel, Aug. 21,
1889, for Fr 15,000; until 1907; Mrs.
H. O. Havemeyer, New York, 1907–29;
MMA 29.100.122.
EXHIBITIONS: 1867 Paris, no. 22(?); 1897
Paris(?); 1919 New York, no. 16.
REFERENCES: Havemeyer 1931, pp. 86f.,
ill.; Havemeyer 1958, p. 17, no. 89; Have-
meyer 1961, p. 194; Sterling and Salinger
1966, p. 122, ill.; Fernier 1977–78,
no. 387; Weitzenhoffer 1982, p. 261, fig.
86; Weitzenhoffer 1986, pp. 117, 257, pl. 72.

141
Gustave Courbet
THE SILENT RIVER
Oil on canvas, 28¹⁄₁₆ x 42⁵⁄₁₆ in.
(71.3 x 107.5 cm)
Signed and dated l.r.: *G. Courbet. / 68.*
PROVENANCE: sale, Hôtel Drouot, Paris,
Dec. 5, 1881, no. 6, as *Les rochers*, for
Fr 3,900; Ferdinand Barbedienne, by 1882–
85; sale, Hôtel Drouot, Paris, Apr. 7, 1885,
no. 20, for Fr 1,050; Martin Landelle,
until 1899; Durand-Ruel, Paris, bought
from Landelle, Feb. 21, 1899, for Fr 2,500
(stock no. 5039, as *Rivière à Ornans*);
Charles Tyson Yerkes, Chicago, bought
from Durand-Ruel, Aug. 29, 1900, for
Fr 11,000; his sale, American Art Associa-
tion, New York, Apr. 5, 1910, no. 29;
bought at sale by Durand-Ruel for Have-
meyer for $3,100; Mrs. H. O. Havemeyer,
New York, 1910–29; her son, Horace
Havemeyer, New York, 1929–41; The
Brooklyn Museum (Gift of Mrs. Horace
Havemeyer), 41.1259.
EXHIBITION: 1882 Paris, no. 71, as
Paysage, Bords de la Loue.
REFERENCES: Havemeyer 1931, p. 357, as
Landscape—The Silent River; Fernier
1977–78, no. 396, as *Bords de la Loue
avec rochers à gauche*, dates it 1864;
Weitzenhoffer 1982, pp. 279f., n. 20.

145

142

146

149

143

147

150

151

144

148

142

Gustave Courbet

WOMAN WITH A CAT

Oil on canvas, 28⅞ x 22½ in.

(73.3 x 57.2 cm)

Signed l.l.: *G. Courbet*

PROVENANCE: Durand-Ruel, Paris, bought from the artist, Feb. 15, 1872; M. d'Ol . . . ; his sale, Hôtel Drouot, Paris, Dec. 9, 1876, no. 22; seized by the state in June 1877; Courbet studio sale, Hôtel Drouot, Paris, Nov. 26, 1877, no. 3; bought at sale by Debrousse for Fr 1,150; Hubert Debrousse, Paris, 1877–1900; his sale, Galerie Georges Petit, Paris, Apr. 4–6, 1900, no. 108; bought at sale by Félix Gérard for Fr 4,000; Mary Cassatt, Paris; Mrs. H. O. Havemeyer, d. 1929; her sale, American Art Association, New York, Apr. 10, 1930, no. 72; bought at sale by R. D. Smith for $2,100; Josef Stransky, New York, d. 1936; his estate, 1936–40; Worcester Art Museum, Worcester, Mass., bought from the Stransky estate, through Wildenstein, Nov. 1940 (Museum purchase), 1940.300.

EXHIBITION: 1882 Paris, no. 161.

REFERENCES: Havemeyer 1931, p. 501, as *Figure Piece—La Femme au Chat*; Havemeyer 1961, p. 195; Fernier 1977–78, no. 431.

143

Gustave Courbet

PORTRAIT OF A MAN

Oil on canvas, 16¼ x 13⅛ in.

(41.3 x 33.3 cm)

Signed l.l.: *G. Courbet.*

PROVENANCE: Félix Gérard père, Paris; his sale, Hôtel Drouot, Paris, Mar. 28–29, 1905, no. 40; bought at sale by Vollard for Fr 280; Ambroise Vollard, Paris, 1905; Mr. and Mrs. H. O. Havemeyer, New York, bought from Vollard, through Cassatt, by Sept. 1905; until 1907; Mrs. H. O. Havemeyer, New York, 1907–29; MMA 29.100.201.

REFERENCES: Havemeyer 1931, p. 100; Havemeyer 1958, p. 17, no. 87; Sterling and Salinger 1966, p. 121, ill.; Fernier 1977–78, no. 445, as *Portrait d'homme, M. Luquet?*; Weitzenhoffer 1986, p. 167, pl. 129.

144

Gustave Courbet

THE DEER

Oil on canvas, 29⅜ x 36⅜ in.

(74.6 x 92.4 cm)

Signed l.l.: *G. Courbet.*

PROVENANCE: Jean-Baptiste Faure, Paris, until 1893; Durand-Ruel, Paris, bought from Faure, Jan. 9, 1893, for Fr 3,000 (stock no. 2583); Mr. and Mrs. H. O.

Havemeyer, New York, bought from Durand-Ruel, Sept. 19, 1895, for Fr 7,000; until 1907; Mrs. H. O. Havemeyer, New York, 1907–29; her son, Horace Havemeyer, New York, 1929; MMA (H. O. Havemeyer Collection, Gift of Horace Havemeyer, 1929), 29.160.34.

REFERENCES: Havemeyer 1931, p. 88, ill.; Havemeyer 1958, p. 16, no. 83; Havemeyer 1961, p. 195; Sterling and Salinger 1966, pp. 119f., ill.; Fernier 1977–78, no. 489, as *Cerf et Biche*; Weitzenhoffer 1982, pp. 241f., fig. 79; Weitzenhoffer 1986, p. 107, pl. 61.

145

Gustave Courbet

WOMAN WITH A PARROT*

Oil on canvas, 51 x 77 in.

(129.5 x 195.6 cm)

Signed and dated l.l.: .66 / *Gustave Courbet.*

PROVENANCE: Jules Bordet, Dijon, bought from the artist, spring 1870, for Fr 15,000; until at least 1889; Haro, Paris(?); Durand-Ruel, Paris, received on deposit from Boudet (Bordet?), Feb. 2, 1895 (deposit no. 8623); Durand-Ruel, New York, received on deposit from Durand-Ruel, Paris, Nov. 4, 1895 (deposit no. 5358); bought from Durand-Ruel, Paris, Apr. 30, 1898, for Fr 20,000 (stock no. 1994); Mr. and Mrs. H. O. Havemeyer, New York, bought from Durand-Ruel, Apr. 30, 1898, for $12,000; until 1907; Mrs. H. O. Havemeyer, New York, 1907–29; MMA 29.100.57.

EXHIBITIONS: 1866 Paris, no. 463; 1867 Paris, no. 10; 1869 Munich; 1870 Antwerp, as *La Courtisane*; 1882 Paris, no. 13; 1889 Paris Universelle, no. 210; 1919 New York, no. 24.

REFERENCES: Havemeyer 1931, pp. 76f., ill.; Havemeyer 1958, p. 18, no. 93; Havemeyer 1961, pp. 184f., 195–97; Sterling and Salinger 1966, pp. 124–27, ill.; Fernier 1977–78, no. 526; Weitzenhoffer 1982, pp. 105f., 118, n. 19, pp. 253, 278, n. 3; Weitzenhoffer 1986, pp. 56, 110, 193, 239, 256, 262, n. 9, colorpl. 143.

146

Gustave Courbet

THE YOUNG BATHER**

Oil on canvas, 51¼ x 38¼ in.

(130.2 x 97.2 cm)

Signed and dated l.l.: 66 / *G. Courbet*

PROVENANCE: Khalil Bey, Paris; his sale, Hôtel Drouot, Paris, Jan. 16–18, 1868, no. 10; bought at sale by Belling for Fr 3,700; Sainctelette, Brussels, in 1878; Mrs. H. O. Havemeyer, New York, bought through Théodore Duret by Feb. 1920, probably for Fr 60,000 (first offered by

Duret, Jan. 16, 1917); d. 1929; MMA 29.100.124.

EXHIBITION: 1878 Brussels.

REFERENCES: Havemeyer 1931, pp. 82f., ill.; Havemeyer 1958, p. 18, no. 95; Sterling and Salinger 1966, pp. 127f., ill.; Fernier 1977–78, no. 535, as *Baigneuse*; Weitzenhoffer 1986, pp. 239, 257, pl. 161.

147

Gustave Courbet

PORTRAIT OF JO (LA BELLE IRLANDAISE)*

Oil on canvas, 22 x 26 in. (55.9 x 66 cm)

Signed and dated l.l.: . . . 66 / *Gustave Courbet.*

PROVENANCE: Félix Gérard père, Paris; sale, Hôtel Drouot, Paris, Feb. 25, 1896, no. 13; bought at sale by M. Gérard fils for Fr 2,020; Brame père, Paris, until 1898; Durand-Ruel, Paris, received on deposit from Brame, June 15, 1898 (deposit no. 9360, as *La femme au miroir*), and bought from him, Sept. 9, 1898, for Fr 4,000 (stock no. 4762, as *Femme au miroir, cheveux rouges*); Durand-Ruel, New York, bought from Durand-Ruel, Paris, Oct. 12, 1898 (Paris stock book), or Oct. 27, 1898 (New York stock book, no. 2042, as *La femme au miroir*, or *La belle Irlandaise*), for Fr 12,000; Mr. and Mrs. H. O. Havemeyer, New York, bought from Durand-Ruel, Dec. 31, 1898, for $2,800; until 1907; Mrs. H. O. Havemeyer, New York, 1907–29; MMA 29.100.63.

EXHIBITIONS: 1898 New York Union, no. 15, as *Woman and Mirror*; 1919 New York, no. 23.

REFERENCES: Havemeyer 1931, pp. 74f., ill.; Havemeyer 1958, p. 16, no. 81; Havemeyer 1961, pp. 187, 212f.; Sterling and Salinger 1966, pp. 128f., ill.; Fernier 1977–78, no. 538; Weitzenhoffer 1982, pp. 307f., 318, n. 49, fig. 121; Weitzenhoffer 1986, pp. 136, 256, colorpl. 99.

148

Gustave Courbet

THE WOMAN IN THE WAVES*

Oil on canvas, 25¾ x 21¼ in.

(65.4 x 54 cm)

Signed and dated l.l.: 68 / *G. Courbet*

PROVENANCE: Jean-Baptiste Faure, Paris, by 1882–93; Durand-Ruel, Paris, bought from Faure, Jan. 9, 1893, for Fr 13,000 (stock no. 2580, as *Femme à la vague*); Durand-Ruel, New York, bought from Durand-Ruel, Paris, Jan. 18, 1893, for Fr 20,000; Mr. and Mrs. H. O. Havemeyer, New York, bought from Durand-Ruel, Jan. 30, 1893, for $5,000; until 1907; Mrs. H. O. Havemeyer, New York, 1907–29; MMA 29.100.62.

EXHIBITIONS: 1868 Ghent; 1869 Munich; 1882 Paris, no. 24; 1919 New York, no. 31.
REFERENCES: Havemeyer 1931, pp. 78f., ill.; Havemeyer 1958, p. 18, no. 94; Havemeyer 1961, pp. 196f.; Sterling and Salinger 1966, pp. 130f., ill.; Fernier 1977–78, no. 628; Weitzenhoffer 1982, p. 198, n. 45(?), pp. 262f., fig. 88; Weitzenhoffer 1986, pp. 112f., 256, pl. 65.

149

Gustave Courbet
WOMAN WITH A DOG
Oil on canvas, 25⅝ x 31⅞ in.
(65.1 x 81 cm)
Signed and dated l.l.: 68 G. Courbet
PROVENANCE: private collection, Worms; Mrs. H. O. Havemeyer, New York,* d. 1929; her sale, American Art Association, New York, Apr. 10, 1930, no. 77; bought at sale by R. D. Smith for $4,000; Ernest Masurel, probably by 1931, until at least 1938; private collection; Musée du Louvre, Paris, from 1979; on deposit at the Musée d'Orsay, Paris, RF 1979–56.
*possibly the picture offered to Mrs. Havemeyer by Théodore Duret, Sept. 26–27, 1911, in letters referring to a female nude of 1868.
EXHIBITIONS: 1868 Ghent; 1912 Berlin, as Le Chien de Léontine Renaude.
REFERENCES: Havemeyer 1931, p. 501, as Nude—La Femme au Chien; Havemeyer 1961, p. 197; Fernier 1977–78, no. 631.

150

Gustave Courbet
THE WAVE
Oil on canvas, 25¾ x 34¾ in.
(65.4 x 88.3 cm)
Signed l.l.: G. Courbet
PROVENANCE: possibly Emil Monteaux, Paris, by 1882; his sale, Hôtel Drouot, Paris, Mar. 10, 1884, no. 11, for Fr 1,800; possibly Ernest May, Paris; possibly Georges Lutz; sale, Galerie Georges Petit, Paris, May 26–27, 1902, no. 39; bought at sale by M. Prayer for Fr 3,700; Jean Dollfus, Paris; his sale, Galerie Georges Petit, Paris, Mar. 2, 1912, no. 24; bought at sale by Durand-Ruel for Havemeyer for Fr 16,000; Mrs. H. O. Havemeyer, New York, 1912–29; her son, Horace Havemeyer, New York, 1929–41; The Brooklyn Museum (Gift of Mrs. Horace Havemeyer), 41.1256.
EXHIBITIONS: 1882 Paris, no. 111, lent by M. Lutz, or 112, lent by M. Monteaux; 1919 New York, no. 28.
REFERENCES: Havemeyer 1931, pp. 358f., ill.; Havemeyer 1961, pp. 185, 195; Fernier 1977–78, no. 688; Weitzenhoffer 1982, p. 199, fig. 55, with erroneous information; Weitzenhoffer 1986, p. 205, pl. 145.

151

Gustave Courbet
THE CALM SEA
Oil on canvas, 23½ x 28¾ in.
(59.7 x 73 cm)
Signed and dated l.l.: .69 / G. Courbet.
PROVENANCE: James Stillman, Paris; Mrs. H. O. Havemeyer, New York, bought from Théodore Duret, fall 1911; d. 1929; MMA 29.100.566.
REFERENCES: Havemeyer 1931, p. 89, as Landscape—Marine; Havemeyer 1958, p. 18, no. 82; Havemeyer 1961, p. 186; Sterling and Salinger 1966, p. 131, ill.; Fernier 1977–78, no. 712.

152

Gustave Courbet
MARINE: THE WATERSPOUT
Oil on canvas, 27⅛ x 39¼ in.
(68.9 x 99.7 cm)
Signed and dated l.r.: G. Courbet / 70
PROVENANCE: sale, Galerie Helbing, Munich, June 26, 1907, no. 8, for Fr 5,750; Mrs. H. O. Havemeyer, New York, bought through Théodore Duret, Dec. 1912, for Fr 16,000, and shipped to her, Jan. 11, 1913; d. 1929; her son, Horace Havemeyer, New York, 1929; MMA (H. O. Havemeyer Collection, Gift of Horace Havemeyer, 1929), 29.160.35.
REFERENCES: Havemeyer 1931, p. 89; Havemeyer 1958, p. 17, no. 86; Havemeyer 1961, p. 195; Sterling and Salinger 1966, pp. 131f., ill.; Fernier 1977–78, no. 756, as La Jetée, marine à la vague.

153

Gustave Courbet
STILL LIFE***
Oil on canvas, 11 x 18½ in. (27.9 x 47 cm)
Inscribed l.l., in another hand: G. Courbet
PROVENANCE: Mr. and Mrs. H. O. Havemeyer, New York, until 1894; Durand-Ruel, New York, bought from Havemeyer, Jan. 16, 1894, for $750 (stock no. 1128, as Nature morte pommes); Durand-Ruel, Paris; Esnault-Pelterie, Paris, in 1906; private collection; sale, Hôtel Drouot, Paris, Mar. 5, 1912, no. 36 not sold.
REFERENCES: Fernier 1977–78, no. 768; Weitzenhoffer 1982, p. 198, n. 45(?), p. 244, n. 8, p. 245, n. 18; Weitzenhoffer 1986, p. 98.

154

Gustave Courbet
STILL LIFE—FRUIT
Oil on canvas, 23⅛ x 28¼ in.
(58.7 x 71.8 cm)
Signed, dated, and inscribed l.l.: 71 Ste. Pélagie / G. Courbet
PROVENANCE: Henri Lambert, Brussels; his sale, Galerie Saint-Luc, Brussels, Apr. 28, 1892, no. 8; Isidore van den Eynde; his sale, Galerie Leroy Frères, Brussels, Dec.

157

161

165

158

162

166

159

164

167

13, 1912, no. 2; bought at sale by Rosenberg for Fr 28,300; Paul Rosenberg, Paris, from 1912; private collection, Austria, bought from Rosenberg; until 1920; Paul Rosenberg, Paris, bought back from the private collection in Austria, Oct. 1920; Mrs. H. O. Havemeyer, New York, bought from Rosenberg, Feb. 1921, for Fr 205,000; d. 1929; her daughter Electra Havemeyer Webb, New York, 1929–60; Shelburne Museum, Shelburne, Vt., from 1960, 27.1.3-23.

REFERENCES: Havemeyer 1931, p. 349, ill.; Havemeyer 1961, p. 195; Fernier 1977–78, no. 776; Weitzenhoffer 1986, p. 239, colorpl. 163.

155
Gustave Courbet
HUNTER IN THE SNOW

Oil on canvas, 23 ½ x 28 ⅜ in. (59.7 x 72.7 cm)
Signed l.l.: *G. Courbet*
PROVENANCE: Brame, Paris, until 1889; Durand-Ruel, Paris, bought from Brame, Oct. 2, 1889, with two other Courbets for Fr 11,000 (stock no. 2521, as *Chasseur à l'affût, neige*); Mr. and Mrs. H. O. Havemeyer, New York, bought from Durand-Ruel, Oct. 10, 1889, for Fr 7,000; until 1907; Mrs. H. O. Havemeyer, New York, 1907–29; her son, Horace Havemeyer, New York, 1929–41; The Brooklyn Museum, 1941–89 (Gift of Mrs. Horace Havemeyer), 41.1257; sale, Sotheby's, New York, May 23, 1989, no. 25, as *Le chasseur d'eau*; bought at sale by Hiroko Saeki (agent) for $275,000; private collection, Japan.
REFERENCES: Havemeyer 1931, pp. 354f.,

ill.; Havemeyer 1961, p. 195; Fernier 1977–78, no. 908.

156
Gustave Courbet
APPLES
Oil on wood, 8 x 14 ¼ in. (20.3 x 36.2 cm)
Signed, dated, and inscribed l.r.: *Ste Pélagie 71. / G.C.*
PROVENANCE: Mrs. H. O. Havemeyer, New York, d. 1929; her sale, American Art Association, New York, Apr. 10, 1930, no. 35, as *Nature morte*; bought at sale by Joseph Brummer for $625; Gallatin, Philadelphia; Margaret Gallatin, Philadelphia; private collection; sale, Sotheby's, New York, Oct. 29, 1981, no. 47; bought at sale by a private collector for $25,000; private collection.

REFERENCES: Havemeyer 1931, p. 502, as *Still Life—Apples*; Havemeyer 1961, p. 195.

157
Gustave Courbet
FOREST IN AUTUMN
Oil on canvas, 19 ¼ x 23 in.
(48.9 x 58.4 cm)
Signed l.l.: *G. Courbet*
PROVENANCE: Mrs. H. O. Havemeyer, New York, d. 1929; her sale, American Art Association, New York, Apr. 10, 1930, no. 68, as *Verdure d'Automne*; bought at sale by Meyer Linker for $550.
REFERENCE: Havemeyer 1931, p. 501.

158
Gustave Courbet
FRUIT AND VEGETABLES
Oil on canvas, 29 x 31 in. (73.7 x 78.7 cm)
Signed l.l.: *G. Courbet*
PROVENANCE: Mrs. H. O. Havemeyer, New York, bought from Théodore Duret; d. 1929; her sale, American Art Association, New York, Apr. 10, 1930, no. 60; bought at sale by Van Diemen Galleries for $1,000.
REFERENCES: Havemeyer 1931, p. 502; Havemeyer 1961, p. 195.

159
Gustave Courbet
HYDRANGEAS
Oil on canvas, 25 x 21 in. (63.5 x 53.3 cm)
Signed l.l.: *G. Courbet*
PROVENANCE: Mrs. H. O. Havemeyer, New York, d. 1929; her sale, American Art Association, New York, Apr. 10, 1930, no. 62; bought at sale by E. and A. Silberman for $800.
REFERENCE: Havemeyer 1931, p. 502.

160
Gustave Courbet
LA POINTE DE VALLIERES
Oil on canvas, 29 ¼ x 49 ¼ in.
(74.3 x 125.1 cm)
Signed: *G. Courbet*
PROVENANCE: Mrs. H. O. Havemeyer, New York, bought through Théodore Duret, Jan.-Feb. 1916, for Fr 15,000; d. 1929; her son, Horace Havemeyer, New York, from 1929.
REFERENCES: Havemeyer 1931, p. 360; Havemeyer 1961, p. 186.

161
Gustave Courbet
THE RUSSET WOOD
Oil on canvas, 46 x 35 ½ in.
(116.8 x 90.2 cm)

Signed l.l.: *Gustave Courbet*
PROVENANCE: Mrs. H. O. Havemeyer, New York, acquired through Théodore Duret, by Apr. 1912, for Fr 18,000; d. 1929; her sale, American Art Association, New York, Apr. 10, 1930, no. 114, as *The Russet Wood*; bought at sale by Van Diemen Galleries for $800; Van Diemen (later Lilienfeld) Galleries, New York, 1930–42; Walker Art Center, Minneapolis, bought from Lilienfeld, Oct. 1942, for $1,400; sale, Sotheby's, New York, Nov. 12, 1970, no. 6; bought at sale by Forbes for $3,500; Malcolm Forbes, Forbes Magazine Collection; sale, Sotheby's, New York, Apr. 28, 1977, no. 143; bought at sale by Shelton for $5,000; Richard Shelton, San Francisco.
REFERENCES: Havemeyer 1931, p. 502, as *Landscape—Autumn Forest at Sunset*; Havemeyer 1961, p. 195; Weitzenhoffer 1986, p. 205, pl. 146.

162
Gustave Courbet
VALLEY IN FRANCHE-COMTE, NEAR ORNANS
Oil on canvas, 22 ½ x 35 ½ in.
(57.2 x 90.2 cm)
Signed l.r.: *G. Courbet*
PROVENANCE: Walter Richmond, Providence, bought from the artist; his sale, American Art Association, New York, Jan. 27, 1899, no. 38; bought at sale by Durand-Ruel for Havemeyer for $1,900; Mr. and Mrs. H. O. Havemeyer, New York, 1899–1907; Mrs. H. O. Havemeyer, New York, 1907–29; her daughter Adaline Havemeyer Frelinghuysen, Morristown, N.J., from 1929; Wildenstein and Co., New York, sold in Japan, about 1991; The Museum of Modern Art, Ibaraki.
REFERENCE: Havemeyer 1931, p. 348, as *Landscape—Town near Ornans*.

163
Gustave Courbet
WOODED LANDSCAPE
Oil on canvas, 31 x 45 in. (78.7 x 114.3 cm)
Signed: *G.C.*
PROVENANCE: possibly Mrs. H. O. Havemeyer, New York, d. 1929; her son, Horace Havemeyer, New York, by 1931–34; The Denver Art Museum, 1934–47 (Gift of Horace Havemeyer), A34–295; deaccessioned Apr. 21, 1947, and sent to New York.
REFERENCE: Havemeyer 1931, p. 355, as *Landscape—Le Forêt*.

164
Gustave Courbet, Copy after
French, 2nd half 19th century
SPRING FLOWERS**

Oil on canvas, 23 ¾ x 32 ¼ in.
(60.3 x 81.9 cm)
Inscribed l.l.: *G. Courbet / . . .*
PROVENANCE: Mrs. H. O. Havemeyer, New York, bought through Théodore Duret in 1911; d. 1929; MMA 29.100.121.
EXHIBITION: 1919 New York, no. 37.
REFERENCES: Havemeyer 1931, p. 101, ill., as by Courbet; Havemeyer 1958, p. 18, no. 90; Havemeyer 1961, p. 195; Sterling and Salinger 1966, p. 112, ill.; Fernier 1977–78, no. 185; Weitzenhoffer 1986, p. 257.

165
Gustave Courbet, Style of
French, 2nd half 19th century
APPLES**
Oil on canvas, 13 x 17 ⅜ in. (33 x 44.1 cm)
Inscribed l.r.: *St. Pélagie / G. Courbet.*
PROVENANCE: Mrs. H. O. Havemeyer, New York, d. 1929; MMA 29.100.123.
REFERENCES: Havemeyer 1931, p. 100, as by Courbet; Havemeyer 1961, p. 195; Weitzenhoffer 1986, p. 257.

166
Gustave Courbet, Style of
French, 2nd half 19th century
PORTRAIT OF A WOMAN, CALLED HELOISE ABELARD**
Oil on canvas, 25 ⅜ x 21 ⅛ in.
(64.5 x 53.7 cm)
Inscribed l.l.: *G. Courbet*
PROVENANCE: Théodore Duret, Paris, until 1921; Mrs. H. O. Havemeyer, New York, bought from Duret, fall 1921–29; MMA 29.100.119.
REFERENCES: Havemeyer 1931, pp. 98f., ill., as by Courbet; Weitzenhoffer 1986, pp. 241f., 257.

167
Gustave Courbet, Style of
French, 19th century
PORTRAIT OF A WOMAN IN BLACK
Oil on canvas, 54 x 39 ½ in.
(137.2 x 100.3 cm)
Inscribed l.l.: *G. Courbet*
PROVENANCE: Mrs. H. O. Havemeyer, New York, bought from Théodore Duret, 1924–29; her sale, American Art Association, New York, Apr. 10, 1930, no. 103, as by Courbet; bought at sale by Kraushaar Galleries for $2,300; Kraushaar Galleries, New York, 1930–35; Josef Stransky, New York, bought from Kraushaar, in Mar. 1935; d. 1936; his estate, 1936–52, as *Portrait of Madame Ollivier*; Wildenstein and Co., New York, bought from Stransky's widow, Marie Stransky, in 1952; sent to Europe in 1976.
REFERENCES: Havemeyer 1931, p. 502, as by Courbet; Weitzenhoffer 1986, p. 247, pl. 168, as style of Courbet.

168

Lucas Cranach the Elder
German, 1472–1553
PORTRAIT OF A MAN WITH A
ROSARY*
Oil on wood, 18¾ x 13⅞ in. (47.7 x
35.2 cm)
PROVENANCE: private collection, England;
Cottier and Co., New York, until 1914;
Mrs. H. O. Havemeyer, New York, bought
from Cottier, Jan. 1914; d. 1929; MMA
29.100.24.
REFERENCES: Havemeyer 1931, p. 14, ill.;
Wehle and Salinger 1947, pp. 199f., ill.;
Havemeyer 1958, p. 33, no. 183; Have-
meyer 1961, p. 20; Friedländer and Rosen-
berg 1978, no. 56; Weitzenhoffer 1982,
p. 166, n. 7; Weitzenhoffer 1986, p. 255.

169

J. Frank Currier
American, 1843–1909
LANDSCAPE
Watercolor, 9½ x 14½ in. (24.1 x 36.8 cm)
Signed and dated l.r.: *Currier 1880*
PROVENANCE: Mrs. H. O. Havemeyer,
New York, d. 1929; her sale, American Art
Association, New York, Apr. 10, 1930,
no. 8, for $40.
REFERENCE: Havemeyer 1931, p. 509.

170

J. Frank Currier
LANDSCAPE
Watercolor, 14¼ x 21¼ in. (36.2 x 54 cm)
Signed and dated l.r.: *Currier 1880*
PROVENANCE: Mrs. H. O. Havemeyer,
New York, d. 1929; her sale, American Art
Association, New York, Apr. 10, 1930,
no. 19, for $30.
REFERENCE: Havemeyer 1931, p. 509.

171

J. Frank Currier
LANDSCAPE
Watercolor, 16¼ x 26 in. (41.3 x 66 cm)
Signed and dated l.l.: *Currier 1880*

PROVENANCE: Goupil, Paris, sold to Havemeyer; Mrs. H. O. Havemeyer, New York,
d. 1929; her sale, American Art Association, New York, Apr. 10, 1930, no. 23;
bought at sale by Joseph Felshin for $55.
REFERENCE: Havemeyer 1931, p. 509.

172

173

172

Aelbert Cuyp
Dutch, 1620–1691
CUYP DESIGNING AFTER NATURE
Oil on wood, 11⅛ x 18 in.
(28.3 x 45.7 cm)
Signed l.l.: *AC* [monogram]
PROVENANCE: The Rt. Hon. Lord Gran-
ville Leveson Gower, first earl Granville,
Stone Park, co. Stafford, by 1835; his sale,
Christie's, London, June 21, 1845, no. 10;
bought at sale by Dunford for £525;
Charles Cope; his sale, Christie's, London,
June 8, 1872, no. 54, for £1,249; John
Waterloo Wilson, Paris; his sale, at his
hôtel, 5, avenue Hoche, Paris, Mar. 14–16,
1881, no. 43; E. Secrétan, Paris; his sale,
Galerie Charles Sedelmeyer, Paris, July 1–
7, 1889, no. 107, as *L'Artiste dessinant
d'après nature*; bought at sale by Durand-
Ruel for Havemeyer for Fr 41,000 (stock
no. 2396); Mr. and Mrs. H. O. Havemeyer, New York, 1889–1907; Mrs.
H. O. Havemeyer, New York, 1907–29;
her son, Horace Havemeyer, New York,
1929–56; The Brooklyn Museum (Gift of
Mr. Horace Havemeyer), 56.191.
EXHIBITIONS: 1835 London, no. 85; 1872
London Winter, no. 153; 1890–91 New
York, no. 14; 1891 New York Metropolitan, no. 2.
REFERENCES: Smith 1829–42, IX, no. 18,
as *The Artist Drawing from Nature*; Hofstede de Groot 1907–27, II, no. 77, as
Cuyp(?) Sketching in the Open; Havemeyer 1931, p. 304; Weitzenhoffer 1982,
pp. 109, 119, n. 24, pp. 127, 131f.;
Weitzenhoffer 1986, p. 64.

173

Aelbert Cuyp
LANDSCAPE
Black chalk and gray and ocher wash, on
wove paper, 5½ x 7⁵⁄₁₆ in. (14 x 18.6 cm)
PROVENANCE: William Russell, London;
Mrs. H. O. Havemeyer, d. 1929; MMA
29.100.931.
REFERENCES: Havemeyer 1931, p. 179;
Havemeyer 1958, p. 5, no. 12.

174

Georges D'Espagnat
French, 1870–1950
SAILBOATS ON THE RIVER
Oil on canvas, 21¾ x 28¾ in.
(55.3 x 73 cm)
Signed l.r.: *D'E*
PROVENANCE: Durand-Ruel, New York,
until 1901; Mr. and Mrs. H. O. Have-
meyer, New York, bought from Durand-
Ruel, Jan. 22, 1901; until 1907; Mrs.
H. O. Havemeyer, New York, 1907–29;
her sale, American Art Association, New
York, Apr. 10, 1930, no. 31, as *Course à la
voile*; bought at sale by Mansfield Ferry
for $220.
REFERENCE: Havemeyer 1931, p. 503, as
La course à la voile.

175

175

Charles-François Daubigny
French, 1817–1878
RIVERBANK
Oil on wood, 15⅜ x 26⅛ in.
(39 x 66.5 cm)
Signed and dated l.r.: *Daubigny 1874*
PROVENANCE: possibly J. E. Chase; con-
signed to M. Knoedler and Co., Oct. 8,
1882, for $3,000, as *Evening*; possibly Mr.
and Mrs. H. O. Havemeyer, New York,
bought from Chase, through Knoedler,
Oct. 23, 1885, for $2,675, as *Evening on
the Marne*; Mrs. H. O. Havemeyer, New
York, d. 1929; her daughter Adaline
Havemeyer Frelinghuysen, Morristown,
N.J., from 1929; Hirschl and Adler, New
York; Rob Noortman, the Netherlands;
sale, Sotheby's, London, July 5, 1973,
no. 11, as *Petit Village au bord de l'Eau*;
bought at sale by Hollinger for £2,900.
REFERENCES: Havemeyer 1931, p. 361, as
Landscape; Hellebranth 1976, no. 830, as

Bords de Rivière; Weitzenhoffer 1982, p. 50, ii. 23(?); Weitzenhoffer 1986, p. 260, n. 10, as *Evening on the Marne*(?).

176
Charles-François Daubigny
LANDSCAPE
Oil on wood, 16 ¼ x 21 ¼ in.
(41.3 x 54 cm)
PROVENANCE: Mrs. H. O. Havemeyer, New York, d. 1929; her sale, American Art Association, New York, Apr. 19, 1930, no. 44, as *The River in the Hills*; bought at sale by O. B. Carrott for $400.
REFERENCE: Havemeyer 1931, p. 502.

177
Honoré Daumier
French, 1808–1879
THE THIRD-CLASS CARRIAGE
Oil on canvas, 25 ¾ x 35 ½ in.
(65.4 x 90.2 cm)
PROVENANCE: Duz, Paris, by 1878–92; Durand-Ruel, Paris, bought from Duz, June 8, 1892 (stock no. 3316); Durand-Ruel, New York, bought from Durand-Ruel, Paris, Apr. 19, 1893 (stock no. 1048); Matthew Chaloner Durfee Borden, New York, bought from Durand-Ruel, Feb. 24, 1896; his sale, American Art Association, New York, Feb. 13–14, 1913, no. 76; bought at sale by Durand-Ruel for Havemeyer for $40,000; Mrs. H. O. Havemeyer, New York, 1913–29; MMA 29.100.129.
EXHIBITION: 1888 Paris, no. 361.
REFERENCES: Havemeyer 1931, pp. 102f., ill.; Havemeyer 1958, p. 19, no. 96; Havemeyer 1961, p. 7; Sterling and Salinger 1966, pp. 37–39, ill.; Maison 1968, I, no. I-165; Weitzenhoffer 1982, pp. 105f., 118, n. 19; pp. 163f., 169, n. 37; Weitzenhoffer 1986, pp. 80f., 209, 258, colorpl. 149.

178
Honoré Daumier
MAN READING IN A GARDEN; verso: preliminary sketch for same
Watercolor over black chalk, with pen and ink, wash, and conté crayon, on wove paper; verso: pen and brown ink, gray wash and conté crayon, 13 ⁵⁄₁₆ x 10 ⅝ in. (33.8 x 27 cm)
Signed l.l.: *h. Daumier*
PROVENANCE: Boussod, Valadon et Cie, Paris; Paul Gallimard, Paris; M. Heymann, until 1890; Durand-Ruel, Paris, bought from Heymann, Jan. 7, 1890, for Fr 450 (stock no. 2601, as *Corot dans son jardin*); Durand-Ruel, New York, bought from Durand-Ruel, Paris, Feb. 25, 1890 (Paris stock book), or Mar. 18, 1890 (New York stock book, no. 1001, as *Portrait de Corot*), for Fr 600; Mr. and Mrs. H. O. Havemeyer, New York, bought from Durand-

177

178

179

Ruel, Apr. 9, 1890, for $240; until 1907; Mrs. H. O. Havemeyer, New York, 1907–29; MMA 29.100.199.
EXHIBITIONS: 1890 New York Union; 1901 Paris, no. 200, as *La Lecture*.
REFERENCES: Havemeyer 1931, pp. 184f., ill., as *Corot Sketching at Ville d'Avray*; Havemeyer 1958, p. 19, no. 98; Havemeyer 1961, p. 7; Maison 1968, II, nos. 359 (verso), 361; Weitzenhoffer 1982, p. 142, n. 13, p. 198, n. 45; Weitzenhoffer 1986, p. 65, pl. 21.

179
Honoré Daumier
THE CONNOISSEUR
Pen and ink, wash, watercolor, conté crayon, and gouache, over black chalk, on wove paper, 17 ¼ x 14 in.
(43.8 x 35.6 cm)
Signed l.l.: *h. Daumier*

PROVENANCE: Jules Dupré, Paris, by 1878–89; his sale, Galerie Georges Petit, Paris, Jan. 30, 1890, probably no. 150; Durand-Ruel, Paris, until 1895 (stock no. 3367); Mr. and Mrs. H. O. Havemeyer, New York, bought from Durand-Ruel, Sept. 19, 1895, for Fr 8,000; until 1907; Mrs. H. O. Havemeyer, New York, 1907–29; MMA 29.100.200.
EXHIBITION: 1878 Paris Daumier, no. 154, as *Un amateur*, lent by M. J. Dupré.
REFERENCES: Havemeyer 1931, pp. 184f., ill.; Havemeyer 1958, p. 19, no. 97; Maison 1968, II, no. 370; Weitzenhoffer 1982, pp. 241f., fig. 77; Weitzenhoffer 1986, p. 107, pl. 59.

180
Jacques-Louis David, Follower of
French, early 19th century
PORTRAIT OF A YOUNG WOMAN IN WHITE
Oil on canvas, 49 ⅜ x 37 ½ in.
(125.4 x 95.3 cm)
PROVENANCE: Gimpel and Wildenstein, Paris, bought from an unknown source in 1914; Mrs. H. O. Havemeyer, New York, bought from Gimpel and Wildenstein, May 1914; d. 1929; her sale, American Art Association, New York, Apr. 10, 1930, no. 79, as by David; bought at sale by Dale for $26,000; Chester Dale, New York, 1930–62; National Gallery of Art, Washington, D.C. (Chester Dale Collection), 1963.10.118.
REFERENCES: Havemeyer 1931, p. 502, as by David; Weitzenhoffer 1986, pp. 219, 258, pl. 153.

181
Mauritz Frederik Hendrik de Haas
American, 1832–1895
HERRING BOATS AT SCHEVENINGEN
Watercolor, 10 x 13 ½ in. (25.4 x 34.3 cm)
Signed and dated l.r.: *M.F.H. de Haas 1880*

PROVENANCE: Mrs. H. O. Havemeyer, New York, d. 1929; her sale, American Art Association, New York, Apr. 10, 1930, no. 14; bought at sale by A. Rudert (agent) for $50.
REFERENCE: Havemeyer 1931, p. 509.

182
Alexandre-Gabriel Decamps
French, 1803–1860
SMYRNA HARBOR
Oil on canvas, 15 x 22 in. (38.1 x 55.9 cm)
PROVENANCE: Baron Papeleu; his sale, Paris, Feb. 17, 1859, for Fr 1,050; Mme F; sale, Hôtel Drouot, Paris, May 11, 1892, no. 7; bought at sale by Durand-Ruel for Fr 3,150; Durand-Ruel, Paris, 1892–93 (stock no. 2207, as *La rade de Smyrne*); Durand-Ruel, New York, bought from Durand-Ruel, Paris, Oct. 4, 1893 (Paris stock book), or Oct. 18, 1893 (New York stock book, no. 1089); Mr. and Mrs. H. O. Havemeyer, New York, bought from Durand-Ruel, Oct. 20, 1893, for $2,800; until 1907; Mrs. H. O. Havemeyer, New York, 1907–29; deposited with Durand-Ruel, Nov. 30, 1908–May 11, 1910 (deposit no. 7494); her sale, American Art Association, New York, Apr. 10, 1930, no. 69; bought at sale by Ferry for $1,100; Mansfield Ferry, New York; Gunther collection, New York.
REFERENCES: Havemeyer 1931, p. 503; Mosby 1977, no. 200, as *La Rade de Smyrne*; Weitzenhoffer 1982, pp. 199, 217, n. 3; Weitzenhoffer 1986, p. 184.

183
Alexandre-Gabriel Decamps
THE EXPERTS
Oil on canvas, 18¼ x 25¼ in. (46.4 x 64.1 cm)
Signed and dated l.: *DE CAMPS.1837*
PROVENANCE: Lord Henry Seymour, London, bought from the artist in 1837; until at least 1855; Colonel de Viterne, in 1860; John Siltzer, London, by 1869; until at least 1886(?); E. Secrétan, Paris; his sale, Galerie Charles Sedelmeyer, Paris, July 1, 1889, no. 11; bought at sale by Durand-Ruel for Havemeyer for Fr 70,000 (stock no. 2386); Mr. and Mrs. H. O. Havemeyer, New York, 1889–1907; Mrs. H. O. Havemeyer, New York, 1907–29; MMA 29.100.196.
EXHIBITIONS: 1839 Paris, no. 504; 1855 Paris, no. 2892; 1860 Paris, no. 141.
REFERENCES: Havemeyer 1931, p. 105; Havemeyer 1958, p. 19, no. 99; Sterling and Salinger 1966, pp. 31f., ill.; Mosby 1977, no. 201; Weitzenhoffer 1982, p. 108, fig. 17; Weitzenhoffer 1986, p. 58.

184
Alexandre-Gabriel Decamps
TRAVELER DRINKING AT SPRING
Oil on canvas, 12¾ x 16 in. (32.4 x 40.6 cm)
Signed l., on rock: *D.C.*
PROVENANCE: Mr. and Mrs. H. O. Havemeyer, New York, by 1890–1907; Mrs. H. O. Havemeyer, New York, 1907–29; consigned to Durand-Ruel, Sept. 24, 1919–Feb. 10, 1928 (deposit no. 7991, as *The Little Traveller [Landscape]*); her sale, American Art Association, New York, Apr. 10, 1930, no. 47, as *Romantic Landscape*; bought at sale by O. B. Carrott for $800; private collection, Riverside, Calif.
EXHIBITIONS: 1890–91 New York, no. 11; 1891 New York Metropolitan, no. 11.
REFERENCES: Havemeyer 1931, p. 503; Mosby 1977, no. 446; Weitzenhoffer 1982, pp. 131f.

185
Alexandre-Gabriel Decamps
THE GOOD SAMARITAN
Oil on canvas, 36⅝ x 29⅛ in. (93 x 74 cm)
PROVENANCE: estate of Decamps; sale, Hôtel Drouot, Paris, Apr. 29–30, 1861, no. 1; bought at sale by Meyer for Fr 24,780 (including 5 percent buyer's premium); Meyer, Vienna, 1861–67; his sale, Hôtel Drouot, Paris, Apr. 27–28, 1866, no. 13, bought in(?) for Fr 14,100; Goupil, Paris, bought in exchange with Meyer,

Dec. 31, 1867, for Fr 14,500 or Fr 14,000 (stock no. 3244); M. Redron, bought from Goupil, Oct. 8, 1869, for Fr 15,000; Gustave Viot, Paris; sale, Galerie Georges Petit, Paris, May 25, 1886, no. 1; Brame, Paris, until 1889; Durand-Ruel, Paris, bought from Brame, July 25, 1889, for Fr 35,000 (stock no. 2370); Mr. and Mrs. H. O. Havemeyer, New York, bought from Durand-Ruel, Aug. 21, 1889, for Fr 55,000; until 1907; Mrs. H. O. Havemeyer, New York, 1907–29; her son, Horace Havemeyer, New York, 1929; MMA (H. O. Havemeyer Collection, Gift of Horace Havemeyer, 1929), 29.160.36.
EXHIBITION: 1883 Paris, no. 23.
REFERENCES: Havemeyer 1931, pp. 104f., ill.; Havemeyer 1958, p. 19, no. 100; Sterling and Salinger 1966, pp. 33f., ill.; Mosby 1977, no. 500; Weitzenhoffer 1982, p. 113, fig. 23; Weitzenhoffer 1986, pp. 61, 158.

186
Alexandre-Gabriel Decamps
TOBIAS AND THE ANGEL***
Oil on wood, 24 x 31⅞ in. (61 x 81 cm)
Signed l.l.: *Decamps*
PROVENANCE: sale, Mar. 14, 1859, for Fr 7,220; sale, Hôtel Drouot, Paris, Mar. 22, 1869, no. 14; bought at sale by Galerie Charles Sedelmeyer for Fr 4,190 or Fr 4,150; Mr. and Mrs. H. O. Havemeyer, New York, deposited with Durand-Ruel, Mar. 1901 and again Feb. 25, 1903; Durand-Ruel, New York, bought from Havemeyer,

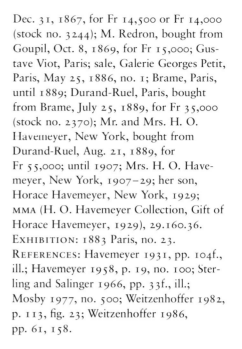

182

184

183

185

194

189

Oct. 28, 1904; Goldschmidt-Przibram, Brussels; sale, Galerie Frederik Muller, Amsterdam, June 17–19, 1924, no. 12.
REFERENCE: Mosby 1977, no. 524.

187
Alexandre-Gabriel Decamps
CHRIST AT EMMAUS
Oil on canvas, 13 x 18 in. (33 x 45.7 cm)
PROVENANCE: possibly Alexandre-Gabriel Decamps; his sale, Hôtel Drouot, Paris, Apr. 29–30, 1861, no. 8(?), as 69 x 95 cm, for Fr 2,800; dealer, bought abroad for $1,000; Mary Jane Morgan, New York, bought for $1,400; her sale, American Art Association, New York, Mar. 3–5, 1886, no. 225; bought at sale by Havemeyer for $3,100; Mr. and Mrs. H. O. Havemeyer, New York, 1886–1907; Mrs. H. O. Havemeyer, New York, 1907–29; her sale, American Art Association, New York, Apr. 10, 1930, no. 66; bought at sale by J. F. Kraushaar for $1,600; Kraushaar Galleries, New York, 1930–before 1947.
REFERENCES: Havemeyer 1931, p. 502; Mosby 1977, no. 531; Weitzenhoffer 1982, pp. 76, 78, 94, n. 6; Weitzenhoffer 1986, pp. 44–46.

188
Alexandre-Gabriel Decamps
CHRIST WITH THE DOCTORS
Watercolor and gouache, 14 x 18 in. (35.6 x 45.7 cm)
Signed below: *Decamps*
PROVENANCE: Paul Périer; his sale, 16, rue des Jeuneurs, Paris, Dec. 19, 1846, no. 52, for Fr 2,400; Lord Henry Seymour, London; his sale, Hôtel Drouot, Paris, Feb. 13,

1860, no. 12, for Fr 7,500; D. G. de Arozarena; his sale, Hôtel des Commissaires-Priseurs, Paris, May 29, 1861, no. 28, for Fr 6,800; John Waterloo Wilson, Paris, in 1881; Secrétan, bought for Fr 2,500; his son, E. Secrétan; his sale, Galerie Charles Sedelmeyer, Paris, July 1, 1889, no. 84; bought at sale by Durand-Ruel for Havemeyer for Fr 28,500 (stock no. 2381); Mr. and Mrs. H. O. Havemeyer, New York, 1889–1907; Mrs. H. O. Havemeyer, New York, 1907–29; her sale, American Art Association, New York, Apr. 10, 1930, no. 65, as *The Youthful Christ in the Temple*; bought at sale by W. Parsons Todd for $1,100; Mrs. Parsons Todd.
EXHIBITION: 1873 Brussels.
REFERENCES: Havemeyer 1931, p. 503; Mosby 1977, no. 535; Weitzenhoffer 1982, pp. 109, 119, n. 23; Weitzenhoffer 1986, p. 58.

189
Alexandre-Gabriel Decamps
THE BATTLE OF JERICHO***
Pastel, 25¼ x 76 in. (64.1 x 193 cm)
PROVENANCE: Alexandre-Gabriel Decamps, Paris; his sale, Hôtel des Ventes Mobilières, Paris, Apr. 21–23, 1853, no. 84; bought at sale by Marquis Maison for Fr 5,300; Veron, in 1855; Francis Petit, Paris, in 1860; MM. Revenaz, by 1869; until at least 1874; Ferdinand Barbedienne; his sale, Durand-Ruel, Paris, June 2–3, 1892, no. 120; bought at sale by Durand-Ruel for Fr 52,600; Durand-Ruel, Paris, 1892 (stock no. 2292, as *Prise de Jericho*); Mr. and Mrs. H. O. Havemeyer, New York, bought from Durand-Ruel, June 17, 1892,

for Fr 52,600; until 1907; Mrs. H. O. Havemeyer, New York, from 1907; deposited with Durand-Ruel, Nov. 30, 1908–May 11, 1910 (deposit no. 7501, as *Prise de Jericho*), Nov. 16, 1911, Dec. 5, 1912–May 24, 1913 (deposit no. 7681), and Nov. 5, 1913–May 29, 1914 (deposit no. 7712).
EXHIBITIONS: 1855 Paris, no. 2895; 1860 Paris, no. 33; 1874 Paris, no. 592.
REFERENCES: Mosby 1977, no. 545, as *Josué arrêtant le soleil*; Weitzenhoffer 1982, pp. 131, 143, n. 18; Weitzenhoffer 1986, pp. 65, 184.

190
Alexandre-Gabriel Decamps
EASTERN FARM
Oil on canvas, 15 x 23 in. (38.1 x 58.4 cm)
PROVENANCE: Mr. and Mrs. H. O. Havemeyer, New York, bought from Durand-Ruel, Feb. 1891, as *Kiosque oriental*; until 1907; Mrs. H. O. Havemeyer, New York, 1907–29; her sale, American Art Association, New York, Apr. 10, 1930, no. 49, as *Rustic Landscape*; bought at sale by Scott and Fowles for $500.
REFERENCES: Havemeyer 1931, p. 503; Weitzenhoffer 1982, pp. 130, 142, n. 14; Weitzenhoffer 1986, p. 65.

191
Alexandre-Gabriel Decamps
EASTERN TRAVELERS
Oil on canvas, 10 x 13 in. (25.4 x 33 cm)
Signed below: *DECAMPS*
PROVENANCE: Mr. and Mrs. H. O. Havemeyer, New York, bought from Durand-Ruel, Feb. 18, 1891, as *Bisque oriental*; until 1907; Mrs. H. O. Havemeyer, New York, 1907–29; her sale, American Art Association, New York, Apr. 10, 1930, no. 38; bought at sale by Scott and Fowles for $450.
REFERENCES: Havemeyer 1931, p. 503; Weitzenhoffer 1982, pp. 130, 142, n. 14; Weitzenhoffer 1986, p. 65.

192
Alexandre-Gabriel Decamps
FERME DU VERRIER***
PROVENANCE: Mr. and Mrs. H. O. Havemeyer, New York, until 1903; Durand-Ruel, New York, bought from Havemeyer, Apr. 13, 1903.
Note: The title of this work is unverified; it is taken from handwritten notes from Durand-Ruel stock books.

193
Alexandre-Gabriel Decamps
NEAR SMYRNA
Oil on wood, 9½ x 13½ in. (24.1 x 34.3 cm)

Signed l.l.: *DECAMPS*
PROVENANCE: Mr. and Mrs. H. O.
Havemeyer, New York, by 1890–1907;
Mrs. H. O. Havemeyer, New York, 1907–
29; her sale, American Art Association,
New York, Apr. 10, 1930, no. 37, as *Environs of Smyrna*; bought at sale by Scott
and Fowles for $450.
EXHIBITIONS: 1890–91 New York,
no. 10; 1891 New York Metropolitan,
no. 10.
REFERENCES: Havemeyer 1931, p. 503;
Weitzenhoffer 1982, pp. 131f.

194
Alexandre-Gabriel Decamps
THE OAK AND THE REED***
Signed and dated l.r.: *D.C. 1842*
PROVENANCE: M. Freret, until 1889;
Durand-Ruel, Paris, received on deposit
from Freret, Oct. 29, 1889 (deposit no.
6930); bought from him, Nov. 4, 1889, for
Fr 8,800 (stock no. 2550); Durand-Ruel,
New York, bought from Durand-Ruel,
Paris, Nov. 4, 1889 (Paris stock book), or
Nov. 29, 1889 (New York stock book,
no. 799); Mr. and Mrs. H. O. Havemeyer,
New York, bought from Durand-Ruel,
Feb. 18, 1891, for $8,000 or Fr 15,000;
until 1907; Mrs. H. O. Havemeyer, New
York, 1907–8; deposited with Durand-
Ruel, Nov. 30, 1908 (deposit no. 7503);
Durand-Ruel, New York, bought from
Havemeyer, Feb. 5, 1909, for $12,000
(stock no. 3299); James J. Hill, St. Paul,
bought from Durand-Ruel, Feb. 5, 1909,
for $13,500.
REFERENCES: Weitzenhoffer 1982,
pp. 130, 142, n. 14; Weitzenhoffer 1986,
pp. 65, 184.

195
Alexandre-Gabriel Decamps
PILGRIM BOY
Oil on canvas, 10 x 8 in. (25.4 x 20.3 cm)
Signed l.l.: *D.C.*
PROVENANCE: Mrs. H. O. Havemeyer, New
York, d. 1929; her sale, American Art Association, New York, Apr. 10, 1930, no. 33,
as *The Peasant Lad*; bought at sale by
Seligmann, Rey and Co. for $225.
REFERENCE: Havemeyer 1931, p. 503.

196
Hilaire-Germain-Edgar Degas
French, 1834–1917
A WOMAN SEATED BESIDE A VASE
OF FLOWERS (MME PAUL
VALPINÇON?)**
Oil on canvas, 29 x 36½ in.
(73.7 x 92.7 cm)
Signed and dated twice l.l.: *Degas / 1865*
[partially illegible] and *1865 / Degas*
PROVENANCE: Boussod, Valadon et Cie,
Paris, bought from the artist, July 22,

1887, for Fr 4,000; deposited at Goupil,
The Hague, Apr. 6–June 9, 1888; Jules-
Emile Boivin, Paris, bought from Boussod,
Valadon, Feb. 28, 1889, for Fr 5,500;
d. 1909; his widow, Mme Jules-Emile
Boivin, Paris, 1909–19; Durand-Ruel,
Paris, received on deposit from her heirs,
June 10, 1920 (deposit no. 12097);
Durand-Ruel, New York, bought from her
heirs, July 3, 1920 (stock no. 4546); received from Durand-Ruel, Paris, Nov. 11,
1920; Mrs. H. O. Havemeyer, New York,
bought from Durand-Ruel, Jan. 28, 1921,
for $30,000; d. 1929; MMA 29.100.128.
REFERENCES: Havemeyer 1931, pp. 108f.,
ill.; Lemoisne 1946, no. 125, as *La Femme
aux chrysanthèmes (Mme Hertel)*; Havemeyer 1958, p. 22, no. 113, ill.; Sterling
and Salinger 1967, pp. 57–60, ill.; Weitzenhoffer 1986, pp. 240, 257, colorpl. 162.

197
Hilaire-Germain-Edgar Degas
THE COLLECTOR OF PRINTS*
Oil on canvas, 20⅞ x 15¾ in. (53 x 40 cm)
Signed and dated l.l.: *Degas / 1866*
PROVENANCE: Mr. and Mrs. H. O. Havemeyer, New York, bought from the artist,
probably spring 1891, for Fr 3,000 or
Fr 5,000; sent to them by Durand-Ruel,
Dec. 13, 1894; probably arrived New
York, Feb. 12, 1895; until 1907; Mrs.
H. O. Havemeyer, New York, 1907–29;
MMA 29.100.44.
REFERENCES: Havemeyer 1931, pp. 112f.,
ill.; Lemoisne 1946, no. 138; Havemeyer
1958, p. 20, no. 102; Havemeyer 1961,
pp. 252f.; Sterling and Salinger 1967,
p. 61, ill.; Weitzenhoffer 1982, pp. 164f.,
169, n. 40, p. 198, n. 45, fig. 48; Weitzenhoffer 1986, pp. 81, 255, pl. 34.

198
Hilaire-Germain-Edgar Degas
MLLE MARIE DIHAU (1843–1935)
Oil on canvas, 8¾ x 10¾ in.
(22.2 x 27.3 cm)
PROVENANCE: Durand-Ruel, Paris, bought
from the sitter, July 19, 1922, for Fr 35,000
(stock no. 12052); Durand-Ruel, New York,
bought from Durand-Ruel, Paris, Nov. 2,
1922 (stock no. 4765); Mrs. H. O. Havemeyer, New York, bought from Durand-
Ruel, Jan. 16, 1923; d. 1929; MMA
29.100.182.
REFERENCES: Havemeyer 1931, p. 115;
Lemoisne 1946, no. 172; Havemeyer 1958,
p. 21, no. 107; Sterling and Salinger 1967,
pp. 61f., ill.; Weitzenhoffer 1986, p. 240,
pl. 167.

199
Hilaire-Germain-Edgar Degas
JOSEPH-HENRI ALTÈS (1826–1895)

Oil on canvas, 10⅝ x 8½ in.
(27 x 21.6 cm)
Signed u.l.: *Degas*
PROVENANCE: Durand-Ruel, Paris, bought
from the artist, Dec. 11, 1902, for Fr 4,000
(stock no. 7200); Durand-Ruel, New York,
bought from Durand-Ruel, Paris, Feb. 12,
1903 (stock no. 2876); Mr. and Mrs. H. O.
Havemeyer, New York, bought from
Durand-Ruel, Mar. 4, 1903; until 1907;
Mrs. H. O. Havemeyer, New York, 1907–
29; MMA 29.100.181.
REFERENCES: Havemeyer 1931, p. 116;
Lemoisne 1946, no. 176; Havemeyer 1958,
p. 20, no. 106; Havemeyer 1961,
pp. 262f.; Sterling and Salinger 1967,
p. 65, ill.; Weitzenhoffer 1986, p. 147.

200
Hilaire-Germain-Edgar Degas
MME THEODORE GOBILLARD (YVES
MORISOT, 1838–1893)*
Oil on canvas, 21¾ x 25⅝ in.
(55.3 x 65.1 cm)
Signed l.l.: *Degas*
PROVENANCE: Michel Manzi, Paris,
d. 1915; Mrs. H. O. Havemeyer, New
York, bought from his widow, Charlotte
Manzi, through Cassatt, Dec. 5, 1916;*
d. 1929; MMA 29.100.45.
*See Chronology, June 26, 1916.
EXHIBITION: 1876 Paris, no. 39.
REFERENCES: Havemeyer 1931, pp. 114f.,
ill.; Lemoisne 1946, no. 213; Havemeyer
1958, p. 21, no. 108; Havemeyer 1961,
pp. 264–67; Sterling and Salinger 1967,
pp. 65f., ill.; Weitzenhoffer 1986,
pp. 230f., 255, pl. 156.

201
Hilaire-Germain-Edgar Degas
SULKING*
Oil on canvas, 12¾ x 18¼ in.
(32.4 x 46.4 cm)
Signed l.r.: *E. Degas*
PROVENANCE: Durand-Ruel, Paris, received on deposit from the artist, Dec. 27,
1895 (deposit no. 8848); bought Apr. 28,
1897, for Fr 13,500 (stock no. 4191);
Durand-Ruel, New York, bought from
Durand-Ruel, Paris (stock no. 1646), for
Havemeyer (this transaction took place before Durand-Ruel, Paris, bought the picture from Degas); Mrs. H. O. Havemeyer,
New York, bought Dec. 15, 1896, for
$4,500; d. 1929; MMA 29.100.43.
EXHIBITIONS: 1896 Paris; 1915 New York
Masterpieces, no. 25, as *The Dispute*.
REFERENCES: Havemeyer 1931, pp. 110f.,
ill.; Lemoisne 1946, no. 335; Havemeyer
1958, p. 21, no. 110, ill.; Sterling and Salinger 1967, pp. 71–73, ill.; Weitzenhoffer
1986, p. 255.

196

200

204

197

201

205

198

202

206

199

203

207

202

Hilaire-Germain-Edgar Degas
THE BALLET FROM "ROBERT LE DIABLE"
Oil on canvas, 26 x 21⅜ in. (66 x 54.3 cm)
Signed and dated l.r.: *Degas / 1872*
PROVENANCE: Durand-Ruel, Paris, bought from the artist, Jan. 1872, for Fr 1,500 (stock no. 978); Edgar Degas, Paris, bought back from Durand-Ruel on his behalf by Jean-Baptiste Faure, Mar. 5 or 6, 1874, for Fr 1,500; Durand-Ruel, Paris, bought from the artist, Aug. 20, 1885, for Fr 800 (stock no. 732); Rouart, Paris, bought from Durand-Ruel, Nov. 10, 1885, for Fr 3,000 and sold back, Dec. 31, 1885, for Fr 3,000; Durand-Ruel, Paris, deposited with Robertson, Dec. 24, 1885–Jan. 11, 1886; Jean-Baptiste Faure, Paris, bought from Durand-Ruel, Feb. 14, 1887, for Fr 2,500; Durand-Ruel, Paris, bought from Faure, Mar. 31, 1894 (stock no. 2981); Durand-Ruel, New York (stock no. 1205); Mr. and Mrs. H. O. Havemeyer, New York, bought from Durand-Ruel, Feb. 14, 1898, for $4,000; until 1907; Mrs. H. O. Havemeyer, New York, 1907–29; MMA 29.100.552.
EXHIBITIONS: 1872 London Fourth, no. 95, as *Robert le Diable*; 1886 New York, no. 17; 1897–98 Pittsburgh, no. 65.
REFERENCES: Havemeyer 1931, pp. 106f., ill.; Lemoisne 1946, no. 294; Havemeyer 1958, p. 20, no. 100; Havemeyer 1961, p. 263; Sterling and Salinger 1967, pp. 66–69, ill.; Weitzenhoffer 1982, p. 315, n. 32; Weitzenhoffer 1986, p. 130.

203

Hilaire-Germain-Edgar Degas
THE DANCING CLASS
Oil on wood, 7¾ x 10⅝ in. (19.7 x 27 cm)
Signed l.r.: *Degas*
PROVENANCE: Durand-Ruel, Paris, bought from the artist, Jan. 1872 (stock no. 943); Premsel, bought from Durand-Ruel, Jan. 16, 1872; Durand-Ruel, Paris, bought back from Premsel, Jan. 30, 1872 (stock no. 979); Edouard Brandon, Paris, bought from Durand-Ruel, Feb. 6, 1872; Durand-Ruel, Paris and London, 1876; Capt. Henry Hill, Brighton, from 1875 or 1876–82; his sale, Christie's, London, May 25, 1889, no. 26, as *A Pas de Deux*; bought at sale by Wallis for 41 or 111 guineas; Wallis, French Gallery, London, from 1889; Michel Manzi, Paris, d. 1915; Mrs. H. O. Havemeyer, New York, bought from his widow, Charlotte Manzi, through Cassatt, Dec. 5, 1916;* d. 1929; MMA 29.100.184.
*See Chronology, June 26, 1916.
EXHIBITIONS: 1874 Paris Capucines, no. 55; 1876 London, no. 2, as *The Practising Room*; 1928 New York, no. 6(?).
REFERENCES: Havemeyer 1931, p. 117, ill.; Lemoisne 1946, no. 297, as *Le Foyer*;

Havemeyer 1958, p. 20, no. 105; Havemeyer 1961, pp. 265f.; Sterling and Salinger 1967, pp. 69–71, ill.; Weitzenhoffer 1986, pp. 230f., pl. 157.

204

Hilaire-Germain-Edgar Degas
THE ARTIST'S COUSIN, PROBABLY MRS. WILLIAM BELL (MATHILDE MUSSON, 1841–1878)*
Pastel on green wove paper, now darkened to brown, 18⅝ x 15⅛ in. (47.3 x 38.4 cm)
Signed and dated l.r.: *Degas / 1873*
PROVENANCE: Edmond Taigny, Paris, until the late 1890s; Mr. and Mrs. H. O. Havemeyer, New York, bought from Taigny through Alphonse Portier, probably in 1896, for Fr 10,000; until 1907; Mrs. H. O. Havemeyer, New York, 1907–29; MMA 29.100.40.
EXHIBITIONS: 1915 New York Masterpieces, no. 40, as *Portrait*; 1922 New York, no. 109.
REFERENCES: Havemeyer 1931, pp. 128f., ill.; Lemoisne 1946, no. 319, as *Mme René de Gas (Estelle Musson)*; Havemeyer 1958, p. 23, no. 122; Havemeyer 1961, pp. 260f.; Weitzenhoffer 1982, pp. 259f., fig. 84; Weitzenhoffer 1986, pp. 115, 255, pl. 69.

205

Hilaire-Germain-Edgar Degas
A WOMAN IRONING*
Oil on canvas, 21⅜ x 15½ in. (54.3 x 39.4 cm)
Signed l.l.: *Degas*
PROVENANCE: Durand-Ruel, Paris, bought from the artist, June 6 or 14, 1873, for Fr 2,000 (stock no. 3132); transferred to Durand-Ruel, London, winter 1873; returned to Durand-Ruel, Paris; Edgar Degas, Paris, bought back on his behalf by Jean-Baptiste Faure, Mar. 5 or 6, 1874, for Fr 2,000; Durand-Ruel, Paris, bought back from the artist, Feb. 29, 1892, for Fr 2,500 (stock no. 2039); deposited with Bernheim-Jeune, Paris, Nov. 3, 1893–Feb. 13, 1894; Durand-Ruel, New York, bought from Durand-Ruel, Paris, Oct. 4, 1894 (stock no. 1204); Mr. and Mrs. H. O. Havemeyer, New York, bought from Durand-Ruel, Dec. 18, 1894, for Fr 2,500; until 1907; Mrs. H. O. Havemeyer, New York, 1907–29; MMA 29.100.46.
EXHIBITIONS: 1873 London, no. 80, as *The Parisian Laundress*; 1876 Paris, no. 49(?); 1915 New York Masterpieces, no. 26, as *The Laundress*.
REFERENCES: Havemeyer 1931, pp. 112f., ill.; Lemoisne 1946, no. 356, as *Repasseuse à contre-jour*; Havemeyer 1958, p. 22, no. 114; Sterling and Salinger 1967, pp. 77f., ill.; Weitzenhoffer 1986, pp. 98, 255, pl. 49.

206

Hilaire-Germain-Edgar Degas
DANCER ADJUSTING HER SLIPPER
Graphite heightened with white chalk, on pink wove paper, now-faded, 12⅞ x 9⅝ in. (32.7 x 24.5 cm)
Signed l.l.: *Degas*; inscribed c.r.: *le bra est enfoncé un / peu dans la / mousseline*
PROVENANCE: Mr. and Mrs. H. O. Havemeyer, New York, bought from the artist; until 1907; Mrs. H. O. Havemeyer, New York, 1907–29; MMA 29.100.941.
EXHIBITION: 1922 New York, no. 11.
REFERENCES: Havemeyer 1931, p. 186; Havemeyer 1958, p. 24, no. 131; Havemeyer 1961, p. 252; Weitzenhoffer 1982, p. 260; Weitzenhoffer 1986, p. 116.

207

Hilaire-Germain-Edgar Degas
TWO DANCERS
Dark brown wash and white gouache on bright pink commercially coated wove paper, now faded to pale pink, 24⅛ x 15½ in. (61.3 x 39.4 cm)
Signed l.r.: *Degas*
PROVENANCE: Boussod, Valadon et Cie, Paris, probably bought from the artist; Mrs. H. O. Havemeyer, New York, probably bought from Boussod, Valadon, by 1922–29; MMA 29.100.187.
EXHIBITION: 1922 New York, no. 90.
REFERENCES: Havemeyer 1931, p. 185; Lemoisne 1946, no. 1005; Havemeyer 1958, p. 24, no. 134.

208

Hilaire-Germain-Edgar Degas
SEATED DANCER
Charcoal and white chalk on pink wove paper, 16½ x 12⅞ in. (41.9 x 32.7 cm)
Signed l.r.: *Degas*
PROVENANCE: Mr. and Mrs. H. O. Havemeyer, New York, bought from the artist; until 1907; Mrs. H. O. Havemeyer, New York, 1907–29; MMA 29.100.942.
EXHIBITION: 1922 New York, no. 13.
REFERENCES: Havemeyer 1931, pp. 186f., ill.; Havemeyer 1958, p. 24, no. 132; Havemeyer 1961, p. 252; Weitzenhoffer 1982, p. 260; Weitzenhoffer 1986, p. 116.

209

Hilaire-Germain-Edgar Degas
DANCERS AT REST
Oil and gouache on paper, laid down on canvas, 18⅛ x 12¾ in. (46 x 32.4 cm)
Signed and dated l.l.: *Degas / 1874*
PROVENANCE: Durand-Ruel, Paris, bought from Camentron, Jan. 24, 1899, for Fr 15,000 (stock no. 4984); Durand-Ruel, New York, bought from Durand-Ruel, Paris, Feb. 21, 1899 (stock no. 2136); Mr.

208

210

212

209

211

213

and Mrs. H. O. Havemeyer, New York, bought from Durand-Ruel, Feb. 20, 1899, for $7,000; until 1907; Mrs. H. O. Havemeyer, New York, 1907–29; her son Horace Havemeyer, New York, from 1929; his sister Electra Havemeyer Webb, New York, d. 1960; her daughter Electra Webb Bostwick, New York, d. 1982; sale, Christie's, New York, Nov. 3, 1982, no. 41; bought at sale by a private collector for $1,320,000; private collection, from 1982.
EXHIBITION: 1915 New York Masterpieces, not in cat.
REFERENCES: Havemeyer 1931, p. 387; Lemoisne 1946, no. 343; Weitzenhoffer 1982, p. 305, fig. 116; Weitzenhoffer 1986, pp. 134f., colorpl. 96.

(stock no. 2116); Mr. and Mrs. H. O. Havemeyer, New York, bought from Durand-Ruel, Feb. 17, 1899; until 1907; Mrs. H. O. Havemeyer, New York, 1907–29; her daughter Electra Havemeyer Webb, New York, 1929–60; her daughter Electra Webb Bostwick, New York, 1960–82; Shelburne Museum, Shelburne, Vt., from 1982, 27.3.1–35A.
EXHIBITIONS: 1879 Paris, no. 65; 1928 New York, no. 6.
REFERENCES: Havemeyer 1931, pp. 374f., ill.; Lemoisne 1946, no. 399; Havemeyer 1961, p. 260; Weitzenhoffer 1982, pp. 303–5, 317, nn. 43, 44, fig. 114; Weitzenhoffer 1986, pp. 133f., colorpl. 95.

from Durand-Ruel, Paris, Jan. 26, 1899 (stock no. 2117); Mr. and Mrs. H. O. Havemeyer, New York, bought from Durand-Ruel, Feb. 17, 1899, for Fr 48,197; until 1907; Mrs. H. O. Havemeyer, New York, 1907–29; MMA 29.100.39.
EXHIBITIONS: possibly 1879 Paris, not in cat.; 1915 New York Masterpieces, no. 38 or not in cat.
REFERENCES: Havemeyer 1931, pp. 124f., ill.; Lemoisne 1946, no. 498; Havemeyer 1958, p. 23, no. 123; Havemeyer 1961, pp. 259f.; Sterling and Salinger 1967, pp. 76f., ill.; Weitzenhoffer 1982, pp. 303–5, 317, nn. 43, 44, fig. 115; Weitzenhoffer 1986, pp. 133f., 255, pl. 93, ill. p. 224.

210
Hilaire-Germain-Edgar Degas
REHEARSAL IN THE STUDIO
Oil and tempera on canvas, 17 ¼ x 23 in. (43.8 x 58.4 cm)
Signed l.r.: *Degas*
PROVENANCE: Ernest May, Paris; his sale, Galerie Georges Petit, Paris, June 4, 1890, no. 30, bought in; his son, Georges May; Durand-Ruel, Paris, bought from May, Jan. 25, 1899, for Fr 47,000 (stock no. 4989); Durand-Ruel, New York, bought from Durand-Ruel, Paris, Jan. 26, 1899

211
Hilaire-Germain-Edgar Degas
THE REHEARSAL ON THE STAGE*
Pastel over brush-and-ink drawing, on thin cream-colored wove paper, laid on bristol board and mounted on canvas, 21 x 28 ½ in. (53.3 x 72.4 cm)
Signed u.l.: *Degas*
PROVENANCE: Ernest May, Paris; his sale, Galerie Georges Petit, Paris, June 4, 1890, no. 75, bought in; his son, Georges May, Paris; Durand-Ruel, Paris, bought from May, Jan. 25, 1899, for Fr 47,000 (stock no. 4990); Durand-Ruel, New York, bought

212
Hilaire-Germain-Edgar Degas
THE REHEARSAL OF THE BALLET ONSTAGE
Oil colors freely mixed with turpentine, with traces of watercolor and pastel over pen-and-ink drawing, on cream-colored wove paper, laid on bristol board and mounted on canvas, 21 ⅜ x 28 ¾ in. (54.3 x 73 cm)
Signed u.l.: *Degas*
PROVENANCE: Charles W. Deschamps, London, sent to him by the artist before Apr. 1876; Capt. Henry Hill, Brighton, d. 1882;

328

214

215

217

216

218

219

his sale, Christie's, London, May 25, 1889, no. 29; bought at sale by Sickert for 66 guineas; Walter Sickert, London, from 1889; his second wife, Ellen Cobden-Sickert, London, given to her by him, until 1902; left in care of her sister, Mrs. T. Fisher-Unwin, London, by summer 1898; deposited with Durand-Ruel, Paris, Jan. 4, 1902 (deposit no. 10185); returned to her in care of Boussod, Valadon, Jan. 25, 1902; Boussod, Valadon et Cie, Paris, bought from her, Jan. 31, 1902, for Fr 75,373 (stock no. 27473); Mr. and Mrs. H. O. Havemeyer, New York, bought from Boussod, Valadon, Feb. 7, 1902, for Fr 82,845; until 1907; Mrs. H. O. Havemeyer, New York, 1907–29; her son, Horace Havemeyer, New York, 1929; MMA (H. O. Havemeyer Collection, Gift of Horace Havemeyer, 1929), 29.160.26.

EXHIBITIONS: 1876 London, no. 130, as *The Rehearsal*; 1877 Paris, no. 61(?); 1891–92 London English, no. 39, as *Répétition*; 1898 London, no. 116, as *Dancers* (pastel); 1900 Paris, no. 210; 1915 New York Masterpieces, no. 38 or not in cat.

REFERENCES: Havemeyer 1931, pp. 122f., ill.; Lemoisne 1946, no. 400; Havemeyer 1958, p. 21, no. 111; Havemeyer 1961, pp. 259f.; Sterling and Salinger 1967, pp. 73–76, ill.; Weitzenhoffer 1986, ill. p. 224.

213
Hilaire-Germain-Edgar Degas
WOMAN ON A SOFA
Oil on pink paper, 19⅛ x 16¾ in. (48.6 x 42.6 cm)
Signed and dated u.r.: *Degas 1875*
PROVENANCE: Michel Manzi, Paris, d. 1915; Mrs. H. O. Havemeyer, New York, bought from his widow, Charlotte Manzi, through Cassatt, Dec. 5, 1916;* d. 1929; MMA 29.100.185.
*See Chronology, June 26, 1916.
EXHIBITION: 1922 New York, no. 108.
REFERENCES: Havemeyer 1931, pp. 185, 187, ill.; Lemoisne 1946, no. 363; Havemeyer 1958, p. 25, no. 136; Havemeyer 1961, pp. 265f.; Weitzenhoffer 1986, pp. 230f.

214
Hilaire-Germain-Edgar Degas
DANCER ONSTAGE WITH A BOUQUET
Pastel over monotype on laid paper, 10⅝ x 14⅞ in. (27 x 37.8 cm)
Signed u.l.: *Degas*
PROVENANCE: Mr. and Mrs. H. O. Havemeyer, New York, bought in 1896 through Alphonse Portier for Fr 4,000; until 1907; Mrs. H. O. Havemeyer, New York, 1907–29; her daughter Adaline Havemeyer Frelinghuysen, Morristown, N.J., 1929–63;

private collection.
REFERENCES: Havemeyer 1931, p. 367; Lemoisne 1946, no. 515, as *Danseuse saluant*; Weitzenhoffer 1986, p. 116.

215
Hilaire-Germain-Edgar Degas
BALLET REHEARSAL
Gouache and pastel over monotype, 21¾ x 26¾ in. (55.3 x 68 cm)
Signed u.r.: *Degas*
PROVENANCE: Louisine W. Elder (later Mrs. H. O. Havemeyer), New York, possibly bought from Julien-François Tanguy in Paris in 1877 for Fr 500; d. 1929; her daughter Adaline Havemeyer Frelinghuysen, Morristown, N.J., 1929–63; her son George G. Frelinghuysen, Beverly Hills, 1963–65; sale, Parke-Bernet, New York, Apr. 14, 1965, no. 49; bought at sale by Simon for $410,000; Norton Simon, Fullerton, Calif., 1965–73; his sale, Sotheby's, New York, May 2, 1973, no. 7; bought at sale by Marlborough for $780,000; Marlborough Gallery, New York, 1973; The Nelson-Atkins Museum of Art, Kansas City, Mo., bought from Marlborough in 1973 (Acquired through The Kenneth A. and Helen F. Spencer Foundation Acquisition Fund), F73-30.
EXHIBITIONS: 1878 New York, no. 233,

220

225

221

226

222

227

223

224

as *A Ballet*, lent by G. N. Elder; 1915 New York Masterpieces, no. 33, as *The Rehearsal with the Dancing Master*. REFERENCES: Havemeyer 1931, pp. 364f., ill.; Lemoisne 1946, no. 365; Havemeyer 1961, pp. 204, 206f., 249–51; Weitzenhoffer 1982, pp. 14f., 18–20, 28f., n. 9, p. 30, n. 24, pp. 45, 47, 198, n. 45, fig. 1; Weitzenhoffer 1986, pp. 21, 23, 26f., 34, colorpl. 1.

216
Hilaire-Germain-Edgar Degas
DANCERS PRACTICING AT THE BAR *
Mixed media on canvas, 29 ¾ x 32 in. (75.6 x 81.3 cm)
Signed l.c.: *Degas*

PROVENANCE: Henri Rouart, Paris, given to him by the artist; d. 1912; his sale, Galerie Manzi-Joyant, Paris, Dec. 10, 1912, no. 177; bought at sale by Durand-Ruel for Havemeyer for Fr 435,000 (Fr 478,500 including buyer's premium); Mrs. H. O. Havemeyer, New York, 1912–29; MMA 29.100.34.
EXHIBITION: 1877 Paris, no. 41.
REFERENCES: Havemeyer 1931, pp. 120f., ill.; Lemoisne 1946, no. 408; Havemeyer 1958, p. 20, no. 103; Havemeyer 1961, pp. 252–54, 257; Sterling and Salinger 1967, pp. 78–81, ill.; Weitzenhoffer 1986, pp. 208f., 255, colorpl. 147.

217
Hilaire-Germain-Edgar Degas
THE SONG OF THE DOG
Gouache and pastel over monotype, on three pieces of paper joined together, 24 ¾ x 20 ⅛ in. (62.9 x 51.1 cm)
Signed l.r.: *Degas*

PROVENANCE: Henri Rouart, Paris; his sale, Galerie Manzi-Joyant, Paris, Dec. 16, 1912, no. 71; bought at sale by Durand-Ruel for Havemeyer for Fr 50,100 (Fr 55,100 including buyer's premium); Mrs. H. O. Havemeyer, New York, 1912–29; her son, Horace Havemeyer, New York, 1929–56; his widow, Doris Dick Havemeyer, New York, 1956–82; her sale, Sotheby's, New York, May 18, 1983, no. 12; bought at sale by Cherry for $3,410,000; Wendell Cherry, Louisville and New York, from 1983; private collection, U.S.A., bought from Cherry through Acquavella, Mar. 1987.
EXHIBITIONS: 1915 New York Masterpieces, no. 35, as *Café Concert, Chanson du chien*; 1917 Paris, no. 25.
REFERENCES: Havemeyer 1931, p. 381; Lemoisne 1946, no. 380; Havemeyer 1961, pp. 245f.; Weitzenhoffer 1986, p. 208, colorpl. 148.

218
Hilaire-Germain-Edgar Degas
DANCERS AT THE BAR

Pastel on paper laid down on board,
26 x 20⅛ in. (66 x 51.1 cm)
Signed u.r.: *Degas*
PROVENANCE: possibly Mr. and Mrs. H. O.
Havemeyer, New York, bought in Paris in
early 1907 and shipped to them, May 11,
1907, by Durand-Ruel (deposit no. 11182
or 11183, both as *Etude de danseuse* [pastel]); Mrs. H. O. Havemeyer, New York,
d. 1929; her daughter Electra Havemeyer
Webb, New York, 1929–60; her daughter
Electra Webb Bostwick, New York, 1960–
82; sale, Christie's, New York, Nov. 3,
1982, no. 44; bought at sale by Acquavella, probably for a private collector, for
$1,045,000.
REFERENCES: Havemeyer 1931, pp. 370f.,
ill.; Lemoisne 1946, no. 460; Havemeyer
1961, pp. 252, 257; Weitzenhoffer 1986,
p. 178, colorpl. 136.

219
Hilaire-Germain-Edgar Degas
DANCER IN YELLOW
Pastel on paper, 28 x 15 in.
(71.1 x 38.1 cm)
Signed l.r.: *Degas*
PROVENANCE: Durand-Ruel, Paris, bought
Aug. 25, 1891, for Fr 1,500 (stock no.
1203); Mr. and Mrs. H. O. Havemeyer,
New York, bought from Durand-Ruel,
Sept. 19, 1895, for Fr 3,500; until 1907;
Mrs. H. O. Havemeyer, New York, 1907–
29; her daughter Electra Havemeyer Webb,
New York, 1929–60; Shelburne Museum,
Shelburne, Vt., from 1960, 27.3.1–32.
REFERENCES: Havemeyer 1931, pp. 372f.,
ill.; Lemoisne 1946, no. 483; Havemeyer
1961, pp. 258f.; Weitzenhoffer 1982,
pp. 241f., fig. 76; Weitzenhoffer 1986,
p. 107.

220
Hilaire-Germain-Edgar Degas
DANCERS IN WHITE
Pastel, 20 x 25 in. (50.8 x 63.5 cm)
Signed u.r.: *Degas*
PROVENANCE: Cottier and Co., New York;
Mr. and Mrs. H. O. Havemeyer, New York,
bought from Cottier; until 1907; Mrs. H. O.
Havemeyer, New York, 1907–29; her
daughter Adaline Havemeyer Frelinghuysen, Morristown, N. J., 1929–63; private collection.
REFERENCES: Havemeyer 1931, p. 368;
Lemoisne 1946, no. 494; Havemeyer 1961,
p. 259.

221
Hilaire-Germain-Edgar Degas
LITTLE GIRL PRACTICING AT THE
BAR
Black chalk heightened with white chalk
on pink laid paper, now faded,
12¼ x 11½ in. (31.1 x 29.2 cm)

Signed l.r.: *Degas*; inscribed u.l.: *bien accuser / l'os du coude*; inscribed l.r.: *battements à la seconde / à la barre*
PROVENANCE: Mr. and Mrs. H. O. Havemeyer, New York, bought from the artist;
until 1907; Mrs. H. O. Havemeyer, New
York, 1907–29; MMA 29.100.943.
EXHIBITION: 1922 New York, no. 24.
REFERENCES: Havemeyer 1931, p. 186;
Havemeyer 1958, p. 24, no. 133; Havemeyer 1961, p. 252; Weitzenhoffer 1982,
p. 260; Weitzenhoffer 1986, p. 116.

222
Hilaire-Germain-Edgar Degas
THREE DANCERS
Charcoal and pastel, 18¼ x 24½ in.
(46.4 x 62.2 cm)
Signed u.r.: *Degas*
PROVENANCE: Mrs. H. O. Havemeyer,
New York, d. 1929; her daughter Electra
Havemeyer Webb, New York, 1929–60;
her daughter Electra Webb Bostwick, New
York, 1960 until at least 1967.
EXHIBITION: 1922 New York, no. 88.
REFERENCES: Havemeyer 1931, p. 380;
Lemoisne 1946, no. 531.

223
Hilaire-Germain-Edgar Degas
FAN MOUNT: BALLET GIRLS
Watercolor, silver, and gold on silk,
7½ x 22¾ in. (19.1 x 57.8 cm)
Signed c.l.: *Degas*
PROVENANCE: Mary Cassatt, Paris, by 1883;
deposited with Durand-Ruel, Paris, Jan. 13–
June 3, 1913 (deposit no. 11640), and
again on Mar. 8, 1918 (deposit no. 11924);
Mrs. H. O. Havemeyer, New York,
bought from Cassatt for $20,000 with two
other Degases (*Woman Bathing in a Shallow Tub*, A239, and *Portrait of a Young
Woman*, A240); shipped to her by Durand-Ruel, May 9, 1919; d. 1929; MMA
29.100.555.
EXHIBITIONS: 1879 Paris, no. 80 or 81;
1922 New York, no. 87 or 89.
REFERENCES: Havemeyer 1931, p. 185;
Lemoisne 1946, no. 566; Havemeyer 1958,
p. 24, no. 130; Weitzenhoffer 1986,
pp. 238, 242.

224
Hilaire-Germain-Edgar Degas
FAN MOUNT: THE BALLET
Watercolor, India ink, silver, and gold on
silk, 6⅛ x 21¼ in. (15.6 x 54 cm)
PROVENANCE: Hector Brame, Paris, probably by 1879; until 1891; Durand-Ruel,
Paris, bought from Brame, Dec. 22, 1891,
for Fr 250 (stock no. 1963); Mr. and Mrs.
H. O. Havemeyer, New York, bought
from Durand-Ruel, Sept. 19, 1895, for

Fr 1,500; until 1907; Mrs. H. O. Havemeyer, New York, 1907–29; MMA
29.100.554.
EXHIBITIONS: 1879 Paris, no. 77(?); 1922
New York, no. 87 or 89.
REFERENCES: Havemeyer 1931, p. 185;
Lemoisne 1946, no. 457; Havemeyer 1958,
p. 24, no. 129; Weitzenhoffer 1982,
pp. 241f.; Weitzenhoffer 1986, pp. 107, 242.

225
Hilaire-Germain-Edgar Degas
THREE DANCERS PREPARING FOR
CLASS
Pastel on buff-colored wove paper,
21½ x 20½ in. (54.6 x 52.1 cm)
Signed l.l.: *Degas*
PROVENANCE: possibly Paul Rosenberg, Paris,
until 1903; possibly Mr. and Mrs. H. O.
Havemeyer, New York, bought from
Rosenberg in early 1903 for Fr 10,000, as
La toilette, and shipped to them by Durand-Ruel, May 7, 1903 (probably this picture);
Mrs. H. O. Havemeyer, New York, d. 1929;
MMA 29.100.558.
EXHIBITION: 1922 New York, no. 86(?).
REFERENCES: Havemeyer 1931, p. 119;
Lemoisne 1946, no. 542; Havemeyer 1958,
p. 23, no. 125; Sterling and Salinger 1967,
p. 85, ill.

226
Hilaire-Germain-Edgar Degas
THE DANCE LESSON
Pastel and black chalk on three pieces of
wove paper joined together,
25⅜ x 22⅛ in. (64.5 x 56.2 cm)
Signed u.r.: *Degas*
PROVENANCE: Gustave Caillebotte, Paris,
probably bought from the 1879 exhibition;
deposited with Durand-Ruel, Paris, Jan.
29–Nov. 30, 1886 (deposit no. 4691);
d. 1894; Pierre-Auguste Renoir, Paris, bequeathed to him by Caillebotte, 1894; deposited with Durand-Ruel, Paris, Mar. 13,
1894–May 13, 1895 (deposit no. 8398);
Durand-Ruel, Paris, bought from Renoir,
Dec. 12, 1898, for Fr 5,000 (stock no.
4879); Durand-Ruel, New York, bought
from Durand-Ruel, Paris, Dec. 31, 1898
(stock no. 2071); Mr. and Mrs. H. O. Havemeyer, New York, bought from Durand-Ruel, Jan. 3, 1899, for Fr 27,750; until
1907; Mrs. H. O. Havemeyer, New York,
1907–29; her son, Horace Havemeyer, New
York, from 1929; MMA (H. O. Havemeyer
Collection, Anonymous Gift, in memory of
Horace Havemeyer, 1971), 1971.185.
EXHIBITIONS: 1879 Paris, no. 74; 1886
New York, no. 63.
REFERENCES: Havemeyer 1931, pp. 386f.,
ill.; Lemoisne 1946, no. 450; Weitzenhoffer
1982, pp. 301f., 315f., n. 37, fig. 111;
Weitzenhoffer 1986, p. 133, pl. 90.

228

232

230

229

231

233

227
Hilaire-Germain-Edgar Degas
TWO DANCERS
Pastel and gouache on paper,
18⅛ x 26¼ in. (46 x 66.7 cm)
Signed u.r.: *Degas*
PROVENANCE: L., Paris; Georges Viau,
Paris; Mr. and Mrs. H. O. Havemeyer,
New York, bought from Viau through
Alphonse Portier, probably in 1896; until
1907; Mrs. H. O. Havemeyer, New York,
1907–29; her daughter Electra Havemeyer
Webb, New York, 1929–60; Shelburne
Museum, Shelburne, Vt., from 1960,
27.3.1–31.
EXHIBITIONS: 1880 Paris Pyramides,
no. 41; 1928 New York, no. 5.
REFERENCES: Havemeyer 1931, pp. 376f.,
ill.; Lemoisne 1946, no. 559; Havemeyer
1961, pp. 233, 259; Weitzenhoffer 1982,
p. 260, fig. 85; Weitzenhoffer 1986, p. 116,
colorpl. 71.

228
Hilaire-Germain-Edgar Degas
THE DANCE EXAMINATION
Pastel and charcoal on heavy gray wove
paper, 25 x 19 in. (63.5 x 48.3 cm)
Signed l.r.: *Degas*
PROVENANCE: Ernest May, Paris; his sale,
Galerie Georges Petit, June 4, 1890,
no. 76, for Fr 2,550; Bernheim-Jeune,

Paris, until 1898; Durand-Ruel, Paris,
bought from Bernheim-Jeune, Mar. 26,
1898, for Fr 10,000 (stock no. 4589);
Durand-Ruel, New York, bought from
Durand-Ruel, Paris, Dec. 22, 1898, for
Fr 22,000 (stock no. 2090); Mr. and Mrs.
H. O. Havemeyer, New York, bought
from Durand-Ruel between Dec. 31, 1898,
and Jan. 3, 1899; until 1907; Mrs. H. O.
Havemeyer, New York, 1907–29; her son,
Horace Havemeyer, New York, 1929–41;
The Denver Art Museum (Anonymous
gift), 1941.6.
EXHIBITIONS: 1880 Paris Pyramides,
no. 40; 1898 London, no. 117, as *Dancers
at Their Toilet*; 1915 New York Masterpieces, not in cat.
REFERENCES: Havemeyer 1931, pp. 384f.,
ill., as *Danseuses à leur toilette*; Lemoisne
1946, no. 576, as *Examen de danse (Danseuses à leur toilette)*; Weitzenhoffer 1982,
pp. 301f., 316, n. 38, fig. 112; Weitzenhoffer 1986, p. 133, pl. 91.

229
Hilaire-Germain-Edgar Degas
TWO DANCERS
Charcoal and white chalk on green com-
mercially coated wove paper, which retains
its original intensity, 25⅛ x 19¼ in.
(63.8 x 48.9 cm)
Signed l.l.: *Degas*

PROVENANCE: possibly Durand-Ruel,
Paris, bought from the artist, Jan. 26,
1882, for Fr 500 (stock no. 2184); possibly
M. Deschamps, bought from Durand-Ruel,
Aug. 31, 1882, for Fr 800; possibly Durand-
Ruel, Paris, bought from Deschamps, June
30, 1890, for Fr 800 (stock no. 567); possi-
bly Durand-Ruel, New York, received from
Durand-Ruel, Paris, Dec. 12, 1893 (stock
no. 1105); possibly Mr. and Mrs. H. O.
Havemeyer, New York, bought from
Durand-Ruel, Jan. 16, 1894; Mrs. H. O.
Havemeyer, New York, definitely by 1922–
29; MMA 29.100.189.
EXHIBITION: 1922 New York, no. 60.
REFERENCES: Havemeyer 1931, pp. 185,
187, ill.; Lemoisne 1946, no. 599; Have-
meyer 1958, p. 25, no. 135; Weitzenhoffer
1982, p. 225(?); Weitzenhoffer 1986, p. 98(?).

230
Hilaire-Germain-Edgar Degas
DANCER IN GREEN (LE PAS SUR
LA SCENE)
Pastel on paper, 28 x 15 in.
(71.1 x 38.1 cm)
Signed l.r.: *Degas*
PROVENANCE: Durand-Ruel, Paris, bought
Aug. 25, 1891, for Fr 1,500 (stock no.
1198); Mr. and Mrs. H. O. Havemeyer,
New York, bought from Durand-Ruel,
Sept. 19, 1895, for Fr 5,500; until 1907;

234

236

237

235

238

Mrs. H. O. Havemeyer, New York, 1907–29; her daughter Electra Havemeyer Webb, New York, 1929 60; Shelburne Museum, Shelburne, Vt. from 1960, 27.3.1–33.
EXHIBITION: 1915 New York Masterpieces, no. 41.
REFERENCES: Havemeyer 1931, pp. 372f., ill.; Lemoisne 1946, no. 591; Havemeyer 1961, pp. 258f.; Weitzenhoffer 1982, pp. 241f., fig. 75; Weitzenhoffer 1986, p. 107.

231
Hilaire-Germain-Edgar Degas
DANCER WITH A FAN
Pastel on gray-green laid paper,
24 x 16½ in. (61 x 41.9 cm)
Signed u.r.: *Degas*
PROVENANCE: Boussod, Valadon et Cie, Paris; Mrs. H. O. Havemeyer, New York, by 1922–29; MMA 29.100.188.
EXHIBITION: 1922 New York, no. 85.
REFERENCES: Havemeyer 1931, p. 186, ill.; Lemoisne 1946, no. 823; Havemeyer 1958, p. 23, no. 119.

232
Hilaire-Germain-Edgar Degas
BEFORE THE ENTRANCE ONSTAGE
Pastel on paper, 23¼ x 17¾ in.
(59.1 x 45.1 cm)
Signed l.r.: *Degas*

PROVENANCE: M. Blanc, Paris, deposited with Durand-Ruel, Paris, Apr. 2–Nov. 26, 1900 (deposit no. 9782); Georges Bernheim, Paris, until 1916; Durand-Ruel, Paris, bought from Bernheim, Oct. 31, 1916, for Fr 62,200 (stock no. 10914, as *Avant l'entrée en scène*); Durand-Ruel, New York, bought from Durand-Ruel, Paris, Nov. 20, 1916 (Paris stock book), or Dec. 12, 1916 (New York stock book, no. 4065), for Fr 40,035; Mrs. H. O. Havemeyer, New York, bought from Durand-Ruel, Jan. 8, 1917, for $30,000; d. 1929; her daughter Adaline Havemeyer Frelinghuysen, Morristown, N.J. from 1929; Mr. and Mrs. Henry Ittleson, Jr., New York, until 1973; Mrs. Henry Ittleson, Jr., New York, 1973–77; private collection, bought from Ittleson through Acquavella Galleries in 1977.
REFERENCES: Havemeyer 1931, pp. 366f., ill., as *Avant l'entrée en scène*; Lemoisne 1946, no. 497, as *Avant l'entrée en scène (Danseuse dans sa loge)*.

233
Hilaire-Germain-Edgar Degas
DANCER TYING HER SLIPPER
Pastel and black chalk on buff-colored paper mounted at the edges on board, 18⅝ x 16⅞ in. (47.3 x 42.9 cm)
Signed l.: *Degas*

PROVENANCE: Boussod, Valadon et Cie, Paris; Mr. and Mrs. H. O. Havemeyer, New York, bought from Boussod, Valadon; until 1907; Mrs. H. O. Havemeyer, New York, 1907–29; her daughter Electra Havemeyer Webb, New York, 1929–60; her daughter Electra Webb Bostwick, New York, from 1960; Hirschl and Adler, New York; Acquavella Galleries, New York, until 1981; Thomas Gibson Fine Art, London, bought from Acquavella, Mar. 13, 1981; Juan Alvarez de Toledo, bought from Gibson, Mar. 24, 1982; his sale, Christie's, New York, Nov. 12, 1985, no. 22; bought at sale by Acquavella for a private collector for $1,045,000; private collection, from 1985.
EXHIBITION: 1922 New York, no. 33.
REFERENCES: Havemeyer 1931, p. 380, as *Drawing—Ballet Girl*; Lemoisne 1946, no. 913; Weitzenhoffer 1986, p. 130, colorpl. 88.

234
Hilaire-Germain-Edgar Degas
JOCKEYS
Oil on canvas mounted on cardboard, 10⅜ x 15¹¹⁄₁₆ in. (26.4 x 39.9 cm)
Signed l.l.: *Degas*
PROVENANCE: Mr. and Mrs. H. O. Havemeyer, New York, until 1907; Mrs. H. O. Havemeyer, New York, 1907–29; her

239

243

249

240

244

250

241

245

251

246

242

248

252

334

daughter Electra Havemeyer Webb, New York, 1929–42; Yale University Art Gallery, New Haven (Gift of J. Watson Webb, B.A. 1907, and Electra Havemeyer Webb), 1942.302.

REFERENCES: Havemeyer 1931, p. 379, as *Horses with Jockeys*; Lemoisne 1946, no. 680; Havemeyer 1961, p. 257.

235

Hilaire-Germain-Edgar Degas
LITTLE MILLINERS
Pastel on paper, 19¼ x 28¼ in.
(48.9 x 71.8 cm)
Signed and dated u.l.: *1882 / Degas*
PROVENANCE: Durand-Ruel, Paris, until 1883; Alexis Rouart, Paris, bought from Durand-Ruel, July 10, 1883, for Fr 3,000; his sale, Hôtel Drouot, Paris, May 8–10, 1911, no. 214; bought at sale by Durand-Ruel for Havemeyer for Fr 51,000; Mrs. H. O. Havemeyer, New York, 1911–29; her daughter Adaline Havemeyer Frelinghuysen, Morristown, N.J., from 1929; her son, Peter H. B. Frelinghuysen, Jr., Morristown, N.J., by 1949; The Nelson-Atkins Museum of Art, Kansas City, Mo., from 1979 (Acquired through the generosity of an anonymous donor), F79-34.
EXHIBITIONS: 1886 Paris, no. 15; 1915 New York Masterpieces, no. 36, as *The Milliners*.
REFERENCES: Havemeyer 1931, pp. 362f., ill.; Lemoisne 1946, no. 681; Havemeyer 1961, p. 258; Weitzenhoffer 1986, ill. p. 224.

236

Hilaire-Germain-Edgar Degas
AT THE MILLINER'S*
Pastel on pale gray wove paper (industrial wrapping paper) adhered to silk bolting in 1951, 30 x 34 in. (76.2 x 86.4 cm)
Signed and dated u.r.: *1882 / Degas*; stamped on verso: *OLD RELIABLE BOLTING EXPRESSLY FOR MILLING*
PROVENANCE: Durand-Ruel, Paris, bought from the artist, July 15–16, 1882, for Fr 2,000 (stock no. 2508); Mme Angello, Paris, bought Oct. 10–12, 1882, for Fr 3,500 or Fr 4,000; until at least 1886; Alexander Reid, London and Glasgow, by 1891; T. G. Arthur, Glasgow, bought Jan. 1892, for £800; Martin et Camentron, Paris, deposited with Durand-Ruel, Paris, Mar. 13–19, 1895 (deposit no. 8637); Durand-Ruel, Paris, bought May 28, 1895, for Fr 15,000 (stock no. 3317); Durand-Ruel, New York, bought from Durand-Ruel, Paris, Jan. 12, 1899, for Fr 50,000 (stock no. 2097); Mr. and Mrs. H. O. Havemeyer, New York, bought from Durand-Ruel, Jan. 24, 1899; until 1907; Mrs. H. O. Havemeyer, New York, 1907–29; MMA 29.100.38.
EXHIBITIONS: 1886 Paris, no. 14; 1891–

92 London, no. 19, as *Chez la Modiste*; 1892 Glasgow; 1892 Glasgow Institute, no. 562.
REFERENCES: Havemeyer 1931, pp. 126f., ill.; Lemoisne 1946, no. 682; Havemeyer 1958, p. 22, no. 116; Havemeyer 1961, pp. 257f.; Sterling and Salinger 1967, pp. 81f., ill.; Weitzenhoffer 1982, pp. 301f., 316, n. 39, fig. 113; Weitzenhoffer 1986, pp. 133, 255, pl. 94.

237

Hilaire-Germain-Edgar Degas
WAITING: DANCER AND WOMAN WITH UMBRELLA ON A BENCH (L'ATTENTE)
Pastel on paper, 19 x 24 in. (48.3 x 61 cm)
Signed u.l.: *Degas*
PROVENANCE: Léon-Marie Clapisson, Paris, until 1892; Durand-Ruel, Paris, bought from Clapisson, Apr. 21, 1892, for Fr 6,000 (stock no. 2124); Mr. and Mrs. H. O. Havemeyer, New York, bought from Durand-Ruel, Sept. 19, 1895, for Fr 15,000; until 1907; Mrs. H. O. Havemeyer, New York, 1907–29; her son, Horace Havemeyer, New York, 1929–56; his widow, Doris Dick Havemeyer, New York, 1956–82; her sale, Sotheby's, New York, May 18, 1983, no. 8; bought at sale by Getty and Norton Simon for $3,740,000; The J. Paul Getty Museum, Malibu, and Norton Simon Museum, Pasadena (Owned jointly by the J. Paul Getty Museum [83.GG.219] and the Norton Simon Art Foundation [M.1983.1.P]).
EXHIBITION: 1915 New York Masterpieces, no. 34, as *Waiting*.
REFERENCES: Havemeyer 1931, pp. 382f., ill., Lemoisne 1946, no. 698; Havemeyer 1961, pp. 246, 258; Weitzenhoffer 1982, p. 241, fig. 74; Weitzenhoffer 1986, p. 107, colorpl. 58.

238

Hilaire-Germain-Edgar Degas
DANCERS IN THE REHEARSAL ROOM, WITH A DOUBLE BASS**
Oil on canvas, 15⅜ x 35¼ in. (39.1 x 89.5 cm)
Signed l.l.: *Degas*
PROVENANCE: Alexander Reid, Glasgow, by 1891–92; Arthur Kay, London, 1892–at least 1893; Martin et Camentron, Paris, until 1895; Durand-Ruel, Paris, bought from Martin et Camentron, May 28, 1895, for Fr 8,000 (stock no. 3318); Durand-Ruel, New York, bought from Durand-Ruel, Paris, Nov. 20, 1895, for Fr 20,000 (stock no. 1445); E. F. Milliken, New York, bought from Durand-Ruel, Mar. 23, 1896, for $6,000; his sale, American Art Association, New York, Feb. 14, 1902, no. 11; bought at sale by Durand-Ruel for Havemeyer for $6,100; Mr. and Mrs.

H. O. Havemeyer, New York, 1902–7; Mrs. H. O. Havemeyer, New York, 1907–29; MMA 29.100.127.
EXHIBITIONS: 1891–92 London, no. 20, as *La Répétition*; 1892 Glasgow; 1893 London, no. 301a; 1896–97 Pittsburgh, no. 86, as *Repetition of the Dance*.
REFERENCES: Havemeyer 1931, p. 119; Lemoisne 1946, no. 905; Havemeyer 1958, p. 22, no. 112; Havemeyer 1961, p. 259; Sterling and Salinger 1967, pp. 84f., ill.; Weitzenhoffer 1986, p. 257.

239

Hilaire-Germain-Edgar Degas
WOMAN BATHING IN A SHALLOW TUB*
Charcoal and pastel on light green wove paper, now discolored to warm gray, adhered to silk bolting in 1951, 32 x 22⅛ in. (81.3 x 56.2 cm)
Signed and dated u.l.: *Degas / 85*
PROVENANCE: Mary Cassatt, Paris, acquired from the artist in exchange for her *Girl Arranging Her Hair* (A51), from about 1886; deposited with Durand-Ruel, Paris, Mar. 8, 1918 (deposit no. 11925); Mrs. H. O. Havemeyer, New York, bought from Cassatt for $20,000 with two other Degases (*Fan Mount: Ballet Girls*, A223, and *Portrait of a Young Woman*, A240); shipped to her by Durand-Ruel, May 9, 1919; d. 1929; MMA 29.100.41.
EXHIBITIONS: 1886 Paris, one of nos. 19–28; 1921 New York, no. 32; 1922 New York, no. 47.
REFERENCES: Havemeyer 1931, p. 132; Lemoisne 1946, no. 816; Havemeyer 1958, p. 24, no. 127; Sterling and Salinger 1967, p. 88, ill.; Weitzenhoffer 1986, pp. 238, 255, pl. 158.

240

Hilaire-Germain-Edgar Degas
PORTRAIT OF A YOUNG WOMAN
Oil on canvas, 10¾ x 8¾ in. (27.3 x 22.2 cm)
Signed l.r.: *D*
PROVENANCE: Mary Cassatt, Paris, by 1917; deposited with Durand-Ruel, Paris, Mar. 8, 1918–May 9, 1919 (deposit no. 11923); Mrs. H. O. Havemeyer, New York, bought from Cassatt for $20,000 with two other Degases (*Woman Bathing in a Shallow Tub*, A239, and *Fan Mount: Ballet Girls*, A223); shipped to her by Durand-Ruel, May 9, 1919; d. 1929; MMA 29.100.183.
REFERENCES: Havemeyer 1931, p. 116; Lemoisne 1946, no. 861; Havemeyer 1958, p. 21, no. 109; Sterling and Salinger 1967, pp. 83f., ill.; Weitzenhoffer 1986, p. 238.

241

Hilaire-Germain-Edgar Degas
WOMAN DRYING HER FOOT*

Pastel on buff-colored wove paper affixed to original pulpboard mount, 19¾ x 21¼ in. (50.2 x 54 cm)
Signed l.l.: *Degas*
PROVENANCE: Goupil (later Boussod, Valadon et Cie), Paris; Mrs. H. O. Havemeyer, New York, by 1915–29; MMA 29.100.36.
EXHIBITIONS: 1886 Paris, one of nos. 19–28, possibly no. 20; 1915 New York Masterpieces, no. 37, as *After the Bath*; 1922 New York, no. 48.
REFERENCES: Havemeyer 1931, pp. 128f., ill.; Lemoisne 1946, no. 875, as *Après le bain*; Havemeyer 1958, p. 22, no. 115; Sterling and Salinger 1967, pp. 89f., ill.; Weitzenhoffer 1986, p. 255.

242
Hilaire-Germain-Edgar Degas
WOMAN HAVING HER HAIR COMBED*
Pastel on light green wove paper, now discolored to warm gray, affixed to original pulpboard mount, 29⅛ x 23⅞ in. (74 x 60.6 cm)
Signed l.l.: *Degas*; l.r.: *Degas* [obscured by the artist]
PROVENANCE: possibly Boussod, Valadon et Cie, Paris, probably bought from the artist about 1888; M. Dupuis, Paris, probably bought from Boussod, Valadon, about 1888–90; sale, Hôtel Drouot, Paris, June 10, 1891, no. 13; bought at sale by Mayer (probably Salvador Meyer) for Fr 2,600; Claude Roger-Marx, Paris, d. 1913; his sale, Galerie Manzi-Joyant, Paris, May 11–12, 1914, no. 125; bought at sale by Durand-Ruel for Havemeyer for Fr 101,000; Mrs. H. O. Havemeyer, New York, deposited with Durand-Ruel, Paris, May 19, 1914 (deposit no. 11710); d. 1929; MMA 29.100.35.
EXHIBITION: 1909 Paris, no. 48, as *La toilette*.
REFERENCES: Havemeyer 1931, pp. 130f., ill.; Lemoisne 1946, no. 847, as *La Toilette*; Havemeyer 1958, p. 24, no. 126; Havemeyer 1961, pp. 261f.; Sterling and Salinger 1967, pp. 86–88, ill.; Weitzenhoffer 1986, pp. 217f., 255, pl. 152.

243
Hilaire-Germain-Edgar Degas
WOMAN DRYING HER ARM
Pastel and charcoal on off-white wove paper, now discolored at the edges, 12 x 17½ in. (30.5 x 44.5 cm)
Signed l.l.: *Degas*
PROVENANCE: Durand-Ruel, Paris, bought from the artist, Nov. 25, 1898, for Fr 2,000 (stock no. 4828); E. F. Milliken, New York, bought from Durand-Ruel, Paris, July 19, 1899, for Fr 5,000; James S. Inglis (president of Cottier and Co.), New

York, bought from Milliken in 1899–1908; his sale, American Art Association, New York, Mar. 10, 1910, no. 63; bought at sale by Durand-Ruel for Havemeyer for $2,500; Mrs. H. O. Havemeyer, New York, 1910–29; MMA 29.100.553.
REFERENCES: Havemeyer 1931, p. 132; Lemoisne 1946, no. 794; Havemeyer 1958, p. 23, no. 121; Havemeyer 1961, p. 261; Sterling and Salinger 1967, p. 90, ill.

244
Hilaire-Germain-Edgar Degas
DANCER AT THE BAR
Pastel on paper, 26¼ x 18½ in. (66.7 x 47 cm)
Signed u.r.: *Degas*
PROVENANCE: Colonel Donop, until 1920; Durand-Ruel, Paris, bought with Bernheim Jeune from Donop, Nov. 15, 1920, for Fr 27,500 (stock no. 11847); Durand-Ruel, New York, received on deposit from Durand-Ruel, Paris, Jan. 1921 (deposit no. 8050); bought from Durand-Ruel, Paris, Feb. 12, 1921 (not entered in New York stock book); Mrs. H. O. Havemeyer, New York, bought from Durand-Ruel, Jan. 28, 1921, for $10,000; d. 1929; her daughter Electra Havemeyer Webb, New York, 1929–60; Shelburne Museum, Shelburne, Vt., from 1960, 27.3.1–34.
REFERENCES: Havemeyer 1931, p. 369; Lemoisne 1946, no. 969.

245
Hilaire-Germain-Edgar Degas
LANDSCAPE WITH COWS
Pastel over monotype on off-white laid paper, 10¼ x 13⅞ in (26 x 35.2 cm)
Signed l.l.: *Degas*
PROVENANCE: Durand-Ruel, Paris, bought from the artist, June 2, 1893, for Fr 1,000; Mr. and Mrs. H. O. Havemeyer, New York, bought from Durand-Ruel 1894 or 1895; until 1907; Mrs. H. O. Havemeyer, New York, 1907–29; her son, Horace Havemeyer, New York, 1929–56; his widow, Doris Dick Havemeyer, New York, 1956–82; her sale, Sotheby's, New York, May 18, 1983, no. 3; bought at sale by a private collector for $110,000; private collection, from 1983.
REFERENCES: Havemeyer 1931, p. 388; Lemoisne 1946, no. 633, as *Paysage*; Weitzenhoffer 1982, pp. 225, 226, or 241f.; Weitzenhoffer 1986, pp. 98, 107(?), colorpl. 46.

246
Hilaire-Germain-Edgar Degas
LAKE AND MOUNTAINS
Pastel over monotype in oil colors on paper, 10 x 13⅜ in. (25.4 x 34 cm)
Signed b.c. and l.r.: *Degas*

PROVENANCE: Durand-Ruel, Paris, bought from the artist, June 2, 1893, for Fr 1,000; Mr. and Mrs. H. O. Havemeyer, New York, bought from Durand-Ruel 1894 or 1895; until 1907; Mrs. H. O. Havemeyer, New York, 1907–29; her son, Horace Havemeyer, New York, 1929–56; his widow, Doris Dick Havemeyer, New York, 1956–82; her sale, Sotheby's, New York, May 18, 1983, no. 16; bought at sale by a private collector for $66,000; private collection.
REFERENCES: Havemeyer 1931, p. 388; Lemoisne 1946, no. 1048; Weitzenhoffer 1982, pp. 225, 226, or 241f.; Weitzenhoffer 1986, pp. 98, 107(?), colorpl. 47.

247
Hilaire-Germain-Edgar Degas
LANDSCAPE***
Pastel over monotype on paper
PROVENANCE: Durand-Ruel, Paris, bought from the artist, June 2, 1893, for Fr 1,000; Mr. and Mrs. H. O. Havemeyer, New York, bought from Durand-Ruel 1894 or 1895.
REFERENCES: Weitzenhoffer 1982, pp. 225, 226, or 241f.; Weitzenhoffer 1986, p. 98 or 107.

248
Hilaire-Germain-Edgar Degas
LANDSCAPE***
Pastel over monotype on paper, 10⅝ x 14⅛ in. (27 x 35.9 cm)
PROVENANCE: Durand-Ruel, Paris, bought from the artist, June 2, 1893, for Fr 1,000 (stock no. 2752); Durand-Ruel, New York, bought from Durand-Ruel, Paris, Nov. 29, 1893 (Paris stock book), or Dec. 12, 1893 (New York stock book, no. 1102), for Fr 1,100; Mr. and Mrs. H. O. Havemeyer, New York, bought from Durand-Ruel, Jan. 16, 1894, for $460; Durand-Ruel, New York, bought back from Havemeyer, Feb. 13, 1894, for Fr 1,100 (stock no. 1161).
EXHIBITION: 1893 Paris Degas.
REFERENCES: Lemoisne 1946, no. 1036, as *Paysage*; Weitzenhoffer 1982, pp. 225f.; Weitzenhoffer 1986, p. 98.

249
Hilaire-Germain-Edgar Degas
LANDSCAPE WITH A FIELD OF CUT GRAIN
Pastel over monotype in oil colors on paper, 10 x 13⅝ in. (25.4 x 34.6 cm)
Signed: *Degas*
PROVENANCE: Durand-Ruel, Paris, bought from the artist, June 2, 1893, for Fr 1,000; Mr. and Mrs. H. O. Havemeyer, New York, bought from Durand-Ruel 1894 or 1895; until 1907; Mrs. H. O. Havemeyer, New York, 1907–29; her son, Horace Havemeyer, New York, 1929–56; his

widow, Doris Dick Havemeyer, New York, 1956–82; her sale, Sotheby's, New York, May 18, 1983, no. 15; bought at sale by Feilchenfeldt for a private collector for $93,500; private collection, Europe, from 1983.

REFERENCES: Havemeyer 1931, p. 388; Lemoisne 1946, no. 1035, as *Champ de blé et ligne d'arbres*; Weitzenhoffer 1982, pp. 225, 226, or 241f.; Weitzenhoffer 1986, p. 98 or 107.

250
Hilaire-Germain-Edgar Degas
OLIVE TREES AGAINST A MOUNTAINOUS BACKGROUND
Pastel over monotype on paper, 10 ⅝ x 14 ⅛ in. (27 x 35.9 cm)
Signed three times l.l. and l.r.: *Degas*
PROVENANCE: Durand-Ruel, Paris, bought from the artist, June 2, 1893, for Fr 1,000; Mr. and Mrs. H. O. Havemeyer, New York, bought from Durand-Ruel 1894 or 1895; until 1907; Mrs. H. O. Havemeyer, New York, 1907–29; her son, Horace Havemeyer, New York, 1929–56; his widow, Doris Dick Havemeyer, New York, 1956–82; her sale, Sotheby's, New York, May 18, 1983, no. 1; bought at sale by Norton Simon for $71,500; Norton Simon Museum, Pasadena, from 1983 (The Norton Simon Foundation), F.1983.2.1.P.
REFERENCES: Havemeyer 1931, p. 388; Lemoisne 1946, no. 1051; Weitzenhoffer 1982, pp. 225, 226, or 241f.; Weitzenhoffer 1986, p. 98 or 107.

251
Hilaire-Germain-Edgar Degas
WHEAT FIELD AND GREEN HILL
Pastel over monotype in oil colors on paper, 10 x 13 ⅝ in. (25.4 x 34.6 cm)
Signed l.l.: *Degas*
PROVENANCE: Durand-Ruel, Paris, bought from the artist, June 2, 1893, for Fr 1,000; Mr. and Mrs. H. O. Havemeyer, New York, bought from Durand-Ruel 1894 or 1895; until 1907; Mrs. H. O. Havemeyer, New York, 1907–29; her son, Horace Havemeyer, New York, 1929–56; his widow, Doris Dick Havemeyer, New York, 1956–82; her sale, Sotheby's, New York, May 18, 1983, no. 2; bought at sale by Norton Simon for $132,000; Norton Simon Museum, Pasadena, from 1983 (The Norton Simon Foundation), F.1983.2.2.P.
REFERENCES: Havemeyer 1931, p. 388; Lemoisne 1946, no. 1034; Weitzenhoffer 1982, pp. 225, 226, or 241f.; Weitzenhoffer 1986, p. 98 or 107.

252
Hilaire-Germain-Edgar Degas
DANCERS, PINK AND GREEN*
Oil on canvas, 32 ⅜ x 29 ¾ in. (82.2 x 75.6 cm)

253

257

254

258

255

259

256

260

Signed l.r.: *Degas*
PROVENANCE: Mrs. H. O. Havemeyer, New York, deposited with Durand-Ruel, New York, Jan. 8–Dec. 21, 1917 (deposit no. 7844); d. 1929; MMA 29.100.42.
EXHIBITION: 1928 New York, no. 7.
REFERENCES: Havemeyer 1931, p. 118, ill.; Lemoisne 1946, no. 1013; Havemeyer 1958, p. 20, no. 104; Havemeyer 1961, p. 259; Sterling and Salinger 1967, pp. 85f., ill.; Weitzenhoffer 1986, p. 255.

253
Hilaire-Germain-Edgar Degas
BATHER STEPPING INTO A TUB
Pastel and charcoal on blue laid paper mounted at perimeter on backing board, 22 x 18¾ in. (55.9 x 47.6 cm)
Signed u.l.: *Degas*
PROVENANCE: Tadamasa Hayashi, Tokyo and Paris, by about 1890–1906; his sale, American Art Association, New York, Jan. 8–9, 1913, no. 85; bought at sale by Durand-Ruel for Havemeyer for $3,100; Mrs. H. O. Havemeyer, New York, 1913–29; MMA 29.100.190.
REFERENCES: Havemeyer 1931, p. 133; Lemoisne 1946, no. 1031 bis, as *La Baigneuse*; Havemeyer 1958, p. 22, no. 118; Havemeyer 1961, p. 261; Sterling and Salinger 1967, pp. 90f., ill.

254
Hilaire-Germain-Edgar Degas
DANCER WITH A FAN
Pastel and charcoal on buff-colored wove tracing paper, 21⅞ x 19¼ in. (55.6 x 48.9 cm)
Signed l.r.: *Degas*
PROVENANCE: Ambroise Vollard, Paris; Mr. and Mrs. H. O. Havemeyer, New York, probably bought from Vollard in summer 1906;* until 1907; Mrs. H. O. Havemeyer, New York, definitely by 1922–29; MMA 29.100.557.
*See Chronology, June 2, 1906.
EXHIBITION: 1922 New York, no. 61.
REFERENCES: Havemeyer 1931, p. 185; Lemoisne 1946, no. 1068; Havemeyer 1958, p. 23, no. 120; Weitzenhoffer 1986, p. 167(?).

255
Hilaire-Germain-Edgar Degas
RACEHORSES IN TRAINING
Pastel on tracing paper, 19¼ x 24¾ in. (48.9 x 62.9 cm)
Signed and dated l.l.: *Degas / 94*
PROVENANCE: Durand-Ruel, Paris, bought from the artist, Aug. 18, 1894, for Fr 5,000 (stock no. 3116); Durand-Ruel, New York, bought from Durand-Ruel,

Paris, Feb. 27, 1895, for Fr 12,000; Mr. and Mrs. H. O. Havemeyer, New York, bought from Durand-Ruel, Mar. 30, 1895; until 1907; Mrs. H. O. Havemeyer, New York, 1907–29; her daughter Electra Havemeyer Webb, New York, 1929–60; her daughter, Electra Webb Bostwick, from 1960; Andrew Crispo Gallery, New York; Baron H. H. Thyssen-Bornemisza, Lugano; sale, Sotheby's, London, June 26, 1984, no. 9, not sold; Thyssen-Bornemisza Collection.
EXHIBITION: 1922 New York, no. 72.
REFERENCES: Havemeyer 1931, pp. 378f., ill., as *L'Entraînement*; Lemoisne 1946, no. 1145, as *L'Entraînement*; Havemeyer 1961, p. 257; Weitzenhoffer 1986, p. 102, colorpl. 53.

256
Hilaire-Germain-Edgar Degas
DANCERS, PINK AND GREEN
Pastel, 26 x 18½ in. (66 x 47 cm)
Signed and dated l.r.: *Degas / 94*
PROVENANCE: Mrs. H. O. Havemeyer, New York, d. 1929; her daughter Adaline Havemeyer Frelinghuysen, Morristown, N.J., from 1929; her son H.O.H. Frelinghuysen, by 1957; his son George L. K. Frelinghuysen, New York; private collection, Tokyo.
REFERENCES: Havemeyer 1931, p. 369; Lemoisne 1946, no. 1149; Havemeyer 1961, p. 259.

257
Hilaire-Germain-Edgar Degas
WOMAN WITH A TOWEL*
Pastel on cream-colored wove paper with red and blue fibers throughout, 37¾ x 30 in. (95.9 x 76.2 cm)
Signed and dated u.r.: *Degas 94*
PROVENANCE: Durand-Ruel, Paris, bought from the artist, Feb. 25, 1901, for Fr 6,000 (stock no. 6226, as *Après le bain*); Mr. and Mrs. H. O. Havemeyer, New York, bought from Durand-Ruel, Apr. 22, 1901, for Fr 10,000 (New York stock book no. 2622, as *Le Bain*, says July 12); until 1907; Mrs. H. O. Havemeyer, New York, 1907–29; MMA 29.100.37.
EXHIBITIONS: 1915 New York Masterpieces, no. 39, as *After the Tub*; 1922 New York, no. 34.
REFERENCES: Havemeyer 1931, p. 133; Lemoisne 1946, no. 1148, as *Après le bain*; Havemeyer 1958, p. 24, no. 128; Sterling and Salinger 1967, p. 91, ill.; Weitzenhoffer 1986, pp. 143, 255, pl. 111.

258
Hilaire-Germain-Edgar Degas
RUSSIAN DANCER
Pastel over charcoal on tracing paper,

24⅜ x 18 in. (61.9 x 45.7 cm)
Signed l.l.: *Degas*
PROVENANCE: Ambroise Vollard, Paris; Mr. and Mrs. H. O. Havemeyer, New York, probably bought from Vollard in summer 1906;* until 1907; Mrs. H. O. Havemeyer, New York, d. 1929; MMA 29.100.556.
*See Chronology, June 2, 1906.
EXHIBITION: 1922 New York, no. 82(?).
REFERENCES: Havemeyer 1931, pp. 185f., ill.; Lemoisne 1946, no. 1184; Havemeyer 1958, p. 23, no. 124; Weitzenhoffer 1986, p. 167(?).

259
Hilaire-Germain-Edgar Degas
DANCERS IN BLUE
Pastel, 19½ x 23¾ in. (49.5 x 60.3 cm)
Signed u.r.: *Degas*
PROVENANCE: Mrs. H. O. Havemeyer, New York, d. 1929; her daughter Adaline Havemeyer Frelinghuysen, Morristown, N.J., 1929–63; private collection.
REFERENCES: Havemeyer 1931, p. 368; Lemoisne 1946, no. 1368.

260
Hilaire-Germain-Edgar Degas
THE BATH
Charcoal and pastel on paper, 12⅝ x 10⅛ in. (32.1 x 25.7 cm)
Signed u.l.: *Degas*
PROVENANCE: sale, to profit Vve. P***, Hôtel Drouot, Paris, May 29, 1895, no. 32; bought at sale by Durand-Ruel; Durand-Ruel, Paris, 1895 (stock no. 3335); Mr. and Mrs. H. O. Havemeyer, New York, bought from Durand-Ruel, Sept. 19, 1895, for Fr 600; until 1907; Mrs. H. O. Havemeyer, New York, 1907–29; MMA 29.100.186.
EXHIBITION: 1922 New York, no. 14.
REFERENCES: Havemeyer 1931, p. 185; Lemoisne 1946, no. 1406; Havemeyer 1958, p. 22, no. 117; Weitzenhoffer 1982, pp. 241f.; Weitzenhoffer 1986, p. 107.

261
Eugène Delacroix
French, 1798–1863
CHRIST ASLEEP DURING THE TEMPEST
Oil on canvas, 20 x 24 in. (50.8 x 61 cm)
Signed l.l.: *Eug. Delacroix*
PROVENANCE: possibly Francis Petit, Paris, from 1853; possibly Bouruet-Aubertot, Paris, by 1860; possibly sale, R.-L. L., Paris, Apr. 22, 1876, no. II; John Saulnier, Bordeaux, by 1873(?); his sale, Hôtel Drouot, Paris, June 5, 1886, no. 35, bought in for Fr 14,000; sale, Galerie Charles Sedelmeyer, Paris, Mar. 25, 1892,

261

264

no. 8; bought at sale by Durand-Ruel for
Fr 26,000; Durand-Ruel, Paris, 1892 (stock
no. 2066); Durand-Ruel, New York, bought
from Durand-Ruel, Paris, Dec. 13, 1892,
for Fr 40,000; Mr. and Mrs. H. O. Have-
meyer, New York, bought from Durand-
Ruel, Jan. 16, 1894; until 1907; Mrs.
H. O. Havemeyer, New York, 1907–29;
MMA 29.100.131.
EXHIBITIONS: 1860 Paris, no. 349(?);
1864 Paris Delacroix, no. 125(?); 1885
Paris, no. 201; 1886 Paris Bayard, no. 78.
REFERENCES: Havemeyer 1931, pp. 134f.,
ill.; Havemeyer 1958, p. 25, no. 137; Ster-
ling and Salinger 1966, pp. 27–30, ill.;
Weitzenhoffer 1982, pp. 225f., fig. 62;
Johnson 1986, no. 454; Weitzenhoffer
1986, pp. 98, 258, pl. 45.

262
Eugène Delacroix
ARAB RIDER***
PROVENANCE: Georges Petit, Paris, until
1882; M. Knoedler and Co., New York,
bought from Petit, Aug. 21, 1882, for
Fr 26,000 (stock no. 4065, as *Cavalier
arabe*); H. O. Havemeyer, New York,
bought from Knoedler, Sept. 4, 1882, as
The Pursuit, for $7,000; returned to
M. Knoedler and Co., New York, by Havemeyer, Dec. 1882 for $7,000 credit (stock
no. 4269); returned to Georges Petit,
Paris, by Knoedler, Oct. 11, 1883, for
Fr 26,000 credit.
REFERENCES: Weitzenhoffer 1982, pp. 41,
49, n. 20; Weitzenhoffer 1986, p. 33.

263
Eugène Delacroix
TIGER***
Pastel
PROVENANCE: Mr. and Mrs. H. O. Have-
meyer, New York, until 1898; Durand-
Ruel, New York, bought from Havemeyer,
Mar. 11, 1898.

264
Eugène Delacroix, Attributed to
DESDEMONA CURSED BY HER
FATHER
Oil on wood, 15¾ x 12⅜ in. (40 x 31.4 cm)
Signed l.l.: *Eug. Delacroix*
PROVENANCE: Edouard Frère; Arnold,
Tripp et Cie, and Tedesco, Paris, bought
Nov. 4, 1882, for Fr 15,000; E. Secrétan,
Paris, bought from them, Oct. 26, 1883,
for Fr 16,000; his sale, Galerie Charles
Sedelmeyer, Paris, July 1, 1889, no. 18;
bought at sale by Durand-Ruel for
Havemeyer for Fr 15,000 (stock no. 2383);
Mr. and Mrs. H. O. Havemeyer, New
York, 1889–1907; Mrs. H. O. Havemeyer,
New York, 1907–29; her sale, American
Art Association, New York, Apr. 10, 1930,
no. 67, as *Desdemona Repulsed by Her Fa-
ther*, by Delacroix; bought at sale by
M. Knoedler and Co. (probably for
Stransky) for $4,100; Josef Stransky, New
York, by 1931–36; Wildenstein and Co.,
New York and London, 1936–57; Alex
Reid and Lefevre, London, bought from
Wildenstein, Feb. 1957; until 1961;
Georges Keller, bought from Reid and
Lefevre in 1961; Laura L. (Mrs. Albert C.)
Barnes, Merion, Pa., d. 1967; The Brook-
lyn Museum (Bequest of Laura L. Barnes),
67.24.22.
REFERENCES: Havemeyer 1931, p. 503,
as *Scene from Shakespeare's Othello*, by
Delacroix; Weitzenhoffer 1982, pp. 108,
115, 119, n. 23; Johnson 1986, no. R47,
as by Pierre Andrieu (1821–1892), proba-
bly after a lost painting by Delacroix;
Weitzenhoffer 1986, p. 58.

265
Eugène Delacroix, Studio of
THE EXPULSION OF ADAM AND EVE
Oil on canvas, 53⅝ x 41⅜ in.
(136.2 x 105.1 cm)
Signed l.l.: *Eug. Delacroix*
PROVENANCE: possibly Félix Gérard, by
1885; Cottier and Co., New York, until
1888; Mr. and Mrs. H. O. Havemeyer,
New York, bought from Cottier, Dec. 8,
1888, for about $10,000; until 1907; Mrs.
H. O. Havemeyer, New York, 1907–29;
her sale, American Art Association, New
York, Apr. 10, 1930, no. 81, as *Expulsion
of Adam and Eve from the Garden*, by

265

Delacroix; bought at sale by Dale for
$3,500; Chester Dale, New York, 1930;
M. Knoedler and Co., New York, 1930;
Alex Reid and Lefevre, London, bought
from Knoedler in 1930; sold to the Trust-
ees of the Hamilton Bequest in 1933; Glas-
gow Art Gallery and Museum (The
Hamilton Bequest, 1933).
EXHIBITIONS: 1885 Paris, no. 118(?);
1890–91 New York, no. 7.
REFERENCES: Havemeyer 1931, p. 503, as
The Expulsion from Eden, by Delacroix;
Weitzenhoffer 1982, pp. 81f., 95, n. 18,
pp. 115, 131f.; Johnson 1986, no. 58;
Weitzenhoffer 1986, pp. 47, 66, 261, n. 9.

266
Narcisse-Virgile Diaz de la Peña
French, 1808–1876
CHILDREN PLAYING WITH A
LIZARD***
PROVENANCE: Georges Petit, Paris, until
1881; M. Knoedler and Co., New York,
bought from Petit, Sept. 1881, for
Fr 42,000 (stock no. 3428, as *Enfants au
Lézard*); H. O. Havemeyer, New York,
bought from Knoedler, Sept. 29, 1881, for
$12,500; until 1899; Durand-Ruel, New
York, bought from Havemeyer, Feb. 4,
1899.
REFERENCES: Weitzenhoffer 1982, pp. 41,
49, n. 19; Weitzenhoffer 1986, p. 33.

267
Narcisse-Virgile Diaz de la Peña
FOREST***
PROVENANCE: Georges Petit, Paris, until
1881; M. Knoedler and Co., New York,
bought from Petit, Sept. 1881, for Fr 9,000
(stock no. 3431, as *Intérieur de forêt*); H. O.
Havemeyer, New York, bought from
Knoedler, Sept. 29, 1881, for $2,500.
REFERENCES: Weitzenhoffer 1982, pp. 41,
49, n. 19; Weitzenhoffer 1986, p. 33.

339

268

Narcisse-Virgile Diaz de la Peña
PAINTING***
Oil
PROVENANCE: H. O. Havemeyer, New
York, acquired through Mary Cassatt,
Paris, in 1880.
REFERENCES: Weitzenhoffer 1982, p. 44,
with incorrect date; Weitzenhoffer 1986,
pp. 33, 260, n. 8.

269

269

Jules Dupré
French, 1811–1889
FARMYARD WITH DUCKS
Charcoal and white chalk on laid paper,
12 x 18 in. (30.5 x 45.7 cm)
Signed l.l.: *Jules Dupré*
PROVENANCE: Mrs. H. O. Havemeyer,
New York, d. 1929; MMA 29.100.930.
REFERENCES: Havemeyer 1931, p. 189;
Havemeyer 1958, p. 25, no. 138.

270

Jules Dupré
THE FOREST***
Oil on canvas
PROVENANCE: Durand-Ruel, Paris and
New York, until 1891; Mr. and Mrs. H. O.
Havemeyer, New York, bought from
Durand-Ruel, Apr. 1891; consigned to
Durand-Ruel, Nov. 1895, as *Paysage route
en forêt*, and sold to it, Mar. 11, 1898.
REFERENCES: Weitzenhoffer 1982,
pp. 130, 142, n. 16; Weitzenhoffer 1986,
pp. 65, 100(?).

271

Jules Dupré
THE PASTURE***
PROVENANCE: Durand-Ruel, Paris, bought
from R. Smit, Feb. 4, 1893, for Fr 70,000
(stock no. 2640); Mr. and Mrs. H. O.
Havemeyer, New York, bought from Durand-
Ruel, Feb. 8, 1893, for Fr 100,000; consigned to Durand-Ruel, Jan. 6, 1896; sold
to Durand-Ruel, Mar. 11, 1898; Durand-
Ruel, New York, from 1898.
REFERENCES: Weitzenhoffer 1982,
pp. 199, 217, n. 2; Weitzenhoffer 1986,
p. 91.

340

272

Jules Dupré
THE WOODCUTTER***
Oil on canvas
PROVENANCE: Durand-Ruel, Paris and
New York, until 1891; Mr. and Mrs. H. O.
Havemeyer, New York, bought from
Durand-Ruel, Apr. 1891, for $13,000;
until 1907; consigned to Durand-Ruel,
Dec. 23, 1898–May 3, 1899, as *Paysage*,
and Jan.–Mar. 1902; Mrs. H. O. Have-
meyer, New York, 1907–12; consigned to
Durand-Ruel as *Le Bûcheron*, Nov. 3,
1909–May 11, 1910, and 1911; returned
to her, May 24, 1911; consigned to
Durand-Ruel again, Nov. 1911; bought by
Durand-Ruel, Apr. 5, 1912, for $15,000;
Durand-Ruel, New York, from 1912.
REFERENCES: Weitzenhoffer 1982,
pp. 130, 142, n. 16; Weitzenhoffer 1986,
p. 65.

273

Albrecht Dürer, Attributed to
German, 1471–1528
SAINT VERONICA'S HANDKERCHIEF
Oil on copper, 5½ x 7 in. (14 x 17.8 cm)
Signed and dated below: *A.D.* [monogram]
1513
PROVENANCE: Mrs. H. O. Havemeyer,
New York, d. 1929; her sale, American Art
Association, New York, Apr. 10, 1930,
no. 34, as *The Handkerchief of Saint Ve-
ronica, with Two Angels*, attributed to
Dürer; bought at sale by A. Michael for
$175.
REFERENCE: Havemeyer 1931, p. 496, as
Sudarium of Saint Veronica, after Dürer,
XVI century.

274

Albrecht Dürer, Copy after
German, 16th or 17th century
PEASANTS AT MARKET
Oil on wood, 13 x 9 in. (33 x 22.9 cm)
Inscribed l.r.: *A.D.* [monogram]
PROVENANCE: possibly Mrs. H. O. Have-
meyer, New York, d. 1929; her son, Hor-
ace Havemeyer, New York, by 1931–34;
The Denver Art Museum, from 1934 (Gift
of Horace Havemeyer), 1934.158.
Note: This is a copy after a Dürer engrav-

ing of 1519 (Bartsch no. 89, as *The Peas-
ant and His Wife at Market*).
REFERENCE: Havemeyer 1931, p. 302, as
Peasants, by school of Dürer.

275

**Dutch or Flemish Painter, Unknown, 16th
century**
PORTRAIT OF A MAN HOLDING
A RING
Oil on wood, 29½ x 20½ in. (74.9 x 52.1 cm)
PROVENANCE: Mrs. H. O. Havemeyer,
New York, d. 1929; her sale, American Art
Association, New York, Apr. 10, 1930,
no. 115, as *Portrait of a Gentleman Hold-
ing a Ring*, attributed to Antonis Mor,
called Antonio Moro (Dutch, 1512–1581);
bought at sale by Hardy for $550.
REFERENCE: Havemeyer 1931, p. 498, as
formerly attributed to Pourbus.

276

G. van Earp; H. Earp, Sr.; or Henry Earp
Dutch or British, 19th century
WATERCOLOR***
PROVENANCE: M. Knoedler and Co., New
York, until 1877; H. O. Havemeyer, New
York, bought from Knoedler, Feb. 21,
1877, for $10.

277

Agustin Esteve
Spanish, 1758–1809

PORTRAIT OF A LADY WITH A
GUITAR
Oil on canvas, 65 ⅝ x 46 in.
(166.7 x 116.8 cm)
Inscribed and dated l., on table: *Fco Goya
Ano 1799* [removed ca. 1940s]
PROVENANCE: Alphonse Oudry, Paris; his
sale, Hôtel des Ventes, Paris, Apr. 16–17,
1869, no. 136, as *Portrait de jeune femme*,
by Goya, for Fr 4,200; Edwards, Paris; his
sale, Hôtel Drouot, Paris, Mar. 7, 1870,
no. 27, as *La Maîtresse de Goya*; bought
at sale by Pommereul for Fr 11,600; Baron
de Pommereul, St. Germain, in 1905;
Durand-Ruel, Paris, until 1906; Mr. and
Mrs. H. O. Havemeyer, New York, bought
from Durand-Ruel between June and Dec.
1906; until 1907; Mrs. H. O. Havemeyer,
New York, 1907–29; her sale, American
Art Association, New York, Apr. 10, 1930,
no. 87, as *La Maîtresse de Goya (The
Lady with a Guitar)*, by Goya; bought at
sale by Ringling for $21,000; John Ring-
ling, Sarasota, 1930–36; The John and
Mable Ringling Museum of Art, Sarasota
(Bequest of John Ringling, 1936), SN358,
as *Portrait of the Duchess of Alba*.
EXHIBITION: 1912 New York, no. 6, as
The Duchess of Alba, by Goya.
REFERENCES: Havemeyer 1931, p. 199, as
Portrait of a Lady with a Guitar, by Goya;
Havemeyer 1961, pp. 163, 177; Weitzen-
hoffer 1986, p. 206.

278
Giovanni Antonio Fasolo, Attributed to
Italian (Venetian), 1530–1572
PORTRAIT OF A LADY**
Oil on canvas, 70 ⅛ x 45 ⁹⁄₁₆ in.
(178.1 x 115.7 cm)
PROVENANCE: possibly Marchese del Car-
pio (probably no. 328 in his inventory of
1692–1704, as "ritratto di donna venezi-
ana palmi 6 e 4 di Paol Veronese"); Martelli
family, Florence, probably bought from
Del Rosso or Gondi, by 1712; Mrs. H. O.
Havemeyer, New York, bought from Nic-
colo, Carlo, and Ugolino Martelli, Flor-

ence, through A. E. Harnisch, summer
1910, for L 110,000; possibly placed on exchange or consignment with Trotti, Paris,
by Nov. 1914 until at least Oct. 1917;*
d. 1929; her sale, American Art Associa-
tion, New York, Apr. 10, 1930, no. 104, as
Portrait of a Lady in a Dantesque Chair,
by Veronese(?); bought at sale by Metropol-
itan Galleries for $800; Chester Dale, New
York, 1930–46; Art Institute of Chicago
(Gift of Chester Dale), 1946.382.
*See Chronology, Nov. 14, 1914.
Note: Early provenance information from
Alessandra Civai, *Dipinti e sculture in casa
Martelli*, Florence, 1990, pp. 64, 71, nn.
122, 123, p. 113, fig. 28.
REFERENCES: Havemeyer 1931, p. 495, as
Portrait of a Woman, by Veronese(?);
Pignatti 1976, no. A48, as attributed to
Veronese; Weitzenhoffer 1986, pp. 256, 258.

279
**Flemish Painter, Unknown, early 16th
century**
THE REST ON THE FLIGHT INTO
EGYPT
Oil on wood, 23 ⅜ x 28 in. (59.4 x 71.1 cm)
PROVENANCE: Mr. and Mrs. H. O. Have-
meyer, New York, bought in Spain for
Pts 20,000, spring 1901; until 1907; Mrs.
H. O. Havemeyer, New York, 1907–29;
MMA 29.100.599.
REFERENCES: Havemeyer 1931, p. 35, ill.;
Havemeyer 1958, p. 9, no. 31, ill.; Have-
meyer 1961, pp. 160–62, as by Patinir.

280
Flemish Painter, Unknown, ca. 1620
PORTRAIT OF A WOMAN WITH A
LAPDOG
Oil on canvas, 43 x 33 ¼ in.
(109.2 x 84.5 cm)
PROVENANCE: Charles Butler, London, in
1901; Durand-Ruel, Paris and New York,
bought in London in 1903, as Dutch
school; Mr. and Mrs. H. O. Havemeyer,
New York, bought from Durand-Ruel,
Aug. 1, 1903, as Dutch school, *Portrait of
a Lady*; until 1907; Mrs. H. O. Have-
meyer, New York, 1907–29; her sale,
American Art Association, New York, Apr.

280

10, 1930, no. 106, as Flemish school, XVI
century, *Portrait of a Lady with Lap Dog*;
bought at sale by W. Seaman (agent) for
$1,300.
EXHIBITIONS: 1895 London, no. 86, as by
Cornelius de Vos; 1901 London, no. 86, as
by Alonso [sic] Sanchez Coello, lent by
Charles Butler, Esq.; 1915 New York Mas-
terpieces, no. 2, as *Portrait of a Spanish
Lady*, by Claudio Coello.
REFERENCES: Havemeyer 1931, p. 498, as
Flemish school, about 1620, *Portrait of a
Woman with a Little Dog*; Weitzenhoffer
1986, p. 176.

281
French Artist, Unknown, 19th century
PORTRAIT OF A WOMAN
Graphite on wove paper, 4 ¾ x 3 in. (12.1
x 7.6 cm)
Inscribed and dated u.r.: *Ingres / 1839*
PROVENANCE: private collection, Paris;
Mrs. H. O. Havemeyer, New York, bought
from the private collection; d. 1929; MMA
29.100.192.
REFERENCES: Havemeyer 1931, p. 190, as
Portrait of Mme de Staël, by Ingres; Have-
meyer 1958, p. 25, no. 139.

282
Thomas Gainsborough
British, 1727–1788
PORTRAIT OF A MAN***
Oil on canvas
PROVENANCE: Edouard Warneck, Paris,
until 1889; Durand-Ruel, Paris, bought
from Warneck, Aug. 1, 1889; Mr. and
Mrs. H. O. Havemeyer, New York, bought

from Durand-Ruel, Aug. 1, 1889, for
Fr 72,000 with four other paintings.
REFERENCES: Weitzenhoffer 1982, p. 128;
Weitzenhoffer 1986, p. 64.

283
**Paul Gavarni (Hippolyte-Sulpice-Guillaume
Chevalier)**
French, 1804–1866
WOMAN SEATED, SEEN FROM BACK
Black chalk on wove paper, 9 ¹¹⁄₁₆ x 6 ⅞ in.
(24.6 x 17.5 cm)
PROVENANCE: Mrs. H. O. Havemeyer,
New York, d. 1929; MMA 29.100.944.
REFERENCES: Havemeyer 1931, p. 189;
Havemeyer 1958, p. 26, no. 140.

284
Théodore Gericault
French, 1791–1824
RIDERLESS RACERS AT ROME***
Oil on paper mounted on canvas,
17 ½ x 23 ⅜ in. (44.5 x 59.4 cm)
PROVENANCE: possibly Amédée Con-
stantin; his sale, Feb. 15, 1830, possibly
no. 193, as *Course de chevaux libres à
Rome, en présence d'un grand nombre de
personnes occupant un amphithéâtre*;
bought at sale by Michel or Monsigny-
Mazarin for Fr 649; Couvreur, Paris, by
1867–at least 1879; Crabbe, Brussels; E.
Secrétan, bought from Crabbe; his sale,
Galerie Charles Sedelmeyer, Paris, July 1,
1889, no. 35; bought at sale by Durand-
Ruel for Havemeyer for Fr 9,200 (stock
no. 2390); Mr. and Mrs. H. O. Havemeyer, New York, 1889–99; Durand-Ruel,
New York, bought from Havemeyer, Feb.
3, 1899; H. S. Henry, Philadelphia, bought

from Durand-Ruel, Feb. 3, 1899; his sale,
American Art Association, New York, Jan.
25, 1907, no. 21; bought at sale by Walters
for $3,000; Henry Walters, Baltimore,
1907–31; Walters Art Gallery, Baltimore,
37.189.
REFERENCE: Bazin 1990, no. 1343.

285
German Painter, Unknown, 15th century
MADONNA AND CHILD
Oil on canvas, 24 x 14 in. (61 x 35.6 cm)
PROVENANCE: de Bonnière, Paris, until
1897; Durand-Ruel, Paris, bought from de
Bonnière, Sept. 4, 1897, for Fr 1,500
(stock no. 4363, as Ecole de Bourgogne,
Vierge et Enfant); Durand-Ruel, New
York, bought from Durand-Ruel, Paris,
Oct. 14, 1897 (Paris stock book), or
Oct. 30, 1897 (New York stock book,
no. 1933, as *Vierge et Enfant*, by Martin
Schoen), for Fr 1,500; Mr. and Mrs. H. O.
Havemeyer, New York, bought from
Durand-Ruel, Mar. 11, 1898, for $4,000;
until 1907; Mrs. H. O. Havemeyer, New
York, 1907–29; her sale, American Art As-
sociation, New York, Apr. 10, 1930,
no. 97, as by Martin Schoen; bought at
sale by Edouard Jonas for $1,900.
Note: "Martin Schoen" can be identified as
Martin Schongauer (German, ca. 1450–
1491), but this attribution to Schongauer is
erroneous.
REFERENCE: Havemeyer 1931, p. 496, as
by Martin Schoen(?).

286
German Painter, Unknown, 16th century
PORTRAIT OF A LADY
Oil on wood, 17 ½ x 12 ½ in.
(44.5 x 31.8 cm)
Dated above: *1532*
PROVENANCE: possibly Prince Demidoff,
San Donato; possibly the family of Count
Filicaja (or Filicaia), Arezzo; Mr. and Mrs.
H. O. Havemeyer, New York, bought
through A. E. Harnisch, fall 1901, for
L 18,000 the pair (with A287), as by Hol-
bein; until 1907; Mrs. H. O. Havemeyer,

286

New York, 1907–29; her sale, American
Art Association, New York, Apr. 10, 1930,
no. 54, as by Ludger Tom Ring; bought at
sale by Dale for $5,200; Chester Dale,
New York, 1930–42; National Gallery of
Art, Washington, D.C. (Chester Dale Collection), 1942.16.3.
REFERENCES: Havemeyer 1931, p. 496, as
school of Cologne, XVI century; Havemeyer 1961, p. 128.

287
German Painter, Unknown, 16th century
PORTRAIT OF A MAN
Oil on wood, 17 x 12 ½ in. (43.2 x 31.8 cm)
Dated above: *1532*
PROVENANCE: possibly Prince Demidoff,
San Donato; possibly the family of Count
Filicaja (or Filicaia), Arezzo; Mr. and Mrs.
H. O. Havemeyer, New York, bought
through A. E. Harnisch, fall 1901, for
L 18,000 the pair (with A286), as by Hol-
bein; until 1907; Mrs. H. O. Havemeyer,
New York, 1907–29; her sale, American
Art Association, New York, Apr. 10, 1930,
no. 55, as by Ludger Tom Ring; bought at
sale by Bohler and Steinmeyer for $1,100.
REFERENCES: Havemeyer 1931, p. 496, as
school of Cologne, XVI century; Have-
meyer 1961, p. 128.

288
Robert Swain Gifford
American, 1840–1905
EL OUTAIA, ALGERIA

Watercolor, 10 x 17 in. (25.4 x 43.2 cm)
Signed and dated l.r.: *R. Swain Gifford 1880*
PROVENANCE: Mrs. H. O. Havemeyer, New York, d. 1929; her sale, American Art Association, New York, Apr. 10, 1930, no. 20, for $25.
REFERENCE: Havemeyer 1931, p. 509.

289
Marie-François-Firmin Girard
French, 1838–1921
LADIES CAUGHT IN THE RAIN***
PROVENANCE: M. Knoedler and Co., New York, bought from the artist, Sept. 16, 1879, for Fr 2,000 (stock no. 1989, as *Surprises par la pluie*); H. O. Havemeyer, New York, bought from Knoedler, Oct. 14, 1879, for $750, as *A Rainy Day*; M. Knoedler and Co., New York, bought back from Havemeyer, Jan. 18, 1887 (stock no. 5545, as *Quai in Paris*); Thomas P. Salter, Portsmouth, N.H., bought from Knoedler, Apr. 30, 1887, as *Rainy Day in Paris*.
REFERENCES: Weitzenhoffer 1982, pp. 40f.; Weitzenhoffer 1986, p. 33.

290
Hugo van der Goes
Flemish, fl. by 1467; d. 1482
PORTRAIT OF A MAN*
Oil on wood, oval, 12½ x 10½ in. (31.8 x 26.7 cm)
PROVENANCE: Signol, Paris; his sale, Hôtel Drouot, Paris, Apr. 1–3, 1878, no. 10, as by Antonello da Messina; bought at sale by Beurnonville for Fr 10,000; Baron E. de Beurnonville, Paris, 1878–81; sale, Paris, May 9–16, 1881, no. 603, as by Antonello da Messina, for Fr 33,000; Paul Mame, Tours; his sale, Galerie Georges Petit, Paris, Apr. 26–29, 1904, no. 1, as by Antonello da Messina; bought at sale by Durand-Ruel for Havemeyer for Fr 50,000; Mr. and Mrs. H. O. Havemeyer, New York, 1904–7; Mrs. H. O. Havemeyer, New York, 1907–29; MMA 29.100.15.
EXHIBITION: 1923 New York, no. 37.
REFERENCES: Havemeyer 1931, p. 34, ill.; Wehle and Salinger 1947, pp. 57f., ill.;

Havemeyer 1958, p. 9, no. 32, ill.; Havemeyer 1961, p. 20; Friedländer 1969, supplement no. 110; Weitzenhoffer 1982, p. 166, n. 7; Weitzenhoffer 1986, pp. 155, 176, 254.

291
Francisco de Goya y Lucientes
Spanish, 1746–1828
BARTOLOME SUREDA Y MISEROL
Oil on canvas, 47⅛ x 31¼ in. (119.7 x 79.4 cm)
PROVENANCE: possibly Pedro Escat, Palma de Mallorca; family of the sitter, Madrid; Durand-Ruel, Paris, until 1897; Mr. and Mrs. H. O. Havemeyer, New York, bought Sept. 28, 1897, for almost Pts 50,000 the pair (with A292); until 1907; Mrs. H. O. Havemeyer, New York, 1907–29; her daughter Adaline Havemeyer Frelinghuysen, Morristown, N.J., 1929–41; National Gallery of Art, Washington, D.C. (Gift of Mr. and Mrs. P.H.B. Frelinghuysen in memory of her father and mother, Mr. and Mrs. H. O. Havemeyer), 1941.10.1.
EXHIBITION: 1912 New York, no. 9.
REFERENCES: Havemeyer 1931, pp. 312f., ill.; Havemeyer 1961, p. 136; Gassier and Wilson 1971, no. 813; Weitzenhoffer 1982, pp. 265, 280f., n. 29, p. 322, fig. 90; Weitzenhoffer 1986, pp. 117, 206, pl. 73.

292
Francisco de Goya y Lucientes
THERESE LOUISE DE SUREDA
Oil on canvas, 47⅛ x 31¼ in. (119.7 x 79.4 cm)
PROVENANCE: possibly Pedro Escat, Palma de Mallorca; family of the sitter, Madrid; Durand-Ruel, Paris, until 1897; Mr. and Mrs. H. O. Havemeyer, New York, bought Sept. 28, 1897, for almost Pts 50,000 the pair (with A291); until 1907; Mrs. H. O. Havemeyer, New York, 1907–29; her daughter Adaline Havemeyer Frelinghuysen, Morristown, N.J., 1929–41; National Gallery of Art, Washington, D.C. (Gift of Mr. and Mrs. P.H.B. Frelinghuysen in memory of her father and mother, Mr. and Mrs. H. O. Havemeyer), 1942.3.1.
EXHIBITION: 1912 New York, no. 10.
REFERENCES: Havemeyer 1931, pp. 314f., ill.; Havemeyer 1961, p. 136; Gassier and Wilson 1971, no. 814; Weitzenhoffer 1982, pp. 265, 280f., n. 29, p. 322, fig. 91; Weitzenhoffer 1986, pp. 117, 206, pl. 74.

293
Francisco de Goya y Lucientes
YOUNG LADY WEARING A MANTILLA AND A BASQUINA
Oil on canvas, 43⅛ x 30½ in. (109.5 x 77.5 cm)
Signed l.l.: *Goya*
PROVENANCE: possibly Serafin Garcia de

la Huerta, Madrid, d. 1839; his inventory, 1840; Marques de Heredia, Madrid, by 1867; Benito Garriga, Madrid, by 1887; his sale, Hôtel Drouot, Paris, Mar. 24, 1890, no. 4; Hubert Debrousse; his sale, Hôtel Drouot, Paris, Apr. 6, 1900, no. 45; Kraemer, Paris; Durand-Ruel, Paris, bought from Kraemer, Mar. 9, 1906, for Fr 35,000 (stock no. 8102, as *Portrait de la Famosa Librera de la calle de las Carretas*); Mr. and Mrs. H. O. Havemeyer, New York, bought from Durand-Ruel, May 4, 1906, for Fr 90,000; until 1907; Mrs. H. O. Havemeyer, New York, 1907–29; her daughter Adaline Havemeyer Frelinghuysen, Morristown, N.J., 1929–63; National Gallery of Art, Washington, D.C. (Gift of Mrs. P.H.B. Frelinghuysen), 1963.4.2.
EXHIBITION: 1912 New York, no. 7.
REFERENCES: Havemeyer 1931, pp. 316f., ill., as *Portrait of a Woman—La Librera*; Havemeyer 1961, pp. 83, 153f., 158f.; Gassier and Wilson 1971, no. 835; Weitzenhoffer 1986, pp. 165, 206.

294
Francisco de Goya y Lucientes
DONA NARCISA BARANANA DE GOICOECHEA*
Oil on canvas, 44¼ x 30¾ in. (112.4 x 78.1 cm)
Signed on ring: *Goya*
PROVENANCE: Don Felipe Modet, Madrid, by 1900–1903; Durand-Ruel, Paris, bought from Modet, Apr. 4, 1903 (stock no. 7344); Mr. and Mrs. H. O. Havemeyer, New York, bought from Durand-Ruel, Apr. 30, 1903; until 1907; Mrs. H. O. Havemeyer, New York, 1907–29; MMA 29.100.180.
EXHIBITIONS: 1900 Madrid, not in cat., supplement no. 170; 1912 New York, no. 11; 1915 New York, no. 14.
REFERENCES: Havemeyer 1931, pp. 44f., ill.; Wehle 1940, p. 248, ill.; Havemeyer 1958, p. 35, no. 189; Havemeyer 1961, p. 177; Gassier and Wilson 1971, no. 889; Weitzenhoffer 1986, pp. 206, 254.

295
Francisco de Goya y Lucientes, Attributed to
DONA MARIA TERESA DE BORBON Y VALLABRIGA, CONDESA DE CHINCHON (THE PRINCESA DE LA PAZ)*
Oil on canvas, 40 x 31 in. (101.6 x 78.7 cm)
PROVENANCE: Marquis de la Vega Inclan; Mrs. H. O. Havemeyer, New York, bought from the Vega family through Ricardo de Madrazo, Apr. 1909; d. 1929; her daughter Electra Havemeyer Webb, New York, 1929–60; Shelburne Museum, Shelburne, Vt., from 1960, 27.1.1–153.
EXHIBITION: 1912 New York, no. 8.

291

293

295

292

294

296

REFERENCES: Havemeyer 1931, pp. 324f., ill., as *Portrait of the Princesa de la Paz*; Havemeyer 1961, pp. 167, 173–78; Gassier and Wilson 1971, under no. 793, as by Agustin Esteve; Weitzenhoffer 1986, pp. 190, 206f., 254, pl. 140.

296
Francisco de Goya y Lucientes,
Attributed to
Spanish, painted between 1827 and 1835
MAJAS ON A BALCONY*
Oil on canvas, 76¾ x 49½ in.
(195 x 125.7 cm)
PROVENANCE: Infante Don Sebastian María Gabriel de Borbón y Braganza, Pau, by 1835–75; his inventory, 1835, no. 48; his son, Don Francisco de Borbón y Borbón, first duke of Marchena, Madrid, 1875–1904; Durand-Ruel, Paris, bought from the

heirs of the duke, Nov. 9, 1904 (stock no. 7813); Mr. and Mrs. H. O. Havemeyer, New York, bought from Durand-Ruel, Nov. 9, 1904; until 1907; Mrs. H. O. Havemeyer, New York, 1907–29; MMA 29.100.10.
EXHIBITIONS: 1854 Madrid(?); 1900 Madrid, no. 112, lent by El Duque de Marchena; 1912 New York, no. 5; 1915 New York, no. 13.
REFERENCES: Havemeyer 1931, pp. 42f., ill.; Wehle 1940, pp. 248–50, ill.; Havemeyer 1958, p. 34, no. 190, ill.; Havemeyer 1961, pp. 83, 138, 144, 153–58; Gassier and Wilson 1971, no. 960; Weitzenhoffer 1986, pp. 141, 154–56, 206, 254, colorpl. 122.

297
Francisco de Goya y Lucientes,
Attributed to

PORTRAIT OF A BOY, MANUEL CANTIN Y LUCIENTES
Oil on wood, 21½ x 16¾ in. (54.6 x 42.6 cm)
PROVENANCE: Don Francisco Cantin Gamboa, Zaragoza; Mrs. H. O. Havemeyer, New York, bought from the Cantin family through Ricardo de Madrazo, June 1910, for Pts 27,500 (including commission of 5 percent); shipped to her, Oct. 19, 1910; d. 1929; her daughter Adaline Havemeyer Frelinghuysen, Morristown, N.J., from 1929.
EXHIBITIONS: 1910 Barcelona, no. 10 in sala III, as *Retrato de D. Manuel Cantin y Lucientes*, lent by D. José Jordan de Uries; 1912 New York, no. 15.*
*There exist two versions of the catalogue for this exhibition; only one version includes this picture.
REFERENCES: Havemeyer 1931, pp. 320f., ill., as by Goya; Havemeyer 1961, pp. 172f.

297

299

298

**Francisco de Goya y Lucientes,
Attributed to**
PORTRAIT OF AN OFFICER ON
HORSEBACK
Oil on canvas, 37 x 30 in. (94 x 76.2 cm)
Signed l.l.: G.
PROVENANCE: Harrington, Boston; M. J.
Rougeron, New York, bought from Har-
rington's daughter; Mrs. H. O. Havemeyer,
New York, bought from Rougeron, 1922–
29; her sale, American Art Association,
New York, Apr. 10, 1930, no. 109, as *An
Officer of Hussars*, attributed to Goya;
bought at sale by W. W. Seaman (agent)
for $400.
REFERENCE: Havemeyer 1931, p. 499, as
by Goya.

299

Francisco de Goya y Lucientes, Copy after
Spanish, after 1792
MARIA LUISA OF PARMA (1751–1819),
QUEEN OF SPAIN*
Oil on canvas, 43 ½ x 33 ½ in.
(110.5 x 85.1 cm)
PROVENANCE: Duke of Rivas, Madrid;
Théodore Duret, Paris; Mr. and Mrs.
H. O. Havemeyer, New York, bought
from Duret; until 1907; Mrs. H. O.
Havemeyer, New York, 1907–29; MMA
29.100.11.
EXHIBITION: 1912 New York, no. 12.
REFERENCES: Havemeyer 1931, pp. 46f.,
ill.; Wehle 1940, pp. 253f., ill.; Havemeyer

1958, p. 34, no. 191; Havemeyer 1961,
pp. 163–66; Gassier and Wilson 1971,
no. 781; Weitzenhoffer 1986, pp. 206, 254.

300

Francisco de Goya y Lucientes, Style of
Spanish, 19th century
A CITY ON A ROCK*
Oil on canvas, 33 x 41 in. (83.8 x 104.1 cm)
PROVENANCE: James S. Inglis, New York,
purchased in Spain between 1882 and
1887; until 1908; his estate, 1908–12; Cot-
tier and Co., New York, bought from
Inglis estate, Nov. 14, 1912; Mrs. H. O.
Havemeyer, New York, bought from Cot-
tier, Nov. 18, 1912, for $8,000; d. 1929;
MMA 29.100.12.
REFERENCES: Havemeyer 1931, pp. 48f.,
ill., as by Goya; Wehle 1940, pp. 252f., ill.;
Havemeyer 1958, p. 34, no. 188, ill.; Gassier and Wilson 1971, no. 955; Weitzenhoffer 1986, pp. 207, 254, 268, n. 17,
pl. 144.

301

Francisco de Goya y Lucientes, Style of
Uncertain date
PORTRAIT OF A MAN, SAID TO
BE THE PAINTER VICENTE LOPEZ
(1772–1850)
Oil on canvas, 22 x 17 ½ in. (55.9 x 44.5 cm)
Inscribed r.c.: *Goya / 1780*
PROVENANCE: Mrs. H. O. Havemeyer,
New York, bought through A. E.
Harnisch, Dec. 1912, for L 30,000;
shipped to her, Jan. 17, 1913; d. 1929;
MMA 29.100.179.

REFERENCES: Havemeyer 1931, pp. 48f.,
ill., as *Portrait of a Man—Lopez*, by
Goya; Weitzenhoffer 1986, p. 258.

302

**Francisco de Goya y Lucientes,
Workshop of**
Spanish, 1746–1828
THE DUKE OF WELLINGTON
Oil on canvas, 41 ½ x 33 in.
(105.4 x 83.8 cm)
Inscribed l.l., in another hand: *A. W. Terror
Gallorum*
PROVENANCE: possibly Miguel de Alava,
Vitoria, Spain; Ricardo Alava, Madrid; Mr.
and Mrs. H. O. Havemeyer, New York,
bought through Joseph Wicht and Cassatt,
Aug. 1901, for Fr 17,975; until 1907; Mrs.
H. O. Havemeyer, New York, 1907–29;
her daughter Adaline Havemeyer Freling-
huysen, Morristown, N.J., 1929–63; Na-
tional Gallery of Art, Washington, D.C.
(Gift of Mrs. P.H.B. Frelinghuysen),
1963.4.1.
EXHIBITION: 1912 New York, no. 14.
REFERENCES: Havemeyer 1931, pp. 318f.,
ill., as by Goya; Havemeyer 1961, pp. 7,
136, 153, 156f.; Gassier and Wilson 1971,
no. 900; Weitzenhoffer 1986, p. 141.

303

El Greco (Domenikos Theotokopoulos)
Greek, 1541–1614
VIEW OF TOLEDO*
Oil on canvas, 47 ¾ x 42 ¾ in.

345

(121.3 x 108.6 cm)
Signed l.r. (in Greek alphabet): *Domenikos Theotokopoulos / made this*
PROVENANCE: possibly Pedro Salazar de Mendoza, Toledo, in 1629; Countess of Anover y Casteneda, Onate Palace, Madrid; Durand-Ruel, Paris, bought from Ricardo de Madrazo (its agent in Spain), June 12, 1907 (stock nos. 6303 and 11454); Mrs. H. O. Havemeyer, New York, bought from Durand-Ruel, Apr. 29, 1909, for Fr 70,000; arrived New York, Oct. 13, 1909; d. 1929; MMA 29.100.6.
EXHIBITIONS: 1912 New York, no. 3; 1915 New York, no. 3; 1920 New York.
REFERENCES: Havemeyer 1931, pp. 52f., ill.; Wehle 1940, pp. 231f., ill.; Havemeyer 1958, p. 33, no. 193; Havemeyer 1961, pp. 132, 139, 153, 156; Wethey 1962, no. 129; Weitzenhoffer 1982, pp. 265f.; Weitzenhoffer 1986, pp. 141, 190f., 206, 245, 254, colorpl. 141.

304
El Greco (Domenikos Theotokopoulos)
PORTRAIT OF A CARDINAL, PROBABLY CARDINAL DON FERNANDO NINO DE GUEVARA (1541–1609)*
Oil on canvas, 67¼ x 42½ in.
(170.8 x 108 cm)
Signed l.c., on paper (in Greek alphabet): *Domenikos Theotokopoulos / made this*
PROVENANCE: The Condes de Anover de Tormes; the Condes de Onate, Madrid; Doña María Josefa de la Cerda, condesa viuda de Onate, Onate Palace, Madrid, until 1884; her inventory, no. 747; Don José Reniero, sixteenth conde de Onate, Onate Palace, Madrid, from 1891; Conde de Paredes de Nava, Onate Palace, Madrid, by 1902 14; Durand-Ruel, Paris, bought from Paredes de Nava, June 1,

1904 (stock no. 7659); Mr. and Mrs. H. O. Havemeyer, New York, bought from Durand-Ruel, June 1, 1904, for Fr 225,000; until 1907; Mrs. H. O. Havemeyer, New York, 1907–29; MMA 29.100.5.
EXHIBITIONS: 1902 Madrid, no. 13, lent by Sr. Conde de Paredes de Nava; 1912 New York, no. 1; 1915 New York, no. 2.
REFERENCES: Havemeyer 1931, pp. 50f., ill.; Wehle 1940, pp. 227–29, ill.; Havemeyer 1958, p. 35, no. 192, ill.; Havemeyer 1961, pp. 132, 138f., 152–59, 177–79; Wethey 1962, no. 152; Weitzenhoffer 1986, pp. 141, 153–55, 206f., 254, colorpl. 121.

306

305
El Greco (Domenikos Theotokopoulos), Copy after
Spanish, ca. 1650
CHRIST CARRYING THE CROSS***
Oil on canvas, 21⅛ x 15 in. (53.7 x 38.1 cm)
PROVENANCE: Mr. and Mrs. H. O. Havemeyer, New York, bought from a Madrid dealer in 1901 for Pts 1,500; until 1907; Mrs. H. O. Havemeyer, New York, 1907–at least 1912.
EXHIBITION: 1912 New York, no. 4.
REFERENCES: Havemeyer 1961, pp. 130, 134f., 137f., 179; Wethey 1962, no. X-39, as a copy after El Greco; Weitzenhoffer 1986, pp. 140f., 206.

307

306
Constantin Guys
French, 1805–1892
A LADY IN A BONNET AND COAT
Pen and brush, brown and black ink and watercolor, over traces of graphite, on wove paper, 15¹¹⁄₁₆ x 10⁷⁄₁₆ in.
(39.9 x 26.5 cm)
PROVENANCE: Ambroise Vollard, Paris; Mrs. H. O. Havemeyer, New York, bought from Vollard, by 1921–29; MMA 29.100.605.
EXHIBITION: 1921 New York Modern, lent by Mrs. H. O. Havemeyer.
REFERENCES: Havemeyer 1931, p. 189; Havemeyer 1958, p. 26, no. 143.

308

307
Constantin Guys
A LADY WITH A VEIL
Brush and black and brown watercolor over graphite, on wove paper, lined, 12⅛ x 8¼ in. (30.8 x 21 cm)
PROVENANCE: Alfred Beurdeley, Paris; his sale, Galerie Georges Petit, Paris, June 3, 1920, no. 189, as *Fille de brasserie*; bought at sale by Gobin for Fr 630; Mrs. H. O. Havemeyer, New York, bought through Théodore Duret, fall 1921–29; MMA 29.100.569.
REFERENCES: Havemeyer 1931, p. 189; Havemeyer 1958, p. 26, no. 144.

309

308
Constantin Guys
DRIVING IN THE BOIS DE BOULOGNE
Pen and brown ink, gray and black wash,
over traces of graphite, on wove paper,
7 11/16 x 11 1/8 in. (19.5 x 28.3 cm)
PROVENANCE: Tadamasa Hayashi, Paris
and Tokyo, d. 1906; his sale, American Art
Association, New York, Jan. 8–9, 1913,
no. 35, as by unknown artist; bought at
sale by Durand-Ruel for Havemeyer for
$52.50; Mrs. H. O. Havemeyer, New
York, 1913–29; MMA 29.100.568.
REFERENCES: Havemeyer 1931, pp. 188f.,
ill.; Havemeyer 1958, p. 26, no. 142.

309
Constantin Guys
OFFICERS OF THE GUARD
Pen and brown ink, watercolor, and black
ink, over traces of graphite, on wove
paper, 9 11/16 x 6 11/16 in. (24.6 x 17 cm)
PROVENANCE: Mrs. H. O. Havemeyer,
New York, d. 1929; MMA 29.100.602.
REFERENCES: Havemeyer 1931, p. 190;
Havemeyer 1958, p. 26, no. 145.

310
Constantin Guys
PORTRAIT OF A LADY
Watercolor over traces of graphite on wove

paper, 9 3/8 x 7 3/16 in. (23.9 x 18.3 cm)
PROVENANCE: Alfred Beurdeley, Paris; his
sale, Galerie Georges Petit, Paris, June 3,
1920, no. 199, as *La Femme au corsage
noir et à la jupe bleue*; Mrs. H. O. Havemeyer, New York, bought through
Théodore Duret, fall 1921–29; MMA
29.100.567.
REFERENCES: Havemeyer 1931, p. 189;
Havemeyer 1958, p. 26, no. 146.

311
Constantin Guys
SAILORS AND WOMEN
Pen and brown ink, gray and some black

310

313

316

311

314

317

312

315

318

wash, over graphite, on wove paper, 6¹⁵⁄₁₆ x 9³⁄₁₆ in. (17.6 x 23.3 cm)
PROVENANCE: Tadamasa Hayashi, Paris and Tokyo, d. 1906; his sale, American Art Association, New York, Jan. 8–9, 1913, no. 33, as by unknown artist; bought at sale by Durand-Ruel for Havemeyer for $27; Mrs. H. O. Havemeyer, New York, 1913–29; MMA 29.100.570.
REFERENCES: Havemeyer 1931, p. 189, as *Sailors and Dancers*; Havemeyer 1958, p. 26, no. 147.

312
Constantin Guys
TWO FAT PEASANT WOMEN
Brush and gray watercolor over traces of graphite, on wove paper, 10¹⁵⁄₁₆ x 8¹⁄₁₆ in. (27.8 x 20.5 cm)
PROVENANCE: Tadamasa Hayashi, Paris and Tokyo, d. 1906; his sale, American Art Association, New York, Jan. 8–9, 1913, no. 36, as by unknown artist; bought at sale by Durand-Ruel for Havemeyer for $25; Mrs. H. O. Havemeyer, New York, 1913–29; MMA 29.100.571.
REFERENCES: Havemeyer 1931, p. 189, as *Two Fat Women*; Havemeyer 1958, p. 26, no. 148.

313
Constantin Guys
TWO GENTLEMEN AND A LADY
Pen and brown ink and watercolor, over traces of graphite, on wove paper, 9⅝ x 7⁵⁄₁₆ in. (24.5 x 18.6 cm)
PROVENANCE: Mrs. H. O. Havemeyer, New York, d. 1929; MMA 29.100.572.
REFERENCES: Havemeyer 1931, p. 190; Havemeyer 1958, p. 27, no. 149.

314
Constantin Guys
TWO GRISETTES
Pen and brown ink, watercolor, and gouache, over traces of graphite, on wove paper, 9³⁄₁₆ x 7¼ in. (23.3 x 18.4 cm)
PROVENANCE: Galerie E. Druet, Paris, until 1922; Mrs. H. O. Havemeyer, New York, bought from Druet through Théodore Duret, summer 1922–29; MMA 29.100.601.
REFERENCES: Havemeyer 1931, p. 190; Havemeyer 1958, p. 27, no. 150.

315
Constantin Guys
TWO SOUBRETTES
Brush and watercolor over traces of graphite, on wove paper, 14½ x 9¹¹⁄₁₆ in. (36.8 x 24.6 cm)
PROVENANCE: Ambroise Vollard, Paris; Mrs. H. O. Havemeyer, New York, bought from Vollard, by 1921–29; MMA 29.100.604.

EXHIBITION: 1921 New York Modern, lent by Mrs. H. O. Havemeyer.
REFERENCES: Havemeyer 1931, p. 189; Havemeyer 1958, p. 27, no. 152.

316
Constantin Guys
TWO WOMEN WITH FANS
Pen and brown ink and watercolor, over slight traces of graphite, on wove paper, lined and varnished, 15⁹⁄₁₆ x 11¼ in. (39.5 x 28.6 cm)
PROVENANCE: Mrs. H. O. Havemeyer, New York, d. 1929; MMA 29.100.600.
REFERENCES: Havemeyer 1931, p. 190; Havemeyer 1958, p. 27, no. 155.

317
Constantin Guys
WOMAN STANDING IN A DOORWAY
Pen and brown ink and watercolor, over traces of graphite, on laid paper, 10½ x 7⅞ in. (26.7 x 18.1 cm)
PROVENANCE: Ambroise Vollard, Paris; Mrs. H. O. Havemeyer, New York, bought from Vollard, by 1921–29; MMA 29.100.603.
EXHIBITION: 1921 New York Modern, lent by Mrs. H. O. Havemeyer.
REFERENCES: Havemeyer 1931, p. 189, as *Déshabillé*; Havemeyer 1958, p. 26, no. 141.

318
Constantin Guys
WOMEN IN A CARRIAGE
Pen and brown ink and watercolor, over traces of graphite, on wove paper, 8³⁄₁₆ x 13⅛ in. (20.8 x 33.3 cm)
PROVENANCE: Ambroise Vollard, Paris; Mrs. H. O. Havemeyer, New York, bought from Vollard, by 1921–29; MMA 29.100.606.
EXHIBITION: 1921 New York Modern, lent by Mrs. H. O. Havemeyer.
REFERENCES: Havemeyer 1931, p. 189, as *Two Ladies in a Carriage*; Havemeyer 1958, p. 27, no. 151.

319
Frans Hals
Dutch, after 1580–1666
ANNA VAN DER AAR (1576/77–d. after 1626)*
Oil on wood, 8¾ x 6½ in. (22.2 x 16.5 cm)
Signed and dated on lower border of painted frame: *FHF 1626*
PROVENANCE: M. J. Caen van Maurick, Oudewater; Etienne Le Roy, Brussels; John Waterloo Wilson, Paris, by 1873; his sale, at his hôtel, 3, avenue Hoche, Paris, Mar. 14–16, 1881, no. 57; bought at sale by Galerie Georges Petit for Fr 80,000 the pair (with A320); E. Secrétan, Paris; his sale, Galerie Charles Sedelmeyer, Paris, July 1–7,

319

320

1889, no. 125; bought at sale by Durand-Ruel for Havemeyer for Fr 45,500 (stock no. 2398); Mr. and Mrs. H. O. Havemeyer, New York, 1889–1907; Mrs. H. O. Havemeyer, New York, 1907–29; MMA 29.100.9.
EXHIBITIONS: 1873 Brussels; 1874 Paris, no. 232; 1890–91 New York, no. 3; 1891 New York Metropolitan, no. 4.
REFERENCES: Havemeyer 1931, pp. 16f., ill.; Havemeyer 1958, p. 5, no. 14; Havemeyer 1961, p. 20; Slive 1974, no. 37; Weitzenhoffer 1982, pp. 109, 119, n. 24; pp. 127, 131f., 149, 166, n. 7; Weitzenhoffer 1986, pp. 58, 64, 77, 158, 254, ill. p. 74.

320
Frans Hals
PETRUS SCRIVERIUS (1576–1660)*
Oil on wood, 8¾ x 6½ in. (22.2 x 16.5 cm)
Signed and dated on lower border of painted frame: *FHF 1626*
PROVENANCE: M. J. Caen van Maurick, Oudewater; Etienne Le Roy, Brussels; John Waterloo Wilson, Paris, by 1873; his sale, at his hôtel, 3, avenue Hoche, Paris, Mar. 14–16, 1881, no. 56; bought at sale by Petit for Fr 80,000 the pair (with A319); E. Secrétan, Paris; his sale, Galerie Charles Sedelmeyer, Paris, July 1–7, 1889, no. 124; bought at sale by Durand-Ruel for Havemeyer for Fr 45,500 (stock no. 2397); Mr. and Mrs. H. O. Havemeyer, New York,

1889–1907; Mrs. H. O. Havemeyer, New York, 1907–29; MMA 29.100.8.
EXHIBITIONS: 1873 Brussels; 1874 Paris, no. 231; 1890–91 New York, no. 2; 1891 New York Metropolitan, no. 3.
REFERENCES: Havemeyer 1931, pp. 16f., ill.; Havemeyer 1958, p. 5, no. 13; Havemeyer 1961, p. 20; Slive 1974, no. 36; Weitzenhoffer 1982, pp. 109, 119, n. 24; pp. 127, 131f., 149, 166, n. 7; Weitzenhoffer 1986, pp. 58, 64, 77, 158, 254, ill. p. 74.

321
Frans Hals, Copy after
Dutch, 17th century
SELF-PORTRAIT
Oil on wood, 11⅜ x 9 in. (28.9 x 22.9 cm)
Inscribed l.c.: *F.H.* [in monogram]
PROVENANCE: possibly Mrs. H. O. Havemeyer, New York, d. 1929; her son, Horace Havemeyer, New York, by 1931–34; The Denver Art Museum, from 1934 (Gift of Horace Havemeyer), 1934.12.
REFERENCES: Havemeyer 1931, p. 305, as *Portrait of the Artist*, by school of Hals; Slive 1974, no. L15–7, as a copy after the lost original.

322
Lucas de Heere
Flemish, 1534–1584
PORTRAIT OF A MAN OF THE ELRINGTON FAMILY
Oil on wood, 26 x 22 in. (66 x 55.9 cm)
Dated u.l.: *Anno 1556*
PROVENANCE: G. S. Hanover, in 1838; Lord de Clifford; Harrington, Boston; M. J. Rougeron, New York, bought from Harrington's daughter; Mrs. H. O. Havemeyer, New York, bought from Rougeron as by Antonio Moro, in 1922–29; her sale, American Art Association, New York, Apr. 10, 1930, no. 93; bought at sale by W. W. Seaman (agent) for $800.
REFERENCE: Havemeyer 1931, p. 498.

323
Jean-Jacques Henner
French, 1829–1905

323

324

LOUISINE W. ELDER, LATER MRS. H. O. HAVEMEYER (1855–1929)
Oil on canvas, 25 x 19 in. (63.5 x 48.3 cm)
Signed and dated l.l.: *JJ HENNER / 1877*
PROVENANCE: Louisine W. Elder (later Mrs. H. O. Havemeyer), New York, commissioned from the artist in 1877–1929; her daughter Adaline Havemeyer Frelinghuysen, Morristown, N.J., 1929–63; private collection.
REFERENCES: Havemeyer 1931, p. 389; Weitzenhoffer 1982, pp. 32f., n. 38; Weitzenhoffer 1986, p. 28, ill. p. 25.

324
Jean-Jacques Henner
MATHILDA W. ELDER (1834–1907)
Oil on canvas, 25 x 19 in. (63.5 x 48.3 cm)
Signed l.l.: *JJ HENNER*
PROVENANCE: Mathilda W. Elder, New York, commissioned from the artist in 1877–1907; her daughter Mrs. H. O. Havemeyer, New York, 1907–29; private collection.
REFERENCES: Havemeyer 1931, p. 389; Weitzenhoffer 1982, pp. 32f., n. 38; Weitzenhoffer 1986, p. 28.

325
Jean-Jacques Henner
WOMAN LYING ON THE GRASS***
PROVENANCE: Boussod, Valadon et Cie, Paris, until 1881; M. Knoedler and Co.,

New York, bought from Boussod, Valadon, Sept. 15, 1881, for Fr 12,000 (stock no. 3511, as *Femme couchée sur le gazon*); H. O. Havemeyer, New York, bought from Knoedler, Sept. 29, 1881, for $3,000; M. Knoedler and Co., New York, bought back from Havemeyer, Dec. 6, 1888, for $1,750 credit (stock no. 6222, as *Sleeping Nymph*); J. V. Parker, New York, bought from Knoedler, Feb. 14, 1889, for $2,000.
REFERENCES: Weitzenhoffer 1982, p. 41; Weitzenhoffer 1986, p. 33.

326
Pieter de Hooch
Dutch, 1629–1684
THE VISIT*
Oil on wood, 26¼ x 23 in. (68 x 58.4 cm)
PROVENANCE: possibly Jacob Odon, Amsterdam; his sale, Arnoldus Dankmeyer en Zoon, Amsterdam, Sept. 6 and following days, 1784, no. 10; bought at sale by Braams Pelsdinge for G 300; Baron François Delessert, Paris; his sale, at his hôtel, Paris, Mar. 15–18, 1869, no. 36, as *Intérieur hollandais*; bought at sale by Narischkine for Fr 150,000; B. Narischkine; his sale, Galerie Georges Petit, Paris, Apr. 5, 1883, no. 16, as *La Consultation*; bought at sale by Cedron for Fr 160,000; E. Secrétan, Paris; his sale, Galerie Charles Sedelmeyer, Paris, July 1–7, 1889, no. 128, as *Intérieur hollandais*; bought at sale by Durand-Ruel for Havemeyer for Fr 276,000 (stock no. 2399); Mr. and Mrs. H. O. Havemeyer, New York, 1889–1907; Mrs. H. O. Havemeyer, New York, 1907–29; MMA 29.100.7.
EXHIBITIONS: 1890–91 New York, no. 4; 1891 New York Metropolitan, no. 6; 1893 New York, no. 16, as *Interior* (probably this picture); 1909 New York Metropolitan, no. 53; 1915 New York Masterpieces, no. 5.
REFERENCES: Havemeyer 1931, pp. 18f., ill.; Havemeyer 1958, p. 5, no. 15, ill.; Havemeyer 1961, p. 19; Sutton 1980, no. 19, as *A Merry Company with Two Men and Two Women*; Weitzenhoffer

1982, pp. 109, 119, n. 24, pp. 127, 131f., 138, 144f., n. 37, pp. 149, 166, n. 7; Weitzenhoffer 1986, pp. 58, 64, 66, 68, 77, 224, 254, ill.

327
Pieter de Hooch
THE CONCERT***
Oil on canvas, 25 ¼ x 29 ⅛ in. (64.1 x 74 cm)
Signed
PROVENANCE: M. X, Cambrai; sale, Hôtel Drouot, Paris, Nov. 25, 1889, no. 9, as *Le Concert*; bought at sale by Durand-Ruel for Fr 8,200; Durand-Ruel, Paris, 1889 (stock no. 2565, as *Le concert*); Durand-Ruel, New York, bought from Durand-Ruel, Paris, Dec. 3, 1889 (Paris stock book), or Dec. 25, 1889 (New York stock book, no. 903, as *Le concert*); Mr. and Mrs. H. O. Havemeyer, New York, bought from Durand-Ruel, Jan. 2, 1890, for $6,000.
REFERENCES: Weitzenhoffer 1982, pp. 126f., 141, n. 4; Weitzenhoffer 1986, pp. 64, 68.

328
Pieter de Hooch
PAINTING***
Oil
PROVENANCE: Durand-Ruel, Paris, until 1889; Mr. and Mrs. H. O. Havemeyer, New York, bought from Durand-Ruel, Aug. 1, 1889, for Fr 15,000 with a van de Cappelle (A47).
REFERENCES: Weitzenhoffer 1982, pp. 127, 141, n. 4; Weitzenhoffer 1986, pp. 64, 68.

329
Jean-Auguste-Dominique Ingres
French, 1780–1867
MME GUILLAUME GUILLON LETHIERE (EARLIER MME PIERRE CHAREN, NEE MARIE-JOSEPH-HONOREE VANZENNE), WITH HER SON, LUCIEN LETHIERE
Graphite on wove paper, 9 ½ x 7 ⅜ in. (24.1 x 18.7 cm)
Signed, dated, and inscribed l.r.: *Ingres. rome / 1808*
PROVENANCE: Mme Guillaume Guillon Lethière, Paris, d. 1838; her daughter from her first marriage, Eugénie Serrières (née Charen), Paris, d. 1855; Mrs. H. O. Havemeyer, New York, bought from a private collection in France; d. 1929; MMA 29.100.191.
REFERENCES: Havemeyer 1931, pp. 188, 190, ill., as *Lady and Boy*; Havemeyer 1958, p. 27, no. 155; Naef 1977–80, no. 51.

330
Jean-Auguste-Dominique Ingres
JOSEPH-ANTOINE MOLTEDO (b. 1775)*

329

330

331

Oil on canvas, 29 ⅝ x 22 ⅞ in. (75.3 x 58.1 cm)
PROVENANCE: possibly Moltedo family, Corsica; Théodore Duret, Paris; Mrs. H. O. Havemeyer, New York, bought from Duret by 1916–29; MMA 29.100.23.
EXHIBITION: 1926 New York, no. 21, as *Portrait of Chevalier X*, lent anonymously.
REFERENCES: Havemeyer 1931, pp. 136f., ill.; Wildenstein 1954, no. 71; Havemeyer 1958, p. 27, no. 154, ill.; Sterling and Salinger 1966, pp. 6f., ill.; Weitzenhoffer 1986, pp. 238f., 255, pl. 160.

331
Jean-Auguste-Dominique Ingres
MARIA LUIGI CARLO ZENOBIA SALVATORE CHERUBINI (1760–1842)***
Oil on canvas, 32 ¼ x 28 in. (81.9 x 71.1 cm)
Signed and dated l.l.: *J. Ingres pinx. 1841.*
PROVENANCE: Mme Cherubini; Mr. and

Mrs. H. O. Havemeyer, New York, until 1907; Mrs. H. O. Havemeyer, New York, consigned to Durand-Ruel, Mar. 10, 1909–May 11, 1910; Galerie Barbazanges, Paris, until 1922; M. Knoedler and Co., New York, bought from Barbazanges, May 15, 1922 (stock no. 15381); Mary M. (Mrs. Thomas J.) Emery, bought from Knoedler, Mar. 1923; Cincinnati Art Museum (Bequest of Mary M. Emery), 1927.386.
REFERENCE: Wildenstein 1954, no. 235.

332
Italian (Ferrarese) Painter, Unknown, 16th century
EPISODE FROM THE ACTS OF THE APOSTLES
Oil on wood, 24 x 17 in. (61 x 43.2 cm)
PROVENANCE: Mrs. H. O. Havemeyer, New York, consigned to Durand-Ruel, Nov. 30, 1908–May 11, 1910 (deposit no. 7500), Jan. 16–May 24, 1911 (deposit no. 7584), Nov. 16, 1911–May 24, 1913 (deposit no. 7621), and Nov. 5, 1913–May 29, 1914 (deposit no. 7716, as *Scène religieuse*, by Vasari); d. 1929; her sale, American Art Association, New York, Apr. 10, 1930, no. 51; bought at sale by Samuel Schepps for $250.
REFERENCES: Havemeyer 1931, p. 494; Weitzenhoffer 1986, p. 184.

333
Italian (Ferrarese) Painter, Unknown, 16th century
THE ROAD TO GOLGOTHA
Oil on wood, 23 ½ x 17 in. (59.7 x 43.2 cm)
PROVENANCE: Mrs. H. O. Havemeyer, New York, consigned to Durand-Ruel, Nov. 30, 1908–May 11, 1910 (deposit no. 7499), Jan. 16–May 24, 1911 (deposit no. 7583), Nov. 16, 1911–May 24, 1913 (deposit no. 7620), and Nov. 5, 1913–May 29, 1914 (deposit no. 7715, as *Jesus Christ Carrying the Cross*, by Vasari); d. 1929; her sale, American Art Association, New York, Apr. 10, 1930, no. 50; bought at sale by Samuel Schepps for $250.
REFERENCES: Havemeyer 1931, p. 494; Weitzenhoffer 1986, p. 184.

334
Italian Painter, Unknown, 15th century
MADONNA AND CHILD IN A ROSE GARDEN
Oil(?) on wood, 15 x 11 ¼ in. (38.1 x 29.9 cm)
PROVENANCE: Mrs. H. O. Havemeyer, New York, d. 1929; her sale, American Art Association, New York, Apr. 10, 1930, no. 52, as *Virgin and Child with Attendants*, by a follower of Fra Filippo Lippi; bought at sale by Ferargil Galleries for $650.
REFERENCES: Havemeyer 1931, p. 494, as Italian school, XV century; Havemeyer 1961, p. 128(?), as by Fra Diamanti.

335

Hans Jordaens III
Flemish, fl. by 1619; d. 1643
INTERIOR OF A PICTURE GALLERY
Pen and brown ink and brown wash, on
laid paper, 7 ¹¹/₁₆ x 9 ⅞ in. (19.5 x 25.1 cm)
PROVENANCE: Robert Prioleau Roupell,
London; Sir Francis Seymour Haden, Wood-
cote, Alresford, Hants; his sale, Sotheby's,
London, June 18, 1891, no. 589, as by
Rembrandt; bought at sale by Durand-
Ruel for Havemeyer; Mr. and Mrs. H. O.
Havemeyer, New York, 1891–1907; Mrs.
H. O. Havemeyer, New York, 1907–29;
MMA 29.100.933.
REFERENCES: Havemeyer 1931, p. 179, as
by Rembrandt; Havemeyer 1958, p. 9,
no. 33, Weitzenhoffer 1982, pp. 141f., n. 12.

336

Willem Kalf
Dutch, 1619–1693
STILL LIFE
Oil on canvas, 25 ⅜ x 21 ¼ in. (64.5 x 54 cm)
PROVENANCE: Cottier and Co., New York,
until 1889; Mr. and Mrs. H. O. Have-
meyer, New York, bought from Cottier in
1889; until 1907; Mrs. H. O. Havemeyer,
New York, 1907–29; her sale, American
Art Association, New York, Apr. 10, 1930,
no. 46; bought at sale by Dale for $3,700;
Chester Dale, New York, 1930–43; Na-
tional Gallery of Art, Washington, D.C.
(Chester Dale Collection), 1943.7.8.
EXHIBITIONS: 1890–91 New York, no. 13;
1891 New York Metropolitan, no. 1.
REFERENCES: Havemeyer 1931, p. 497;

Grisebach 1974, no. 102; Weitzenhoffer 1982,
pp. 127, 131f.; Weitzenhoffer 1986, p. 64.

337

Eugen Johann Georg Klimsch
German, 1839–1896
WATERCOLOR***
PROVENANCE: M. Knoedler and Co., New
York, until 1877; H. O. Havemeyer, New
York, bought from Knoedler, Feb. 21,
1877, for $60.

338

Ferdinand Kobell
German, 1740–1799
LANDSCAPE WITH FIGURES
Oil on canvas, 86 x 76 in. (218.4 x 193 cm)
Signed and dated l.l.: *Ferd. Kobell 1780*
PROVENANCE: Mrs. H. O. Havemeyer,
New York, bought through A. E. Harnisch
for L 3,000 the pair (with A339), by sum-
mer 1909–29; her sale, American Art Asso-
ciation, New York, Apr. 10, 1930, no. 117;
bought at sale by Metropolitan Galleries
for $550.
REFERENCE: Havemeyer 1931, p. 496.

339

Ferdinand Kobell
THE STORM
Oil on canvas, 86 x 67 ½ in.
(218.4 x 171.5 cm)
PROVENANCE: Mrs. H. O. Havemeyer,
New York, bought through A. E. Harnisch
for L 3,000 the pair (with A338), by summer 1909–29; her sale, American Art Association, New York, Apr. 10, 1930, no. 118;
bought at sale by Metropolitan Galleries
for $200.
REFERENCE: Havemeyer 1931, p. 496.

340

Fra Filippo Lippi, Follower of
Italian (Florentine), 15th century
MADONNA AND CHILD WITH TWO
ANGELS*
Tempera on wood, oval, 39 ¼ x 28 in.
(99.7 x 71.1 cm)
PROVENANCE: Removed from the parish

church of San Tommaso, Castelfranco di
Sopra, near Florence, late 18th century; the
counts Baglioni, Baglioni Villa, Cerreto,
from the late 18th century; Mr. and Mrs.
H. O. Havemeyer, New York, acquired
from the Baglioni family through A. E.
Harnisch by summer 1903, probably for
L 115,000; until 1907; Mrs. H. O. Havemeyer, New York, 1907–29; MMA
29.100.17.
REFERENCES: Havemeyer 1931, pp. 6f.,
ill., as by Lippi; Havemeyer 1961, pp. 113,
115–23; Zeri and Gardner 1973, pp. 93f.,
ill.; Weitzenhoffer 1986, p. 255.

341

**Fra Filippo Lippi, Imitator of, possibly
19th century**
MADONNA AND CHILD, WITH
BISHOP ADORING***
Oil on canvas, 24 ½ x 19 ½ in.
(62.2 x 49.5 cm)
PROVENANCE: Mr. and Mrs. H. O. Havemeyer, New York, bought in Italy; until
1907; Mrs. H. O. Havemeyer, New York,
1907–9; consigned to Durand-Ruel, Nov.
30, 1908 (deposit no. 7493, as school of
Lippi); Durand-Ruel, New York, bought
from Havemeyer, Feb. 1, 1909, for $6,500
(stock no. 3300, as Fra Filippo Lippi);
Mrs. Collis P. Huntington (later Mrs
Henry E. Huntington), New York, bought
from Durand-Ruel, Feb. 1, 1909, for
$8,000; d. 1924; her son, Archer M. Hunt-
ington, New York, 1924–26; Henry E.
Huntington Library and Art Gallery, San
Marino, Calif. (Gift of Archer Huntington,
1926).
REFERENCE: Weitzenhoffer 1986, p. 184.

342

Eugenio Lucas y Padilla
Spanish, 1824–1870
SCENE FROM THE WAR OF
INDEPENDENCE
Oil on canvas, 24 ½ x 36 in.
(62.2 x 91.4 cm)
PROVENANCE: Raimundo Madrazo, Spain;

343

345

347

344

346

348

Ambassador Gerinen,* ambassador to Spain, bought in Spain; M. J. Rougeron, New York, bought from Gerinen's widow; Mrs. H. O. Havemeyer, New York, bought from Rougeron as by Goya, in 1924–29; her sale, American Art Association, New York, Apr. 10, 1930, no. 45, as *Scene from the War of Independence*, by Eugenio Lucas the Elder, XIX century; bought at sale by DeMotte for $500.

*All information on this collector is taken from Havemeyer "Notes" [1974] and is unverified.

REFERENCE: Havemeyer 1931, p. 500, as *War Scene*, by Eugenio Lucas, XIX century.

343
Edouard Manet
French, 1832–1883
COPY AFTER DELACROIX'S "BARK OF DANTE"**
Oil on canvas, 13 x 16⅛ in. (33 x 41 cm)
PROVENANCE: Ambroise Vollard, Paris, bought from Mme Manet, the artist's widow, Oct. 30, 1894, for Fr 150; Durand-Ruel, Paris, bought from Vollard, Aug. 27, 1895, for Fr 350 (stock no. 3392); Mr. and Mrs. H. O. Havemeyer, New York, bought

from Durand-Ruel, Aug. 27, 1895, for Fr 400; until 1907; Mrs. H. O. Havemeyer, New York, 1907–29; MMA 29.100.114.
EXHIBITION: 1895 Paris Vollard.
REFERENCES: Havemeyer 1931, p. 150; Havemeyer 1958, p. 27, no. 156; Sterling and Salinger 1967, pp. 24f., ill.; Rouart and Wildenstein 1975, I, no. 3; Weitzenhoffer 1982, p. 240, fig. 72; Weitzenhoffer 1986, pp. 105, 257.

344
Edouard Manet
MLLE V . . . IN THE COSTUME OF AN ESPADA*
Oil on canvas, 65 x 50¼ in. (165.1 x 127.6 cm)
Signed and dated l.l.: *éd. Manet. / 1862*
PROVENANCE: Durand-Ruel, Paris, bought from the artist, Jan. 1872, for Fr 3,000; Jean-Baptiste Faure, Paris, bought from Durand-Ruel, Feb. 16, 1874, for Fr 5,000; deposited with Durand-Ruel, Nov. 11, 1896–Jan. 9, 1897 (deposit no. 9021, as *Femme torero*), and Sept. 11, 1897–Aug. 30, 1898 (deposit no. 9182, as *Toréador*); Durand-Ruel, Paris, bought from Faure,

Dec. 22, 1898, for Fr 45,000 (stock no. 4906, as *Femme toréador*); Durand-Ruel, New York, bought from Durand-Ruel, Paris, Dec. 28, 1898 (Paris stock book), or Jan. 21, 1899 (New York stock book, no. 2095, as *Mlle V. en costume d'espada*); Mr. and Mrs. H. O. Havemeyer, New York, bought from Durand-Ruel, Dec. 31, 1898, for $15,000; until 1907; Mrs. H. O. Havemeyer, New York, 1907–29; MMA 29.100.53.
EXHIBITIONS: 1863 Paris, no. 365; 1867 Paris Manet, no. 12; 1884 Paris, no. 15.
REFERENCES: Havemeyer 1931, pp. 146f., ill.; Havemeyer 1958, p. 28, no. 159, ill.; Havemeyer 1961, pp. 224f.; Sterling and Salinger 1967, pp. 33–35, ill.; Rouart and Wildenstein 1975, I, no. 58; Weitzenhoffer 1982, pp. 295f., 313, n. 22, fig. 104; Weitzenhoffer 1986, pp. 129, 212, 255, colorpl. 82.

345
Edouard Manet
YOUNG MAN IN THE COSTUME OF A MAJO*
Oil on canvas, 74 x 49⅛ in. (188 x 124.8 cm)
Signed and dated l.r.: *éd. Manet. 1863*

PROVENANCE: Durand-Ruel, Paris, bought from the artist, Jan. 1872, for Fr 1,500 (stock no. 960, as *L'Espagnol*; in 1877, stock no. 1363, as *L'Espagnol*); Ernest Hoschedé, Paris, bought from Durand-Ruel, Jan. 29, 1877, with 28 other works for Fr 18,500; his sale, Hôtel Drouot, Paris, June 6, 1878, no. 43; bought at sale by Faure for Fr 650; Jean-Baptiste Faure, Paris, 1878–98; on deposit with Durand-Ruel, Nov. 11, 1896–Jan. 9, 1897 (deposit no. 9183); Durand-Ruel, Paris, bought from Faure, Dec. 31, 1898, for Fr 20,000 (stock no. 4933, as *Portrait de son frère, costume de majo*); Durand-Ruel, New York, bought from Durand-Ruel, Paris, Jan. 24, 1899 (Paris stock book), or Feb. 9, 1899 (New York stock book, no. 2107, as *Le majo*); Mr. and Mrs. H. O. Havemeyer, New York, bought from Durand-Ruel, Feb. 24, 1899, for $10,000; until 1907; Mrs. H. O. Havemeyer, New York, 1907–29; MMA 29.100.54.

EXHIBITIONS: 1863 Paris, no. 364; 1867 Paris Manet, no. 13; 1874 London, no. 4(?), as *A Spaniard*; 1884 Paris, no. 11; 1913 New York, no. 4; 1928 New York, no. 9.

REFERENCES: Havemeyer 1931, pp. 142f., ill.; Havemeyer 1958, p. 28, no. 161; Havemeyer 1961, p. 224; Sterling and Salinger 1967, pp. 35f., ill.; Rouart and Wildenstein 1975, I, no. 70; Weitzenhoffer 1982, pp. 295f., fig. 103; Weitzenhoffer 1986, pp. 129, 256, pl. 83.

346
Edouard Manet
THE DEAD CHRIST AND THE ANGELS*
Oil on canvas, 70⅝ x 59 in. (179.4 x 149.9 cm)
Signed l.l.: *Manet*; inscribed l.r., on rock: *évang[ile]. sel[on]. S! Jean / chap[itre]. XX v. XII [John 20:12]*
PROVENANCE: Durand-Ruel, Paris, bought from the artist, Jan. 1872, for Fr 3,000 (or Fr 4,000, according to Manet's account book; old stock no. 1178, as *Le Christ*); Durand-Ruel, Paris, bought from an unidentified collector in 1881 (stock no. 19, as *Le Christ aux anges*); Durand-Ruel, New York, received on deposit from Durand-Ruel, Paris, Feb. 27, 1895 (deposit no. 5253); bought from Durand-Ruel, Paris, Nov. 16, 1900 (Paris stock book), or Nov. 27, 1900 (New York stock book, no. 2411), for Fr 4,050; Mr. and Mrs. H. O. Havemeyer, New York, bought from Durand-Ruel, Feb. 7, 1903, for $17,000; until 1907; Mrs. H. O. Havemeyer, New York, 1907–29; MMA 29.100.51.

EXHIBITIONS: 1864 Paris Salon, no. 1281; 1867 Paris Manet, no. 7; 1872 London Fourth, no. 91, as *Christ in the Sepulchre*;

1883 Boston, no. 1; 1895 New York, no. 8; 1902–3 Pittsburgh, no. 94, as *Angels at the Tomb of Christ*, lent by Messrs. Durand-Ruel and Company.

REFERENCES: Havemeyer 1931, pp. 140f., ill.; Havemeyer 1958, p. 28, no. 158; Havemeyer 1961, pp. 220, 236f.; Sterling and Salinger 1967, pp. 36–40, ill.; Rouart and Wildenstein 1975, I, no. 74; Weitzenhoffer 1982, p. 234; Weitzenhoffer 1986, pp. 102, 147, 255, pl. 118.

347
Edouard Manet
THE KEARSARGE AT BOULOGNE
Oil on canvas, 32 x 39¼ in. (81.3 x 99.7 cm)
Signed l.l.: *Manet*
PROVENANCE: Boussod, Valadon et Cie, Paris, bought from Gatti, Mar. 10, 1890, for Fr 2,000; Gustave Goupy, Paris, bought from Boussod, Valadon, Mar. 10, 1890, for Fr 4,000; his sale, Hôtel Drouot, Paris, Mar. 30, 1898, no. 20; bought at sale by Durand-Ruel for Havemeyer; Mr. and Mrs. H. O. Havemeyer, New York, 1898–1907; Mrs. H. O. Havemeyer, New York, 1907–29; her daughter Adaline Havemeyer Frelinghuysen, Morristown, N.J., 1929–63; private collection.

EXHIBITIONS: 1865 Paris(?); 1867 Paris Manet, no. 34 or 45.

REFERENCES: Havemeyer 1931, pp. 390f., ill., as *L'Alabama au large de Cherbourg*; Havemeyer 1961, pp. 222f., confuses it with Manet's *Port of Calais* (A353); Rouart and Wildenstein 1975, I, no. 75; Weitzenhoffer 1982, pp. 296, 313, n. 19, p. 314, n. 23, fig. 105; Weitzenhoffer 1986, pp. 129, 158.

348
Edouard Manet
A MATADOR*
Oil on canvas, 67⅜ x 44½ in. (171.1 x 113 cm)
Signed l.l.: *Manet*
PROVENANCE: Théodore Duret, Paris, bought from the artist in 1870 for Fr 1,200; his sale, Galerie Georges Petit, Paris, Mar. 19, 1894, no. 20; bought at sale by Durand-Ruel and Faure for Fr 10,500; Durand-Ruel, Paris, owned jointly with Jean-Baptiste Faure until Faure sold his half share to Durand-Ruel, Dec. 21, 1898 (stock no. 2965); Durand-Ruel, New York, bought from Durand-Ruel, Paris, Oct. 25, 1894 (stock no. 1223); Durand-Ruel, Paris, bought back from Durand-Ruel, New York, Aug. 31, 1895; on deposit with Durand-Ruel, New York, from Durand-Ruel, Paris, Aug. 31, 1895–Dec. 31, 1898 (deposit no. 5350); bought again from Durand-Ruel, Paris, Dec. 21, 1898 (Paris stock book), or Dec. 31, 1898 (New York stock book, no. 2073), for Fr 20,000; Mr.

and Mrs. H. O. Havemeyer, New York, bought from Durand-Ruel, Dec. 31, 1898, for $8,000; until 1907; Mrs. H. O. Havemeyer, New York, 1907–29; MMA 29.100.52.

EXHIBITIONS: 1866 Paris Manet; 1867 Paris Manet, no. 16; 1884 Paris, no. 34; 1895 New York, no. 24; 1896 Buffalo, no. 56; 1897–98 Pittsburgh, no. 139; 1898 Boston, no. 58.

REFERENCES: Havemeyer 1931, pp. 144f., ill.; Havemeyer 1958, p. 28, no. 160; Havemeyer 1961, pp. 223f.; Sterling and Salinger 1967, pp. 43f., ill.; Rouart and Wildenstein 1975, I, no. 111; Weitzenhoffer 1982, pp. 234, 295, fig. 102; Weitzenhoffer 1986, pp. 102, 128f., 255, pl. 81.

349
Edouard Manet
LUNCHEON IN THE STUDIO***
Oil on canvas, 46⅝ x 60⅝ in. (118.4 x 154 cm)
Signed lower center, on tablecloth: *É. Manet*
PROVENANCE: Jean-Baptiste Faure, Paris, bought from the artist, Nov. 18, 1873, for Fr 4,000; deposited with Durand-Ruel, Jan. 2, 1893 [1894?] (deposit no. 8166, as *Le déjeuner*); shipped to New York, Feb. 7, 1895; Durand-Ruel, New York, received on deposit from Durand-Ruel, Paris, Feb. 23, 1895 (deposit no. 5236, as *Le déjeuner dans l'atelier*); bought from Durand-Ruel, Paris, Apr. 8, 1895, for Fr 18,000 (stock no. 1388, as *Le déjeuner dans l'atelier*); Mr. and Mrs. H. O. Havemeyer, New York, bought from Durand-Ruel, Apr. 8, 1895, for $7,000; Durand-Ruel, Paris, bought back from Havemeyer, Oct. 28, 1895, for Fr 35,000; Durand-Ruel, New York, received on deposit from Durand-Ruel, Paris, Nov. 11, 1895–Dec. 18, 1897 (deposit no. 5359, as *Le déjeuner*); Durand-Ruel, Paris, bought from Faure, Jan. 5, 1898, for Fr 25,000 (stock no. 4522, as *Le déjeuner à l'atelier*); Auguste Pellerin, Paris, bought from Durand-Ruel, Jan. 10, 1898, for Fr 35,000; Bernheim-Jeune, Paul Cassirer, and Durand-Ruel, Paris, bought Feb. 2, 1911 (Durand-Ruel stock no. 9477, as *Le déjeuner dans l'atelier*); Georg Ernst Schmidt-Reissig, Starnberg, bought from them in 1911, in memory of Hugo von Tschudi, for the Bayerische Staatsgemäldesammlungen, Munich; Neue Pinakothek, Munich, inv. 8638.

EXHIBITIONS: 1869 Paris, no. 1617; 1869 Brussels, no. 755; 1884 Paris, no. 48; 1891 Munich, no. 923; 1895 New York, no. 11; 1900 Paris, no. 447; 1910 Munich, no. 10; 1910 Paris, no. 2, as *Le déjeuner dans l'atelier*; 1913 Stuttgart, no. 309, as *Das Frühstück*, lent by Kgl. Pinakothek, Munich.

349

352

355

350

353

356

351

354

357

REFERENCES: Havemeyer 1961, p. 225; Rouart and Wildenstein 1975, I, no. 135; Weitzenhoffer 1982, p. 198, n. 45(?), p. 245, n. 18, pp. 246f., n. 29; Weitzenhoffer 1986, p. 102, colorpl. 52.

350
Edouard Manet
THE SALMON
Oil on canvas, 28 ¼ x 35 ⅜ in. (71.8 x 89.9 cm)
Signed l.r.: *Manet*
PROVENANCE: Durand-Ruel, Paris, bought from Basset, Apr. 1872, for Fr 250 (stock no. 1228, as *Le saumon*); Jean-Baptiste Faure, Paris, bought from Durand-Ruel, Nov. 16, 1874, for Fr 1,500; Durand-Ruel, Paris, received on deposit from Faure, Feb. 2, 1886 (deposit no. 4716, as *Nature morte*); bought from Faure, Aug. 24, 1886, for Fr 5,000 (stock no. 847, as *Le saumon*); Durand-Ruel, New York, bought

from Durand-Ruel, Paris, Aug. 24, 1886, for Fr 5,000; Mr. and Mrs. H.O. Havemeyer, New York, bought from Durand-Ruel from the 1886 exhibition for Fr 15,000; until 1907; Mrs. H. O. Havemeyer, New York, 1907–29; on deposit with Durand-Ruel, Nov. 22–Dec. 15, 1913 (deposit no. 7733); her daughter Electra Havemeyer Webb, New York, 1929–60; Shelburne Museum, Shelburne, Vt., from 1960, 27.1.3–24.
EXHIBITIONS: 1864 Paris; 1867 Paris Manet, no. 36(?); 1872 London, no. 105, as *Still Life*; 1884 Paris, no. 50; 1886 New York, no. 23, as *Still Life*; 1895 New York; 1913 New York, no. 8; 1928 New York, no. 11.
REFERENCES: Havemeyer 1931, pp. 396f., ill.; Havemeyer 1961, pp. 220f.; Rouart and Wildenstein 1975, I, no. 140; Weitzenhoffer 1982, pp. 65, 75f., 198, n. 45;

p. 233, fig. 7; Weitzenhoffer 1986, pp. 41, 44, 101f., colorpl. 10.

351
Edouard Manet
IN THE GARDEN
Oil on canvas, 17 ½ x 21 ¼ in. (44.5 x 54 cm)
Signed l.r.: *Manet*
PROVENANCE: Giuseppe de Nittis, given to him by the artist; d. 1884; Suzanne Manet, the artist's widow, Paris, received in an exchange with de Nittis's widow; Alphonse Portier, Paris, bought from Mme Manet in 1889; sold to Eugène Blot on credit for Fr 2,000, but returned when Blot could not raise this sum; Gustave Goupy, Paris, bought from Portier; his sale, Hôtel Drouot, Paris, Mar. 30, 1898, no. 21; bought at sale by Durand-Ruel for Havemeyer for Fr 22,000; Mr. and Mrs. H. O. Havemeyer, New York, 1898–1907; Mrs. H. O. Havemeyer, New

York, 1907–29; her daughter Electra Havemeyer Webb, New York, 1929–60; her daughter Electra Webb Bostwick, New York, 1960–82; Shelburne Museum, Shelburne, Vt., from 1982, 27.1.1–200.
EXHIBITIONS: 1884 Paris, no. 58; 1913 New York, no. 9.
REFERENCES: Havemeyer 1931, pp. 392f., ill.; Havemeyer 1961, p. 222; Rouart and Wildenstein 1975, I, no. 155; Weitzenhoffer 1982, pp. 296, 314, n. 23; fig. 106; Weitzenhoffer 1986, pp. 129, 158, colorpl. 84.

352
Edouard Manet
MANET'S FAMILY AT HOME IN ARCACHON
Oil on canvas, 15 ½ x 21 ⅛ in. (39.4 x 53.7 cm)
Signed r.: *Manet*; inscribed on book: *Manet*[?]
PROVENANCE: Mr. and Mrs. H. O. Havemeyer, New York, by 1902–7; Mrs. H. O. Havemeyer, New York, 1907–29; her daughter Electra Havemeyer Webb, New York, 1929–43; on deposit with Durand-Ruel, Feb. 13–16, 1931 (deposit no. 8471, as *Intérieur [homme et femme]*), by Mrs. Havemeyer (Webb?); M. Knoedler and Co., New York, consigned by Webb, Apr. 1, 1943 (stock no. CA1983); Robert Sterling Clark, New York, bought from Knoedler, Apr. 12, 1943; until 1955; Sterling and Francine Clark Art Institute, Williamstown, Mass., from 1955, inv. no. 552.
REFERENCES: Havemeyer 1931, p. 400, as *Interior*; Havemeyer 1961, pp. 221f.; Rouart and Wildenstein 1975, I, no. 170, as *Intérieur à Arcachon*; Weitzenhoffer 1982, p. 257, fig. 81; Weitzenhoffer 1986, p. 112, pl. 63.

353
Edouard Manet
THE PORT OF CALAIS
Oil on canvas, 32 ⅛ x 39 ⅝ in. (81.6 x 100.7 cm)
Signed and inscribed on boat: *Édouard Manet Calais*
PROVENANCE: Jean-Baptiste Faure, Paris, bought from the artist, Mar. 1882, for Fr 1,500; Durand-Ruel, Paris, bought from Faure, May 12, 1893 (stock no. 2741, as *Le port de Calais*); Harris Whittemore, Naugatuck, Conn., bought from Durand-Ruel, May 12, 1893; Durand-Ruel, New York, bought from Whittemore, Mar. 10, 1896, for $2,200 (stock no. 1605, as *Marine, Port de Calais*); Mr. and Mrs. H. O. Havemeyer, New York, bought from Durand-Ruel, Jan. 20, 1898, for $3,500; until 1907; Mrs. H. O. Havemeyer, New York, 1907–29; her son, Horace Havemeyer, New York, 1929–56; his widow, Doris Dick Havemeyer, New York, 1956–82; her sale, Sotheby's, New York, May 18, 1983, no. 14; bought at sale by a private collector for $1,045,000; private collection.
EXHIBITION: 1884 Paris, not in cat.
REFERENCES: Havemeyer 1931, p. 403; Havemeyer 1961, pp. 222f., confuses it with Manet's *Kearsarge at Boulogne* (A347); Rouart and Wildenstein 1975, I, no. 174; Weitzenhoffer 1982, pp. 210, 218, n. 24, pp. 294f., 313, n. 19, fig. 101; Weitzenhoffer 1986, p. 128, colorpl. 80.

354
Edouard Manet
YOUNG WOMAN WITH LOOSENED HAIR
Oil on canvas, 24 x 19 ¾ in. (61 x 50.2 cm)
PROVENANCE: possibly bought by Mr. and Mrs. Havemeyer from Clemenceau in fall 1896 at the same time they acquired Manet's portrait of Clemenceau (A363); Mrs. H.O. Havemeyer, New York, d. 1929; her sale, American Art Association, Apr. 10, 1930, no. 123, as *Buste de Femme*, French school, Contemporary; bought at sale by M. Knoedler and Co. for $200; Etienne Bignou, Paris; Bernheim-Jeune, Paris; J. K. Thannhauser, Berlin and New York; sale, Parke-Bernet, New York, Apr. 12, 1945, no. 106; bought at sale by Friedman; C. Friedman, New York, from 1945.
REFERENCES: Havemeyer 1931, p. 504, as *Buste de jeune femme*, French school, XIX or XX century; Havemeyer 1961, pp. 231f.(?), misleadingly described; Rouart and Wildenstein 1975, I, no. 206.

355
Edouard Manet
PORTRAIT OF MARGUERITE DE CONFLANS
Oil on canvas, 21 x 17 ½ in. (53.3 x 44.5 cm)
Signed and dated l.l.: *Manet / 1873*
PROVENANCE: Manet's posthumous inventory, 1883, no. 53; Ignace Ephrussi, Paris; Alexandre Rosenberg, Paris, in 1898; Paul Rosenberg, Paris, until 1903; Mr. and Mrs. H. O. Havemeyer, New York, bought from Rosenberg in early 1903 for Fr 28,000; shipped to them by Durand-Ruel, May 7, 1903; until 1907; Mrs. H. O. Havemeyer, New York, 1907–29; her sale, American Art Association, New York, Apr. 10, 1930, no. 73; bought at sale by Durand-Ruel for $10,500 or R. D. Smith for $10,000; Paul Rosenberg, New York; Smith College Museum of Art, Northampton, Mass. (Purchased, Drayton Hillyer Fund, 1945), 1945.6.
EXHIBITION: 1913 New York, no. 11.
REFERENCES: Havemeyer 1931, p. 504; Havemeyer 1961, pp. 231f., with erroneous acquisition information; Rouart and Wildenstein 1975, I, no. 203.

356
Edouard Manet
GARE SAINT-LAZARE
Oil on canvas, 36 ¼ x 45 ⅛ in. (92.1 x 114.6 cm)
Signed and dated l.r.: *Manet / 1873*
PROVENANCE: Jean-Baptiste Faure, Paris, bought from the artist in 1873; until 1881; Durand-Ruel, Paris, bought from Faure, June 29, 1881, for Fr 5,400 (stock no. 1137, as *Enfant regardant le chemin de fer*; later stock no. 236, as *Le pont de l'Europe*); Durand-Ruel, New York, bought from Durand-Ruel, Paris, July 11, 1888 (stock no. 174, as *A la gare St. Lazare*; later stock no. 73, as *Gare St. Lazare*); Mr. and Mrs. H. O. Havemeyer, New York, bought from Durand-Ruel, Dec. 31, 1898, for $15,000; until 1907; Mrs. H. O. Havemeyer, New York, 1907–29; her son, Horace Havemeyer, New York, 1929–56; National Gallery of Art, Washington, D.C. (Gift of Horace Havemeyer in memory of his mother, Louisine W. Havemeyer), 1956.10.1.
EXHIBITIONS: 1874 Paris Salon, no. 1260; 1883 London, no. 46, as *Le Pont de l'Europe*, marked for sale for £400; 1884 Paris, no. 68; 1895 New York, no. 25; 1898 Boston, no. 58; 1913 New York, no. 12.
REFERENCES: Havemeyer 1931, pp. 406f., ill., as *Le Chemin de fer—Gare St. Lazare*; Havemeyer 1961, pp. 220, 237–40; Rouart and Wildenstein 1975, I, no. 207; Weitzenhoffer 1982, pp. 234, 296, fig. 107; Weitzenhoffer 1986, pp. 102, 129, 212, colorpl. 85.

357
Edouard Manet
BALL AT THE OPERA
Oil on canvas, 23 ¼ x 28 ½ in. (59.1 x 72.4 cm)
Signed l.r., on dance program: *Manet*
PROVENANCE: Jean-Baptiste Faure, Paris, bought from the artist, Nov. 18, 1873, for Fr 6,000; his sale, Hôtel Drouot, Paris, Apr. 29, 1878, no. 40, bought in for Fr 6,000; Durand-Ruel, Paris, bought from Faure, Jan. 9, 1893, for Fr 15,000 (stock no. 2582, as *Bal de l'Opéra*); Durand-Ruel, New York, bought from Durand-Ruel, Paris, Jan. 18, 1894 (stock no. 1131, as *Bal à l'Opéra*); Mr. and Mrs. H. O. Havemeyer, New York, bought from Durand-Ruel, Jan. 16, 1894, for $8,000; until 1907; Mrs. H. O. Havemeyer, New York, 1907–29; her son, Horace Havemeyer, New York, 1929–56; his widow, Doris Dick Havemeyer, New York, 1956–82; National Gallery of Art, Washington, D.C. (Gift of Mrs. Horace Havemeyer in memory of her mother-in-law, Louisine W. Havemeyer), 1982.75.1.

EXHIBITIONS: 1884 Paris, no. 69; 1895 New York, no. 29.
REFERENCES: Havemeyer 1931, pp. 404f., ill.; Havemeyer 1961, pp. 218–20, 227; Rouart and Wildenstein 1975, I, no. 216; Weitzenhoffer 1982, pp. 225f., 233, 244, n. 9, fig. 61; Weitzenhoffer 1986, pp. 98, 101f., 176, colorpl. 44.

358
Edouard Manet
BOATING**
Oil on canvas, 38 1/4 x 51 1/4 in. (97.2 x 130.2 cm)
Signed l.r.: *Manet*
PROVENANCE: Victor Desfosses, Paris, bought from the 1879 Salon for Fr 1,500; until 1895; Durand-Ruel, Paris, bought from Desfosses, May 7, 1895, for Fr 25,000 (stock no. 3267, as *En bateau*); Mr. and Mrs. H. O. Havemeyer, New York, bought from Durand-Ruel, Sept. 19, 1895, for Fr 55,000; until 1907; Mrs. H. O. Havemeyer, New York, 1907–29; MMA 29.100.115.
EXHIBITIONS: 1876 Paris Manet; 1879 Paris Salon, no. 2011; 1884 Paris, no. 76; 1889 Paris Universelle, no. 498; 1913 New York, no. 13.
REFERENCES: Havemeyer 1931, pp. 138f., ill.; Havemeyer 1958, p. 28, no. 157, ill.; Havemeyer 1961, p. 225; Sterling and Salinger 1967, pp. 45–47, ill.; Rouart and Wildenstein 1975, I, no. 223; Weitzenhoffer 1982, pp. 105f., 118, n. 19, pp. 241f., 281, n. 30, fig. 78; Weitzenhoffer 1986, pp. 56, 107, 117, 177, 257, 262, n. 9, colorpl. 60.

359
Edouard Manet
THE GRAND CANAL, VENICE (BLUE VENICE)
Oil on canvas, 23 1/8 x 28 1/8 in. (58.7 x 71.4 cm)
Signed r., below pole: *Manet*
PROVENANCE: James Tissot, London, bought from the artist in 1875, possibly for Fr 2,500; Durand-Ruel, Paris, by Aug. 25, 1891 (stock no. 1163); Durand-Ruel, New York (stock no. 1389, as *Vue de Venise*); Mr. and Mrs. H. O. Havemeyer, New York, bought from Durand-Ruel, Apr. 8, 1895, for $12,000; until 1907; Mrs. H. O. Havemeyer, New York, 1907–29; her daughter Electra Havemeyer Webb, New York, 1929–60; Shelburne Museum, Shelburne, Vt., from 1960, 27.1.5–30.
EXHIBITIONS: 1884 Paris, no. 79; 1895 New York, no. 16; 1913 New York, no. 15.
REFERENCES: Havemeyer 1931, pp. 394f., ill., as *Blue Venice*; Havemeyer 1961, pp. 225–29; Rouart and Wildenstein 1975, I, no. 231; Weitzenhoffer 1982, pp. 233f., 247, n. 31, fig. 67; Weitzenhoffer 1986, pp. 102, 232, colorpl. 51.

360
Edouard Manet
GEORGE MOORE (1852–1933)*
Pastel on canvas, 21 3/4 x 13 7/8 in. (55.3 x 35.2 cm)
Signed l.l.: *Manet*
PROVENANCE: Edouard Manet, Paris, d. 1883; his sale, Hôtel Drouot, Paris, Feb. 5, 1884, no. 96; bought at sale by Jacob for Fr 1,800; Mr. and Mrs. H. O. Havemeyer, New York, bought from a private collection, Paris, through Alphonse Portier, probably in 1896, for Fr 10,000; until 1907; Mrs. H. O. Havemeyer, New York, 1907–29; MMA 29.100.55.
EXHIBITIONS: 1880 Paris, no. 15; 1884 Paris, no. 153.
REFERENCES: Havemeyer 1931, pp. 148f., ill.; Havemeyer 1958, p. 29, no. 162; Havemeyer 1961, pp. 233–36; Sterling and Salinger 1967, pp. 48–50, ill.; Rouart and Wildenstein 1975, II, no. 11; Weitzenhoffer 1986, pp. 115f., 256, colorpl. 70.

361
Edouard Manet
MLLE LUCIE DELABIGNE (1859–1910), CALLED VALTESSE DE LA BIGNE
Pastel on canvas, 21 3/4 x 14 in. (55.3 x 35.6 cm)
Signed r.c.: *Manet*
PROVENANCE: Mlle Delabigne, Paris; her sale, Haro and Bloche, Paris, June 2–7, 1902, no. 78; Mrs. H. O. Havemeyer, New York, possibly bought through Alphonse Portier;* d. 1929; MMA 29.100.561.
*Portier died on June 24, 1902.
EXHIBITIONS: 1880 Paris, no. 13 or 19; 1884 Paris, no. 138.
REFERENCES: Havemeyer 1931, p. 150; Havemeyer 1958, p. 29, no. 164; Havemeyer 1961, p. 232; Sterling and Salinger 1967, pp. 51f., ill.; Rouart and Wildenstein 1975, II, no. 14.

362
Edouard Manet
MLLE ISABELLE LEMONNIER*
Pastel on canvas, 22 x 18 1/4 in. (55.9 x 46.4 cm)
PROVENANCE: Mlle Lemonnier, Paris; Durand-Ruel, Paris, bought from van Wisselingh, Mar. 8, 1899, for Fr 1,000 (stock no. 5081); Mr. and Mrs. H. O. Havemeyer, New York, bought from Durand-Ruel, Apr. 22, 1901; until 1907; Mrs. H. O. Havemeyer, New York, 1907–29; MMA 29.100.56.
EXHIBITION: 1880 Paris, no. 13 or 19.
REFERENCES: Havemeyer 1931, pp. 148f., ill.; Havemeyer 1958, p. 29, no. 163; Havemeyer 1961, p. 232; Sterling and Salinger 1967, pp. 47f., ill.; Rouart and Wildenstein 1975, II, no. 15; Weitzenhoffer 1986, pp. 143, 256.

363
Edouard Manet
GEORGES CLEMENCEAU (1841–1929)
Oil on canvas, 37 x 29 1/4 in. (94 x 74.3 cm)
PROVENANCE: Georges Clemenceau, Paris, given to him by Suzanne Manet, widow of the artist, July 11, 1883; Mr. and Mrs. H. O. Havemeyer, New York, bought from Clemenceau in fall 1896 for Fr 10,000; until 1907; Mrs. H. O. Havemeyer, New York, 1907–27; Musée du Louvre, Paris (given by Havemeyer, July 4, 1927); Musée d'Orsay, Paris, RF 2641.
EXHIBITION: 1913 New York, no. 16.
REFERENCES: Havemeyer 1931, pp. 292f., ill.; Havemeyer 1961, pp. 229–31; Rouart and Wildenstein 1975, I, no. 330; Weitzenhoffer 1982, pp. 257–59, 279, n. 14, fig. 83; Weitzenhoffer 1986, p. 243.

364
Edouard Manet
MLLE SUZETTE LEMAIRE
Pastel on paper, 21 3/8 x 17 3/4 in. (54.3 x 45.1 cm)
Signed r.: *Manet*
PROVENANCE: Madeleine Lemaire, mother of the sitter, Paris, acquired through Charles Ephrussi, Paris; Durand-Ruel, Paris, bought from Lemaire, May 8, 1906, for Fr 12,000 (stock no. 8154); Mr. and Mrs. H. O. Havemeyer, New York, bought from Durand-Ruel, May 8, 1906, for Fr 15,000; until 1907; Mrs. H. O. Havemeyer, New York, 1907–29; her daughter Electra Havemeyer Webb, New York, 1929–60; her daughter Electra Webb Bostwick, New York, 1960–82; Shelburne Museum, Shelburne, Vt, from 1982, 27.3.1–36.
EXHIBITION: 1884 Paris, no. 126.
REFERENCES: Havemeyer 1931, pp. 400f., ill.; Havemeyer 1961, pp. 232f.; Rouart and Wildenstein 1975, II, no. 42; Weitzenhoffer 1986, p. 165, pl. 128.

365
Edouard Manet
CONSTANTIN GUYS (1802–1892)
Pastel on fine weave linen, 21 1/4 x 13 3/8 in. (54 x 34 cm)
Signed and dated l.r.: *Manet 187[?]*
PROVENANCE: Charles Ephrussi, Paris, bought from the artist in 1880; until at least 1884; Ignace Ephrussi, Paris; Paul Rosenberg, Paris, until 1903; Mr. and Mrs. H. O. Havemeyer, New York, bought from Rosenberg in early 1903 for Fr 22,000; shipped to them by Durand-Ruel, May 7, 1903; until 1907; Mrs. H. O. Havemeyer, New York, 1907–29; her daughter Electra Havemeyer Webb, New York, 1929–60; Shelburne Museum, Shelburne, Vt., from 1960, 27.3.1–35.
EXHIBITIONS: 1880 Paris, no. 14; 1884 Paris, no. 140, as *Vieillard*, lent by M.

358

359

362

360

363

367

361

364

Charles Ephrussi; 1889 Paris Universelle, no. 400; 1903 Vienna.
REFERENCES: Havemeyer 1931, pp. 398f., ill.; Havemeyer 1961, p. 232; Rouart and Wildenstein 1975, II, no. 28.

366
Edouard Manet
ROSES IN A CRYSTAL VASE
Oil on canvas, 22 x 13¾ in. (55.9 x 34.9 cm)
Signed r.: *Manet*
PROVENANCE: Mr. and Mrs. H. O. Havemeyer, New York, by 1902–7; Mrs. H. O. Havemeyer, New York, 1907–29; her son, Horace Havemeyer, New York, 1929–56; his widow, Doris Dick Havemeyer, New York, 1956–82; her sale, Sotheby's, New York, May 18, 1983, no. 5; bought at sale by Cherry for $1,540,000; Wendell Cherry, Louisville and New York, from 1983; private collection, Japan.
EXHIBITION: 1884 Paris, no. 116.
REFERENCES: Havemeyer 1931, p. 402, as *Still Life—Flowers*; Havemeyer 1961, p. 222; Rouart and Wildenstein 1975, I, no. 429; Weitzenhoffer 1982, p. 257, fig. 82; Weitzenhoffer 1986, p. 112, colorpl. 64.

367
Edouard Manet
STILL LIFE—FLOWERS
Oil on canvas, 23½ x 19 in. (59.7 x 48.3 cm)
Signed: *Manet*
PROVENANCE: Mr. and Mrs. H. O. Havemeyer, New York, by 1902–7; Mrs. H. O. Havemeyer, New York, 1907–29; her daughter Electra Havemeyer Webb, New York, from 1929.
REFERENCES: Havemeyer 1931, p. 402; Rouart and Wildenstein 1975, I, no. 430.

368
Emile van Marcke
Belgian, 1827–1890
MILKING***
PROVENANCE: Mr. and Mrs. H. O. Havemeyer, New York, consigned to Durand-Ruel, New York, May 8, 1895; bought by Durand-Ruel, Mar. 11, 1898.
REFERENCE: Weitzenhoffer 1986, p. 100.

369
Emile van Marcke
RETURN TO THE FARM***
PROVENANCE: Mr. and Mrs. H. O. Havemeyer, New York, consigned to Durand-Ruel, New York, Nov. 1895; bought by Durand-Ruel, Jan. 20, 1898.
REFERENCE: Weitzenhoffer 1986, p. 100.

370
Jacob Maris
Dutch, 1837–1899
DUTCH TOWN ON A RIVER***

PROVENANCE: Mr. and Mrs. H. O. Havemeyer, New York, until 1899; Durand-Ruel, New York, bought from Havemeyer, Feb. 11, 1899.

371
Alfred H. Maurer
American, 1868–1932
STILL LIFE—FLOWERS
Oil on canvas, 21¼ x 18 in. (54 x 45.7 cm)
Signed and dated u.r.: *A.H. Maurer 26*
PROVENANCE: Mrs. H. O. Havemeyer, New York, d. 1929; her sale, American Art Association, New York, Apr. 10, 1930, no. 26; bought at sale by Ferargil Galleries for $60.
REFERENCE: Havemeyer 1931, p. 509.

372
Gabriel Metsu
Dutch, 1629–1667
THE FISH SELLER***
PROVENANCE: Edouard Warneck, Paris, until 1889; Durand-Ruel, Paris, bought from Warneck, Aug. 1, 1889; Mr. and Mrs. H. O. Havemeyer, New York, bought from Durand-Ruel, Aug. 1, 1889, for Fr 72,000 with four other works; deposited with Durand-Ruel, New York, Mar. 20, 1895.
REFERENCE: Weitzenhoffer 1986, p. 100.

373

373
Louis-Félix-Victor Mettling
French, 1847–1904
THE DOMESTIC
Oil on wood, 16 x 12½ in. (40.6 x 31.8 cm)
Signed and dated l.l.: *Mettling 73*
PROVENANCE: Cottier and Co., New York, until 1889; Mr. and Mrs. H. O. Havemeyer, New York, bought from Cottier in 1889; until 1907; Mrs. H. O. Havemeyer, New York, 1907–29; her sale, American Art Association, New York, Apr. 10, 1930, no. 36; bought at sale by N. S. Goetz for $200.
REFERENCE: Havemeyer 1931, p. 504, as *La Domestique*.

374
Francisque Millet
French, 1642–1679
MERCURY AND BATTUS*
Oil on canvas, 40 x 70 in. (119.4 x 177.8 cm)
PROVENANCE: François de Laborde-Méréville, Paris, 1761–1802; sale, Le Brun, Paris, 22 thermidor, an XI (Aug. 10, 1803), no. 76; bought at sale by Le Brun for 4,800 livres; Viliers; sale, Le Brun, Paris, Mar. 30, 1812, no. 34; bought at sale by Le Brun; possibly Fabre; sale, Paris, Jan. 6, 1813, possibly no. 23; Lafontaine, Paris; sale, Henry and Laneuville, Paris, May 28, 1821, no. 50, bought in by Henry for 8,000 livres; second sale, Henry, Paris, Dec. 10–12, 1822, no. 29; Mr. and Mrs. H. O. Havemeyer, New York, bought in Italy, through A. E. Harnisch, after Jan. 30, 1907, as by Poussin, for L 15,000 the pair* (with A434); shipped to them July 13, 1907; Mrs. H. O. Havemeyer, New York, 1907–29; MMA 29.100.21.
*In a letter of Jan. 30, 1907, Harnisch wrote Cassatt that he believed the pair came from the Talleyrand collection.
EXHIBITION: 1920 New York.
REFERENCES: Havemeyer 1931, pp. 164f., ill., as *Orpheus Asking the Way to Hades*, by Poussin; Sterling 1955, pp. 92–94, ill.; Havemeyer 1958, p. 29, no. 165; Weitzenhoffer 1986, pp. 178, 245, 255.

375
Jean-François Millet
French, 1814–1875
MOTHER AND CHILD (LES ERRANTS)
Oil on canvas, 20 x 16 in. (50.8 x 40.6 cm)
Signed l.r.: *J.F. Millet*
PROVENANCE: Arnold and Tripp, Paris, until 1881; M. Knoedler and Co., New York, bought from Arnold and Tripp, Aug. 31, 1881, for Fr 13,000 (stock no. 3388, as *The Storm*); H. O. Havemeyer, New York, bought from Knoedler, Nov. 28, 1881, for $3,800; d. 1907; Mrs. H. O. Havemeyer, New York, 1907–29; her son, Horace Havemeyer, New York, 1929–34; The Denver Art Museum (Gift of Horace Havemeyer in memory of William D. Lippitt), 1934.14.
REFERENCES: Havemeyer 1931, p. 410, as *The Coming Storm*; Weitzenhoffer 1982,

375

378

382

376

379

383

377

381

385

pp. 41, 49, n. 19; Weitzenhoffer 1986, p. 33, pl. 5, as *Mother and Child (Les Errants)*.

376

Jean-François Millet
SPRING (DAPHNIS AND CHLOE)***
Oil on canvas, 92¾ x 53 in.
(235.6 x 134.6 cm)
Signed l.r.: *J.F. Millet*
PROVENANCE: one of a series of the Four Seasons painted for Thomas de Colmar, Paris, in 1865; Marquis d'Urre, Paris, until 1901; Durand-Ruel, Paris, bought from d'Urre, Apr. 22, 1901, for Fr 55,000 (stock no. 6305, as *Le printemps*); Mr. and Mrs. H. O. Havemeyer, New York, bought from Durand-Ruel, Apr. 22, 1901, for Fr 100,000;* Durand-Ruel, New York, bought back from Havemeyer, Feb. 4, 1903, for $21,500 (stock no. 2857, as *Le printemps, Daphnis et Chloé*); Felix Isman, Philadelphia, bought from Durand-Ruel, Feb. 13, 1905, for $21,500; his sale, American Art Association, New York, Feb. 3, 1911, no. 25, as *Spring, Daphnis and Chloe*; bought at sale by Durand-Ruel for $5,300; K. Matsukata, Tokyo; sequestered by the French government in 1944 and returned to Japan in 1959; National Museum of Western Art, Tokyo, P.1959-146.
*New York stock book no. 2597 states that Durand-Ruel, New York, bought the picture from Durand-Ruel, Paris, June 11, 1901, and sold it to the Havemeyers, June 17, 1901, for Fr 100,000.
REFERENCE: Weitzenhoffer 1986, p. 143.

377

Jean-François Millet
PEASANT CHILDREN AT GOOSE POND
Pastel on paper, 15¼ x 20½ in.
(38.7 x 52.1 cm)
Signed l.l.: *J.F. Millet*
PROVENANCE: Emile Gavet, Paris; his sale, Hôtel Drouot, Paris, June 11–12, 1875, no. 33, as *Petite fille gardant des oies près d'une métairie*; Alfred Sensier, Paris; his sale, Hôtel Drouot, Paris, Dec. 10–15, 1877, no. 195; Durand-Ruel, Paris, bought from Bourdariat, Nov. 3, 1892, for Fr 18,000 (stock no. 2483, as *Enfants conduisant des oies*); Durand-Ruel, New York, bought from Durand-Ruel, Paris, Apr. 19, 1893 (stock no. 1028, as *Gardeuse d'oies*); Mr. and Mrs. H. O. Havemeyer, New York, bought from Durand-Ruel, Mar. 31, 1893, for $7,000; until 1907; Mrs. H. O. Havemeyer, New York, 1907–29; her daughter Electra Havemeyer Webb, New York, 1929–42; Yale University Art Gallery, New Haven (Gift of J. Watson Webb, B.A. 1907, and Electra Havemeyer Webb), 1942.298.

REFERENCES: Havemeyer 1931, pp. 408f., ill., as *Little Girl with Geese*; Weitzenhoffer 1982, p. 199, fig. 53; Weitzenhoffer 1986, p. 91, pl. 36.

378

Jean-François Millet
PEASANT GIRL DRIVING GEESE
Pastel on paper, 18⁹⁄₁₆ x 22³⁄₁₆ in.
(47.2 x 56.4 cm)
Signed l.r.: *J.F. Millet*
PROVENANCE: Emile Gavet, Paris; his sale, Hôtel Drouot, Paris, June 11–12, 1875 no. 29, as *Paysanne pourchassant des oies*; Emile Dehau; his sale, Hôtel Drouot, Paris, Mar. 21, 1885, no. 61, as *La Mare*, for Fr 4,000; Doidatz, Paris, by 1887; sale, Hôtel Drouot, Paris, Mar. 15, 1888, no. 61, as *La Gardeuse d'oies*, for Fr 5,000; Mrs. H. O. Havemeyer, New York, d. 1929; her daughter Electra Havemeyer Webb, New York, 1929–42; Yale University Art Gallery, New Haven (Gift of J. Watson Webb, B.A. 1907, and Electra Havemeyer Webb), 1942.300.
EXHIBITION: 1887 Paris Millet, no. 87, as *Gardeuse d'oies*, lent by Doidatz.
REFERENCE: Havemeyer 1931, p. 410, as *Peasant Girl and Geese*.

379

Jean-François Millet
PEASANT WATERING HIS COWS ON THE BANKS OF THE ALLIER RIVER, DUSK
Pastel on paper, 28¼ x 37 in. (71.8 x 94 cm)
Signed l.r.: *J.F. Millet*
PROVENANCE: Emile Gavet, Paris; his sale, Hôtel Drouot, Paris, June 11–12, 1875, no. 51, as *Paysan menant boire ses vaches, bords de l'Allier, Effet de soir*; Charles Sedelmeyer, Paris; his sale, Hôtel Drouot, Paris, Apr. 30–May 2, 1877, no. 71; E. Secrétan, Paris; his sale, Galerie Charles Sedelmeyer, Paris, July 1, 1889, no. 100; bought at sale by Durand-Ruel for Havemeyer for Fr 26,000 (stock no. 2380); Mr. and Mrs. H. O. Havemeyer, New York, 1889–1907; Mrs. H. O. Havemeyer, New York, 1907–29; her daughter Electra Havemeyer Webb, New York, 1929–42; Yale University Art Gallery, New Haven (Gift of J. Watson Webb, B.A. 1907, and Electra Havemeyer Webb), 1942.299.
EXHIBITIONS: 1875 Paris Gavet, no. 9; 1875 London; 1887 Paris Millet, no. 101, as *Vaches à l'abreuvoir, Environs de Vichy*.
REFERENCES: Havemeyer 1931, pp. 408f., ill.; Weitzenhoffer 1982, pp. 108, 115, fig. 18; Weitzenhoffer 1986, p. 58, pl. 16.

380

Jean-François Millet
ALLEY OF CHESTNUT TREES***
Pastel

PROVENANCE: Mr. and Mrs. H. O. Havemeyer, New York, until 1900; Durand-Ruel, New York, bought from Havemeyer, Dec. 14, 1900.

381

Jean-François Millet
GIRL BURNING WEEDS
Pen and brown ink and watercolor, over traces of black chalk, on laid paper, 15⁵⁄₁₆ x 9¾ in. (38.9 x 24.8 cm)
Signed l.r.: *J.F. Millet*
PROVENANCE: Mr. and Mrs. H. O. Havemeyer, New York, bought through Durand-Ruel, by July 18, 1895, for Fr 7,000; until 1907; Mrs. H. O. Havemeyer, New York, 1907–29; MMA 29.100.560.
REFERENCES: Havemeyer 1931, p. 190, as *Peasant Girl Burning Weeds*; Havemeyer 1958, p. 30, no. 167; Weitzenhoffer 1982, p. 239; Weitzenhoffer 1986, p. 105.

382

Jean-François Millet
GIRL WITH SHEEP**
Black chalk over charcoal on laid paper, 12¹⁵⁄₁₆ x 18⅜ in. (32.9 x 46.7 cm)
Signed l.r.: *J.F. Millet*
PROVENANCE: Jean-Baptiste Faure, Paris; R. B. Angus, until 1893; Durand-Ruel, New York, bought from Angus, Mar. 30, 1893, for $2,000 (stock no. 1042, as *La Bergère* or *Bergère et moutons*); Mr. and Mrs. H. O. Havemeyer, New York, bought from Durand-Ruel, Mar. 31, 1893, for $3,000; until 1907; Mrs. H. O. Havemeyer, New York, 1907–29; MMA 29.100.116.
REFERENCES: Havemeyer 1931, pp. 190f., ill., as *La Bergère*; Havemeyer 1958, p. 30, no. 168; Weitzenhoffer 1982, p. 199, fig. 54; Weitzenhoffer 1986, pp. 91, 257.

383

Jean-François Millet
THE SHEPHERDESS
Pastel on laid paper, 15 x 11⅛ in.
(38.1 x 28.3 cm)
Signed l.r.: *J.F. Millet*
PROVENANCE: Durand-Ruel, Paris, bought from Guyotin, July 19, 1895, for Fr 4,500 (stock no. 3376, as *Paysanne*); Mr. and Mrs. H. O. Havemeyer, New York, bought from Durand-Ruel, Sept. 19, 1895, for Fr 7,000; until 1907; Mrs. H. O. Havemeyer, New York, 1907–29; MMA 29.100.559.
REFERENCES: Havemeyer 1931, p. 190; Havemeyer 1958, p. 29, no. 166; Weitzenhoffer 1982, pp. 239, 241f.; Weitzenhoffer 1986, p. 107.

384

Jean-François Millet
SUNSET OVER A PLAIN***

Pastel
PROVENANCE: Mr. and Mrs. H. O. Have-
meyer, New York, until 1900; Durand-
Ruel, New York, bought from Havemeyer,
Dec. 14, 1900.

385
Jean-François Millet
TEMPTATION OF SAINT HILARION
Pastel crayon, 14 x 16½ in. (35.6 x 41.9 cm)
Signed l.l.: *J.F.M.*
PROVENANCE: Edouard Gros, Paris, in
1887; Durand-Ruel, Paris, until 1889; Mr.
and Mrs. H. O. Havemeyer, New York,
bought from Durand-Ruel, Oct. 1889;
until 1907; Mrs. H. O. Havemeyer, New
York, 1907–29; her sale, American Art
Association, New York, Apr. 10, 1930,
no. 29, for $350.
EXHIBITION: 1887 Paris Millet, no. 75,
lent by Gros.
REFERENCES: Havemeyer 1931, p. 504;
Weitzenhoffer 1982, pp. 113, 115; Weitzen-
hoffer 1986, p. 61.

386

386
Luigi Miradori (called Genovesino)
Italian (Cremonese), 1601–1661
A SAINT PERFORMING A MIRACLE
FOR A NEWBORN
Oil on canvas, 47⅝ x 42⅞ in.
(121 x 108.9 cm)
PROVENANCE: Mrs. H. O. Havemeyer,
New York, d. 1929; her sale, American Art
Association, New York, Apr. 10, 1930,
no. 108, as *The Conspiracy*, Spanish
school, about 1600; bought at sale by W. C.
Loring for $2,100; private collection,
Milan, in 1985.
Note: The current attribution was supplied
by Marco Bona Castellotti in his *La
pittura lombarda del '600*, Milan, 1985,
pl. 378.
REFERENCE: Havemeyer 1931, p. 500, as
Interior with Figures, attributed to
Zurbarán.

387
Claude Monet
French, 1840–1926
THE GREEN WAVE**
Oil on canvas, 19⅛ x 25½ in.
(48.6 x 64.8 cm)
Signed and dated l.r.: *Cl. Monet 65*
PROVENANCE: possibly Théodore Duret,
Paris, in 1879; M. Oudard, until 1882;
Durand-Ruel, Paris, bought from Oudard,
July 19, 1882, for Fr 150 (stock no. 2512,
as *Marine*); Mary Cassatt, Paris, bought
from Durand-Ruel for her brother, Oct. 8,
1883, for Fr 800; her brother, J. Gardner
Cassatt, Philadelphia, 1883–98; Durand-
Ruel, New York, received on deposit from
Cassatt, Feb. 2, 1898 (deposit no. 5658, as
Marine); bought from him, July 1, 1898,
for $1,000 (stock no. 2012, as *Marine*);
Mr. and Mrs. H. O. Havemeyer, New
York, bought from Durand-Ruel, July 1,
1898, for $1,000; until 1907; Mrs. H. O.
Havemeyer, New York, 1907–29; MMA
29.100.111.
EXHIBITION: 1879 Paris, no. 140(?).
REFERENCES: Havemeyer 1931, p. 151,
ill.; Havemeyer 1958, p. 30, no. 171; Sterling and Salinger 1967, p. 124, ill.; Wildenstein 1974–85, no. 73; Weitzenhoffer
1982, pp. 22, 31, n. 28, p. 70, n. 6, p. 306,
fig. 117; Weitzenhoffer 1986, pp. 135,
257, colorpl. 97.

388
Claude Monet
GARDEN OF THE PRINCESS, LOUVRE
Oil on canvas, 36⅛ x 24⅜ in.
(91.8 x 61.9 cm)
Signed l.r.: *Claude Monet*
PROVENANCE: Charles de Bériot, Paris,
bought from the artist in 1873; his sale,
Hôtel Drouot, Paris, Mar. 11, 1901,
no. 76; bought at sale by Bernheim-Jeune;
Durand-Ruel and Rosenberg, Paris, in
1908; Frederic Bonner, New York; his sale,
Plaza Hotel, New York, Jan. 24, 1912,
no. 36; bought at sale by Durand-Ruel for
Havemeyer for $4,100; Mrs. H. O. Have-
meyer, New York, 1912–29; her son, Horace Havemeyer, New York, 1929–48;
consigned to M. Knoedler and Co., New
York, by Havemeyer, Sept. 1948 (stock no.
CA3142); Allen Memorial Art Museum,
Oberlin College, Oberlin, Ohio, bought
from Havemeyer through Knoedler, Dec.
1948 (R. T. Miller, Jr., Fund, 1948), 48.296.
EXHIBITIONS: 1907 Stuttgart, no. 169;
1907 Strasbourg, no. 186.
REFERENCES: Havemeyer 1931, pp. 420f.,
ill.; Wildenstein 1974–85, no. 85.

389
Claude Monet
LA GRENOUILLERE**
Oil on canvas, 29⅜ x 39¼ in.

(74.6 x 99.7 cm)
Signed l.r.: *Claude Monet*
PROVENANCE: possibly Edouard Manet,
Paris, d. 1883; possibly his widow, Mme
Edouard Manet, Paris, until 1886; Durand-
Ruel, Paris, possibly bought from Mme
Manet in 1886, definitely by 1891 (stock
no. 1586); Mr. and Mrs. H. O. Havemeyer,
New York, bought from Durand-Ruel,
Sept. 27, 1897, for Fr 12,500; until 1907;
Mrs. H. O. Havemeyer, New York, 1907–
29; MMA 29.100.112.
REFERENCES: Havemeyer 1931, pp. 152f.,
ill.; Havemeyer 1958, p. 30, no. 172, ill.;
Sterling and Salinger 1967, pp. 126f., ill.;
Wildenstein 1974–85, no. 134; Weitzen-
hoffer 1982, p. 120, n. 32, pp. 267, 280f.,
n. 29, fig. 94; Weitzenhoffer 1986, pp.
117, 257, colorpl. 76.

390
Claude Monet
THE RIVER ZAAN AT ZAANDAM
Oil on canvas, 18¼ x 26 in. (46.4 x 66 cm)
Signed l.l.: *Claude Monet*
PROVENANCE: Jean-Baptiste Faure, Paris;
Durand-Ruel, Paris, bought from Faure,
Mar. 18, 1901, for Fr 6,000 (stock no.
6256); Mr. and Mrs. H. O. Havemeyer,
New York, bought from Durand-Ruel,
Apr. 22, 1901 (New York stock book says
July 12, 1901); until 1907; Mrs. H. O.
Havemeyer, New York, 1907–29; her son,
Horace Havemeyer, New York, 1929–56;
his widow, Doris Dick Havemeyer, New
York, 1956–82; her sale, Sotheby's, New
York, May 18, 1983, no. 6; bought at sale
by a private collector for $1,540,000; pri-
vate collection, from 1983.
REFERENCES: Havemeyer 1931, p. 422, as
Canal aux environs d'Amsterdam; Wilden-
stein 1974–85, no. 187; Weitzenhoffer
1986, p. 143, colorpl. 112.

391
Claude Monet
SAILBOAT ON A BRANCH OF THE
SEINE, ARGENTEUIL
Oil on canvas, 20½ x 25 in. (52.1 x 63.5 cm)
Signed and dated l.r.: *75 Claude Monet*
PROVENANCE: Leclanche, about 1889; Mr.
and Mrs. H. O. Havemeyer, New York,
1901–7; Mrs. H. O. Havemeyer, New
York, 1907–29; her daughter Adaline
Havemeyer Frelinghuysen, Morristown,
N.J., from 1929; private collection.
EXHIBITIONS: 1889 Paris Monet, no. 30,
as *Printemps, Argenteuil, 1875*; 1899
Paris, no. 45.
REFERENCES: Havemeyer 1931, p. 412;
Wildenstein 1974–85, no. 200.

387

392

395

388

393

396

389

394

397

390

391

398

362

392
Claude Monet
IN THE GARDEN
Oil on canvas, 25 x 31¼ in. (63.5 x 79.4 cm)
Signed and dated l.r.: *Claude Monet.72*
PROVENANCE: possibly Durand-Ruel, Paris, bought from the artist in 1872, as *Lilas en fleurs*; Ernest Hoschedé, Paris; his sale, Hôtel Drouot, Paris, June 5–6, 1878, no. 52; bought at sale by Kim . . . , 18, rue de Mauberge; A. Nunès; his sale, Hôtel Drouot, Paris, Apr. 16, 1894, no. 35; bought at sale by Durand-Ruel; Mrs. H. O. Havemeyer, New York, bought from Durand-Ruel, Jan. 17, 1911; d. 1929; her daughter Adaline Havemeyer Freling-huysen, Morristown, N.J., from 1929; private collection.
EXHIBITIONS: 1895 New York Monet, no. 34; 1895 Boston, no. 21.
REFERENCES: Havemeyer 1931, p. 413; Wildenstein 1974–85, no. 202.

393
Claude Monet
VIEW OF ROUEN
Oil on canvas, 20⅝ x 28 in. (52.4 x 71.1 cm)
Signed and dated l.r.: *Claude Monet 72*
PROVENANCE: Michel-Lévy, Paris, bought from the artist, Jan. 1873; his sale, Hôtel Drouot, Paris, Apr. 7, 1892, no. 12; bought at sale by Bellino for Fr 9,200; American Art Association, New York; their sale, American Art Association, New York, Apr. 25–30, 1895, no. 146; bought at sale by Havemeyer for $2,600; Mr. and Mrs. H. O. Havemeyer, New York, 1895–1907; Mrs. H. O. Havemeyer, New York, 1907–29; her son, Horace Havemeyer, New York, 1929–49; consigned to M. Knoedler and Co., New York, by Havemeyer, Sept. 1948 (stock no. CA3144); Mrs. Charles S. Payson, New York and Manhasset, N.Y., bought from Havemeyer through Knoedler, Oct. 18, 1949; private collection, Great Britain, about 1969.
EXHIBITION: 1883 Paris Durand-Ruel, no. 30.
REFERENCES: Havemeyer 1931, p. 423; Wildenstein 1974–85, no. 217; Weitzen-hoffer 1982, p. 237, fig. 70; Weitzenhoffer 1986, p. 104.

394
Claude Monet
BARGES AT ASNIERES
Oil on canvas, 22 x 29½ in. (55.9 x 74.9 cm)
Signed l.r.: *Claude Monet*
PROVENANCE: possibly sold by the artist in June 1875 through M. Dombasle; Count Armand Doria, Orrouy, France; his sale, Georges Petit, Paris, May 4–5, 1899, no. 193; bought at sale by Bernheim-Jeune; Bernheim-Jeune et fils, Paris, 1899–1901; Boussod, Valadon et Cie, Paris, bought

from Bernheim-Jeune, Apr. 23, 1901, for Fr 8,500 (stock no. 27157, as *Le Seine à Asnières*); Mr. and Mrs. H. O. Havemeyer, New York, bought from Boussod, Valadon, May 24, 1901, for Fr 20,000 ($3,846); until 1907; Mrs. H. O. Havemeyer, New York, 1907–29; her daughter Adaline Havemeyer Frelinghuysen, Morristown, N.J., 1929–63; private collection.
REFERENCES: Havemeyer 1931, p. 412; Wildenstein 1974–85, no. 270; Weitzen-hoffer 1986, p. 143, colorpl. 115.

395
Claude Monet
THE DRAWBRIDGE
Oil on canvas, 21 x 25 in. (53.3 x 63.5 cm)
Signed l.r.: *Claude Monet*
PROVENANCE: Louisine Elder (later Mrs. H. O. Havemeyer), New York, bought in Paris, possibly in 1877, for Fr 300; d. 1929; her daughter Electra Havemeyer Webb, New York, 1929–60; Shelburne Museum, Shelburne, Vt., from 1960, 27.1.2–109.
EXHIBITION: 1886 New York, no. 308, as *View in Holland*.
REFERENCES: Havemeyer 1931, pp. 416f., ill.; Havemeyer 1961, pp. 204, 206; Wildenstein 1974–85, no. 306; Weitzen-hoffer 1982, pp. 15, 29, n. 12, pp. 45, 64, 198, n. 45, fig. 2; Weitzenhoffer 1986, pp. 21f., 34, 41, colorpl. 2.

396
Claude Monet
PETIT GENNEVILLIERS
Oil on canvas, 21½ x 29 in. (54.6 x 73.7 cm)
Signed l.r.: *Claude Monet*
PROVENANCE: Victor Chocquet, Paris, d. 1898; his widow, d. 1899; her sale, Georges Petit, Paris, July 1–4, 1899, no. 77; bought at sale by M. D'Hauterive; L. Crist Delmonico, until 1901; Boussod, Valadon et Cie, Paris, bought from Delmonico, Apr. 3, 1901, for Fr 13,000 (stock no. 27113, as *Gennevilliers*); Mr. and Mrs. H. O. Havemeyer, New York, bought from Boussod, Valadon, Apr. 19, 1901, for Fr 20,000 ($3,846); until 1907; Mrs. H. O. Havemeyer, New York, 1907–29; her daughter Adaline Havemeyer Freling-huysen, Morristown, N.J., 1929–63; private collection.
REFERENCES: Havemeyer 1931, p. 411, as *Landscape—Argenteuil*; Wildenstein 1974–85, no. 337.

397
Claude Monet
SNOW AT ARGENTEUIL
Oil on canvas, 20 x 25¾ in. (50.8 x 65.4 cm)
Signed l.r.: *Claude Monet*
PROVENANCE: Georges Petit, Paris, until 1892; Boussod, Valadon et Cie, Paris, bought from Petit, Oct. 19, 1892, for

Fr 2,500 (stock no. 22538, as *Entrée de village neige*); Mr. and Mrs. H. O. Havemeyer, New York, bought from Boussod, Valadon, Apr. 15, 1898, for Fr 1,864 ($358); until 1907; Mrs. H. O. Havemeyer, New York, 1907–29; her sale, American Art Association, New York, Apr. 10, 1930, no. 85, as *Village Street*; bought at sale by H. E. Russell for Heyman for $5,500; Ruth S. and David M. Heyman, 1930–84; sale, Christie's, New York, May 16, 1984, no. 8, as *Neige à Argenteuil*, for $313,500; Alex Reid and Lefevre, London, in 1988.
REFERENCES: Havemeyer 1931, p. 504, as *Landscape—Village Street*; Wildenstein 1974–85, no. 349, as *Neige à Argenteuil*; Weitzenhoffer 1982, pp. 317f., n. 48; Weitzenhoffer 1986, pp. 130, 237, colorpl. 86.

398
Claude Monet
FLOATING ICE
Oil on canvas, 38¼ x 58¼ in. (97.2 x 148 cm)
Signed and dated l.r.: *Claude Monet 1880*
PROVENANCE: Mme Georges Charpentier, Paris, bought from the artist in 1880 for Fr 1,500; until at least 1889; American Art Association, New York; their sale, American Art Association, New York, Apr. 25–30, 1895, no. 163; bought at sale by Havemeyer for $4,250; Mr. and Mrs. H. O. Havemeyer, New York, 1895–1907; Mrs. H. O. Havemeyer, New York, 1907–29; her daughter Electra Havemeyer Webb, New York, 1929–60; Shelburne Museum, Shelburne, Vt., from 1960, 27.1.2–108.
EXHIBITIONS: refused by the Paris Salon of 1880; 1880 Paris Monet, no. 1; 1882 Paris Saint-Honoré, no. 58; 1889 Paris Monet, no. 46.
REFERENCES: Havemeyer 1931, pp. 416f., ill.; Wildenstein 1974–85, no. 568; Weitzenhoffer 1982, p. 237, fig. 71; Weitzenhoffer 1986, p. 104, colorpl. 55.

399
Claude Monet
BOUQUET OF SUNFLOWERS**
Oil on canvas, 39¾ x 32 in. (101 x 81.3 cm)
Signed and dated u.r.: *Claude Monet 81*
PROVENANCE: Durand-Ruel, Paris, bought from the artist, Oct. 1881; Alden Wyman Kingman, New York, bought from the 1886 Impressionist exhibition; Durand-Ruel, New York, bought from Kingman in 1892; Catholina Lambert, Paterson, N.J., bought from Durand-Ruel in 1892; Durand-Ruel, New York, bought from Lambert in 1899 (stock no. 2120); Mr. and Mrs. H. O. Havemeyer, New York, bought from Durand-Ruel, Mar. 10, 1899; until 1907; Mrs. H. O. Havemeyer, New York, 1907–29; MMA 29.100.107.
EXHIBITIONS: 1882 Paris Saint-Honoré,

399

401

403

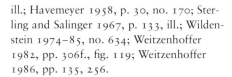

400

402

404

no. 78; 1883 Paris Durand-Ruel, no. 14; 1886 Brussels, no. 7, lent by M. Durand-Ruel; 1886 New York, no. 293; 1891 New York Monet, no. 48.

REFERENCES: Havemeyer 1931, p. 154; Havemeyer 1958, p. 31, no. 176; Sterling and Salinger 1967, pp. 132f., ill.; Wildenstein 1974–85, no. 628; Weitzenhoffer 1982, pp. 306f., fig. 118; Weitzenhoffer 1986, pp. 135, 256.

400
Claude Monet
CHRYSANTHEMUMS**

Oil on canvas, 39 ½ x 32 ¼ in. (100.3 x 81.9 cm)
Signed and dated l.l.: *Claude Monet 82*
PROVENANCE: Durand-Ruel, Paris, bought from the artist, Dec. 1883; Alden Wyman Kingman, New York, bought from the 1886 Impressionist exhibition; Durand-Ruel, New York, bought from Kingman in 1892; Catholina Lambert, Paterson, N.J., bought from Durand-Ruel in 1892; Durand-Ruel, New York, bought from Lambert, Feb. 28, 1899 (stock no. 2121); Mr. and Mrs. H. O. Havemeyer, New York, bought from Durand-Ruel, Mar. 10, 1899; until 1907; Mrs. H. O. Havemeyer, New York, 1907–29; MMA 29.100.106.
EXHIBITIONS: 1883 Paris Durand-Ruel, no. 18; 1886 Brussels, no. 6, lent by M. Durand-Ruel; 1886 New York, no. 294; 1891 New York Monet, no. 50.
REFERENCES: Havemeyer 1931, pp. 154f.,

ill.; Havemeyer 1958, p. 30, no. 170; Sterling and Salinger 1967, p. 133, ill.; Wildenstein 1974–85, no. 634; Weitzenhoffer 1982, pp. 306f., fig. 119; Weitzenhoffer 1986, pp. 135, 256.

401
Claude Monet
CUSTOMS HOUSE AT VARENGEVILLE

Oil on canvas, 26 x 32 in. (66 x 81.3 cm)
Signed and dated l.r.: *82 Claude Monet*
PROVENANCE: possibly Durand-Ruel, Paris, bought from the artist, July 28, 1883 (stock no. 2984); possibly Durand-Ruel, Paris (stock no. 1305; stock book for 1884–88 missing); Durand-Ruel, New York, probably bought from Durand-Ruel, Paris; Mr. and Mrs. H. O. Havemeyer, New York, bought from Durand-Ruel, Jan. 16, 1894; until 1907; Mrs. H. O. Havemeyer, New York, 1907–29; her son, Horace Havemeyer, New York, 1929–41; The Brooklyn Museum (Gift of Mrs. Horace Havemeyer), 41.1260.
EXHIBITIONS: 1883 Boston, no. 10; 1887 New York, no. 155(?).
REFERENCES: Havemeyer 1931, p. 422, as *Landscape—Marée montante à Pourville*; Wildenstein 1974–85, no. 740; Weitzenhoffer 1982, p. 225, fig. 58; Weitzenhoffer 1986, p. 98, pl. 41, as *High Tide at Pourville*.

402
Claude Monet
HAYSTACKS AT GIVERNY

Oil on canvas, 26 x 32 ⅛ in. (66 x 81.6 cm)
Signed and dated l.r.: *84 Claude Monet*
PROVENANCE: Durand-Ruel, Paris, bought from the artist, Nov. 1884; Frederic Bonner, New York; sale, American Art Association, New York, Apr. 10, 1900, no. 66; bought at sale by Durand-Ruel for Havemeyer for $2,300; Mr. and Mrs. H. O. Havemeyer, New York, 1900–1907; Mrs. H. O. Havemeyer, New York, 1907–29; her son, Horace Havemeyer, New York, 1929–56; his widow, Doris Dick Havemeyer, New York, 1956–82; her sale, Sotheby's, New York, May 18, 1983, no. 11; bought at sale by Acquavella for $605,000; Acquavella Galleries, New York, 1983–88; Galerie Nichido, Tokyo, bought from Acquavella, May 1988; private collection, bought from Nichido, Sept. 30, 1988.
REFERENCES: Havemeyer 1931, p. 419; Wildenstein 1974–85, no. 902; Weitzenhoffer 1986, p. 143, colorpl. 114.

403
Claude Monet
MORNING HAZE

Oil on canvas, 29 ⅛ x 36 ⅝ in. (74 x 93 cm)
Signed l.l.: *Claude Monet*
PROVENANCE: James F. Sutton, New York, 1892–1917; sale, Hotel Plaza, New York, Jan. 16–17, 1917, no. 151; bought at sale by Durand-Ruel, probably for Havemeyer, for $2,500; Mrs. H. O. Havemeyer, New York, 1917–29; her sale, American Art Association, New York, Apr. 10, 1930,

405

407

409

406

408

410

no. 71; bought at sale by Dale for $2,600; Chester Dale, New York, 1930–58; National Gallery of Art, Washington, D.C., from 1958 (Chester Dale Collection), 1958.12.1.
REFERENCES: Havemeyer 1931, p. 504, as *Landscape—Fog*; Wildenstein 1974–85, no. 1196.

404
Claude Monet
GERMAINE HOSCHEDÉ IN THE GARDEN AT GIVERNY
Oil on canvas, 28¼ x 36 in. (71.8 x 91.4 cm)
Signed and dated l.l.: *Claude Monet 88*
PROVENANCE: Tadamasa Hayashi, Tokyo and Paris, d. 1906; his sale, American Art Association, New York, Jan. 8–9, 1913, no. 160; bought at sale by Durand-Ruel for Havemeyer for $3,100; Mrs. H. O. Havemeyer, New York, 1913–29; her daughter Adaline Havemeyer Frelinghuysen, Morristown, N.J., from 1929; French Art Galleries, New York; Mr. and Mrs. Robert E. Eisner, U.S., from 1946; sale, Sotheby's, New York, May 11, 1977, no. 29; bought at sale by a private collector for $310,000; private collection.
REFERENCES: Havemeyer 1931, p. 413, as *Little Girl in a Garden*; Wildenstein 1974–85, no. 1207.

405
Claude Monet
HAYSTACKS IN THE SNOW

Oil on canvas, 23 x 39 in. (58.4 x 99.1 cm)
Signed and dated l.l.: *Claude Monet 91*
PROVENANCE: Durand-Ruel, Paris, bought from the artist, July 2, 1891 (stock no. 1061); Potter Palmer, Chicago, bought from Durand-Ruel, July 2, 1891; Durand-Ruel, New York, bought from Palmer in early 1892 (stock no. 863); Alfred Atmore Pope, Cleveland, bought from Durand-Ruel, Jan. 31, 1892; lent to Durand-Ruel, New York, by Pope, for their Monet exhibition, Jan. 1895 (deposit no. 5146); bought from Pope, Jan. 28, 1895 (stock no. 1337), but sold Jan. 12, 1895, to Havemeyer; Mr. and Mrs. H. O. Havemeyer, New York, 1895–1907; Mrs. H. O. Havemeyer, 1907–29; her daughter Electra Havemeyer Webb, New York, 1929–60; Shelburne Museum, Shelburne, Vt., from 1960, 27.1.2–106.
EXHIBITIONS: 1891 Paris, no. 6; 1895 New York Monet, no. 16.
REFERENCES: Havemeyer 1931, p. 418, ill.; Wildenstein 1974–85, no. 1274; Weitzenhoffer 1982, p. 229, fig. 66; Weitzenhoffer 1986, p. 100, colorpl. 50.

406
Claude Monet
HAYSTACKS (EFFECT OF SNOW AND SUN)**
Oil on canvas, 25¾ x 36¼ in. (65.4 x 92.1 cm)
Signed and dated l.l.: *Claude Monet 91*
PROVENANCE: Potter Palmer, Chicago,

until 1893; Durand-Ruel, New York, bought from Palmer, Jan. 24, 1893 (stock no. 1016); Mr. and Mrs. H. O. Havemeyer, New York, bought from Durand-Ruel, Jan. 16, 1894; until 1907; Mrs. H. O. Havemeyer, New York, 1907–29; MMA 29.100.109.
EXHIBITION: 1891 Paris, no. 7.
REFERENCES: Havemeyer 1931, pp. 158f., ill., as *Landscape—Meules, effet de neige*; Havemeyer 1958, p. 31, no. 173; Sterling and Salinger 1967, pp. 137f., ill.; Wildenstein 1974–85, no. 1279; Weitzenhoffer 1982, pp. 225, 244, n. 6, fig. 60; Weitzenhoffer 1986, pp. 98, 257, pl. 42.

407
Claude Monet
POPLARS**
Oil on canvas, 32¼ x 32⅛ in. (81.9 x 81.6 cm)
Signed and dated l.l.: *Claude Monet 91*
PROVENANCE: M. Knoedler and Co., New York; their sale, American Art Association, New York, Apr. 14, 1893, no. 362; bought at sale by Durand-Ruel for $1,175; Durand-Ruel, New York, 1893–95 (stock no. 1063); Mr. and Mrs. H. O. Havemeyer, New York, bought from Durand-Ruel, Jan. 12, 1895; until 1907; Mrs. H. O. Havemeyer, New York, 1907–29; MMA 29.100.110.
EXHIBITIONS: 1892 Paris, no. 10; 1895 New York Monet, no. 14.
REFERENCES: Havemeyer 1931, p. 160, ill., as *Landscape—Les Quatre arbres*;

411

413

415

412

414

416

Havemeyer 1958, p. 31, no. 175; Sterling and Salinger 1967, pp. 136f., ill.; Wildenstein 1974–85, no. 1309, as *Les Quatre arbres*; Weitzenhoffer 1982, p. 229, fig. 65; Weitzenhoffer 1986, pp. 100, 257.

408
Claude Monet
ICE FLOES**
Oil on canvas, 26 x 39½ in. (66 x 100.3 cm)
Signed and dated l.r.: *Claude Monet 93*
PROVENANCE: Durand-Ruel, Paris, bought from the artist, with I. Montaignac, Feb. 3, 1897, for Fr 11,400 (stock no. 4067); Mr. and Mrs. H. O. Havemeyer, New York, bought from Durand-Ruel and Montaignac, Feb. 3, 1897; until 1907; Mrs. H. O. Havemeyer, New York, 1907–29; MMA 29.100.108.
REFERENCES: Havemeyer 1931, pp. 158f., ill., as *Landscape—Les Glaçons*; Havemeyer 1958, p. 31, no. 174; Sterling and Salinger 1967, p. 138, ill.; Wildenstein 1974–85, no. 1335; Weitzenhoffer 1982, pp. 266f., fig. 92; Weitzenhoffer 1986, pp. 117, 257.

409
Claude Monet
ICE FLOES, BENNECOURT
Oil on canvas, 25½ x 39⅜ in. (64.8 x 100 cm)
Signed and dated l.r.: *Claude Monet 93*
PROVENANCE: Boussod, Valadon et Cie, Paris, bought from the artist, Dec. 1, 1893, for Fr 6,000 (stock no. 23239, as *Glaçons effet rose*); Henri Vever, Paris; bought from Boussod, Valadon, Dec. 2, 1893, for Fr 8,000; his sale, Galerie Georges Petit,

Paris, Feb. 1–2, 1897, no. 82; bought at sale by Montaignac for Fr 12,600; Galerie Montaignac, Paris, 1897; Durand-Ruel, Paris, bought half share from Montaignac, Feb. 3, 1897 (stock no. 4069), and sold back to Montaignac, Sept. 23, 1897; Mr. and Mrs. H. O. Havemeyer, New York, bought from Montaignac, Sept. 23, 1897; until 1907; Mrs. H. O. Havemeyer, New York, 1907–29; her son, Horace Havemeyer, New York, 1929–56; his widow, Doris Dick Havemeyer, New York, 1956–82; her sale, Sotheby's, New York, May 18, 1983, no. 13, for $605,000; private collection.
EXHIBITION: 1895 Paris Monet, no. 40.
REFERENCES: Havemeyer 1931, p. 419, as *Landscape—Les glaçons*; Wildenstein 1974–85, no. 1336; Weitzenhoffer 1982, pp. 267, 280f., n. 29, fig. 93; Weitzenhoffer 1986, p. 117, colorpl. 75.

410
Claude Monet
MORNING ON THE SEINE
Oil on canvas, 28⅛ x 35⅝ in. (71.4 x 90.5 cm)
Signed and dated l.l.: *Claude Monet 93*
PROVENANCE: Durand-Ruel, Paris, bought from the artist, Dec. 1893; Mr. and Mrs. H. O. Havemeyer, New York, bought from Durand-Ruel, New York, Jan. 16, 1894; until 1907; Mrs. H. O. Havemeyer, New York, 1907–29; her daughter Adaline Havemeyer Frelinghuysen, Morristown, N.J., 1929–63; her son H.O.H. Frelinghuysen, 1963–89; sale, Christie's, New York, May 10, 1989, no. 52, as *Matin sur*

la Seine à Giverny, for $4,620,000.
REFERENCES: Havemeyer 1931, p. 414; Wildenstein 1974–85, no. 1365; Weitzenhoffer 1982, p. 225, fig. 59; Weitzenhoffer 1986, p. 98.

411
Claude Monet
OLD CHURCH AT VERNON
Oil on canvas, 25½ x 35½ in. (64.8 x 90.2 cm)
Signed and dated l.l.: *Claude Monet 94*
PROVENANCE: possibly James F. Sutton, New York; Frederic Bonner, New York; sale, American Art Association, New York, Apr. 10, 1900, no. 63; bought at sale by Durand-Ruel for Havemeyer for $3,100; Mr. and Mrs. H. O. Havemeyer, New York, 1900–1907; Mrs. H. O. Havemeyer, New York, 1907–29; her daughter Electra Havemeyer Webb, New York, 1929–60; Shelburne Museum, Shelburne, Vt., from 1960, 27.1.2–107.
EXHIBITION: 1895 Paris Monet, no. 22 or 23.
REFERENCES: Havemeyer 1931, p. 415; Wildenstein 1974–85, no. 1390; Weitzenhoffer 1986, p. 143.

412
Claude Monet
THE SEINE NEAR VERNON
Oil on canvas, 28¼ x 36 in. (71.8 x 91.4 cm)
Signed and dated l.l.: *Claude Monet 97*
PROVENANCE: Boussod, Valadon et Cie, Paris, bought from the artist, Jan. 20, 1898, for Fr 6,000 (stock no. 25253, as *Bords de Seine matin*); Mr. and Mrs. H. O.

Havemeyer, New York, bought from
Boussod, Valadon for Fr 7,800 ($1,500);
until 1907; Mrs. H. O. Havemeyer, New
York, 1907–29; her daughter Adaline
Havemeyer Frelinghuysen, Morristown,
N.J., 1929–63; private collection.
REFERENCES: Havemeyer 1931, p. 414;
Wildenstein 1974–85, no. 1492.

413
Claude Monet
WATER LILIES AND JAPANESE
BRIDGE***
Oil on canvas, 35 3/8 x 35 3/8 in. (89.9 x 89.9 cm)
Signed and dated l.r.: *Claude Monet 99*
PROVENANCE: Petit, Bernheim-Jeune,
and Montaignac, Paris, bought from the
artist, Dec. 1899; Durand-Ruel, Paris
and New York, bought in 1900; Mr. and
Mrs. H. O. Havemeyer, New York, bought
from Durand-Ruel in 1901; on deposit
with Durand-Ruel, New York, Jan.–July
10, 1901; Durand-Ruel, New York, bought
back from Havemeyer in 1902; William
Church Osborn, New York, bought from
Durand-Ruel in 1905; d. 1951; his son,
Earl D. Osborn, 1951–72; The Art Museum, Princeton University, Princeton, N.J.
(From the Collection of William Church
Osborn, Class of 1883, Trustee of Princeton University [1914–51], President of the
Metropolitan Museum of Art [1941–47];
given by his Family), 72–15.
EXHIBITION: 1900 Paris Durand-Ruel,
no. 7.
REFERENCES: Wildenstein 1974–85,
no. 1509; Weitzenhoffer 1986, p. 143.

414
Claude Monet
BRIDGE OVER A POOL OF WATER
LILIES**
Oil on canvas, 36 1/2 x 29 in. (92.7 x 73.7 cm)
Signed and dated l.r.: *Claude Monet / 99*
PROVENANCE: Durand-Ruel, Paris, bought
from the artist, Jan. 25, 1900 (stock no.
5632); Durand-Ruel, New York, bought
from Durand-Ruel, Paris, Jan. 9, 1901
(stock no. 2458); Mr. and Mrs. H. O.
Havemeyer, New York, bought from
Durand-Ruel, Jan. 26, 1901; until 1907;
on deposit with Durand-Ruel, Jan.–July
10, 1901; Mrs. H. O. Havemeyer, New
York, 1907–29; on deposit with Durand-
Ruel, Nov. 30, 1908–Aug. 20, 1909; MMA
29.100.113.
EXHIBITION: 1900 Paris Durand-Ruel,
no. 12.
REFERENCES: Havemeyer 1931, pp. 156f.,
ill., as *Landscape—Bridge and Pond Lilies*; Havemeyer 1958, p. 30, no. 169; Sterling and Salinger 1967, pp. 141f., ill.;
Wildenstein 1974–85, no. 1518; Weitzenhoffer 1986, pp. 143, 184, 257, pl. 113.

415
Claude Monet
THE THAMES AT CHARING CROSS
BRIDGE
Oil on canvas, 25 1/2 x 35 3/8 in.
(64.8 x 89.9 cm)
Signed and dated l.r.: *Claude Monet 99*
PROVENANCE: Boussod, Valadon et Cie.
Paris, bought from the artist, Nov. 1899;
Bernheim-Jeune, Paris, bought from
Boussod, Valadon in 1900; Durand-Ruel,
Paris, bought from Bernheim-Jeune, Oct.
28, 1902 (stock no. 7172); Durand-Ruel,
New York, bought from Durand-Ruel,
Paris, Jan. 8, 1903 (stock no. 2856); Mr.
and Mrs. H. O. Havemeyer, New York,
bought from Durand-Ruel, Jan. 27, 1903;
until 1907; Mrs. H. O. Havemeyer, New
York, 1907–29; her daughter Electra
Havemeyer Webb, New York, 1929–60;
Shelburne Museum, Shelburne, Vt., from
1960, 27.1.4–70.
REFERENCES: Havemeyer 1931, p. 415;
Wildenstein 1974–85, no. 1521; Weitzen-
hoffer 1986, p. 147, pl. 120.

416
Claude Monet
THE HOUSES OF PARLIAMENT,
SEA GULLS***
Oil on canvas, 31 7/8 x 36 1/4 in. (81 x 92.1 cm)
Signed and dated l.r.: *Claude Monet 1903*
PROVENANCE: Durand-Ruel, Paris, bought
from the artist, Oct. 30, 1905 (stock no.
8010); Mr. and Mrs. H. O. Havemeyer,
New York, bought from Durand-Ruel, Jan.
26, 1906, until 1907; Mrs. H. O. Have-
meyer, New York, 1907–8; consigned to
Durand-Ruel, Nov. 30, 1908; Durand-
Ruel, New York, bought from Havemeyer,
Dec. 1908, for $5,000; William Church Os-
born, New York, from 1908; Mrs. Vander-
bilt Webb, from about 1968; The Art
Museum, Princeton University, Princeton,
N.J. (Bequest of Mrs. Vanderbilt Webb,
1979), 79–54.
REFERENCES: Wildenstein 1974–85,
no. 1612; Weitzenhoffer 1986, p. 184,
pl. 138.

417
Francesco Montemezzano
Italian (Venetian), ca. 1540–after 1602
PORTRAIT OF A WOMAN**
Oil on canvas, 46 3/4 x 39 in. (118.7 x 99.1 cm)
PROVENANCE: William Coningham; sale,
Christie's, London, June 9, 1849, no. 7, as
*The Wife of the Painter, in a crimson and
white dress, seated with a poodle dog in
her lap, and a handkerchief in her hand*,
by Veronese, for £818s.6d.; bought at sale
by Anthony; Donna Rosalia Velluti-Zati,
countess Fossi, Florence; Mr. and Mrs.

417

H. O. Havemeyer, New York, bought from
Countess Fossi through A. E. Harnisch by
summer 1901; until 1907; Mrs. H. O.
Havemeyer, New York, 1907–29; possibly
placed on exchange or consignment with
Trotti, Paris, by Nov. 1914 until at least
Oct. 1917;* MMA 29.100.104.
*See Chronology, Nov. 14, 1914.
REFERENCES: Havemeyer 1931, pp. 8f.,
ill., as *Portrait of the Artist's Wife*, by Veronese; Wehle 1940, pp. 206f., ill., with no
firm attribution; Havemeyer 1958, p. 33,
no. 186; Havemeyer 1961, pp. 110–13;
Zeri and Gardner 1973, p. 44, pl. 49,
as by Montemezzano; Pignatti 1976,
no. A226, as *Dama con Cagnolino*, by
Montemezzano; Weitzenhoffer 1986,
p. 256.

418
Mihály de Munkácsy
Hungarian, 1844–1900
THE HAYMAKERS***
Oil on canvas, 39 x 23 in. (99.1 x 58.4 cm)
PROVENANCE: Erwin Davis, New York;
his sale, Ortgies and Co., Chickering Hall,
New York, Mar. 20, 1889, no. 103; possi-
bly bought at sale by Havemeyer for
$2,000; possibly Mr. and Mrs. H. O. Have-
meyer, New York, from 1889.
REFERENCE: Weitzenhoffer 1982, p. 100.

419
Aert van der Neer
Dutch, 1603/4–1677
LANDSCAPE AT SUNSET
Oil on wood, 9 1/4 x 14 in. (23.5 x 35.6 cm)
Signed l.r.: *A.V.D.N.* [monogram]
PROVENANCE: Edouard Warneck, Paris, un-
til 1889; Durand-Ruel, Paris, bought from
Warneck, Aug. 1, 1889, for Fr 10,000
(stock no. 2402, no title); Mr. and Mrs.
H. O. Havemeyer, New York, bought from
Durand-Ruel, Aug. 1, 1889, for Fr 72,000
with four other works; until 1907; Mrs.
H. O. Havemeyer, New York, 1907–29;

419

her sale, American Art Association, New York, Apr. 10, 1930, no. 53, as *Sunset Landscape*; bought at sale by Bohler and Steinmeyer for $1,100.

REFERENCES: Havemeyer 1931, p. 497, as *Landscape*; Weitzenhoffer 1982, p. 127; Weitzenhoffer 1986, p. 64.

420

421

420
Robert Noir
French, 1864–1931
PORTRAIT OF A GIRL
Oil on canvas, 25 x 19 in. (63.5 x 48.3 cm)
Signed l.l.: *Robert Noir*
PROVENANCE: possibly Mrs. H. O. Havemeyer, New York, d. 1929; her daughter Electra Havemeyer Webb, New York, by 1931–60; Shelburne Museum, Shelburne, Vt., from 1960, 27.1.1–156.
REFERENCE: Havemeyer 1931, p. 423.

421
Robert Noir
PORTRAIT OF TWO CHILDREN
Oil on canvas, 25 x 19 in. (63.5 x 48.3 cm)
Signed l.l.: *Robert Noir*
PROVENANCE: possibly Mrs. H. O. Havemeyer, New York, d. 1929; her daughter Electra Havemeyer Webb, New York, by 1931–60; Shelburne Museum, Shelburne, Vt., from 1960, 27.1.1–155.
REFERENCE: Havemeyer 1931, p. 423.

422
Adriaen van Ostade
Dutch, 1610–1685
PEOPLE PLAYING BOWLS***
PROVENANCE: Mr. and Mrs. H. O. Havemeyer, New York, possibly by Feb. 1892; consigned to Durand-Ruel, New York, Mar. 13, 1895.
Note: Either this work or the following one can probably be identified as the Ostade that Durand-Ruel, Paris, bought from Edouard Warneck, Paris, Aug. 1, 1889, and sold that same day to the Havemeyers for Fr 72,000 with four other works.
REFERENCES: Weitzenhoffer 1982, p. 127(?); Weitzenhoffer 1986, pp. 64(?), 100.

423
Adriaen van Ostade, Style of
Dutch, 17th century
MAN WITH A TANKARD
Oil on wood, 10⅛ x 8½ in. (25.7 x 21.6 cm)
PROVENANCE: Mr. and Mrs. H. O. Havemeyer, New York, possibly by Feb. 1892; until 1907; Mrs. H. O. Havemeyer, New York, 1907–29; MMA 29.100.198.
Note: See preceding work.
REFERENCES: Havemeyer 1931, p. 19; Havemeyer 1958, p. 6, no. 16; Weitzenhoffer 1982, p. 127(?); Weitzenhoffer 1986, p. 64(?).

424
Juan Pantoja de la Cruz, Attributed to
Spanish, 1551–1608/9
PORTRAIT OF A YOUNG WOMAN
Oil on canvas, 25 x 22 in. (63.5 x 55.9 cm)
PROVENANCE: Mrs. H. O. Havemeyer, New York, consigned to Durand-Ruel, Nov.

424

30, 1908–May 11, 1910 (deposit no. 7495), Jan. 16–May 24, 1911 (deposit no. 7585), Nov. 16, 1911–May 24, 1913 (deposit no. 7619), and Nov. 5, 1913–May 29, 1914 (deposit no. 7717), as *Buste de femme, Ecole espagnole*); d. 1929; her sale, American Art Association, New York, Apr. 10, 1930, no. 107, as by Pantoja de la Cruz; bought at sale by Ferry for $850; Mansfield Ferry, New York, from 1930; his wife, Jean Ferry, New York, until 1955; MMA (Gift of Jean Ferry, in memory of her husband, Mansfield Ferry, 1955), 55.174.
EXHIBITION: 1928 New York Metropolitan, no. 49, as by Pantoja de la Cruz.
REFERENCES: Havemeyer 1931, p. 499, as by Claudio Coello; Weitzenhoffer 1986, p. 184.

425
Giovanni Battista Piazzetta
Italian (Venetian), 1682–1754
MADONNA***
PROVENANCE: Mrs. H. O. Havemeyer, New York, consigned to Durand-Ruel, New York, Nov. 3, 1909–May 11, 1910, from Nov. 16, 1911, again in 1912; returned to her, May 24, 1913; at Durand-Ruel again from Nov. 6, 1913.

426
Ludovic Piette-Montfoulcault
French, 1826–1877
LANDSCAPE WITH FIGURES
Gouache, 7¼ x 7¼ in. (18.4 x 18.4 cm)
Signed and dated l.r.: *L. Piette 1874*
PROVENANCE: Mrs. H. O. Havemeyer, New York, d. 1929; her sale, American Art Association, New York, Apr. 10, 1930, no. 2; bought at sale by W. Willett for $100.
REFERENCE: Havemeyer 1931, p. 505.

427
Camille Pissarro
French, 1830–1903
THE CABBAGE GATHERERS
Gouache on silk, 6½ x 20½ in. (16.5 x 52.1 cm)
Signed l.l.: *C. Pissarro*

PROVENANCE: Mary Cassatt, Paris, until about 1879; Louisine Elder (later Mrs. H. O. Havemeyer), New York, probably bought from Cassatt about 1879; d. 1929; her sale, American Art Association, New York, Apr. 10, 1930, no. 32; bought at sale by Laporte for $650; Mr. and Mrs. William F. Laporte, Passaic, N.J., 1930–44; their sale, Parke-Bernet, New York, Mar. 30, 1944, no. 57, as *La Récolte des choux*; bought at sale by a private collector for $1,300; private collection, from 1944; sale, Sotheby's, London, June 30, 1992, no. 6, as *La Récolte des choux*, bought in.

EXHIBITION: 1886 New York, no. 307, as *Peasant Girls at Normandy*.

REFERENCES: Havemeyer 1931, p. 505, as *Landscape—Cabbage Gatherers*; Pissarro and Venturi 1939, no. 1624, as *La Récolte des choux*; Havemeyer 1961, p. 206; Weitzenhoffer 1982, pp. 15, 29, n. 12, pp. 45, 64, 198, n. 45, p. 281, n. 31; Weitzenhoffer 1986, pp. 22, 27, 34, 41, 117f., as *Peasant Girls at Normandy*.

428
Camille Pissarro
POTATO GATHERERS
Oil on canvas, 18⅛ x 21¾ in. (46 x 55.3 cm)
Signed and dated l.l.: *Pissarro 81*
PROVENANCE: Erwin Davis, New York, until 1901; Durand-Ruel, New York, bought from Davis, May 15, 1901, for $300 (stock no. 2548, as *Récolte des pommes de*

terre); Mrs. H. O. Havemeyer, New York, bought from Durand-Ruel, Jan. 10, 1913, for $3,000; d. 1929; her son, Horace Havemeyer, New York, 1929–48; consigned to M. Knoedler and Co., New York, by Havemeyer, Sept. 20, 1948 (stock no. CA3145); Robert Lehman, Port Washington, N.Y., bought from Havemeyer through Knoedler, Nov. 15, 1948, for $6,000; d. 1969; MMA (Robert Lehman Collection, 1975), 1975.1.197.

REFERENCES: Havemeyer 1931, p. 425; Pissarro and Venturi 1939, no. 516, as *Récolte de pommes, Pontoise*.

429
Camille Pissarro
GIRL WITH A GOAT
Oil on canvas, 32½ x 25½ in. (82.6 x 64.8 cm)
Signed and dated l.r.: *C. Pissarro 81*
PROVENANCE: Durand-Ruel; Ryerson, bought from Durand-Ruel in 1891; Durand-Ruel, New York, bought back from Ryerson, July 29, 1902, for $4,000 (stock no. 2814, as *Femme à la chèvre*); Hugo Reisinger, New York, bought from Durand-Ruel, Jan. 26, 1907, for $2,250; his sale, American Art Association, New York, Jan. 18–20, 1916, no. 74; bought at sale by Durand-Ruel for Havemeyer for $5,100; Mrs. H.O. Havemeyer, New York, 1916–29; her daughter Adaline Havemeyer Frelinghuysen, Morristown, N.J., from 1929; private collection.

EXHIBITION: 1882 Paris Saint-Honoré, no. 120, as *La gardeuse de chèvres*.
REFERENCES: Havemeyer 1931, p. 424; Pissarro and Venturi 1939, no. 546, as *La Femme à la chèvre*.

430
Camille Pissarro
FLOOD AT PONTOISE
Oil on canvas, 20½ x 25 in. (52.1 x 63.5 cm)
Signed and dated l.r.: *C. Pissarro/1882*
PROVENANCE: Mr. and Mrs. H. O. Havemeyer, New York, deposited with Durand-Ruel in 1901 (deposit no. 6058); until 1907; Mrs. H. O. Havemeyer, New York, 1907–29; her daughter Adaline Havemeyer Frelinghuysen, Morristown, N.J., 1929–63; private collection.
REFERENCES: Havemeyer 1931, p. 425, as *Landscape—View of Pontoise*; Pissarro and Venturi 1939, no. 557, as *Inondation à Pontoise*.

431
Camille Pissarro
HAYMAKERS RESTING
Oil on canvas, 26 x 32 in. (66 x 81.3 cm)
Signed and dated l.l.: *C. Pissarro 1891*
PROVENANCE: Tadamasa Hayashi, Tokyo and Paris, d. 1906; his sale, American Art Association, New York, Jan. 8–9, 1913, no. 157; bought at sale by Durand-Ruel for Havemeyer for $2,800; Mrs. H. O. Havemeyer, New York, 1913–29; her

428

429

431

428

430

432

427

369

daughter Adaline Havemeyer Freling-
huysen, Morristown, N.J., from 1929.
REFERENCES: Havemeyer 1931, p. 424;
Pissarro and Venturi 1939, no. 773.

432

Camille Pissarro
BATHER IN THE WOODS**
Oil on canvas, 23¾ x 28¾ in. (60.3 x 73 cm)
Signed and dated l.l.: *C. Pissarro.1895*
PROVENANCE: Alphonse Portier, Paris,
1895; Tadamasa Hayashi, Tokyo and
Paris, 1895–1906; his sale, American Art
Association, New York, Jan. 8–9, 1913,
no. 146; bought at sale by Durand-Ruel
for Havemeyer for $4,200; Mrs. H. O.
Havemeyer, New York, 1913–29; MMA
29.100.126.
REFERENCES: Havemeyer 1931, p. 161,
ill.; Pissarro and Venturi 1939, no. 904;
Havemeyer 1958, p. 31, no. 177; Sterling
and Salinger 1967, pp. 19f., ill.; Weitzenhoffer 1986, p. 257.

433

Peeter, Frans I, or Frans II Pourbus
Flemish, 1523–1584, 1545–1581, or
1569–1622
PORTRAIT OF A WOMAN***
PROVENANCE: Mr. and Mrs. H. O. Have-
meyer, New York, consigned to Durand-
Ruel, New York, Feb. 3, 1897; bought by
Durand-Ruel, Feb. 14, 1898.

434

Nicolas Poussin, Style of
French, 3rd quarter 17th century
ORPHEUS AND EURYDICE*
Oil on canvas, 47½ x 70¾ in.
(120.7 x 179.7 cm)
PROVENANCE: General Craig, London;
sale, Christie's, London, Apr. 18, 1812,
no. 73, for 181 guineas; Earls of Dunmore,
Dunmore Park, near Falkirk, by 1835–66;
Mr. and Mrs. H. O. Havemeyer, New
York, bought through A. E. Harnisch in
Italy, after Jan. 30, 1907, for L 15,000 the
pair* (with A374); shipped to them, July
13, 1907; Mrs. H. O. Havemeyer, New
York, 1907–29; MMA 29.100.20.

*In a letter of 1/30/07, Harnisch wrote Cas-
satt that he believed the pair came from
the Talleyrand collection.
EXHIBITIONS: 1857 Manchester, no. 600;
1866 London, no. 21; 1920 New York.
REFERENCES: Smith 1829–42, VIII, no. 303;
Havemeyer 1931, pp. 162f., ill., as by
Poussin; Sterling 1955, pp. 78f., ill.; Havemeyer 1958, p. 31, no. 178, ill.; Blunt 1966,
no. R91, as by an imitator of Poussin;
Weitzenhoffer 1986, pp. 178, 245, 255,
pl. 135.

435

Pierre-Paul Prud'hon
French, 1758–1823
CHARLES-HUBERT MILLEVOYE
(1782–1816)
Watercolor(?) on ivory, oval, 6¼ x 4¾ in.
(15.9 x 12.1 cm)
Signed and dated r.: *P.P. Prud'hon 1803*
PROVENANCE: Eugène Tondu; sale, Paris,
Apr. 3–29, 1865, no. 795; M. Furby, Aix-
en-Provence, until 1880; Charles Bayard,
Lyon, bought from Furby in 1880; Mrs.
H. O. Havemeyer, New York, d. 1929; her
sale, American Art Association, New York,
Apr. 10, 1930, no. 56; bought at sale by
M. Sloug for $800.
REFERENCES: Guiffrey 1924, no. 578;
Havemeyer 1931, p. 505.

436

Pseudo Pier Francesco Fiorentino
Italian (Florentine), fl. late 15th century
MADONNA AND CHILD WITH SAINT
JOHN
Tempera and gold on wood, 33 x 22½ in.
(83.8 x 57.2 cm)
PROVENANCE: Mrs. H. O. Havemeyer,
New York, bought through A. E.
Harnisch, for L 15,750 (including 5 per-
cent commission), as Sienese school, spring
1911–29; her sale, American Art Associa-
tion, New York, Apr. 10, 1930, no. 112, as
by Pier Francesco Fiorentino; bought at
sale by Ferargil for $750; Ferargil Galler-

436

ies, New York, until at least Dec. 1934;
sale, Parke-Bernet, New York, Nov. 15,
1945, no. 77, as by Master of the Blonde
Madonnas (Florentine, fl. 1475); bought at
sale by Ferargil for $450.
Note: The current attribution was provided by Everett Fahy.
REFERENCES: Havemeyer 1931, p. 494, as
Florentine school, XV century; Havemeyer
1961, p. 128.

437

Pierre Puvis de Chavannes
French, 1824–1898
TAMARIS
Oil on canvas, 10 x 15½ in. (25.4 x 39.4 cm)
Signed l.l.: *P. Puvis de Chavannes*
PROVENANCE: Durand-Ruel, Paris, from
1887; Robert de Bonnières, Paris, in 1895;
Paul Rosenberg, Paris, until 1903; Mr. and
Mrs. H. O. Havemeyer, New York, bought
from Rosenberg, Apr. 21, 1903, for
Fr 10,000; shipped to them by Durand-
Ruel, May 7, 1903; until 1907; Mrs. H. O.
Havemeyer, New York, 1907–29; her
daughter Electra Havemeyer Webb, New
York, 1929–30; MMA (H. O. Havemeyer
Collection, Gift of Mrs. J. Watson Webb,
1930), 30.20.
EXHIBITION: 1887 Paris, no. 23.
REFERENCES: Havemeyer 1931, p. 167;
Havemeyer 1958, p. 32, no. 180; Sterling
and Salinger 1966, pp. 228f., ill.

438
Pierre Puvis de Chavannes
THE ALLEGORY OF THE
SORBONNE**
Oil on canvas, 32 ⅝ x 180 ¼ in.
(82.9 x 457.9 cm)
Signed and dated l.r.: *P. Puvis de
Chavannes. 1889*
PROVENANCE: Durand-Ruel, Paris, 1889
(stock no. 2546); Mr. and Mrs. H. O.
Havemeyer, New York, bought from
Durand-Ruel, Oct. 30, 1889; until 1907;
Mrs. H. O. Havemeyer, New York, 1907–
29; MMA 29.100.117.
REFERENCES: Havemeyer 1931, pp. 166f.,
ill.; Havemeyer 1958, p. 32, no. 179; Ster-
ling and Salinger 1966, pp. 229f., ill.;
Weitzenhoffer 1982, pp. 112f., 132, 143,
n. 21, fig. 21; Weitzenhoffer 1986, pp. 60,
66, 177, 257.

439
Jean-François Raffaëlli
French, 1850–1924
WINTER LANDSCAPE WITH THE
FIGURE OF JEAN VALJEAN
Watercolor(?) on paper, 18 ½ x 12 ½ in.
(47 x 31.8 cm)
Signed and dated l.l.: *J.F. Raffaelli 79*
PROVENANCE: Day et Cie, Paris; Louisine
Elder (later Mrs. H. O. Havemeyer), New
York, probably bought from Day in 1879;
d. 1929; her sale, American Art Associa-
tion, New York, Apr. 10, 1930, no. 41, as
Un Paysan; bought at sale by Edouard
Jonas for $250.
EXHIBITION: 1880 New York, no. 747, as
Jean Valjean, lent by Mrs. A.S.W. Elder.
REFERENCES: Havemeyer 1931, p. 505;
Weitzenhoffer 1982, p. 250, n. 53.

440
Henry Ward Ranger
American, 1858–1916
WINTER STREET SCENE
Watercolor, 11 ½ x 15 in. (29.2 x 38.1 cm)
Signed and dated: *H.W. Ranger 86*
PROVENANCE: Mrs. H. O. Havemeyer,
New York, d. 1929; her daughter Adaline
Havemeyer Frelinghuysen, Morristown,
N.J., from 1929.
REFERENCE: Havemeyer 1931, p. 438.

441
Henry Ward Ranger
AUTUMN
Watercolor, 13 ½ x 10 ½ in. (34.3 x 26.7 cm)
Signed and dated l.l.: *H.W. Ranger 88*
PROVENANCE: Mr. and Mrs. H. O. Havemeyer, New York, bought from the artist
from the 1889 exhibition for $125; until
1907; Mrs. H. O. Havemeyer, New York,
1907–29; her sale, American Art Association, New York, Apr. 10, 1930, no. 6;
bought at sale by Meade for $125.
EXHIBITION: 1889 New York Watercolor,
no. 390.
REFERENCE: Havemeyer 1931, p. 509.

442
Henry Ward Ranger
EVENING AT LYDD
Watercolor, 10 ½ x 13 ½ in. (26.7 x 34.3 cm)
Signed and dated l.l.: *H.W. Ranger 88*
PROVENANCE: Mr. and Mrs. H. O. Havemeyer, New York, bought from the artist
from the 1889 exhibition for $125; until
1907; Mrs. H. O. Havemeyer, New York,
1907–29; her sale, American Art Association, New York, Apr. 10, 1930, no. 11;
bought at sale by Joseph Durst for $120.
EXHIBITION: 1889 New York Watercolor,
no. 458.
REFERENCE: Havemeyer 1931, p. 510.

443
Raphael (Raffaello Sanzio or Santi),
Copy after
Uncertain date
BINDO ALTOVITI
Oil on wood, 25 x 18 ½ in. (63.5 x 47 cm)
PROVENANCE: Altoviti collection, Italy;
Mr. and Mrs. H. O. Havemeyer, New

York, bought through A. E. Harnisch before 1903; until 1907; Mrs. H. O. Havemeyer, New York, 1907–29; her sale,
American Art Association, New York, Apr.
10, 1930, no. 122, as *Portrait of the Artist*, after Raphael; bought at sale by W. W.
Seaman (agent) for $325.
Note: This is a copy of a picture now in
the National Gallery of Art, Washington,
D.C.
REFERENCES: Havemeyer 1931, p. 494,
as *Portrait of the Artist*, after Raphael;
Havemeyer 1961, pp. 113, 115, 128f.

444
Marie Magdeleine Real del Sarte
French, d. 1928
LA REVERENCE***
Watercolor, 47 ¾ x 28 ¾ in. (121.3 x 73 cm)
PROVENANCE: Mr. and Mrs. H. O. Havemeyer, New York, until 1907; consigned to
Durand Ruel, Sept. 1, 1907 (deposit no.
5100); Mrs. H. O. Havemeyer, New York,
1907–29.
Note: In a letter of 2/19/32, to Horace
Havemeyer, Durand-Ruel wrote that this
work was still on consignment with them
and asked what should be done with it,
mentioning that Mrs. Havemeyer had several times asked that it be destroyed. See
also A483.

445
Rembrandt Harmensz. van Rijn
Dutch, 1606–1669
PORTRAIT OF A MAN*
Oil on canvas, 44 x 35 in. (111.8 x 88.9 cm)
Signed and dated l.r.: *RHL van Rijn / 1632*
PROVENANCE: G. van Beresteyn van
Maurick, Kasteel Maurik, Vught; sale,
L.G.N. van Dullemen, 's Hertogenbosch,
Netherlands, Oct. 24, 1884, probably
among nos. 17–46b, bought in by Jacob
van Beresteyn for G 75,000 with pendant
(A446); Jacob van Beresteyn, Gorssel; sale,
Casino, 's Hertogenbosch, Netherlands,
June 28, 1887; Félix Gérard, Paris, 1887–
88; Cottier and Co., New York, 1888; Mr.
and Mrs. H. O. Havemeyer, New York,
bought from Cottier, Dec. 8, 1888, for
$60,000 with pendant (A446); until 1907;
Mrs. H. O. Havemeyer, New York, 1907–
29; MMA 29.100.3.

445

449

453

446

450

454

447

451

455

448

452

EXHIBITIONS: 1890–91 New York, no. 5;
1891 New York Metropolitan, no. 5.
REFERENCES: Havemeyer 1931, pp. 20f.,
ill., as *Portrait of Christian Paul van
Beresteijn*; Havemeyer 1958, p. 6, no. 17;
Havemeyer 1961, p. 19; Weitzenhoffer
1982, pp. 81f., 94f., nn.14, 16, 18, pp. 97,
127f., 131f., 143, n. 23, pp. 149, 155,
166, n. 7, fig. 8; Bruyn et al. 1982–89,
no. C68, as workshop of Rembrandt;
Weitzenhoffer 1986, pp. 47, 64, 254, 261,
n. 9, ill. p. 74, pl. 11.

446

Rembrandt Harmensz. van Rijn
PORTRAIT OF A WOMAN*
Oil on canvas, 44 x 35 in. (111.8 x 88.9 cm)
Signed and dated l.r.: *RHL van Rijn / 1632*

PROVENANCE: G. van Beresteyn van
Maurick, Kasteel Maurik, Vught; sale,
L.G.N. van Dullemen, 's Hertogenbosch,
Netherlands, Oct. 24, 1884, probably
among nos. 17–46b, bought in by Jacob
van Beresteyn for G 75,000 with pendant
(A445); Jacob van Beresteyn, Gorssel;
sale, Casino, 's Hertogenbosch, Netherlands,
June 28, 1887; Félix Gérard, Paris, 1887–
88; Cottier and Co., New York, 1888; Mr.
and Mrs. H. O. Havemeyer, New York,
bought from Cottier, Dec. 8, 1888, for
$60,000 with pendant (A445); until 1907;
Mrs. H. O. Havemeyer, New York, 1907–
29; MMA 29.100.4.
EXHIBITIONS: 1890–91 New York, no. 8;
1891 New York Metropolitan, no. 9.
REFERENCES: Havemeyer 1931, pp. 22f.,
ill., as *Portrait of Volkera van Beresteijn*;
Havemeyer 1958, p. 6, no. 18; Havemeyer
1961, p. 19; Weitzenhoffer 1982, pp. 81f.,
94f., nn. 14, 16, 18, pp. 97, 127f., 131f.,
143, n. 23, pp. 149, 155, 166, n. 7, fig. 9;
Bruyn et al. 1982–89, no. C69, as workshop of Rembrandt, possibly with limited
involvement by Rembrandt; Weitzenhoffer
1986, pp. 47, 64, 254, 261, n. 9.

447

Rembrandt Harmensz. van Rijn
TWO STUDIES OF A WOMAN
READING
Pen and brown ink on tan laid paper,
6¾ x 5⅞ in. (17.2 x 14.9 cm)

PROVENANCE: Jonathan Richardson, Sr.,
London; William Mayor, London; Sir Francis Seymour Haden, Woodcote, Alresford,
Hants; his sale, Sotheby's, London, June
18, 1891, no. 582, as *Two Women Seated*;
bought at sale by Durand-Ruel for Havemeyer; Mr. and Mrs. H. O. Havemeyer,
New York, 1891–1907; Mrs. H. O. Havemeyer, New York, 1907–29; MMA
29.100.932.
REFERENCES: Havemeyer 1931, p. 180;

Havemeyer 1958, p. 7, no. 25; Benesch
1973, no. 249; Weitzenhoffer 1982,
pp. 141f., n. 12.

448

Rembrandt Harmensz. van Rijn
SEATED MAN WEARING A FLAT CAP
Pen and brown ink, brown wash, and white
gouache, on wove paper, 5¹³/₁₆ x 5⁷/₁₆ in.
(14.8 x 13.8 cm)

PROVENANCE: Sir Joshua Reynolds, London; Sir Thomas Lawrence, London; William Esdaile, London; his sale, Christie's,
London, June 17, 1840, no. 13, as *A
Portly Man in a Cap, seated before the
door of a house*, for £3 5s.; Sir Francis Seymour Haden, Woodcote, Alresford, Hants;
his sale, Sotheby's, London, June 18, 1891,
no. 584, as *A Man Seated on a Doorstep*;
bought at sale by Durand-Ruel for Havemeyer; Mr. and Mrs. H. O. Havemeyer,
New York, 1891–1907; Mrs. H. O. Havemeyer, New York, 1907–29; MMA
29.100.935.
REFERENCES: Havemeyer 1931, p. 180,
ill., as *Man Seated on a Doorstep*; Benesch
1973, no. 324; Weitzenhoffer 1982,
pp. 141f., n. 12.

449

Rembrandt Harmensz. van Rijn
HERMAN DOOMER (ca. 1600–1654)*
Oil on wood, 29⅝ x 21¾ in. (75.3 x 55.3 cm)
Signed and dated l.r.: *Rembrandt / f 1640*

PROVENANCE: Baertje Martens, wife of H
Doomer, Amsterdam, 1654–62; her son,
Lambert Doomer, Amsterdam, 1662–1700;
his nephew, Herman Vorster the Younger,
Amsterdam, from 1700; possibly private
collection, Geneva; Anthony Cousin, London, by 1730–35; his sale, London, Feb. 8,
1750, probably no. 53, as *A Man's Head,
3 qrs*, for £55 13s.; H. Wolters; sale, Amsterdam, May 4, 1757, no. 61; Peregrine,
third duke of Ancaster, by 1769–78; his
widow, Mary, dowager duchess of Ancaster; her sale, Christie's, London, May 16–
18, 1791, probably no. 84, as *A Portrait*;
bought at sale by Tapant for £49 7s.; Van
Eyl Sluyter, Amsterdam; sale, Paris, Jan.
25, 1802, no. 145; bought at sale by
Urique; possibly anonymous sale, Paris,
1836; Mme Gentil de Chavagnac, Geneva
or Paris, before 1854; Charles-Auguste-
Louis-Joseph Demorny, first duc de Morny,
Paris, by 1854; his sale, Palais de la
Présidence du Corps Législatif, Paris, May
31, 1865, no. 68; bought at sale by Sala-
manca(?) for the duke's widow for
Fr 155,000; Sophie Troubetskoi, duchesse
de Morny, later duquesa de Sexto, Madrid,
1865–82; Mme de Cassin, Paris, 1882–83;
Auguste de Morny, second duc de Morny,

Paris, by 1883; William Schaus, New York,
bought from Morny, Nov. 19, 1884, for
Fr 210,000; Mr. and Mrs. H. O. Havemeyer, New York, bought from Schaus,
Mar. 7, 1889, reputedly for between
$70,000 and $100,000; until 1907; Mrs.
H. O. Havemeyer, New York, 1907–29;
MMA 29.100.1.
EXHIBITIONS: 1883 Paris, no. 95; 1890–
91 New York, no. 9; 1891 New York Metropolitan, no. 8; 1893 New York, no. 15,
as *The Gilder*; 1909 New York Metropolitan, no. 88; 1915 New York Masterpieces,
no. 9.
REFERENCES: Havemeyer 1931, pp. 24f.,
ill., as *Portrait of the Gilder, Herman
Doomer*; Havemeyer 1958, p. 6, no. 19,
ill.; Havemeyer 1961, pp. 19, 24, 142;
Weitzenhoffer 1982, pp. 97–100, 117,
nn. 2, 3, pp. 127f., 131f., 138, 143, n. 23,
pp. 149, 155, 166, n. 7, fig. 14; Bruyn et
al. 1982–89, no. A140; Weitzenhoffer
1986, pp. 53f., 64, 68, 209, 254, ill.
p. 224, pl. 12.

450

Rembrandt Harmensz. van Rijn
A COTTAGE AMONG TREES
Pen and brown ink on tan laid paper; artist
extended the sheet by joining a vertical
strip of paper at the right margin,
6¾ x 10¹³/₁₆ in. (17.2 x 27.5 cm)

PROVENANCE: Jan Pietersz. Zoomer, Am-
sterdam; Sir Thomas Lawrence, London;
William Esdaile, London; his sale, Christie's,
London, June 17, 1840, no. 119, as *A
Farmhouse Surrounded by Trees*, for £7;
John Heywood Hawkins, London; his sale,
Sotheby's, London, Apr. 29, 1850, no.
1022; Sir Francis Seymour Haden,
Woodcote, Alresford, Hants; his sale,
Sotheby's, London, June 18, 1891, no. 587,
as *A Landscape with a Cottage in a Clump
of Trees*; bought at sale by Durand-Ruel
for Havemeyer; Mr. and Mrs. H. O. Have-
meyer, New York, 1891–1907; Mrs. H. O.
Havemeyer, New York, 1907–29; MMA
29.100.939.
REFERENCES: Havemeyer 1931, pp. 178f.,
ill., as *Landscape with a Barn Among
Trees*; Havemeyer 1958, p. 7, no. 22;
Benesch 1973, no. 1249; Weitzenhoffer
1982, pp. 141f., n. 12.

451

Rembrandt Harmensz. van Rijn
GROUP OF FARM BUILDINGS
Pen and brown ink, brown wash, and
white gouache, on tan prepared laid paper,
4¹/₁₆ x 6¹⁵/₁₆ in. (10.3 x 17.6 cm)

PROVENANCE: Sir Francis Seymour Haden,
Woodcote, Alresford, Hants; his sale,
Sotheby's, London, June 18, 1891, no.

590, as *Landscape with low thatched cottages*; bought at sale by Durand-Ruel for Havemeyer; Mr. and Mrs. H. O. Havemeyer, New York, 1891–1907; Mrs. H. O. Havemeyer, New York, 1907–29; MMA 29.100.936.
REFERENCES: Havemeyer 1931, p. 179; Havemeyer 1958, p. 7, no. 20; Benesch 1973, no. 1271; Weitzenhoffer 1982, pp. 141f., n. 12.

452
Rembrandt Harmensz. van Rijn
HOUSES BY THE WATER
Pen and brown ink on beige laid paper, 3 ¹⁵⁄₁₆ x 6 ⅛ in. (10 x 15.6 cm)
PROVENANCE: Jonathan Richardson, Sr., London; Sir Joshua Reynolds, London; Sir Francis Seymour Haden, Woodcote, Alresford, Hants; his sale, Sotheby's, London, June 18, 1891, no. 573, as *An Open Place in a Town*; bought at sale by Durand-Ruel for Havemeyer; Mr. and Mrs. H. O. Havemeyer, New York, 1891–1907; Mrs. H. O. Havemeyer, New York, 1907–29; MMA 29.100.938.
REFERENCES: Havemeyer 1931, p. 179; Havemeyer 1958, p. 7, no. 21; Benesch 1973, no. 1307; Weitzenhoffer 1982, pp. 141f., n. 12.

453
Rembrandt Harmensz. van Rijn
NATHAN ADMONISHING DAVID
Pen and brown ink, brown wash, and white gouache, on laid paper, 7 ⁵⁄₁₆ x 10 in. (18.6 x 25.4 cm)
PROVENANCE: Jonathan Richardson, Sr., London; Sir Thomas Lawrence, London; William Esdaile, London; his sale, Christie's, London, June 17, 1840, no. 98, as *Nathan Reproving David*, for £2 12s.6d.; Samuel Woodburn, London, d. 1853; his sale, Christie's, London, June 4, 1860, no. 750; Sir Francis Seymour Haden, Woodcote, Alresford, Hants; his sale, Sotheby's, London, June 18, 1891, no. 586, as *David and Nathan*; bought at sale by Durand-Ruel for Havemeyer; Mr. and Mrs. H. O. Havemeyer, New York, 1891–1907; Mrs. H. O. Havemeyer, New York, 1907–29; MMA 29.100.934.
REFERENCES: Havemeyer 1931, pp. 178f., ill.; Havemeyer 1958, p. 7, no. 24; Benesch 1973, no. 948; Weitzenhoffer 1982, pp. 141f., n. 12.

454
Rembrandt Harmensz. van Rijn
WOMAN HANGING ON A GIBBET
Pen and brown ink and brown wash, on tan laid paper, lined, 6 ¾ x 3 ⁹⁄₁₆ in.

(17.2 x 9.1 cm)
PROVENANCE: possibly Jacob de Vos, Amsterdam; Sir Thomas Lawrence, London; William Esdaile, London; Sir Francis Seymour Haden, Woodcote, Alresford, Hants; his sale, Sotheby's, London, June 18, 1891, no. 577, as *A Malefactor on a Gibet* [sic]; bought at sale by Durand-Ruel for Havemeyer; Mr. and Mrs. H. O. Havemeyer, New York, 1891–1907; Mrs. H. O. Havemeyer, New York, 1907–29; MMA 29.100.937.
REFERENCES: Havemeyer 1931, p. 180; Havemeyer 1958, p. 7, no. 26; Benesch 1973, no. 1105; Weitzenhoffer 1982, pp. 141f., n. 12.

455
Rembrandt Harmensz. van Rijn, Copy after
Uncertain date
PORTRAIT OF REMBRANDT IN A CAP AND A POLISH JACKET
Oil on wood, 25 x 20 in. (63.5 x 50.8 cm)
Inscribed and dated r.: *Rembrandt f. 1632* [or *1634*]
PROVENANCE: Thomas Agnew and Son, Liverpool; Harrington, Boston; M. J. Rougeron, New York, bought from Harrington's daughter; Mrs. H. O. Havemeyer, New York, bought from Rougeron, in 1922–29; her sale, American Art Association, New York, Apr. 10, 1930, no. 102, as *Rembrandt with Short Hair in a Cap and a Polish Jacket*, by Rembrandt(?); bought at sale by J. M. Hardy for $4,500.
Note: This is a copy after a painting now in the Norton Simon Museum, Pasadena. The museum attributes its picture to Rembrandt, but this is rejected by Bruyn et al., who suggest an attribution to Carel Fabritius.
REFERENCES: Havemeyer 1931, p. 497, as by Rembrandt(?); Weitzenhoffer 1982, p. 142, n. 12; Bruyn et al. 1982–89, copy no. 4 under no. C97.

456
Rembrandt, Style of
Dutch, 17th century
PORTRAIT OF A MAN—THE TREASURER
Oil on canvas, 44 x 36 in. (111.8 x 91.4 cm)
Inscribed and dated l.r.: *R. van Ryn / 1632*
PROVENANCE: John Hinchcliff, in 1836; John Nieuwenhuys; A. J. Boesch, Vienna, in 1885; Durand-Ruel, Paris; Durand-Ruel, New York, Nov. 1890; Mr. and Mrs. H. O. Havemeyer, New York, bought from Durand-Ruel, Nov. 1890; until 1907; Mrs. H. O. Havemeyer, New York, 1907–29; her daughter Electra Havemeyer Webb, New York, 1929–60; Shelburne Museum, Shelburne, Vt., from 1960, 27.1.1–151.

156

EXHIBITION: 1891 New York Metropolitan, no. 7.
REFERENCES: Havemeyer 1931, pp. 306f., ill.; Havemeyer 1961, p. 19; Bredius/Gerson 1969, no. 168, as *Portrait of a Man with Gloves*, rejects attribution to Rembrandt; Weitzenhoffer 1982, pp. 125–28, 132, 149, 155, 166, n. 7; Weitzenhoffer 1986, pp. 64, 66.

457
Rembrandt, Style of
Dutch, 17th century
PORTRAIT OF A MAN WITH A BREASTPLATE AND PLUMED HAT**
Oil on canvas, 47 ¾ x 38 ¾ in. (121.3 x 98.4 cm)
PROVENANCE: Baron de Seillière, Paris; possibly Chevalier Sebastien Erard, Boulogne; Princesse de Sagan, Paris; Durand-Ruel, Paris, bought from the princess for Havemeyer, June 1892; Durand-Ruel, New York, 1892 (stock no. 966); Mr. and Mrs. H. O. Havemeyer, New York, bought from Durand-Ruel, Sept. 7, 1892; until 1907; Mrs. H. O. Havemeyer, New York, 1907–29; MMA 29.100.102.
REFERENCES: Havemeyer 1931, pp. 28f., ill., as *Portrait of an Admiral*; Havemeyer 1958, p. 8, no. 27; Havemeyer 1961, pp. 19f.; Bredius/Gerson 1969, no. 223, as

by Bol; Weitzenhoffer 1982, pp. 129, 141, n. 11, pp. 149, 155, 166, n. 7, p. 168, n. 34, fig. 26; Sumowski 1983, IV, p. 2884, n. 40, as school of Rembrandt; Weitzenhoffer 1986, pp. 65, 256, 262, n. 5.

458
Rembrandt, Style of
Dutch, 17th century
PORTRAIT OF A WOMAN**
Oil on canvas, 47⅝ x 38⅝ in. (121 x 98.1 cm)
Inscribed and dated l., on chair: *Rembrandt f / 1643*
PROVENANCE: Baron de Seillière, Paris; possibly Chevalier Sebastien Erard, Boulogne; Princesse de Sagan, Paris; Durand-Ruel, Paris, bought from the princess for Havemeyer, June 1892; Durand-Ruel, New York, 1892 (stock no. 967); Mr. and Mrs. H. O. Havemeyer, New York, bought from Durand-Ruel, Sept. 7, 1892; until 1907; Mrs. H. O. Havemeyer, New York, 1907–29; MMA 29.100.103.
REFERENCES: Havemeyer 1931, pp. 30f., ill., as *Portrait of the Admiral's Wife*; Havemeyer 1958, p. 8, no. 28; Havemeyer 1961, pp. 19f.; Bredius/Gerson 1969, no. 364, as by Bol; Weitzenhoffer 1982, pp. 129, 141, n. 11, pp. 149, 155, 166, n. 7, p. 168, n. 34, fig. 27; Sumowski 1983, IV, p. 2884, n. 41, as school of Rembrandt; Weitzenhoffer 1986, pp. 65, 256, 262, n. 5.

459
Rembrandt, Style of
Dutch, 17th century
PORTRAIT OF A YOUNG MAN IN A BROAD-BRIMMED HAT
Oil on canvas, 45⅞ x 36 in. (116.5 x 91.4 cm)
Signed and dated l.r.: *Rembrandt f. 1643*
PROVENANCE: Stiers d'Aertselaer, Antwerp, in 1822; Baron von Mecklenburg, Berlin; his sale, Hôtel des Commissaires-Priseurs, Paris, Dec. 11, 1854, no. 14, as *Portrait de bourguemestre Six, ami de Rembrandt*; bought at sale by Seillière for

459

Fr 28,000; Baron de Seillière, Paris, 1854 until at least 1861; Princesse de Sagan, Paris, by 1874–about 1892; Mr. and Mrs. H. O. Havemeyer, New York, bought from the princess through Durand-Ruel; until 1907; Mrs. H. O. Havemeyer, New York, 1907–29; her daughter Electra Havemeyer Webb, New York, 1929–60; Shelburne Museum, Shelburne, Vt., from 1960, 27.1.1–150.
EXHIBITION: 1874 Paris, no. 413.
REFERENCES: Havemeyer 1931, pp. 308f., ill.; Havemeyer 1961, p. 19; Weitzenhoffer 1982, pp. 129, 149, 155, 166, n. 7; Weitzenhoffer 1986, p. 65.

460
Pierre-Auguste Renoir
French, 1841–1919
BY THE SEASHORE**
Oil on canvas, 36¼ x 28½ in. (92.1 x 72.4 cm)
Signed and dated l.l.: *Renoir. 83.*
PROVENANCE: possibly Durand-Ruel, Paris, bought from the artist, Jan. 9, 1884, as *Young Woman Knitting by the Sea*; P. de Kuyper, The Hague, until 1891; Durand-Ruel, Paris, bought from de Kuyper, Oct. 14, 1891; Catholina Lambert, Paterson, N.J., bought from Durand-Ruel, New York, Apr. 2, 1892, for $1,800; Durand-Ruel, New York, bought from Lambert, Feb. 28, 1899 (stock no. 2123); Mr. and Mrs. H. O. Havemeyer, New York, bought from Durand-Ruel, Mar. 10, 1899, for $4,000; until 1907; Mrs. H. O. Havemeyer, New York, 1907–29; MMA 29.100.125.
REFERENCES: Havemeyer 1931, pp. 168f., ill.; Havemeyer 1958, p. 32, no. 181; Sterling and Salinger 1967, pp. 155–57, ill.; Daulte 1971, no. 448; Weitzenhoffer 1982, p. 281, n. 31, pp. 306f., fig. 120; Weitzenhoffer 1986, pp. 135, 151, 226f., 257, pl. 98.

460

461

462

461
Pierre-Auguste Renoir
YOUNG WOMAN READING***
Pastel on paper
PROVENANCE: Durand-Ruel, Paris, bought from the artist in 1889 for Fr 500; Mr. and Mrs. H. O. Havemeyer, New York, bought from Durand-Ruel, Oct. 1889, for Fr 1,500; until 1907; Mrs. H. O. Havemeyer, New York, 1907–8; Durand-Ruel, New York, bought from Havemeyer, Dec. 1908, for $500; private collection, U.S.
REFERENCES: Weitzenhoffer 1982, pp. 113, 120f., n. 34, p. 198, n. 45, fig. 22; Weitzenhoffer 1986, pp. 60f., 184, pl. 19.

462
Pierre-Auguste Renoir
YOUNG WOMAN WITH A MUFF
Red, black, and white chalk on light pink
laid paper, 20¾ x 14¼ in. (52.7 x 36.2 cm)
Signed l.r.: *Renoir*
PROVENANCE: Mrs. H. O. Havemeyer,
New York, d. 1929; MMA 29.100.195.
REFERENCES: Havemeyer 1931, pp. 190f.,
ill.; Havemeyer 1958, p. 32, no. 182.

463
José Ribelles y Helip, Attributed to
Spanish, 1778–1835
FERDINAND VII (1784–1833), KING
OF SPAIN
Oil on canvas, 25 x 20½ in. (63.5 x 52.1 cm)
PROVENANCE: Harrington, Boston, M. J.
Rougeron, New York, bought from Har-
rington's daughter; Mrs. H. O. Havemeyer,
New York, bought from Rougeron as by
Goya, in 1922–29; her sale, American Art
Association, New York, Apr. 10, 1930,
no. 119, as *King Ferdinand VII of Spain*,
Spanish school, early XIX century; bought
at sale by J. M. Hardy for $500.
REFERENCE: Havemeyer 1931, p. 500, as
Portrait of Ferdinand VII, attributed to
Ribelles, XIX century.

464

464
José Ribelles y Helip, Attributed to
PORTRAIT OF A SPANISH OFFICER
Oil on canvas, 38 x 28½ in. (96.5 x 72.4 cm)
PROVENANCE: Mrs. H. O. Havemeyer, New
York, d. 1929; her sale, American Art Asso-
ciation, New York, Apr. 10, 1930, no. 99,
as *Portrait of Major Z*, by Goya(?); bought
at sale by Metropolitan Galleries for
$1,600.
REFERENCE: Havemeyer 1931, p. 500, as
attributed to Ribelles, XIX century.

465
Roman Ribera
Spanish, b. 1848
THE CONCERT***
PROVENANCE: F. Reitlinger, Paris, until

1880; M. Knoedler and Co., New York,
bought from Reitlinger, Sept. 14, 1880, for
Fr 3,500 (stock no. 2864, as *The Concert*
or *Spanish Tavern*); H. O. Havemeyer,
New York, bought from Knoedler, Apr. 1,
1882, for $875; returned to M. Knoedler
and Co., New York, by Havemeyer, Dec.
7, 1886, for $850 credit (stock no. 5495);
George F. Baker, New York, bought from
Knoedler, Dec. 14, 1886, for $3,200.

466
Lucius (or Lucio), or Luigi Rossi
French or Swiss, 1846–1913 or
1853–1923
WATERCOLOR***
PROVENANCE: M. Knoedler and Co., New
York, until 1877; H. O. Havemeyer, New
York, bought from Knoedler, Feb. 21,
1877, for $250, as by Louis Rossi.

467
Théodore Rousseau
French, 1812–1867
AUTUMN
Oil on wood, 7⅛ x 9¼ in. (18.1 x 23.5 cm)
Signed: *Rousseau*[?]
PROVENANCE: possibly Mrs. H. O. Have-
meyer, New York, d. 1929; her son, Hor-
ace Havemeyer, New York, by 1931.
REFERENCE: Havemeyer 1931, p. 426.

468
Théodore Rousseau
FARM IN SOLOGNE
Oil on wood, 6¼ x 8⅜ in. (15.9 x 22 cm)
Signed: *Th. Rousseau*
PROVENANCE: Mr. and Mrs. H. O. Have-
meyer, New York, until 1907; consigned to
Durand-Ruel, Nov. 1895–Jan. 1896; Mrs.
H. O. Havemeyer, New York, 1907–29;
her son, Horace Havemeyer, New York,
from 1929.
Note: This picture may be the one bought
by H. O. Havemeyer in 1881, as *Paysage,
arbres et cabanes*, which has the following
provenance: M. Teese, Paris, until 1881;
Boussod, Valadon et Cie, Paris, bought
from Teese, May 20, 1881, for Fr 6,000
(stock no. 15396); M. Knoedler and Co.,
New York, bought from Boussod, Valadon, May 25, 1881 (Boussod, Valadon
stock book), or June 1881 (Knoedler stock
book, no. 3311, as *Paysage, arbres et cabanes*), for Fr 8,000; H. O. Havemeyer,
New York, bought from Knoedler, Nov.
28, 1881, for $2,200.
REFERENCES: Havemeyer 1931, p. 426;
Weitzenhoffer 1982, pp. 41, 49, n. 19(?);
Weitzenhoffer 1986, pp. 33(?), 100.

469

470

469
Théodore Rousseau
A HAMLET IN NORMANDY***
Oil on wood, 8½ x 12½ in. (21.6 x 31.8 cm)
Signed l.r.: *Th. Rousseau*
PROVENANCE: John Waterloo Wilson,
Paris; his sale, at his hôtel, 3, avenue
Hoche, Paris, Mar. 14–16, 1881, no. 180,
as *Un Hameau en Normandie*; E. Secrétan,
Paris; his sale, Galerie Charles Sedelmeyer,
Paris, July 1–7, 1889, no. 72, as *Un Ha-
meau en Normandie*; bought at sale by
Durand-Ruel for Havemeyer for Fr 22,000
(stock no. 2382); Mr. and Mrs. H. O.
Havemeyer, New York, from 1889.
Note: This work can probably be identified
with one of two landscapes by Rousseau
consigned to Durand-Ruel by the Havemeyers, Nov. 1895; one was bought back
by Durand-Ruel, Dec. 15, 1896, and sold
by it to Samuel P. Avery, Jr., New York, in
1899, and the other was bought back by
Durand-Ruel, Mar. 11, 1898.
REFERENCE: Weitzenhoffer 1986, p. 100.

470
Théodore Rousseau
LANDSCAPE SKETCH
Oil on canvas, 35 x 46¾ in.
(88.9 x 118.8 cm)
PROVENANCE: William Merritt Chase, New
York; James S. Inglis, New York, bought
from Chase; d. 1908; his sale, American
Art Association, New York, Mar. 10, 1910,
no. 99; bought at sale by Durand-Ruel for
Havemeyer for $500; Mrs. H. O. Have-
meyer, New York, 1910–29; her sale,
American Art Association, New York,
Apr. 10, 1930, no. 111, for $600.
REFERENCE: Havemeyer 1931, p. 505.

471
Peter Paul Rubens, Workshop of
Flemish, 1577–1640
SAINT CECILIA*
Oil on canvas, 47⅞ x 40¾ in.
(121.6 x 103.5 cm)
PROVENANCE: possibly Richard Plantagenet
Campbell Temple-Nugent-Brydges-Chandos-
Grenville, Third Duke of Buckingham and
Chandos and Tenth Lord Kinloss, Stowe,
Buckinghamshire; Charles Sedelmeyer; sale,
Galerie Charles Sedelmeyer, Vienna, Dec.
20–21, 1872, no. 141; Baron Etienne Mar-
tin de Beurnonville, Paris; sale, Paillet,
Paris, May 9–16, 1881, no. 437; bought at
sale by Tabourier for Fr 4,950; Antoine
François Marmontel, Paris; his sale, Hôtel
Drouot, Paris, Mar. 28–29, 1898, no. 3,
for Fr 11,000; Mrs. H. O. Havemeyer,
New York, bought through Trotti, Apr. 26,
1909; d. 1929; MMA 29.100.14.
REFERENCES: Havemeyer 1931, pp. 38f.,
ill., as by Rubens; Havemeyer 1958, p. 9,
no. 34; Vlieghe 1972, no. 81(2), as copy
after Rubens; Liedtke 1984, I, pp. 222–24,
II, pl. 84; Weitzenhoffer 1986, pp. 158,
191, 254.

472
Peter Paul Rubens, Workshop of
LADISLAS SIGISMUND IV (1595–1648),
KING OF POLAND*

Oil on canvas, 49¼ x 39¾ in.
(125.1 x 101 cm)
PROVENANCE: John Campbell, Lord Glen-
orchy, Third Earl of Breadalbane and Holland, London, until 1737; Sir Henry William
Dashwood, Fifth Baronet, Kirtlington Hall,
Oxfordshire; sale, Christie's, London, Apr.
23, 1887, no. 138, bought in; d. 1889; Sir
George John Egerton Dashwood, Sixth Baronet; sale, Knight, Frank and Rutley, London, Oct. 22, 1909, no. 3; possibly Eyles,
1909; Mrs. H. O. Havemeyer, New York,
bought through Trotti, May 1914; d. 1929;
MMA 29.100.13.
EXHIBITION: 1915 New York Masterpieces, no. 14, as by Rubens.
REFERENCES: Havemeyer 1931, pp. 36f.,
ill., as by Rubens; Havemeyer 1958, p. 10,
no. 35; Liedtke 1984, I, pp. 220–22, II,
pl. 83; Weitzenhoffer 1986, pp. 219, 254;
Vlieghe 1987, no. 113(1), as Copy after
Rubens.

473
William Sartain
American, 1843–1924
HEAD OF AN ITALIAN GIRL
Oil on canvas, 18½ x 15 in. (47 x 38.1 cm)
Signed, dated, and inscribed l.r.: *W. Sartain
Paris 79*
PROVENANCE: Samuel Colman; his sale,
American Art Association, New York,
Mar. 25, 1903, no. 76; bought at sale by
Havemeyer for $240; Mr. and Mrs. H. O.
Havemeyer, New York, 1903–7; Mrs.
H. O. Havemeyer, New York, 1907–29;
her sale, American Art Association, New
York, Apr. 10, 1930, no. 15; bought at sale
by A. Rudert (agent) for $175.
REFERENCE: Havemeyer 1931, p. 510.

474
**Andrea del Sarto (Andrea d'Agnolo),
Attributed to**
Italian (Florentine), 1486–1530
MADONNA AND CHILD WITH SAINT
JOHN*
Oil(?) on wood, 35 x 25 in. (88.9 x 63.5 cm)
PROVENANCE: Mr. and Mrs. H. O. Have-
meyer, New York, bought through A. E.
Harnisch in summer 1901 for L 75,000;
until 1907; Mrs. H. O. Havemeyer, New
York, 1907–29; her sale, American Art As-
sociation, New York, Apr. 10, 1930, no.
105; bought at sale by Metropolitan Galler-
ies for $550.
REFERENCES: Havemeyer 1931, p. 494;
Havemeyer 1961, pp. 113, 115, 128;
Weitzenhoffer 1986, pp. 254, 258.

475
Julius Schrader
German, 1815–1900
BARON ALEXANDER VON
HUMBOLDT (1769–1859)***

475

Oil on canvas, 62½ x 54⅜ in.
(158.8 x 138.1 cm)
Signed and dated l.r.: *Julius Schrader.1859.*
PROVENANCE: commissioned from the art-
ist by a member of the Havemeyer family
in 1859; by descent to H. O. Havemeyer,
New York, until Apr. 1889; MMA (Gift of
H. O. Havemeyer, 1889), 89.20.
REFERENCES: Weitzenhoffer 1982, pp. 102f.,
118, n. 13; Weitzenhoffer 1986, p. 55.

476
Sarah C. Sears
American, b. 1858
FLOWERS
Watercolor, 10 x 13¾ in. (25.4 x 34.9 cm)
Signed and dated l.r.: *Sarah C. Sears 1922*
PROVENANCE: Copley Galleries, Boston,
sold to Havemeyer; Mrs. H. O. Have-
meyer, New York, d. 1929; her sale, Ameri-
can Art Association, New York, Apr. 10,
1930, no. 3, for $30.
REFERENCE: Havemeyer 1931, p. 510.

477
Alfred Sisley
British, 1839–1899
BANKS OF THE SEINE, NEAR THE
ISLAND OF SAINT-DENIS
Oil on canvas, 16 x 25¾ in.
(40.6 x 65.4 cm)
Signed l.l.: *Sisley*
PROVENANCE: Durand-Ruel, Paris, bought
from the artist in 1877; Mr. and Mrs. H. O.
Havemeyer, New York, bought from
Durand-Ruel, Jan. 16, 1894; until 1907;
Mrs. H. O. Havemeyer, New York, 1907–
29; her sale, American Art Association,
New York, Apr. 10, 1930, no. 76; bought
at sale by Jonas for $4,500; Edouard
Jonas, Paris, from 1930; Wildenstein and
Co., Paris, bought, Feb. 1977, from a Euro-
pean collector; sold to a European collector
in 1981; Mme J. Carmona, Paris; private
collection, Switzerland; private collection,
Germany.
REFERENCES: Havemeyer 1931, p. 505, as

477

Bords de la Seine; Daulte 1959, no. 48;
Weitzenhoffer 1982, pp. 225, 281, n. 31;
Weitzenhoffer 1986, p. 98, pl. 43.

478

Alfred Sisley
ALLEE OF CHESTNUT TREES
Oil on canvas, 19¾ x 24 in. (50.2 x 61 cm)
Signed and dated l.r.: *Sisley 78*
PROVENANCE: Tadamasa Hayashi, Paris
and Tokyo, d. 1906; his sale, American Art
Association, New York, Jan. 8–9, 1913,
no. 138; bought at sale by Durand-Ruel
for Havemeyer for $2,100; Mrs. H. O.
Havemeyer, New York, 1913–29; her son,
Horace Havemeyer, New York, 1929–48;
consigned to M. Knoedler and Co., New
York, by Havemeyer, Sept. 20, 1948 (stock
no. CA3143); Robert Lehman, Port Wash-
ington, N.Y., bought from Havemeyer
through Knoedler, Nov. 15, 1948, for
$8,000; d. 1969; MMA (Robert Lehman
Collection, 1975), 1975.1.211.
REFERENCES: Havemeyer 1931, p. 427, as
Allée près d'un fleuve; Daulte 1959,
no. 286; Weitzenhoffer 1982, p. 281, n. 31.

479

George Henry Smillie
American, 1840–1921
OAKS NEAR PORTLAND, MAINE
Watercolor, 12 x 21 in. (30.5 x 53.3 cm)
Signed and dated l.r.: *Geo. H. Smillie 1880*
PROVENANCE: Mrs. H. O. Havemeyer, New
York, d. 1929; her sale, American Art Asso-
ciation, New York, Apr. 10, 1930, no. 21;
bought at sale by A. Rudert (agent) for $60.
REFERENCE: Havemeyer 1931, p. 510.

480

Henry Pember Smith
American, 1854–1907
OFF FASTNET LIGHT, IRELAND
Watercolor, 11¼ x 10¾ in. (28.6 x 27.3 cm)
Signed and dated l.r.: *Henry P. Smith 1880*
PROVENANCE: Mrs. H. O. Havemeyer, New
York, d. 1929; her sale, American Art Asso-
ciation, New York, Apr. 10, 1930, no. 10,
for $40.
REFERENCE: Havemeyer 1931, p. 510.

481

**Spanish (Castilian) Painter, Unknown, 17th
century**
HEAD OF A MAN
Oil on canvas, 14 x 10¾ in. (35.6 x 27.3 cm)
Inscribed l.l.: */38*
PROVENANCE: Spanish nobleman (possibly
Benito Garriga or Garriga family, Madrid);
Mr. and Mrs. H. O. Havemeyer, New
York, by 1902*–7; bought for them by
Raimundo de Madrazo through a dealer
called Berringham, as by Velázquez; Mrs.
H. O. Havemeyer, New York, 1907–29;
MMA 29.100.607.

481

*In a letter of 1/26/03, Mary Cassatt men-
tioned to Mrs. Havemeyer a Velázquez
head already in their collection (Cassatt's
description should be compared to that of
Mrs. Havemeyer in her memoirs).
REFERENCES: Havemeyer 1931, p. 54, ill.,
as by José Leonardo; Wehle 1940, p. 242,
ill.; Havemeyer 1958, p. 34, no. 187; Havemeyer 1961, pp. 159f., as by Velázquez;
López-Rey 1963, no. 567, as a fragment,
and questionable owing to condition.

482

Spanish Painter, Unknown, 16th century
SAINT FRANCIS IN ECSTASY
Oil on wood, 21¼ x 17¾ in. (54 x 45.1 cm)
PROVENANCE: Ambassador Gerinen,*
bought in Malines, Belgium; M. J. Rouge-
ron, bought from the ambassador's widow;

Mrs. H. O. Havemeyer, New York, bought
from Rougeron as by van Dyck, about
1924–29; her sale, American Art Association, New York, Apr. 10, 1930, no. 120, as
Saint Francis in Prayer, Spanish school,
early XVII century; bought at sale by
Metropolitan Galleries for $200.
*All information on this collector is taken
from Havemeyer "Notes" [1974] and is
unverified.
REFERENCE: Havemeyer 1931, p. 500, as
Spanish school, XVI century, style of
Morales.

483

A. Stalk
FAN SHAPE***
PROVENANCE: Mr. and Mrs. H. O. Havemeyer, New York, until 1907; consigned to
Durand-Ruel, Sept. 1, 1907 (deposit no.
5100a); Mrs. H. O. Havemeyer, New York,
1907–29.
Note: In a letter of 2/19/32, to Horace
Havemeyer, Durand-Ruel wrote that this
work was still on consignment with it and
asked what should be done with the work,
mentioning that Mrs. Havemeyer had several times asked that it be destroyed. See
also A444.

484

Gilbert Stuart
American, 1755–1828
GEORGE WASHINGTON (1732–1799)***
Oil on canvas, 29⅛ x 24⅛ in. (74 x 61.3 cm)
PROVENANCE: Daniel Carroll, Duddington
Manor, Washington, D.C., from about
1803–49; his daughters, the Misses Car-
roll, at Duddington Manor until 1884,
then on loan to The Corcoran Gallery of
Art until 1888; sent to James T. Swift, Apr.
11, 1888, for examination for possible pur-
chase; H. O. Havemeyer, New York,
bought from the Misses Carroll through
Swift, Apr.–May 1888; MMA (Gift of H. O.
Havemeyer, 1888), 88.18.
EXHIBITION: 1896 New York, no. 167.
REFERENCES: Gardner and Feld 1965,
pp. 92f., ill.; Weitzenhoffer 1982, pp. 82,
95, n. 19; Weitzenhoffer 1986, p. 47.

484

487

485

Justus Sustermans
Flemish, 1597–1681
ELIZABETTA MARTELLI, WIDOW OF
DON HERNANDO RAMIRES DE
MONTALVO

Oil on canvas, 81 x 45 in. (205.7 x 114.3 cm)
PROVENANCE: S.A. Alberigo XII D'Este,
prince of Barbiano; Mrs. H. O. Havemeyer, New York, d. 1929; her sale, American Art Association, New York, Apr. 10,
1930, no. 100, as by Juan de Pareja, Spanish, 1606–1670; bought at sale by J. M.
Hardy for $1,000.
REFERENCE: Havemeyer 1931, p. 498, as
by Justus Sustermans, formerly attributed
to Velázquez and to Juan de Pareja.

486

David Teniers the Younger
Flemish, 1610–1690
THE INN—DRINKERS AND
SMOKERS***
Oil

PROVENANCE: Edouard Warneck, Paris,
until 1889; Durand-Ruel, Paris, bought
from Warneck, Aug. 1, 1889, for Fr 32,000
(stock no. 2401, no title); Mr. and Mrs.
H. O. Havemeyer, New York, bought from
Durand-Ruel, Aug. 1, 1889, for Fr 72,000
with four other paintings; Durand-Ruel,
New York, bought back from Havemeyer,
Jan. 2, 1890, for $6,000 (stock no. 910,
as *L'Estaminet—buveurs et fumeurs*);
Durand-Ruel, Paris, bought from Durand-
Ruel, New York, June 2, 1890.
REFERENCES: Weitzenhoffer 1982, p. 127;
Weitzenhoffer 1986, p. 64.

487

Giovanni Battista Tiepolo
Italian (Venetian), 1696–1770
THE GLORIFICATION OF
FRANCESCO BARBARO***

Oil on canvas, irregular oval, 96 x 183 ¾ in.
(243.8 x 466.7 cm)
PROVENANCE: the Barbaro family, Palazzo
Barbaro, Venice; Marcantonio Barbaro, Pa-
lazzo Barbaro, Venice, until 1860; Elisa
Bassi, Palazzo Barbaro, Venice, 1860–66;
Vicenzo Favenza, Venice, 1866; private col-
lection, France; sale, Hôtel Drouot, Paris,
Feb. 9, 1875, no. 1, for Fr 25,000; Count
Isaac de Camondo, Paris, 1875–93; sale,
Galerie Georges Petit, Paris, Feb. 1, 1893,
no. 25, for Fr 30,000; Camille Groult, Paris,
1893–1908; Manuel de Yturbe, Paris, about
1910; possibly Heilbronner, Paris; Stanford
White, New York, about 1910; Col. Oliver
H. Payne, New York, about 1917; Mrs.
H. O. Havemeyer, New York, until 1923;
MMA (Anonymous Gift, in memory of
Oliver H. Payne, 1923), 23.128.
REFERENCES: Morassi 1962, p. 33; Zeri
and Gardner 1973, pp. 56f., pl. 61 (whole
and detail).

488

Tintoretto (Jacopo Robusti), Workshop of
Italian (Venetian), 1518–1594
DOGE GIROLAMO PRIULI (ca. 1486–
1567)

Oil on canvas, 39 ⅜ x 31 ¹⁵⁄₁₆ in.
(100 x 81.1 cm)
PROVENANCE: S.A.R. la Duchesse de Berri,
Venice; Harrington, Boston; M. J. Rougeron, New York, bought from Harrington's
daughter; Mrs. H. O. Havemeyer, New
York, bought from Rougeron in 1922–29;
her sale, American Art Association, New
York, Apr. 10, 1930, no. 113, as *A Doge*,
by school of Titian; bought at sale by
Valentiner for $400; The Detroit Institute
of Arts, from 1930 (Gift of Dr. Wilhelm R.
Valentiner), 30.300.

488

REFERENCES: Havemeyer 1931, p. 495, as
Portrait of a Doge, attributed to Titian;
Rossi [1974], p. 103, fig. 104, as by
Tintoretto; Weitzenhoffer 1986, pp. 247,
270, n. 38.

489

Titian (Tiziano Vecellio), Style of
Italian (Venetian), 16th century
SAINT CECILIA

Oil on canvas, 41 x 38 ½ in. (104.1 x 97.8 cm)
PROVENANCE: S.A.R. la Duchesse de Berri,
Venice; Harrington, Boston; M. J. Rougeron, New York, bought from Harrington's
daughter; Mrs. H. O. Havemeyer, New
York, bought from Rougeron as by Titian,
in 1922–29; her sale, American Art Association, New York, Apr. 10, 1930, no. 110,
as by a follower of Veronese; bought at
sale by Metropolitan Galleries for $300.
REFERENCE: Havemeyer 1931, p. 495, as
style of Titian, XVI century.

490

Eduardo Tofano
Italian, 1838–1920
REVERIE***

PROVENANCE: possibly Louisine W. Elder
(later Mrs. H. O. Havemeyer), New York,
in 1878.

379

EXHIBITION: 1878 New York, no. 252, as *Reverie*, by Edward Tofano, lent by G. N. Elder.
Note: This work was lent to the 1878 exhibition by "G. N. Elder," the same name under which Louisine Elder lent her Degas *Ballet Rehearsal* (A215).
REFERENCES: Weitzenhoffer 1982, pp. 18f.; Weitzenhoffer 1986, pp. 23, 26.

491
Constant Troyon
French, 1810–1865
LANDSCAPE AT SUNSET
Oil on wood, 13½ x 18 in. (34.3 x 45.7 cm)
Signed and dated l.l.: *C. Troyon 1851*
PROVENANCE: George I. Seney, New York; his sale, American Art Association, New York, Feb. 11–13, 1891, no. 233; bought at sale by Durand-Ruel for Havemeyer for $2,900; Mr. and Mrs. H. O. Havemeyer, New York, 1891–1907; Mrs. H. O. Havemeyer, New York, 1907–29; her sale, American Art Association, New York, Apr. 10, 1930, no. 63; bought at sale by Charles S. McVeigh for $700.
REFERENCES: Havemeyer 1931, p. 506; Weitzenhoffer 1982, pp. 130, 142, n. 14; Weitzenhoffer 1986, p. 65.

492
Constant Troyon
LANDSCAPE WITH CATTLE
Chalk, 12 x 17¾ in. (30.5 x 45.1 cm)
Signed l.r.: *C.T.*
PROVENANCE: Mrs. H. O. Havemeyer, New York, d. 1929; her sale, American Art Association, New York, Apr. 10, 1930, no. 28, for $150.
REFERENCE: Havemeyer 1931, p. 506.

493
Constant Troyon
RETURN FROM MARKET***
PROVENANCE: R. Smit, until 1893; Durand-Ruel, Paris, bought from Smit, Feb. 4, 1893, for Fr 170,000 (stock no. 2634); Mr. and Mrs. H. O. Havemeyer, New York, bought from Durand-Ruel, Feb. 8, 1893.

REFERENCES: Weitzenhoffer 1982, pp. 199, 217, n. 2; Weitzenhoffer 1986, p. 91.

494
Constant Troyon
THE WATER CART***
PROVENANCE: Mr. and Mrs. H. O. Havemeyer, New York, consigned to Durand-Ruel, New York, Jan. 31–May 31, 1899.
EXHIBITION: 1890–91 New York, no. 1.
REFERENCE: Weitzenhoffer 1982, pp. 131f.

495
Dwight W. Tryon
American, 1849–1925
COUNTRY LANDSCAPE
Watercolor, 16¾ x 28¼ in. (42.6 x 71.8 cm)
Signed and dated l.r.: *D.W. Tryon 1887*
PROVENANCE: Mr. and Mrs. H. O. Havemeyer, New York, bought from the artist from the 1889 exhibition for $100; until 1907; Mrs. H. O. Havemeyer, New York, 1907–29; her sale, American Art Association, New York, Apr. 10, 1930, no. 24; bought at sale by Mrs. M. Heyman for $150.
EXHIBITION: 1889 New York Watercolor, no. 372, as *Afternoon*.
REFERENCE: Havemeyer 1931, p. 510.

496
Dwight W. Tryon
CRESCENT MOON
Pastel, 8½ x 10 in. (21.6 x 25.4 cm)
Signed and dated l.l.: *D.W. Tryon 1889*
PROVENANCE: Mrs. H. O. Havemeyer, New York, d. 1929; her sale, American Art Association, New York, Apr. 10, 1930, no. 9, for $130.
REFERENCE: Havemeyer 1931, p. 510.

497
Diego Rodríguez de Silva y Velázquez, Copy after
Spanish, of uncertain date
PHILIP IV (1605–1665), KING OF SPAIN
Oil on canvas, 21 x 17 in. (53.3 x 43.2 cm)
PROVENANCE: J. de Munoz de Ortiz, Va-

lencia; sale, R. Lepke, Berlin, Dec. 12, 1911, no. 83, bought in or withdrawn; until at least 1914; Mrs. H. O. Havemeyer, New York, bought from the Munoz family in 1923/24–29; her sale, American Art Association, New York, Apr. 10, 1930, no. 96, as by Velázquez; bought at sale by J. M. Hardy for $6,100.
EXHIBITION: 1913–14 London, no. 60, as *Portrait of Don Fernando of Austria*, lent by Señor Don José M. Munoz.
REFERENCES: Havemeyer 1931, p. 500, as attributed to Velázquez; López-Rey 1963, no. 233, as copy after Velázquez.

498
Adriaen van de Velde
Dutch, 1636–1672
SWINE SLEEPING
Black chalk on laid paper, 4½ x 6¾ in. (11.4 x 17.2 cm)
Signed l.l.: *Velde fc.*
PROVENANCE: Jacob de Vos, Amsterdam; Mrs. H. O. Havemeyer, New York, d. 1929; MMA 29.100.940.
REFERENCES: Havemeyer 1931, p. 180; Havemeyer 1958, p. 8, no. 30.

499
Louis-Mathieu Verdilhan
French, 1875–1928
THE OLD PORT, MARSEILLE
Oil on canvas, 24 x 28½ in. (61 x 72.4 cm)
Signed foreground: *Verdilhan Mathieu*
PROVENANCE: Kraushaar Galleries, New York, bought from the artist; Mrs. H. O. Havemeyer, New York, bought from Kraushaar; d. 1929; her sale, American Art Association, New York, Apr. 10, 1930, no. 43; bought at sale by Kraushaar for $150; Kraushaar Galleries, New York, 1930–47; sale, Parke-Bernet, New York, Apr. 9–10, 1947, no. 179, for $150.
REFERENCE: Havemeyer 1931, p. 506.

500
Louis-Mathieu Verdilhan
STILL LIFE
Oil on canvas, 35 x 25 in. (88.9 x 63.5 cm)
Signed l.r.: *Verdilhan Mathieu*
PROVENANCE: Kraushaar Galleries, New York, bought from the artist; Mrs. H. O. Havemeyer, New York, bought from Kraushaar; d. 1929; her sale, American Art

Association, New York, Apr. 10, 1930, no. 61; bought at sale by Kraushaar for $100; Kraushaar Galleries, New York, 1930–47; sale, Parke-Bernet, New York, Apr. 9–10, 1947, no. 62, for $60.
REFERENCE: Havemeyer 1931, p. 506.

501
Louis-Mathieu Verdilhan
STILL LIFE
Oil on canvas, 29 x 20 in. (73.7 x 50.8 cm)
Signed l.r.: *Verdilhan Mathieu*
PROVENANCE: Kraushaar Galleries, New York, bought from the artist; Mrs. H. O. Havemeyer, New York, bought from Kraushaar; d. 1929; her sale, American Art Association, New York, Apr. 10, 1930, no. 39; bought at sale by Kraushaar for $100; Kraushaar Galleries, New York, 1930; Mrs. Edwin G. Manning, bought from Kraushaar in 1930.
REFERENCE: Havemeyer 1931, p. 506.

502
Jan Cornelisz. Vermeyen
Dutch, 1500–1559
JEAN DE CARONDELET (1469–1545)
Oil on wood, 30¾ x 24½ in. (78.1 x 62.2 cm)
PROVENANCE: Count Charles Marie-Tanneguy Duchâtel, Paris, from about 1836 or 1846; his daughter, Duchesse de la Trémoïlle, Paris, until 1896; Mr. and Mrs. H. O. Havemeyer, New York, bought from Duc and Duchesse de la Trémoïlle in 1896 for Fr 110,000; until 1907; their son, Horace Havemeyer, New York, 1907–47; The Brooklyn Museum (Gift of Mr. Horace Havemeyer), 47.76.
EXHIBITION: 1866 Paris Industrie.
REFERENCES: Havemeyer 1931, pp. 300f., ill., as by Holbein; Havemeyer 1961, pp. 20, 24, 231; Weitzenhoffer 1982, p. 166, n. 7; Weitzenhoffer 1986, pp. 176, 267, n. 29; Horn 1989, no. A19.

503
Paolo Veronese (Paolo Caliari)
Italian (Venetian), 1528?–1588
BOY WITH A GREYHOUND**

503

Oil on canvas, 68⅜ x 40⅛ in. (173.7 x 101.9 cm)
PROVENANCE: Mr. and Mrs. H. O. Havemeyer, New York, acquired from the Martinengo family, Brescia, through A. E. Harnisch, about 1904; until 1907; Mrs. H. O. Havemeyer, New York, 1907–29; MMA 29.100.105.
REFERENCES: Havemeyer 1931, pp. 10f., ill.; Wehle 1940, p. 206, ill.; Havemeyer 1958, p. 33, no. 185; Havemeyer 1961, pp. 103f., 123–27; Zeri and Gardner 1973, p. 87, pl. 98; Pignatti 1976, no. 109; Weitzenhoffer 1986, pp. 140, 256, pl. 102.

504
Paolo Veronese, Style of
Italian (Venetian), 16th century
PORTRAIT OF A WOMAN**
Oil on canvas, 49 x 37½ in. (124.5 x 95.3 cm)
PROVENANCE: Colleoni, Bergamo; Mrs. H. O. Havemeyer, New York, consigned to Durand-Ruel, Feb. 11–May 31, 1913 (deposit no. 7699), and Nov. 5, 1913–May 29, 1914 (deposit no. 7714, as *Portrait d'un membre de la famille Colleone [Bergame]*, by Veronese); possibly placed on exchange or consignment with Trotti, Paris, by Nov. 1914 until at least Oct.

1917;* d. 1929; her sale, American Art Association, New York, Apr. 10, 1930, no. 116, as *Portrait of a Venetian Lady*, school of Veronese; bought at sale by Weitzner for $450.
*See Chronology, Nov. 14, 1914.
REFERENCES: Havemeyer 1931, p. 495, as *Portrait of a Woman*, style of Veronese, XVI century; Weitzenhoffer 1986, pp. 256, 258.

505
Jehan Georges Vibert
French, 1840–1902
WATERCOLOR***
PROVENANCE: M. Knoedler and Co., New York, until 1877; H. O. Havemeyer, New York, bought from Knoedler, Feb. 21, 1877, for $205.

506
Jacobus Victors
Dutch, 1640–1705
PIGEONS
Oil on canvas, 13¼ x 19 in. (33.7 x 48.3 cm)
PROVENANCE: Marques de la Ensenada y del Buen Retiro, in 1789; Mrs. H. O. Havemeyer, New York, d. 1929; her sale, American Art Association, New York, Apr. 10, 1930, no. 48; bought at sale by W. C. Loring for $375.
REFERENCE: Havemeyer 1931, p. 497, as formerly attributed to Velázquez.

507
Antoine Vollon
French, 1833–1900
INTERIOR WITH STILL LIFE
Oil on canvas, 24 x 19½ in. (61 x 49.5 cm)
Signed l.l., with dedication: *A. Vollon*
PROVENANCE: Mrs. H. O. Havemeyer, New York, d. 1929; her sale, American Art Association, New York, Apr. 10, 1930, no. 40; bought at sale by Dale for $250; Chester Dale, New York, from 1930.
REFERENCE: Havemeyer 1931, p. 506.

508
Jean Antoine Watteau, Style of
French, 18th century
MASQUERADE
Oil on canvas, 14 x 11¾ in. (35.6 x 29.9 cm)
PROVENANCE: Edouard Warneck, Paris,
until 1890; Durand-Ruel, Paris, received
on deposit from Warneck, June 13, 1890
(deposit no. 7128, as *Divertissement*);
bought from him, Oct. 4, 1890, for
Fr 25,000 (stock no. 661); Durand-Ruel,
New York, bought from Durand-Ruel, Paris,
Oct. 4, 1890 (stock no. 1062, as *Comé-
diens*); Mr. and Mrs. H. O. Havemeyer,
New York, bought from Durand-Ruel,
Nov. 29, 1890, for $8,000; until 1907;
Mrs. H. O. Havemeyer, New York, 1907–
29; her sale, American Art Association,
New York, Apr. 10, 1930, no. 57, as *Mas-
querade*, French school, XVIII century;
bought at sale by Samuel Schepps for $600.
REFERENCES: Havemeyer 1931, p. 506, as
La Comédie Italienne, style of Watteau,
XVIII century; Weitzenhoffer 1982,
pp. 128, 141, n. 8; Weitzenhoffer 1986,
p. 64.

509
Julian Alden Weir
American, 1852–1919
FRUIT
Oil on canvas, 21⅛ x 17⅛ in.
(53.7 x 43.5 cm)
PROVENANCE: sale of works by J. Alden
Weir, Ortgies, New York, Feb. 7, 1889,

no. 75; bought at sale by Clarke for $130;
Thomas B. Clarke, New York, 1889–99;
his sale, American Art Association, New
York, Feb. 14–18, 1899, no. 75; bought at
sale by Cottier for $300; James S. Inglis
(president of Cottier and Co.), New York,
1899–1908; his sale, American Art Association, New York, Mar. 10, 1910, no. 101;
bought at sale by Durand-Ruel for Havemeyer for $325; Mrs. H. O. Havemeyer, New
York, 1910–29; her sale, American Art Association, New York, Apr. 10, 1930,
no. 61; bought at sale by Weir for $600;
the artist's daughter, Dorothy Weir, New
York and Ridgefield, Conn., 1930–about
1948; her husband, Mahonri M. Young,
New York and Ridgefield, Conn., about
1948–57; Brigham Young University,
Provo, Utah, bought from Young estate
through M. Knoedler and Co., after 1958;
until about 1972; private collection, Salt
Lake City, bought from a Salt Lake City
dealer; Peter H. Davidson and Co., bought
from the private collection, Salt Lake City;
MMA, bought from Davidson in 1980 for
$27,500 (Purchase, Gift of Robert E. Tod,
by exchange, 1980), 1980.219.
EXHIBITIONS: 1891 New York, no. 32;
1891 Philadelphia, no. 189; 1892 New
York Union, no. 70; 1924 New York,
no. 18, lent anonymously.
REFERENCE: Havemeyer 1931, p. 511.

510
Julian Alden Weir
THE QUAY
Chalk, 10½ x 13¾ in. (26.7 x 34.9 cm)
Signed l.l.: *J. Alden Weir*
PROVENANCE: Mrs. H. O. Havemeyer,
New York, d. 1929; her sale, American Art
Association, New York, Apr. 10, 1930,
no. 22, for $100.
REFERENCE: Havemeyer 1931, p. 511.

511
James Abbott McNeill Whistler
American, 1834–1903
CAMPO S. MARTA: WINTER EVENING
Crayon and pastel on brown paper,
8³⁄₁₆ x 11 in. (20.8 x 27.9 cm)
Signed l.r. with butterfly
PROVENANCE: Louisine Elder (later Mrs.
H. O. Havemeyer), New York, bought
from the artist, summer 1881, for £30 for
the set of 5; until 1917; Charles Lang
Freer, Detroit, received from Havemeyer,
Jan. 1917; d. 1919; Freer Gallery of Art,
Smithsonian Institution, Washington, D.C.,
from 1919, 17.7.
EXHIBITION: 1881 London, no. 51, as
Campo Sta. Martin—Winter Evening,
marked for sale for 30 guineas.
REFERENCES: Havemeyer 1931, p. 295;
Havemeyer 1961, pp. 204–9; Weitzen-

hoffer 1982, pp. 17f., 30, n. 21, pp. 45,
100; Weitzenhoffer 1986, pp. 23, 34, 54,
259, nn. 14, 16.

512
James Abbott McNeill Whistler
THE GREEK SLAVE GIRL
Pastel on brown paper, 10¼ x 7⅛ in.
(26 x 18.1 cm)
Signed with butterfly
PROVENANCE: H. Wunderlich and Co.,
New York, until 1889; Mr. and Mrs. H. O.
Havemeyer, New York, bought from Wun-
derlich, Mar. 1889; until 1907; Mrs. H. O.
Havemeyer, New York, 1907–29; her
daughter Electra Havemeyer Webb, New
York, 1929–60; Shelburne Museum, Shel-
burne, Vt., from 1960, 27.3.1–40.
EXHIBITIONS: 1886 London, probably
no. 21, as *Variations in Violet and Rose*;
1889 New York, no. 46, as *Pink & Violet*;
1904 Boston, no. 124, as *Greek Girl*, lent
by H. O. Havemeyer, Esq.
REFERENCES: Havemeyer 1931, p. 438, as
Greek Girl; Weitzenhoffer 1982, p. 101,
fig. 15; Weitzenhoffer 1986, pp. 55, 159,
pl. 13.

513
James Abbott McNeill Whistler
GREY AND GREEN
Watercolor, 4⅝ x 8¼ in. (11.8 x 21 cm)
Signed with butterfly
PROVENANCE: H. Wunderlich and Co.,
New York, until 1889; Mr. and Mrs. H. O.
Havemeyer, New York, bought from Wun-
derlich, Mar. 1889; until 1907; Mrs. H. O.
Havemeyer, New York, 1907–29; her
daughter Adaline Havemeyer Freling-
huysen, Morristown, N.J., from 1929.
EXHIBITION: 1889 New York, no. 36, as
Grey and Green—Dortrecht [sic].
REFERENCES: Havemeyer 1931, p. 439;
Weitzenhoffer 1982, pp. 101, 118, n. 10;
Weitzenhoffer 1986, p. 55.

514
James Abbott McNeill Whistler
GREY AND SILVER
Watercolor, 4¼ x 7⅞ in. (10.8 x 20 cm)
Signed l.r. with butterfly
PROVENANCE: probably H. Wunderlich and
Co., New York; Mr. and Mrs. H. O. Have-
meyer, New York, probably bought from
Wunderlich, Mar. 1889; until 1907; Mrs.
H. O. Havemeyer, New York, 1907–29;
her daughter Adaline Havemeyer Freling-
huysen, Morristown, N.J., 1929–63; pri-
vate collection.
EXHIBITION: 1889 New York, no. 8, as
Grey and Silver—the Beach—Holland(?).
REFERENCES: Havemeyer 1931, p. 439;
Weitzenhoffer 1982, pp. 101, 118,
n. 10(?); Weitzenhoffer 1986, p. 55(?).

515
James Abbott McNeill Whistler
MARINE
Gouache and watercolor, 4¾ x 8⅛ in.
(12.1 x 20.6 cm)
Signed l.l. with butterfly
PROVENANCE: probably H. Wunderlich and
Co., New York; Mr. and Mrs. H. O. Have-
meyer, New York, probably bought from
Wunderlich, Mar. 1889; until 1907; Mrs.
H. O. Havemeyer, New York, 1907–29;
her daughter Adaline Havemeyer Freling-
huysen, Morristown, N.J., from 1929; pri-
vate collection.
EXHIBITION: 1889 New York, no. 24, as
Grey and Green—Cornwall(?).
REFERENCES: Havemeyer 1931, p. 439;
Weitzenhoffer 1982, pp. 101, 118, n. 10(?);
Weitzenhoffer 1986, p. 55(?).

516
James Abbott McNeill Whistler
NOCTURNE: SAN GIORGIO
Chalk and pastel on gray paper,
8 x 11⅞ in. (20.3 x 30.2 cm)
Signed l.r. with butterfly
PROVENANCE: Louisine Elder (later Mrs.
H. O. Havemeyer), New York, bought
from the artist, summer 1881, for £30 for
the set of 5; until 1917; Charles Lang
Freer, Detroit, received from Havemeyer,
Jan. 1917; d. 1919; Freer Gallery of Art,
Smithsonian Institution, Washington, D.C.,
from 1919, 17.6.
EXHIBITION: 1881 London, no. 18, as
Nocturne—San Giorgio, marked for sale
for 30 guineas.
REFERENCES: Havemeyer 1931, p. 295;
Havemeyer 1961, pp. 204–9; Weitzen-
hoffer 1982, pp. 17f., 30, n. 21, pp. 45,
100; Weitzenhoffer 1986, pp. 23, 34, 54,
259, nn. 14, 16.

517
James Abbott McNeill Whistler
THE STEPS
Crayon and pastel on gray paper,
7⅝ x 11⅞ in. (19.4 x 30.2 cm)
Signed r. with butterfly
PROVENANCE: Louisine Elder (later Mrs.
H. O. Havemeyer), New York, bought
from the artist, summer 1881, for £30 for
the set of 5; until 1917; Charles Lang
Freer, Detroit, received from Havemeyer,
Jan. 1917; d. 1919; Freer Gallery of Art,
Smithsonian Institution, Washington, D.C.,
from 1919, 17.4.
EXHIBITION: 1881 London, no. 23, as
The Steps, marked for sale for 30 guineas.
REFERENCES: Havemeyer 1931, p. 295;
Havemeyer 1961, pp. 204–9; Weitzen-
hoffer 1982, pp. 17f., 30, n. 21, pp. 45,
100; Weitzenhoffer 1986, pp. 23, 34, 54,
259, nn. 14, 16, colorpl. 4.

511

517

512

518

514

519

515

516

520

518

James Abbott McNeill Whistler
WHITE AND PINK (THE PALACE)
Pastel on paper, 7¾ x 12 in.
(19.7 x 30.5 cm)
Signed r. with butterfly
PROVENANCE: Mr. and Mrs. H. O. Have-
meyer, New York, by 1904–7; Mrs. H. O.
Havemeyer, New York, 1907–29; her
daughter Adaline Havemeyer Freling-
huysen, Morristown, N.J., from 1929;
private collection.
EXHIBITIONS: 1881 London, no. 15; 1904
Boston, no. 123, as *The Palace—Pink and
White*, lent by H. O. Havemeyer, Esq.
REFERENCES: Havemeyer 1931, p. 439;
Weitzenhoffer 1986, p. 159.

519

James Abbott McNeill Whistler
SUNSET IN RED AND BROWN
Chalk and pastel on brown paper, 11⅞ x
8 in. (30.2 x 20.3 cm)
Signed l.r. with butterfly
PROVENANCE: Louisine Elder (later Mrs.
H. O. Havemeyer), New York, bought
from the artist, summer 1881, for £30 for
the set of 5; until 1917; Charles Lang
Freer, Detroit, received from Havemeyer,
Jan. 1917; d. 1919; Freer Gallery of Art,
Smithsonian Institution, Washington, D.C.,
from 1919, 17.8.
EXHIBITION: 1881 London, no. 25,
marked for sale for 20 guineas.
REFERENCES: Havemeyer 1931, p. 295;
Havemeyer 1961, pp. 204–9; Weitzen-
hoffer 1982, pp. 17f., 30, n. 21, pp. 45,
100; Weitzenhoffer 1986, pp. 23, 34, 54,
259, ns. 14, 16.

520

James Abbott McNeill Whistler
WINTER EVENING
Crayon and pastel on gray paper,
11¹³⁄₁₆ x 7¹⁵⁄₁₆ in. (30 x 20.2 cm)
Signed l.l. with butterfly
PROVENANCE: Louisine Elder (later Mrs.
H. O. Havemeyer), New York, bought
from the artist, summer 1881, for £30 for
the set of 5; until 1917; Charles Lang
Freer, Detroit, received from Havemeyer,
Jan. 1917; d. 1919; Freer Gallery of Art,

Smithsonian Institution, Washington, D.C.,
from 1919, 17.5.
EXHIBITION: 1881 London, no. 50, as
Winter Evening, marked for sale for 25
guineas.
REFERENCES: Havemeyer 1931, p. 295;
Havemeyer 1961, pp. 204–9; Weitzenhoffer 1982, pp. 17f., 30, n. 21, pp. 45,
100; Weitzenhoffer 1986, pp. 23, 34, 54,
259, nn. 14, 16.

521

James Abbott McNeill Whistler
WINTER LANDSCAPE
Watercolor, 10 x 7¼ in. (25.4 x 18.4 cm)
Signed with butterfly
PROVENANCE: Mrs. H. O. Havemeyer,
New York, d. 1929; her daughter Adaline
Havemeyer Frelinghuysen, Morristown,
N.J., from 1929.
REFERENCE: Havemeyer 1931, p. 439.

522

Carleton Wiggins
American, 1848–1932
LANDSCAPE
Watercolor, 11 x 15 in. (27.9 x 38.1 cm)
Signed l.l.: *Carleton Wiggins*
PROVENANCE: Mr. and Mrs. H. O. Havemeyer, New York, bought from the artist
from the 1889 exhibition for $35; until
1907; Mrs. H. O. Havemeyer, New York,
1907–29; her sale, American Art Association, New York, Apr. 10, 1930, no. 12;
bought at sale by Charles Henry for $80.
EXHIBITION: 1889 New York Watercolor,
probably no. 293, as *Plains of Meudon*.
REFERENCE: Havemeyer 1931, p. 511.

523

Carleton Wiggins
NEAR FONTAINEBLEAU
Watercolor, 15½ x 21½ in. (39.4 x 54.6 cm)
Signed l.l.: *Carleton Wiggins*
PROVENANCE: Mr. and Mrs. H. O. Havemeyer, New York, bought from the artist
from the 1889 exhibition for $200; until
1907; Mrs. H. O. Havemeyer, New York,
1907–29; her sale, American Art Association, New York, Apr. 10, 1930, no. 18;
bought at sale by A. Rudert (agent) for $60.

EXHIBITION: 1889 New York Watercolor,
no. 333.
REFERENCE: Havemeyer 1931, p. 511.

524

Félix Ziem
French, 1821–1911
CANAL IN HOLLAND
Oil on canvas, 27 x 41¼ in.
(68.6 x 104.8 cm)
Signed: *Ziem*
PROVENANCE: E. Secrétan, Paris; his sale,
Galerie Charles Sedelmeyer, Paris, July 1,
1889, no. 83; bought at sale by Durand-
Ruel for Havemeyer for Fr 20,500 (stock
no. 2388); Mr. and Mrs. H. O. Havemeyer,
New York, 1889–1907; Mrs. H. O. Have-
meyer, New York, 1907–29; her daughter
Adaline Havemeyer Frelinghuysen, Morris-
town, N.J., from 1929; private collection;
sale, Sotheby's, New York, Oct. 3, 1975,
no. 159, not sold; sale, Sotheby's, New
York, May 14, 1976, no. 282, as *Canal
Scene*; bought at sale by Karr for $2,500;
Mr. and Mrs. Bernard Karr, New York,
from 1976.
EXHIBITION: 1890–91 New York, no. 12.
REFERENCES: Havemeyer 1931, p. 428;
Miquel 1978, no. 1271; Weitzenhoffer 1982,
pp. 108f., 119, n. 23, pp. 131f.; Weitzenhoffer 1986, p. 58.

525

Félix Ziem
VENICE***
PROVENANCE: N. L. Lepke, Berlin, until
1880; M. Knoedler and Co., New York,
bought from Lepke, Aug. 11, 1880, for
DM 2,500 (stock no. 2559); H. O. Have-
meyer, New York, bought from Knoedler,
Apr. 1, 1882, for $875.

Selected Bibliography

Adhémar, Jean. "Before the Degas Bronzes." *Art News* 54 (November 1955), pp. 34–35, 70.

Artistic Houses, Being a Series of Interior Views of a Number of the Most Beautiful and Celebrated Homes in the United States. 2 vols. New York, 1883–84.

Baccheschi 1973
Baccheschi, Edi. *L'Opera completa del Bronzino.* Milan, 1973.

Ballu, Roger. *L'Oeuvre de Barye.* Paris, 1890.

Barnes, Albert C. "How to Judge a Painting." *Arts and Decoration* 5 (April 1915), pp. 217–20, 246, 248–50.

Bauch, Kurt. *Rembrandt: Gemälde.* Berlin, 1966.

Bazin 1990
Bazin, Germain. *Théodore Gericault: Etude critique, documents et catalogue raisonné.* Vol. 4. Paris, 1990.

Bean, Jacob. *100 European Drawings in The Metropolitan Museum of Art.* New York, 1964.

Beattie, May H. *Carpets of Central Persia.* London, 1976.

Benesch 1973
Benesch, Otto. *The Drawings of Rembrandt.* Enlarged and edited by Eva Benesch. 6 vols. London, 1973.

Benge, Glenn F. *Antoine-Louis Barye, Sculptor of Romantic Realism.* University Park, Pa., 1984.

Bergman, Sidney M. "Azeez Khayat (1875–1943): A Noted Collector of Ancient Glass." *Carnegie Magazine* 48 (June 1974), pp. 238–44.

Beruete y Moret, Aureliano de. *Goya as Portrait Painter.* 2nd ed. New York and Boston, 1922.

Biddle, George. "Some Memories of Mary Cassatt." *The Arts* 10 (August 1926), pp. 107–11.

Bing, S. "Artistic America," trans. of the 1895 French version, "La Culture artistique en Amérique," by Benita Eisler. In *Artistic America, Tiffany Glass, and Art Nouveau*, intro. by Robert Koch, pp. 12–191. Cambridge, Mass., and London, 1970.

Blankert 1978
Blankert, Albert. *Vermeer of Delft: Complete Edition of the Paintings.* Oxford, 1978.

Blunt 1966
Blunt, Anthony. *The Paintings of Nicolas Poussin.* London, 1966.

Boggs et al. 1988
Boggs, Jean Sutherland, et al. *Degas.* Exh. cat., MMA. New York, 1988.

B[osch] R[eitz], S. C. "The Magnolia Screen by Koyetsu." *Bulletin of The Metropolitan Museum of Art* 11 (January 1916), pp. 10–12.

B[reck], J[oseph]. "Sculptures by Degas on Loan." *Bulletin of The Metropolitan Museum of Art* 18 (March 1923), p. 59.

Bredius/Gerson 1969
Bredius, A. *Rembrandt: The Complete Edition of the Paintings.* 3rd ed. Revised by H. Gerson. London, 1969.

Breeskin 1948
Breeskin, Adelyn D. *The Graphic Work of Mary Cassatt: A Catalogue Raisonné.* New York, 1948.

Breeskin 1970
Breeskin, Adelyn Dohme. *Mary Cassatt: A Catalogue Raisonné of the Oils, Pastels, Watercolors, and Drawings.* Washington, D.C., 1970.

Brimo, René. *L'Evolution du goût aux Etats-Unis.* Paris, 1938.

Brown, Jonathan, et al. *El Greco of Toledo.* Exh. cat., Toledo Museum of Art. Boston, 1982.

Brown, Jonathan, and Dawson A. Carr. "Portrait of a Cardinal: Niño de Guevara or Sandoval y Rojas?" *Studies in the History of Art* 11 (National Gallery, Washington, D.C., 1982), pp. 33–42.

Bruyn et al. 1982–89
Bruyn, J., et al. *A Corpus of Rembrandt Paintings.* 3 vols. The Hague and Dordrecht, 1982–89.

Burke, Doreen Bolger, et al. *In Pursuit of Beauty: Americans and the Aesthetic Movement.* Exh. cat., MMA. New York, 1986.

Burnett, Robert N. "Henry Osborne Havemeyer." *Cosmopolitan* 34 (April 1903), pp. 701–4.

B[urroughs], B[ryson]. "Loan Exhibition of the Arts of the Italian Renaissance." *Bulletin of The Metropolitan Museum of Art* 18 (May 1923), pp. 107–10.

Burroughs, Bryson. "Un Portrait inédit attribué à Hugo van der Goes." In *Mélanges Hulin de Loo*, pp. 71–73. Brussels and Paris, 1931.

Catlin, Daniel, Jr. *Good Work, Well Done: The Sugar Business Career of Horace Havemeyer, 1903–1956.* New York, 1988.

C[larke], T[homas] B. "The Havemeyer Collections." *American Art News* 6 (December 21, 1907), p. 4.

Cohen, Warren J. *East Asian Art and American Culture.* New York, 1992.

Constable, William George. *Art Collecting in the United States of America*. London, 1964.

Cortissoz, Royal. "M. Degas and Miss Cassatt: Types Once Revolutionary Which Now Seem Almost Classical." *New York Tribune*, April 4, 1915, p. 3.

Cossío, Manuel B. *El Greco*. Edited by Natalia Cossío de Jiménez. Barcelona, 1972.

Craven, Wayne. "Samuel Colman (1832–1920): Rediscovered Painter of Far-Away Places." *American Art Journal* 8 (May 1976), pp. 16–37.

Dam, Peter van. "Wakai Kenzaburo, the Connoisseur." *Andon* 5 (1985), pp. 35–41.

Daulte 1959
Daulte, François. *Alfred Sisley: Catalogue raisonné de l'oeuvre peint*. Lausanne, 1959.

Daulte 1971
Daulte, François. *Auguste Renoir: Catalogue raisonné de l'oeuvre peint*. Lausanne, 1971.

Dimand, Maurice S. "The Horace Havemeyer Bequest of Islamic Art." *Metropolitan Museum of Art Bulletin* 15 (May 1957), pp. 208–12.

Dimand, M. S., and Jean Mailey. *Oriental Rugs in The Metropolitan Museum of Art*. New York, 1973.

Eisen, Gustavus Augustus, and Fahim Kouchakji. *Glass, its Origin, History, Chronology, Technic and Classification to the Sixteenth Century*. 2 vols. New York, 1927.

The Estate of Mrs. H. O. Havemeyer: [Part I] Oil Paintings. Sale cat. American Art Association, Anderson Galleries, New York, April 10, 1930.

The Estate of Mrs. H. O. Havemeyer: [Part II] Roman, Syrian, & Egyptian Glass, Hispano-Moresque Lustre Ware, Mohammedan Pottery and Italian Majolica, Fine Rugs. Sale cat. American Art Association, Anderson Galleries, New York, April 10–12, 1930.

The Estate of Mrs. H. O. Havemeyer: [Part III] Japanese & Chinese Art. Sale cat. American Art Association, Anderson Galleries, New York, April 14–19, 1930.

Etchings and English Sporting Prints with Other Prints in Color Together with a Fine Group of Rowlandson Drawings from the Estate of Mrs. H. O. Havemeyer and Other Owners. Sale cat. American Art Association, Anderson Galleries, New York, April 16, 17, 1930.

"The Exhibition of the H. O. Havemeyer Collection." *Bulletin of The Metropolitan Museum of Art* 25 (March 1930), pp. 54–76.

Failing, Patricia. "The Degas Bronzes Degas Never Knew." *Art News* 78 (April 1979), pp. 38–41.

Failing, Patricia. "Cast in Bronze: The Degas Dilemma." *Art News* 87 (January 1988), pp. 136–41.

Faude, Wilson H. "Associated Artists and the American Renaissance in the Decorative Arts." *Winterthur Portfolio* 10 (1976), pp. 101–30.

Faxon, Alicia. "Painter and Patron: Collaboration of Mary Cassatt and Louisine Havemeyer." *Woman's Art Journal* 2 (Fall 1982/Winter 1983), pp. 15–20.

Fenollosa, Ernest. *Epochs of Chinese and Japanese Art*. 2 vols. London, 1912.

Fernier 1977–78
Fernier, Robert. *La Vie et l'oeuvre de Gustave Courbet: Catalogue raisonné*. 2 vols. Lausanne and Paris, 1977–78.

"The Fine Arts: The French Impressionists." *The Critic* 5 (April 17, 1886), pp. 195–96.

Fink, Lois Marie. "French Art in the United States, 1850–1870, Three Dealers and Collectors." *Gazette des Beaux-Arts* 92 (September 1978), pp. 87–100.

Fong, Wen, and Maxwell K. Hearn. "Silent Poetry: Chinese Paintings in the Douglas Dillon Galleries." *Metropolitan Museum of Art Bulletin* 39 (Winter 1981/82), pp. 4–80.

Frelinghuysen, Alice Cooney. "Aesthetic Forms in Ceramics and Glass." In *In Pursuit of Beauty: Americans and the Aesthetic Movement*, by Doreen Bolger Burke et al., pp. 199–229. Exh. cat., MMA. New York, 1986.

Friedländer 1969
Friedländer, Max J. *Early Netherlandish Painting*. Vol. 4, *Hugo van der Goes*. New York, 1969.

Friedländer and Rosenberg 1978
Friedländer, Max J., and Jakob Rosenberg. *The Paintings of Lucas Cranach*. Rev. ed. Ithaca, N.Y., 1978.

Furnishings and Decorations from the Estate of Mrs. H. O. Havemeyer, on the premises, 1 East 66th Street. Sale cat. American Art Association, Anderson Galleries, New York, April 22, 1930.

Gardner and Feld 1965
Gardner, Albert Ten Eyck, and Stuart P. Feld. *American Paintings: A Catalogue of the Collection of The Metropolitan Museum of Art*. Vol. 1, *Painters Born by 1815*. New York, 1965.

Garlick 1989
Garlick, Kenneth. *Sir Thomas Lawrence: A Complete Catalogue of the Oil Paintings*. Oxford, 1989.

Gassier and Wilson 1971
Gassier, Pierre, and Juliet Wilson. *The Life and Complete Work of Francisco Goya, with a Catalogue Raisonné of the Paintings, Drawings, and Engravings*. Rev. ed. New York, 1971.

Gonse, Louis. *L'Art Japonais*. 2 vols. Paris, 1883.

Grisebach 1974
Grisebach, Lucius. *Willem Kalf: 1619–1693*. Berlin, 1974.

Grose, David Frederick. *Early Ancient Glass*. New York, 1989.

Gsell, Paul. "Edgar Degas, Statuaire." *La Renaissance de l'art français et des industries de luxe* 1 (December 1918), pp. 373–78.

Gudlaugsson 1959
Gudlaugsson, Sturla Jonasson. *Gerard ter Borch*. 2 vols. The Hague, 1959–60.

Guiffrey [1907]
Guiffrey, Jean. "Catalogue raisonné de l'oeuvre peint et dessiné de J.-B. Siméon Chardin." In *J.-B. Siméon Chardin*, by Armand Dayot. Paris [1907].

Guiffrey 1924
Guiffrey, Jean. *L'Oeuvre de Pierre-Paul Prud'hon*. Archives de l'art français, vol. 13. Paris, 1924.

Hall, Helen. *Hill-Stead Museum House Guide*. Farmington, Conn., 1988.

Hart, Ernest. "Ritsuō et son école." *Le Japon Artistique* 11 (1889).

Havemeyer, Louisine. Remarks on Edgar Degas and Mary Cassatt. Speech read at M. Knoedler and Co., New York, April 6, 1915.

Havemeyer 1922a
Havemeyer, Louisine W. "The Suffrage Torch: Memories of a Militant." *Scribner's Magazine* 71 (May 1922), pp. 528–39.

Havemeyer 1922b
Havemeyer, Louisine W. "The Prison Special: Memories of a Militant." *Scribner's Magazine* 71 (June 1922), pp. 661–76.

Havemeyer, Louisine W. "The Freer Museum of Oriental Art, with Personal Recollections of the Donor." *Scribner's Magazine* 73 (May 1923), pp. 529–40.

Havemeyer, Louisine W. "Mary Cassatt." *The Pennsylvania Museum Bulletin* 22 (May 1927), pp. 377–82.

Havemeyer 1930
The H. O. Havemeyer Collection: A Catalogue of the Temporary Exhibition. Exh. cat., MMA. New York, 1930.

Havemeyer 1931
H. O. Havemeyer Collection: Catalogue of Paintings, Prints, Sculpture and Objects of Art. Portland, Me., 1931.

Havemeyer 1944
Havemeyer, Henry O. *Biographical Record of the Havemeyer Family (1600–1943), More Particularly the Descendants of Frederick Christian Havemeyer (1774–1841) and Their Sugar Refining Interests*. New York, 1944.

Havemeyer 1958
The H. O. Havemeyer Collection: The Metropolitan Museum of Art. 2nd ed. New York, 1958.

Havemeyer 1961
Havemeyer, Louisine W. *Sixteen to Sixty: Memoirs of a Collector*. New York, 1961.

Havemeyer "Notes" [1974]
Havemeyer, Louisine. "Notes to Her Children." Typescript [1974]. MMA Archives.

Held 1980
Held, Julius S. *The Oil Sketches of Peter Paul Rubens: A Critical Catalogue*. Princeton, N.J., 1980.

Hellebranth 1976
Hellebranth, Robert. *Charles-François Daubigny, 1817–1878*. Morges, France, 1976.

Hofstede de Groot 1907–27
Hofstede de Groot, C. *A Catalogue Raisonné of the Works of the Most Eminent Dutch Painters of the Seventeenth Century*. 8 vols. London, 1907–27.

Horn 1989
Horn, Hendrik J. *Jan Cornelisz Vermeyen*. 2 vols. Doornspijk, 1989.

Hosley, William. *The Japan Idea: Art and Life in Victorian America*. Exh. cat., The Wadsworth Atheneum. Hartford, 1990.

[Interview]. *Sun*, August 21, 1895. Reprinted as "Raffaëlli on American Art." *Collector* 6 (September 1, 1895), pp. 294–95.

Jenkins, Marilyn. "Early Medieval Islamic Pottery: The Eleventh Century Reconsidered." *Muqarnas* 9 (forthcoming).

Johnson 1986
Johnson, Lee. *The Paintings of Eugène Delacroix: A Critical Catalogue*. Vols. 3 and 4. Oxford, 1986.

Johnson, Marilynn. "The Artful Interior." In *In Pursuit of Beauty: Americans and the Aesthetic Movement*, by Doreen Bolger Burke et al., pp. 110–41. Exh. cat., MMA. New York, 1986.

Junior League of Greenwich. *The Great Estates: Greenwich, Connecticut, 1880–1930*. Canaan, N.H., 1986.

Kelekian, Dikran Khan. *The Potteries of Persia: Being a Brief History of the Art of Ceramics in the Near East*. Paris, 1909.

Kelekian, Dikran Khan. *The Kelekian Collection of Persian and Analogous Potteries, 1885–1910*. Paris, 1910

Kennedy, Edward G. *The Etched Work of Whistler*. New York, 1910.

M. Knoedler and Co. *Loan Exhibition of Paintings by El Greco and Goya* (Benefit for the American Women War Relief Fund and the Belgian Relief Fund). Exh. cat. New York, 1912.

M. Knoedler and Co. *Loan Exhibition of Masterpieces by Old and Modern Painters* (Benefit for the Women's Political Union). Exh. cat. New York, 1915.

Larsen 1988
Larsen, Erik. *The Paintings of Anthony van Dyck*. Freren, Germany, 1988.

Lemoisne, Paul-André. "Les Statuettes de Degas." *Art et Décoration* 36 (July–August 1919), pp. 109–17.

Lemoisne 1946
Lemoisne, P. A. *Degas et son oeuvre*. 4 vols. Paris, 1946.

Liedtke 1984
Liedtke, Walter A. *Flemish Paintings in The Metropolitan Museum of Art*. 2 vols. New York, 1984.

Liedtke, Walter. "Dutch Paintings in America: The Collectors and Their Ideals." In *Great Dutch Paintings from America*, pp. 14–59. Exh. cat., Mauritshuis. The Hague, 1990.

López-Rey 1963
López-Rey, José. *Velázquez: A Catalogue Raisonné of His Oeuvre*. London, 1963.

McCabe, James D. *The Illustrated History of the Centennial Exhibition*. 1876. Reprint. Philadelphia, 1975.

McKean, Hugh F. *The "Lost" Treasures of Louis Comfort Tiffany*. New York, 1980.

Maison 1968
Maison, K. E. *Honoré Daumier: Catalogue Raisonné of the Paintings, Watercolours and Drawings*. 2 vols. Greenwich, Conn., 1968.

Marks, Montague. "My Note Book." *Art Amateur* 29 (September 1893).

Mather, Frank Jewett, Jr. "The Havemeyer Pictures." *The Arts* 16 (March 1930), pp. 444–83.

Mathews 1984
Mathews, Nancy Mowll, ed. *Cassatt and Her Circle: Selected Letters*. New York, 1984.

Mathews, Nancy Mowll, and Barbara Stern Shapiro. *Mary Cassatt: The Color Prints.* Exh. cat., Williams College Museum of Art. Williamstown, Mass., 1989.

Mayor, A. Hyatt. "The Gifts That Made the Museum." *Metropolitan Museum of Art Bulletin* 16 (November 1957), pp. 85–107.

Meech, Julia, and Gabriel Weisberg. *Japonisme Comes to America: The Japanese Impact on the Graphic Arts 1876–1925.* New York, 1990.

Meech-Pekarik, Julia. "Early Collectors of Japanese Prints and The Metropolitan Museum of Art." *Metropolitan Museum Journal* 17 (1982), pp. 93–118.

The Metropolitan Museum of Art. *Loan Exhibition of the Works of Gustave Courbet.* Exh. cat. New York, 1919.

MMA 1983
The Metropolitan Museum of Art. *Manet: 1832–1883.* Exh. cat. New York, 1983.

Miquel 1978
Miquel, Pierre. *Félix Ziem: 1821–1911.* 2 vols. Maurs-la-Jolie, France, 1978.

Mirviss, Joan B. "Jewels of *Ukiyo-e*: Hayashi's *Spring Rain Collection* of *Surimono* Albums." *Orientations* 20 (February 1989), pp. 26–37.

"Modern American Residences." *Architectural Record* 1 (January–March 1892), n.p.

Montezuma. "My Note Book." *Art Amateur* 22 (May 1890), pp. 112–13.

Morassi 1962
Morassi, Antonio. *A Complete Catalogue of the Paintings of G. B. Tiepolo.* London, 1962.

Mosby 1977
Mosby, Dewey. *Alexandre-Gabriel Decamps, 1803–1860.* 2 vols. New York, 1977.

Naef 1977–80
Naef, Hans. *Die Bildniszeichnungen von J.-A.-D. Ingres.* 5 vols. Bern, 1977–80.

Norton, Thomas E. *100 Years of Collecting in America: The Story of Sotheby Parke Bernet.* New York, 1984.

Pantazzi, Michael. "The First Monotypes." In *Degas*, by Jean Sutherland Boggs et al., pp. 257–60. Exh. cat., MMA. New York, 1988.

Pignatti 1976
Pignatti, Terisio. *Veronese.* 2 vols. Venice, 1976.

Pingeot 1991
Pingeot, Anne. *Degas Sculptures.* Paris, 1991.

Pissarro and Venturi 1939
Pissarro, Ludovic Rodo, and Lionello Venturi. *Camille Pissarro: Son art, son oeuvre.* 2 vols. Paris, 1939.

Pivar 1974
Pivar, Stuart. *The Barye Bronzes: A Catalogue Raisonné.* 2nd ed. Woodbridge, Suffolk, 1974.

Randall, Lilian M. C. *The Diary of George A. Lucas: An American Art Agent in Paris 1857–1909.* 2 vols. Princeton, N.J., 1979.

Reitlinger, Gerald. *The Economics of Taste.* 3 vols. London, 1961–70.

Rewald, John. "Foreword." In *Edgar Degas 1834–1917: Original Wax Sculptures*, n.p. Exh. cat., M. Knoedler and Co., New York, 1955.

Richardson, Leslie. "The Spring Rain Collection of Japanese Surimono in the H. O. Havemeyer Collection." *Bulletin of The Metropolitan Museum of Art* 26 (July 1931), pp. 171–74.

Robaut 1905
Robaut, Alfred. *L'Oeuvre de Corot: Catalogue raisonné et illustré.* 5 vols. Paris, 1905.

Robinson, Lilien Filipovitch. "Barye and Patronage." In *Antoine-Louis Barye: The Corcoran Collection*, by Lilien F. Robinson and Edward J. Nygren, pp. 66–70. Exh. cat., The Corcoran Gallery of Art. Washington, D.C., 1988.

Rossi [1974]
Rossi, Paola. *Jacopo Tintoretto.* Vol. 1. Venice [1974].

Roth, Linda Horvitz, ed. *J. Pierpont Morgan, Collector: European Decorative Arts from the Wadsworth Atheneum.* Exh. cat., The Wadsworth Atheneum. Hartford, 1987.

Rouart and Wildenstein 1975
Rouart, Denis, and Daniel Wildenstein. *Edouard Manet: Catalogue raisonné.* 2 vols. Lausanne and Paris, 1975.

Rowlands 1985
Rowlands, John. *Holbein: The Paintings of Hans Holbein the Younger.* Oxford, 1985.

Saarinen, Aline B. *The Proud Possessors.* New York, 1958.

Schmit 1973
Schmit, Robert. *Eugène Boudin, 1824–1898.* 3 vols. Paris, 1973.

Slive 1974
Slive, Seymour. *Frans Hals.* Vol. 3, *Catalogue.* London, 1974.

Smith 1829–42
Smith, John. *Catalogue Raisonné of the Works of the Most Eminent Dutch, Flemish, and French Painters.* 9 vols. London, 1829–42.

Sonnabend, Martin. *Antoine-Louis Barye (1795–1875).* Munich, 1988.

Spassky et al. 1985
Spassky, Natalie, et al. *American Paintings in The Metropolitan Museum of Art.* Vol. 2, *A Catalogue of Works by Artists Born between 1816 and 1845.* New York, 1985.

Stadler 1936
Stadler, Franz. *Hans von Kulmbach.* Vienna, 1936.

Sterling 1955
Sterling, Charles. *The Metropolitan Museum of Art: A Catalogue of French Paintings XV–XVIII Centuries.* Cambridge, Mass., 1955.

Sterling and Salinger 1966
Sterling, Charles, and Margaretta M. Salinger. *French Paintings: A Catalogue of the Collection of The Metropolitan Museum of Art.* Vol. 2, *XIX Century.* New York, 1966.

Sterling and Salinger 1967
Sterling, Charles, and Margaretta M. Salinger. *French Paintings: A Catalogue of the Collection of The Metropolitan Museum of Art.* Vol. 3, *XIX–XX Centuries.* New York, 1967.

Sumowski 1983
Sumowski, Werner. *Gemälde der Rembrandt-Schüler.* 5 vols. Landau, 1983.

Sutton, Denys. "The Discerning Eye of Louisine Havemeyer." *Apollo* 82 (September 1965), pp. 230–35.

Sutton 1980
Sutton, Peter C. *Pieter de Hooch*. Ithaca, N.Y., 1980.

Sweet, Frederick A. *Miss Mary Cassatt, Impressionist from Pennsylvania*. Norman, Okla., 1966.

Taki, Seiichi. "Ga ryû setsu" (On the painting of dragons). *Kokka*, no. 550 (September 1936), pp. 251–56.

Tomita, Kojiro. *Portfolio of Chinese Paintings in the Museum (Han to Sung Periods)*. Cambridge, Mass., 1933.

Tomkins, Calvin. *Merchants and Masterpieces: The Story of The Metropolitan Museum of Art*. New York, 1970.

Ushikubo, Daijiro. *Life of Koyetsu*. Kyoto, 1926.

Veblen, Thorstein. *The Theory of the Leisure Class: An Economic Study of Institutions*. 1899. Reprint. New York, 1953.

Venturi 1936
Venturi, Lionello. *Cézanne: Son art, son oeuvre*. 2 vols. Paris, 1936.

Vlieghe 1972
Vlieghe, Hans. *Saints*. Vol. 1. Corpus Rubenianum Ludwig Burchard, pt. 8. London, 1972.

Vlieghe 1987
Vlieghe, Hans. *Rubens Portraits of Identified Sitters Painted in Antwerp*. Corpus Rubenianum Ludwig Burchard, pt. 19. London, 1987.

Weber, Charles D. *Chinese Pictorial Bronze Vessels of the Late Chou Period*. Ascona, 1968.

Wehle 1940
Wehle, Harry B. *The Metropolitan Museum of Art: A Catalogue of Italian, Spanish and Byzantine Paintings*. New York, 1940.

Wehle and Salinger 1947
Wehle, Harry B., and Margaretta Salinger. *The Metropolitan Museum of Art: A Catalogue of Early Flemish, Dutch and German Paintings*. New York, 1947.

Weisberg, Gabriel. *Art Nouveau Bing: Paris Style 1900*. New York, 1986.

Weitzenhoffer 1982
Weitzenhoffer, Frances. "The Creation of the Havemeyer Collection, 1875–1900." Ph.D. diss., The City University of New York, 1982. University Microfilms International, Ann Arbor, Mich., 1982.

Weitzenhoffer, Frances. "The Earliest American Collectors of Monet." In *Aspects of Monet: A Symposium on the Artist's Life and Times*, edited by Frances Weitzenhoffer, pp. 73–92. New York, 1986.

Weitzenhoffer 1986
Weitzenhoffer, Frances. *The Havemeyers: Impressionism Comes to America*. New York, 1986.

Wethey 1962
Wethey, Harold E. *El Greco and His School*. 2 vols. Princeton, N.J., 1962.

Wethey 1975
Wethey, Harold E. *The Paintings of Titian*. 3 vols. London, 1975.

Wildenstein 1974–85
Wildenstein, Daniel. *Claude Monet: Biographie et catalogue raisonné*. 4 vols. Lausanne and Paris, 1974–85.

Wildenstein 1933
Wildenstein, Georges. *Chardin*. Paris, 1933.

Wildenstein 1954
Wildenstein, Georges. *Ingres*. [London?], 1954.

Wilson, Richard. *The Art of Ogata Kenzan*. New York and Tokyo, 1991.

Wilson, Richard L. "Aspects of Rimpa Design." *Orientations* 21 (December 1990), pp. 28–35.

Yarnall, James L., and William H. Gerdts, comps. *The National Museum of American Art's Index to American Art Exhibition Catalogues*. 6 vols. Boston, 1986.

Young et al. 1980
Young, Andrew McLaren, et al. *The Paintings of James McNeill Whistler*. New Haven, 1980.

Zeri and Gardner 1971
Zeri, Federico, and Elizabeth E. Gardner. *Italian Paintings: A Catalogue of the Collection of The Metropolitan Museum of Art, Florentine School*. New York, 1971.

Zeri and Gardner 1973
Zeri, Federico, and Elizabeth E. Gardner. *Italian Paintings: A Catalogue of the Collection of The Metropolitan Museum of Art, Venetian School*. New York, 1973.

Zieseniss 1953
Zieseniss, Charles Otto. *Les Aquarelles de Barye: Etude critique et catalogue raisonné*. Paris, 1953.

Key to Exhibition Abbreviations

1835 London — British Institution for Promoting the Fine Arts in the United Kingdom, from May, *Pictures by Italian, Spanish, Flemish, Dutch, and French Masters, with which the Proprietors have Favoured the Institution*

1839 Paris — Musée Royal, from March 1, Salon

1844 Paris — Musée Royal, from March 15, Salon

1854 Madrid — Museo Nacional de la Trinidad, Calle Atocha

1855 Paris — Palais des Beaux-Arts, from May 15, *Exposition universelle de 1855* (Salon)

1855 Paris Courbet — Pavillon du réalisme, 7, avenue Montaigne, from June 26, *Exposition et vente de 40 tableaux et 4 dessins de l'oeuvre de M. Gustave Courbet*

1857 Manchester — *Art Treasures of the United Kingdom Collected at Manchester*

1857 Paris — Palais des Champs-Elysées, from June 15, Salon

1858 Dijon — July

1860 Paris — 26, boulevard des Italiens [Francis Petit], *Tableaux tirés de collections d'amateurs et exposés au profit de la caisse de secours des artistes peintres, sculpteurs, architectes et dessinateurs*

1863 Paris — Salon annexe, Palais des Champs-Elysées, from May 15, Salon des Refusés

1863 Saintes — Hôtel de Ville, from January 15, *Ouvrages de peintures et de sculpture exposés dans les salles de la Mairie au profit des pauvres*

1864 Paris — Société Nationale des Beaux-Arts, April (group show)

1864 Paris Delacroix — Société Nationale des Beaux-Arts, 26, boulevard des Italiens, *Exposition des oeuvres d'Eugène Delacroix*

1864 Paris Salon — Palais des Champs-Elysées, from May 1, Salon

1865 Paris — Galerie Martinet, from February 19, Société Nationale des Beaux-Arts

1866 Lille — July–August

1866 London — British Institution for Promoting the Fine Arts in the United Kingdom, from June, *Pictures by Italian, Spanish, Flemish, Dutch, French and English Masters, with which the Proprietors have Favoured the Institution*

1866 Paris — Palais des Champs-Elysées, from May 1, Salon

1866 Paris Industrie — Palais de l'Industrie, Salon

1866 Paris Manet — Manet's studio, rue Guyot

1867 Paris — Rond-Point du Pont de l'Alma, *Exposition des oeuvres de M. G. Courbet*

1867 Paris Manet — Avenue de l'Alma, from May 22, *Tableaux de M. Edouard Manet*

1867 Paris Universelle — Palais du Champ de Mars, *Exposition universelle de 1867*

1868 Ghent — Salon

1869 Brussels — July 29–September 30, *Exposition générale des beaux-arts*

1869 Munich — Glaspalast, July 20–October 31, *Première exposition internationale des beaux-arts dans le Palais de l'Industrie à Munich*

1869 Paris — Palais des Champs-Elysées, from May 1, Salon

1870 Antwerp — Salon

1871 Pau — Musée des Beaux-Arts, *Exposition de la Société des Amis des Arts de Pau*

1872 London — Durand-Ruel, 168 New Bond Street, spring, *Third Exhibition of the Society of French Artists*

1872 London Fourth — Durand-Ruel, 168 New Bond Street, summer, *Fourth Exhibition of the Society of French Artists*

1872 London Winter — Royal Academy of Arts, *Exhibition of the Works of the Old Masters, Together with Works of Deceased Masters of the British School* (winter exhibition)

1873 Brussels — Cercle artistique et littéraire, *Collection de M. John W. Wilson exposée dans la Galerie du cercle artistique et littéraire de Bruxelles au profit des pauvres de cette ville*, unnumbered catalogue

1873 London — Durand-Ruel, 168 New Bond Street, from November 3, *Seventh Exhibition of the Society of French Artists*

1873 Vienna	Cercle de Vienna, _238^e et 239e Exposi-tions de l'Association d'Art Autrichien_	1880 Paris	Galerie de la Vie Moderne, April 8–30, _Exposition d'oeuvres nouvelles d'Edouard Manet_
1874 London	Durand-Ruel, 168 New Bond Street, spring, _Eighth Exhibition of the Society of French Artists_	1880 Paris Monet	Galerie de la Vie Moderne, _Monet_
1874 Paris	Palais de la Présidence du Corps Législatif, from April 23, _Ouvrages de peinture exposés au profit de la colonisation de l'Algérie par les Alsaciens-Lorrains_	1880 Paris Pyramides	10, rue des Pyramides, April 1–30, _5^{me} exposition de peinture_ (5th Impressionist exhibition)
1874 Paris Capucines	35, boulevard des Capucines, April 15–May 15, _Première exposition_ (1st Impressionist exhibition)	1881 London	Fine Art Society, from January 29, _Private View of 53 Venice Pastels_
1874 Paris Salon	Palais des Champs-Elysées, from May 1, Salon	1882 Paris	Ecole Nationale des Beaux-Arts, May, _Exposition des oeuvres de Gustave Courbet_
1875 London	McLean Gallery, autumn, no catalogue	1882 Paris Saint-Honoré	251, rue Saint-Honoré, probably March 1–31, _7^{me} exposition des artistes indépendants_ (7th Impressionist exhibition)
1875 Paris	Ecole Nationale des Beaux-Arts, _Oeuvres de Antoine-Louis Barye_	1883 Boston	Mechanics' Building, September 1 or 3 December, _American Exhibition of Foreign Products, Arts and Manufactures_
1875 Paris Corot	Ecole Nationale des Beaux-Arts, _Exposition de l'oeuvre de Corot_		
1875 Paris Gavet	7, rue Saint-Georges, April 6–May 6, _Dessins de Millet provenant de la collection de M. G[avet] et exposés au profit de la famille de l'artiste_	1883 London	Durand-Ruel, Dowdeswell and Dowdeswells', 133 New Bond Street, spring–summer, _Paintings, Drawings and Pastels by Members of "La Société des Impressionnistes"_
1876 London	Deschamps Gallery, 168 New Bond Street, spring, _Twelfth Exhibition of Pictures by Modern French Artists_	1883 Paris	Galerie Georges Petit, from June 12, _Cent chefs-d'oeuvre des collections parisiennes_
1876 Paris	11, rue Le Peletier, April, _2^e exposition de peinture_ (2nd Impressionist exhibition)	1883 Paris Durand-Ruel	Galerie Durand-Ruel, March 1–25 or 27, _Claude Monet_
1876 Paris Manet	Manet's studio, 4, rue de Saint-Pétersbourg, April 15–May 1, Paintings rejected by the Salon, and other works	1884 Paris	Ecole Nationale des Beaux-Arts, January 6–28, _Exposition des oeuvres de Edouard Manet_
1877 Paris	6, rue Le Peletier, April, _3^e exposition de peinture_ (3rd Impressionist exhibition)	1885 Paris	Ecole Nationale des Beaux-Arts, March 6–April 15, _Exposition Eugène Delacroix au profit de la souscription destinée à élever à Paris un monument à sa mémoire_
1878 Brussels	Galerie du cercle artistique et littéraire, _14 tableaux de Gustave Courbet exposés appartenant à des collectionneurs belges_		
1878 New York	National Academy of Design, February 3–March 3, _Eleventh Annual Exhibition of the American Water Color Society_	1885 Paris Louvre	Musée du Louvre, _Exposition de tableaux, statues et objets d'art au profit de l'oeuvre des orphelins d'Alsace-Lorraine_
1878 Paris	_Exposition universelle internationale de 1878_	1886 Brussels	From February 6, _Les XX_ (3rd annual exhibition of Les XX)
1878 Paris Daumier	Galerie Durand-Ruel, _Exposition des peintures et dessins de H. Daumier_	1886 London	Messrs. Dowdeswell, 133 New Bond Street, May, _"Notes"—"Harmonies"—"Nocturnes,"_ second series
1878 Paris Durand-Ruel	Galerie Durand-Ruel, _Exposition rétrospective de tableaux et dessins des maîtres modernes_	1886 New York	American Art Association, April 10–28, and National Academy of Design, from May 25, _Works in Oil and Pastel by the Impressionists of Paris_
1879 Paris	26, avenue de l'Opéra, April 10–May 11, _4^{me} exposition de peinture_ (4th Impressionist exhibition)	1886 Paris	1, rue Laffitte, May 15–June 15, _8^{me} exposition de peinture_ (8th Impressionist exhibition)
1879 Paris Salon	Palais des Champs-Elysées, from May 12, Salon	1886 Paris Bayard	3, rue Bayard (former studio of Gustave Doré), April–May, _Maîtres du siècle_
1880 New York	National Academy of Design, until March 1, _Thirteenth Annual Exhibition of the American Water Color Society_	1887 New York	National Academy of Design, May 25–June 30, _Celebrated Paintings by Great_

	French Masters, Brought to this Country from Paris, for Exhibition Only	1891 Paris	Galerie Durand-Ruel, May, *Exposition Claude Monet*
1887 Paris	Galerie Durand-Ruel, November 20– December 20, *Exposition de tableaux, pastels, dessins par M. Puvis de Chavannes*	1891 Paris Cassatt	Galerie Durand-Ruel, April, *Exposition de tableaux, pastels, et gravures par Mlle Mary Cassatt*
1887 Paris Millet	Ecole Nationale des Beaux-Arts, *Exposition des oeuvres de J. F. Millet*	1891 Philadelphia	The Pennsylvania Academy of the Fine Arts, October 15–November 28, *Thomas B. Clarke Collection of American Pictures*
1887 Pittsburgh	Carnegie Institute		
1888 Paris	Ecole des Beaux-Arts, *Exposition des peintures, aquarelles, dessins et lithographies des maîtres français de la caricature et de la peinture de moeurs au XIXe siècle*	1891–92 London	La Société des Beaux-Arts, Mr. Collie's Rooms, 39B Old Bond Street, December–January, *A Small Collection of Pictures by Degas and Others*
1889 Brussels	*Portraits du siècle (1789–1889)*	1891–92 London English	New English Art Club, winter, *Seventh Exhibition*
1889 New York	H. Wunderlich and Co., March, *Notes— Harmonies—Nocturnes*	1892 Glasgow	La Société des Beaux-Arts, February (expanded version of 1891–92 London exhibition), no catalogue
1889 New York Watercolor	National Academy of Design, until March 2, *Twenty-second Annual Exhibition of the American Water Color Society*	1892 Glasgow Institute	Glasgow Institute of the Fine Arts, 31st *Exhibition of Works of Modern Artists*
1889 Paris	Ecole des Beaux-Arts, April, *Oeuvres de Barye*	1892 New York	Union League Club, January 14–16, *Paintings by American Artists*
1889 Paris Boudin	Galerie Durand-Ruel, July 8–August 14, *Exposition de tableaux, pastels, fusains par E. Boudin*	1892 Paris	Galerie Durand-Ruel, February 29– March 10, *Monet*
1889 Paris Monet	Galerie Georges Petit, June 21–August, *Claude Monet, A. Rodin*	1893 Chicago	World's Columbian Exposition, Department K, Fine Arts, May 1–October 30, *Loan Collection: Foreign Masterpieces Owned in the United States*
1889 Paris Universelle	Palais du Champ de Mars (Galerie des Beaux-Arts), May–November, *Exposition universelle de 1889, beaux-arts: 1789–1889 (Exposition centennale des beaux-arts)*	1893 London	Grafton Galleries, from February 18, *First Exhibition, Consisting of Paintings & Sculpture, by British & Foreign Artists of the Present Day*
1890 New York	Avery's Art Gallery, February, *Collection of Pictures by Samuel Colman, N.A.*	1893 New York	American Fine Arts Society, February 13–March 31, *Loan Exhibition*
1890 New York Grolier	Grolier Club, April, *A Whistler Exhibition*, no catalogue	1893 Paris	Galerie Durand-Ruel, November– December, *Exposition de tableaux, pastels et gravures de Mary Cassatt*
1890 New York Union	Union League Club, spring		
1890 Tours	Eglise de Saint François, *Exposition rétrospective*	1893 Paris Degas	Galerie Durand-Ruel, *Paysages de Degas*
1890–91 New York	The Metropolitan Museum of Art, November–April, *Loan Collection of Paintings*	1895 Boston	St. Botolph's Club, February, *Monet*
		1895 London	Burlington Gallery
1891 Munich	Glaspalast, *Münchener Jahresausstellung von Kunstwerken aller Nationen*	1895 New York	Durand-Ruel, March, *Paintings by Edouard Manet*
1891 New York	Union League Club, January, *Exhibition of Art Objects at the Union League*	1895 New York Cassatt	Durand-Ruel, April 16–30, *Exhibition of Paintings, Pastels, and Etchings by Miss Mary Cassatt*
1891 New York Metropolitan	The Metropolitan Museum of Art, May– November, *Loan Collection of Paintings*	1895 New York Monet	Durand-Ruel, January 12–27, *Monet*
1891 New York Monet	Union League Club, February 12–14, *Paintings by Old Masters, and Modern Foreign and American Painters, Together with an Exhibition of the Work of Claude Monet the Impressionist*	1895 Paris	Musée Galliera, *Exposition du centenaire de Corot*
		1895 Paris Monet	Galerie Durand-Ruel, May 10–31, *Exposition de tableaux de Claude Monet*
		1895 Paris Vollard	Galerie Vollard

1896 Buffalo	Buffalo Society of Artists, Library Building, March 23–April 11, *5th Annual Exhibition*, no catalogue
1896 New York	The Metropolitan Museum of Art [May], Hand-Book No. 6, [including] *Retrospective Exhibition of American Paintings: Loan Collections and Recent Gifts to the Museum*
1896 Paris	Galerie Durand-Ruel, *Degas*
1896–97 Pittsburgh	Carnegie Art Galleries, November 5– January 1, *First Annual Exhibition*
1897 Paris	Galerie Durand-Ruel, *Exposition rétrospective des oeuvres de G. Courbet aux artistes franc-comtois*
1897–98 Pittsburgh	Carnegie Institute, November 4–January 1, *Second Annual Exhibition*
1898 Boston	Copley Society of Boston, Copley Hall, March 7–27, *Loan Exhibition of Pictures by Modern Painters*
1898 London	Prince's Skating Ring, The International Society of Sculptors, Painters and Gravers, April 26–September 22, *Exhibition of International Art*
1898 New York	Durand-Ruel, from February 28, *Cassatt*
1898 New York Union	Union League Club, November, *Old Master and Modern Paintings*
1899 Paris	Galerie Georges Petit, February 16– March 8, *Exposition de tableaux par P.-A. Besnard, J.-C. Cazin, C. Monet, A. Sisley, F. Thaulow, et de Poteries par E. Chaplet*
1900 Madrid	Ministerio de Instrucción Publica y Bellas Artes, May, *Catalogo de la obras de Goya*
1900 Paris	Grand Palais, Exposition universelle de 1900, May–November, *Exposition centennale de l'art français de 1800 à 1889*
1900 Paris Durand-Ruel	Galerie Durand-Ruel, November 22– December 15, *Oeuvres récentes de Claude Monet*
1901 London	Art Gallery of the Corporation of London (Guildhall), April 30–August 28, *Exhibition of the Works of Spanish Painters*
1901 Paris	Syndicat de la Presse Artistique, Palais de l'Ecole des Beaux-Arts, May, *Exposition Daumier*
1902 Madrid	Museo Nacional de Pintura y Escultura, *Exposición de las obras de Domenico Theotocopuli, llamado El Greco*
1902–3 Pittsburgh	Carnegie Institute, November 6–January 1, *Loan Exhibition of Paintings*
1903 Vienna	*Entwicklung des Impressionismus in der Malerei und Plastik* (16th exhibition of the Wiener Secession)
1904 Boston	Copley Society of Boston, Copley Hall, from February 23, *Oil Paintings, Water Colors, Pastels, & Drawings, Memorial Exhibition of the Works of Mr. J. McNeill Whistler*
1904 Paris	Musée du Louvre (Pavillon de Marsan), April–July, *Exposition des primitifs français: La Peinture en France sous les Valois*
1907 Paris	Société Nationale des Beaux-Arts, Palais du domaine de Bagatelle, May 15–July 14, *Portraits de femmes (1870 à 1900)*
1907 Strasbourg	Château des Rohan, March 2–April 2, *Art français contemporain*
1907 Stuttgart	Museum der Bildenden Künste, May 1– 31, *Französischer Kunstwerke*
1908 Paris	Galerie Durand-Ruel, November 3–28, *Tableaux et pastels par Mary Cassatt*
1909 Boston	St. Botolph's Club, February 8–22, *Cassatt*
1909 New York	Grolier Club, March 11–27, *Exhibition of Bronzes and Paintings by Antoine-Louis Barye*
1909 New York Metropolitan	The Metropolitan Museum of Art, September–November, *The Hudson-Fulton Celebration*
1909 Paris	MM. Bernheim-Jeune et Cie, May 3–15, *Aquarelles & Pastels de Cézanne, H.-E. Cross, Degas, Jongkind, Camille Pissarro, K.-X. Roussel, Paul Signac, Vuillard*
1910 Barcelona	Until June 15 or 20, *Exposición de retratos y dibujos antiguos y modernos*
1910 Munich	Moderne Galerie [Thannhauser], from May 1, *Edouard Manet (Aus der Sammlung Pellerin)*
1910 Paris	MM. Bernheim-Jeune et Cie, June 1–17, *Manet: Trente-cinq tableaux de la Collection Pellerin*
1911 New York	Durand-Ruel
1912 Berlin	Galerie Bernheim, then Galerie Cassirer
1912 London	Royal Academy of Arts, January 1– March 9, *Exhibition of Works by the Old Masters and Deceased Masters of the British School Including a Collection of Pictures and Drawings by Edwin Austin Abbey, R.A.* (winter exhibition)
1912 New York	M. Knoedler and Co., April 2–20, *Paintings by El Greco and Goya*
1912 St. Petersburg	Institut Français, *Exposition centennale de l'art français*
1913 New York	Durand-Ruel, November 29–December 13, *Loan Exhibition of Paintings by Edouard Manet*

1913 Stuttgart — Kgl. Kunstgebäude, Schlossplatz, May–October, *Grosse Kunstausstellung*

1913–14 London — Grafton Galleries, October–January, *Exhibition of Spanish Old Masters in Support of National Gallery Funds and for the Benefit of the Sociedad de Amigos del Arte Espanola*

1914 Paris — Galerie Durand-Ruel, June 8–27, *Tableaux, pastels, dessins, et pointes-sèches par Mary Cassatt*

1915 New York — M. Knoedler and Co., January 12–23, *Loan Exhibition of Paintings by El Greco and Goya*

1915 New York Masterpieces — M. Knoedler and Co., April 6–24, *Loan Exhibition of Masterpieces by Old and Modern Painters*

1915 San Francisco — Fine Arts Palace, February 20–December 4, *Panama-Pacific International Exposition, Department of Fine Arts*

1917 New York — Arden Gallery, unnumbered catalogue(?)

1917 Paris — Galerie Rosenberg, June 25–July 13, *Exposition d'art français du XIXᵉ siècle*

1919 New York — The Metropolitan Museum of Art, April 7–May 18 (extended to June 1), *Loan Exhibition of the Works of Gustave Courbet*

1920 New York — The Metropolitan Museum of Art, May 7–October 3, *Fiftieth Anniversary Exhibition*, unnumbered catalogue

1920 Philadelphia — The Pennsylvania Academy of the Fine Arts, April 17–May 9, *Exhibition of Paintings and Drawings by Representative Modern Masters*

1921 New York — The Metropolitan Museum of Art, May 3–September 15, *Loan Exhibition of Impressionist and Post-Impressionist Paintings*

1921 New York Modern — The Metropolitan Museum of Art, May 17–September 15, *Modern French Exhibition*, no catalogue

1922 New York — The Grolier Club, January 26–February 28 (extended through the week of March 18), *Prints, Drawings and Bronzes by Degas*

1923 New York — The Metropolitan Museum of Art, May 7–September 9, *Loan Exhibition of the Arts of the Italian Renaissance*

1924 New York — The Metropolitan Museum of Art, March 17–April 20, *Memorial Exhibition of the Works of Julian Alden Weir*

1924 Paris — Galerie Durand-Ruel

1926 New York — Museum of French Art, French Institute in the United States, *Special Dedication Exhibition of French Art*

1926–27 Chicago — The Art Institute of Chicago, December 21–January 24, *A Memorial Collection of the Works of Mary Cassatt*

1927 Philadelphia — The Pennsylvania Museum, April 30–May 30, *Memorial Exhibition of the Work of Mary Cassatt*

1928 Buffalo — Albright Art Gallery, *22nd Annual Exhibition*

1928 New York — Durand-Ruel, March 20–April 10 (extended to April 14), *Loan Exhibition of French Masterpieces of the Late XIX Century*

1928 New York Metropolitan — The Metropolitan Museum of Art, February 17–April 1 (extended to April 15), *Spanish Paintings from El Greco to Goya*

1928 Pittsburgh — Carnegie Institute, *Memorial Exhibition of the Works of Mary Cassatt*

Contributors to the Catalogue

Unless otherwise noted, contributors are members of departments of The Metropolitan Museum of Art.

MWA   Maryan W. Ainsworth   *Senior Research Fellow, Paintings Conservation*

DA   Dorothea Arnold   *Lila Acheson Wallace Curator in Charge, Egyptian Art*

KB   Katharine Baetjer   *Curator, European Paintings*

JSB   Janet S. Byrne   *Former Curator, Prints and Illustrated Books*

KC   Keith Christiansen   *Jayne Wrightsman Curator, European Paintings*

HMC   Hyung-min Chung   *Lecturer, Seoul National University*

BBF   Barbara B. Ford   *Associate Curator, Asian Art*

JHF   James H. Frantz   *Conservator in Charge, Objects Conservation*

ACF   Alice Cooney Frelinghuysen   *Associate Curator, American Decorative Arts*

MKH   Maxwell K. Hearn   *Curator, Asian Art*

CI   Colta Ives   *Curator in Charge, Prints and Illustrated Books*

MJ   Marilyn Jenkins   *Curator, Islamic Art*

WL   Walter Liedkte   *Curator, European Paintings*

Julia Meech   *Consultant, Christie's, New York, and free-lance author*

JRM   Joan R. Mertens   *Curator, Greek and Roman Art*

HBM   Helen B. Mules   *Associate Curator, Acting in Charge, Drawings*

MO   Morihiro Ogawa   *Research Associate, Arms and Armor*

HO   Hiroshi Onishi   *Research Curator, Asian Art*

Rebecca A. Rabinow   *Assistant, European Paintings*

Susan Alyson Stein   *Special Exhibitions Associate, European Paintings*

Gary Tinterow   *Engelhard Associate Curator, European Paintings*

SGV   Suzanne G. Valenstein   *Research Curator, Asian Art*

CV   Clare Vincent   *Associate Curator, European Sculpture and Decorative Arts*

DW   Daniel Walker   *Curator in Charge, Islamic Art*

JCYW   James C. Y. Watt   *Brooke Russell Astor Senior Curator, Asian Art*

HBW   H. Barbara Weinberg   *Curator, American Paintings and Sculpture*

Gretchen Wold   *Research Associate, European Paintings*

Index

COMPILED BY SUSAN BRADFORD

Note: Page numbers given in italic type are those with illustrations of works in the Appendix.

as collector, 220, 223, 250, 379; correspondence from Cassatt, 89, 91; death of, 280; donation of painting to Metropolitan Museum of Art, by Louisine Havemeyer, in memory of, 280; Havemeyers' role in the collecting practices of, 220, 223, 239, 253, 256

Payson, Mrs. Charles S., 363

Peabody and Stearns, 194, 195

Peabody Museum, Salem Massachusetts, 132

peachbloom ware (China), 147–48; pls. 141, 142

peacock vase (Tiffany Glass and Decorating Co.), 105, 123; pl. 114

Pedestal Fund Art Loan Exhibition, New York (1883), 76, 205

Pellerin, Auguste, 254, 268, 353

Pelsdinge, Braams, 349

Pennsylvania Academy of the Fine Arts, Philadelphia, 277

Pennsylvania Museum of Art, Philadelphia, 282

Pennsylvania Sugar Refining Co., 246, 251

Périer, Paul, 324

Perry, Commodore, 141

Persian art, 108, 110, 111, 253, 282; pls. 99, 101

Peters, Adaline, 218, see also Elder, Adaline

Peters, Samuel, 218

Petit, Francis, 324, 338

Petit, Georges, 339, 363, 367

Philadelphia Museum of Art, 141, 150, 300

Philip II, 58

Piazzetta, Giovanni Battista, 368; work by: *Madonna* (A425), 252, 368

Picasso, Pablo, 6, 82

Pier Francesco Fiorentino, 370

Pierpont Morgan Library, New York, interior view of West Room, 100; fig. 14

Piette-Montfoulcault, Ludovic, 368; work by: *Landscape with Figures* (A426), 368

pillar prints (Japanese), 135; pl. 124

Pillet, 306

Pinart, 309

Pissarro, Camille, 6, 203, 210, 256, 368–70; art dealer of, 8; correspondence of, 52; exhibition of the work of, 206; in the Faure collection, 49; in the Havemeyer collection, 6, 8, 51, 52, 203, 261–62, 270; works by: *Bather in the Woods* (A432), 261, 370; 369; pl. 259; *Cabbage Gatherers, The* (A427), 6, 8, 203, 206, 368–69; 369; pl. 4; *Flood at Pontoise* (A430), 52, 369; 369; pl. 54; *Girl with a Goat* (A429), 270, 369; 369; pl. 265; *Haymakers Resting* (A431), 261–62, 369–70; 369; "Peasant Girls at Normandy" (A427), 206; *Potato Gatherers* (A428), 262, 369; 369

Pommereul, Baron de, 341

Pope, Alfred Atmore, 33, 216, 217, 248, 298, 365

Pope, Mrs. Alfred, 94, 248, 267

Pope, Arthur Upham, 282

Pope, Theodate, 248

Portier, Alphonse, 219–20, 327, 329, 332, 354, 356, 370

Post, George B., 213

Pourbus, Frans I, or Frans II, or Peeter, 285, 370; work by(?): *Portrait of a Woman* (A433), 221, 222, 370

Poussin, Nicolas, 10, 244, 276, 277, 358, 370

Poussin, Nicolas, Style of: *Orpheus and Eurydice* (A434), 244, 277, 358, 370; 370; pl. 241

Prado, Madrid, 229, 264

Prayer, M., 318

Premsel, 327

Price, James, 218

Priest, Alan, 147

Promayet, Alphonse, 312; portrait of (Courbet), 23, 266, 284, 312; 313; pl. 23

Proskauer, Edith H., 298

Proskauer, Richman, 298

Prud'hon, Pierre-Paul, 274; work by: *Charles-Hubert Millevoye (1782–1816)* (A435), 370; 370

Pseudo Pier Francesco Fiorentino, work by: *Madonna and Child with Saint John* (A436), 256, 370; 370; pl. 253

Putnam Foundation/Timken Museum of Art, San Diego, 302

Puvis de Chavannes, Pierre, 370–71; works by: *Allegory of the Sorbonne, The* (A438), 210, 371; 371; *Tamaris* (A437), 235, 286, 370; 370

Q

Qianlong period (China): ceramics from, 169; pl. 162

Qing dynasty (China): bronzes from, 146; ceramics from, 130, 147–48, 169; pls. 119, 141, 142, 162

Quiroga, Gaspar de, 58, 60

R

Raffaëlli, Jean François, 197, 203, 217, 371; work by: *Winter Landscape with the Figure of Jean Valjean* (A439), 203, 371; 371

Ranger, Henry Ward, 207, 371; works by: *Autumn* (A441), 207, 371; *Evening at Lydd* (A442), 207, 371; *Winter Street Scene* (A440), 371

Raphael (Raffaello Sanzio or Santi), Copy after: *Bindo Altoviti* (A443), 371

Raqqa ware (Syria), 110, 120; pls. 88, 110

Real del Sarte, Marie Magdeleine, 371; work by: *Révérence, La* (A444), 283, 371

Redron, M., 323

Reed, Luman, 192

Reichart and Co., 296

Reid, Alex, and Lefevre, London, 312, 339, 363

Reid, Alexander, Glasgow and London, 335

Reisinger, Hugo, 270, 369

Reitlinger, F., 376

Rembrandt Harmensz. van Rijn, 10, 24, 62–69, 283, 286, 292, 371–75; bankruptcy of, 68; classical period of, 67; as collector, 67; drawings by, 66; etchings by, 68–69, 286; exhibition of the work of, 91, 92, 95; fakes and forgeries of, 10, 62–63, 65, 66, 211, 212, 213, 286, 292; in the Havemeyer collection, 3, 4, 8, 10, 36, 39, 62–63, 65–69, 207, 211, 212, 213, 214, 280; influenced by Venetian painting, 67; landscapes by, 67; mature period of, 67; portraits by, 68; price paid for the work of, 260; self-portraits by, 68; subject matter of, 66; techniques of, 67, 68, 69; works by: "Admiral and His Wife, The," 63; *Christ and His Parents Returning from the Temple*, 206; pl. 183; *Christ with the Sick Around Him, Receiving Little Children (The "Hundred Guilder Print")*, 68; pl. 68; *Cottage Among Trees, A* (A450), 66–67, 212, 286, 373; 372; pl. 66; *David Playing Before Saul*, 63, 65, 211; *Group of Farm Buildings* (A451), 212, 286, 373–74; 372; *Herman Doomer (The Gilder)* (A449), 36, 39, 49, 62, 91, 207, 214, 252, 260, 373; 372; pl. 63; fig. 10; *Houses by the Water* (A452), 212, 286, 374; 372; *Landscape with Three Gabled Cottages Beside a Road*, 68–69; pl. 69; *Landscape with Trees, Farm Buildings and a Tower*, 206; *Nathan Admonishing David* (A453), 66, 212, 286, 374; 372; *Portrait of a Man*, 94; *Portrait of a Man* (A445), 62, 63, 207, 371, 373; 372; pl. 61; *Portrait of an Elderly Man*, 94; *Portrait of a Woman*, 94; *Portrait of a Woman* (A446), 62, 63, 207, 371, 373; 372; pl. 62; *Portrait of Himself*, 91, 94; *Portrait of Rembrandt with Plumed Cap*, 206; *Portrait of Thomas Jacobsz. Haaringh (The "Old Haaringh")*, 68; pl. 67; *Seated Man Wearing a Flat Cap* (A448), 212, 286, 373; 372; *Three Crosses*, 69; *Two Studies of a Woman Reading* (A447), 212, 286, 373; 372; *Woman Hanging on a Gibbet* (A454), 212, 286, 374; 372

Rembrandt Harmensz. van Rijn, works by(?): *Polish Rider, The*, 63; *Seated Man Wearing a Flat Cap* (A448), 66

Rembrandt Harmensz. van Rijn, Copy after: *Portrait of Rembrandt in a Cap and a Polish Jacket* (A455), 280, 374; 372

Rembrandt Harmensz. van Rijn, Style of: *Portrait of a Man—The Treasurer* (A456), 63, 211, 374; 374; *Portrait of a Man with a Breastplate and Plumed Hat* (A457), 63, 213, 374–75;

374; pl. 192; *Portrait of a Woman* (A458), 63, 213, 375; 375; pl. 193; *Portrait of a Young Man in a Broad-Brimmed Hat* (A459), 10, 63, 65, 213, 375; 375

Reni, Guido, 237

Reniero, José, 346

Renoir, Pierre-Auguste, 8, 52, 210, 225, 226, 245, 263, 279, 331, 375–76; works by: *By the Seashore* (A460), 8, 52, 53, 226, 248, 279, 375; 375; pl. 6; *Young Woman Reading* (A461), 210, 248–49, 375; 375; *Young Woman with a Muff* (A462), 285, 376; 375

Revenaz, 324

Reynolds, Joshua, 239, 373, 374

Ribalier, 315

Ribelles y Helip, José, 376

Ribelles y Helip, José, Attributed to: *Ferdinand VII (1784–1833), King of Spain* (A463), 280, 376; *Portrait of a Spanish Officer* (A464), 376; 376

Ribera, Jusepe de, 263; works by: "Flaying of Saint Bartholomew," 258; "Martyrdom of Saint Peter," 258

Ribera, Roman, 376; work by: *Concert, The* (A465), 205, 206, 376

Richardson, Jonathan, Sr., 373, 374

Richmond, Walter, 225, 320

Richter, Gisela M. A., 104, 116, 118, 285

Riddle, Mrs. Robert Moore, portrait of (Cassatt), 265; fig. 95

Rimpa school (Japan), 144, 145, 146; screens from, 142, 160–61; fig. 24; pl. 153

Ring, Ludger Tom, 342

Ringling, John, 341

Ringling, John and Mable, Museum of Art, Sarasota, 341

Ritsuō (or Ogawa Haritsu), 146, 150, 163; lacquerware box by, 163; pl. 156

ritual wine vessel (*hu*) (Chinese bronze), 146, 166–67; pl. 160; radiograph of, 166; fig. 25

Rivas, Duke of, 345

Robaut, Alfred, 247, 306, 311

Robertson, 327

Robertson, R. Austin, 149

Robiano, comte de, 292

Robinson, Edward, 236–37, 253, 254, 277, 284

Robinson, Theodore, 217

Rockefeller family, 207

Rodin, Auguste, 33, 70, 208

Roman art: ceramics, 117; pl. 106; coins, 116; glass, 99, 103, 104–5, 116–17, 148, 211; pls. 93, 94, 104, 105

Romanoff, Nicolai Dmitrivitch, 312

Romanoff family, 312

Rosenberg, Alexandre, 355

Rosenberg, Paul, New York, 355

Rosenberg, Paul, Paris, 220, 235, 261, 266, 278, 312, 319, 331, 355, 356, 361, 370

Rossellino, Antonio: work by: *Young Saint John the Baptist*, 249, 259; fig. 92

Rossi, Louis, 203

Rossi, Lucius, or Lucio, or Luigi, 376; work by: *Watercolor* (A466), 203, 376

Rosso, del, 341

Photograph Credits

Acquavella Galleries, New York: A232

Photograph by David Allison, Courtesy The Metropolitan Museum of Art: pl. 89

Archival photograph, The Metropolitan Museum of Art: figs. 6, 7, 27–30, 32–37, 101, 103

Courtesy Archives of The Pierpont Morgan Library, New York: fig. 14

© 1992, The Art Institute of Chicago. All Rights Reserved: pl. 247; figs. 66, 93; A61

Bayerische Stattsgemäldesammlungen: pl. 201

The Brooklyn Museum, photograph by Pat Bazelon: pl. 189

Tyler Campbell: pl. 75

Courtesy Christie's: pl. 170; A410

The Chrysler Museum, Norfolk, Virginia, photograph by Scott Wolff: pl. 199

Documentation photographique de la réunion des musées nationaux: figs. 5, 52, 76

Durand-Ruel Document Archives, Paris: pl. 190, figs. 49, 55, 91; A118, 341, 376, 461, 504

Richard L. Feigen and Co., Inc., New York: A222, 256

Courtesy Thomas Feist: A233

Courtesy Free Library of Philadelphia, Print and Picture Department, Centennial Photographic Collection: fig. 18

Courtesy Freer Gallery of Art, Smithsonian Institution, Washington, D.C., Charles Lang Freer Papers, Freer Gallery of Art/Arthur M. Sackler Gallery Archives, Smithsonian Institution, Photographer, S. Matsubara: fig. 21

Courtesy George G. Frelinghuysen: fig. 100

Courtesy Horace Havemeyer, Jr.: pl. 179; fig. 47

Courtesy William E. Havemeyer: fig. 57

Courtesy The Historical Society of the Town of Greenwich: fig. 51

Courtesy The Historical Society of the Town of Greenwich by permission of the Trustees of the Boston Public Library (Peabody and Stearns Collection, Fine Arts Department): fig. 40

Courtesy Jozuka Taketoshi: fig. 22

Courtesy M. Knoedler and Co., New York: figs. 10–13

Courtesy The Museum of the City of New York, The Byron Collection: fig. 53

© 1992 National Gallery of Art, Washington, D.C.: pls. 10, 11, 29, 196, 226, 272; figs. 77, 92; A51, 60, 109, 126, 180, 286, 291–93, 336, 356, 357, 403

Courtesy The New-York Historical Society: fig. 94

Courtesy Pennsylvania Academy of the Fine Arts archives, Philadelphia: fig. 46

Photographie Sidman, rights reserved, Durand-Ruel Document Archives, Paris: fig. 54

Eric Pollitzer, Hempstead, New York: fig. 43

Shelburne Museum, Shelburne, Vermont, photograph by Ken Burris: pls. 3–5, 12, 16, 28, 30, 36, 37, 70–72, 85, 98, 171, 172, 184, 191, 200, 203, 214, 258, 274; fig. 17; A110, 113, 154, 210, 219, 227, 230, 350, 351, 359, 364, 365, 395, 398, 405, 411, 420, 421, 456, 459

United States History, Local History & Genealogy Division, The New York Public Library, Astor, Lenox and Tilden Foundations: fig. 26

University of Michigan, Museum of Art, Ann Arbor, photograph by Pat Young: pls. 97, 163–67, 169, 174, 176, 178

Courtesy J. Watson Webb, Jr.: figs. 9, 39, 43, 44, 48, 50, 58, 65, 70–74, 78–80, 82, 83, 87, 89, 96

Courtesy Linden Havemeyer Wise: fig. 90